P9-BIR-086

LIFE
IN THE MIDDLE AGES

SELECTED
TRANSLATED AND ANNOTATED
BY

G. G. COULTON

ADULT
940.1
COULTON
1967
V2
no.3+4

III & IV
MEN AND MANNERS

MONKS, FRIARS AND NUNS

BEVERLY HILLS PUBLIC LIBRARY

3 5048 00013 5408

Beverly Hills Public Library
WITHDRAWN
444 North Rexford Drive
Beverly Hills, California 90210

CAMBRIDGE
AT THE UNIVERSITY PRESS
1967

PUBLISHED BY
THE SYNDICS OF THE CAMBRIDGE UNIVERSITY PRESS

Bentley House, 200 Euston Road, London, N.W.1
American Branch: 32 East 57th Street, New York, N.Y. 10022

First edition in one volume	1910
(Constable & Co. Ltd)	
Second edition in four volumes	1928
(Cambridge University Press)	
Reissued in two volumes	1967
First paperback edition	1967

First printed in Great Britain at the University Press, Cambridge
Reprinted by photolithography in Great Britain by
Butler & Tanner Ltd, Frome and London

8-72

c
1967
v. 2
cop. 3

To

MY WIFE

202839

PREFACE

TO THE SECOND EDITION
(January 1928)

THE original volume was felt by some readers to be rather bulky; here, therefore, it is divided into separately purchasable parts, arranged roughly according to subject. The first and largest deals with *Religion, Folk-Lore and Superstition*; the second, with *Chronicles, Science and Art*; the third, with *Men and Manners*; the fourth, with *Monks, Friars and Nuns*. The first is enlarged by the addition of three extracts which were not in the first edition, two of which refer to subjects of considerable recent interest, St Joan and the Inquisition. The fourth volume is considerably enlarged, especially by the inclusion of *My Lord Abbot* from *Petit Jean de Saintré*. I have been able to correct a few mistakes and add a few notes; otherwise, there has been little opportunity of bringing the book up to date. For the re-arrangement of the extracts and the revision of the proofs, and much other help, I am indebted to my wife.

G. G. C.

ST JOHN'S COLLEGE
CAMBRIDGE

PREFACE

TO THE FIRST EDITION
(May 1910)

THIS book appeals to the increasing body of readers who wish to get at the real Middle Ages; who, however impatient of mere dissertations and discussions, are glad to study genuine human documents, and to check the generalizations of historians by reference to first-hand facts. The Author has, therefore, attempted to compile a catena of such documents, each more or less complete in itself, but mostly too long for full quotation by historians. Moreover, he claims to cover a wider ground than most of the formal histories. The records here printed represent thirty years' study among all kinds of medieval writings, and could scarcely be outdone in this respect but by scholars who have better work to do. They have been chosen as specially characteristic of the period, and as appealing also to that deeper humanity which is common to all minds in all periods. They treat of clergy and laity, saints and sinners; spiritual experiences, love, battles, pageants, and occasionally the small things of everyday life. Drawn from six different languages, the large majority of these extracts are here translated for the first and perhaps the last time, since they are only the cream from bulky and often inaccessible volumes. A few are from manuscripts. If, on the whole, religious life is more fully represented here, and that life itself in its least conventional aspects, this want of strict proportion is more or less inherent in the plan of the work. We do not go abroad to meet Englishmen, or into the Middle Ages for the commonplace; though an occasional touch of this kind may help to show us the essential uniformity of little things in all ages. We most want to hear of those who, for good or evil, stand apart from the rest; and in the Middle Ages, as now, the evil generally lent itself best to picturesque description. The Author has, however, done all he can, consistently with any measure of historical truth, to avoid those darkest sides of all upon which the scope of his *From St Francis to Dante* compelled him to dwell at some length.

Several of the best books, being easily accessible elsewhere, are omitted here. From one or two more, only just enough is given to indicate the value of the rest, already sufficiently translated. It was impossible, within any reasonable compass, to exploit the rich mine of Franciscan and Dominican records also; a small fraction of these have already been printed in *From St Francis to Dante*, and the rest are reserved for a later volume. With these necessary exceptions, it is hoped that the present selection may be in some real sense representative. How far it is from being exhaustive, those will know best who have read most widely. From such critics the Author can only claim indulgence for this first attempt in English to cover Medieval Life as a whole.

G. G. C.

40 MILL ROAD
EASTBOURNE

PREFACE

TO THE SECOND EDITION OF PART IV
(*December 1929*)

This volume is very considerably enlarged in the present edition; it has been increased by more than a hundred pages. The additional matter consists of extracts which I had made for a volume planned ten years ago, which was to illustrate every side of monastic life. A good deal of that material will be summarized in the third volume of my *Five Centuries of Religion*, which I hope to bring out in the course of 1930; but many passages were too long for that volume, yet too valuable to abridge farther than they will be found abridged here. The story of *How Friar Michael was burned*,

A*

and the *Abbot, Lady, and Knight* from *Petit Jean de Saintré*, are of this character. Friar Michael's story has been far too much neglected by historians of the Inquisition; and if, as in the Saintré case and in that of Caesarius of Heisterbach, I give long extracts from books which can now be procured in their completeness, this is because I made my own versions long ago, and because the stories seemed too important to be omitted from any collection of this kind. They may, after all, send some readers on from the present volume to the full translations of the books from which they are taken.

One valuable criticism which has reached me must be met by a frank confession. In thus splitting my old *Garner* into four volumes for the reader's convenience, I ought to have followed my first impulse, and divided them by order of time, not according to their subject-matter, which, moreover, was sometimes rather difficult to decide; one and the same story might be counted with equal truth as illustrating Monasticism or Adventure. Within each volume, the chronological order has indeed been kept, roughly at least; but in the book as a whole it has been broken. This, as my kind critic points out, has the great disadvantage that the reader does not see for himself, with sufficient clearness, how things progressed from generation to generation in the Middle Ages; my arrangement may deceive him into a too static view of these five centuries. For this I must here apologize; yet, even thus, it may be permissible to suggest some sort of remedy for any really determined student who has been extravagant enough to buy all four volumes. Dates, exact or approximate, are given for every extract; he may therefore follow the chronological order by skipping from volume to volume. This, however, I point out not in excuse but only in palliation of an error which I now see plainly enough.

CAMBRIDGE

G. G. C.

CONTENTS

PART III: MEN AND MANNERS

CONTENTS

PART IV: MONKS, FRIARS AND NUNS

CONTENTS

LIST OF ILLUSTRATIONS
IN PART III

IN PART IV

PART III
MEN AND MANNERS

From the Chronicle of Gervase, a monk of Canterbury, R.S. vol. I, p. 258. A Church Council held in Westminster Abbey (A.D. 1176) brought to a head the inveterate rivalry for precedence between the sees of Canterbury and York.

1. ARCHIEPISCOPAL MANNERS

IN the month of March, about Mid-Lent, the king came to London with his son Henry and the Lord Uguccione, Legate of the Pope, who purposed to call together the clergy of England and hold a Council. When therefore the Papal Legate had taken his seat on a raised throne in the midst, and Richard Archbishop of Canterbury, by right of his primacy, had sat down on his right, then Roger Archbishop of York, puffed up with his own innate arrogance to reject the left-hand throne that was destined for him, strove irreverently to sit down between the Legate and his Grace of Canterbury, thrusting with the more uncomely quarters of his body so that he sat down upon the lap of his own Primate. Yet scarce had he struck my lord of Canterbury with that elbow of his wherewith he had been accustomed to fight, when he was ignominiously seized by certain bishops, clerics, and laymen, and torn from the Archbishop's lap, and cast upon the floor. But, when staves and fists were now wielded on both sides, the Archbishop of Canterbury sprang up and returned good for evil, snatching away from this disastrous conflict his own rival and the inveterate enemy of his see. At length the contumacious Archbishop of York, rising from the pavement with his cape torn ignominiously by the struggle, fell down at the king's feet and belched forth lying[1] calumnies against the Archbishop of Canterbury.

---

[1] *Mendosam* should probably be *mendacem.*

Peter of Blois, descended from a noble Breton family, distinguished himself greatly at the Universities of Paris and Bologna, and was invited by Henry II to England, where he became successively Archdeacon of Bath and of London, and died in 1200. He earned a world-wide reputation by his Letters, the popularity of which called forth spurious imitations. The following extract is from his fourteenth letter, "to the Royal Chaplains of Henry II." He relates how his recent illness has opened his eyes to the miseries of court life, where "these martyrs of the world, through many tribulations, enter into the kingdom of hell." He therefore exhorts his friends to retire likewise from a place not only so perilous to the soul, but so comfortless to the body. Bad enough are the racket and disorder, the weariness of constant travel from manor to manor; but, to any man of delicate perceptions, the meals are worst of all.

2. A ROYAL INFERNO

FOR all who fight in the camp of ambition have been taken prisoners by Nahash the Ammonite, and have lost their right eyes [1 Sam. xi, 2]; for they are keen-sighted to acquire worldly things, but pay no heed to the loss of this passing life and to the imminent torments of everlasting death.... They are wise (saith the Prophet) to do evils, but to do good they have no knowledge.... This I marvel most, how any man can suffer the miseries of court life who hath long been used to the warfare of learning and the camp of university discipline. For (to return to the courtiers) they know neither order nor reason nor measure in their meals, or in their ridings abroad, or in their nightly watchings. Court chaplains and knights are served with bread hastily made, without leaven, from the dregs of the ale-tub—leaden bread, bread of tares, bread unbaken. The wine is turned sour or mouldy; thick, greasy, stale, flat, and smacking of pitch [from the cask]. I have sometimes seen even great lords served with wine so muddy that a man must needs close his eyes and clench his teeth, wry-mouthed and shuddering, and filtering the stuff rather than drinking. The ale which men drink in that place is horrid to the taste and abominable to the sight. There also, (such is the concourse of people), sick and whole beasts are sold at random, with fishes even four days old; yet shall not all this corruption and stench abate one penny of the price; for the servants reck not whether an unhappy guest fall sick or die, so that their lords' tables be served with a multitude of dishes; we who sit at meat must needs fill our bellies with carrion, and become graves (as it were) for sundry corpses. Many more would die of such corrupt stuff, but that the ravenous clamour of our maw, and the Scyllaean whirlpool of that dark abyss, with the help of laborious exercise, consumeth all at last. Yet even so, if the court dwell longer than usual in any town, some courtiers are ever left behind to die. I cannot endure (to say nothing of others) the vexations of the royal stewards— fawning flatterers, wicked backbiters, unprincipled extor- tioners: wearisome with their importunities for gifts, ungrate- ful for benefits received, malignant to all such as are loth to give again and again. I have known many who have dealt liberal largesse to such stewards; yet, when with much labour they had sought their lodging after a long day's journey, while their supper was yet half-cooked, or again while they sat at meat—nay, even while they slept on their bed, these stewards would come swelling with pride and contumely, cut the horses' halters, cast forth the baggage recklessly and perchance not without grievous loss, and expel the guests with so little ceremony that these, (for all their wealth and their provision of travelling bed-gear) had not where to lay their heads that night. This again addeth to the courtiers' misery, that if the king have promised to stay anywhere, and especially if the herald have publicly proclaimed this as the royal will, then be sure that he will set out at daybreak, mocking all men's expectation by his sudden change of purpose. Whereby it cometh frequently to pass that such courtiers as have let themselves be bled, or have taken some purgative, must yet follow their prince forthwith without regard to their own bodies, and, setting their life on the hazard of a die, hasten blindfold to ruin for dread of losing that which they have not, nor never shall have. Then may ye see men rush forth like madmen, sumpter-mules jostling sumpter-mules and chariots clashing against chariots in frantic confusion, a very Pande- monium made visible. Or again, if the Prince have proclaimed his purpose of setting out for a certain place with the morrow's dawn, then will he surely change his purpose; doubt not but that he will lie abed till mid-day. Here wait the sumpters

3

standing under their loads, the chariots idly silent, the outriders asleep, the royal merchants in anxious expectation, and
all murmuring together: men flock round the court prostitutes
and vintners, (a kind of courtiers who often know the palace
secrets), to get tidings of the king's journey. For the king's
train swarms with play-actors and washerwomen, dicers and
flatterers, taverners, waferers,[1] buffoons, barbers, tumblers,
and all birds of that feather. Oftentimes have I seen how,
when the king slept and all things were in quiet silence, there
leapt down a word from the royal quarters, not almighty
indeed, yet all-awakening,[2] and naming that city or town for
which the court must now set out. After the long weariness
of delay and suspense, we solaced ourselves with the expectation of sleeping there, where (as we hoped) lodging and
food would abundantly be found: for so great was the press,
so confused and tumultuous the wandering crowds of horse
and foot, that the abyss seemed to have been opened, and hell
to vomit forth his legions. Yet, when our outriders had now
well-nigh or fully gone the whole day's journey, then again
would the king change his purpose and lodge elsewhere,
having perchance a single house and victuals enough for
himself alone, whereof no other might share: yea, and I verily
believe (if I may dare so to speak) that he hath found in our
anguish a keener zest to his own pleasures. We therefore,
wandering for three or four miles through unknown forests,
and oftentimes in the black darkness, esteemed ourselves
fortunate if perchance we fell upon some vile and sordid hovel.
Oftentimes the courtiers would fight bitterly and obstinately
for mere huts, and contend with drawn swords for a lair which
had been unworthy of contention among swine. How we
and our beasts fared meanwhile on such a night may well be
imagined: I myself was so divided from my train that it was
scarce possible to collect the scattered remnants within three
days. Almighty God on high, Thou Who art King of kings
and Lord of lords, and terrible with the kings of earth, Who
takest away the spirit of princes, Who givest health to kings,

---

Makers of wafers (Fr. *gaufres*), or thin sweet cakes. It appears that they
enjoyed no very good reputation; see *Piers Plowman*, A, vi, 120.
  [2] This is parodied from Wisdom xviii, 14.

in Whose hand is the king's heart and Who turnest it whither-soever Thou wilt, turn now and convert the king's heart from this his pestilent custom, that he may know himself to be but a man, and may learn by use to show the grace of royal liberality and the kindness of human compassion to those men who are drawn after him not by ambition but by necessity!

Ralph Higden, a monk of Chester, died in 1364. His *Polychronicon* is not only a digest of such chronicles as the author could get hold of, but also a popular encyclopaedia: it has no original merit, but is most valuable as showing a learned man's outlook on the world during Chaucer's boyhood. The book was translated in 1367 by John Trevisa, chaplain to Lord Berkeley; and is printed in the Rolls Series.

3. FAIR ROSAMUND
(R.S. vol. VIII, p. 53.)

But when King Henry had visited meekly Thomas the martyr's tomb, William the king of Scotland and the two earls of Chester and of Lincoln were taken at Alnwick. This mischief endured two years, and was unnethe ceased, and he accounted the ceasing thereof to his own strength, and not to God's mercy, and he that had imprisoned his wife Eleanor the queen, and was privily a spouse-breaker, liveth now openly in spouse-breach, and is not ashamed to misuse the wench Rosamund. To this fair wench the king made at Woodstock a chamber of wonder craft, wonderly y-made by Daedalus' work, lest the queen should find and take Rosamond: but the wench died soon, and is buried in the chapter-house at Godstowe beside Oxenford with such a writing on her tomb:

Hic jacet in tumba rosa mundi, non rosa munda.
Non redolet, sed olet, quae redolere solet,

that is, Here lieth in tomb the rose of the world, nought a clean rose; it smelleth nought sweet, but it stinketh, that was wont to smell full sweet. This wench had a little coffer, scarcely of two feet long, made by a wonder craft, that is yet y-seen there. Therein it seemeth that giants fight, beasts

5

startle, fowls flee, and fishes move without men's hand-moving. . . .

(viii, 99.) In the year of our Lord God 1192, St Hugh, bishop of Lincoln, making visitations by religious places in his diocese, came to the monastery of Godstowe nigh to Oxenford. Which, entering into the church to make his prayers, saw a tomb in the midst of the choir before the high altar covered with cloths of silk, and lamps and tapers burning about it. And the bishop inquired anon what person was buried there; people present answered, saying that [it was] Rosamond, friend to king Henry II, for whom the king had done many great benefits to their church. Then the bishop commanded that she should be buried out of the church with other people, saying that she was an harlot, lest the religion of Christ decrease, that ill-disposed women may take example by her to avoid the sin of adultery and of lechery.

4. A PLAIN-SPOKEN PATRIARCH

(Ib. p. 69.)

THAT time [A.D. 1185] came Heraclius, patriarch of Jerusalem, into England to king Henry, and prayed him help against the Saracens in the name of all the Christian men of the eastern lands, and proffered him the keys of the holy city and of our Lord's grave, with the king's banner, and letters of Lucius the pope (that counselled and charged him that he should take that journey, and had mind of the oath that he had made); but the king put over his answer before he came to London; and, by the presence of the patriarch and of Baldwin the archbishop, many took the cross to the Holy Land. But Henry answered and said that he might not forsake and leave his lands without ward and keeping, neither set them to be prey to be robbed of Frenchmen; but he would give largely of his to men that would thither go. "King," quoth the patriarch, "it is nought that thou dost; we seek and ask a prince, and not money; nigh every land of the world sendeth us money, but no land sendeth us a prince; therefore

6

we ask a man that needeth money, and not money that needeth a man"; and so the patriarch goeth his way, and his hope is lost; and the king followeth him anon to the sea, for he would with fair words, as he could well, please the patriarch that was grieved. But the patriarch spake to the king and said, "Hitherto thou hast reigned gloriously, but hereafter He will forsake thee That thou hast forsaken. Think and have mind what our Lord hath given thee, and what thou hast given Him again; how thou wert false to the king of France, and slewest St Thomas, and now thou forsakest the defence and protection of Christian men." The king was wroth with these words; the patriarch saw that, and proffered him his head and his neck, and said, "Do by me right as thou didst by Thomas, for me is as lief be slain of thee in England as of Saracens in Syria, for thou art worse than any Saracen." "Though all my men," quoth the king, "were one body and spake with one mouth, they durst not speak to me such words!" "No wonder," quoth the patriarch, "for they love thine, and not thee. This people followeth prey, and not a man." Then the king said, "I may not go out of my lands, for mine own sons would arise against me when I was absent." "No wonder," quoth the patriarch, "for of the devil they come, and to the devil they shall" . . . Also that year [1188] fell strife between the kings of England and of France, and all the money was wasted that was gathered in tithes for the journey in going to Jerusalem; for at the city of Le Mans the king of France and Richard earl of Poitou came against the king of England, and king Henry set the suburbs afire, for a device that his enemies should have no succour therein; but the strength of the wind drove the flame of the fire into the town, and burnt up all the city, and compelled king Henry to go out of the city; and the king in his going from the city spake such words and said: "For that Thou, God, hast taken from me this day the city that I most loved in this world, I shall requite Thee. For after this time I shall take from Thee the thing that should most please Thee in me, that is mine heart."

Roger de Hoveden, R.S. vol. III, p. 35; laws published by Richard I for those who sailed on his crusade. Similar and more elaborate legislation for crusaders may be found in A. Schultz, *Höfisches Leben, etc.* Band II, S. 220 ff.

5. SHIPMAN'S LAW

MEANWHILE [A.D. 1190] King Richard went into Gascony, and laid siege to the castle of William de Chisi and took it, and hanged William himself, the lord of that castle, for that he had robbed pilgrims to Compostella and others that passed over his domains. Then the king went to Chinon in Anjou, where he appointed Gerard bishop of Auch, and Bernard bishop of Bayonne, and Robert de Sablun, and Richard de Camville, and William de Forz of Oleron as leaders and constables over his whole fleet which was to sail for Silves;[1] unto whom he gave a charter in this form following: "Richard by the grace of God king of England, Duke of Normandy and Aquitaine, and Count of Anjou, to all his men who are about to go to Jerusalem by sea, greeting. Know that we, by the common counsel of honourable men, have made these rules of justice here following. Whosoever shall kill a man on board ship, let him be bound to the corpse and cast into the sea; but if he kill him on land, let him be bound to the corpse and buried alive. Whosoever hath been convicted by lawful witnesses of drawing his knife to strike another, or of striking him even to the shedding of blood, let him lose his hand: but if he have struck him with the palm, and shed no blood, let him be thrice dipped in the sea. If any cast upon his fellow either contumely or reviling or God's curse, then, so often as he have reviled him, so many ounces of silver let him pay. If any robber be convicted of theft, let him be shorn like a champion, and boiling pitch be poured over his head, and let the feathers of a feather-bed be shaken over his head that all men may know him; and at the first spot where the ships shall come to land, let him be cast forth. Given at Chinon, under

[1] Near Cape St Vincent, where they were to land on their way to Palestine. The tale of their doings at Lisbon (Hoveden, p. 45) suggests that Richard's laws were scarcely more strictly kept than those of other medieval sovereigns. Schultz (*l.c.*) gives other evidence to the same effect.

our own hand." Moreover the king enjoined in another brief under his own hand, that all his men who were to go by sea should obey the words and precepts of these aforesaid justiciars of his fleet.

The account of the journey itself, though too long for insertion here, is extremely interesting. It may be found in Riley's translation of Hoveden (Bohn, 1853, vol. II, pp. 143 ff.). I subjoin as an illustration of the above ship-laws, some extracts from T. D. Wunderer's account of his voyage on a great Hanse Ship from Riga to Tramünd in 1590 (Fichard, *Frank-furtisches Archiv*, Band II, S. 245). Though the date is late, the main features of the ordinances there described had doubtless been handed down from very early times.

6. LIFE ON A HANSE SHIP

AFTER we had driven half a day under full sail [from Riga], then the Skipper, Bernhard Schultz of Lübeck, called us together according to custom and made the usual speech to us, who were forty-seven all told, to the following purport: "Seeing that we are now at the mercy of God and the elements, each shall henceforth be held equal to his fellows, without respect of persons. And because, on this voyage, we are in jeopardy of sudden tempests, pirates, monsters of the deep and other perils, therefore we cannot navigate the ship without strict government. Wherefore I do hereby most earnestly warn and instantly beseech every man, all and singular, that we hear first of all a reading of God's word from the Scriptures, both text and notes; and then that we approach God steadfastly with prayer and hymn that He may vouchsafe us fair winds and a prosperous journey. After which we will set about to ordain and establish a government by the most prudent according to the customary sea-laws; which office (as sea-law hath it) no man may refuse to undertake, but must rather be ready to exercise it strictly and without respect of persons, even as each desireth that God may deal with him at his last end and at that dreadful day, truly and without flinching, and with all diligence that may be." Then followed the preaching and prayers; after which the aforesaid Skipper, by universal consent, chose as our judge or Reeve a noted citizen of Riga, Dietrich Finger by name: after whom he chose four assessors, firstly Herr Albrecht Veldthusen, a Councillor of Mittau, the capital of Curland; secondly and thirdly me and my fellow-traveller Conrad Dasypodius of Strassburg; and fourthly Elias Kiesel, bailiff of the castle of Candau in Curland. Lastly, to serve these, he chose two Procurators, a Watchmaster, a Scribe, an Executor or Masterman, and a Provost-Marshal with two servants. After which ordinance of our government, then the following sea-laws were read out from the written text, that men might obey them. [A few of these regulations may here be given: *e.g.* IV. Let every man beware of sleeping on his watch; if he be caught sleeping, let him be punished by common sea-law: that is, let him be hauled through under the keel: yet this law must be interpreted with due respect of persons. VI. No man shall cause tumult or disturbance on board, under penalty of the common mariners' punishment; that is, let him be hauled through under the keel, yet with due respect of circumstances and persons. IX. No man shall draw his sword in anger against another on board ship, whether the weapon be long or short, under penalty of sea-law: that is, let the weapon be struck through the offender's hand into the foremast, so that, if he will go free, he must himself draw the sword out of his hand: yet this should be interpreted with due respect to circumstances. X. No man shall promise another to fight or quarrel with him when he is come to land, under penalty of the [land] court when the fact is established. XII. No man shall spill or pour away more beer than he can cover with his foot, under penalty of a cask of beer, or less according to the circumstances.]...When therefore we were come within near half a day's sail of the port of Tramünd, in the territory of Lübeck, then the Keel-master or Skipper made his reckoning according to custom, after which the Bailiff resigned the command which he had held with the following words: "Whatsoever hath passed and befallen on shipboard all this time, each man should forgive to every man his fellow, overlook it, and let it be dead and gone, even as I for my part am glad to do; for, whatsoever doom I and my assessors may have given, all must needs be so dealt and kept for judgment's and justice' sake. Wherefore I beseech all and singular, with regard to all our honest judgments, that each will lay aside such enmity as he may have conceived against another, and swear an oath by salt and bread that he will never more think bitterly of that matter. If however any yet thinketh that any matter have been unwarrantably judged, let him speak out now when we can yet dispute of that matter; whereunto I for my part will give all possible diligence to settle the dispute, and leave no stone unturned. Otherwise, let him appeal to the Portreeve at Tramünd, as hath been the custom from time immemorial unto this day, and claim a judgment before this day's sundown. And may God Almighty hear me now and grant me further good fortune, health, and all well-being in all future voyages; which also I wish from the bottom of my heart to all here present." Then each man took forthwith salt and bread, in token of hearty forgiveness for all that might have befallen.

The following extract, while illustrating that phrase in King Richard's laws, "shorn like a champion," will also throw light on one of the most characteristic customs of the earlier Middle Ages. It is from the book which goes under the name of Britton, a Norman-French legal compilation made from authoritative sources about the year 1290. The translation here quoted is that of the standard edition (F. M. Nichols, Clarendon Press, 1865, vol. I, pp. 104 ff. For further references to this subject, see Extract 40).

7. TRIAL BY BATTLE

IF the defendant cannot abate the appeal, then it shall be in his election, whether he will defend himself by his body or by the country,[1] and so in all felonies prosecuted by private persons, except in special cases, as of women, persons maimed, and others who neither can nor ought to wage battle. And if he says, by his body, and it be in the case of felony at the prosecution of another, then let the matter be examined before battle is joined, whether the cause be trespass or felony; and if trespass, let the appeal be abated by the Justices *ex officio*.

[1] *I.e.* by referring the case to a jury.

But if felony, then let the defendant give security to defend himself, and the appellor security to prove the cause; next let a day be given them to provide themselves with arms, and let the defendant in the meantime remain in prison.

When they appear armed in Court, let the plaintiff repeat his appeal word for word as he did before, and the defendant

CHAMPIONS FIGHTING

From a thirteenth-century encaustic tile found on the site of Chertsey Abbey.
(H. Shaw's *Specimens of Tile Pavements*, pl. XVII.)

defend himself as before; and afterwards let them take each other by the hand, and let the defendant swear first in this manner, and the appellor afterwards as shall be presently more fully set forth. "Hear this, you man whom I hold by the hand, who call yourself John by your name of baptism, that I, Peter, did not in such a year, nor on such a day, nor in such a place, compass or propose the death aforesaid, nor did assent to such felony as you have charged me with, so help me God and the Saints." Afterwards the appellor shall swear thus. "Hear this, you man whom I hold by the hand, who call yourself Peter by your name of baptism, that you are perjured, inasmuch as on such a day, in such a year, and in such a place, you did propose such a treason or such a death as I have said against you in the appeal, so help me God and the Saints."

Then let them both be brought to a place appointed for that purpose, where they must swear thus. "Hear this, ye Justices, that I John (or I Peter) have neither eaten nor drunk anything, nor done or caused to be done for me any other thing, whereby the law of God may be abased, and the law of the devil advanced or exalted." And thus let it be done in all battles in appeals of felony. And let proclamation be immediately made, that no one, except the combatants, whatever thing he see or hear, be so bold as to stir, or cry aloud, whereby the battle may be disturbed; and whosoever disobeys the proclamation shall be imprisoned a year and a day.

Next, let them go to combat, armed without iron and without the slightest armour, their heads uncovered, their hands and feet bare, with two staves tipped with horn of equal length, and each of them a target of four corners, without any other arms, whereby either of them may annoy the other; and if either of them have any other arms concealed about him, and therewith annoy or offer to annoy his adversary, let it be done as shall be mentioned in treating of battle in a plea of land.

If the defendant can defend himself until the stars can be seen in the firmament, and demands judgment whether he ought to combat any longer, our will is, that judgment pass for the defendant, and so in all battles between champions; and in the case of felony the appellor shall be committed to prison. And if the defendant will confess the felony before he is otherwise attainted, and appeal others of consenting to the same, we allow him to be admitted thereto.

And if the defendant be vanquished, let the judgment be this, that he be drawn and hanged, or put to such other painful death as we shall direct, and that all his movable goods be ours, and his heirs disinherited; and his children shall be incapable of ever holding land in our realm. And let not any, unless they would be suspected themselves of the felony, presume to intercede for him; and let the accuser, who without delay shall prosecute such felony with good effect, receive from us a notable reward.

Walther v. der Vogelweide was born of a knightly stock, perhaps in Tyrol. He tells us himself that he learnt his art in Austria. He lived some time at the Court of Vienna, but fell out of favour at the death of his patron in 1198. For the next twenty years or more he took to the profession of a wandering minstrel—perhaps he was the first nobleman who ever did so. In 1203 we find him at the court of the Bishop of Passau, where he receives clothes in the capacity of "singer," just as Chaucer did from other patrons in that of page. At another time he was at the Wartburg, where he knew Wolfram von Eschenbach and perhaps St Elizabeth. He was attached to the Emperors Philip of Swabia, Otto of Brunswick, and Frederick II, from the last of whom he received after many years a fief of his own (1220), and was no longer obliged to live from hand to mouth. The third of the pieces here translated alludes to the Emperor's excommunication in 1227, as he was on the point of starting for his crusade: Walther probably started next year in the Emperor's train, and died soon after his return in 1229. He is certainly one of the greatest lyric poets of the Middle Ages; and his poems are so cheaply procurable, either in the original or in modern German versions, that I subjoin these brief specimens in the hope of tempting more readers to independent study.

8. FLOWERS AND FAIR LADIES

(*So die bluomen uz dem grase dringent*, Lachmann, 45, 37.)

On a May morning at daybreak, when the blossoms crowd forth from the grass like laughing faces in the merry sunshine, and little fowls sing the sweetest lays that their hearts can find, what joy may then be compared to this? It is well half a kingdom of heaven! Shall I confess what this is like? Then I say what hath oftentimes brought still more bliss to mine eyes, and would bring it yet again, could I but see it.

When a noble lady, fair and clean, daintily clad, daintily kempt and tired, moveth for pastime among a crowd of folk, in courtly pride and with a courtly train, looking round her now and again even as the sun standeth in comparison with the stars—then let May bring her best marvels, what hath she among them all so enchanting as this lady's lovely shape, to gaze at whom we turn our backs on all the flowers of spring?

See here then, will ye know the truth?—go we now to May's bridal feast, for the merry month is come with all her charms! Look here on the fields and there on the worshipful ladies, which may outshine the other, and see whether I have not chosen the better part! If, to my woe, any man should bid me choose; if indeed I must leave the one to cleave unto the other, how straight and sheer should be my choice! Lady May, thou mightest be March for me, ere I would leave my lady there!

9. LOVE AND DREAM

(*Nemt, frouwe, disen kranz*, Lachmann, 74, 20.)

"TAKE, Lady, this garland": thus spake I to a maid in fair attire: "then will you grace the dance with these bright flowers in your hair. Had I many jewels of price, by your gracious leave all should be set on your head; mark my troth, that I mean it well.

"Lady, you are so comely clad that I rejoice to give you my coronet, the best of all that I have. Flowers know I many, white and red, that stand hard by on yonder heath: so sweetly they spring, and so sweet the birds sing, there shall we twain pluck them together."[1]

---

[1] *Blumen brechen*, "to pluck flowers" was a time-honoured poetic phrase for courting in the fields: cf. the first two stanzas of Walther's *Nightingale* ("Under der Linden," Lachmann, 39, 11):

> Under the linden
>   Amid the heather,
> There where our place of resting was,
> There might ye finden,
>   Fair together,

She took that I offered her, even as a child that is honoured; her cheeks flushed red, as a rose in a bed of lilies; then her bright eyes were ashamed, yet she sweetly bowed in greeting to me. This was my guerdon; if I had more reward, that I keep to mine own heart.

Methought I had never greater bliss than this content of mind. The blossoms from the trees fell all the while around us on the grass; lo! then must I laugh aloud for joy. Yet, even while I was so merry and so rich in my dream, then the day dawned and I must needs awake!

This hath she wrought in me, that all this summer long I must look well-nigh all maidens in the eyes; thus perchance might I find mine own, and then my care were gone! What if she pace this very dance? Ladies, of your gracious kindness raise the chaplets on your brows.—Alas, would that I could see her under some garland!

10. A WORLD GROWING OLD

(*Ouwe war sint verswunden alliu miniu jar?* Lachmann, 124, 1.)

ALAS! whither then are all my years fled? Hath this life of mine been but a dream, or is it true? That which I ever held for truth, was it naught all this while? then have I slept this many a year, and knew it not myself! Now am I awakened, and all is far and strange, yea though it were heretofore more homely to me than my two hands. Land and folk, where I was nurtured from my childhood up, are become as unknown

> Broken flowers and broken grass
> By the wood-side in a dale;
>   *Tandaradei,*
> Sweetly sang the nightingale.
>
> To our field-meeting
>   Stole I at even;
> There was my true love come before!
> So sweet was his greeting
>   (Lady of heaven!)
> That I am blessed for ever more.
>   Kissed he me? Yea, thousandfold!
>   *Tandaradei,*
> See, my red lips are not yet cold.

to me as were it all a lie! They that were my playfellows are
waxen dull and old; tilled is the fallow field, felled is the forest;
but that the water floweth as it flowed of yore, then methinks
my mishap would be sore indeed. Many a man is slow to
greet me, whom once I knew right well; the world on all
sides is full of ungrace. When now I think on many a joyous
day that is passed from me as the stroke passeth when men
smite the sea, then evermore alas!

Alas! how miserably thrive the young folk, whose minds
once felt no rue! In these days they know naught but care;
alas! why go they thus? Whithersoever I turn in the world,
no man is merry; dancing, singing, are all perished for sorrow;
never saw Christian folk so wretched a year. Mark now how
the wimple sitteth on the noble lady, and how the haughty
knights go clad in village weeds! Unsoft letters are come to
us from Rome; we have license to mourn, but our joy is taken
clean away. That wringeth my heart so sore (for of old we
lived in peace) that I must now choose weeping for my
laughter that was of yore. The very fowls of the air are
troubled by our lamentations; what wonder if I myself am
in despair? Why speak I thus like a fool in my bitter wrath?
Whoso followeth after present bliss hath lost the joys of
heaven for evermore, alas!

Alas! how vainly have we spent ourselves upon the sweets
of earth! I see the bitter gall floating amidst the honey. Fair
is the world to outward show, white and green and red, yet
inwardly she is black of hue, and dismal as death. He whom
she hath seduced, let him look now to his comfort, for great
trespass may be atoned by little penance. Think thereon, ye
knights, for this is your concern, ye who bear glittering helms
and many a hard ring of steel, and stout shields withal and
hallowed blades. Would God that I too were worthy of this
victory! for then would I, poor and needy as I am, earn a rich
reward. I mean not fiefs or barons' gold, but I myself would
bear an everlasting crown, such as any soldier might win with
his good spear. If I might once go this dear journey over sea,
then would I thenceforth sing O joy! and never more Alas!

The so-called *Lanercost Chronicle*, from which these extracts are taken, was not written at the monastery of that name, as earlier antiquaries supposed, but by a Grey Friar, probably of Carlisle. It extends in its original form to 1307, but is partly based on older materials. Like nearly all compilations by the early friars, it is full of picturesque anecdotes and human touches. It was edited for the Maitland Club by Father Stevenson in 1839. A translation of the greater part of it by Sir Herbert Maxwell was printed in the *Scottish Historical Review*; though not always accurate, it is very readable and interesting.

11. A ROYAL NEMESIS
(p. 48, A.D. 1241.)

IN this same year, Alexander [II] King of the Scots had a son, whom he called after his own name, born of his second wife, Marie de Coucy, whom he had brought from beyond the seas. And because, though it be good to keep close the secret of a king, yet it is honourable to publish God's works abroad, therefore I will briefly touch upon a noteworthy event which came to pass at that boy's birth. We know how it is written, "God will not despise the supplication of the fatherless, nor the widow when she poureth out her complaint." This I record because, when the said King Alexander had prepared his departure from Edinburgh Castle, where he had stayed for a while, then as he rode through his borough there met him an old woman, the widow of a certain burgher; who, drawing nigh to the king's bridle, held out to him a handful of wooden tallies,[1] crying, "Behold, my lord king, I who was once rich and am now sunken in poverty have received the whole revenues of my possessions in these tallies, which thy servants have given me again and again for food to thine household, and which I now give up to thee; only beseeching thee to pay me for the one hen wherein I thought myself rich until yester-morn, when thy vassals tore her from me; pay me that alone, for I scorn the rest of my losses." Then the king, flushed with shame, replied, "Lady, they shall be well paid unto thee; bear for the present with this debt and that

---

[1] Two exactly corresponding pieces of wood, for keeping and checking accounts. The buyer kept one, the seller another; at each fresh transaction the two were fitted together so that a single fresh notch with a knife left a corresponding record on each tally.

debt." With that he spurred his horse, but she followed after him with this grievous curse: "The God of heaven," quoth she, "grant thee the same joy in thine only-begotten son, as I had yesterday when I saw my hen with her neck wrung." At which the prince in terror stretched out his open hands to heaven, saying: "O God, I beseech thee for my part that Thou pay no heed to her prayers." The Almighty, to Whom each side had cried for judgment, deferred in His patience to inflict the imprecated curse; yet He who saith *I will repay*, after a long interval of respite, fulfilled it more clearly than daylight.[1] Thus, as saith the Scripture, "Do not the tears run down the widow's cheeks; and is not her cry against him that causeth them to fall."

12. DEATH OF ALEXANDER III

(p. 115.)

IN the course of this year (1285–6) a sudden death removed Alexander King of Scotland, after a reign of 36 years and 9 months. He departed this world on the 19th day of March, on a Monday night, on the eve of St Cuthbert, Bishop and Confessor, the liberties and boundaries of whose see he and his vassals had harried for the last three years....Moreover, all that year and throughout that province a boding word was current among the Scots, that on that day would be the day of judgment; whereat many feared but some scoffed. Moreover, in the December next preceding, under the sign of Capricorn, men heard terrible thunder and saw lightning, which in wise men's judgment foreboded the fall of princes, wherefore he was warned to beware; but all these bodings, with many more, availed not to teach him, so that God punished him through his own sins. For his wont was to spare for neither time nor tempest, for perils of waters nor for rugged cliffs; but by night or day, even as the humour took him, he would sometimes change his guise, and often ride

---

[1] The editor's or scribe's *interpretatum* should obviously be *imprecatum*. The fulfilment is described in the next piece.

with a single companion to visit, in no way of honour, matrons or nuns, maidens or widows. Wherefore, on this same day whereon the judgment hung over him, yet he knew it not, so grievous a tempest burst upon the land that to me and many other men it seemed too bitter to uncover our faces against the north wind, the rain, and the snow. On this day, in his high Maidens' Castle [of Edinburgh], with a great throng of barons, he held a council concerning the answer to be given to the king's messengers of England, who on the third day were to come to Norham, bringing with them Thomas of Galloway, whose deliverance from prison was then demanded by John de Baliol the younger. When dinner-time was come, then the king's brow cleared amid the meat and drink, and he sent a present of fresh lampreys to one of his barons, bidding him through the squire that brought it to feast merrily, and remember that this day was the day of judgment. He, with many thanks, answered jestingly to his lord: "If to-day be the day of judgment, then shall we soon rise with full bellies!" When the long feast was ended, and night began to fall, then neither the foul weather nor the lords' persuasion could withhold the king from hastening forth to the Queen's Ferry, there to visit his new bride, daughter to the Count of Dreux, Yolette by name, whom he had brought shortly before this from beyond the sea, to his own woe and the eternal affliction of the whole country; for she dwelt then at Kinghorn, and (as many tell) before her espousal she had taken the veil beyond the sea in a convent of nuns, but had looked backwards from the plough through feminine fickleness and ambition for the crown. When the king came to the hamlet by the ferry-side, the master of the boats overtook him and warned him of his peril, and would have persuaded him to return. "Fearest thou then," quoth the king, "to stay with me?" "God forbid," quoth he, "for it is just and fitting that I should go with thy father's son to the death." So the king came in black darkness to the town of Inverkennan, with only three squires in his train; when the master of his salt-pans, a married man of that town, knew his voice and cried: "Lord, what do you here at such a time and in this darkness? Oftentimes have I warned you that your night journeys would have an evil issue; now therefore tarry with me, where we will provide you with honourable lodging and all that you need until morning light." "Nay," said the king, and laughed; "we have no need of thy lodging but lend me two of thy servants to go on foot and show us the way." When therefore they had gone some two miles forward, then both these and those lost the way, save only that the horses, by natural instinct, knew the trodden path. While they thus straggled apart, and he last, though the squires followed the right way, yet the king (to speak briefly) fell from his horse into Sisera's sleep, and thus bade farewell to his kingdom.[1] In token whereof we may cite that proverb of Solomon's, "Woe to him that is alone when he falleth, for he hath not another to help him up." He lieth alone at Dunfermline, in a grave on the south side of the presbytery. While therefore we saw the multitude bewailing not only his sudden death but also the destitution of his kingdom, those alone suffered no tears to wet their cheeks who had clung most closely to his friendship and his benefits while yet he lived.

13. WILL OF THE GRISKIN[2]
(p. 51, A.D. 1244.)

ABOUT this time, as I think, there thus grew up in France, from small beginnings, a man of substance and of worthy memory. There lived in Norfolk a simple countryman who had many children, among whom he specially loved a little boy named William, for whom he set aside a pigling and the profits thereof, in order that, grown to manhood, he might provide for himself without burdening his parents, wheresoever Fortune might favour him. The boy followed his father's bidding; and, leaving his fatherland, he hastened to France with naught else in his purse but the profits of that pig; for at home his playfellows were wont to call him the Boy of the Griskin. Now it came to pass, amidst the miseries

---

[1] The text seems a little corrupt here, but the main sense is plain enough. Alexander, as we know from other sources, fell down the cliff and broke his neck.

[2] Little pig.

and evils of those folk, he so advanced himself as to espouse an honourable matron, the widow of a man of some substance; with whom he had wealth and honour and a household of servants. This he did; and, being a man of diligence in all his works, he profited much, and was oftentimes summoned to business councils by the king and his great men. From hence-forward, even as this honest man grew in substance, so did the fickle favour of the people grow with him; and, lest he should find his prosperity as false and perilous as adversity, he caused a most comely chamber to be built and painted within according to his own choice; whereof he committed the key to none save unto his own care, nor suffered any other, not even his wife, to enter therein. It was his wont, whensoever he returned from the courts of the great, forth-with to neglect all other business and enter into this secret chamber, wherein he would stay as long as he desired, and return in melancholy mood to his family. In process of time, as this custom became inveterate, all were amazed and agape to know what this might mean that they saw; wherefore, having taken counsel, they called all his friends together to solicit this wise man for the reason of his so strange behaviour in this chamber. At last, besieged and importuned by their complaints, he unlocked the door and called them all together to see his secret, the monument of his poverty thus set forth. Amid other ornaments of this chamber, he had caused a pigling to be painted and a little boy holding him by a string; above whose heads was written, in the English tongue—

> Willé Gris, Willé Gris,
> Thinche cwat you was, and qwat you es!

Which may be confirmed by that saying of St Gregory: "We can then keep our present state well, when we never neglect to consider what we were."

14. THE ARCHDEACON'S PURSE
(p. 99, A.D. 1276.)

I WILL here insert, for mirth's sake also, a certain piece of evidence which I learned through Lord Robert of Roberstone, knight of the king of Scotland, and which he repeated before many trustworthy witnesses at my instance. That nobleman had a manor in Annandale, in the diocese of Glasgow, that was let out on farm to the peasants; who, being dissolute by reason of their wealth, and waxing wanton after their visits to the tavern, commonly sinned in adultery or incontinence, and thus frequently filled the Archdeacon's purse; for their relapses kept them almost perpetually on his roll. When therefore the lord of the manor demanded the rent due for the lands, they either pleaded their poverty or besought a respite; to whom this kindly and just man said: "Why do ye, more than all my other tenants, fail to pay your yearly rent? If it be too dear, I may lessen it; but if ye cannot till it, return it to me." Then one made answer jeering and laughing aloud, "Nay, my lord, the cause is not as thou sayest; but our frequent incontinence maketh us so poor that it falleth both upon ourselves and upon thee our lord." He therefore made answer: "I make this law among you, that, whosoever shall thus sin in future, he shall quit my manor forthwith." The peasants, terrified at this strict penalty, amended their transgressions, busied themselves with field-labour, and waxed beyond all expectation in wealth, while they decreased from day to day in the Archdeacon's roll. When therefore one day he enquired why he found no man of that manor upon his roll, then they told him what manner of law the lord had made; whereat he was moved to indignation and, meeting the knight on the road, he asked with lofty brow: "Who, my lord Robert, hath constituted thee Archdeacon or Official?" "Nay, no man," quoth the lord. "Yet," replied he, "thou dost exercise such an office, in restraining thy tenants by penal statutes." "Nay," quoth the knight; "for the statute that I have made is of mine own land and not of men's sins; but thou, with thy ransom for sin, hast sucked out the revenues

23

of my farms; and now I see that thou wouldst reck little who should take the souls, if only thou couldst ever fill thy purse." With such words he silenced this exactor of crimes and lover of transgressions.

15. THE SIEGE OF CARLISLE

(p. 230, A.D. 1315.)

Soon afterwards in that same year, on the feast of St Mary Magdalene (July 22), the king of Scotland assembled all his forces and came to Carlisle, where he compassed the city round about and besieged it for ten days, treading all the crops under foot, ravaging the suburbs with the surrounding country, and burning throughout all those parts; moreover he drove a vast spoil of cattle to feed his army, from Allerdale and Coupland and Westmoreland. So on each day of the siege they made an assault against one of the three city gates, and sometimes at all three together, yet never with impunity. For we cast upon them from the wall javelins and arrows and stones, both then and at other times, in such multitude and number that they enquired one of the other, "Do stones increase and multiply, then, within these walls?" Moreover on the fifth day of the siege they set up an engine for casting stones hard by Trinity Church, where their king had pitched his tent; and they threw great stones without intermission against the wall and the Calden gate; yet with all this they did little or no harm to the townsfolk, save only that they slew one man. For we had seven or eight such engines in the city, without reckoning other engines of war, namely, the so-called springalds, for hurling long javelins, and slings on staves for casting stones, which wrought much terror and havoc among the besiegers. So in the meanwhile the Scots set up a great Belfry, like a tower, which far overtopped the town walls; whereupon the city carpenters, upon one tower against which this belfry must have been set if it had been brought up to the wall, built another tower of wood that overtopped that belfry. But the Scottish engine never came

BELFRY AND ASSAULT

From Viollet-le-Duc's *Dict. de l'Architecture*, vol. I, p. 365.

against the wall; for when men dragged it on its wheels over the wet and miry ground, there it stuck fast with its own weight, nor could they draw it forward or harm us. Moreover the Scots had made long ladders, which they had brought with them for scaling the wall in divers places, and a sow for undermining the town wall if possible; but neither ladders nor sow availed them. Again, they made a multitude of fascines of corn and hay to fill the water-moat without the wall towards the east, that they might thus cross it dry-shod; and long wooden bridges that ran on wheels, which they hoped to draw so strongly and swiftly with ropes as to pass that broad moat. Yet, for all the time of this siege, neither could the fascines fill the ditch nor those bridges pass it; but their weight dragged them to the bottom. So on the ninth day, when all their engines were ready, they made a general assault on all the city gates and around the whole wall; manfully they came on, and our townsfolk also defended themselves like men; and likewise again on the morrow. Now the Scots here used that same wile whereby they had taken the castle of Edinburgh; for they caused the greater part of their host to make an assault upon the eastern part of the city, against the Franciscan Friary, that they might draw the defenders thither. Meanwhile the lord James Douglas, a bold and crafty knight, with others of the doughtiest and most active of that army, arrayed themselves on the west against the convents of the Canons and of the Friars Preachers, where the defences were so high and difficult of access that no assault was expected. There they reared long ladders whereby they climbed up; and they had a great host of archers who shot thick and close, that no man might show his head over the wall. Yet, blessed be God! they found such a welcome there that they and their ladders were flung to the earth; at which place and elsewhere around the wall some were slain and some taken and some wounded; yet on the English side, during that whole siege, save only that man of whom we have already spoken, there was but one man smitten with an arrow, and but few were even wounded. So on the eleventh day, to wit on the feast of St Peter *ad vincula*, either because they had tidings of an English host coming to raise the siege, or because they despaired of further success, the Scots retired in confusion at daybreak to their own land, leaving behind all their engines of war aforesaid.

Jacques de Vitry studied at Paris, was ordained priest in 1210, and devoted himself to preaching by the advice of the Blessed Mary of Oignies, whose Life he also wrote. After her death in 1213 he preached the crusade first against the Albigensians and then against the Saracens. In 1214 he was elected Bishop of Acre; here he worked many years with his accustomed zeal, until at last, disheartened by the vices and failures of the crusaders, he resigned in or about 1227. Next year he was made a cardinal, and in 1239 elected Patriarch of Jerusalem; but the Pope was unwilling to spare him. He probably died in 1240. A passage from one of his letters, recording his enthusiasm for the new-born Franciscan Order, may be found in Sabatier's *St François d'Assise*, c. xiii, p. 261. His *Historia Occidentalis* and *Historia Orientalis* describe the age in language even more unfavourable than that of Roger Bacon and others quoted in this book; but the main human interest of his works is contained in the *Exempla*, or stories for the use of preachers, published by Prof. Crane for the Folk-Lore Society in 1890. A good many of these had already appeared anonymously among T. Wright's *Latin Stories*. Prof. Crane's edition, though of very great value, contains a good many misreadings which I have been able to amend by collations procured from the Paris MS. References are to folios of the MS. Lat. 17,509 of the Bibliothèque Nationale, and to pages in Crane's edition.

16. A VOLUNTARY NEBUCHADNEZZAR
(fol. 50, p. 21.)

I HAVE heard of one man who, wishing to do penance, even as he had likened himself to the beasts in sin, so he would make himself like to a beast in his food; wherefore he rose up at dawn and browsed on grass without touching it with his hands; and thus he would oftentimes eat daily. When therefore he had long lived thus, he began to ponder within himself, wondering of what Order of Angels he should be, seeing that he had done so great a penance; until at length it was answered to him through an angel: "By such a life thou hast not deserved to be of the Order of Angels, but rather of the Order of Asses." For, as saith St Bernard: "He who hath not lived as a man shall live as a beast"; so this man fell from discretion into presumption.

17. THE STINGY KNIGHT
(fol. 123, p. 77.)

I HAVE heard how, when a certain covetous knight ate at the court of a certain noble, and asked after dinner for his mantle, which his servant had laid among the other garments, then, seeing that it could not at once be found, he began to revile him before all that stood by, saying: "Son of a ——, bring my mantle forthwith! knowest thou it not?" The servant, offended and moved to indignation, answered in all men's hearing, "Lord, I know it well; I have known it these seven years past; yet I have not yet been able to find it." The other knights hearing this, began to laugh and to scoff at this covetous knight, who was covered with confusion.

18. THE PILGRIMS' PERILS
(fol. 130, p. 130.)

I HAVE heard how certain abominable traitors, having received payment to furnish the pilgrims with victuals even to the port [of their destination], have stocked their ships with but little meat, and then, after a few days' journey, have starved their pilgrims to death and cast them ashore on an island, or (most cruel of all) have sold them as manservants or maidservants to the Saracens. I have known certain sailors bound for the city of Acre who had hired a ship from a man on condition that, if it perished on the sea, they should be bound to pay naught. When therefore they were within a short distance of the haven, without the knowledge of those pilgrims and merchants who were on board, they pierced the hold and entered into a boat while the ship was sinking. All the passengers were drowned; and the sailors, having laden their boats with the money and goods of the pilgrims, put on feigned faces of sadness when they drew near unto the haven. Therefore, having drowned the pilgrims and carried away their wealth, they paid not the hire of the ship, saying that they were not bound thereunto unless the vessel should come safe and sound to haven.

19. THE JEW AND THE BLASPHEMER
(fol. 134, p. 91.)

I HAVE heard that a certain Jew, playing at dice with a Christian and hearing how he blasphemed God when he lost, stopped his ears and rose from the game and fled, leaving his money on the table. For the Jews not only will not blaspheme God, but will not even listen to blasphemers. How wretched are those taverners who, for a little gain, suffer such blasphemous fellows, worse than Jews, to revile God in their houses! Would they not lose all patience and give rein to wrath, if as many injurious words were spoken against their wives as are spoken against the Blessed Virgin and the Saints? If such things were said of their parents or any one of their kinsfolk, as are said of God, they would not suffer it, but would cast the fellows forth from their houses.

20. WEDDING CUSTOMS
(fol. 145, p. 112.)

IN some parts I have seen how, when women came home from the church after a wedding, others threw corn in their faces as they entered their house, crying in the French tongue, *plenté, plenté,* (which is being interpreted *abundance*); yet for all this, before the year was past, they remained poor and needy for the most part, and had no abundance of any goods whatsoever.[1]

21. BROKEN VOWS
(fol. 147, p. 116.)

I HAVE heard how certain folk promise much to God, binding themselves by vows which they afterwards violate to the detriment of their souls, and seeking to mock Him with

---

[1] Compare the Bologna statute of 1289, re-enacted four times within the next seventy years, against those who at weddings threw "snow, grain, paper-cuttings, sawdust, street-sweepings and other impurities" (Frati, *La Vita Privata di Bologna*, p. 50).

deceit. Such were a man and his wife who vowed to God that they would not drink wine save on solemn feast-days or when they had chanced to make a bargain. When therefore they had drunk water for a few days, then the man began to say to his wife: "We cannot abstain altogether to-day; let us make a bargain, that we may drink wine." So he sold his ass to the wife. Next day the wife said to her good man, "Buy back thine ass, and let us drink wine." Thus they bargained daily, that they might drink wine.

This fraud is committed by many. Such was the man who had vowed that he would eat no flesh save when he had guests; wherefore he invited guests for every day whereon men are wont to eat flesh. Such also are certain monks who, being forbidden to eat any flesh save hunted game, set hounds to chase their own home-bred swine through the monastery after the fashion of a hunting-party; and who thus, eating such flesh, fraudulently break their vows.

Collection des poètes français du M.A., *La Chanson du Chevalier du Cygne et de Godefroid de Bouillon*, p. 26. Count Eustace of Boulogne married Ydain or Yde, daughter of the Knight of the Swan; she bore him three sons, Eustace, Godfrey and Baldwin, all of whom, in her extreme devotion, she always suckled at her own breast. Godfrey became Duke of Lorraine and (if he had willed it) King of Jerusalem; Baldwin, again, King of Jerusalem; while Eustace (through a misfortune here recounted) remained a mere Count.

22. A SUCKING-PRINCE

NEVER did Countess Yde, who was so good and fair, suffer that one of her three sons, for any cause whatsoever, should be suckled by waiting-woman or damosel; all three were suckled at her own breast. One day the lady went to hear mass at her chapel, and commended her three sons to one of her maidens. One of the three, awakening, wailed sore and howled; wherefore the maiden called a damosel and bade her suckle the child. Better had it been for her that she had been at Nivelles that day! The Countess came back and called the maiden: "Tell me now wherefore this child hath wetted his chin?" "My lady, he awoke but now; sore and loud were his cries, and I bade a damosel give him of her milk." When the Countess heard this, all her heart shook; for the pain that she had, she fell upon a seat; sore gasped her heart under her breast, and when she would have spoken, she called herself a poor leper![1] Swiftly she flew, all trembling with rage, and caught her child under the arms: the child of tender flesh, she caught him in her hands, her face was black as a coal with the wrath that seethed within.... There on a mighty table she bade them spread out a purple quilt, and hold the child: there she rolled him and caught him by the shoulders, that he delayed not to give up the milk which he had sucked. Yet ever after were his deeds and his renown the less, even to the day of his death. The maiden stood more benumbed than a worm in winter-time: full dearly shall she pay this antic to her lady! nevertheless she fled before the bursting of the storm; not until August was past, and September in its train, only then did she dare to return to court and face the lady Countess. Then this saintly and devout countess laid the child in the place where he should be, and suckled him so long until she had laid him to rest, and all three were covered with her ermine mantle.

[1] *I.e.* looked upon this defilement as hopeless.

"This Romance [of Flamenca]," writes Paul Meyer, "occupies a place by itself in Provençal literature.... It is the creation of a clever man who wished to write a pretty book representing court life in the twelfth century on its most brilliant side. It was a romance of contemporary manners." Later critics, while dating the book rather from the early thirteenth century, have otherwise endorsed Meyer's verdict. Archambaut, Lord of Bourbon, married the good and beautiful Flamenca, against whom a jealous queen soon poisoned his mind. He therefore shut her up in a tower, which she left for moments only to go to church on Sundays and feast-days under the husband's own eye. The most handsome, liberal, learned and adventurous young knight of the day, Guillaume de Nevers, heard of this oppressed lady, to whom he vowed love and deliverance. By a series of ingenious subterfuges he first came to speech with her and then arranged a series of stolen interviews almost under the eyes of the jealous monster; and finally Flamenca was suffered to go free like other ladies, after swearing to her husband on the holy relics the subtly equivocal oath, "that she would keep herself henceforth as surely as he, the husband, had hitherto guarded her." The following passage (ll. 2232 ff.) describes how Guillaume came to stay at Bourbon under pretext of the famous medicinal baths which still exist there; and how, after talk with the host of his inn, Pierre Gui, he managed at last to catch sight of his lady's face at church.

23. THE COURSE OF TRUE LOVE

MEANWHILE came Master Pierre Gui into his room and cried: "Good Sir, I give you good morning and may God give you other good hours! but lo! how early you are arisen! There will be a long hour yet ere mass be sung; men delay it for my lady's sake, who would fain hear it."[1] Then Guillaume fetched a sigh and said: "Fair host, yet let us go straightway to the church and pray there; then will we go forth and

[1] One of the worst misstatements in Abbot Gasquet's *Parish Life in Medieval England* is that on p. 7, "To 'Holy Mother Church' all were the same; and within God's house the tenant, the villein, and the serf stood side by side with the overlord and master." English church synods enact that the great man alone might claim a sitting in church for his own; he alone might sit in the chancel among the clergy; he alone might be buried within the church. For him or his lady the whole parish had often to wait for hours before mass could be said; cf. the two very curious tales in La Tour-Landry (chaps. xxx and xxxi) referred to even in such a well-known book as Cutt's *Parish Priests and Their People*: "I haue herde of a knight & of a lady that in her youthe delited hem to rise late. And so they used longe, tille many tymes that thei loste her masse, and made other of her parisshe to lese it, for the knight was lorde and patron of the chirche, and therfor the preest durst not disobeye hym," etc., etc.

desport ourselves till the bell shall ring for mass." Both went straight to the minster; but the thoughts of their hearts were far apart; for Guillaume had set his thoughts all on love, since he had no other mind; while the host thought of gain and how he would prepare his bath; for he doubted not but that his guest would bathe there on the morrow. Into the minster went Guillaume; and, kneeling before St Clement's altar, he prayed devoutly to God and our Lady St Mary, to St Michael and all his company, and all the Saints, that they would be his good helpers. Then said he three *Paternosters* and a little prayer that a holy hermit had taught him: a little prayer of the seventy-and-two names of God, even as men say it in Hebrew and Latin and Greek.[1] This prayer keepeth a man fresh and hearty in the love of God, that he may do nought but good every day: every man who sayeth it with faith shall find mercy from the Lord God; nor shall he ever come to an evil end if in his heart he trust therein or carry it written about him. When Guillaume had said this prayer, he took a psalter and opened it; a verse he found whereof he was right joyful, the verse, "I have loved, because the Lord will hear the voice of my prayer" [Ps. cxiv, 1. Vulg.]. "God knoweth my heart's desire!" cried he as he shut the book. Then he kept his eyes fixed on the ground; and, ere he left the church, he looked well at the lady's customary seat when she came thither; but little he dreamed how she was kept immured in that church![2] Then said mine host, "Ey, sir! thou knowest to pray many prayers. We have here a rich and holy altar and many glorious relics; this you have doubtless seen well, since you know much of letters." "Host,

---

[1] On this Prof. Meyer notes (p. 316), "This petition still exists. It has been preserved in a collection of prayers often printed since the sixteenth century, both in Latin and French, under the name of Pope Leo III, and has become at last a chap-book.... In this little book, which is still bought by country-folk, the prayer of the seventy-two names of God is preceded by this following rubric: 'Here are the names of Jesus Christ; whosoever shall carry them upon him on a journey, whether by land or sea, shall be preserved from all kinds of dangers and perils, if he say them with faith and devotion.'"

[2] Cf. l. 1426 above. "And there was neither knight nor clerk who could speak with her; for in the minster [Archambaut] made her sit in a dark, dark corner with walls on either side; and in front he had fixed a screen, tall and close, which reached well to her chin."

I know them well, but I am not therefore too lifted up in heart, that I can read my psalter aright, or sing a responsory, or say a lesson from a legendary." "My Lord, you are all the better for that...."

With this they passed over the public square, and went forth into a garden where the nightingale took his disport for the sweet season's sake and for the spring green. Guillaume cast himself down in the cool shade beneath a fair apple-tree in flower. Mine host marked how all his colour was gone, and believed him to be pale with that sickness whereof he had spoken the other day; he prayed fast to God that He might restore his health and grant him his heart's desire. Guillaume heard only the nightingale, and not the host's prayers: for in truth Love bereaveth a man of sight and hearing, and maketh men to take him for a fool when he thinketh to have his best mind. Guillaume had nor sight nor hearing nor sense; with eyes unmoved and open mouth he felt a sweet pain pierce his heart with the song of that nightingale.... At last the gentle bird lowered his voice, and soon left his song when the bells began to ring for mass. "My Lord, it is high time to pray," quoth the host; "let us now go to mass." Guillaume heard him, for his thoughts were fled, and said, "Host, at thy good pleasure; for I would fain be at church ere the mass begin, that the crowd of folk hinder us not." "My Lord, we shall be in good time, and you and I will go into the choir; for I know somewhat of reading and chant, though not too plainly." "Ah, fair Host, may good hap befall thee! wherefore didst thou conceal this from me? For thy love I will sing there with thee, for I know to chant right well."

To the minster went they both, and met neither man nor woman but said to them, "God save thee!" for it is a custom at Eastertide that each man gladly greeteth his fellow. When they were come to the minster they entered together into the choir, where Guillaume could spy unseen through a little hole. There he watched and waited till Flamenca should come in, fully persuaded that he would know her at once.... There he waited with sore beatings of heart; for at each shadow that darkened the portal he thought to see the Lord Archambaut.

THE COURSE OF TRUE LOVE

The people took their places one by one; all were come in,
and the third bell had sounded, when that fierce devil entered,
haggard, staring, and shaggy; had he but borne a boar-spear
in his hand, men might have taken him for those scarecrow
figures that the peasants make with old rags to affright the
wild boars in the mountains. By his side went his spouse, the
fair Flamenca; yet she held her as far as might be from her
husband, for the grief that he made her. Under the portal she
stayed a moment and bent in deep humility; then, for the
first time, did Guillaume de Nevers see her, so far as she might
be seen.... Then he lowered his gaze, for the lady was come
into her closet, and knelt down. The priest sang *Asperges me*;
Guillaume fell in at the *Domine*, and sang the whole versicle
as it had never been sung before in that minster. Then the
priest went out of the choir, and a villein bare the holy water:
to Archambaut he went with his hand raised to sprinkle first.
Then all the chant remained with Guillaume and mine host
his helper; yet this hindered not but that his eyes dwelt still
on the loophole in the closet screen. The chaplain sprinkled
with the hyssop, casting the salt water, as best he could,
straight upon Flamenca's head; who for her part made an
opening right in the midst of her parted hair, that she might
the better receive it. Her skin was white and tender as a
babe's, her hair was fair and radiant; and the sun did her great
courtesy, lighting straight down upon her at that moment
with one of his golden rays. When Guillaume saw this fair
sample of the rich treasure which Love held in store, then his
heart laughed and leapt for joy, and he chanted forth the
Signum salutis.... Then Nicholas, [the little clerk], took a
breviary wherein were psalms, hymns, gospels, prayers,
responses, versicles, and lessons; with which book he gave the
pax[1] to Flamenca. As she kissed it, Guillaume saw her sweet
vermeil mouth through the loophole, though one might have
filled it with one's little finger.... When Nicholas had

[1] All exchanged the kiss of peace at the mass by applying their lips to the same
object in turn—usually an engraved tablet of metal or marble, but here a book.
"It was introduced into England about the middle of the thirteenth century....
But the use was almost extinct [about A.D. 1700] on account of the absurd contentions for precedency to which it gave rise" (Arnold and Addis, *Catholic Dictionary*, s.v. *Pax*).

35

fulfilled his round, then Guillaume thought in his heart how he might get that book.... He hath found a subtle device. "It is good that I teach others in order that I may be taught myself: Clerk, wherewith giveth thou the *pax*? for thou shouldst give it with the Psalter, if it may be." "Yea, lord, so I do, and it is thus that I give it," and showed him the leaf and the place withal. Guillaume needed no more: he fell into prayer and kissed the book more than a thousand times: the whole world seemed his, and his cup of joy was wellnigh full; if only he might have kept his eyes on the page and on the loophole at the same moment, his bliss had been the greater. In these thoughts he dwelt so long, and took such delight in that contemplation, that he heard no word until the priest sang *Ite, missa est*; sore was he then abashed.

A GOOD CANON

Caesarius of Heisterbach was possibly born, and certainly educated, at Cologne, then one of the richest and busiest cities of Europe. After some inward struggles, he was at last converted by the story of the harvester-monks and the Virgin Mary (vol. IV, no. 16); upon which he entered the Cistercian monastery of Heisterbach in the Siebengebirge. In this house, then at the height of its efficiency and influence, he finally became prior and teacher of the novices, for whose special guidance he wrote his de-lightful *Dialogus Miraculorum*, one of the most intimate documents of the Middle Ages. He also wrote a few biographical and chronological treatises, and a book of Homilies. All these were apparently written between 1220 and 1235: the last dated event he mentions occurred in 1233. The *Dialogue* was printed five or six times between 1475 and 1605; the Homilies only once, in 1615. The author's faults are those of his time; his virtues of earnestness and vividness will perhaps be apparent even from these extracts. Father B. Tissier, reprinting him in 1662 in the *Biblio-theca Patrum Cisterciensium*, praises him as just the author to arouse the slumbering embers of strict Cistercian observance, and adds "yet it is lamentable that this authority, who has deserved so excellently of the Church, should now at last, after so many centuries, be called not only fabulous but even erroneous; whereas, if he be attentively read even by a jealous critic, nothing can be found in him strange to Catholic doctrine" (t. II, Preface). The modern view is rather that of Father Karl Unkel: "The almost scrupulous love of truth which Caesarius shows in his anecdotes is well known, but equally so is his great credulousness" (*Annalen des Historischen Vereins f. d. Niederrhein*, Heft 34, 1879, p. 5). The interlocutors in the *Dialogue* are Caesarius himself, and a novice whom he is instructing. I quote by volume and page from Joseph Strange's critical edition (Cologne, 1851).

24. A GOOD CANON

(Vol. I, p. 345.)

ENSFRID, Dean of St Andreas at Cologne, was born in that same bishopric, a simple and upright man and foremost in works of mercy. What his life was before his ordination to the priesthood or what he did in his youth I know not; but that mercifulness grew and increased with him I gather from his later acts. That he was of docile mind and eager to learn was shown by the effect; for even in his boyish years he laid so good a foundation of learning that, as I have heard from his own mouth, he became Master of the Schools as a mere youth, and instructed many both in word and in example, not only to learn but, what is more, to live well. Having been ordained priest, he received the rectory of a church at Siegburg, a good parish that is rich in oblations, wherein he put his learning to effect. The pilgrim remained not without, for his door was open to the wayfarer. He was the father of widows, the consoler of orphans, the snibber of sinners. He nourished many scholars in his house; and, being of a dove-like simplicity, at that season when the cherries were ripe he said to his cellarer: "Good man, give the boys leave to climb the trees, that they may eat of cherries as many as they will and as they can; then thou needest to give them no other food; for there is no other food wherein they take such delight." This he said not as a niggard, but from the abundant kindliness of his heart. When therefore they had done this for some days, and the freedom given to the boys pleased their boyish hearts, the cellarer said to Ensfrid: "Of a truth, my lord, unless these boys eat other food also, they will soon fail": wherefore he straightway suffered himself to be persuaded. After this he was made canon of the church of St Andreas in Cologne; and not long after, for the goodness of his life, he was raised to the Deanery; where, although he was of blameless life and strong in the virtue of chastity, yet was he specially fervent in works of mercy. In the parish of St Paul, which adjoins the church of St Andrew, there was no poor widow whose cottage he knew not, and whom he failed to visit with his alms. So much bread was given from his table to those who begged from door to door; so much money passed from his hands into Christ's treasury—that is, into the hands of the poor—that many who knew his annual revenues marvelled thereat. Now he had a kinsman, Frederick by name, a canon of the same church, who held the office of cellarer; this man was wont oftentimes to rebuke his uncle for his indiscreet liberality, and the uncle in turn blamed him for his too great niggardliness; for they kept house in common, and therefore Frederick was much grieved that the Dean was wont to give secretly to the poor whatsoever he could seize. It came to pass that this Frederick, having many and great swine in virtue of his office, slew them and made them into flitches which he hung in the kitchen to be kept until the time appointed; these the Dean would often-times consider, and, grudging sore that they should hang there, knowing at the same time that he could not or dared not beg any part thereof from his nephew, he contrived a holy fraud, a pious fraud, a fraud worthy of all memory! So often as he knew that no man was in the kitchen, he would steal secretly thither, and sometimes seize the occasion to send the servants forth. Then would he mount the ladder and cut from the flitches on the side next to the wall until all were wasted away almost to the midst; but the forepart he left untouched, that none might mark how the rest had been taken. This he did for many days, distributing the flesh thus cut away to widows, and poor folk, and orphans. In brief, the theft of this household property was at last discovered, the thief was sought and found without delay. The cellarer raged, the Dean held his peace; and when the other complained that he had lost the sustenance of the brethren and the stock of a whole year, the holy man sought to soothe him with such words as he could, saying: "Good kinsman, it is better that thou shouldst suffer some little want than that the poor should die of hunger. The Lord will indeed reward thee." At which words the other was soothed and held his peace. Another time as he went to St Gereon's (methinks, on the feast-day of that martyr,) a poor man followed him with importunate cries; and he, having nought to give him, bade the cellarer who followed him to go on for a little space: then, retiring apart to the corner hard by the church of St Mary, the Blessed Mother of God, where bishops are wont to give indulgences to the people on Palm Sunday, having there no other garment which he could take off, in the sight of the poor man he loosened his breeches and let them fall; and the other, raising them from the ground, went his way rejoicing. The man of God would fain have hidden this virtuous act, but at God's will it was set upon a candlestick as an example to posterity, as I shall here relate. When he was come from St Gereon's and was sitting by the embers, seeing that he raised not up the skirt of his fur cloak to warm himself according to his wont, the aforesaid Frederick said unto him: "Raise your cloak and warm yourself": for it was cold and he was an old man: to which he replied: "There is no need": and Frederick: "Verily I believe that ye have no breeches," for he read this in the shamefaced colour of his countenance. At last he confessed that they had fallen from him, saying no word of his charity. Whereupon his nephew laughed and published the matter abroad. ¶ *Novice.* We read of no such charity in the acts of St Martin; it was a greater thing to give his breeches than cut his cloak in half. ¶ *Monk.* For these and other like deeds some said that they had never read of a man who was so compassionate, so merciful, and so pitiful to the poor.... On a certain solemn festival when the lord Adolf, Dean of the cathedral church and afterwards Archbishop, had invited him to his feast, Ensfrid refused, saying that he had noble guests. So, when mass had been said and the blessed man was hastening homewards, then Gottfried, his fellow-canon and notary of the cathedral deanery (who told me this story himself) looked forth from the window of the upper chamber of the clergy-house and saw many poor following him, whereof some were halt and others blind; and since they could not cross the stepping-stones which there divide the square, he, aged and decrepit as he was, was giving his hand to each in turn. Forthwith the clerk called his master to the window and said: "Behold, lord, these are the noble guests whom our friend the Dean said that he had invited"; and both were no little edified. I myself have seen another like work of his mercy. On the anniversary of the lord Bruno, Archbishop of Cologne, when all the chapters of the conventual churches flocked together to the church of St Pantaleon which this same Bruno had built, after mass had been said for his soul, and the priors as had been ordained were entering the refectory, I know not how many poor folk followed the lord Ensfrid to the very refectory door. When therefore the refectorer would have admitted him and cast out the poor, he was moved with indignation and cried: "I will not enter to-day without them": for, as a most prudent man, he knew that the poor are God's friends and door-keepers of heaven, and he kept well in his memory that counsel of the Son of God: "Make unto you friends of the mammon of iniquity, that when you shall fail they may receive you into everlasting dwellings." Hence one day when he had been set to stand beside the relics and to warn those who came in to give alms for the building of that church whereof he was then custos, he spake to the people in these words: "Good folk, ye see well what noble buildings stand here around you! ye will do well indeed in giving your alms to them, yet ye expend them better and more safely on the poor." This sermon of his was heard by Frederick of blessed memory, our fellow monk, who at that moment entered the church of St Andreas with certain knights, and who afterwards was often wont to repeat it to me.... A certain citizen of Cologne, named Lamprecht, was his familiar friend and near neighbour; who, sitting one day with the aforesaid Gottfried the notary, as they spake together of the lord Ensfrid's almsgivings, said in my hearing: "I will tell you how he treated me. One day he had invited me and my wife to sup with him. We sat down to table with him and waited long in expectation that some meat would be set before us, for nought was there but dry bread; then I, knowing well his ways, called one of the servants and whispered in his ear: "Tell me, good fellow, shall we have anything to eat?" The man answered: "We have nothing; for a goodly repast had been prepared for you, but my master entered the kitchen before the hour of supper and divided among the poor all that we had prepared, in spite of all our cries." Then I smiled and sent the same servant to mine own house, and he brought enough meat to suffice for all our guests. Another day I came into his kitchen and saw I know not how many geese roasting on the spit; then said I in my heart: "Of a truth this Dean nourishes his household well!" but when the geese were roasted he himself came in and cut them down, and dividing them plate by plate, sent them round to the widows and poor even unto the last fragment. Oftentimes geese and hens were sent to him both for his office of Dean and for a personal gift by the many who respected him, knowing his charity; and, because he was most pitiful, therefore whatsoever he would send of them to his brethren or other neighbours, he sent it not alive but dead, that they might eat it forthwith. So great, as I have often said, was his compassion towards the poor that sometimes he did that which seemed scarce just according to the judgment of men. A certain citizen of Cologne, as one of the priests of St Andreas related to me, loved his own wife little and afflicted her often, wherefore she stole much money from him. When therefore her husband accused her and she stoutly denied, then, fearing to be caught by him, she cast the money into the cesspool; after which, grieving at that which she had done, she came to the Dean and told him, under seal of confession, of her theft and its cause; and methinks that the holy man must have persuaded her to bring forth the money to her husband; but she, for that she had denied the deed to him with an oath, dared not do thus, fearing lest he should afflict her all the more on this account. The Dean therefore answered her: "If I may get the money secretly, wilt thou that I give it to the poor?" "Yea," said she, "that is all my desire." Wherefore, a few days afterwards, the Dean said to this citizen: "Wilt thou give me leave to cleanse thy cesspool and take thence whatsoever the Lord shall give me there?" He, knowing the Dean to be a holy man, and thinking moreover that God had revealed something to him, gave him leave. The place was purged, the money was found, and within a few days was spent among the poor by the hands of this man of God. ¶ *Novice.* Herein might some detractor fix his tooth. ¶ *Monk.* Three things would seem to excuse him here from sin: first that this same money, as it was the husband's, so also was it the wife's: secondly, that it was already lost and might not be brought forth on account of the seal of confession: thirdly, that he gave it to the poor. To this may be added lastly, that it was charity which impelled him to the deed; for priests are wont oftentimes to give wives leave that they may take from their covetous and merciless husbands and distribute among the poor. The Dean did one more deed which was yet more disputable. Having nought to eat, he entered the bakery of the brethren, and seeing there the loaves set in order upon a table to be borne away, he asked the baker whose was this or that loaf; and when the man had answered him in each case as the truth was, he bade that the loaves of those whom he knew to be rich should be brought to his home, saying: "They are in abundance, and I have nought to eat." ¶ *Novice.* How should this deed be excused? ¶ *Monk.* Many things are lawful to the saints which are unlawful to such as are no saints, for where the Spirit of the Lord is, there is liberty." Whence the Author saith: "have charity, and do whatsoever thou wilt."....Now when his failing body and his ripe old age warned him that the day of his death was near, lest any earthly possession should burden his poor spirit on its journey to its heavenly home, he sold his house and divided its price—not among his kinsfolk, not among his friends, but with his own hands among Christ's poor; for he knew that his fellow-canons, however faithful to his face, would be less faithful after his death. When, therefore, the man who had bought his house, a certain priest and canon of the same church named Conrad, said unto him: "Lord, I would fain have my house," then Ensfrid answered in all simplicity: "Good Conrad, I am a decrepit old man: my day of death is at hand: wait a little while and ye shall have it. Where wouldest thou have me dwell in the meanwhile?" Conrad, as a good man, made a virtue of necessity and awaited his death in all patience. The blessed man was so pitiful that oftentimes, as he sat in the porch of his church and watched the poor creeping up laden with moss which they had collected in the woods, he himself would buy it, not that it was of any use to him, but that he might free the poor from their labour....One day, passing by the schools and hearing the cries of a certain canon[1] who had committed a grievous fault and was being held by four scholars to be scourged, he rushed into the schools all breathless, and coming up like a lion, brandishing his staff (as I myself saw) against the master of the schools and his fellow-canon, he released the boy from his hand, saying: "What dost thou, tyrant? Thou art set here to teach the scholars, not to slay them." At which word the other was confounded and held his peace. The following story will declare how patient he was. One day as he sat in the church according to his wont, between nones and vespers as I believe, a wretch named Scothus, who was oftentimes drunken and utterly unworthy of the honour of the priesthood, found him alone there, and seizing him by the hood drew out his knife and threatened him, saying: "Give me somewhat, or I will slay thee." By God's providence a certain young and lusty canon came up at that moment and dragged this

---

[1] Boys were frequently promoted to canonries; see vol. 1, nos. 29 and 55.

Scothus roughly from him; then, when he would have beaten him as one whom he judged worthy of death, this meekest of men withheld him, saying: "Be not troubled, brother! beware lest thou hurt him, for he did this in jest." He never returned evil for evil, for the simplicity of a dove reigned in him; but, though he was so exceeding merciful, as I have said, yet he burned with the zeal of justice. One day he met the abbess of the holy Eleven Thousand Virgins: before her went her clerks, wrapped in mantles of grey fur like the nuns; behind went her ladies and maid-servants, filling the air with the sound of their unprofitable words; while the Dean was followed by his poor folk that besought him for alms. Wherefore this righteous man, burning with the zeal of discipline, cried aloud in the hearing of all: "Oh, lady Abbess, it would better befit your profession, it would better adorn your religion, that ye, like I, should be followed not by buffoons but by poor folk!" Whereat she was much ashamed, not presuming to answer so worthy a man. So great was his love of justice that one day when some other spake in his hearing of the evil lives of the clergy, he answered abruptly: "It is all one howsoever they live!" which was as if to say: "A good tree cannot spring from an evil root": for he knew that there were few clergy who had entered by canonical ways: few who were not either blood-clerks (that is, foisted in by their kinsfolk); or jester-clerks (that is, such as had been thrust in by the power of great folks); or simoniacs who had crept in through money or through worldly services.... ¶ *Novice.* How is it that thou tellest no miracle of so holy a man? ¶ *Monk.* Who was greater than John the Baptist? Yet we read not that he worked any miracles, as the Gospel telleth of Judas who betrayed the Lord.[1] Know therefore that to some who now work miracles in Christ's name He will say in the end: "I know you not whence you are: depart from me, all ye workers of iniquity." All miracles are not of the *essence* of holiness, but only *signs* of holiness.

[1] Mark vi, xiii.

25. A SIMPLE SOUL
(*Ib.* p. 357.)

THERE lived in our days, in the church of St Gereon the Martyr in Cologne, a certain canon called Werinbold, of noble race and great wealth of church revenues; yet was he so simple-minded that he could not comprehend the sum-total of anything, except so far as it could be understood from the evenness or oddness of the number. Once upon a time, therefore, having many flitches hanging in his kitchen, and fearing lest any should be stolen from him, he went in and counted them thus: "Here is a flitch, and there is his wife! here is a flitch, and there is his wife!" and so forth. When one of these had been stolen by a wicked servant, then this Werin-bold, entering once more and numbering them as he had done aforetime, found the number odd, and cried out: "I have lost one of my flitches!" to whom his servants answered smiling: "Master, it shall soon be found." So they led him forth; and, taking away another, made the number even. When there-fore he had been brought again into his kitchen and counted them afresh, finding the number even, he said to them with much cheerfulness: "Lo now, masters, I might have held my peace too long!"

When his servants would fain fare sumptuously, they would say to him: "Master, wherefore do ye not care for yourself, for ye are exceeding sick?" He then would answer: "How know ye that, good fellows?" and they: "We see it well in your hairs, for they are swollen." Then, putting him to bed, they would prepare delicate meats as for his infirmity, and make good cheer for themselves. A certain country-fellow, wily and cunning, hearing of his simplicity, feigned to be an hereditary serf of his from ancestor to ancestor, and said: "I cannot suffer, my lord, that your goods should be thus wasted or neglected, for I am your serf. It is meet that I should serve your worship and guard your goods with all faithfulness." In short, all things were committed to him: he then would sit drinking over the fire with the servants by night, when his master had gone to sleep. One night he let a wandering minstrel in, whose merry fiddle awakened the sleeping canon. When, therefore, he arose from his bed, the servant met him and asked: "Where will ye go, lord?" He answered: "I hear an excellent merry tune, but I know not where it is." Then answered the servant: "Return to your bed; it is the monks of Deutz who sing to their organs."[1] . . . ¶ *Novice.* Methinks that this man was rather foolish than simple-minded, for simplicity should not be without prudence. ¶ *Monk.* Prudence consisteth in warding against evil, in which virtue he was not altogether lacking; wherefore by Divine Providence he was made cellarer of the church of St Gereon, whose revenues are many and abundant; and we may say of him as it is written of the Holy Joseph: "Neither knew he any other thing, but the bread which he ate"; nor even that fully; therefore the Lord, who loveth simplicity, fulfilled his defects and blessed everything whereto he put his hand. Yet one day he entered the church-barn and saw many cats running hither and thither among the corn; whereupon he could scarce contain himself until the hour of Chapter. Then, falling at the feet of the Dean, he gave up his keys and begged to be absolved from his office. When therefore the Dean of the brethren said: "Good Master Werinbold, what ails you? why do ye do thus?" he answered: "For I cannot suffer to see the waste of this church." "What waste?" said they: and he: "This day I saw your barn full of cats, who will surely devour your whole store." When they had enquired further of him, even though they told him how cats devour not the store, but rather cleanse it," yet even so they could scarce prevail on him to take back the keys. For they had learned by experience that the Lord blessed them for his simplicity's sake. . . . ¶ *Novice.* Such men would not be chosen for cellarers in our day. ¶ *Monk.* Times are changed, and men are changed with them; yet even in our days it cometh to pass oftentimes that houses of religion profit in worldly things under simple-minded prelates and officials, and fail under wily men trained in the school of the world.

[1] The Rhine separates Cologne from Deutz.

THE CASTLE OF LOVE

Rolandino of Padua was born in 1200, studied at Bologna, and became a renowned notary in his native city. He began his Chronicle in 1260, and read it publicly two years later, with great applause, before the University of Padua. He died in 1276. The following extract is from bk I, chap. xiii (Muratori, *Scriptt. Ital.* vol. VIII, p. 180).

26. THE CASTLE OF LOVE

In the year 1214 Albizzo da Fiore was Podesta of Padua, a prudent and discreet man, courteous, gentle, and kindly; who, though in his government he was wise, lordly, and astute, yet loved mirth and solace. In the days of his office they ordained at Treviso a Court of Solace and Mirth, whereunto many of Padua were called, both knights and footmen. Moreover, some dozen of the noblest and fairest ladies, and the fittest for such mirth that could be found in Padua, went by invitation to grace that Court. Now the Court, or festivity, was thus ordered. A fantastic castle was built and garrisoned with dames and damsels and their waiting-women, who without help of man defended it with all possible prudence. Now this castle was fortified on all sides with skins of vair and sable, sendals, purple cloths, samites, precious tissues, scarlet, brocade of Bagdad, and ermine. What shall I say of the golden coronets studded with chrysolites and jacinths, topaz and emeralds, pearls and pointed headgear, and all manner of adornments wherewith the ladies defended their heads from the assaults of the beleaguerers? For the castle itself must needs be assaulted; and the arms and engines wherewith men fought against it were apples and dates and muscat-nuts, tarts and pears and quinces, roses and lilies and violets, and vases of balsam or ambergris or rosewater, amber, camphor, cardamums, cinnamon, cloves, pomegranates, and all manner of flowers or spices that are fragrant to smell or fair to see. Moreover, many men came from Venice to this festival, and many ladies to pay honour to that Court; and these Venetians, bearing the fair banner of St Mark, fought with much skill and delight. Yet much evil may spring sometimes from good beginnings; for, while the Venetians strove in sport with the Paduans, contending who should first press into the castle gate, then discord arose on either side; and (would that it had never been!) a certain unwise Venetian who bare the banner of St Mark made an assault upon the Paduans with fierce and

A CASTLE OF LOVE

From a carved ivory casket of the thirteenth century
(A. Schultz, *Höfisches Leben*, Band 1, S. 449).

wrathful mien; which when the Paduans saw, some of them waxed wroth in turn and laid violent hands on that banner, wherefrom they tore a certain portion; which again provoked the Venetians to sore wrath and indignation. So the Court or pastime was forthwith broken up at the bidding of the other stewards of the court and of the lord Paolo da Sermedaula, a discreet Paduan citizen of great renown who was then King of the Knights of that court, and to whom with the other stewards it had been granted, for honour's sake, that they should have governance and judgment over ladies and knights and the whole Court. Of this festival therefore we might say in the words of the poet, "The sport begat wild strife and wrath; wrath begat fierce enmities and fatal war." For in process of time the enmity between Paduans and Venetians waxed so sore that all commerce of trade was forbidden on either side, and the confines were guarded lest anything should be brought from one land to the other: then men practised robberies and violence, so that discord grew afresh, and wars, and deadly enmity.

Matthew Paris, monk of St Albans and Historiographer Royal to Henry III, is unquestionably the greatest of the English medieval chroniclers, and has few rivals in Europe during this period. He was a man of many and various accomplishments—diplomatist, mathematician, poet, theologian, and artist, though the best authorities ascribe to other hands nearly all the beautiful drawings which illustrate the MSS. of his works. Far more extracts would have been given here, but that a complete translation of his Chronicle, uninspired but otherwise satisfactory, has been published in Bohn's Antiquarian Library. He died in or about the year 1259.

27: AN OXFORD BRAWL

In this year [1238] the pope's legate came to Oxford and was received as was fitting with the highest honours; he was lodged in the house of the canons, that is, the Abbey of Oseney. Now the clerks of the University sent him before dinner-time an honourable present of meat and drink: and after dinner, they came to his lodging to salute him and pay him a visit of respect. But when they came to his lodging, a certain Italian doorkeeper, with most unbecoming and deplorable levity, holding the door just ajar, and raising his voice as these Romans are wont to do, cried: "What seek

ye here?" To which the clerks replied: "We seek the lord
legate, for we would fain salute him"; believing naturally
that they should receive honour in return for honour. But
the porter railed at them, refusing rudely, and with proud and
evil words, to admit any one. The clerks, seeing this, forced
their way in by an impetuous rush. Then the Romans, wishing
to drive them back, began to smite them with rod and with
fist; and while these contending parties exchanged abuse and
blows, it fell out that a certain poor Irish chaplain was standing
at the kitchen door, begging importunately enough, in God's
name, for a morsel of food, like a poor half-starved wretch
that he was. Now the legate, to guard against poison, which
he feared greatly, had appointed his own brother, as one
whom he could trust, to the post of chief cook; which man
now hearing the poor chaplain, yet in his wrath not waiting
to hear him to the end, cast into his face hot water from the
caldron in which fat flesh was seething. At this outrage, a
certain clerk from the Welsh marches cried aloud: "For
shame, why endure we thus far?" and, drawing the bow
which he bare (for, as the tumult waxed hotter, some of the
clerks had caught up such arms as lay to hand) he smote the
cook (whom the clerks called in jest Nabuzardan, that is,
the chief cook)[1] with an arrow through the body. The man
sank dead to the ground, and a tumult arose. The legate,
dismayed, caught up his canonical cope and fled to the church
tower, locking all the doors behind him.... The infuriated
clerks ceased not to seek him even in the secret recesses of the
private chambers, shouting as they went: "Where is that
usurer, that simoniac, robber of revenues and insatiate of
money, who, perverting our king and subverting our kingdom,
plunders us to fill strangers' coffers?" While the fugitive
legate, in his hiding-place, heard still the shouts of such as
sought him, then he said within himself in the words of the
poet: "When madness hath its course, yield to the course of
madness": and, bearing all in patience, he became as a man
that heareth not, and that hath no reproofs in his mouth....
So when, as we have said, he had with difficulty crossed the
river with few followers, since the ferry was small and the

---

[1] 2 Kings xxv, 8; but both A.V. and Douay translate this as a military office.

rest of his men hid in the abbey, then came he breathless and troubled to the king's presence, and set forth all things in order as they had happened both to the king and those that sat with him, with tears and sobs that interrupted his speech, complaining most bitterly of those things. The king was amazed; and, moved to great pity by his lamentable speech, he sent Earl de Warenne with a troop of armed men to Oxford to rescue the Romans from their hiding-places, and to arrest the scholars, among whom Master Odo, Doctor of Laws, was truculently seized and cast ignominiously into chains, with thirty others, in the castle-dungeons of Wallingford, which is hard by Oxford. Meanwhile the legate, having broken the snare and escaped, called together certain bishops and laid Oxford under an interdict, and excommunicated all those who had consented to so enormous a misdeed. Afterwards these scholars were carried to London in tumbrils, like robbers, at the legate's command, where again they were cast into prison and bonds and strict guard, and despoiled of their revenues, and smitten with excommunication. The legate, though his purpose had been to ride northwards, turned now and came back to London, and scarce dared to dwell in the royal hostel of the bishop of Durham, where he was commonly lodged. The king, for his part, sent word to London that the mayor and all the citizens should keep that legate by a sure and armed watch, as the apple of their eye. Meanwhile the legate, in virtue of his authority from the Pope, commanded straitly that the archbishop of York and all the bishops of England should assemble in London to treat in common of the perilous state of the church and clergy on the 17th of May; on which day they came together, and the bishops sought earnestly how they might safeguard the clerical status of the University as scarce less precious than the church itself; to whom the legate consented, saving always the honour of the Roman church, lest it should be said to his dishonour that he who had come to reform the clergy and church was rather deforming them. At length the bishops and all the clergy present pleaded that the riot had been begun by his own household, and that the scholars had at last been worsted in the struggle. "Already," said they, "many of them are cast into prison at your will; and the rest, obeying your commands, are ready humbly to submit in any place not more than three days' journey from Oxford. Ye should therefore lean to mercy at the petition of so many and so grave men. At length it was agreed that the legate should forgive them on these terms following: that all the scholars there assembled, attended by the bishops on foot, should go themselves on foot from St Paul's Cathedral, which was about a mile distant from the legate's lodging: then, as soon as they came to the house of the bishop of Carlisle, from that spot onward they should advance even to the legate's lodging without their copes and mantles, ungirt and barefooted, begging humbly for pardon, whereupon they should have pardon and mercy: and thus it was done.

From a thirteenth century MS. printed in *Reliquiae Antiquae*, vol. 1, p. 162.

28. A RHYME OF FAIR LADIES

Ici commence la geste des dames.

WHAT shall we say of the ladies when they come to feasts? Each marks well the other's head; they wear bosses like horned beasts, and if any have no horns, she is a laughing stock for the rest. Their arms go merrily when they come into the room; they display their kerchiefs of silk and cambric, set on their buttons of coral and amber, and cease not their babble so long as they are in the bower. There they send for brewis[1] and sit down to dine; they put aside their wimples to open their mouths; if a wanton squire would enter at that moment, he could not well fail of privy mockery. Two nimble valets have their hands full with serving all these ladies, each to her own fancy: the one is busy fetching their meats from the kitchen, and the other drawing good wine from the buttery. When therefore they have dined at their good leisure, then they herd together to babble in secret; one tickles the other's heart, if by chance she may entice some secret from thence. Then, when dinner-hour is come, they descend

[1] Pottage.

the steps and trip daintily into the hall hand in hand; then doth a man see so many of the fair creatures together, that he may not pass the day without sighing for them! But when they are set down to meat, they touch no morsel of all that is spread before them; right coyly they sit there and show their faces; she whom men most gaze upon is she who bears away the prize. When therefore they have shown all that is in front, then they find some occasion to sweep the bench-backs, that men may see the costly workmanship on their backs, which was hidden in front. When they arise from table (I say not from meat, for they have eaten but little and yet have well dined) then go they to their bower to entertain each other with subtleties of needlework whereof they love to talk; then comes up the frilled work and the open-work, the German and the Saracen work, the pinched work, the scalloped and the wool-work, the perroun[1] and the melice and the diaper-work, the rod-work, and the peynet and the gernettée; nor is the double samite forgotten, nor do they fail to handle again and again the redener-work. She who knows most of these things shall be their lecturess, to whom the rest hearken without sluggardy; none sleeps here as they do at mass, for all are cheerful champions in these lists of vanity. Then go they homewards, back from the feast; and forthwith they put away their sleek and comely heads; she who was even now so fresh, becomes so restive that the merchant repents the day when he bought this beast. Then they play the folly that costs so dear; for, when they are bidden again to some feast, then for a long while before they are busy unravelling their wreaths and plaited tresses, to make all new again. Thus all their heraldry is changed, both field and device: here they put beads where spangles were before, they cut up a lion and make thereof a soaring eagle, or pare a swan into the form of a hare couchant. But, however well their attire be fashioned, when the feast is come it pleases them nought; so great is their envy now and so high grows their pride, that the bailiff's daughter counterfeits the lady.

Ici finit la geste des dames.

[1] Several of these Anglo-Norman terms of millinery are difficult to identify nowadays.

St Douceline, born about 1214 of a rich merchant family at Digne in Provence, was sister to the celebrated Franciscan preacher Hugues de Digne; for whom see Joinville (§ 657 ff.), Miss A. Macdonell's *Sons of Francis*, and Salimbene's chronicle. At the age of twenty-six, she founded at Marseilles, and under the direction of the Franciscans, a house of Béguines which was spared when Clement V and John XXII abolished the majority of such houses, and which only perished of inanition in 1407. Douceline died 1 September, 1274; her worship began from that moment among the people; an office was composed for her day, the tomb became a great resort of pilgrims; and (like many other saints) she enjoyed every honour but that of papal canonization. Her Life, published with a translation by Abbé Albanès in 1879, was written in Provençal probably by Douceline's disciple and friend Philippine de Porcellet, sister to the only Frenchman whose life was spared in the Sicilian Vespers.

29. SAINT DOUCELINE
(Pp. 10, 50, 73, 80, 56, 186, 82, 196.)

[EVEN while she was yet in the world] she wore in secret a shirt of pigskin, hard and rough, which galled her to the quick, so that she was oftentimes unable to remove it; and when it was taken off it left her body all torn and covered with sores. It befell one day that this shirt was so ingrown into her flesh as to defy all her efforts to tear it away; whereupon she was fain to call her handmaid, in whom she put her trust, and who drew off the shirt by main force, tearing her flesh with the hide. She was wont to gird her waist so straitly with a knotted cord, that worms would oftentimes breed where the knots entered into her flesh. Moreover, she wore an iron hoop night and day...over which she showed fair and choice garments, as though she loved gay stuffs. She lay, for penance' sake, on a little straw in the corner of her room; and, lest she should rest in sleep, she bound a cord above her bed with one end, and with the other round her own waist; so that, whensoever she stirred, the cord would drag and awake her. Then would she rise forthwith to say her matins with all devotion, and to read....Such then was her life so long as she lived in the world....

[During her life as a Béguine] she ordained the avoidance not only of all familiarity with men, but also of all speech and interchange of glances; and this she demanded strictly not only from her spiritual daughters but of all who would live under her direction. For herself, she knew no man's face; and if she saw one of her sisterhood raise her head to look upon any man, even though he were a near relation, then she would rebuke her sharply, and chastise her with severity. It befell one day that a girl of the house, who was but seven years old, had looked upon some men who were there at work. When the holy mother knew this, she beat her so shrewdly that the blood ran down her ribs, saying meanwhile that she would sacrifice her to God. . . .

She could not hear speak of God or St Francis, or the Saints, but that she fell forthwith into a trance. Oftentimes she was caught up into so high contemplation, that she remained rapt the whole day long; in which state she felt things beyond all human sense, knowing and perceiving naught of what was done around her. This was oftentimes proved, and in manifold ways, by all manner of persons who, seeing her thus ravished, thrust or drew her violently, and even did her much harm, yet without being able to make her stir. Sometimes she was raised up in the air, leaning on nothing nor touching the earth with her feet, save with her two big toes alone; and she was raised so high, held up in the air by the virtue of her marvellous trance, that there was a whole handsbreadth betwixt her and the ground; so that, while she stayed thus, we oftentimes kissed the soles of her feet. . . . The first time that king Charles [of Anjou] saw her thus ravished, he desired to prove the truth (and he was then but Count of Provence, and thus he proved her): he let men bring much molten lead and cast it boiling upon her bare feet, under his own eyes; and she felt it not. Wherefore the king felt such love towards her that he made her godmother to a child of his. Nevertheless at her awakening she felt great pain in her feet, and anguish that might scarce be endured. . . .

When men brought her presents of living fowls, then she would not suffer them to be killed, but would disport herself a space with them, speaking meanwhile of our Lord Who made them; then her mind would rise to God and she would let them go, saying, "Praise now the Lord Who created thee!" . . . As she sat at meat, if anyone brought her a flower, a bird, a fruit, or any other thing that gave her pleasure, then she fell straightway into an ecstasy, and was caught up to Him Who had made these fair creatures.... When one read before her at meat, if some devout word came in the lesson, she was ravished forthwith even as she sat at table, and could eat no more. If she heard an air which aroused her devotion, or pleased her, then she was forthwith drawn to her Lord; so that she could at last support no sweet sound, and scarce any song, not even the singing of birds, but that she was rapt beside herself. One day she heard a lonely sparrow sing, whereupon she said to her companions, "How lonely is the song of that bird!" and in the twinkling of an eye she was in an ecstasy, drawn up to God by the bird's voice....

On the day after her death, the body was removed to the Franciscan church for burial.

The whole people flocked together and rushed upon the sacred body with incredible ardour, so that the guards could by no means keep them at arm's length. Before the procession had reached the church, three tunics had been cast upon her, one after the other, for each in turn was cut into pieces: moreover, one of the Friars having spread his frock over the corpse, this was forthwith cut piecemeal by the people. Thrice, on the way, was the cloth renewed that covered her; for men left nought of that which was laid upon her, but all was torn into a thousand shreds. The soldiers, who did all they might to defend her with swords and maces, could scarce hinder the people from cutting her body itself to pieces, in their excess of devotion.[1] We had thus all the pains in the world to bring her holy body decently to the church; and it was the chief men of the town who, out of respect, desired to carry the bier.

[1] When St Elizabeth of Hungary was carried to her grave, the people did actually cut her flesh for relics. "Quaedam autem aures illius truncabant; etiam summitatem mamillarum ejus quidam praecidebant," etc. (I. B. Mencken, *Scriptores*, vol. II, col. 2032).

Berthold von Regensburg, or of Ratisbon, was born about 1220 of a well-to-do citizen family. He joined the Franciscans while still a youth, and became the favourite pupil of David of Augsburg, whose writings were often attributed in the Middle Ages to St Bonaventura. He was already famous as a preacher in 1250; until his death in 1272 he tramped from village to village, like a Whitefield or a Wesley, through Bavaria, Rhineland, Switzerland, Swabia, Austria, Moravia, Bohemia, Silesia, Thuringia and Franconia. His fame spread all over Europe; he is enthusiastically extolled in the chronicles of Salimbene and the XXIV Generals; and Roger Bacon, speaking of contemporary preaching in words which do not err on the side of compliment, expressly excepts Berthold as one who "alone maketh more excellent profit in preaching than almost all the other Friars of either Order" (*Opp. Inedd.* R.S. p. 310). A thick volume of Berthold's sermons, translated into modern German, is in its third edition as a book of living theology (Regensburg, Manz, 1873). The text here used is that of Franz Pfeiffer (2 vols. Vienna, 1862). In the first extract, I put together in an abbreviated form what Berthold says on the same subject in three different sermons. The abrupt changes from *thou* to *ye* are in the original.

30. TRICKS OF TRADE
(Band 1, S. 146, 285, 478.)

THE first are ye that work in clothing, silks, or wool or fur, shoes or gloves or girdles. Men can in no wise dispense with you; men must needs have clothing, therefore should ye so serve them as to do your work truly; not to steal half the cloth, or to use other guile, mixing hair with your wool or stretching it out longer, whereby a man thinketh to have gotten good cloth, yet thou hast stretched it to be longer that it should be, and makest a good cloth into useless stuff. Nowadays no man can find a good hat for thy falsehood; the rain will pour down through the brim into his bosom. Even such deceit is there in shoes, in furs, in curriers' work; one man sells an old skin for a new, and how manifold are your deceits no man knoweth so well as thou and thy master the devil. Why should I come here to teach thee frauds? Thou knowest enough thyself.

The second folk are all such as work with iron tools, goldsmiths, penny-smiths, and other smiths, and carpenters or blacksmiths, and all manner of men that smite, and stone-masons and turners, and all such as use handicrafts with iron.

Such should all be true and trustworthy in their office, whether they work by the day or the piece, as many carpenters and masons do. When they labour by the day, they should not stand all the more idle that they may multiply the days at their work. If thou labourest by the piece, then thou shouldest not hasten too soon therefrom, that thou mayest be rid of the work as quickly as possible, and that the house may fall down in a year or two; thou shouldest work at it truly, even as it were thine own. Thou smith, thou wilt shoe a steed with a shoe that is naught; and the beast will go perchance scarce a mile thereon when it is already broken, and the horse may go lame, or a man be taken prisoner or lose his life. Thou art a devil and an apostate; thou must go to the apostate angels. They fell not from one Order only, but from all ten Orders; and so fall many thousand from these nine Orders. The tenth is utterly fallen beyond recall; I bar no man from contrition and repentance, but, otherwise, such as beat out the long knives wherewith men slay their fellowmen, such may use deceit or not, may sell dear or cheap as they will, yet for their soul there is no help.

The third are such as are busied with trade; we cannot do without them. They bring from one kingdom to another what is good cheap there, and whatsoever is good cheap beyond the sea they bring to this town, and whatsoever is good cheap here they carry over the sea. Thus some bring us from Hungary, others from France; some on ships, some on waggons; driving beasts or bearing packs. Howsoever that be, they all follow the same office. Thou, trader, shouldst trust God that He will find thee a livelihood with true winnings, for so much hath He promised thee with His divine mouth. Yet now thou swearest so loudly how good thy wares are, and what profit thou givest the buyer thereby; more than ten or thirty times takest thou the names of all the saints in vain—God and all His saints, for wares scarce worth five shillings! That which is worth five shillings thou sellest, maybe, sixpence higher than if thou hadst not been a blasphemer of our Lord, for thou swearest loud and boldly: "I have been already offered far more for these wares": and that is a lie, and so often as thou swearest by God and His saints, so often hast thou

broken one of the Ten Commandments; that is a great mortal
sin, whereof thou committest perchance ten or more at one
little bargain. Now see how many those sins become ere a
year is past, and how many in ten years! And all those sins
together thou couldst well have forborne, for many men are
so prudent of evil that, the more thou swearest, the less they
are willing to buy from thee; and thy worldly profit is small
thereby, while all the time thou damnest away thine own
salvation; for he goeth oftentimes away without buying, howsoever thou mayest have sworn to him. And if thou wilt buy
anything from simple folk, thou turnest all thy mind to see
how thou mayest get it from him without money, and weavest
many lies before his face; and thou biddest thy partner go to
the fair also, and goest then a while away and sayest to thy
partner what thou wilt give the man for his wares, and
biddest him come and offer less. Then the simple country-
fellow is affrighted, and will gladly see thee come back; so
thou gettest it untruly from him, and swearest all the while:
"Of a truth," thou sayest, "by all the saints, no man will give
thee so much for these as I!" yet another would have given
more. If thou wouldst keep thyself free from mortal sin in
trade, see that thou swear not. Thou shouldst say: "If thou
wilt not buy it, perchance another will": and should thus sell
honestly without lie or deceit. Thus should a man keep himself in trade; for many thousand souls are damned thereby,
seeing that there is so much fraud and falsehood and blasphemy
that no man can tell it. Ye yourselves know best what lies
and frauds are busy in your trade!

The fourth are such as sell meat and drink, which no man
can disregard. Wherefore it is all the more needful that thou
shouldst be true and honest therein; for other deceit dealeth
only with earthly goods, but this deceit with a man's body,
which many would not give for all the goods in the world.
If thou offerest measly or rotten flesh that thou hast kept so
long until it be corrupt, then art thou guilty perchance of one
man's life, perchance of ten. Or if thou offerest flesh that was
unwholesome before the slaughter, or unripe of age, which
thou knowest well and yet givest it for sale, so that folk eat
it into their clean souls which are so dear a treasure to

Almighty God, then dost thou corrupt the noble treasure which God hath buried in every man; thou art guilty of the blood of these folk. The same say I to him who selleth fish. Thou keepest thy fish captive in water until Friday come, then they are corrupt, and a man eateth his death by them, or some great sickness. So are certain innkeepers and cooks in the town, who keep their sodden flesh too long, whereof a guest eateth and falleth sick thereafter for his life long. So also do certain others betray folk with corrupt wine or mouldy beer, or unsodden mead, or give false measure, or mix water with the wine. Certain others, again, bake rotten corn to bread; whereby a man may lightly eat his own death: and they salt their bread, which is most unwholesome. We read not that salt is so unwholesome and harmful in any other food as in bread: and, the better it is salted, the nearer to great sickness or death.

The fifth folk are such as till the earth for wine or corn. Such should live truly towards their lords and towards their fellows, and among each other; not plough one over the other's landmark, nor trespass nor reap beyond the mark, nor feed their cattle to another's harm, nor work any other deceit, one on the other, nor betray their fellows to the lord. Fie, traitor! untrue man! Where sittest thou before mine eyes, thou Chusi, thou Achithophel? And thou shouldst be true to thy lord; yet thou dost thy service so sparingly and so slothfully and with such constraint! and, when he chideth thee, then dost thou leave him and flee to some other master. Sometimes the lords also are guilty here. Ye lords, ye deal sometimes so ill with your poor folk, and can never tax them too high; ye would fain ever tax them higher and higher. It is far better for you that ye should take small taxes every year, and take these all the more straitly. Ye cannot till the land yourselves, therefore should ye so deal with your folk that they gladly serve you; and it is their duty too to serve you truly and live truly one with the other and sell truly among themselves.— Thou boor, thou bringest to the town a load of wood that is all full of crooked billets beneath; so sellest thou air for wood! and the hay thou layest so cunningly on the waggon that no man can profit thereby; thou art a right false deceiver. Moreover, thou layest fine corn at the top of the sack, and the evil corn beneath; and all thy work is spoiled with deceit and hate and envy.

The sixth folk are all that deal with medicine, and these must take great heed against untruth, for in that office standeth no less at stake than body and soul. He who is no good master of that art, let him in no wise undertake it, or folks' blood will be on his head, the blood of all men to whom he giveth his medicines at a venture. Yet such as are not learned and understand nothing—nay not even to deal with a wound —such men presume to possess and exercise the inward art, and must needs give drinks to folk. Take heed, thou doctor, and keep thyself from this as thou lovest the kingdom of heaven. For thou hast not the right knowledge that a man should have; thou wert as easily hit upon the wrong as upon the right, for even learned masters have enough to do here. —"O, Brother Berthold, four times already have I had all success!" Lo! that was but a blow at a venture. Therefore if thou wilt not let this matter go and study further in the inward art, then the rulers of this world should forbid it thee on pain of curse and banishment. We have murderers enough without thee, to slay honest folk. Deal with thy wounds for the present, and practise the rest until thou be past master. Whether they be children or old folk, thou hast much need of good art before thou canst well cut them for the stone....

Almighty God send in His Grace that these nine Orders be kept safe, for the tenth Order is utterly fallen from us and become apostate. These are buffoons, fiddlers, and timbrelplayers, and all such folk, whatsoever their name be, that sell their honour for money. Such should have made up the tenth Order; but now they are apostate from us through their falsehood. For such a man speaketh to another the best words that he can before his face, and when his back is turned he speaketh of him all evil that he can or may; and blameth full many a man who is upright before God and the world, and praiseth another who liveth to God's harm and the world's. For such men have turned their whole lives only to sins and shame. They blush not for any sin or shame; yea, thou buffoon, whatsoever the devil is ashamed to speak, that speakest thou; and all that the devil may pour into thee thou lettest fall from thy mouth. Alas, that ever Holy Baptism came upon thee, since thou hast denied thy Baptism and thy Christendom! And all that men give to thee they give sinfully, and must answer for it to God at the Last Day. If there be such here, forth with him!

So are some men deceivers and liars like the craftsmen. The shoemaker saith: "See, these are two most excellent soles"; and he hath burned them before the fire, and lieth and cheateth thee of thy money. And the baker floods his dough with yeast, so that thou, who dreamest to have bought bread, thou hast bought mere air for bread. And the huxter pours beer sometimes, or water, into his oil; and the butcher will sell calves' flesh at times, saying: "It is three weeks old": and it is scarce a week old.... Ye fishers, ye must catch fish with manifold devices; and these fish betoken the poor folk; for the fish is a very poor and naked beast; it is ever cold, and liveth ever in the water, and is naked and cold and bare of all graces. So are also the poor folk; they, too, are helpless. Wherefore the devils have set the bait for them that is called untruth, because they are poor and helpless; with no bait could the devil have taken so many of them as with this. Because the fishes are poor and naked, therefore they devour one another in the water; so do also poor folk; because they are helpless, therefore have they divers wiles and invent many deceits. When such a man would sell anything, he doth it untruly, lying and deceiving and stealing. But the poor naked folk that are called menservants and maidservants and that serve your needs, such will steal your salt and your bacon, your meal and your corn. Thou servant, thou stealest eggs and cheese, thou stealest bread; if thou canst not steal a whole loaf thou stealest the fragments and the half loaves and the half joints of flesh! And those too are false to whom thou bringest thy thefts, for if they took it not thou wouldst have left it alone. Thus many a man betrayeth another for his life or his possessions; but none are so false as the countryfolk among each other, who are so untrue that for envy and hatred they can scarce look upon one another. One will drive another's cattle to his harm and damage, and another will buy his fellow-peasant out of his farm, all from untruth.

31. WOMEN'S DRESS

(*Ib.* S. 408 abbreviated; the description of ladies' dresses is completed from
Band I, S. 253, 397, and Band II, S. 242.)

I AM come here to speak of these words, how you should beware of these snares of the devil, for the holy saint saw so many thereof that he said: "Alas, Lord! is there any who may avoid all these snares?" He saw well that the whole of the world was full of the devil's snares. They go by night to towns and villages in great companies and multitudes and lay their snares and gins of many kinds; for the devils have nought else to do than daily to set more and more of such snares.— "But, Brother Berthold, thou sayest much to us of these devils and of their manifold guiles, and we never see a single devil with our eyes, nor hear we any, nor grasp, nor feel them."—Lo, now! that is even the worst harm that they do thee; for, didst thou see but once a single devil as he is, then wouldst thou surely never commit one sin again; that itself is one of their snares the worst of all that they have, that they deal so stealthily with us. Now see how dead a silence they keep, albeit there are many thousand of them here in this place! Ye devils, ye hear me well enough preaching here, yet ye would not take all the wealth that is under heaven (I except a man's soul) that only one of you should let himself once be seen; for then all your cunning and your snares would avail you no more. Now see, ye young folk, what a deadly snare that is, that no man may ever see a devil! Behold now what silence they keep, though so many are here with us; for if ye saw them but once ye would never sin more, since they are so foul of form that, if we could but see one single devil as he is, all mankind would die of fear. As little as a man may endure the sight of Almighty God with his fleshly eyes for excess of joy, so little may one ever see the devil for fear. And if it were so that a man might see the devil with his bodily eyes and not die of horror, and if the devil were to come out at this moment from that forest yonder,[1] and this town here

---

[1] Many sentences in these sermons testify to Berthold's habit of preaching in the open air; chroniclers reckoned the numbers of his hearers somewhat wildly at 60,000, or even 100,000 men.

before us were a burning fiery furnace heated through and through, there would yet be the greatest throng of men pressing into that fiery furnace that ever there was in the world, or ever will be!...

The second snare which the devils set so perilously for us Christian folk, they have set specially for women. Women are as well created for the Kingdom of Heaven as men, and they need it also as much as men, and many more of them would come into the Kingdom of Heaven but for this one snare. Fie! ye wicked devils! How many thousand poor women's souls would now be in heaven but for the single snare which ye have laid so cunningly for them! Ye women, ye have bowels of compassion, and ye go to church more readily than men, and ye pray more readily than men, and come to hear preaching and to earn indulgences more readily than men; and many of you would be saved but for his one snare, which is called vain glory and empty honour. In order that ye may compass men's praise ye spend all your labour on your garments—on your veils and your kirtles. Many of you pay as much to the sempstress as the cost of the cloth itself; it must have shields on the shoulders, it must be flounced and tucked all round the hem; it is not enough for you to show your pride in your very buttonholes, but you must also send your feet to hell by special torments, ye trot this way and that way with your fine stitchings; and so many ye make, and with so much pains, that no man may rehearse it all. At the least excuse ye weary yourselves with your garments; all that wherewith ye busy yourselves is nought but vanity. Ye busy yourselves with your veils, ye twitch them hither, ye twitch them thither; ye gild them here and there with gold thread, and spend thereon all your time and trouble. Ye will spend a good six months' work on a single veil, which is sinful great travail,—and all that men may praise thy dress: "Ah, God! How fair! Was ever so fair a garment?" Yea, our Lady was far fairer than thou, yet was she exceeding humble of heart; and St Margaret, and many other saints.—"How, Brother Berthold! we do it only for the goodman's sake, that he may gaze the less on other women." No, believe me, if thy goodman be a good man indeed he would far rather see thy chaste conversation than thine outward adorning, so that the folk point their fingers at thee and gape: "See, who is she?" or "Whose wife is she?" Or if he be a lewd fellow, then all thy crimple-crispings and christy-crosties and thy gold thread are of no avail; and they help thee only to hell for ever and ever, unless thou come to contrition and true penitence. Every woman's excuse is: "I do it not for vain glory's sake; I do it only for my goodman!" But many husbands are heartily sorry for your dressing; and then more especially when ye leave them no rest. Now ye will have this, now ye will have that; and when thou shouldest be busy in the house with something needful for the goodman, or for thyself, or thy children, or thy guests, then art thou busy instead with thy hair or thy wimple! thou art careful whether thy sleeves sit well, or thy veil, or thy headdress, wherewith thy whole time is filled—the days and the weeks and the whole year long. Now see, ye women, to how little purpose ye lose the Kingdom of Heaven! Believe me, whatsoever thou doest with thy dress, yet in all the world it is nought but a little dust and a bit of cloth. With all the crimple-crispings here and the christy-crosties there, and the gold thread here and there, yet again I say, it is nought but a bit of cloth after all! Only the Jewesses and the parsons' lemans and the lost women who walk outside the town walls—only such should wear these yellow scarves, that they may be known from the rest. Ye men might put an end to this and fight against it doughtily, first with good words, and if they are still obdurate, then ye should step valiantly in.—"Ah, Brother Berthold, yet that is a perilous enemy whom the goodman must always keep in his house! I have oftentimes besought my wife kindly and commanded her straitly, yet would she never forbear. Now therefore, were I to pull one veil from her, I fear lest she should do me all the greater harm behind my back, and go buy another twice as dear."—Lo, now, thou shouldst take heart of grace. Thou art a man after all, and bearest a sword, yet thou art easily conquered with a distaff. Take courage, and pluck up heart and tear it from her head, even though four or ten hairs should come away with it, and cast it into the fire! Do thus not thrice or four times only; and presently she will forbear.

It is fitting that the man should be the woman's lord and master.

Thomas Cantimpratanus (of Chantimpré in Brabant) was the son of a noble who had fought under our Richard I in the Holy Land. A hermit near Antioch, to whom the father had confessed his sins, warned him that some of them would keep him long in purgatory unless he bred up one of his sons to the priesthood. The child Thomas was therefore sent to school at Liège, where (as he tells us in no. 69 in vol. I) he spent eleven years. At the age of fifteen he was much impressed by Jacques de Vitry's preaching. In early manhood he became a Canon Regular at Chantimpré, but passed over to the stricter Dominicans about 1231. He became a very distinguished preacher, a suffragan bishop, and a fairly voluminous writer. By far the most valuable of his works is the *Bonum Universale de Apibus*, a treatise on virtues and vices by analogy with the life of the bee, illustrated by personal and historical anecdotes. This was written somewhere about 1260; my extract is from the Douay edition of 1597.

32. HUNTERS AND FARMERS
(Lib. II, c. 49, p. 373.)

THERE is also a fourth kind of game, of those who sport with the fowls of the air and the hounds of the earth; whereof the damnation is most manifest in clerics, who wander about after such sports and neglect their due service to Christ. Yet even in noble laymen those things may be seen to be damnable, if on this account they neglect and despise their daily prayers and masses.... A certain knight of high degree was wont to compel many of his tenants daily to wander and spend their labour in hunting with him; whereby very many left their own business of tilling the fields, and fell with their wives and children into poverty and want. It befel therefore one day that he went into the forest to chase the stag with his own body-servants and his household, and the hounds were in full cry, and he followed the game with all his might on horseback. But when he had ridden all day in vain, and still saw the stag fleeing ever before his face, then his mind was turned to madness, and he pursued after him all night long with his whole train; so that from that day forward no man ever saw or knew what had become of them, or whither they were gone. Some said (and we easily believe it) that the earth opened her jaws to swallow them up like Dathan and Abiram, and sucked them down to hell.

Ulrich von Lichtenstein, an Austrian knight of great distinction in his own day, was an ancestor of the present princely house of that name. Born shortly before 1200, he died in 1275 or 1276. His name first occurs in 1227 as witness to an important document; in 1241 he was Steward of his native Styria, and later on we find him Grand Marshal of that province. His wife, who plays a very subordinate rôle in his autobiography, was Bertha von Weitzenstein; she bore him two sons and two daughters.

Ulrich's poem entitled *Frauendienst* is, however we take it, one of the strangest monuments of medieval love; it bridges the gulf between the *Vita Nuova* and *Don Quixote*. We have sufficient collateral evidence to prove it partly true and partly imaginary, but not enough to unravel the two threads: yet even the purely poetical additions have a real value as indications of contemporary manners. If Ulrich did not act and suffer exactly as he tells us, yet he shows us clearly how he would wish to have acted and suffered as a perfect lover. The question has been fully discussed, without any very definite conclusion, by Reinhold Becker in his *Wahrheit und Dichtung in U. v. L.'s Frauendienst* (Halle, 1888). The following extracts are from R. Bechstein's edition (Leipzig, 1888, 2 vols.) numbered according to stanzas.

33. CALF-LOVE
(Stanza 8.)

WHEN I was yet a little child, I heard oftentimes how men would read, and wise men would say, that no man may come to any worth his whole life long, but if he be ready stead-fastly to serve good women; for such men have their high reward. Moreover, (said the wise men) no man is so truly glad and happy in this world, as he who loveth a pure and virtuous lady no less than his own self, and they said that all men had done so who would fain come to honour. I was then but a child, and so foolish that I yet rode hobby-horse; neverthe-less [I thought in my simplicity]: "Since pure women do thus exalt a man, then will I ever serve the ladies with body, goods, spirit and life." In such thoughts I grew until my twelfth year. Then I thought to and fro within my childish heart, enquiring after the manners and beauty, the wit and virtue of all ladies throughout the land. When any man praised good women, then would I, softly smiling, follow at his heels; for my delight was in their praise. So it befel that I heard of a lady whose praise was in the best men's mouths of the land, and in whom men found most goodness. She was high of birth, fair and good, chaste and pure, and fulfilled of all virtues. In this lady's service I abode wellnigh five years. Then said my heart unto me: "Good friend, good fellow, wilt thou give thyself up to one woman? then must it be to this one, for she is free in all her ways." "Heart, I will follow thy bidding; yet is it too much for both of us to serve for such guerdon as a man hath from a woman; for she is too high-born for us; so may it befal that we both alike lose our service." "Peace, body! no woman was ever so high and so rich but that a noble knight who served her with mind, heart, and body, might win her in the end." "Heart, I swear to thee by all mine hopes of heaven that she is dearer to me than mine own self; wherefore, in this same loving mind which I now hold towards her, therein will I serve her for ever."

When therefore soul and body were thus resolved to woo this fair lady, then went I and stood before her, and looked lovingly upon her, saying within myself: "O bliss! shall this be mine own sweet lady? But how may I serve as beseemeth her worth, better than so many other noble boys in her service? It may be that one of them will serve her better, and that my lady will hate me; for I have no other wit than to serve her early and late; yet it may be that some other who loves her less will serve her better; nevertheless in love at least will I excel them all." Oftentimes in summer I plucked fair flowers, and brought them to my lady; and when she took them in her white hand I thought with joy: "Where thy hand is now, there hath mine own hand been." When I came and saw others pour water upon the lily-white hands of my beloved, then would I bear away secretly this water which she had touched, and drink it for love of her. Thus in my childish fashion I served her well, even as a child may serve, until my father took me from her; on which day I knew heartfelt mourning and the power of love. My body did indeed depart from thence; but my heart abode there still, for it would not come with me. Little rest had I by night or by day; wheresoever I went or rode, my heart was ever with her; and, how far soever I might be removed from her, yet her mild light shone by night into mine heart. I was sent unto a lord rich in all virtues, the Markgraf Heinrich of Austria. He served the ladies right loyally, and spake well of them as beseemeth a knight; he was mild, bold, and magnanimous; he bare himself as a wise man with wise men and as a fool with fools; he suffered hardships for honour's sake, and his tongue spake no word of villainy; to all his friends was he ever honest and true, and loved God with all his heart. This worthy lord said unto me that whosoever would fain live in worthiness must give himself wholly to some lady. He taught me much of his own sweet virtue; he taught me to speak of ladies, to ride a horse, and to write sweet words in letters— saying that a young man is of more worth when he can speak sweetly of ladies; "for," quoth he, "never shalt thou fare well with good women, if thy heart be set upon flattery and lies." Had I followed all his precepts in deed, then had I been a worthier man than I now am.

Meanwhile Ulrich is knighted, and sends to the lady his first song. He begs his aunt (who acts as go-between) to tell the lady how he loves her; the latter answers that, even though he were otherwise her equal, yet no lady could abide his hare-lip. Ulrich immediately promises that he will undergo an operation (stanza 85).

34. MEDIEVAL SURGERY

THEN said mine aunt, "I counsel thee in all loyalty, spoil not thine own self; live as God hath bid thee live, and be willingly content with that which He hath given; for if so thou doest, thy sense is sound; but thou art overweening if thou willest otherwise than God willeth." "God bless thee, fair Aunt; but know that mine own purpose is fixed, and I will duly tell thee how it goeth or prospereth with me;

meanwhile I beseech thee, by thy true affection, bear tidings whereof to my beloved lady." "Thereto plight I my troth; yet know, nephew, it grieveth me sore that thou wilt not desist from thy purpose." So I took leave of my good kinswoman, and rode to Gratz in Styria, where I found many a good master-leech; to the best of whom I told my purpose forthwith. "Nay," quoth he, "that may not be as yet; I will not cut thee before the month of May; but come to me in the May-days, and I swear upon my troth so to deal with thy mouth as that thou shalt have good cause to rejoice; for in these matters I am past-master." Wherefore I rode thence, since those were winter-days, to see fair ladies; until winter was past, and the sweet summer came, and I heard the little fowls' song. Then thought I within myself: "Now may it well be time that I betake me to Gratz again; God help me there!" So thence I rode in God's hand, and lo! on the way I met with my lady's squire. I knew him well and he knew me, and he asked whither I rode and whereon my purpose was set. "Comrade, I will tell thee true, nor will I hide the strange tidings; know now that I am whole and sound, yet I am freely purposed to wound myself; the leech in Gratz will cut me." Then the good squire crossed himself and said, "Why, lord, where shalt thou be cut?" "Lo, comrade, these lips whereof I have three, and I will now have one cut away." "And if that be true, then God help you; so say I in all earnest, for this is a wondrous tale; my lady doubtless knoweth nought thereof; I will tell it her now for very wonder's sake. God knoweth, ye must needs be beside yourself, that ye will hazard this venture uncompelled, whereby ye may lightly take your death." "Nay, tell the tale freely to whom thou wilt, for so I am resolved it shall come to pass on this journey of mine." "Truly then will I be there to see, if that be your good pleasure, and will report to my lady that ye would fain have me with you to behold how ye fare." Wherefore I rode on my way to Gratz, where my business lay, and where I found my Master. He took me in hand forthwith, and went about to cut me on a Monday morning. He would fain have bound me, but I would not; then said he, "Ye may lightly take harm thereby; for, an ye stir but a hair's breadth, then the

fungul de nare
fic enclocaur

5

A SURGICAL OPERATION

om MS. Harl. 1585, fol. 18 b (Strutt, *Horda Angel Cynnan*, pl. xxxiii). The legend runs:
"Thus is a polypus of the nose cut."

harm is done, I speak no lie!" "Nay," quoth I, "I will have no such gear; of mine own free will rode I hither to you; and, howsoever ye deal with me now, though it were to my death, no man shall see me blench." Yet in truth I was sore afraid, and sat me down on a bench before his face. Then he took a knife in his hand and cut my mouth clean through above my teeth; all which I bore with so great patience that, when all the cutting was done, I had stirred no whit. Master-like he cut me, and manlike I bore it all. Forthwith my mouth swelled; it was far bigger than a tennis ball, and he dressed the wounds as befitted his office. Then said my lady's squire (for he had seen it all): "If ye come to your health again, then am I glad to have been here. When I rode from you of late and told my lady how the man would cut you here, then she would never believe me; 'Nay,' quoth she, 'Of a surety he will not, trust my word; for methinks that were a fool's deed to let himself thus be cut.' Now have I seen right well with mine own eyes what marvels have been done; wherefore I will ride hence again; may the God of bounty keep you and make you whole in good time; meanwhile I will report to my lady how your mouth was cut and how manlike ye have borne it." "Nay, thou shalt tell my lady nought but to speak of my service, for I dare tell her no more; yet do thou tell whom thou wilt, as from me, how these bodily pains of mine were endured for a lady's sake who said that my mouth beseemed me ill. That is the cause of these my pains; for I have served her all my life (thus much I tell thee openly); whatsoever therefore displeaseth her is hateful to me, and if my right hand stood ill in her eyes, then by God! I would smite it off forthwith! Thereof will I speak little; for my will standeth in her will alone." Then rode the squire forth from me; and I must needs lie on my sickbed five and a half weeks or more; there lay I in much weal and in sore woe:—woe for the wound of my body, but comfort for the gladness of heart. Love constrained me so that I was both sad and merry. Yet was I ever glad for all my pains, though sore disquieted with hunger and thirst; nought could I take to myself for my sore pain of teeth and lips, and therewithal my mouth was anointed with an ointment greener than grass and ranker to the smell than any hound.[1] Then did love-need constrain me; for, whensoever I would have eaten or drunken for my need, then came this ointment into my belly withal; and my body took such a smack thereof that I loathed all meat and drink. Therefore I lived as those live who eat nought for very sickness of body; whereby I was sore weakened.... In Gratz I abode until I was whole again.

Shortly after this, Ulrich got speech of his lady, for the first time in his life; he then sent her a "little book" in verse. He next goes on to tell of the tourneys at Frisach and Brixen, in the latter of which he lost his little finger. Shortly after this, he cut off a finger of his own accord and sent it to his lady with another "little book." Then, with her leave, he went Romewards in garb of a pilgrim: but at Venice he took the guise of a Queen, issued a letter as from "Frau Venus" inviting all knights to joust by the way, and rode twenty-eight days' journey into Bohemia, with veiled face and muffled hands, speaking to no man. He writes (stanza 472): "At Venice I lay all winter through; hear now what I wrought there. I caused ladies' garments to be made; twelve gowns were made for me and thirty fair ladies' sleeves sewn upon little shirts; such was my device.[2] Therewithal I got me two comely-braided tresses of hair, which I richly entwined with pearls whereof I found great plenty for sale in Venice; at the same time they made me there white samite mantles; silverwhite were my saddles, wrought by the master with much labour and cunning craft; and their trappings were of white cloth, long and broad and of masterly work, with bridles of great cost." After this long and somewhat aimless adventure, and another tourney at Kornneuburg, Ulrich determined to venture to his lady's castle in the guise of a leper (stanza 1124).

35. ULRICH AND HIS DULCINEA

On Saturday at dawn I went forthwith on my journey with two followers, taking good care that none should know whither I went.... That day I rode six-and-thirty miles,

---

[1] The German editor, taking this to be a popular ointment of marjoram, is at a loss to account for its rankness. But the stuff would probably be a very common medieval salve for wounds which was compounded mainly of verdigris. See p. 39 of the fifteenth-century translation of Lanfrank's *Science of Cirurgie* (Early English Text Society).

[2] *I.e.* a fresh sleeve daily for his journey. We learn from stanza 511 that the tresses hung down to his saddle, and that he therefore wore them in a net.

and was sore wearied with so great and hasty a journey; two of my horses (I lie not) fell dead on the road, yet small heed had I thereof. By nightfall I came to a town where I got me basins such as lepers bear, and wretched garments. Thus I and my messenger disguised ourselves next day; no fouler clothes could have been; yet we bare long knives upon us, if perchance our lives might come into jeopardy. That Sunday morning I rode two miles thence in such wretched array; then I left our horses in a secret place, and went with my messenger two miles further to the gates of a glorious castle, where the virtuous lady abode with her household—mine own good lady, whom I never forgot! To that castle I went forthwith; and without the gates I found many poor folk sitting there beyond all number; if I shall tell truth, a good thirty lepers or more sat there, in their miserable sores. Many were pained with grievous torments. I must needs go sit with them (which I would fain have avoided, but my comrade bade me thither), as though I too had been sick. Then that crowd of lepers greeted us with a mighty snort of welcome. I will not lie; grievously sick were many of that crew, and I sat down among them on the grass. Therewith all asked with one voice whence we were; whereat I was abashed and said, "We are two strangers, that have never yet been here; poverty hath urged us, if perchance some man would give us help." Then said they: "Happily are ye come hither; perchance ye know not that the lady of this house lieth sick, wherefore folk give us oftentimes our fill of food and pennies withal; a maiden hath even now brought us bread and wine (may she be blessed for ever!) and ye also should have gifts if your coming were known, believe us well. Knock therefore boldly and beg after the wont of us poor folk; wine and bread shall ye have for your pains, wherewith ye may still your ravening hunger; and, if perchance no pennies to-day, yet to-morrow at least without fail." So I departed from these lepers and went to stand by an oriel window that was hung with fair tapestry, such as men hang oftentimes at a window against overmuch wind or light. . . . Thither I took my basin, that rang like a bell, and knocked so loud that it sounded even into the ladies' parlour; after which I miserably besought a morsel of bread for the sore hunger that beset me. As I prayed thus, a maiden looked forth from the window and beheld us twain standing alone and apart from the rest; whereupon she closed it again and went to tell her lady how we stood there; and the pure saint looked out upon us. After a while this maiden came forth from the gate and gave unto each of the lepers a penny; and when she was come to us, the sweet maiden spake from her red mouth: "Tell me, when came ye hither? I have not yet seen you here." Then I made my voice strange unto her and answered, "We suffer sore discomfort of sickness and poverty; whosoever will help us aught for God's sake may work his own eternal bliss, for we are come hither in great poverty and are well nigh dead for hunger and for stress of want." Then drew she nearer to us and said, "Let me know who ye are; I may no longer tarry here; if ye be come for my lady's sake, tell it me forthwith and conceal not the truth." Then said I to that fair damsel: "Lady, in truth, your lady bade me come hither; and know that I am he whose joy standeth in her grace, and who hath ever served her and will ever truly serve her unto my life's end." Then answered she forthwith: "If thou art high-minded for ladies' sake, then shall your stout and worthy arms enfold a worthy lady: ye sit here with little likeness to one who hath broken spears for his lady's grace and borne himself with knightly strength; yet will I tell my lady from you that ye are come hither for her sake; when she hath heard of your good coming, then will I return and tell how ye shall fare here." Therewithal she departed to find my Fair, and said forthwith in all truth how I was here. Then said my pure and sweet lady, "Truly I am right glad thereof; bid him welcome for me, for I have gladly heard of his coming; go again secretly and bring him somewhat; bid the proud knight go down the hill and take good heed lest he be discovered, and spare mine honour as he loveth his own life. Bid him come up again in the evening, then will I let him know what I have bethought and wherefore I have brought him hither: take to him now flesh of capons, bread, and wine, and bid him be right welcome." The maid went swiftly thence and found me yet waiting there; she and another maiden brought me meat and wine in plenty; seeing therefore that there was another with her, I set my bowl far from me and said, "Lady, set the meat therein; for alas! my sickness lieth hard on me." Then the one maiden halted, but the other drew near to me, saying, "I fear not thy sickness; my worthy lady hath bidden you God-welcome; she would fain see you, if so it may be without shame. She hath bidden you through me (wherefore ye must willingly obey), to go down forthwith and beware of discovery and keep yourself well; this must needs be, or you are but a dead man: your own sense will tell you that, and I counsel you well, foolish as I stand here. Then at nightfall shall ye come up again hither; then will I discover to you my lady's mind; I ween well that she is gracious to you; be sure that she hateth you not, for such favour hath she never yet shown to any knight." With this she departed from me; and when she was gone I took my meat and drink and bare it to the lepers, saying: "My lady hath given us great plenty of meat and drink to-day! God grant her a long and happy life! Never did I get so great alms, wherefore I will share it with you, and we will hold it in common, and ye shall do likewise to us when ye get good meat." "Yea," said they, "So be it; for men oftentimes give us flesh and bread and wine, which we will share in turn with thee and live in good fellowship." So we sat all in a ring and set there the good flesh and wine; I saw in that dish many a hand such as I dare not here speak of; yea, I must needs restrain my words for very courtesy; the hair stood straight on my head to see that filth. . . . With such folk must I now eat; rather would I have lost my life than sit there among them; yet care for my good lady's good name constrained me. Had I not gone in among these folk, then had I been discovered without fail. Now know I that many will say, I could not have dwelt among these lepers but that they had discovered me to be free from their sickness. To such an one would I answer that he knoweth not the virtue of simples, which can work many wonders. I have not yet forgot the herb which, if a man take it in his mouth, will make him swell forthwith and change the fashion of his countenance so that no man may know him; he may wander unknown throughout the whole earth; this art I know, simple as I am.[1] Those same herbs had I there; I had coloured my hair grey, yet methinks I needed it not; for ye might already see me grey with care before my time....

When we sick folk had eaten, I went forthwith down the hill into the village, and begged for alms in the guise of a sick man. Men gave me much broken meat, which I took for my lady's sake; they gave me enough and to spare, but I bare it forth and laid it in a furrow, nor know I who took it thence; I know well that it profited me not. So I went about begging for pastime until evening came on, and the setting sun cast his rays athwart the hill; then went I again to the castle-gate and sat in my place among the lepers, who gave me a ready welcome. Then asked I whether they had yet eaten. "Nay," said they, "we eat even now, ye are come in good time; for now they will bring our evening dole at so timely an hour that each may creep away to his own shelter." Here sat I a good space, until the fair maid came again to us, with attendants that bore meat and wine in plenty. Then said she to me, "Get you down without delay and come again to-morrow for the morning meal; take good heed meanwhile." "Nay," quoth I, "what boots it to my lady that I am here in so wondrous wise, if she will not see me secretly?" "Not so," quoth she, "for that may not be until the morrow. She hath surely purposed to see you before your departure; only take heed that none discover you." When the maiden was gone, I ate among the lepers sore against my will, for their company was loathsome unto me....After our meal was done, then each vied with the other to bid me to his own hut; but I made answer: "One of my fellows lieth sore sick: I will go thither and spend the night with him for God's sake, and for mine own troth." So I departed straightway from the castle unto a field afar off, where I found the corn both thick and high; thither I and

---

[1] Compare the following extract from a fourteenth-century book of medicine and magic preserved in the Communal Library of Siena and alluded to on pp. 320 ff. of Mr W. Heywood's *Ensamples of Fra Filippo*. I owe the transcript from the Italian text to Mr Heywood's good offices. "*Chapter 235. To make a man appear a Leper.* Take the husks of fresh walnuts, and draw out the juice, and wash in the said juice, and thou shalt appear a leper. And then shalt thou wash in water of bean-leaves and of elder, and thou shalt return to thy right colour." It must be remembered that all forms of skin disease were commonly confounded under the one name of leprosy.

my fellow fled from the lepers, and the corn must needs be our inn for that night. There spent I a most evil night, believe me; for with the sunset and darkness arose a great wind, and the rain beat down in torrents; there was I in sore straits, for a ragged worn-out coat and mantle were all my shelter against the rain, and I was half frozen to death. Moreover, my need was greater still; for (I will not lie) the worm that hath no name bit me so sore throughout the night that I burst well nigh out of my body; many a guest tormented me that night, both he and she.[1] Heartily glad was I to see the glimmer of day: then ran I hither and thither until I was warm again. Believe me, when Ereck lay in Enid's arms, it was better with him than with me on that most evil night. Had I not lived on thoughts of love, I had never been whole again: but sweet hope upheld me. Though bodily comfort be good, yet thoughts of love are better still; he who hath such amid his troubles may well be comforted and glad.

When the sun stood high, then went I again without delay to my place at the castle gates, where I knocked and begged piteously for alms; all my garments were wet to the skin, and I was in sore distress. Then came the maiden again with much meat; I thought within myself: "My lady will fain make me sick indeed!" Then came the maiden and said, "Where were ye yesternight in that wicked weather? for ye must needs have suffered sore distress if ye had no roof." "Yea," quoth I, "much discomfort have I suffered, and was well nigh dead for cold and other pains which I dare not tell; yet I suffer all gladly and joyfully if but my lady will do me grace, for therein standeth my life." "Eat then," quoth she, "and go down the hill again; but come again at eventide, for (by my troth I swear it) my most worthy lady will leave you there no more: to-night she will see you." Then she departed from me, and her tale rejoiced me much; wherefore I went amongst the sick folk, among whom I must needs eat again, with however evil will. Then I went into a wood where many fowls sang; there I set my body in the sun and clean forgot the cold; my fellow meanwhile picked most busily; he picked here and

[1] The Florentines (according to Bechstein) still use the nicknames *boy* and *girl* for *pulce* and *cimice*: this suits the German genders, if not the Italian.

picked there throughout that livelong day; no Italian could have done it better or more cunningly, yet to me no day was ever so long as this. . . . Thus sat I here in the forest until it drew towards evening; then I arose and went up in high hope, right as a man whose heart hath high desire of love, and who deemeth that it is returned; rightly may his heart then stand high, and thus it was with me. I sat again at the castle gate, as ye may well believe, but I was too early; men had not yet begun to flock thither as they do towards sunset: yet there I sat in high hopes and thought within myself: "Well is me, if I shall indeed this night see my lady!" So high stood my hopes of love, when this virtuous maiden came demurely again to me, saying: "Ye have done right well to come so early; I know not if ye have heard it, but one of the sick folk saith that ye be no true leper, for he saith that ye wear undergarments of so fine linen as any nobleman might be honoured to possess; I know not how he hath seen it, yet thus hath he said to me, and I fear sore lest he may say the same to others." Then said I, "If I be discovered, that is by my lady's fault; why would she have me sit here and go all day hence? and how could they otherwise have seen and suspected me? Counsel me now, lady, what I should do." "Go then forthwith, and tarry no longer here, for that is my lady's purpose: yet mark me now. At the parting of day and night, come hither again and hide thee in the castle ditch,[1] conceal yourself well, as ye are wise, for the need is great; that may ye well see. Mark me now well; see ye yon high oriel? When a light shall be shown thence, tarry no longer, but come swiftly beneath the window, and ye shall find bedclothes hanging, knotted in a loop, whereby ye shall be drawn up."

So I did as she bade me, and went forthwith into the forest again; my mood was turned again to gladness and I thought: "Now, well is me for evermore, since I shall see my beloved lady this night, whereof I will rejoice!" In that forest I tarried until day was gone and dark night had chased the light away; then I hastened to the ditch and swiftly walled myself in with stones that no man might see me; my fellow did like-

---

[1] Which would of course be a dry ravine hewn in the rock, as this was a hill-castle.

wise; then must we lie as still as death. As we lay thus hidden, the seneschal himself went seven times around the castle hither and thither, seeking diligently whether any man were come to hide: full closely did he peer around.... Then he went into the castle, and I marked the light shining from the oriel: forthwith I rose up and drew off the ragged garments wherein I was disguised and hid them full fast. Swiftly I crept under the window, where I found the coverlet hanging; wherein I set myself willingly; my fellow was full handy and shoved after me with a right good will; my heart beat in haste until white hands drew me somewhat upwards. But when I was come so high that my trusty fellow might help me no further, then know that they could draw me no higher, whereof both they and I were sorry. With this they let me suddenly fall; then they strove afresh, and drew me as high as before: yet no hair's breadth further might they bring me, to their sorrow and mine. Thus it befel me three times; when therefore I came thus for the third time to earth, I stepped forth in anger from the coverlets and said, "Good fellow mine, thou mayest well be lighter than I; step thou in, that they may draw thee up." He stepped in, and thus they did forthwith; I shoved after him with a right good will; they drew him swiftly up, and I was glad. As he stepped into the chamber, he was greeted with a kiss: for my good aunt kissed him for me, whereof she hath oftentimes since been ashamed. When this undesigned kiss had been given, my fellow let down the noose to me again; I stepped in with hearty good will, for thereto was all my desire; and forthwith they drew me up to the oriel.

As I came through the window, my aunt pressed her red mouth with hearty love to mine; then that fair and virtuous lady drew me into a corner and clad me in a robe of Bagdad brocade, wherein I went forthwith to find my lady. Chaste and sweet and merry sat she there upon a bed and greeted me right modestly; she bade me welcome. I tell you how she was clad: she bare a white sark, that was full strait. Over this had my noble and fair and pure lady a robe of scarlet furred with ermine; no feather could be softer. Her mantle was green as grass, lined with soft vair, and with skirts neither too wide nor too close. By her stood eight ladies, right nobly clad; upon the bed lay a fair mattress of samite whereon were two quilts of silk, better there might not be, and over all such a bed-cover as no knight saw ever a fairer. There too lay a precious bolster and two most comely pillows. The floor could nowhere be seen, for it was bespread with many a fair carpet; at the bed's foot burned two great tapers in their candlesticks, and a good hundred tapers on the walls. The eight ladies of that bower were fair and lovely: richly were they clad; yet, sooth to say, methought the ladies were too many, their presence irked me, and I grieved in my heart to see them.

Here sat my worthy lady before me, no fairer or more virtuous could be seen. Then knelt I before her and said: "Lady, for your virtue and your worshipful youth's sake, for your pure sweet mind, be kind and gracious to me! Think now on my heart's desire which is turned towards your love, whom I hold dear above all other women. You are dearer to me than aught else; if therefore I may have your love *par amours*, then have I all the bliss that ever I longed for; here may you grant me high courage and worshipful life for all my days to come." Then said that pure and gentle lady: "Nay, your courage may not aspire so far as that I should lay you here by my side. Be warned, nor desire that which may not be; if I have gladly seen you here in my secret bower, that is only for your honour; since ye have so demeaned yourself as that every woman should ever honour you therefore. If therefore I could grant you honour, ye should have it from me: take it for honour that I have brought you into my chamber, a thing that hath never yet befallen any knight. My lord and master shall live ever free from fear lest I should love another man than he; for (even though I feared it not for God's honour and mine own), yet my lord would keep close watch over me; nevertheless, even though his watch were away, mine own honour is a yet stronger defence; and my pure mind helpeth him here more than aught else. If therefore I set mine honour thus in jeopardy, and neglect my homage to him, that is to honour you; for, if any man in this castle were aware of your presence, then were mine own honour tarnished; wherefore ye should thank me for this venture." "Ever will I thank you, dear Lady, whatsoever ye do unto me; for I know ye are so good and pure and blessed that ye alone stand betwixt me and mourning; and doubtless ye will here grant me your love this night." Then said she, "No more of this, but if ye would lose my grace...." At this threat I was afraid and rose and went to mine aunt saying: "How shall this be? If I get no profit of my coming, then shall I be crestfallen: I will not believe so ill of her goodness, for that were a great ungrace and mischief; my lady shall bethink herself. Nay, aunt, I will not go hence, befall what may, until my lady grant me her love...." Then said mine aunt, "Nephew, I know in truth that she hath summoned thee for no more than she saith; therefore hath she so many of us in attendance, that thou mayest do her no violence, as many men are wont to do: and I know well that, if thou but touch a hair of her head against her will, then will she never be gracious to thee, nor shalt thou ever have thy will: yet one thing have I heard her say, that thou shalt yet get her love if thou blench not in her service."

Here follow nearly 40 stanzas more of three-cornered discussions between Ulrich, the lady, and the aunt.

Then came my lady to me and said, "God knoweth that I have seen no man so witless as ye are...if ye tarry here till morning light, then must ye surely be slain; ye should be glad to get hence as I bid you; if ye will not bear yourself mannerly towards me, then sue me not for your friend, and know that your promised troth is naught. They told me that ye would be at my service, but therein have they deceived me and belied you, as I see by your bearing: for whatsoever I pray you this night ye deny me; wherefore I esteem you but lightly." Then spake I, "Nay, dear lady, but I will ever serve you truly until my dying day. Your love shall bind me to all eternity: wherefore, dear lady of all my bliss, grant me your grace that I may love you *par amours*; for, an we must now part, then truly ye use me worse than any knight was ever used of his lady." "Follow me," quoth she, "do as I bid now, and it shall be well with you. Step once more into the coverlet: then shall I let you down but a little and draw you up again, and greet you well according to your desire. When I have thus received you again, I will be wholly your subject unto whatsoever end ye will; for I have chosen you above all other knights to be my friend." "Lady," quoth I, "were I well assured of that, then would I do all your will; yet I fear lest ye let me down and draw me never up again; then were I crestfallen and unhappy that ever I was born!" "Nay," quoth she, "but I will give you a pledge; for I grant that ye hold me fast by the hand; ye are no true servant of mine an ye trust me not, and yet have I chosen you to be my friend above all other knights; by my womanhood I lie not!" "Dear lady, I will commend myself wholly to your grace, as my duty biddeth; ye may deal well or evil with me as ye will, since ye say ye have chosen me above all others for friend." "Yea, and it shall be well with you if ye do after my will; in the end ye shall love me *par amours*." Therewith my good lady took me by the hand and led me until she found the coverlet that hung at the window: there she bade me step in, saying, "Fear not; trust my faith that I will not suffer you, my chosen friend, to part thus from me." Anxiously I stepped in the coverlet, and they let me down so far that they should have raised me again; then said my good lady with subtle intent, "God knoweth that I never saw so dear a knight as this who now hath me by the hand! wherefore be thou welcome to me; I will comfort thy sorrow and thou shalt be God-welcome!" Therewith she caught me by the chin and said, "Friend, kiss me now!" at which word I was so overjoyed that I let go her hand: swift then was my downward journey; and, had not God been with me, I had lightly broken my neck. When I reached the earth, the coverlet was drawn up again, and I must needs sit there in sorrow with a bitter aching heart. Then waxed I almost beside myself with grief, and cried aloud, "Alas, alas, and ever alas! woe is me, that ever I was born! now have I lost both life and honour!" Then I sprang to my feet in a frenzy, and ran down a steep path to a deep water, wherein I would have drowned myself in sin; of a truth I had died there had not my fellow come to me, whom they had let down swiftly after me. When this faithful courteous servant heard my cries, he was cut to the heart and ran after and caught me even as I would have leapt into the water for my death. "Alas," quoth he, "what may this be? Dear friend and master, if ye will slay yourself, then are ye lost, body and soul; better wert thou unborn Up, then, and play the man." "Nay," quoth I, "here must my life be spilled; for I have lost my pure, worthy, sweet lady through an evil subtlety, wherefore will I no longer live!" "Nay," quoth he, "but ye should be glad to live on, for thy lady sendeth you her own pillow, whereon her cheek hath lain this many a night; she had thought to have had your love this night, and now would she fain comfort you." When he spake thus, and I saw the pillow, then my senses came somewhat back to me: sadly I sat on the ground and gazed on the trusty fellow through my tears, and said, "Alas! I am in evil case, for my pure, sweet, worthy lady hath deceived me; she bade me trust her faith that she would not let me down; a noble pledge she gave me, her own soft white hand; with subtlety she hath overcome me, which was not well done!" Then said he, "Master, ye should be glad; believe me well, to-night will she greet you with love for your delight, that ye may have your will of her. But let us tarry here no longer; the day dawneth, and it will soon be light, and ye must needs see to your young simple squire, whether he be still there with our horses, or whether he have been discovered." . . . So we went forth and found the horses. . . . Then said my fellow, "Master, now that ye are in your right mind, I dare no longer hold my peace. . . . Your lady sendeth you word, ye shall come to her this day three weeks (mark well what I say); then will she give you such welcome that you may be glad thereof your whole life long. Sore against her will hath she let you depart, as she said to me; one lady was there in her train for whose sake she must needs send thee forth; that lady will soon depart, whereof your own lady is heartily glad; then shall ye come again, and she will keep you ten days at the castle (on my troth I swear it), and deal with you as lovingly as a good lady should deal with her friend."

The lady next attempted to get rid of Ulrich by a too common device which Chaucer reprobates; she bade him go and fight the heathen overseas. The knight promised obedience, but in due time found a good excuse; finally, however, "she dealt so with me as it beseemeth me not to tell for shame"; so he cast her off and found another love. One of the latest episodes in the book shows our hero imprisoned by the treachery of certain private enemies, assisted by his "housewife" to the best of her power, and consoling himself by composing fresh poems to his second anonymous lady-love, to whom in a few verses of epilogue he dedicated this whole book of *Frauendienst*.

The following are from the collection of *Latin Stories* published by T. Wright for the Percy Society in 1842. They are from preachers' manuals of the thirteenth and fourteenth centuries, to be used as illustrations in sermons.

36. A MERCIFUL ARCHBISHOP

(p. 30.)

BALDWIN, monk and abbot and afterwards archbishop, was wont to eat no flesh. A certain old woman therefore asked him whether he ate flesh; whereunto he replied: "No." But she: "It is false, my lord; for thou hast eaten my flesh to the bones, and thou hast drunken my blood to the very heart. Behold how lean am I! for thy reeves have seized my cow, the only one that I had, wherefrom I and my children had our sustenance." To whom the Archbishop answered, "I will see that they shall give thee back thy cow, and from henceforth I will beware of such flesh-food."[1]

37. A JONGLEUR'S REVENGE[2]

(p. 40.)

I HAVE heard of a certain monastery that, whereas at its first foundation it had but few possessions, the brethren were then hospitable and kind to the poor; but when they had become

[1] Mr Wright notes, "I suppose the Baldwin mentioned here, was Baldwin archbishop of Canterbury, the preacher of the crusade in which Richard I distinguished himself. He was abbot of Ford in Devonshire, previous to being bishop of Worcester, from which see he was promoted to the archbishopric of Canterbury in 1184."

[2] This is also given in Crane's *Exempla of Jacques de Vitry*, p. 28, from which I have made one or two corrections in this text.

rich they did the very opposite. One of their abbots, being most hard-hearted and inhuman himself, put men like unto himself into the monastic offices, the most evil whom he could find. It befel then that a jongleur was benighted on his journey and came to this monastery for entertainment; where he found neither cheerful welcome nor any pity, but got with difficulty the blackest of bread, and herbs with salt and water, and a hard pallet. Whereat he was so grieved that he began to think within himself how he might take vengeance on the heartless guestmaster. So when the day had dawned, he turned aside by the way whereby he hoped that the abbot would come back to his monastery; and, meeting him, he cried, "Welcome, my lord, my good and liberal abbot! I thank you and your whole community, for that the brother guestmaster entertained me royally last night; he set before me most excellent fish and wine of price, and so many dishes that we know not their number; and even now as I departed he gave me a pair of shoes, a belt, and a knife." The abbot, hearing this, was moved to indignation and hastened back to his abbey, where he accused the aforesaid monk in Chapter as for a grievous crime. The guestmaster denied in vain; for he was sore scourged and driven forth from his office; and the abbot set in his place another whom he believed to be still worse.

38. A WOMAN'S OATHS
(p. 61.)

NOT only men, however, but some women also are grown into such a habit of swearing that they can scarce even speak without an oath.... Whence I have heard of a woman whom, in confession, the priest commanded to swear no more: to whom she answered, "Sir, I will swear no more, so help me God!" And he: "Lo, thou swearest already." "Nay, by God," quoth she, "but I will indeed abstain from henceforth." Then said the priest, "But let your speech be yea, yea! no, no! as the Lord biddeth: and that which is over and above these, is of evil." Then said she, "Sir, ye say it again, and I say unto you, by the blessed Virgin and all the saints!

I will swear no more, but do your bidding, and ye shall never hear me swear again." So that accursed woman gave many promises, yet contradicted them in deed.

39. THE PRIEST'S FATE

(p. 124.)

I T is told on good authority how, in a very well-known town, a certain priest was returning from his leman in the dusk, and heard a lamentable voice proceeding from a ruined house; whereupon he drew near and enquired who cried thus in that place. "Who art thou," said the voice, "that enquirest of me?" "A priest," answered he. "What, a priest!" cried that voice in great astonishment, repeating the word twice or thrice. When therefore the priest had enquired wherefore he spake in such tones of wonder, then said the voice, "They come down so thick among us into hell, that methought no priest could be left on earth; wherefore I cried aloud in wonder to hear that one was still alive; for I deemed they were all gone down to hell!"

From *Bishop Cantilupe's Register*, f. 32 b (Cantilupe Soc. p. 104), or *Roll of Bishop Swinfield* (Camden Soc., Append. No. 1). This champion was not in fact called on to fight in this particular dispute for the Chases of Colwall and Ledbury; St Thomas Cantilupe won his case in the ordinary course of justice, and a trench along the crest of the Malvern Hills still marks the boundary set between his chase and Gilbert de Clare's. Thomas appears in fact to have drawn double the covenanted salary: cf. the entry printed in Swinfield's Roll, p. 125: "Paid to the Champion Thomas de Brugge for his three terms' fee—viz. for Michaelmas 1288, the following Easter, and for the following Michaelmas—20 shillings."

40. A BISHOP'S CHAMPION

To all faithful in Christ, Thomas, by the grace of God Bishop of Hereford, prayeth eternal salvation in the Lord. Know ye all that we are bound to Thomas de Bruges [or

Brydges] our Champion, for his homage and service, in the sum of 6s. 8d. sterling, to be paid yearly from our treasury, wheresoever we may then be, on the feast of St Michael, so long as the said Thomas is able to do the work of a Champion; and the said Thomas hath promised to us upon oath that he will fight for us, whensoever called upon, against the Lord Gilbert earl of Gloucester and Hereford, or any other man, those lords only excepted to whom he was bound before the making of this present deed. And we for our part will fully satisfy the said Thomas, when he must fight for us, according as may be agreed upon between us and him, both in wages and in supply of victuals and all other necessaries. In testimony whereof we have caused our seal to be set on this deed. Given at Westminster, on the Tuesday next following the feast of All Saints, in the year of Grace 1276.

The accompanying illustration, from Waller's *Monumental Brasses*, gives the brass of Bishop Wyvil, who held the See of Salisbury from 1330 to 1375 and built the cathedral spire. He recovered the castle of Sherborne, which had been unjustly seized by the Crown since 1139, and had now been transferred to the Earl of Salisbury. "This involved trial by battle. At the appointed time, the champions of the respective parties appeared; but at the last moment letters were brought from the king postponing the combat, and the object was ultimately attained by a payment on the bishop's part of 2500 crowns." The proud and grateful bishop wished his champion to go down to posterity together with himself, armed with the double-pointed pick which the law prescribed for such combats. The inscription ran: "Here lieth Robert Wyvill of blessed memory, bishop of this church of Salisbury, who ruled this church peacefully and laudably for more than five-and-forty years. The scattered possessions of the see he prudently gathered together, and kept them when gathered like a watchful shepherd; among his lesser good deeds he recovered, like an intrepid champion, the castle of Sherborne, which had been violently occupied by force of arms for more than two hundred years; and he procured also the restoration to the said church of its Chase of Bere. On the fourth day of September in the year of our Lord 1375, and in the 46th year of his consecration, it pleased the Most High that he should pay his debt to mortality in the Castle aforesaid: upon whose soul may the Almighty have mercy, in Whom he hoped and believed." This extract (from the *Year Books of Edward III*, Anno XXIX, Hilary Term, Case No. 34) gives the story in full; the *Salisbury* castle of this report is evidently a clerical error for *Sherborne*. For similar incidents we may compare the entry of the Worcester annalist under the year 1275 (*Anglia Sacra*, vol. I, p. 501): "On the 26th of June there was a duel in Hardwick meadow for the church of Tenbury; but peace was made and the church left in possession of the Abbot of Lyre. On the 9th of July a duel was fought for the bailiwick of Hembury, and the bishop's champion conquered the champion of Philip de Stock." Many other interesting details as to judicial duels may be found in George Neilson's *Trial by Combat* (1890) and J. Hewitt's *Ancient Armour*, vol. I, p. 375, vol. II, p. 342.

41. WAGER OF BATTLE AND WITCHCRAFT

A BRIEF of Right was brought by the Bishop of Salisbury against the Earl of Salisbury, whereby the bishop claimeth the castle of Salisbury with its appurtenances. And last term they joined issue between the champions, Robert S. being the bishop's champion and Nicholas D. the earl's; and the fight was fixed for the morrow of the Purification. And the

Court bade them have their champions harnessed in leather and ready to do battle that same day. And early on the morrow the bishop came first, and his champion followed him to the bar clad in white leather next his skin, and over it a coat of red sendal painted with the bishop's arms, and a knight to bear his staff and a serving-man to bear his target, which was of like colour with his coat, painted with images both without and within; and the bishop stood at the bar with his champion by his side, the knight bearing his staff. And [Justice] Thorp made the champion raise the target upon his back, so that the top of the target once passed the crown of his head, and thus it was held on the champion's back so long as he stood at the bar. Then came the earl on the other part leading by the hand his champion who was clad in white leather, over which a coat of red sendal with the earl's coat-of-arms, and two knights bearing two white staves in their hands; and the target was held on the champion's back even as the target of the bishop's champion. [Then said] Knyvet, "For plaintiff ye have here Robert Bishop of Salisbury with his free man, Robert son of John de S., in leather harness, to prove and perform, with God's grace, that which the court of our Lord the king hath already awarded or shall award; this I proffer now to William Earl of Salisbury, and we pray that he be summoned." [Then said] Fyff, "Ye have here William Earl of Salisbury with his free man N. son of D., all ready harnessed, willing to perform, by God's grace, whatsoever the court of our lord King awardeth or shall award." [Then said Justice] Grene, "My lord bishop, go and take a chamber within this palace and strip your champion, and leave there all his harness under ward of the palace-warden, and the court will see to it, so that there may be neither fraud nor deceit. And you, sir Earl, go in like manner into another chamber"; (and it was commanded to the palace-warden to give them rooms;) "and keep your days here on Monday." And the court said, "Go and retire ye from the bar at one time, so that neither go before the other": and, since neither would withdraw before the other, they stood there until the Justices removed them; which they had much ado to perform. At the day appointed came the bishop and the earl with their champions, as before; but meanwhile the Justices had viewed all the harness, so that the staves might be of one length, that is of five quarters [of an ell?], and the targes of the same length and breadth, and the images. And two men stripped both champions of their harness. And the lord Thomas Beauchamp came to the place and set forth a letter under privy seal to the Justices, rehearsing the matter of the plea betwixt the parties: and, seeing that this toucheth somewhat on the king's right, he commanded the justices to adjourn that plea in the same state wherein it now standeth, until the Thursday next following. [Then said] Grene, "Seeing that the King hath bidden us adjourn this plea, and considering also that in searching the harness of you champions we have found certain defects whereof we know not yet whether they have been amended or no, keep your day here on Thursday next in the same plight as now." And it was said that the Justices had found in Shawel's coat, (who was the bishop's champion), several rolls of prayers and witchcrafts. Wherefore Grene said as aforesaid, "and withdraw now from the bar"; and since neither would part before the other, they stood there long until the justices removed them as before. And Grene said to the claimant, "Sir Bishop, withdraw now from the bar under pain of losing your plea"; whereupon he withdrew. And, before the day appointed, they accorded together, so that the bishop paid the earl 1,500 marks. So on Thursday the bishop came with his champion in leather harness as before; and the earl was called, and came not, and his default was recorded.... Wherefore it was awarded by the Court that the bishop should recover the Castle of Salisbury, as the right of the church of Our Lady of Salisbury, for himself and his successors, quit of all claim from the earl and his heirs in all perpetuity.

LIFE IN THE MIDDLE AGES

Robert de Graystanes, Subprior of Durham, was canonically elected and actually consecrated to that bishopric in 1333; but the Pope had meanwhile "provided" Richard de Bury with the prize, and the king gave his assent. Bury, one of the most learned of the English bishops and the probable author of the *Philobiblon*, honourably commends the learning and worth of his unsuccessful rival; and Robert himself tells the story with great impartiality. He did not long outlive his disappointment; his *Chronicle* ends in 1336. The following extracts are from the Surtees Society edition, *Hist. Dunelm. Scriptt. Tres.*

42. THE BISHOP AND HIS MOTHER

(Robert of Holy-Isle, Bishop from 1274 to 1283, p. 57.)

IT is said that, when raised to the bishopric, he honoured his mother, who had been a very poor woman, with menservants and maidservants and respect and luxury. So upon a time he went to visit her, saying, "How is it with thee, Mother?" "Nay, ill indeed," quoth she. "What, dear Mother, is there aught that you lack, in menservants or maidservants or necessary expenses?" "Nay," quoth she, "I have enough: but when I say to this man '*Go!*' he hasteneth thither; and to another '*Come!*' then he will fall on his knees before me; and all are so obedient to my slightest nod, that I have not wherewith to let my heart swell. When I was a poor old woman, and came down to the waterside to wash tripe or clothes or the like, then some neighbour would come, and the occasion would soon be given; first we would scold, and then tear each other's hair, and fight with fists and chitterlings and monifauldes;[1] nor can those precious electuaries or syrups which you send unto me work as those things worked for the expanding and purging of my heart; nay, when the poison is suppressed then it is all the more harmful, but when we can belch it forth we are relieved by the very act."

This same bishop came once to Norham, where the Lord Scremerston sent him a present of ale; which though the bishop had never drunk for many years now past, yet for reverence of the sender and for the noble report of the ale he tasted thereof: then, unable to bear it, he was seized with

[1] "The intestines or bowels; *spec.* the manyplies, or third stomach of a ruminant" (*O.E.D.*).

92

a sickness and must needs hasten from the table. Wherefore, after dinner, he called together his familiars and said, "Ye know how humble was my origin, and how neither my birth nor my country taught me to love wine, but only use and long custom. Yet now I am so accustomed thereunto that I cannot taste this ale, my natural drink; for custom is a second nature." When he was Prior of Finchale, he had a special friendship for a certain forester, John Madur by name, who would oftentimes bring him venison [from the bishop's parks]; but, when he was promoted to the see, and this same man looked to have had some reward from the bishop for the service that he had done to the prior, then his lordship cast him forth from his office, saying, "He would serve me as unfaithfully as he served my predecessor: as the poet saith, 'Such base deeds as were done yesterday, the same may be done to-morrow.'"

43. A LORDLY BISHOP
(p. 64.)

THIS Anthony [Bek, bishop 1283–1311] was great hearted, second to none in the realm, save the king only, in pomp and bearing and might of war, busy rather about the affairs of the kingdom than of his diocese, a powerful ally to the king in battle, and prudent in counsel. In the Scottish war he had once 26 knights-banneret in his own train, and he had commonly 140 knights in his following, so that men deemed him rather a secular prince than a priest or bishop. Moreover, though he delighted to be thus surrounded with knights, yet he bore himself towards them as though he heeded them not. For to him it was a small thing that the greatest earls and barons of the realm should kneel before him, or that, while he remained seated, knights should stand long and tediously before him like servants. Nothing was too dear for him, if only it might magnify his glory. He once paid forty shillings[1] in London for forty fresh herrings, because the other great folk there assembled in Parliament said that they were too

_____
[1] *I.e.* £40 modern money.

dear and cared not to buy them. He bought cloth of the rarest and costliest, and made it into horse-cloths for his palfreys, because one had said that he believed Bishop Anthony dared not buy so precious a stuff. Impatient of repose, and scarce resting on his bed beyond his first sleep, he said that they who turned from side to side deserved not the name of man. He settled in no place, but would go round perpetually from manor to manor, from north to south and back again; he was a mighty hunter with hawk and hound. Moreover, despite his great and manifold expenses, he was never in want, but abounded in all things unto the day of his death. He scarce ate in company; he lived most chastely, scarce gazing fixedly on any woman's face; wherefore, when the body of St William of York was translated, while the other bishops feared to touch his bones, their conscience pricking them for past sins, he laid his hand boldly on the holy relics, and wrought reverently all that the matter required.... On the second summons [of the Pope], the bishop came to the court of Rome, but with such magnificence and so lordly a bearing that all marvelled at his retinue and his lavish generosity. One day when he was riding through the city of Rome to the court, a certain count of those parts, coming in the other direction and passing the bishop's train, stood a while in admiration and asked one of the citizens: "Who is this that goeth by?" "A foe to money," quoth that citizen. To a certain cardinal who desired one of his palfreys (for he had the fairest in the world) he sent two, that the cardinal might take his choice; and he, seduced by their beauty, retained both. When this was reported to the bishop, he said, "So save me God! he hath not failed to choose the better of the two!" He was so high-minded that he thought he might without blame do whatsoever he would; therefore he refrained not for the cardinals' presence from giving benediction, nor for the Pope's presence from playing with his hawks. As he went towards Rome, and lodged in a certain city, there arose a discussion between his men and the townsfolk. At last, when the whole city was risen up against him and his men could not longer hold out in their lodging, then the door of the bishop's chamber was broken open and the Podesta rushed in with the great men of that city, bearing swords and staves as against a thief, and crying, "Yield thee, yield thee!" He therefore neither rose from his seat nor deferred to them in any wise, but said, "So save me God! ye have failed to say to whom I am to yield me: certainly to none of you." All his followers looked for no issue but death; yet he answered as boldly as though there had been no danger, though he would indeed have been slain but that there came by chance [*hiatus in MS.*]. It was on this same journey that, when one of his train asked of the price of a very costly cloth, the merchant answered that he believed the bishop would not buy so precious a stuff; which when the bishop heard, he bought the cloth, and under the merchant's eyes made horse-cloths thereof for his palfreys. Wherefore the Pope and cardinals honoured him for his highmindedness and lavishness....[He gained his cause and] returned to England with an honourable farewell from the Pope and his court.

The *Gesta Abbatum S. Albani* is a chronicle of the abbots of that great house compiled about 1350 by Thomas Walsingham, precentor of the abbey and last of the great English chroniclers. The writer had access to the wide collection of documents in his abbey; the *Gesta* extends from 793 to 1349, and Walsingham's own *Historia Anglicana* goes down to 1422. The edition of the *Gesta* here used is that published in the Rolls Series; it is brilliantly summarized by Froude in one of his *Short Studies* (Annals of an English Abbey).

William de Somerton, whose Priory of Binham in Norfolk was a cell to St Albans, rebelled in 1327 with six of his monks against the abbot's extortions. The six monks were clapped into prison at St Albans, but Somerton escaped to Rome.

44. A MONASTIC ALCHEMIST
(Vol. II, p. 132.)

FOR the benefit of posterity I have thought fit to describe here the manners of the aforesaid William of Somerton, that those to come might beware of being branded with the same. He was greedy above measure, hunting after money as eagerly as he wasted it lavishly, whence it chanced that he contracted a familiar friendship with a certain mendicant friar, who promised to multiply his moneys beyond all computation by the art which men call Alchemy, if only the prior spared none of the needful expenses at the beginning of his art. To whose words the prior lent too credulous an ear, and lavished such sums of gold and silver as might have brought even the richest to poverty. Yet even so he learned not to beware of the perils of false brethren; for, having lost once, he continued even unto the third time, pouring such plenty of gold and silver into this unprofitable work, that now scarce anything was left of the whole substance of his monastery, wherewith he might have made a fourth contribution. Wherefore it came about that, what with the abbot's former extortions from that priory, and what with the prior's present waste of its substance, nothing more was left in the house to supply the monks' necessities. So this William, slipping off into apostasy, fled hastily to the court of Rome: where, in so far as opportunity served him, he sought to prosecute his cause, and to thwart the abbot to the best of his ability, now by falsehoods, now by colourable pleas, now by the prayers of noble persons, especially of the Earl of Hereford. . . . When however he heard [that the abbot had obtained a sentence of outlawry against him] then, grieving not so much for his priory as for his banishment from England, he presently plied gifts, promises, and prayers all at once, and enticed to his side everyone of the cardinals or others whom he knew to be thirsty for gold, giving much and promising more, until he had obtained from the Apostolic See a personal citation of the abbot himself to Rome. . . . But the abbot escaped by a miracle (if I may so speak) from the need of undertaking so arduous a journey, to the grievous harm both of his monastery and of his body. Wherefore the aforesaid William (after a long and dispendious stay at the Roman Court, after much and unavailing waste of money, after many bulls obtained on his behalf, . . . seeing that his wiles profited him little or naught in all these matters,) obtained, as it is reported, other bulls more favourable to his part, wherewith he purposed to return home. When therefore he was come to London, he was searched and arrested by the king's serjeants, who favoured the abbot and had perchance been hired by him for this purpose; and by royal command he was brought before the king at Marlborough. So he was caught in the manner and city aforesaid, in a secular habit and without tonsure. The king sent him back by the sheriff to London, there to be kept in ward till he had sent word to the abbot of his royal pleasure in this matter. Soon afterwards he caused him to be delivered to the abbot's custody, to be guarded body for body, until the abbot should hear further from the king concerning this matter. But what those bulls contained which he is said to have brought, the abbot alone knoweth, and He to Whom all things are known. ...[Meanwhile powerful friends pleaded for Somerton, not without covert threats.] Wherefore after no long interval, at the instance of the Lady Isabella our queen, and others to whose prayers it were unsafe not to defer, since (as the poet saith) the great man supplicates with naked sword—therefore the aforesaid William was loosed from prison and restored to his Priory of Binham, albeit the abbot had been firmly purposed to deal otherwise with him.

These things we record, not as defending the aforesaid cause, which indeed is criminal and damnable, but that posterity may see how great dissensions, what hatred, what damages, follow from the greed and covetousness of prelates. For both the lord abbot wasted the substance of St Albans with grievous expenses for the prosecution of his cause, and the prior himself did irreparable harm to his priory in defence of his own case. In truth, he alienated the two best chalices of his church, which were worth far more than all those that were left; together with six copes, three chasubles, two mass-phials and a silver censer, cloths of silk, and seven golden rings which had been offered aforetime by pious folk, and silver goblets and spoons, alas! nor did he spare the silver cup and crown wherein the Lord's Body was wont to hang over the high altar; these also he alienated for the aforesaid cause.

Nevertheless, though this William was restored to Binham Priory as aforesaid; yet after that he had dwelt there a few years in great poverty, and had marked how the priory goods sufficed not for paying the pensions which he had so lavishly promised to the knights and other gentles of the countryside for the defence of his cause, then [in 1335] he was pierced with the dart of shame and fled, repeating (horrible to relate!) his former apostasy, and leaving that priory in abject poverty; [stripped of farms and churches to the value of 900 marks, and burdened with a debt of £400].

[P. 203.] Yet, within a brief space, this William of Somerton, wearied with his wicked life, and touched by God's grace after his second apostasy, came back as a suppliant to the gate of St Albans Abbey, and there threw himself down according to the custom.[1] When therefore he had sat there some hours, the Abbot Michael, a man of abundant bowels of mercy, was moved with compassion for him and sent his seneschal, John of Munden, to bring him into the almonry. There he dwelt five weeks by reason of a sickness which fell upon him; after which time he recovered and came to the abbey gate, there to begin his public penance, casting himself on the ground and deploring his wretched state. The abbot therefore pitied his infirmity, and (contrary to the wonted custom of the abbey) suffered him to lie in his woollen shirt; but for which he must have lain there naked save only his drawers.[2] So then he was received and admitted to mercy, after that he had earned his absolution from the major excommunication which by his apostasy he had incurred; and a penance was inflicted upon him according to the Rule and in proportion to the heinousness of his offences; which when he had humbly laboured to fulfil, he was afterwards fully absolved from the same.

[1] For an apostate begging readmission, see Martène, *Comment. in Regulam*, pp. 389 ff.
[2] The editorial side-note misinterprets this passage, as if it referred to the dormitory and not to the public penance.

45. A POET'S COMPLAINT OF THE BLACKSMITHS

From MS. Arundel, 292, f. 72 vo, fourteenth century.

(Reliquiae Antiquae, vol. 1, p. 240.)

SWART smutted smiths, smattered with smoke,
Drive me to death with din of their dints;
Such noise on nights ne heard men never,
What [with] knaven cry and clattering of knocks!
The crooked caitiffs cryen after col! col!
And blowen their bellows that all their brain bursteth.
Huf! puf! saith that one; haf! paf! that other;
They spitten and sprawlen and spellen many spells.[1]
They gnawen and gnashen, they groan all together,
And holden them hot with their hard hammers.
Of a bull-hide be their barm-fells;[2]
Their shanks be shackled for the fiery flinders;
Heavy hammers they have that hard be handled,
Stark strokes they striken on a steely stock,
Lus! bus! las! das! snore they by the row,
Such doleful a dream the devil it to-drive!
The master loungeth a little, and catcheth a less,
Twineth them twain and toucheth a treble,[3]
Tik! tak! hic! hac! tiket! taket! tyk! tyk!
Lus! bus! lus! das!...Christ them give sorrow!
May no man for brenn-waters[4] on night have his rest.

[1] Tell many tales.
[2] Leathern apron.
[3] The master pauses, catches up a smaller hammer, and intertwines [or perhaps separates] the bass of the sledge-hammer with his own lighter treble.
[4] For the hissing of the steel in the trough of water.

The fullest details of du Guesclin's life are recorded in the lengthy poem of the Picard trouvère Cuvelier (23,000 lines). This has come down to us in a longer and a shorter text; I have taken the liberty of choosing one or the other as it suited my present purpose, and of omitting here and there the trouvère's digressions or repetitions.

46. THE UGLY DUCKLING

(T. I, p. 5.)

[The Knight] Renaud du Guesclin was Bertrand's father, and his mother a most gentle lady and most comely; but for the boy of whom I tell you, methinks there was none so hideous from Rennes to Dinant. Flat-nosed he was and dark of skin, heavy and froward; wherefore his parents hated him so sore that often in their hearts they wished him dead, or drowned in some swift stream; *Rascal*, *Fool*, or *Clown* they were wont to call him; so despised was he, as an ill-conditioned child, that squires and servants made light of him; but we have oftentimes seen, in this world of vain shadows, that the most despised have been the greatest....

So when he had fulfilled eight or nine years, he took a custom of his own, as I will here tell. Many a time and oft he would go play in the fields, gathering around him forty or fifty boys, whom he would divide into companies and make them fight as at a tournament—yea, and so fiercely that one would rudely overthrow the other. When therefore Bertrand saw his fellows overthrown before his face, to their great hurt, then would he run and help them to rise, saying, "Haste now, avenge yourself well and boldly on that other!" Thus he skilfully kept up the fight and the tourney by thrusting himself among them; as hounds tear wolves with their teeth, so he would overthrow even the great ones and bruise them sore, and they knew him by this token, that all his clothes were torn and his body bleeding. Truly I declare that he made no account of his own blood; thus would he cry aloud, "Guesclin to the rescue!" and maintain the fight so long that none knew which side had the victory. When therefore all were glutted with fighting, then he would bid them cease, and say in a soft voice: "Come, good fellows all, let us go privily and drink all together as good friends; I will pay, so long as there is a penny in my purse. If any have not wherewithal, I will cheerfully stand surety for him; if I lend to any, and he repay it, then will I never love him so long as my youth shall last; if mine host will trust me, soon shall he be paid, even though I must take a silver cup from my father's house or go sell a good mare at Rennes; my lord [father] would ransom more than an hundred." "God!" said the boys within themselves, "to what wisdom will this Bertrand grow! God Almighty send him good speed, that this good beginning may come to full honour!"

When Bertrand came back from such company all bruised and torn and merry at heart, then his mother would say in grief and wrath: "In sooth, wretched boy, this is a foul life that you lead; little does it show of the noble lineage from which you come...! If ever again you return in this guise, you shall repent it all the days of your life...." But on the morrow Bertrand would do half as ill again....When his father Renaud knew the truth, whence he was come and what he wrought there, then he straitly charged the peasants that no child in all the country round should follow his son; or if any so follow him, then shall the father pay a fine of five pounds. Then all the children were so sad and so abashed that they fled at Bertrand's approach; and when he saw this, he would catch and assail them and oftentimes compel them to wrestle against their will. So his father heard complaints on all sides, and oftentimes the mother that bare him cursed her child, shedding bitter tears, and saying to her lord that naught would ever avail until he should cast his son into prison. So to prison he went, where they brought him meat and drink and all that he needed: a good four times was he thus in ward, but little he recked for all that. It befel that a chambermaid brought his dinner and unlocked the door; forthwith he seized her, and took her keys, and shut her in and took his leave. The bird was gone; so cunningly did he hide that none could find him, wheresoever they might search. Then one morning he fled hastily till he came to a field that he knew full well; there he found a ploughman toiling in the furrow with two of Sir Renaud's mares. Bertrand bestrode the one and fled; yet as he went the bondman cried: "Alas, Bertrand!" quoth he, "this is an ill deed; I dare not now look your father in the face; bring back the mare, for St Benet's sake!" But Bertrand laughed aloud, for he made little account of such words.

Then rode Bertrand full gallop on his mare, that had neither shoes nor bridle, harness nor saddle: he rode on the rough hair, and galloped as though he would break her back. When his father knew this, his head grew hot with anger, and he would gladly have seen his son drowned in the salt sea. Meanwhile Bertrand rode as one who recked nought of all this, and came to stately Rennes to an uncle who had married his aunt, a wealthy dame and well furnished with worldly goods. When his aunt saw him, she was grieved in her soul and said, "Bertrand, you have such a repute as cuts your mother to the heart, and your father too—God keep him whole! This is great folly, by the glorious Virgin, that you live so wayward a life and so unworthy of your lineage." "Lady," quoth the husband, "you speak as a simple woman; it is meet and right that youth should have his way; for all that we may say, it must slough its first skin. He is young enough yet, by the glorious Virgin! to have sense and honour in days to come. He hath done neither crime nor lawless deed; we have good wine and well-salted meat, whereof he shall have his part so long as it shall last." "Uncle," said Bertrand, "I hold with you! Your will shall be done both morn and even." "Truly," said his aunt, "ye have found a fair word; but, so God help me! my heart and mind tell me well that you will trouble us before six months be past."

Bertrand dwelt peaceably with his uncle; he constrained himself as best he could to wander neither hither nor thither; oftentimes he rode abroad with his uncle, and kept good company to his aunt also. Thus three months were well-nigh past, and he had joined in no sport. Then it came to pass that a prize was proclaimed for the best wrestler; and when he heard this tidings—the day was fixed for Sunday after dinner, and the place was ordained—then Bertrand's fair aunt called to her nephew, and prayed him softly to go with her to church and hear the sermon, whereof she had a pious thirst. Bertrand, will-he, nill-he, went with his aunt: but he slipped from her side when the sermon began, and came to the place where the wrestling was already begun. Some comrades were there who knew him: "Ho, Bertrand!" they cried, "your jolly body shall wrestle here; look ye, my masters, here is he who will throw all the rest!" "Gentles," said Bertrand, "I may not wrestle to-day, unless ye all pledge your faith, so many as are here, to say no word to mine aunt; for in truth, should she hear thereof, she would beat me." The good fellows swore to discover him neither thus nor otherwise; then began the wrestling, and long it endured. Bertrand was still a stripling under age—he had but seventeen years, if the tale be true— but he was short and thickset and big of bone. He beheld a Breton, a proud wrestler, who had thrown many of his fellows; twelve had he thrown, himself unconquered! Then came Bertrand and gripped him without more ado: now stood he not long unmoved, for Bertrand played on him a subtle trip; by force and wily craft he laid him on the ground: yet he drew Bertrand with him; but the Breton was undermost, grieved at heart, and Bertrand had the upper hand and the mastery over him. Yet went it ill with him in his fall, for he fell upon a rough sharp flint-stone, which cut through his knee, that the blood ran down. Hastily he rose to his feet; but he could no longer hold himself up for his weight in silver: "Ay me!" quoth Bertrand, "now am I in evil case, for my fair aunt will know all the trick I played her; it were better for me to be even at the sermon! Gentles," (quoth Bertrand) "for God's majesty let me be borne to mine aunt's house: but first of all my wound must be dressed."[1] Then they bore him to a leech with the noble prize on his head—a fair chaplet of gold and silver and cunning workmanship. "Ha, God!" quoth Bertrand, "by God's majesty take off this chaplet, for I am in no dancing mood!"...

Now was Bertrand in bed for all his fretting; then came his aunt and began to cry fie upon him: "Certes, Bertrand," said she, "you are nothing worth! You shame your knightly birth in wrestling thus with common folk: better to take your joy and solace in following tourneys, since you are thus bent

---

[1] Here and again on p. 39, where the Editor reads the verb *remuer* this is an obvious misreading for *remirer*.

upon showing your prowess." "Lady," said Bertrand, "I pray you be not wroth, and I swear to the just God our Father, so soon as I may well ride again I will follow jousts and tourneys, and wrestle no more; you shall see me fully whole again in eight days." There the gentle squire spake truth; for on the ninth day he was hale and sound. Then they made peace between Bertrand and his father, and his mother also, whom Bertrand loved right heartily. Bertrand went to see them in their high hall, and came right close to his mother; for he is bent on having jewels, silver, and fine gold to buy harness and a noble war-horse withal. Yea, he said openly that, if his mother set not her money thereto, he would break her coffer and take her jewel-casket. So spake Bertrand, and worked so well that his mother, his aunt, and his friends gave him harness, a shield, and a spear, with an ambling hackney that was not too good. Not a joust nor a tourney was held now in Brittany, if only Bertrand heard tidings thereof, but he would ride thither on the best mare that his father had: for his little hackney endured but a brief while; so soon as he lacked money, he sold his own steed, and then fell back on his father for a mare; jewels too he would take where he knew to find them, and freely he would sell them when he came to the lists. If he heard of a dinner of noble array, then he would take wine and send it to the house where he knew the squires: in the name of Bertrand du Guesclin the wine would be served up; all then made him good cheer, all feasted him well. He was but seventeen years old when he bore himself thus; so he won much acquaintance, and all men honoured him.

The most brilliant exploit of Du Guesclin's earlier career, (while he was only a guerilla captain in his thirtieth year,) was this capture, at a moment when the castellan, Robert Brembro, was absent on an expedition. Bertrand and his men disguised themselves as a party of wood-cutters with their wives, bringing faggots for sale at the castle.

47. CAPTURE OF THE CASTLE OF FOUGERAY

(*Ib.* p. 35, A.D. 1350.)

THEN each man hid his armour and his sword, and loaded himself with brushwood bound in faggots. Full thirty of them are together in the main band, and several more are posted in the valley; the band divides into four parts, and their plan is clearly ordered. Bertrand, in front, bore on his shoulders a great load of true faggots, as all would say who had seen him that day: manfully he strode forward to reach the castle. The men of the castle are aware now of the strangers, and the watchman has sounded his horn; Bertrand's comrades hear them assemble, and many among them would rather be now in the salt sea. But they mark how Bertrand has quickened his step; it were better to go on in good faith without faltering; already in his forward thoughts Bertrand saw himself in the castle, seated in the tapestried room and setting the flesh to roast before the great fire! Meanwhile his comrades, straggling behind, carrying their brushwood and faggots, dare neither to turn back nor to fall away for Bertrand's sake, whom they see drawing near to the castle. "Gentles!" said Bertrand, "have a care that ye do your work; this night ye shall sup with me in the castle, and I will give you wine of the best in the cellar." Yet some said, "God vouchsafe us His help! methinks they will sell us this wine right dearly": for the watchman with his horn dismayed them all; wherefore Bertrand began to sing for the comfort of their spirits.

Meanwhile the men of the castle took counsel together: "We must open the castle," said they, "to take these faggots in, for we have need thereof. These are the woodmen who come and supply us, and their wives also, straight come from church; lo! they are clad in white. Let us go and unbar the doors; these are no folk that know aught of war; great folly would it be to fear them." Then they gave word forthwith to the porter, who went to open the gate and let down the bridge; hastily he went, with but three men at his back; soon the gate was unbarred, and the chains fell. Then Bertrand came first under the vaulted arch, and cast down his load at the gate; right on the threshold he cast down his great load of faggots, so that none could bar his further entry. Then he cried, "Ah, whoreson knaves! ye shall buy this wood dear; I will heat the vessels for your bath, but it shall be in your own blood, which I will draw from your veins!" Therewith he drew his blade of tempered steel and smote the porter withal; little he spared him, but cleft through brainpan and half-way to the chine: then he cried his rough war-cry, "Guesclin!—forward, my friends, leave your loads, cast all to earth and come to my succour: here is good wine within, that needs but the tapping." Then said his fellows, "He is a good stark warrior!" Over the bridge they came like good knights: now the gate is won, and they pain them to press on. Down rushed the English in hot wrath, full a hundred men in all—cooks and turnspits, boys and varlets, and good men at arms: they came about Bertrand like bees, and cast great flint-stones to smite him down. . . . An English squire raised his axe and smote one of Bertrand's comrades on the ear; wherewith he fell asleep on the highroad, never to wake again for all that men might cry in his ear. To him Bertrand came without more ado, and drove with his bright sword through lungs and liver at a single thrust: down he fell dead. Bertrand seized the axe; he would not have given it up for all the gold of Pavia; "Guesclin!" he cried, "the day is ours!" He drove the English into a sheep-pen; there was he shut in on every side with cooks and buttery-boys, pantlers and grooms and suchlike rabble; one wielded a pitchfork, another a pointed pole; many a shrewd stroke he had from spit and pestle, but all his fellows gave him good help. Then it might have sped ill with their bodies and lives, but up there rode a troop of horse, drawn to the castle by the shouting of the fray. When therefore the horsemen were come by the gate where Bertrand's men had mounted, then these cried aloud to them:

CAPTURE OF THE CASTLE OF FOUGERAY

"Enter not herein but if ye be of the party of Charles de Blois! If ye be English, go your way with all speed, ye are but dead men if ye tarry here; for here is the noble du Guesclin with five hundred French, confessing the English of their sins!" "Ha, God!" cried these French, "it is he whom we sought!" ...Meanwhile Bertrand was hard bested: not a shred of his harness but was broken in pieces, and his blood reddened the earth; for the English smote upon him with axe and spear, thrusting and hewing to make an end of his life; "Guesclin!" he cried, for he had sore need of help. Then said one to another: "Mark his fury! never was such a squire as this in the wide world!" Then, seeing how hard he was pressed, they said: "Let us go straight to him; ours were the blame if such a champion were slain." Bertrand was now at such a pass as no tongue can tell; he had lost his axe, and defended himself with his two hands; then came a knight who knew him well, and broke through the press sword in hand; he cleared around him so wide a space that he came to Bertrand and cried, "Squire, come hither and follow me forthwith." Bertrand saw nought for the blood that blinded his eyes. Men drew him apart, and all were fain to dress his wounds; one would have bound up his sores, another wiped his face, but he was so wroth to be thus held that he would not suffer them to do him good. Yet when this troop was come to the rescue, then they slew outright all that they found in the castle...then forthwith they closed the gates, let down the bridge, and sent for wine to pass round among themselves....Each made ready to eat and drink; Bertrand drank the good wine and took good heart, for he had good wine to his fill, and drank with the rest.

John of France was prisoner in England; the castle of Melun had been surprised by Charles the Bad, King of Navarre, who was now an ally of the English. Three queens were in the castle, which was defended by Bertrand's old enemy the Bascon de Mareuil. The Dauphin, or Duke of Normandy, soon to be King Charles the Wise, commanded the siege in person; the still existing treasury-accounts show that he drew from his arsenal 20,000 crossbow-bolts, 10,000 arrows, and two great cannons for this occasion; and here for the first time he witnessed the prowess of du Guesclin, who in later years was his chief instrument in driving the English out of France.

48. THE SIEGE OF MELUN

(Ib. p. 126, A.D. 1359.)

T H E N the Duke of Normandy prepared for a general assault. ...On the morrow his men were drawn up on the sand; in the van were ranged the good crossbowmen, having great shields to cover themselves withal; and the garrison for their part took their appointed posts. Then began the general assault, that it was wonder to see. The Bastard of Mareuil and all his soldiers stood unabashed on the wall; they hurled down stones to maim our men, and shot their bolts as stout crossbowmen; thicker flew the bolts than winter rain. The Bastard spared nought: down he cast the stones like a stout workman; none could behold him without dismay. Bertrand at last perceived the Knight, and cried: "Ha, God! good Father of Justice, never was I so thirsty for drink nor for meat as my soul thirsteth now to come to hand-grips with that man; gladly would I try his flesh with this dagger of mine!"

Valiantly our men maintained the assault; stoutly men shot, and down they cast their stones; into the moat they plunged, some four hundred or more, bearing ladders to set against the walls; but many a man went up who was sore grieved at heart. The Bastard, fulfilled of all valour, cried aloud, "Shoot ye down there, or ye are lost!" But sore was the assault, and long was it sustained. The Duke leaned at his window hard by and made his complaint to the one true God: "Now is this realm of France confounded; now is the King my father, the noble, the redoubtable, kept a prisoner in England....Now forward!" said the Duke, "and labour with a good will; assault them sore, cost what cost may!"

THE SIEGE OF MELUN

Then might ye see many a noble knight rush mightily to the assault with shot of shaft and javelin, and strive to rear the ladders against the walls. Those within the castle defended

STORM OF AUBENTON

From an early fifteenth-century MS. reproduced in Viollet-le-Duc's *Dict. de l'Architecture*, t. 1, p. 383. (Note the *barriers*, or outwork of palisades.)

themselves like wild boars; long will the memory live in men's minds. Our Frenchmen must needs give wholly backwards, for the stones that men rolled down from the walls. Bertrand beheld them plunge into the moat to break the wall;

but all in vain, they could not make a mine. Then looked he at the Bastard, at whose sight our men were wholly dismayed: "Ha, God!" cried Bertrand, "may I find thee? By the faith that I ought to bear to Jesus Christ, either ye shall deal with my body in such wise that no succour nor comfort shall ever avail, or I will mount to those battlements, and speak with thee face to face!"

Then Bertrand withdrew a space; a ladder he chose, and reared it in his arms: swiftly and nimbly he laid it on his neck; and, what with others' help, what with his own travail, he set it up to the wall and seized a shield to cover his head. When the Duke saw him, he asked of his people: "Who is this man" (said the Duke) "who thus mounteth yonder?" To whom a knight replied, "Ye have heard long since of Bertrand du Guesclin, whose prowess is so great, and who endured such travail in the wars of Brittany for your cousin Charles the lord of that land." "Is that he," said the Duke, "by God who created us all?" "Yea, sire, by God, never was there so doughty a warrior." "By my head!" said the Duke, "there is a good knight!" Meanwhile Bertrand hath not tarried; he is mounted fearlessly on the ladder. The Bastard of Mareuil was aware of his coming, and cried to his men, who stood thick around him, "Good sirs, do quickly and stay not your hands; bring me forthwith a stone of weight, the weightiest of all that ye can find." Then answered they, "What say ye? Behold, all that ye require is before you: on one side great beams and stout, and on the other barrels filled to the brim with stones; ye may not fail, smite at a venture upon this boor who mounts so sturdily. See how great and short and square he is, big and bulging like a hog in armour! Ah God! how properly he would fall into the moat, and how his heart would burst with the fall! Give him good measure and running over; for in very truth he is fashioned like a Paris street-porter, all bloated under his canvas slop!"

Meanwhile Bertrand came up: small account they made of him; yet those who scoffed knew him but ill. With his shield at his neck and the good blade in his hand, he cried aloud to the Bastard of Mareuil: "Ho, Bastard! let me come forthwith to the battlements, and I will prove that thou commandest here against all right! or come thou down hither into this alder-grove, there will we fight with a right good heart! for I will prove to thee, if that hour come, that thou dost ill and unjustly towards the Duke of Normandy." To this the Bastard gave no friendly word: without further ado he discharged a mighty herring-barrel full of stones plump upon Bertrand as he mounted his ladder. So boisterous was the blow that the ladder brake, and Bertrand fell headlong to the ground: head-foremost plunged he into the moat, where he had leisure to drink his fill: thus he tarried awhile with his two feet in the air. Bertrand was stunned; he knew not where he was; loud cried the Duke: "Succour me my Bertrand, to whom all honour is due; certes, it would be pity that he should die thus!" Then came a squire and drew him by the feet; so long he drew, and so lustily, that he dragged him forth from the water. Forth came Bertrand's head all covered with mud; so stunned was he that he knew not where he was; sooth to say, he seemed more dead than alive. Forth from thence they bore him by main force, and laid him for his comfort within a warm dung-heap, until he came to himself again and stretched his limbs, and asked aloud of those who kept him: "Lordings, what vile devil hath brought me hither? Is our assault come to nought? We must hasten to the front!" "Alas!" said a squire who knew him well: "you have your belly-full, Bertrand; be ye content therewith!" Lightly rose he then from his dung-heap, with a good will to join in the assault. Already some of the French retreated; and men said to Bertrand, "Sir, be advised; go no more to the assault, for within a little while all will be finished." But Bertrand answered that he would go to the barriers; truly he spake it, and truly he went. There was no man so hardy, of all who were there, who would have dared to go whither Bertrand thrust himself forward; sword in hand, and by main force, he drove the foe back to the barriers; many he felled to the earth: then they closed their barriers and raised the drawbridge. Thus long did the assault last; then at nightfall they sounded the retreat until to-morrow's sunrising. Then they held a parley; a treaty was made, and the noble Duke went back to Paris.

Eustache Deschamps, Chaucer's French contemporary and panegyrist, is a voluminous poet who, without much inspiration, gives many vivid pictures of contemporary life. The first of the *balades* here translated voices the complaint, (at least as old as that great growth of material prosperity which marks the thirteenth century) of the growing power of money in the world. The edition quoted is that of the *Société des Anciens Textes Français*.

49. THE ALMIGHTY DOLLAR

(T. I, p. 229.) Balade.

That all men in these days seek only to grow rich.

I FEAR sore that dear times will come, and that we shall have an evil year, when I see many men gather corn together and store it apart. I see the fields fail, the air corrupted, the land in disarray, evil plowing and rotting seed, weakling horses whose labour drags; on the other hand the rich man crieth *Check*! Wherefore poor folk must needs go begging, for no man careth but to fill his bags.

Each man is selfish and covetous in his own fashion; their lives are disordered; all is snatched away by violence of great men, nor doth any creature under the sun seek the common good. Do men govern the land according to reason? Nay! for law is perished, Truth faileth, I see Lying reign among us, and the greatest men are drowned in this lake [of sin]; the earth is ruined by covetise, for no man careth but to fill his bags.

Therefore the innocent must die of hunger, with whom these great wolves daily fill their maw; those who heap up false treasures by the hundred and the thousand. This grain, this corn, what is it but the blood and bones of the poor folk who have ploughed the land? wherefore their spirit crieth on God for vengeance. Woe to the lords, the councillors, and all who steer us thus, and woe to all such as are of their party; for no man careth now but to fill his bags.

L'ENVOY

Prince, short is the span of this life, and a man dieth as suddenly as one may say "clac"; whither will the poor abashed soul go? for no man careth now but to fill his bags.

50. UNIVERSITY EXPENSES

(T. VIII, p. 96.) Balade.

Of the Scholars at Orleans.

THUS runs the Orleans Scholar's Letter: "Well-beloved father, I have not a penny, nor can I get any save through you, for all things at the University are so dear: nor can I study in my Code or my Digest, for they are all tattered. Moreover, I owe ten crowns in dues to the Provost, and can find no man to lend them to me; I send you word of greetings and of money.[1]

The Student hath need of many things if he will profit here; his father and his kin must needs supply him freely, that he be not compelled to pawn his books, but have ready money in his purse, with gowns and furs and decent clothing, or he will be damned for a beggar; wherefore, that men may not take me for a beast, I send you word of greetings and of money.

Wines are dear, and hostels, and other good things; I owe in every street, and am hard bested to free myself from such snares. Dear father, deign to help me! I fear to be excommunicated; already have I been cited, and there is not even a dry bone in my larder. If I find not the money before this feast of Easter, the church door will be shut in my face: wherefore grant my supplication, for I send you word of greetings and of money.

L'ENVOY

Well-beloved father, to ease my debts contracted at the tavern, at the baker's, with the doctor and the bedells, and to pay my subscriptions to the laundress and the barber, I send you word of greetings and of money."

---

[1] There is a pun here: *Salux* meant a kind of gold coin as well as greetings.

Geoffrey de la Tour-Landry fought in the Hundred Years' War at least as early as 1346 and as late as 1383. He wrote in 1371, for the instruction of his daughters, a book which became the most popular educational treatise of the Middle Ages. This "Book of the Knight of the Tower" was translated into German, and at least twice into English; it had passed through seven editions in the three languages before 1550. After Caxton's edition of 1483 there was none in English until it was reprinted in 1868 by T. Wright for the Early English Text Society, from a MS. of Henry VI's reign. It is from this edition that the following extracts are taken.

51. MARITAL AMENITIES
(p. 23.)

I WILL say an ensample that it is an evil thing to a woman to be in jealousy. There was a gentlewoman that was wedded to a squire, and she loved him so much that she was jealous over all women that he spake with; for the which he blamed her often, but it was never the better. And among other she was jealous of a woman that had a great and high heart; and so on a time she reproved that woman with her husband, and she said she said not true; and the wife said she lied. And they ran together and pulled off all that ever was on their heads, and plucked each other by the hair of the head right evil. And she that was accused, caught a staff, and smote the wife on the nose such a stroke that she brake her nose, and that all her life after she had her nose all crooked, the which was a foul maim and blemishing of her visage; for it is the fairest member that man or woman hath, and sitteth in the middle of the visage. And so was the wife fouled and maimed all her life, and her husband said often to her, that it had been better that she had not been jealous, than for to have undone her visage as she had. And also for that defouling of her visage her husband might never find in his heart to love her heartily as he did before, and he took other women, and thus she lost his love through her jealousy and folly. And therefore here is a good example to all good women, that they ought to leave all such fantasies, and suffer and endure patiently their anger, if they have any; ... Also, a woman ought not to strive with her husband, nor give him no displeasance nor answer her husband before strangers, as did once a woman that did answer her husband before strangers like a rampe,[1] with great

[1] Virago, vixen.

villainous words, dispraising him and setting him at nought; of the which he was often ashamed, and bade her hold her peace for shame, but the more fair he spake, the worse she did. And he, that was angry of her governance, smote her with his fist down to the earth; and then with his foot he struck her in the visage and brake her nose, and all her life after she had her nose crooked, the which shent[1] and disfigured her visage after, that she might not for shame show her visage, it was so foul blemished. And this she had for her evil and great language, that she was wont to say to her husband. And therefore the wife ought to suffer and let the husband have the words, and to be master, for that is her worship; for it is shame to hear strife between them, and in especial before folk. But I say not but when they be alone, but she may tell him with goodly words, and counsel him to amend if he do amiss....

It happened once there were iij merchants that went homeward from a fair, and as they fell in talking, riding on the way, one of them said, "It is a noble thing for a man to have a good wife that obeyeth and doth his bidding at all times." "By my troth," said that other, "my wife obeyeth me truly." "By God," said that other, "I trow mine obeyeth best to her husband." Then he that began first to speak said, "Let us lay a wager of a dinner, and whose wife that obeyeth worst, let her husband pay for the dinner"; and thus the wager was laid. And they ordained among them how they should say to their wives, for they ordained that every man should bid his wife leap into a basin that they should set before her, and they were sworn that none should let his wife have witting of their wager, save only they should say, "Look, wife, that whatsoever I command be done." However it be, after one of them bade his wife leap into the basin that he had set afore her on the ground, and she answered and asked: "Whereto?" and he said, "for it is my lust, and I will that ye do it." "By God," quoth she, "I will first wit whereto ye will have me leap into the basin." And for nothing her husband could do she would not do it. So her husband up with his fist, and gave her ij or iij great strokes; and then went they to the second

___
[1] Spoiled, discomfited.

merchant's house, and he commanded that whatever he bade do it should be done, but it was not long after but he bade his wife leap into the basin that was afore her on the floor, and she asked: "Whereto?" and she said she would not for him. And then he took a staff, and all to-beat her; and then they went to the third merchant's house, and there they found the meat on the board, and he whispered in one of his fellows' ears, and said, "After dinner I will assay my wife, and bid her leap into the basin." And so they set them to their dinner. And when they were set, the good man said to his wife, "Whatever I bid, let it be done, however it be." And she, that loved him and dreaded him, heard what he said, and took heed to that word; but she wist not what he meant; but it happed that they had at their dinner rere-eggs,[1] and there lacked salt on the board, and the good man said, "Wife, *sele sus table*"; and the wife understood that her husband had said, "*seyle sus table*," the which is in French, "*leap on the board*." And she, that was afraid to disobey, leapt upon the board, and threw down meat, and drink, and brake the glasses, and spilt all that there was on the board. "What," said the good man, "then can ye none other play, wife?" "Be ye mad, sir," she said, "I have done your bidding, as ye bade me to my power, notwithstanding it is your harm and mine; but I had liever ye had harm and I both, than I disobeyed your bidding. For ye said, '*seyle sus table*.'" "Nay," quoth he, "I said, '*sele sus table*,' that is to say, salt on the board." "By my troth," she said, "I understood that ye bade me leap on the board," and there was much mirth and laughing. And the other two merchants said it was no need to bid her leap into the basin, for she obeyed enough; wherefore they consented that her husband had won the wager, and they had lost both. And after she was greatly praised for her obeisance to her husband, and she was not beat, as were that other ij wives that would not do their husband's commandment. And thus poor men can chastise their wives with fear and strokes, but a gentlewoman should chastise herself with fairness, for otherwise they should not be taught.

[1] The editor of the E.E.T.S. volume offers no explanation of this word; it represents the *œu s molés, i.e.* "scrambled eggs" of the French original.

52. THE LOST MARRIAGE
(p. 165.)

I SHALL tell you of an ensample of a knight's daughter that
lost her marriage by her nicety. There was a knight that had
iij daughters, of the which the eldest was wedded, and there
was a knight that axed the second daughter both for land and
marriage; insomuch that the knight came for to see her that
should be his wife, and for to be assured and affianced together,
if they were pleased each with other, for neither of them had
seen other before that time. And the damosel, that knew of
the knight's coming, she arrayed herself in the best guise
that she could for to have a slender and a fair-shapen body,
and she clothed her in a cote-hardie[1] unfurred, the which sat
right strait upon her, and it was great cold, great frost, and
great wind; and for the simple vesture that she had upon, and
for the great cold that was at that time, the colour of the maid
was defaced, and she waxed all pale and black of cold. So this
knight that was come for to see her, and beheld the colour
of her all dead and pale, and after that he looked upon that
other sister that she had, and saw her colour fresh and ruddy
as a rose, (for she was well clothed, and warm against the
cold, as she that thought not upon no marriage at so short a
time) the knight beheld first that one sister and after that
other. And when he had dined, he called two of his friends
and of his kin, and said unto them, "Sirs! we be come hither
for to see the daughters of the lord of this place, and I know
well that I should have which that I would choose, wherefore
I would have the third daughter." And his friends answered
him, that it was more worship unto him for to have the elder.
"Fair friends," said the knight, "ye see but little advantage
therein,[2] for ye know well they have an elder sister, the which
is wedded; and also I see the youngest, the fairest and freshest
of colour, more pleasant than her second sister, for whom
I was spoken unto for to have in marriage; and therefore my

[1] Close-fitting gown for ladies, or tunic for men.
[2] *I.e.* apparently the wedded sister had taken the lion's share of the inheritance,
so that there would be little pecuniary difference between the second and the third.

pleasaunce is to have her." And the knight axed the third daughter, which was granted him; whereof folk were marvelled, and in especial the maid that weened for to have been wedded unto the same knight. So it happed within short time after, they married the young damosel, the which the knight had refused because the cold had paled her colour and withdrawn her fairness; after when she was well clothed and furred, and the weather was changed to warmer, her colour and fairness was come again, so that she was fresher and fairer an hundred part than was her sister, the knight's wife; and so the knight said unto her, "My fair sister, when I was to wed, and I came for to see you, ye were not so fair by the seventh part as ye be now, for ye be now right fair and well coloured, and then ye were all pale and of other colour, and now ye pass your sister my wife in fairness, whereof I have great marvel." And then the knight's wife answered, "My lord, I shall tell you how it was; my sister thought well that ye should come for to affiance her as for your wife; and for to make her gentle, and small, and fair bodied, she clothed her in a simple cote-hardie, not doubled; and it was cold winter, and great frost, and great wind, and that permuted her colour, and I, that thought as much to have such wealth and worship as for to have you unto my lord without any nicety, I was well clothed with furred gowns that kept my body warm, wherefore I had better colour than she had; whereof I thank God, for therefore I gat your love; and blessed be the hour that my sister clothed herself so light, for if it had not been so, ye had not taken me for to have left her." Thus lost, as ye have heard, the elder daughter her marriage because she quainted herself.

The British Museum Royal MS. 6. E. vi, is a great theological dictionary in two volumes, compiled at the beginning of the fourteenth century from many earlier authors of repute. The book illustrates in many passages the ideas of Dante's age: *e.g.* on fol. 37 b the friars are spoken of in much the same terms as in *Par.* xii, 112 ff. and the author refers to the damnation of Pope Anastasius for heresy (f. 360 b; cf. *Inf.* xi, 8).

53. TRAIN UP A WIFE IN THE WAY SHE SHOULD GO

(f. 214 a, under the rubric *Castigare*.)

MOREOVER, a man may chastise his wife and beat her for her correction; for she is of his household, and therefore the lord may chastise his own, as it is written in Gratian's *Decretum*, part 2. c. VII q. 1. under the gloss *judicari*.[1] Also a master in the schools may chastise or beat his disciple, even though this latter be a clerk, provided only that he exceed not due measure; nor doth he thereby incur the stigma of excommunication,[2] even though his disciple be in Holy Orders, if the chastisement be for discipline's sake....And note that clerics may be beaten with rods.

John Gower, Chaucer's friend, was probably a London merchant and a country squire: the reader should consult G. C. Macaulay's admirable essay on him in the *Camb. Hist. Eng. Lit.* vol. II, chap. vi. His poems are frankly satirical, but gain much force as evidence from his frequent protest that he simply voices what the public is saying around him. The following extract is from his *Mirour de l'Omme*, ed. Macaulay, lines 25,213ff.

54. TRICKS OF TRADE

ALL men know that of our bounden duty we must preach to vices for their amendment.... The good are good, the evil are evil; if therefore we preach to the dishonest, the honest

[1] "He may chastise her temperately, for she is of his household." The same doctrine is laid down in part I, dist. xxv, c. 3, s.v. *servum.* "So likewise the husband is bound to chastise his wife in moderation...unless he be a clerk, in which case he may chastise her more severely." The Wife of Bath's last husband, being a clerk of Oxford, was possibly conscious of this privilege. Gratian's *Decretum*, though never recognized as absolutely authoritative on all points, was throughout the Middle Ages the great text-book of Canon Law.

[2] Under the rubric *siquis suadente diabolo.* See note to vol. I, no. 71.

man need take no heed thereof; for each shall have reward or blame according to his work. Sooth to say, there is a difference betwixt the merchant whose thoughts are set on deceit, and him whose day is spent in honest work; both labour alike for gain, but one would sort ill with the other. There is one merchant in these days whose name is on most men's tongues: Trick is his name, and guile his nature: though thou seek from the East to the going out of the West, there is no city or good town where Trick doth not amass his ill-gotten wealth. Trick at Bordeaux, Trick at Seville, Trick at Paris buys and sells; he hath his ships and his crowd of servants, and of the choicest riches Trick hath ten times more than other folk. Trick at Florence and Venice hath his counting-house and his freedom of the city, nor less at Bruges and Ghent; to his rule, too, hath the noble city on the Thames bowed herself, which Brutus founded in old days, but which Trick stands now in the way to confound, fleecing his neighbours of their goods: for all means are alike to him whether before or behind; he followeth straight after his own lucre, and thinketh scorn of the common good. . . . In the mercer's trade also doth Trick, of his cunning, practise often divers guiles. . . . Birds of that feather never want a tongue, and Trick is more clamorous than any sparrowhawk: when he seeth strange folk, then shalt thou see him pluck and draw them by the sleeve, calling and crying: "Come," quoth he, "come in without demur! Beds, kerchiefs, and ostrich feathers—sandals, satins, and stuffs from oversea—come, I will show you all. What d'ye lack? Come buy, ye need go no further, for here is the best of all the street. . . ." Sometimes Trick is a draper . . . men tell us, (and I believe it) that whatsoever is dark by nature hateth and avoideth the light: wherefore when I see the draper in his house, methinks he hath no clear conscience. Dark is the window where he bargaineth with thee, and scarce canst thou tell the green from the blue; dark too are his ways, none may trust his word for the price of his goods. Darkly will he set thee his cloth at double price, and clinch it with an oath; darkly thus will he beguile thee all the worse, for he would persuade that he hath done thee a friendship, wherein he hath the more cozened thee, saying that he hath given thee the

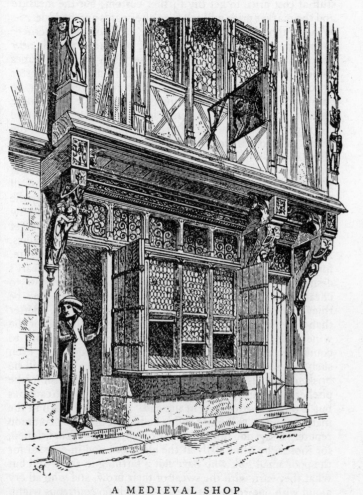

A MEDIEVAL SHOP

From Viollet-le-Duc's *Dict. de l'Architecture*, t. II, p. 239.

stuff at cost price to get thy further custom; but the measure and the market price will tell thee afterwards another tale. . . . Wouldst thou have closer knowledge of Trick the Taverner? thou shalt know him by his piment, his clarée, and his new ypocras, that help to fatten his purse when our City dames come tripping at dawn to the tavern as readily as to minster or to market. Then doth Trick make good profit; for be sure that they will try every vintage in turn, so it be not mere vinegar. Then will Trick persuade them that they may have Vernage, Greek wine and Malvesie if they will but wait; the better to cajole them of their money, he will tell them of divers sorts—wines of Crete, Ribole and Roumania, of Provence and Monterosso; so he boasteth to sell Riviera and Muscadel from his cellar, but he hath not a third part of all these; he nameth them but for fashion's sake, that he may the better entice these dames to drink. Trust me, he will draw them ten sorts of wine from one barrel, when once he can get them seated in his chairs. Then will he say, "Dear ladies, *Mesdames*, make good cheer, drink freely your good pleasure, for we have leisure enough!" Then hath Trick his heart's desire, when he hath such chamberers who know how to cheat their husbands; little doth he care whether they be thieves or no, so that he but make his profit of them. Better than any master of magic, Trick knoweth all the arts of the wine-trade; all its subtilties and its guile. He is crafty to counterfeit Rhine wine with the French vintage; nay, even such as never grew but by Thames shore, even such will he brisk up and disguise, and baptize it for good Rhenish in the pitcher: so quaintly can he dissemble, that no man is so cautious but Trick will trick him in the end. And if he be evil in the matter of wine, still more evil is he in that of ale, by common repute. I say not this for the French, but for Englishmen, for those who drink daily at the alehouse; and in especial for the poor small folk who have not a farthing in the world but what they earn with the sweat of their brow, and who all cry aloud with one voice that the ale-seller is no courteous wight.

A MORTUARY CASE

The mortuary system is so curious, yet has been so neglected by historians, that the reader may be glad to see an actual case from a fifteenth-century book of precedents (Brit. Mus. MSS., Harl. 862, f. 5 a). On a peasant's death, the lord of the manor had frequently a claim upon his best beast or other possession as *mortuary* or *heriot*. Side by side with this grew up a similar claim from the parish priest. It was presumed that the dead man must have failed to some extent in due payment of tithes during his lifetime, and that a gift of his second best possession to the Church would therefore be most salutary to his soul. This claim had admittedly no foundation in law, but was maintained already in 1305 as a custom which, being pious and reasonable, must therefore have the binding force of law. I have dealt more fully with this system, which did much to precipitate the Reformation, in *Priests and People in Medieval England* (Simpkin, Marshall, 1s. nett). It will be noticed that the compiler of this Formulary, though he has copied actual cases into his book, often abbreviates for his own convenience or supplies alternative phraseology, as the reader will see from the brackets throughout this piece. Bp Stafford's Register shows that Robert Tayllour was instituted to the Vicarage of Morwenstow, 23 February, 1408.

55. A MORTUARY CASE

In God's name, Amen. In the presence of you, lord Bishop of Exeter, (whoever he may be, by God's etc., etc.), I, the proctor of Sir R. T. perpetual Vicar of the parish of Morstow in Cornwall, of the Diocese of Exeter, [plead] against John Martyn executor of the will (or administrator of the goods) of Richard Martyn, father of the aforesaid John, now dead, and against all who may legally appear for him, affirming that according to laudable and reasonable custom for the last (10 or 20 or 30 or 40 or 60) years last past, more or less, and indeed from a time and for a time whereunto the memory of man goeth not to the contrary, used, approved, and generally observed, and legitimately prescribed, in the said parish of Morstow, the right of taking and holding the best possession appertaining to every customary[1] parishioner who may die in that same parish, and especially whose heriot hath been paid to his worldly lord after the death of the said defunct, pertained, pertaineth, and should pertain even in future to the Vicars for the time being of the said church of Morstow,

---

[1] Subject to certain manorial burdens; most customary tenants were themselves serfs.

predecessors of the said Sir Robert, as by his lawful right of taking tithes of cut timber or of taking and having the aforesaid mortuary, in the manner and form aforesaid, for all and every time etc. (as aforesaid in its own place already alleged): Nevertheless the said John Martyn, executor or administrator of the goods of the said Richard Martyn deceased, knowingly seized and still holdeth without and against the will of the said Sir Robert, one ox of black colour, valued by the common reckoning at thirteen shillings,[1] which ox at the death of the said R. Martyn had been (after the heriot paid to the Prior and Convent of Launceston, his temporal lords, on the occasion of his death) his next best possession, and thus owing to the said Vicar Sir Robert as a mortuary, in virtue of the said custom, as aforesaid, (or at least, "by means of the guile and fraud of this same John, in this matter, the Vicar hath failed to take the said ox.") And, albeit the aforesaid executor or administrator John hath been oftentimes required, in due form of law, on the part of the said Sir Robert, to deliver the said ox to the said Sir Robert and to satisfy him from his possessions in this matter according to the above estimate; yet this John *etc.* hath hitherto refused to deliver the ox as aforesaid to this same Sir Robert and to satisfy him according to his own estimate as aforesaid, and expressly refuseth it still, without form of justice, thus wickedly robbing *etc.* the said Vicar Sir Robert, and his aforesaid Vicarage of his right and possessions (or "as it were robbing him of his rights as aforesaid in the aforesaid things") in the aforesaid parish of Morstow, in the month of February and the year of our Lord 1414; seeing also that the right of taking and having this his best possession as a mortuary, in the manner and form aforesaid, pertained, pertaineth, and ought to pertain in future also to the said Vicar of the aforesaid Vicarage, (whosoever for the time being may be its Vicar, by name) in virtue of the custom aforesaid, [We pray therefore] that you, our lord Judge aforesaid, may pronounce and declare finally and definitely for the aforesaid custom and the future keeping of its observance in the aforesaid parish, and that the said executor or administrator John Martyn may be condemned to render the said

---

[1] From £7. 10s. to £10 modern money.

A MORTUARY CASE

ox, if he still exist, or otherwise according to the aforesaid valuation of his possessions, or some other (*etc.* as in the aforesaid place).

There are two other mortuary cases in the Formulary, fols. 5 b and 16 b. In the first (undated) the vicar of Morstow claims a blue coat value 10s. from John Baldwin executor of Nicholas Day, in virtue of a custom which gave him, by way of mortuary, "the best day-garment of each parishioner that dieth in the said parish, (excepting only servants working for a certain annual wage in the same parish and also inhabiting the borough or village of Morstow)." In the second, dated 1468, "the reverend man John Snyffemore, rector of the parish church of Silverton" claims that, from time immemorial, "if the wife of any parishioner of the aforesaid parish die, in what place or manner soever, forthwith the right of taking and having her husband's second best possession or beast, which the said husband had in his wife's lifetime, under the name of a mortuary and as a mortuary, belonged belongeth and should belong even in future to the rector of the aforesaid parish church." He therefore demands one red ox, valued at 18s., which John Laven, having lost his wife Matilda, had hitherto refused to render "to God and to the aforesaid church." Prebendary Hingeston-Randolph, whose knowledge of this diocese in the Middle Ages is unrivalled, has kindly supplied me with the following note: "John Snyffemore was presented to Silverton (on the Resignation of John Coke) by William Wadham, Esquire, and was instituted by Bishop Lacy, at Clyst, 11 Feb., 1444/5. On his death, William Somaster was instituted, 2 March, 1479/80. Snyffemore built the north aisle of Silverton Church at his own cost. His will, dated 18 June, 1479, is entered in Bishop Courtenay's Register. He directed that his body should be buried in the Chancel of Silverton 'afore our Ladie.' He bequeathed £40 to build a new ambulatory in the north side of the church, and all the issues and profits of all his lands and tenements in Silverton were to be paid yearly in sustentation of a priest to sing in the said north aisle. Moreover, he gave £38 towards the support of the foundation." To illustrate the above-mentioned cases, I subjoin an extract from the accounts of the Collegiate Church of St Mary Ottery for 1437/8 (Oliver, *Monast. Dioc. Exon.* p. 282); and a petition to the Pope extracted from Father Denifle's *Désolation des Eglises, etc.* t. I, p. 472.[1]

---

[1] I can only draw attention briefly here to the value of this book as a mine for the student of fifteenth-century manners. I had once thought of translating from it, as an illustration of medieval warfare, the letter of Bishop des Ursins to the Etats Généraux assembled at Blois in 1433 (t. I, p. 497); but the document is too painful to publish in naked English, and the reader will only find a far milder description of the same sort in vol. II, no. 63. It is a partial consolation to find that, on the repeated testimony of their enemies, the English soldiers were on the whole more humane to the French peasants than their own fellow-countrymen and nominal defenders. Another passage (t. I, p. 500) shows clearly, as Denifle notes, that the French themselves—or French rulers and statesmen, at least—

56. MORTUARY PROFITS

RECEIPTS from mortuaries. He accounteth for 9s. for an ox, mortuary of the wife of Thomas Glade and sold to the same Thomas:—6s. for a cow, the mortuary of John Harbelyn's wife and sold to the same John:—6d. for an ewe, the mortuary of Matilda Byre, sold to John At-the-Welle:—12d. for a pig, the mortuary of John Benyne sold to the widow of the same John:—1s. 6d. for a calf, the mortuary of Richard Swayne at Wakkesway:—6s. 4d. for a cow, the mortuary of William Reymond, sold to the said William's widow:—1s. 2d. for a ram, the mortuary of Roger At-the-Welle's wife's mother:—6s. for a cow, the mortuary of Richard Calley of Wygdon. Whereof the sum total is £1. 11s. 8d.

Complaint from the Abbot and monks of Cerisy in the Diocese of Bayeux to the Pope, A.D. 1445.

57. MORTUARY RESULTS

WHEREAS from time immemorial, as often as any tenants that were heads of families dwelling on our manors of Cerisy or Littry chanced to die, then if they had no wives or children the monastery had the right of taking to itself and applying to its own uses all their moveable goods; if, however, they had wives and children, then such goods were divided into three equal parts between the abbot and convent, the wife, and the children; moreover, the garments also of the said householders thus deceased were applied to the use and profit of the said monastery—those of Cerisy to the benefit of the sacristy and those of Littry to the granary; and whereas the said parishioners and tenants, having become sorely diminished in their possessions and impoverished by reason of the wars and other miseries which had so long wasted those parts, began to desert

"were ashamed to speak of Joan of Arc after her execution," until the lapse of a score of years had brought out her greatness more plainly; but for this again the reader must consult the original.

the manors aforesaid and betake themselves elsewhere for fear of this burden and servitude; whereas they refused also to marry their daughters on that manor[1] to the great, (nay, to the very greatest) damage and loss of the aforesaid monastery; and also, by reason of the aforesaid chattels, very many of the inhabitants aforesaid incurred, and [long] had incurred, the sentence of excommunication by not giving over faithfully the aforesaid moveable goods, but hiding them and thus defrauding the said monastery...[therefore the Abbot and monks have agreed with the tenants to commute these dues for a yearly tribute of 20 *livres tournois*, until such time as the sum of 300 gold pieces might be collected for the final redemption of the burden].

Extracts 58–69 are from Dr Gairdner's 1900 edition of the *Paston Letters*, which are probably the fullest and most remarkable collection of medieval family letters existing in any language.

58. WIFE TO HUSBAND

(Margaret Paston to John Paston, 28 Sept. 1443; vol. 1, p. 48.)

To my right worshipful husband, John Paston, dwelling in the Inner Temple at London, in haste.

RIGHT worshipful husband, I recommend me to you, desiring heartily to hear of your welfare, thanking God of your amending of the great disease that ye have had; and I thank you for the letter that ye sent me, for by my troth my mother and I were not in heart's ease from the time that we wist of your sickness, till we wist verily of your amending. My mother behested another image of wax, of the weight of you, to our Lady of Walsingham; and she sent iiij nobles to the iiij

[1] By marrying their daughters elsewhere, the serfs would withdraw them from the heavy burdens of this manor; but they would have to pay a heavy fine for doing so. This was an inevitable consequence of the social system which made one-half of the population the property of a few great landowners. It would of course be unjust to blame the individual landlord; but it is equally unhistorical to blink the fact that such regulations tended to foster those vices of which medieval moralists complain among the rural population. See Léopold Delisle, *Études sur la Classe Agricole*, 1903, p. 187.

Orders of Friars at Norwich to pray for you; and I have behested to go on pilgrimage to Walsingham and to Saint Leonard's[1] for you; by my troth I had never so heavy a season as I had from the time that I wist of your sickness till I wist of your amending; and sith my heart is in no great ease, nor nought shall be, till I wot that ye be very whole. Your father and mine was this day se'nnight at Beccles for a matter of the Prior of Bromholme; and he lay at Gelderstone that night, and was there till it was ix of the clock, and the t'other day. And I sent thither for a gown, and my mother said that I should have then, till I had been there anon, and so they could none get.

My father Garneys sent me word that he should be here the next week, and my uncle also, and playen them here with their hawks, and they should have me home with them; and, so God help me! I shall excuse me of mine going thither if I may; for I suppose that I shall readilier have tidings from you here than I should have there. I shall send my mother a token that she took me, for I suppose the time is come that I should send her, if I keep the behest that I have made; I suppose I have told you what it was. I pray you heartily that ye will vouchsafe to send me a letter as hastily as ye may, if writing be no disease to you, and that ye will vouchsafe to send me word how your sore doth. If I might have had my will, I should have seen you ere this time; I would ye were at home, (if it were your ease, and your sore might be as well looked to as it is where ye be,) now liever than a gown, though it were of scarlet! I pray you, if your sore be whole, and so that ye may endure to ride, when my father come to London, that ye will asken leave, and come home when the horse shall be sent home again; for I hope ye should be kept as tenderly here as ye be at London. I may none leisure have to do writen half a quarter so much as I should say to you if I might speak with you. I shall send you another letter as hastily as I may. I thank you that ye would vouchsafe to remember my girdle, and that ye would write to me at the time, for I suppose that writing was none ease to you.

[1] St Leonard's Priory at Norwich, where there was a wonder-working shrine of King Henry VI, sainted by popular acclamation.

Almighty God have you in His keeping, and send you health. Written at Oxnead, in right great haste, on St Michael's Even.

Yours,

M. PASTON.

My mother greets you well, and sendeth you God's blessing and hers; and she prayeth you, and I pray you also, that ye be well dieted of meat and drink; for that is the greatest help that ye may have now to your health-ward. Your son fareth well, blessed be God.

59. HUSBAND TO WIFE

(John Paston to Margaret Paston, 21 Sept. 1465; vol. II, p. 235.)

To my Cousin Margaret Paston.

MINE own dear sovereign lady, I recommend me to you, and thank you of the great cheer that ye made me here to my great cost and charge and labour. No more at this time, but that I pray you ye will send me hither ij clue of worsted for doublets, to wrap me this cold winter; and that ye inquire where William Paston bought his tippet of fine worsted, which is almost like silk, and if that be much finer than that he should buy me after vij. or viij. shillings,[1] then buy me a quarter and the mail thereof for collars, though it be dearer than the other, for I would make my doublet all worsted for worship of Norfolk, rather than like Gonnore's doublet....

Item, on the day after your departing, I received letters by Will. Ros from your sons to me, and to you, and to Ric. Calle, etc.[2]

Item, I shall tell you a tale,
Pampyng and I have picked your mail   *[trunk*

---

[1] *I.e.* "if that [of W. P.'s] be much finer than could be bought for 7 or 8 shillings, then etc."

[2] This *etc.*, as the reader will presently see, was the frequent refuge of writers unaccustomed to express themselves at length on paper: it occurs with tantalizing frequency all through these letters.

And taken out pieces five.
For upon trust of Calle's promise, we may soon unthrive;
And, if Calle bring us hither twenty pound
Ye shall have your pieces again, good and round;
Or else, if he will not pay you the value of the pieces, there
To the post do nail his ear;
Or else do him some other wrongs,[1]
For I will no more in his default borrow;
And, but if the receiving of my livelihood be better plied
He shall Christ's curse and mine clean tried;
And look ye be merry and take no thought,
For this rhyme is cunningly wrought.
My Lord Percy and all this house
Recommend them to you, dog, cat, and mouse,
And wish ye had been here still;
For they say ye are a good gille:
No more to you at this time,
But God him save that made this rhyme.
Writ the [day] of Saint Mathee
By your true and trusty husband,   J. P.

60. BUSINESS MATCHES

(Elizabeth Clere to John Paston, junr., about 1449; vol. I, p. 89.)

To my Cousin, John Paston, be this letter delivered.

TRUSTY and well-beloved cousin, I commend me to you, desiring to hear of your welfare and good speed in your matter, the which I pray God send you to his pleasance and to your heart's ease.

Cousin, I let you wit that Scrope hath been in this country to see my cousin your sister, and he hath spoken with my cousin your mother, and she desireth of him that he should show you the indentures made between the knight that hath his daughter and him, whether that Scrope, if he were married and fortuned to have children, if those children should inherit his land, or his daughter the which is married. Cousin, for

---

[1] *Query, sorrow?*

this cause take good heed to his indentures, for he is glad to show them, or whom ye will assign with you; and he saith to me he is the last in the tail of his livelihood, the which is cccl marks and better, as Watkin Shipdam saith, for he hath taken account of his livelihood divers times; and Scrope saith to me if he be married, and have a son and heir, his daughter that is married shall have of his livelihood i marks and no more; and therefore, cousin, meseemeth he were good for my cousin your sister, without that ye might get her a better. And if ye can get her a better, I would advise you to labour it in as short time as ye may goodly, for she was never in so great sorrow as she is nowadays, for she may not speak with no man, whosoever come, nor may not see nor speak with my man, nor with servants of her mother's, but that she [*the mother*] beareth her on hand otherwise than she meaneth. And she hath since Easter the most part been beaten once in the week or twice, and sometimes twice on one day, and her head broken in two or three places. Wherefore, cousin, she hath sent to me by Friar Newton in great counsel, and prayeth me that I would send to you a letter of their heaviness, and pray you to be her good brother, as her trust is in you; and she saith, if ye may see by his evidences that his children and hers may inherit, and she to have reasonable jointure, she hath heard so much of his birth and his conditions, that an ye will she will have him, whether that her mother will or will not, notwithstanding it is told her his person is simple,[1] for she saith men shall have the more duty of her if she rule her to him as she ought to do.

Cousin, it is told me there is a goodly man in your Inn, of the which the father died lately, and if ye think that he were better for her than Scrope, it would be laboured, and give Scrope a goodly answer that he be not put off till ye be sure of a better; for he said when he was with me, but if he have some comfortable answer of you, he will no more labour in this matter, because he might not see my cousin your sister, and he saith he might 'a seen her an she had been better than she is; and that causeth him to demur that her mother was not well willing, and so have I sent my cousin your mother word.

[1] *I.e.* plain.

Wherefore, cousin, think on this matter, for sorrow often-time causeth women to beset them otherwise than they should do; and if she were in that case, I wot well ye would be sorry. Cousin, I pray you burn this letter, that your men nor none other man see it; for an my cousin your mother knew that I had sent you this letter, she should never love me. No more I write to you at this time, but Holy Ghost have you in keeping. Written in haste, on St Peter's Day, by candle light.

By your Cousin,

ELIZABETH CLERE.

61. THE COURSE OF LOVE

(A.D. 1476? John Paston to Margery Brews; vol. III, p. 159.)

MISTRESS, though so be that I, unacquainted with you as yet, take upon me to be thus bold as to write unto you without your knowledge and leave, yet mistress, for such poor service as I now in my mind owe you, purposing, ye not displeased, during my life to continue the same, I beseech you to pardon my boldness, and not to disdain, but to accept this simple billet to recommend me to you in such wise as I best can or may imagine to your most pleasure. And, mistress, for such report as I have heard of you by many and divers persons, (and specially by my right trusty friend, Richard Stratton, bearer hereof, to whom I beseech you to give credence in such maters as he shall on my behalf commune with you of, if it like you to listen him,) and that report causeth me to be the more bold to write unto you, so as I do; for I have heard oft-times Richard Stratton say that ye can and will take every-thing well that is well meant, whom I believe and trust as much as few men living, I assure you by my troth. And, mistress, I beseech you to think none otherwise in me, but that I will and shall at all seasons be ready with God's grace to accomplish all such things as I have informed and desired the said Richard on my behalf to give you knowledge of; unless it so be that against my will it come of you that I be cast off from your service and not willingly by my desert, and that I am and will be yours and at your commandment in every wise during my life. Here I send you this billet written with my lewd hand and sealed with my signet to remain with you for a witness against me, and to my shame and dishonour if I contrary it. And, mistress, I beseech you, in easing of the poor heart that sometime was at my rule, which now is at yours, that in as short time as can be that I may have knowledge of your intent and how ye will have me demeaned in this matter, and I will be at all seasons ready to perform in this matter and all others your pleasure, as far forth lieth in my power to do, or in all theirs that aught will do for me, with God's grace, Whom I beseech to send you the accomplishment of your most worshipful desires, mine own fair lady, for I will no further labour but to you, unto the time ye give me leave, and till I be sure that ye shall take no displeasure with my further labour.

62. THE SAME

(The same John Paston to his elder brother, Sir John Paston, 6 May, 1476; vol. III, p. 163.)

To the right worshipful Sir John Paston, Knight, lodged at the George, by Paul's Wharf, in London.

AFTER all duties of recommendation, liketh you to wit, that to my power ye be welcome again into England. And as for the Castle of Sheen, there is no more in it but Colle and his mate, and a goose may get it; but in no wise I would not that way, and my mother thinketh the same. Take not that way, if there be any other.

I understand that Mistress Fitzwalter hath a sister, a maid, to marry. I trow, an ye entreated him, she might come into Christian men's hands. I pray you speak with Master Fitzwalter of that matter for me; and ye may tell him, since that he will have my service, it were as good, and such a bargain might be made that both she and I awaited on him and my mistress his wife at our own cost, as I alone to await on him

133

at his cost; for then I should be sure that I should not be flitting, an I had such a quarry[1] to keep me at home. An I have his good will, it is none impossible to bring about.

I think to be at London within a xiiij days at the farthest, and peradventure my mistress also, in counsel be it clattered. God keep you and yours.

At Norwich, the vj. day of May, anno E. iiijti xvj.

J. P.

63. THE SAME

(Dame Elizabeth Brews to John Paston, Feb. 1477; vol. III, p. 169.)

To my worshipful cousin, John Paston, be this billet delivered, etc.

COUSIN, I recommend me unto you, thanking you heartily for the great cheer that ye made me and all my folks, the last time that I was at Norwich; and ye promised me, that ye would never break the matter to Margery until such time as ye and I were at a point. But ye have made her such advocate for you, that I may never have rest night nor day, for calling and crying upon [me] to bring the said matter to effect, etc. And cousin, upon Friday is St Valentine's Day, and every bird chooseth him a mate; and if it like you to come on Thursday at night, and so purvey you, that ye may abide there till Monday, I trust to God that ye shall so speak to mine husband; and I shall pray that we shall bring the matter to a conclusion, etc. For, cousin,

> It is but a simple oak,
> That [is] cut down at the first stroke.

For ye will be reasonable, I trust to God, Which have you ever in His merciful keeping, etc.

> By your cousin, Dame ELIZABETH BREWS,
> otherwise shall be called by God's grace.

[1] Prize: the game at which a hawk flies.

THE COURSE OF LOVE

64. THE SAME

(Margery Brews to John Paston, Feb. 1477; vol. III, p. 170.)

Unto my right well-beloved Valentine, John Paston,
Squire, be this billet delivered, etc.

RIGHT reverend and worshipful, and my right well-beloved
Valentine, I recommend me unto you, full heartily desiring
to hear of your welfare, which I beseech Almighty God long
for to preserve unto His pleasure, and your heart's desire.
And if it please you to hear of my welfare, I am not in good
heal of body nor of heart, nor shall be till I hear from you;

> For there wotteth no creature what pain that I endure,
> And for to be dead, I dare it not discure.   *[discover*

And my lady my mother hath laboured the matter to my
father full diligently, but she can no more get [of dowry]
than ye know of, for the which God knoweth I am full sorry.
But if that ye love me, as I trust verily that ye do, ye will not
leave me therefore; for if that ye had not half the livelihood
that ye have, for to do the greatest labour that any woman on
live might, I would not forsake you.

> And if ye command me to keep me true wherever I go,
> I wis I will do all my might you to love and never no mo.
>   And if my friends say, that I do amiss,
>   They shall not let me so for to do,
> Mine heart me bids ever more to love you
>   Truly over all earthly thing,
> And if they be never so wroth,
> I trust it shall be better in time coming.

No more to you at this time, but the Holy Trinity have
you in keeping. And I beseech you that this billet be not seen
of none earthly creature save only yourself, etc.

And this letter was indited at Topcroft, with full heavy
heart, etc.

By your own,

MARGERY BREWS.

65. THE SAME

(Sir John Paston to his brother, John Paston, 9 March, 1477;
vol. III, p. 177.)

To John Paston, Esquire, in haste.

I HAVE received your letter, and your man, J. Bykerton, by whom I know all the matter of Mistress Brews, which if it be as he saith, I pray God bring it to a good end.

Item, as for this matter of Mistress Barly, I hold it but a bare thing. I feel well that it passeth not [*blank*] mark.[1] I saw her for your sake. She is a little one; she may be a woman hereafter, if she be not old now; her person seemeth xiij year of age; her years, men say, be full xviij. She knoweth not of the matter, I suppose; nevertheless she desired to see me as glad as I was to see her.

I pray you send me some writing to Calais of your speed with Mistress Brews. Bykerton telleth me that she loveth you well. If I died, I had liever ye had her than the Lady Wargrave; nevertheless she singeth well with an harp.

Clopton is afeard of Sir T. Grey, for he is a widower now late, and men say that he is acquainted with her of old.

No more. Written on Sunday, the ix. day of March, anno E. iiijti xvij to Calais-ward.

If ye have Mistress Brews, and E. Paston Mistress Bylyngford, ye be like to be brethren.

J. PASTON, Kt.

66. THE SAME

(Margery Paston (*née* Brews) to her husband, John Paston, 18 Dec. 1477;
vol. III, p. 214.)

To my right reverend and worshipful husband,
John Paston.

RIGHT reverend and worshipful husband, I recommend me to you, desiring heartily to hear of your welfare, thanking you for the token that ye sent me by Edmund Perys, praying you

---

[1] *I.e.* there is no more to be got out of it but this (unintentionally omitted) sum of money.

to wit that my mother sent to my father to London for a gown-cloth of musterdevillers[1] to make of a gown for me; and he told my mother and me when he was come home that he charged you to buy it, after that he were come out of London. I pray you, if it be not bought, that ye will vouchsafe to buy it, and send it home as soon as ye may, for I have no gown to wear this winter but my black and my green a Tyer,[2] and that is so cumbrous that I am weary to wear it. As for the girdle that my father behested me, I spake to him thereof a little before he went to London last, and he said to me that the fault was in you, that ye would not think thereupon to do make it; but I suppose that is not so; he said it but for a 'scusation. I pray you, if ye dare take upon you, that ye will vouchsafe to do make it against ye come home, for I had never more need thereof than I have now, for I am waxed so shapely that I may not be girt in no bar of no girdle that I have, but of one. Elizabeth Peverel hath lain sick xv. or xvj. weeks of the sciatica, but she sent my mother word by Kate that she should come hither when God sent time, though she should be wheeled in a barrow. John of Damm was here, and my mother discovered me to him, and he said, by his troth that he was not gladder of nothing that he heard this twelvemonth than he was thereof. I may no longer live by my craft, I am discovered of all men that see me. Of all other things that ye desired that I should send you word of, I have sent you word of in a letter that I did write on Our Lady's Day last was. The Holy Trinity have you in His keeping. Written at Oxnead in right great haste, on the Thursday next before St Thomas's Day.

I pray you that ye will wear the ring with the image of St Margaret, that I sent you for a remembrance, till ye come home; ye have left me such a remembrance that maketh me to think upon you both day and night when I would sleep.

Yours,

M. P.

[1] A grey cloth made at Montivilliers in Normandy, and very popular here in the fourteenth and fifteenth centuries.
[2] This word has baffled both editors of the letters. It may be simply *attire*.

67. AN ETONIAN'S ROMANCE

(William Paston, junr. (aged 19), to John Paston, 23 Feb. 1479;
vol. III, p. 240.)

*To his worshipful brother, John Paston, be this
delivered in haste.*

RIGHT reverend and worshipful brother, after all duties of
recommendation, I recommend me to you, desiring to hear
of your prosperity and welfare, which I pray God long to
continue to His pleasure, and to your heart's desire; letting
you wit that I received a letter from you, in the which letter
was viijd. with the which I should buy a pair of slippers.
Furthermore certifying you, as for the xiijs. iiijd. which ye
sent by a gentleman's man, for my board, called Thomas
Newton, was delivered to mine hostess, and so to my creditor
Mr Thomas Stevenson; and he heartily recommended him
to you. Also he sent me word in the letter of xij.lb. figs and
viij.lb. raisins. I have them not delivered, but I doubt not
I shall have, for Alwether told me of them, and he said that
they came after in another barge. And as for the young
gentlewoman, I will certify you how I first fell in acquaintance with her. Her father is dead; there be ij. sisters of them;
the elder is just wedded; at the which wedding I was with
mine hostess, and also desired by the gentleman himself, called
William Swan, whose dwelling is in Eton. So it fortuned that
mine hostess reported on me otherwise than I was worthy;
so that her mother commanded her to make me good cheer,
and so in good faith she did. She is not abiding there she is
now; her dwelling is in London; but her mother and she
came to a place of hers v. miles from Eton, where the wedding
was, for because it was nigh to the gentleman which wedded
her daughter. And on Monday next coming, that is to say,
the first Monday of Clean Lent, her mother and she will go
to the pardon at Sheen, and so forth to London, and there to
abide in a place of hers in Bow Churchyard; and if it please
you to inquire of her, her mother's name is Mistress Alborow,
the age of her is by all likelihood xviij. or xix. year at the

furthest. And as for the money and plate, it is ready when-soever she were wedded; but as for the livelihood, I trow not till after her mother's decease; but I cannot tell you for very certain, but you may know by inquiring. And as for her beauty, judge you that when ye see her, if so be that ye take the labour; and specially behold her hands, for an if it be as it is told me, she is disposed to be thick.[1]

And as for my coming from Eton, I lack nothing but versifying, which I trust to have with a little continuance.

> Quare, Quomodo non valet hora, valet mora,
> Unde di' [*dictum*, vel *deductum?*]
> Arbore jam videas exemplum. Non die possunt,
> Omnia suppleri; sed tamen illa mora.

And these two verses aforesaid be of mine own making. No more to you at this time, but God have you in His keeping. Written at Eton the Even of St Matthias the Apostle in haste, with the hand of your brother.

WILLIAM PASTON, Junr.

68. ON WITH THE NEW

(Edmund Paston to William Paston, about 1481; vol. III, p. 278.)

To my brother, William Paston, be this delivered.

I HEARTILY recommend me to you. Here is lately fallen a widow in Worsted, which was wife to one Bolt, a worsted-merchant, and worth a thousand pounds, and gave to his wife a hundred marks in money, stuff of household, and plate to the value of an hundred marks, and ten pounds by year in land. She is called a fair gentlewoman. I will for your sake see her. She is right sister, of father and mother, to Harry Ynglows. I purpose to speak with him to get his good will. This gentle-woman is about xxx. years, and has but ij. children, which shall be at the dead's charge; she was his wife but v. years. If she be any better than I write for, take it in woothe [sic] I shew the least. Thus let me have knowledge of your mind

---

[1] Is likely to grow stout.

as shortly as ye can, and when ye shall moun [sic] be in this country. And thus God send you good health and good aventure.

From Norwich, the Saturday after xij^{the} day.

Your,

E. Paston.

69. A SAD ENDING

(The Earl of Oxford to Sir John Paston, some time after 1495; vol. III, p. 391.)

To the right worshipful and my right entirely
well-beloved Sir John Paston, Knight.

Right worshipful and right entirely beloved, I commend me heartily to you. And whereas your brother William, my servant, is so troubled with sickness and crazed in his mind, that I may not keep him about me, wherefore I am right sorry, and at this time send him to you; praying especially that he may be kept surely and tenderly with you, to such time as God fortune him to be better assured of himself and his mind more sadly[1] disposed, which I pray God may be in short time, and preserve you long in good prosperity.

Written at my place in London, the xxvj. day of June.

Oxynford.

70. GOOD ALE

(From a fifteenth century MS. printed in T. Wright's *Songs and Carols* (Percy Society), p. 63.)

Bring us in no brown bread, for that is made of bran,
Nor bring us in no white bread, for therein is no game.
But bring us in good ale, and bring us in good ale;
For our blessed Lady's sake, bring us in good ale!

Bring us in no beef, for there is many bones,
But bring us in good ale, for that goeth down at once;
And bring us in good ale, etc.

[1] Seriously, responsibly.

GOOD ALE

Bring us in no bacon, for that is passing fat,
But bring us in good ale, and give us enough of that;
    And bring us in good ale, etc.

Bring us in no mutton, for that is often lean,
Nor bring us in no tripës, for they be seldom clean;
    But bring us in good ale, etc.

Bring us in no eggës, for there are many shells,
But bring us in good ale, and give us nothing else;
    And bring us in good ale, etc.

Bring us in no butter, for therein are many hairs;
Nor bring us in no piggës flesh, for that will make us boars;
    But bring us in good ale, etc.

Bring us in no puddings, for therein is all God's good;
Nor bring us in no venison, for that is not for our blood;
    But bring us in good ale, etc.

Bring us in no capon's flesh, for that is often dear;
Nor bring us in no duck's flesh, for they slobber in the mere;
But bring us in good ale, and bring us in good ale,
For our blessed Lady's sake, bring us in good ale!

71. WIVES AT THE TAVERN

(Ib. p. 91.)

Now, gossip mine, gossip mine,
When will ye go to the wine?

I will you tell a full good sport,
How gossips gather them on a sort,
Their sick bodies for to comfort,
    When they meet, in a lane or street.

But I dare not, for their displeasance,
Tell of these matters half the substance;
But yet somewhat of their governance,
    As far as I dare, I will declare.

"Good gossip mine, where have ye be?
It is so long sith I you see.
Where is the best wine? tell you me.
      Can you ought tell, [then say] full well.

"I know a draught of merry-go-down,
The best it is in all this town;
But yet would I not, for my gown,
      My husband it wist, ye may me trist![1]

Call forth your gossips by and by,
Elinor, Joan, and Margery,
Margaret, Alice, and Cecily;
      For they will come both all and some.

And each of them will somewhat bring,
Goosë, pig, or capon's wing,
Pasties of pigeons, or some other thing;
      For a gallon of wine they will not wring."

"Go before by twain and twain,
Wisely, that ye be not seen;
For I must home, and come again,
      To wit ywis where my husband is.

A stripe or two God might send me,
If my husband might here see me.
She that is afearëd, let her flee."
      Quoth Alice then, "I dread no man."

"Now we be in tavern set,
A draught of the best let him go fet,[2]
To bring our husbands out of debt;
      For we will spend, till God more send."

Each of them brought forth their dish;
Some brought flesh, and some [brought] fish.
Quoth Margaret meek: "Now with a wish,
      I would Anne were here, she would make us cheer."

"How say you, gossips, is this wine good?"
"That it is," quoth Elinor, "by the rood;
It cherisheth the heart, and comforteth the blood;
      Such junkets among shall make us live long!

                [1] Trust.   [2] Fetch.

WIVES AT THE TAVERN

"Anne, bid fill a pot of muscadel;
For of all wines I love it well,
Sweet winës keep my body in heal;
    If I had of it nought, I should take great thought."

"How look ye, gossip, at the board's end?
Not merry, gossip? God it amend.
All shall be well, else God it forfend;
    Be merry and glad, and sit not so sad."

"Would God I had done after your counsel!
For my husband is so fell,
He beateth me like the devil of hell;
    And the more I cry, the less mercy!"

Alice with a loud voice spake then,
"Ywis," she said, "little good he can,
That beateth or striketh any woman,
    And specially his wife; God give him short life!"

Margaret meek said, "So mot I thrive,
I know no man that is alive,
That give me two strokes, but he shall have five;
    I am not afeard, though I have no beard!"

One cast down her shot, and went her way.
"Gossip," quoth Elinor, "what did she pay?"
"Nought but a penny." "Lo, therefore I say,
    She shall no more be of our lore.

Such guestës we may have y-now,
That will not for their shot allow.
With whom came she? gossip, with you?"
    "Nay," quoth Joan, "I came alone."

"Now reckon our shot, and go we hence,
What? cost it each of us but three pence?
Pardé, this is but a small expence,
    For such a sort, and all but sport.

Turn down the street where ye came out,
And we will compass round about."
"Gossip," quoth Anne, "what needeth that doubt?
    Your husbands be pleased, when ye be reised.[1]

[1] Raised, exalted in liquor.

Whatsoever any many think,
We come for nought but for good drink.
Now let us go home and wink;
    For it may be seen, where we have been."

This is the thought that gossips take,
Once in the week merry will they make,
And all small drink they will forsake;
    But wine of the best shall have no rest.

Some be at the tavern once in a week;
And so be some every day eke;
Or else they will groan and make them sick.
    For thingës used will not be refused.

What say you, women, is it not so?
Yes, surëly, and that ye well know;
And therefore let us drink all a row,
    And of our singing make a good ending.

Now fill the cup, and drink to me;
And then shall we good fellows be.
And of this talking leave will we,
    And speakë then good of women.

The medieval "freshman" was called *bejaunus* or *beanus* (=bec-jaune=
greenhorn). According to the convenient fiction of his seniors, he came
up from home in the shape of an uncouth and offensive wild beast, horned,
tusked, and rough-haired: nor could he take place in decent society until
all these deformities had been removed. The rough horseplay and black-
mail for which this *Depositio Cornuum* gave excuse are set forth at length
in a *Scholars' Manual* composed for Heidelberg university about A.D. 1480,
and frequently printed before the Reformation. This has been reprinted
by F. Zarncke (*Die Deutschen Universitäten im Mittelalter*, Leipzig, 1857);
I give it here in an abbreviated form. For the similar ordeals at other
universities see Dr H. Rashdall, *Universities of Europe in the Middle Ages*,
vol. II, pp. 628 ff.

72. THE FRESHMAN'S ORDEAL

CAMILLUS. What is this stench which fills the whole place?
Faugh! it must either be some decaying corpse or a goat, most
unsavoury of beasts. Good masters and excellent fellows all,

how can ye sit in the midst of this stench? It availeth not even to hold one's nose: I must needs go forth or die! Come, Berthold!

Berthold. Tarry awhile, and we shall see whence it cometh.

Camillus. Well said! Search we every nook and cranny of the building till we find the source of this hog-stye odour.... Ha! what do I see? What monster is this?...Horned like a bull, tusked like a wild swine, beaked like an owl, with red and inflamed eyes that bespeak his furious mood! Didst thou ever see a devil? Methinks this is worse still. Flee, lest he fall upon us!

Berthold. Nay, I will gaze upon him, even at mine own peril! What say'st thou, Camillus? here we have a *beanus*!

Camillus. What, a beanus?

Berthold. If I be not altogether deceived, a beanus it is.

Camillus. Never before have I seen a beast which giveth so plain a promise of cruelty and ferocity as this uncouth creature!

Berthold. Peace, I will address him. Master Johann, when didst thou come hither? Of a truth thou art a fellow-countryman of mine, hold forth thy hand. What, ruffian! wilt thou tear me with thy claws? A man must be clad in mail to accost thee safely....What, thou sittest, wild ass of the desert! Seest thou not here Masters of the University, reverend seniors, before whom thou shouldst humbly stand?...Good God! see him stand like a block of wood, stock still, shameless, though all men's eyes be upon him!...Mark now, good folk, how soon his hind legs grow weary; he hath raised himself up but a few minutes, and already he boweth again like a crooked old hag. See how he draweth in his neck!

Camillus. Thou hast no pity: wherefore terrify him thus? I will suffer it no more, for he is a landsman of mine. Be of good cheer, Johann, for I will defend thee; take a glass and pluck up heart of grace....O butcherly boor! fearest thou not to dip thy venomous beak into the cup wherefrom thy most learned masters drank even now! Thy drink should be muddy water, where the beasts go down to the river.

Berthold. Enough now! is it a small thing that this tenderly-nurtured youth should be treated like an ox? What if his mother saw this, whose only darling he is? See, weepeth he not already? indeed his eyes are wet: he was moved at the sound of his mother's name.

Camillus. What can we make of him?

Berthold. He is doubtless come hither to be purged of his deformities and join the laudable company of students: go fetch a surgeon. Ha! what say I? for thou, Camillus, art a noble and renowned student in surgery. Rejoice, O Johann, and bless this happy day; for now thine hour of salvation is near, wherein thou shalt be purged of all grossness in body and mind, and shalt have thy part in every privilege of this our university. Haste thee, Camillus.

Camillus. First I will remove his horns; Berthold, reach me yonder saw. How, ass! thou kickest against thy physician!

Berthold. Hold him like an untamed horse; beware lest he hurt thee with talon or horn.

Camillus. How tough and deep-rooted are these horns! my saw is gapped, and half its stinking teeth are gone! (*producing a pair of ox-horns*): See here, thy horns, thou froward beast, which before thou couldst not see and therefore believedst not! Where now are my tooth-pincers? Hold out thy mouth.... Berthold, here is one tooth—here now is the second.

Berthold. I will keep these to show at a fair, as men do with sea-monsters!

Camillus. Bring a bowl and water, and odorous herbs for his beard—herbs grown at the spot where the sewer disgorges into our garden. Hold thy chin still!... The beard is soaked enough: where now is my razor of stout oak-splinter?... See John, here now is thy beard, black as the beard of Judas that betrayed Christ!

Berthold. He grows faint; he is unaccustomed to such downright surgery.

Camillus. True: his hue is gone, and the fashion of his countenance is changed, which is the token of a fragile complexion. Reach hither the ointment and the pills. [*The unsavoury ingredients of these medicines have been duly enumerated higher up.*]...Our remedies profit little, it seems: lest he die on our hands, it were safer that he should confess his sins. Lo! he is half dead already: his knees bow under him.

Berthold. I too am in holy orders; that shall be my care. But where have I laid my surplice?...Now begin, good Johann, to confess all thy sins, and without doubt thou shalt be saved. What do I hear?...geese and chickens?...horrid crime! And what next? tell me without fear....kissed? —and thy mother's maid?—Why, this is far more grievous! ...Nevertheless, seeing that pardon must not be denied to a man truly confessed; yet again that a merciful confessor (as I am) must still enjoin some penance, this then shall be thine. For these and thine other sins, and for thy most unsavoury odour, thou shalt refresh these masters here with a right plenteous repast. But mine office is only to enjoin penance, and not to give absolution; wherefore I send you to the masters who have this authority to assoil thee. [*Here the tormentor introduces the victim to each in turn, saying*]: "Reverend master, behold the chief of sinners, whose crimes are not to be told; I am he who hath authority to enjoin his penance, wherefore I have determined that he should give his goods to be scattered broadcast; and where better than among us? He hath promised to refresh us with most excellent wine, and to spend all the silver which his father hath wrung from the ancestral farm, together with every coin which his mother abstracted from her goodman and hid in her own hoard. Go therefore, Johann, to this master, and thou shalt obtain his pardon.

[*When the whole ceremony is over, then shall all draw near and cry* Prosit, Johann!]

73. A FARMER'S WILL

(Madox, *Formulare Anglicanum*, 1702, p. 435.)

IN Dei nomine Amen. Vicesimo octavo die mensis *Novembris*, Anno Domini Millesimo cccclxviii. Y *Custans Pothyn*, hoole & fresch, make my Wille in this maner. First I bequeth my sowle to Almyghty God, to owre blessed Lady, and to all the Holy Company of hevyn; My body to be beryed in

Chalke chirche. Also y be quethe to the hy Auter viii. *d.* Also to the Rode lyght a Cowe with v Ewes. Also to owre *Lady of Peté* iii. Ewes. Also to the Lyght of Seynt *John* Baptyste iiii. Ewes. Also to a Torche vi *s.* viii *d.* Also to *Alson Potkyn* iiii quarter barly; Also a Cowe with iiii shepe, iiii peyre shets parte of the best, with a bord cloth of diapur, Another of playne, iii Towels of diapur with ii Keverletts, iii blanketts, a mattras, a bolster, iiii pelewes, vi Candelstikes. To *Marget Crippis* ii Candelstikes, a peyre shetis, a quarter barly. To *Thomas Harry* iii quarter barly, a peyre shetis, with a blanket. To Thomas Crippe a peyre shetis. To John Martyn a peyre shetis. To every gode-child a bushel barly. The residue of my godes I will that *Richard* and *John* my Sones, myn Executours, have and dispose for the helthe of my Sowle as they see that best ys.

74. ANOTHER

(Ib.)

In the name of God Amen. The ix day of the moneth of *February*, the yere of our Lord God a Mcccclxxiii; Y *Thomas Martyn* of the parish of *Chalke* in the shire of *Kent*, hooll of mynde & in good wit, make my testament in the manere that foluyth. First y bequethe my Sowle to Almighti God my Creatur, to our Lady Seint [Mary], & to all the blessed Seints of hevene; My body to be beryed in the Cherche of our Lady of *Chalke* forsaid. Item y bequethe to the hye Awter of the same Cherche, for tythes for geten, xii *d.* Item I bequethe to the Hye Cros Lyght v modershepe. Item to the Lyght of Seint *John* in the same Cherche v modershepe. Item to the Lyght of our Lady Pety v modershepe. Item to the Lyghts of our Lady & of *Mary Magdaleyn* v modershepe. Item y bequethe a blak yonge cowe to the Sustentacion of the Lyghtys of Seint *Anne*, Seint *Jame*, and Seint *Margarete* in the forsaid Cherche. Item to the Lyght of the Lampe in the hye Chauncell v modershepe. Item y bequethe to the reparacions of the said Cherche xxvi *s.* viii *d.* Item to eche of my Godchildron xii *d.* Item y bequethe to *Margarete* my

A FARMER'S WILL

Dowghter my grete bras pot, & my grettist Cawdron. Item y will that a honest Preste synge Masses in the forsaid parish of *Chalke* for my Sowle, & for the Sowle of my Fader, and for all my Frendys Sowlys, by halff a yere; and y bequethe to hym his Sallayre v marc. Item y bequethe to a Mass book to serve in the same Cherche v. marc. The Residewes of all my godes and cattels not bequethen, after my detts ben paid, my beryeng don, and thys my present Testament fulfilled, y bequethe to *Alys* [my] wiff, & to *Margarete* my Doughter. Item y will that yff hit happe the said *Margarete* with in the age of xvi yere deye, that y will that the part of all the Mevabill godes to the same *Margarete* bequethen, remayne to *Alys* hir moder. Item hit is my will, that all my bequests & all other things that shall bee don for me, be rulyd and governyd by the advys and discrescion of *Thomas Page* my Fader in Lawe, and of my moder his wiff. And to this my present Testament y make and ordeyne my trewe Executors the forsaid *Alys* my Wiff, *Stephene Charlys* of *Hoo*, & *William Banaster* of *Derteforde*; & y bequethe to eche of theym for her Labour vi *s*. viii *d*. Also y will that the said *Thomas Page* my Fader be over seer; & y bequethe to hym for hys Labour vi *s*. viii *d*. Dat. daye and yere abovesaid.

John Morton, afterwards cardinal, became Bishop of Ely in 1478. He walked barefoot the two miles from his palace at Downham to the cathedral; whence, after the installation ceremonies, he repaired to his other palace of Ely with many distinguished guests, "and a great multitude of common people, for the Banquet was great and costly." The *menu* may be found in J. Bentham's *History and Antiquities of Ely*, Appendix, p. 35. I have ventured on a few necessary emendations, and omit all but the first of the long doggerel "rehearsals" inscribed on the "subtleties," or elaborate symbolical structures of sugar, etc., of which the degenerate descendants may still be seen on wedding-cakes. I have also ventured on one or two necessary emendations of the text. *Leche*, according to the *Oxford English Dictionary*, was "a dish consisting of sliced meat, eggs, fruits and spices in jelly or some other coagulating material." *Leche damaske* would be either made of damsons, or damson-coloured. *Stoker* might possibly be stock-fish, or a kind of apple called *stoken*. *Semeca* seems unintelligible as it stands. *Boateur* is probably botargo, a kind of caviare. *Bounce* is probably connected with *bun* and the French *beignet*, a kind of pancake: "*bugne* is said to be used at Lyons for a kind of fritter" (*O.E.D. s.v. bun*).

75. A BISHOP'S INSTALLATION BANQUET

¶ THE FIRST COURSE FOR THE ESTATES.

A Subtlety of a White Lion: rehearsal.

THINK and thankë, Prelate of greatë price,
That it hath pleasëd the abundant grace
Of King Edward, in all his actës wise,
Thee to promoten hither to his place.
This little I see, while thou hast time and space,
For to repair do aye thy busy cure;
For thy reward of heaven thou shalt be sure.

Pure pottage—Frumenty and Venison—Cygnet roasted—Great pike in sauce—Roe roasted regardant—Pheasant roasted—Venison in paste—Great custard—Leche purple.

A Subtlety of the Nativity of St John.

* * * *

¶ THE SECOND COURSE.

A Subtlety of the Glebe of Ely.

Jelly to [*for*] pottage—Stoker roasted—Peacock flourished—Carp in sops—Rabbits roasted—Bream freshwater—

A BISHOP'S INSTALLATION BANQUET

Fritter Semeca (?)—Orange in paste—Tart borboyne—
Leche damaske.

A Subtlety of God as Shepherd.

* * * *

¶ THE THIRD COURSE.

A Subtlety of Saints Peter, Paul, and Andrew.

Cream of Almonds to pottage—Boateur roasted—Perch
in jelly—Curlew—Plover roasted—A mould of jelly
flourished—Crayfish of freshwater—Larks roasted—Fresh
sturgeon— Quinces in paste—Tart poleyn—Fritter bounce
—Leche royal.

A Subtlety of the Eagle on the Tun.[1]

* * * *

Sitting at the High Dais: my Lord of Ely in the midst.

On the right hand: The Abbots of Bury and Ramsey, the
Prior of Ely, the Master of the Rolls, the Priors of Barnwell
and Anglesey.

On the other hand: Sir Thomas Howard, Sir John Donne,
Sir John Wyngelfield, Sir Harry Wentworth, John Sapcote,
Sir Edward Wodehouse, Sir Robert Chamberlain, Sir John
Cheyne, Sir William Brandon, Sir Robert Fynes, John
Fortescue.

The Abbot of Thorney, and my Lady Brandon, and other
estates, in the Chamber.

The future cardinal's installation-feast was a poor thing compared with
that of a prior of St Augustine's, Canterbury, in 1309, as recorded by
a monk of that house and quoted on p. 83 of W. Fleetwood's *Chronicon
Preciosum.* Six thousand guests sat down to meat, and the bill (including
presents and gratuities) amounted to £287, or some £5000 of modern
money. The guests consumed 53 quarters of wheat, 58 quarters of malt,
11 tuns of wine, 36 oxen, 100 hogs, 200 little pigs, 200 sheep, 1000 geese,
973 capons, hens, and pullets, 24 swans, 600 rabbits, 16 shields of brawn,
9600 eggs, with game, spice, and almonds to the price of more than
£1000 modern. The sole economy was in secondary appliances; the
dishes, plates and trenchers amounted only to 3300 for the six thousand,
and the drinking cups to 1400.

[1] Apparently a punning rebus on Morton's name.

The following is one of the many formal trials and executions of homicidal animals reported in full, from contemporary records of the fourteenth and fifteenth centuries, by Berriat-Saint-Prix in *Mémoires de la Soc. des Antiquaires de France* (t. VIII, 1829, pp. 403 ff.). The author quotes many other abbreviated notices of similar trials: *e.g.* the mayor of Bâle, in 1474, condemned a cock to be burned alive for having laid an egg, in derogation of its proper sex. The last instance quoted is from the year 1679, when the Parliament of Aix condemned a mare to the stake. Another very amusing instance is recorded in Didron's *Annales Archéologiques*, t. VI, p. 313; and there is an article on the subject in *Merry England* for December, 1887.

76. ANIMALS BEFORE THE LAW

To all who shall see or hear these presents, Jean Lavoisier, Licentiate of Laws, and Grand Mayor of the church and monastery of my lord Saint Martin at Laon, of the Order of Prémontré, together with the bailiffs of the place aforesaid. Whereas it had been reported and affirmed to us by the Procurator-fiscal or Syndic of the monks, abbot, and convent of St Martin at Laon, that on the manor [*cense*] of Clermont-lez-Montcornet, to the said monks with all rights of high, mean, and low justice appertaining, a young pig had strangled and mutilated a young child in its cradle, son of Jehan Lenfant, cowherd of the aforesaid domain of Clermont, and of Gillon his wife, calling upon us and requiring us to proceed in this case as justice and reason desired and required; whereas further, in order to learn and know the truth of the aforesaid case, we had heard and examined upon oath the said Gillon Lenfant, with Jean Benjamin, and Jean Daudancourt, tenants of the aforesaid farm, who testified and affirmed to us upon their oath and conscience that on Easter Monday last past the said Lenfant being abroad with his cattle, the said Gillon his wife departed from the farm aforesaid in order to go to the village of Dizy, leaving the said child in her house, under charge of a daughter of hers nine years of age: in and during which time the aforesaid girl went away to play around the said farm, leaving the said child in his cradle; during which said time the pig aforesaid entered the said house and mutilated and devoured the face and throat of the child aforesaid; so that within a brief space the aforesaid child, by means of the bites and mutilations inflicted by the hog aforesaid, departed this life: wherefore we make known that we, in detestation and horror of this case aforesaid, and in order to keep exemplary justice, have bidden, judged, sentenced, pronounced and appointed that the said hog, being now bound in prison under lock and key in the Abbey aforesaid, shall by the common hangman be hanged by the neck until he be dead, upon a wooden gibbet near and adjoining to the standing gallows and place of execution of the aforesaid monks, which are hard by their manor of Avin. In witness whereof, we have sealed these presents with our own seal.

Johann Geiler, born at Kaisersberg near Schaffhausen in 1445, became Doctor of Theology at Bâle and Freiburg, but accepted, at the invitation of bishop and chapter, the cathedral preachership at Strasbourg (1478). Here his spiritual fervour, his hatred of abuses, and the raciness of his style, raised him to a unique position among contemporary preachers. He died at his work in 1510, looking forward to an impending catastrophe from which his strict orthodoxy shrank, while he fully recognized its necessity. See L. Dacheux, *Jean Geiler*, Paris, 1876, from which this extract is taken (app. XXXVI, letter of Geiler in 1486 to his former pupil, Count Friedrich von Zollern, now Bishop-Elect of Augsburg).

77. A NOBLE BISHOP

I KNOW that, if thou wert now here, thou wouldst say, "Well, what thinkest thou? Counsel me; shall I or shall I not undertake this burden from which even an angel's shoulders might shrink?" I would first say that (like St Bernard when a bishop-elect consulted him in a similar case) I say nothing. For St Bernard would give no advice to such a prelate-elect, but left him to his own conscience; so also will I. In short I say nothing, because if I shall tell you (as Jesus said to those who said to Him, "tell us") you will not believe me nor let go. But perchance thou urgest me and wilt have me speak. If therefore thou wilt have it, I tell thee again and again, without hesitation: if thou wilt follow in the footsteps of the bishops of our days, saying within thyself, "Lo, I will have so many horses!" and acting accordingly, then [fear] that which thou hast so often heard from my lips. Again, if thou wilt follow the counsel of men of this world, holding on thy course with excommunications and such other things as are commonly done in bishops' courts, not visiting thy diocese nor effectually extirpating vices, not spending thy goods on the poor to whom indeed they pertain, not seeing to spiritual things thyself and leaving worldly things to others, but on the contrary neglecting ordinations and such duties—in short, unless thou wilt become as it were a prodigy among bishops, a phoenix, single of thine own kind, then would it be better for thee that thou hadst never been born!

78. DUKE AND BISHOP

(Geiler, *Navicula Fatuorum*, turba XLIII, nola 2.)

SOME men, when they are about to enter a church, equip themselves like hunters, bearing hawks and bells on their wrists, and followed by a pack of baying hounds, that trouble God's service. Here the bells jangle, there the barking of dogs echoes in our ears, to the hindrance of preachers and hearers, of all who do their masses and of all who say their prayers. Brother, this is no ground for *huntsmen*, but for *bedesmen*! Such conduct is most reprehensible in all men, but especially in the clergy, albeit some of these would fain excuse many things in themselves under pretext of their noble birth, claiming the right to do that which would be clearly unlawful for the commonalty, and saying that they must show themselves nobles at one time, clerics at another.[1] Against whom I am reminded of that shrewd answer which is recorded from a peasant to a bishop. This prelate, as he rode through the fields escorted by a noisy army of knights, saw a boor who had left his plough and stood on the mound that fenced his field,

---

[1] In the cathedrals of Auxerre and Nevers, for instance, the treasurers had the legal right of coming to service with hawk on wrist. This was because those particular canonries were hereditary in noble families; but already in the middle of the fifteenth century we find this permission causing scandal among the faithful (*Ménagier de Paris* (1846), t. I, p. 296). The abuse of conferring high church offices on nobles was worse in Germany, however, than in most other countries.

staring at him with open mouth and goggling eyes of wonder. To whom the Bishop said, "What thinkest thou, to stand staring thus with gaping throat and cheeks cleft to the ears?" "I was thinking," quoth he, "whether St Martin, who himself also was a bishop, was wont to go along the high road with all this din of arms and all this host of knights." Whereunto the Bishop replied, with somewhat of a blush, "I am not only a Bishop, but a Duke of the Empire, wherefore I now play the Duke. But if thou wouldst fain see the Bishop, come to the Church on such a day," (and therewith he named him a day), "and I will show you the prelate." To which the rustic made answer, with a little laugh, "But if (which Heaven forfend!) the Duke were to go and find his deserts in hell, what then would become of our Bishop?"

In *Memorials of King Henry VII* (R.S. pp. 223 ff.), Dr James Gairdner printed a paper of great interest. Henry's queen had died in February 1503. He thought of marrying again, and "his first thoughts were directed to the young queen of Naples, widow of Ferdinand the Second. To ascertain how far she was likely to prove a suitable match for him, he sent three gentlemen into Spain on a very confidential mission." Their report, which was drawn up in 1505, is here given, with their instructions, almost in full.

79. AMBASSADORS TAKE MEASURE OF A PRINCESS

H. R.

Instructions given by the King's Highness to his trusty and well beloved servants, Francis Marsin, James Braybroke, and John Stile, showing how they shall order themselves when they shall come to the presence of the old Queen of Naples and the young Queen her daughter.

1. *First, after presentation and deliverance of such letters as they shall have with them to be delivered to the said queens from the lady Catherine, Princess of Wales,[1] making her*

---

[1] Widow of prince Arthur, and already contracted now to the future Henry VIII.

recommendation and declaration of such charges and words as shall be showed and committed unto them by the said princess to be opened and declared on her behalf to the said queens, they shall well note and mark the estate that they keep, and how they be accompanied with nobles and ladies.

Pleaseth your Grace, at our coming to the city of Valencia, the which was in the xxii^d day of June in the evening, at which time the Queens of Naples, both the old and the young, sojourned and kept their households together jointly in the King's palace, that is a little without the said city of Valencia, the which palace is called the Reyalls; . . . at the hour and time appointed we came unto the said palace, where by a servant of the said queens we were conveyed and brought through divers chambers, the which were bare and not hanged, and so unto a chamber that was hanged with black cloth, and but one window open, and on the floor there was a great carpet spread, whereon by the window side sat the old queen, and on her left hand from the window-wardes sat the young queen. Both the said queens were clothed in black cloth and also in black kerchers as mourners, and in like case were all they that waited on the said queens. On the right hand of the queens in the window stood an ancient duke in a long beard, whose name is the duke Fernandin of Naples, and two of his sons, and other knights and gentlemen to the number of twenty persons or thereabouts, and on the left hand of the queens there sat the duchess, the wife of the said Fernandin, and a duchess of the parties of Greece and the Marchesa de Chara, the Countessa de Tortona, and the Countessa de Montorio, and Donia Maria de Enrykes, the old queen's niece, and three daughters of the duke Fernanderies, and other ladies and gentlewomen to the number of xviii or xx^{tie} persons. . . .

2. *Item, to take good heed and mark that estate the said queens keep, and whether they keep their estates and households apart or in one house together and how they be accompanied, and what lords and ladies they have about them.*

As touching this article the principal points be rehearsed in the first article before rehearsed. . . .

3. *Item, if it shall fortune the said King's servants to find the said queens keeping their estates together, they shall well and assuredly note and mark the manner of keeping and ordering them in their estates, with the countenance and manner of every of them, and such answer as they shall make upon the speech and communication as they shall have with them at the deliverance of the said letters and declaration of the other matters before mentioned, and to mark her discretion, wisdom, and gravity in her said communication and answer in every behalf.*

4. *Item, they shall in likewise endeavour to understand whether the young queen speak any other languages but Spanish and Italian, and whether she can speak any French or Latin.*

As to this article, as far as that we can understand and know that the said young queen can speak no languages except Spanish and Italian. It is said that she understands both Latin and French, but she speaketh none.

5. *Item, specially to mark and note well the age and stature of the said young queen, and the features of her body.*

As to this article, as to the age of the said young queen, it is seven and twenty years and not much more; and as to the stature of her person we cannot perfectly understand nor know, for commonly when that we came into her presence her grace was sitting on a pillow, and other ii times we saw her going on her foot going overthwarte a chamber that was not broad, where she came in at a door and came unto the queen her mother, being in the same chamber and sat down by her, at the which both times she wore slippers after the manner of the country in such wise that we could not come to any perfect knowledge of the height of the said queen. And as to the features of her body of the said young queen, forasmuch as that at all times that we have seen her grace ever she had a great mantle of cloth on her in such wise after the manner of that country that a man shall not lightly perceive anything except only the visage, wherefore we could not be in certain of any such features of her body, but as far as that we can perceive and judge that she is of no high stature but of a middle stature after our judgment by the reason of the height of her slippers whereof we have seen an ensample.

6. *Item, specially to mark the favor of her visage, whether she be painted or not, and whether it be fat or lean, sharp or round, and whether her countenance be cheerful and amiable, frowning or melancholy, stedfast or light, or blushing in communication.*

As to this article, as far as that we can perceive or know, that the said queen is not painted, and the favor of her visage is after her stature, of a very good compass and amiable, and somewhat round and fat, and the countenance cheerful, not frowning, and stedfast, and not light nor bold-hardy in speech, but with a demure womanly shamefaced countenance, and of a few words, as that we could perceive as we can think that she uttered the fewer words by cause that the queen her mother was present, which had all the sayings, and the young queen sat as demure as a maiden, and some time talking with ladies that sat about her with a womanly laughing cheer and countenance, and with a good gravity, always the ladies talking with her having their countenances towards her grace with reverences and honor and obedience.

7. *Item, to note the clearness of her skin.*

As to this article, the said queen is very fair and clear of skin as far as we could perceive by her visage neck and hands, the which we saw and well perceived.

8. *Item, to note the colours of her hair.*

As to this article, by that we could see and perceive by the brows of the said queen, and by the ends of some of her hairs that we perceived through her kerchers, it should seem her hair to be a brown hair of colour.

9. *Item, to note well her eyes, brows, teeth and lips.*

As to this article, the eyes of the said queen be of colour brown, somewhat greyish; and her brows of a brown hair and very small like a wire of hair; and her teeth fair and clean, and as far as we could perceive, well set; and her lips somewhat round and thick, according to the proportion of her visage, the which right well becometh the said queen.

10. *Item, to mark well the fashion of her nose and the height and breadth of her forehead.*

As to this article, the fashion of her nose is a little rising in the midward, and a little coming or bowing towards the end, and she is much like nosed unto the queen her mother. And as to her forehead, the height or the breadth thereof we could not perfectly discern, for the manner of the wearing of the kerchers or tuckas in that country is such that a man cannot well judge it, for their kerchers coming down to their brows, and much the less we could come by the very knowledge of that cause for that the queen weared black kerchers.

11. *Item, specially to note her complexion.*

As to this article, as far as we can perceive the said queen is of a very fair sanguine complexion and clean.

12. *Item, to mark her arms, whether they be great or small, long or short.*

As to this article, as that we can perceive and know, that the arms of the said queen be somewhat round and not very small, by that we could perceive when that she putteth forth her hand when that we did kiss it; and as to the length of her arm, to our understanding, it is of a good proportion unto her personage and stature of height.

13. *Item, to see her hands bare, and to note the fashion of them, whether the palm of her hand be thick or thin, and whether her hands be fat or lean, long or short.*

As to this article, we saw the hands of the said queen bare at three sundry times that we kissed her said hands, whereby we perceived the said queen to be right fair handed, and according to her personage, they be somewhat fully and soft and fair and clean skinned.

14. *Item, to note her fingers, whether they be long or short, small or great, broad or narrow before.*

As to this article, the fingers of the said queen be right fair and small, and of a meetly length and breadth before, according unto her personage very fair handed.

15. *Item, to mark whether her neck be long or short, small or great.*

As to this article, the neck of the said queen is fully and comely, and not misshapen, nor very short nor long, but meetly after the proportion of her personage; but her neck seemeth for to be shorter because that her breasts be fully and somewhat big.

16. *Item, to mark her breasts and paps, whether they be big or small.*

As to this article, the said queen's breasts be somewhat great and fully, and inasmuch as that they were trussed somewhat high, after the manner of the country, the which causeth her grace for to seem much the fullyer and her neck to be the shorter.

17. *Item, to mark whether there appear any hair about her lips or not.*

As to this article, as far as that we can perceive and see, the said queen hath no hair appearing about her lips or mouth, but she is very clear skinned.

18. *Item, that they endeavour them to speak with the said young queen fasting, and that she may tell unto them some matter at length, and to approach as near to her mouth as they honestly may, to the intent that they may feel the condition of her breath, whether it be sweet or not, and to mark at every time when they speak with her if they feel any savour of spices, rosewater, or musk by the breath of her mouth or not.*

To this article: we could never come unto the speech of the said queen fasting, wherefore we could nor might not attain to knowledge of that part of this article, notwithstanding at such other times as we have spoken and have had communication with the said queen, we have approached as nigh unto her visage as that conveniently we might do, and we could feel no savour of any spices or waters, and we think verily by the favour of her visage and cleanness of her complexion and of her mouth that the said queen is like for to be of a sweet savour and well eyred.

19. *Item, to note the height of her stature and to inquire whether she wear any slippers, and of what height her slippers be, to the intent that they be not deceived in the very height and*

stature of her; and if they may come to the sight of her slippers,
then to note the fashion of her foot.

As to this article of the height and stature of the said young
queen, as in the vth article of this book it is answered that we
could not come by the perfect knowledge of her height, forasmuch as that her grace weareth slippers after the manner
of the country whereof we saw the fashion the which be of
vi fingers breadth, of height large, and her foot after the
proportion of the same is but small, but by the slipper the
greatness of her foot cannot be known, notwithstanding by
the height of her slipper, considering the height that she
appeared unto our sight being a-foot, her grace seemed not
to be of high stature, and also by cause of the manner of the
clothing that women do use and wear after the manner of
the country, and also she of herself is somewhat round and
well liking, the which causeth her grace for to seem lesser in
height.

20. *Item, to inquire whether she have any sickness of her*
nativity, deformity or blemish in her body, and what that should
be, or whether she hath been commonly in health or sometimes
sick and sometimes whole, and to know the specialties of such
diseases and sickness.

As to this article we have inquired for to come by the
knowledge thereof to the best that we can, and as it hath been
by us considered that such secret causes be unto all persons
unknown, except unto her physicians, apothecary, or secret
women of her chamber, and for the next remedy for to come
by any knowledge thereof we acquainted ourselves with one
Pastorell, a Neapolitan, the which is a wise man, and he is
apothecary and in manner physician to the said queens, both
to the old and young, with the which apothecary we had
divers times pastimes and communications, amongst the which
sometimes we asked such questions if that the said young
queen had any such infirmities as in the said articles before
be specified; whereunto the said apothecary said, "I have
served the said queen many years, being her grace a little child
hitherunto, and ever she hath been in as much health as any
gentlewoman that ever I had known, and of so noble a nature

and complexion, having in her person no disconformity nor cause of sickness."

21. *Item, whether she be in any singular favour with the King of Arragon her uncle, and whether she have any resemblance in visage, countenance, or complexion to him.*

As to this article, we have understood by the sayings of many and divers persons the King of Arragon favoureth and right much loveth the old queen his sister, the which queen is alike unto the said King her brother, as any man and woman may be like unto another, and also right much he loveth and favoureth the young queen his niece, and that the said king intendeth for to promote her unto some excellent marriage, and that she shall have as much or more of his gift than any of his own daughters had, for somewhat of favour the said young queen is like unto the King her uncle and especially in the fashion of her nose and complexion. Moreover a common saying is in all Spain and in the King's court that the said young queen shall be married unto the King of England our sovereign lord by the means and labor of the King her uncle.

22. *Item, to inquire of the manner of her diet and whether she be a great feeder or drinker, and whether she useth often to eat or drink, and whether she drinketh wine or water or both.*

As to this article, it hath been shown unto us by one Pastorell, the which is apothecary unto the said queen, and also by one Sorya, the which is a household servant, the which two persons be much in the presence of the said queen when that she eateth and drinketh and as they do report and say that the said queen is a good feeder, and eateth well her meat twice on a day, and that her grace drinketh not often, and that she drinketh most commonly water, and sometimes that water is boiled with cinnamon, and sometimes she drinketh ipocras, but not often.

23. *Item, the King's said servants shall also at their coming to the parties of Spain diligently inquire for some cunning painter having good experience in making and painting of visages and portraitures, and such one they shall take with them*

*to the place where the said queens make their abode, to the intent
that the said painter may draw a picture of the visage and
semblance of the said young queen, as like unto her as it can or
may be conveniently done, which picture and image they shall
substantially note and mark in every point and circumstance, so
that it agree in similitude and likeness as near as it may possible
to the very visage, countenance and semblance of the said queen.
And in case they may perceive that the painter at the first or
second making thereof hath not made the same perfect to her
similitude and likeness, or that he hath omitted any feature or
circumstance, either in colours or other proportions of the said
visage, then they shall cause the same painter, or some other the
most cunning painter that they can get, so often times to renew
and reform the same picture till it be made perfect and agreeable
in every behalf with the very image and likeness of visage of the
said queen.*

There is no answer to this article.

24. *Item, the said King's servants, by the wisest ways that
they can use, shall make inquisition and ensearch what land or
livelihood the said young queen hath or shall have after the
decease of her mother, either by the title of jointure or otherwise,
in the realm of Naples, or in any other place or country, what is
the yearly value thereof, and whether she shall have the same to
her and her heirs for ever or else during her life only, and to
know the specialities of the title and value thereof in every behalf
as near as they can.*

Here the ambassadors pumped Pastorell again, and one "Martyn
de Albistur, master of a ship"; but neither could give a satisfactory answer
to this all-important question. As the editor puts it (p. xlix): "The young
queen appears to have had but one disqualification. She was healthy,
beautiful, and well formed, but moneyless." Henry VII remained a
widower.

80. A HEALTHY APPETITE
(*Lübeckische Chronik* (ed. J. F. Faust, 1619). Appendix P, p. 292,
"Of Eaters"—apparently about A.D. 1550.)

I T is recorded by men worthy of belief that a man came to
a hostelry in Lübeck a few years since, and bade the Host
prepare for certain persons whom he had bidden to a supper;

for which, (as he said) he would honourably pay. When all had been done as he had bidden, and the supper-time was come, no guests appeared; whereat the Host was sore troubled. But the guest desired him to serve up all the food that he had cooked, and for as many persons as he had ordered it; "which," (said he) "I will honourably pay." It was done as he had bidden; whereupon he ate up all that was set before him, and passed back the empty dishes to the Hostess. When the Host had marked this, and the time of reckoning was now come, then said he to the guest, "Ye shall have this meal for a free gift, if only ye will see to it that I lose not by making a wager in trust upon you." "Yea," said the Guest, "so much may ye boldly do in trust upon me; I am he who can help you out"; and the Host knew that he was safe. Now it befel that a Shipman came to Lübeck with a load of butter from Sweden; to whom the Host went to bargain for a tub of butter, saying in mocking words to the Shipman, "What shall I give thee for this little keg of butter?" Then answered the Shipman in wrath at his mockery: "Holdest thou this for a little keg? Methinks it is a full barrel of butter." To whom the Host: "yea, verily, a pitiful barrel, that a man might eat up at a single meal!" Whereupon the Shipman was sore troubled, and spake: "Bring me the man who can eat up this barrel of butter at a meal, and I will give thee my ship with all my goods that are in her, if thou too will set as much to wager for thine own part!" Thereupon they accorded, and each gave pledges to the other. Then the Host brought his guest, who bade him be of good cheer, for he would help him loyally out of his need: as also he did, to the astonishment of all that saw him, and at last begged for one or two halfpenny-rolls wherewith to wipe the staves clean. Then began the Shipman to rage like one possessed, and to call down all the curses in the world upon this Eater's head, saying, "Is it a small thing that thou hast lost me my ship and my goods, but wilt thou also scrape the staves clean?" I would never have recorded so strange a story, but that it is plainly reported as true by common testimony.

[The curious reader may compare this with the tract by John Taylor, the Water-Poet, on Nicholas Wood, "the great

Eater of Kent," who in later life lost nearly all his teeth "in eating a quarter of mutton, bones and all, at Ashford." Wood far outstripped his predecessor Wolner of Windsor, who digested iron, glass, and oyster-shells, but was at length "by a raw eel over-mastered."]

More's English Works (as Principal Lindsay writes on p. 17 of the third volume of the *Camb. Hist. Eng. Lit.*) "deserve more consideration than they usually receive." Yet he vouchsafes them no further consideration; and later on Mr Routh mentions one of them only to disparage it (p. 80). Since they are practically inaccessible to the general reader (for the folio costs from £25 to £50 according to its condition) I give in these volumes some stories which show him at his best as a raconteur, and of which no. 61 in vol. IV is doubly interesting for the use that Shakespeare made of it. In the *Dialogue* More is arguing in his own person against a disputant of quasi-heretical leanings, generally alluded to as the *Messenger* or *your Friend*.

81. FEMININE PERVERSITY

(p. 1187. Anthony speaks.)

THERE was here in Buda in king Ladislaus' days a good poor honest man's wife. This woman was so fiendish that the devil, perceiving her nature, put her in the mind that she should anger her husband so sore that she might give him occasion to kill her, and then should he be hanged for her. *Vincent.* This was a strange temptation indeed. What the devil should she be the better then? *Anthony.* Nothing but that it eased her shrewd stomach before, to think that her husband should be hanged after. And peradventure if you look about the world and consider it well, you shall find more such stomachs than a few. Have you never heard no furious body plainly say, that to see some such man have a mischief, he would with good will be content to lie as long in hell as God lieth in heaven? *Vincent.* Forsooth and some such have I heard of. *Anthony.* This mind of his was not much less mad than hers, but rather haply the more mad of the twain; for the woman peradventure did not cast so far peril therein. But to tell you now to what good pass her charitable purpose came.

As her husband (the man was a carpenter) stood hewing with his chip-axe upon a piece of timber, she began after her old guise so to revile him that the man waxed wroth at last, and bade her get her in, or he would lay the helve of his axe about her back, and said also that it were little sin even with the axe-head to chop off that unhappy head of hers, that carried such an ungracious tongue therein. At that word the devil took his time, and whetted her tongue against her teeth. And when it was well sharped she sware to him in very fierce anger, "By the mass, villain husband, I would thou wouldest: here lieth mine head, lo!" (and therewith down she laid her head upon the same timber log) "if thou smite it not off, I beshrew thy villainous heart!" With that likewise, as the devil stood at her elbow, so stood (as I heard say) his good angel at his, and gave him ghostly courage, and bade him be bold and do it. And so the good man up with his chip-axe, and at a chop chopped off her head indeed. There were standing other folk by, which had a good sport to hear her chide, but little they looked for this chance, till it was done ere they could let it. They said they heard her tongue babble in her head and call villain, villain! twice after that the head was from the body. At the least wise afterwards unto the king thus they reported all, except only one, and that was a woman, and she said that she heard it not. *Vincent.* Forsooth, this was a wonderful work. What came, uncle, of the man? *Anthony.* The king gave him his pardon. *Vincent.* Verily, he might in conscience do no less. *Anthony.* But then was it farther almost at another point, that there should have been a statute made, that in such case, there should never after pardon be granted, but the truth being able to be proved, none husband should need any pardon, but should have leave by the law to follow the example of the carpenter, and do the same. *Vincent.* How happed it, uncle, that that good law was left unmade? *Anthony.* How happed it? as it happeth, Cousin, that many more be left unmade as well as it, and within a little as good as it too, both here and in other countries, and sometimes some worse made in their stead. But, as they say, the let of that law was the Queen's grace (God forgive her soul)! It was the greatest thing, I ween, good lady, that she had to answer for when she died. For surely, save for that one thing, she was a full blessed woman. But letting now the law pass, this temptation in procuring her own death was unto this carpenter's wife no tribulation at all, as far as ever men could perceive. For it liked her well to think thereon, and she even longed therefore. And therefore if she had before told you or me her mind, and that she would so fain bring it so to pass, we could have had none occasion to comfort her as one that were in tribulation. But, marry! counsel her (as I told you before) we might to refrain and amend that malicious devilish mind. *Vincent.* Verily that is truth. But such as are well willing to do any purpose that is so shameful, will never tell their mind to no body for very shame. *Anthony.* Son, men will not indeed. And yet are there some again that, be their intent never so shameful, find some yet whom their heart serveth them to make of their counsel therein. Some of my folk here can tell you that, no longer ago than even yesterday, one that came out of Vienna showed us among other talking that a rich widow (but I forgat to ask him where it happened) having all her life an high proud mind and a fell, as those two virtues are wont alway to keep company together, was at debate with another neighbour of hers in the town. And on a time she made of her counsel a poor neighbour of hers, whom she thought for money she might induce to follow her mind. With him she secretly brake, and offered him ten ducats for his labour, to do so much for her as in a morning early to come to her house, and with an axe, unknown, privily strike off her head; and when he had so done, then convey the bloody axe into the house of him with whom she was at debate, in some such manner wise as it might be thought that he had murdered her for malice, and then she thought she should be taken for a martyr. And yet had she further devised, that another sum of money should after be sent to Rome, and there should be means made to the Pope that she might in all haste be canonized. This poor man promised, but intended not to perform it; howbeit, when he deferred it, she provided the axe herself, and he appointed with her the morning when he should come and do it; and thereupon into her house he came. But then set he such other folk as he would should know her frantic fantasy, in such place appointed as they might well hear her and him talk together. And after that he had talked with her thereof what he would, so much as he thought was enough, he made her lie down, and took up the axe in his own hand, and with the other hand he felt the edge, and found a fault that it was not sharp, and that therefore he would in no wise do it till he had grounden it sharp; he could not else, he said, for pity, it would put her to so much pain. And so, full sore against her will, for that time she kept her head still. But because she would no more suffer any more deceive her so and food her forth with delays, ere it was very long after, she hung herself [with] her own hands. *Vincent.* Forsooth, here was a tragical story, whereof I never heard the like. *Anthony.* Forsooth, the party that told it me sware that he knew it for a truth; and himself is, I promise you, such as I reckon for right honest and of substantial truth.

Now here she letted not, as shameful a mind as she had, to make one of her counsel yet; and yet, as I remember, another too, whom she trusted with the money that should procure her canonization. And here I wot well, that her temptation came not of fear but of high malice and pride. But then was she so glad in the pleasant device thereof, that, as I showed you, she took it for no tribulation, and therefore comforting of her could have no place; but if men should anything give her toward her help it must have been, as I told you, good counsel. And therefore, as I said, this kind of temptation to a man's own destruction, which requireth counsel, and is out of tribulation, was out of our matter, that is to treat of comfort in tribulation.

PART IV
MONKS, FRIARS AND NUNS

The first really historical figure in Christian monasticism is Antony, who died in 356 and whose life was written less than ten years afterwards by St Athanasius. Though he created no regular organization, the colonies of hermits whom his fame gathered round him were called *monasteria*. Towards the end of his long life, he retired still farther into a wilderness near the Red Sea. St Jerome, in his *Life of St Hilarion*, recounts how that Palestinian hermit, who had known St Antony in life, paid a pilgrimage to his cell after his death. The original is in Migne, *Pat. Lat.* vol. 23, col. 44: the translation is from p. 33 of the second part of *Certaine Selected Epistles of S. Hierome*, Paris, 1630.

I. A HERMIT'S PARADISE

...But Hilarion going from thence, after three other days, came to the town called Aphroditos, where, meeting with Baysanes the Deacon (who by reason of the usual great want of water in that desert was wont to hire out camels and dromedaries to such as went to visit Antony, and so conduct them to him), he confessed to those brothers that the anniversary of Antony's death was at hand, and that he was then to celebrate the same to him by watching all that night, in that very place where he died. After three days therefore of travel through that vast and horrible desert, at length they came to a huge high mountain, where they found two monks, Issac and Pelusianus, which Issac had been Antony's interpreter. And because occasion is here so fairly offered, and that already we are upon the place, I will in few words describe the habitation of so great a person as Antony was.

There is a high and stony mountain, of a mile in circuit, which hath abundance of springing water at the root thereof. The sand drinketh up part and the rest, sliding downwards, grows by little and little to make a brook; upon the banks whereof, on both sides, the innumerable palm-trees which grow there, give both great commodity and beauty to the place. There you might have seen our old man pass nimbly up and down with the disciples of Blessed Antony; here they said he sang; here he prayed, here he wrought; here, when he was weary, he used to rest. These vines, and these little trees did he plant himself; this little bed of earth did he compose with his own hands; this pool did he contrive with much labour for the watering of his garden; with this rake did he use to break up the earth many years. He lay in the lodging of Antony, and kissed that place of his repose which, as a man may say, was yet warm; his cell was of no larger measure than such a square wherein a sleeping man might extend himself. Besides this, in the very highest top of the mountain, which is very steep and could not be ascended but by circling, there were two other cells of the same proportion wherein he would stay sometimes when he had a mind to fly from the frequent recourse of comers and the conversation of his disciples. Now these two were hewn out of freestone, and had no addition but of doors. But when they were come to his garden, "Do you see," said Issac, "that part thereof, which is the orchard, set with young trees and so green with herbs? Almost three years since, when a herd of wild asses came to destroy it, he willed one of the leading asses to stay, and beating the sides of it with his staff, 'How chanceth it,' saith he, 'that you eat of that which you did not sow?' And from henceforth, when they had drunk their water for which they came, they would never touch tree or fruit any more." Our old man desired besides, that they would show him the place of Antony's tomb: but they leading him apart, we are yet uncertain whether they showed it or not. They say that the reason why Antony commanded it to be concealed, was for fear lest one Pergamus, who was a very rich man in those parts, should carry the saint's body to his village and so there erect a shrine.

The *Lives of the Fathers* (*Vitaspatrum*) was commonly ascribed in the Middle Ages to St Jerome. The book contains early material of very unequal historical value, ranging from contemporary and trustworthy descriptions to evidently legendary matter. It is accessible to English readers in Dr Wallis Budge's translation from the Syriac version, *The Paradise of the Fathers* (Chatto and Windus, 1907, 2 vols.). The following extract is translated from Migne's edition (*Pat. Lat.* vol. 73, col. 1119).

2. FROM ROBBER TO SAINT

THERE was a man named Moses, Ethiopian by race, a black slave, whom his master, a certain governor, cast forth on account of his dishonesty and theft. Nay, he was said even to have proceeded to murder; for I must needs rehearse his wickedness, that I may proceed to set forth his acts of penitence. It is said, therefore, that he was the chief of a great band of robbers. Among his other deeds they tell this of him, that he once vowed revenge against a shepherd who, with his dogs, had hindered him in one of his evil deeds. Therefore, having resolved to slay this shepherd, he spied after the spot where the man kept his sheep; and it was told him that this was beyond the Nile. The river was then in flood, a good mile in breadth, but Moses folded his tunic on his head, took his sword in his teeth, and swam thus from bank to bank. But the shepherd, seeing what was in store for him, had time to hide himself while his enemy was yet in the water. Moses therefore, frustrated of his purpose, slew the four fattest rams, bound them with a rope, and swam the Nile again. Then, coming to a small village, he flayed the rams, ate all the choicest morsels, and sold the fleeces for wine. Of this he drank, to the last drop, a great measure containing about eighteen pints, and then rose up and went fifty miles to join his band.

At length, by some strange chance, this robber-chief was touched by a late-born spirit of compunction, and gave himself up to monastic life, wherein he advanced to such a pitch of penitence as may be seen in the very facts of his life. It is told, among other things, how four robbers once burst in upon him as he sat in his cell, not knowing him to be Moses. The saint bound all four like a truss of straw and carried them on his shoulders unto the church of the brethren, where he said, "Here are four men who have set upon me; I may not now hurt any man; what then shall I do with these?" The robbers, caught, confessed their sin; and, finding this saint to be that same Moses who had once been a famous chief of robbers, they gave glory to Christ for his sake, and renounced the world on account of his penitence, and became most excellent monks. For they reasoned thus within themselves: "If this so strong and famous robber hath cast away theft for such fear of God, why then should we longer defer our own salvation?"

Thenceforward the Blessed Moses (for so we must call him) was assailed by demons who tempted him to fornication.... Wherefore he shut himself in his cell and used the greatest abstinence, especially in food, eating daily only twelve ounces of dry bread, and labouring hard, and saying fifty prayers in the day. Yet, with all this maceration of the body, he was still hard beset....Then for six years he dwelt in his cell, standing on his feet all night, with open eyes and assiduous prayer to God; yet still he could not conquer the demon of desire....Then said Isidore, the priest and servant of Christ, "In the name of our Lord Jesus Christ, thine evil delusions shall cease from this hour forth." And so it was; for this saint was endowed with such grace against demons that, even as we despise the flies in summer, so and even more did the great man Moses despise the demons....He died in Skete at the age of threescore years and fifteen, a consecrated priest; and he left threescore and fifteen disciples.

Many of his sayings have been recorded; two of them are here subjoined (Migne, *Pat. Lat.* vol. 73, cols. 781, 782).

A certain brother besought Abbot Moses for a word of advice. Then said the old man, "Go and sit in thine own cell; the cell will teach thee all wisdom, if thou do but dwell therein. For as a fish, drawn from the water, dieth forthwith, so also doth the monk perish if he desire to tarry outside his cell."[1]

A certain judge of the province wished to worship Abbot Moses, but he, learning this, fled from his cell [into the marshes]. Yet it befell by chance that he met the judge by the way, who enquired of him, "Tell us where is the cell of Abbot Moses?" To whom he made answer, "Wherefore

[1] This saying is ascribed elsewhere to St Antony, and is enshrined in Canon Law. Cf. Chaucer's *Prologue*.

wouldst thou see that fool, that heretic?" The judge, hearing these words, went to the church and reported them to the clerics, saying, "I had heard so much of Abbot Moses that I desired his blessing; but a monk hath even now met me who reported of him that he is a heretic!" The clerics, troubled at these words, enquired of him what sort of monk had thus spoken: whereunto he made reply, "An old man, tall and black, clad in the most ancient of garments." Then, learning from their report that this was Moses himself, the judge departed in great wonder.

St Jerome (Hieronymus Sophronius Eusebius) was the most learned of all the Latin Fathers and is mainly responsible for the Vulgate translation of the Bible. He was born of Christian parentage at Stridon in Dalmatia about A.D. 340 and baptized in 360. About 374, in consequence of the dream referred to in the subjoined extract, he deserted profane learning for exclusively theological studies. Soon afterwards he tried a life of extreme asceticism in a desert S.E. of Antioch, but his health broke down under these austerities. He returned to Rome, whence in 385 he finally departed with Paula and Eustochium to end his days in semi-conventual life at Bethlehem. He died in 420.

Paula was a noble and wealthy Roman who, having lost her husband and one of her five children, put herself and her daughter Eustochium under Jerome's guidance. She built four convents at Bethlehem; her own life was abridged by her austerities and her endowments were hampered by her indiscriminate almsgiving; but Eustochium, with Jerome's help, put the convents upon a sounder footing. It was for Eustochium, and her niece, the younger Paula, that Jerome wrote many of his most important works. The *Letter to Eustochium*, from which the following extract is compressed, was written at Rome in A.D. 384 on the occasion of her taking the vow of virginity; it may almost be called the Magna Carta of medieval nunnery life. Though it is far from being the most pessimistic of monastic pleas, Jerome's eloquence and power of satire here bring out, with great clearness, the pessimistic side of the ascetic ideal. A great deal of less relevant matter is here omitted, including some highly imaginative Biblical exegesis; but any passage may easily be identified by the paragraph references. The letter is in Migne, *Pat. Lat.* vol. 22, cols. 394 ff.; but I have translated from the more recent edition of I. Hilberg (1910, vol. I, p. 143). There is an excellent translation of all St Jerome's letters, and many of his other works, by the late Dean Fremantle (Oxford and New York, 1893).

3. THE IDEAL NUN

(§ 1) "Hear, O daughter, and consider, and incline thine ear; forget also thine own people and thy father's house, and the king shall desire thy beauty." In this 44th Psalm[1] doth God call upon man's soul to follow the example of Abraham, who went forth from his own land and kindred, and from those Chaldaeans who, mystically interpreted, signify *demons*, in order to dwell in the land of the living. (§ 2) Wherefore, my lady Eustochium (for *lady* must I call the Spouse of my Lord), know now from the very first that I am not about to sing the praises of virginity, which thou hast excellently proved by thine own pursuit of that virtue, nor to tell the long tale of woe that dwells in married life—how the belly swelleth, the child crieth, the husband's concubine tormenteth, the care of the house vexeth ever, and death at last cutteth off all that seemed to be good—for even married women have their own order, their honourable espousals and their undefiled couch. Upon this, then, I will not dwell, but only show thee how, having gone forth from Sodom, thou must fear the example of Lot's wife.

(§ 4) So long as we are bound in this frail body, so long as we have this treasure in earthen vessels, while the spirit lusteth against the flesh and the flesh against the spirit, no man's victory is assured. Our adversary the Devil, as a roaring lion, walketh about seeking whom he may devour.

(§ 5) If the Apostle Paul, that chosen vessel prepared for the gospel of Christ, was constrained by a thorn in the flesh and by vicious desires to keep under his body and bring it into subjection, lest, when he had preached to others, he himself should become a castaway—if even he saw another law in his members, warring against the law of his mind and bringing him into captivity to the law of sin—if, even after nakedness, hunger, prison, scourging and torments he could return upon himself and cry aloud, "O wretched man that I am! who shall deliver me from the body of this death?"—if this be so, dost thou dream of security? Beware, I pray thee, lest God say of thee some day, "The virgin of Israel is fallen; she shall no more rise." I speak boldly: with God all things are possible, yet He cannot raise a virgin after her fall. He can indeed free her from her punishment, yet He cannot crown her, once corrupted. Let us fear lest in ourselves that prophecy be

[1] A.V. Ps. xlv, 10, 11.

THE IDEAL NUN

fulfilled: "The good virgins shall fail."[1] (§ 6) While our enemy is yet small, slay him; let iniquity be crushed in the bud. What saith the Psalmist? "O daughter of Babylon, who art to be destroyed, happy shall he be that rewardeth thee as thou hast served us; happy shall he be, that taketh and dasheth thy little ones against the rock!" For, since it cannot be but that the natural heat of sense should creep into man's marrow, therefore he is praised and blessed who, at the first unfolding of such thoughts, doth slay these cogitations by dashing them against the rock: for that Rock is Christ.

(§ 7) O how often, in that wilderness, in that abode of monks, in that vast and sun-scorched solitude, have I dreamed myself back among the flesh-pots of Rome! There I sat in solitude and overflowing bitterness of soul. My limbs were clad in rough and unsightly sackcloth; my squalid skin, through neglect, had become as black as an Ethiop's. Daily I wept and groaned; and, whensoever sleep crept upon me and overcame my struggles, then I dashed to the ground my naked and almost disjointed limbs. Of food and drink I speak not; for even the sick drink cold water in that wilderness, and it is a luxury to get a morsel of cooked food. Yet I, who had condemned myself to this prison for fear of hell, and who had no companions but scorpions and wild beasts—even I often dreamed myself among companies of girls. My face was pale with hunger, yet in that shivering body my mind seethed with hot desire; in this flesh of mine, already dead before its earthly death, the fires of lust alone burst forth. Thus, destitute of all help, I would cast myself at Jesus' feet, washing them with tears and wiping them with the hairs of my head; by weeks of fasting I would subdue my rebellious flesh. I blush not at my misery; nay, rather, I mourn now that I am no longer what I have been. I remember how, in my crying, I often added night to day, nor ceased from beating my breast until, at the Lord's rebuke, peace and stillness returned. I feared my very cell as the accomplice of my thoughts; wroth and severe with myself, I would oftentimes plunge alone into the desert. Wheresoever I could find hollow

[1] Amos viii, 13: different in the A.V.

valleys, steep mountains, beetling precipices, there I chose
my place for prayer and there I punished my wretched flesh
with labour; until (the Lord Himself is my witness!) after
many tears, after the straining of eyes to heaven, I seemed at
times to be among the angelic host, and sang in joyful
jubilation: "We run after thee in the savour of thy good
ointments."[1]

(§ 8) If such, then, are the pains of those who have wasted
their bodies and have no adversary save their thoughts, what
must a maiden suffer who is fed with the good things of this
world? [As Paul saith to Timothy:] "She that liveth in
pleasure is dead while she liveth." Wherefore, if there be any
counsel in mine experience, believe me; for thus in the first
place I warn and beseech, that the Spouse of Christ should
flee from wine as from poison.[2] Wine is the foremost weapon
of devils against the young; less does avarice shake us than wine,
less does pride puff us up, or ambition charm us. Other vices
we easily avoid; but this is a familiar foe, an enemy whom we
carry whithersoever we go. Wine and youth supply double

---

[1] Song of Solomon, i, 3: different in A.V.

[2] It is instructive to go forward a century, and compare this with chap. 40
of St Benedict's Rule: "Every man hath his proper gift of God, one after this
manner and another after that; wherefore we are somewhat scrupulous in providing a measure for other men's meat and drink. Nevertheless, considering the
infirmities of the weak, think that a *hemina* of wine daily is sufficient for each man.
But to whomsoever God giveth the gift of abstinence, let such know that they
will have their own reward. If, however, more be required either by the necessity
of the monastery or by the labour or heat of summer, let this be left to the Superior's
judgment, who shall consider in every case that no surfeiting or drunkenness
creep in. We read indeed that wine is altogether unfit for monks; yet, seeing that
the monks of our day cannot be persuaded of this, we do at least consent so far
as that we should not drink to fulness, but somewhat sparingly; for 'wine will
make even men of understanding to fall away' (Ecclus. xix, 2). Yet when the
necessity of the monastery requireth that not even the aforesaid measure can be
furnished, but far less, or none at all, then let those who dwell therein bless God
and refrain from murmuring. For this we warn you strictly, that there be no
murmuring among you." The *hemina*, according to the most probable opinion,
which was Mabillon's, contained 18 ounces, or nearly a pint. Cardinal Gasquet,
in his translation of the *Rule of St Benedict* (King's Classics), has not only taken
the liberty of expurgating the text considerably, but made a significant blunder.
Not realizing that *infirmorum imbecillitatem* is a quotation from the Vulgate
(Rom. xv, 1) he mistranslates it altogether. The saint's allowance of wine for his
monks was applied to nuns also; see the early fifteenth-century translation published
by the E.E.T.S. (1902), p. 28.

fuel to sensuality; wherefore then do we add oil to the flame? wherefore do we heap fresh fuel upon this miserable burning body of ours? [St Jerome here quotes at length from Noah, Lot, and other scriptural examples.] (§ 11) But if thou wilt answer that thou, born of a noble stock, and nourished ever in feather-beds and luxurious fare, canst not abstain from wine and more delicate meats, nor live by this stricter rule of life, to that I make reply: "Live then by thine own law, if thou mayst not endure the law of God." Not that the Creator and Lord of all things delighteth in the roaring of our empty bowels or in our fevered lungs; but He loveth these things as the only safeguards to chastity. Job was dear to God, who bore witness that he was perfect and upright; yet what saith Job of the Devil? "His strength is in his loins, and his force is in the navel of his belly";[1] under the decent obscurity of which words, he signifieth the uncomely parts of man and woman. Wherefore all the Devil's strength against man is in the loins, all his power against women is in the navel. [Examples of Samson, David, Solomon and Tamar.]

(§ 13) I can scarce bring myself to say how many virgins fall daily, how many Mother Church loseth from her bosom, over how many stars of God the proud enemy doth exalt his throne, how many rocks the serpent doth hollow out, that he may lurk in the clefts thereof. Thou mayst see many such unmarried widows, cloaking their conscious sin under a lying garb, and tripping through the streets with their heads in the air, until their teeming womb and the cry of the new-born babe betray them. Others, again, court barrenness by protecting drinks, and murderously prevent conception. Some, finding themselves big with a guilty offspring, compass abortion by a poisonous draught; whereby they oftentimes die themselves, and go down to hell with three crimes upon their head—slayers of their own selves, adulteresses of Christ, and murderesses of their unborn children. These are they who

---

[1] Job xl, 16. The Behemoth and Leviathan of this and the next chapter were commonly interpreted as signifying the powers of darkness; St Bernard's favourite text against sinners who conspire against visitatorial authority was Job xli, 15–17, and especially: "They stick together, that they cannot be sundered."

are wont to say, "To the clean all things are clean; mine own conscience is my safeguard. It is a clean heart that God desireth; why then should I abstain from meats which God hath created for man's use?" Moreover, whensoever they would fain show themselves pleasant and merry, and have drenched themselves in wine, then they add sacrilege to drunkenness, saying, "God forbid that I should abstain from that which is Christ's blood!" These are they who, when they see a maiden sad and pale, call her *wretched nun*, or *Manichaean*; and herein they speak consistently, for to such a purpose as theirs there is heresy in all fasting. These are they who flaunt abroad among the people and with furtive and sidelong glances entice a crowd of youths to follow them; yet of such the prophet saith truly: "Thou hast a whore's forehead, thou refusest to be ashamed." Let them but have a narrower purple edge to their robe [than secular folk]; let their head-band be looser, that their hair may fall down; let them be more roughly shod and their cloak fly loosely over their shoulders; let their sleeves fit closely to their arms; let them amble with bowed knees; in these things doth all their virginity consist. Yet such have their own admirers, and go more dearly to perdition under the precious name of *virgin*; such as these I seek not to please.

(§ 14) It is a shame to speak—fie, fie upon the lamentable truth!—whence hath this plague of spiritual sisters[1] crept into the churches? Whence have we these wives, without the name or sacrament of matrimony? say rather, whence this new kind of concubines? nay, I will speak more plainly; whence these one-man harlots? In one and the same house and bedchamber—nay, oftentimes, in one bed—and they call us suspicious if we bode anything amiss here! The brother deserts his maiden sister, the maiden scorns her unmarried blood-brother; and, each professing the same purpose, they seek spiritual consolation elsewhere as a cloak for fleshly commerce at home. These are they whom God rebuketh in the Proverbs of Solomon: "Can a man take fire in his bosom, and his clothes not be burned? Can one go upon hot coals, and his feet not be burned?"

---

[1] *Agapetae*, literally, "beloved ones," women who kept house for the unmarried clergy, and who are anathematized in several of the early Councils.

(§ 15) Wherefore, casting forth ignominiously these who wish not to be virgins, but to seem, let me now turn all my words to thee. Seeing that thou hast begun as the first Roman virgin of noble birth, so much the more must thou now labour lest thou lose not only the goods of this world, but the wealth of that which is to come. In truth, thou hast learned by home experience both the troubles of marriage and the uncertain chances of the conjugal state. For thy sister Blesilla, above thee in age but below thee in holy purpose, hath taken a husband and hath found herself a widow in the seventh month of her marriage. O unhappy and shortsighted condition of mankind! She hath lost both the crown of virginity and the pleasures of married life. Though she stand but in the second rank of chastity, yet how great must be the torments which beset her at intervals, beholding daily in her sister that which she herself hath lost, and expecting the less reward for her continence in proportion as she yearneth still for past pleasures! Yet let her be assured, let her rejoice; the hundredfold fruit and the sixtyfold fruit are of the same seed of chastity.[1]

(§ 16) I desire that thou consort not with married women, nor go to the houses of the noble, nor see frequently those things which it is part of thy virgin purpose to contemn. If silly women are wont to pride themselves that their husbands are judges or in other honourable offices, if the ambitious troop flocks to the levee of the Empress, wherefore dost thou disparage thine own Husband? Spouse of God, wherefore dost thou wait upon the wife of a man? Learn here an holy pride; know that thou art better than they. (§ 17) Let those be thy companions, whom thou seest lean with fasting, pale of face, approved both by age and by life; those who sing daily in their hearts: "Tell me, [O thou whom my soul loveth,] where thou feedest, where thou makest thy flock to rest at noon"; those who cry passionately "I desire to depart and be with Christ." Be subject to thy parents; imitate here thy Spouse. Go seldom in public; if thou wouldst seek the

---

[1] The parable of Matt. xiii, 8 was thus interpreted in the Middle Ages: the reward of virgins in heaven shall be an hundredfold, of continent widows sixtyfold, of righteous married folk, thirtyfold.

martyrs, seek them in thine own chamber. If thou art to go abroad both with and without necessity, then shalt thou never lack an excuse for leaving thy retreat. Let thy food be moderate, thy stomach never full. There are many women who, though sober in their cups, are drunken with superfluity of food. When thou risest to midnight prayer, let thy belly groan not with repletion but with emptiness. Read assiduously; learn many things. Let sleep come upon thee book in hand, and let thy sinking cheek rest upon the holy page. Fast daily: let thy refection avoid satiety; for it profiteth not to go empty for two or three days, if the fast be buried and outweighed by succeeding gluttony. Repletion deadens the mind; a ground well-watered buddeth forth into the thorns of lust. If ever thou feelest the outer man sigh for the flower of youth; if, as thou liest on thy couch after eating, the sweet pageants of fleshly lusts allure thee, then seize the shield of faith, wherewith thou shalt quench all the fiery darts of the Devil.

(§ 18) Be as a nightly grasshopper;[1] all the night make thy bed to swim; and water thy couch with thy tears; watch, and be as the sparrow upon the housetop. Sing with the spirit, and sing with the understanding also. As saith the Psalmist, "I have eaten ashes like bread and mingled my drink with weeping." Should I not rightly weep and groan, when the serpent would again tempt me to forbidden fruit? when he would dash me forth from the paradise of my virginity and clothe me with garments of skin? Let marriage have its proper time and title; my virginity is dedicate in Mary and in Christ.

(§ 19) Some man may say "dost thou then dare to speak ill of marriage, which our Lord hath blessed?" We speak no ill of marriage in preferring virginity; between bad and good there is no comparison. Let married folk glory in being next after virgins. "Be fruitful and multiply," said the Lord; "and replenish the earth." Let him be fruitful and multiply who hath a mind to replenish the earth; thy company, O Eustochium, is in heaven. The command "be fruitful and multiply" was fulfilled only after paradise, when the fig-

---

[1] *I.e.* sing psalms all night long.

leaves that covered their nakedness foreboded sexual passion. Let those marry and be given in marriage who eat their bread in the sweat of their brow, for whom the earth bringeth forth thorns and thistles, and whose green herb is choked with brambles; my seed shall bring forth fruit an hundredfold. Let those sew for themselves earthly garments, who have lost their seamless robe; those who delight in the cries of children bewailing, on the very threshold of life, that hour wherein they were born. Eve in Paradise was a virgin; after the garments of skins came marriage; thy home, Eustochium, is Paradise. (§ 20) I praise marriage and the married state, but because they breed virgins for me; thus do I pluck roses from thorns, gold from clay, pearls from oyster-shells.

(§ 22) What troubles beset the conjugal state, and in what anxieties the married are entangled, I have briefly expressed in that book which I wrote against Helvidius, in defence of the perpetual virginity of Mary. It would be tedious to repeat it here; and those who wish may draw from that source[1] [reference to similar treatises by Tertullian, Cyprian, Pope Damasus, and Ambrose]. (§ 23) Our way is different; it is not our task to extol virginity, but to keep it; nor doth it suffice to know the good, unless it be chosen and strictly kept. For to know is a mere matter of judgment, common to many; the labour is, to keep, and here we have but few on our side. It is written, "He that endureth to the end shall be saved"; and "many are called, but few are chosen." Wherefore I adjure thee, before the face of God and Christ Jesus and His elect Angels, that thou bear not too lightly abroad those vessels of the Temple which it is lawful only for the priests to behold, lest some profane person should see the sanctuary of God. Thou indeed speakest with simplicity, and in thy courtesy thou dost not scorn unknown folk; but unchaste eyes see differently; such know not to behold the beauty of souls, but only of bodies.

(§ 25) May the secrets of thy couch ever guard thee; ever may the Bridegroom play with thee in thy retirement. In prayer, thou speakest to Him; in reading, He speaketh to thee.

---

[1] Those two passages formed, naturally, a source for the medieval misogynist as well as for the monk; the *Wife of Bath's Prologue* is deeply indebted to St Jerome.

When sleep hath overcome thee, then shall he come behind thy wall and put his hand through the key-hole, and thy bowels shall be moved at his touch.[1] Then shalt thou rise trembling, and say, "I languish with love"; and he shall make reply, "My sister, my spouse is a garden enclosed, a garden enclosed, a fountain sealed up." Beware that thou go not forth from thine house, as one who would fain see the daughters of another land, though she rejoice in Israel for a father and in patriarchs for brethren; Dinah went forth and was defiled. I would not have thee seek thy spouse through the streets, nor go about the corners of the city. Thou mayest indeed plead, "I will rise and go about the city: in the street and the broad ways I will seek Him whom my soul loveth"; thou mayest indeed ask, "Have you seen Him whom my soul loveth?" No man will vouchsafe thee an answer. The Bridegroom is not to be found in the street—strait is the gate and narrow is the way which leadeth unto life—and then in the Song follow these words: "I sought him and found him not; I called, and he did not answer me." Nay, would to God that there were no worse than this *I found him not*! For thou shalt be wounded and stripped naked; thou shalt groan and cry aloud, "The keepers that go about the city found me; they struck me and wounded me; they took away my veil from me." Such, when she went abroad, was the fate even of her who said, "I sleep, and my heart watcheth"; and again, "A bundle of myrrh is my beloved to me; he shall abide between my breasts." How, then, shall we fare, who are yet unripe, and who remain without when the Bridegroom goeth in with the Bride? Jesus is a jealous Spouse; He would not that others should see thy face.

(§ 26) Wherefore, O Eustochium, my daughter in age, my lady in merit, my fellow-servant in religion and my sister in charity—hear now what Esaias saith, "Come, my people, enter thou into thy chambers, and shut thy doors about thee; hide thyself as it were for a little moment, until the indignation be overpast." Let the unwise virgins wander abroad;

---

[1] The quotations are, of course, from Solomon's Song (ii, 9, v, 4, iv, 12, iii, 2, v, 6, 7, v, 2, i, 13). I quote here according to the Douay version; the expressions in the original Latin are somewhat cruder.

do thou abide within with thy Spouse; for, if thou shut thy door—if, at the Gospel bidding, thou pray to thy Father which is in secret—then shall He come and knock, saying, "Behold, I stand at the door and knock; if any man hear my voice and open the door, I will come in to him and will sup with him, and he with me." And thou shalt forthwith make eager answer, as in the Song of Solomon: "The voice of my beloved knocking! Open to me, my sister, my love, my dove, my undefiled." Nor wilt thou find reason to add, "I have put off my garment, how shall I put it on? I have washed my feet, how shall I defile them?" Nay, arise straightway and open, lest, if thou tarry, He turn aside, leaving thee to bewail, "I opened the bolt of my door to my beloved; but he had turned aside and was gone."

(§ 27) Moreover, thou must take especial heed lest thou be caught with the flame of vainglory. When thou givest alms, let God alone see thee. Bear a cheerful countenance. Let thy dress be neither unwontedly neat nor slovenly, nor notable for any singularity, lest the crowd of passers-by stand still and point a finger at thee. I warn thee not against glorying in thy wealth or noble birth, nor against claiming precedence on that account, for I know thine humility. But I warn thee not to find vainglory herein and that thou hast scorned the vain glory of this world. Let not such thoughts steal into thine heart, that thou, who hast ceased to please men in gold-woven garments, shouldst seek to please in vile attire. When thou comest into the congregation of the brethren or the sisters, sit not on a lowly stool, nor plead thine unworthiness, nor studiously lower thy voice as one weak from fasting, nor feign a fainting gait and lean on another's shoulders. Some virgins there are who disfigure their faces that they may appear unto men to fast; who have no sooner caught sight of you than they force a groan; who lower their eyelids, cover their face, and scarce free half an eye to gaze withal; their garments are black, girt with sack-cloth; their hands and feet are unwashen; their belly alone, which no man can see, seethes with a superfluity of food. It is for such as these that we sing daily in the Psalms: "God hath scattered the bones of them that please men." Others change their garb to appear like men; they blush to be the women that God made them; they cut their hair short, and shamelessly uplift a eunuch's face. Others are clad in sack-cloth of hair and cowls such as a carpenter would fashion; they go back to the unshapely garb of childhood, and disguise themselves as owls or night-hawks.

(§ 28) But (lest I seem to arraign women only) flee from men also; from such as thou seest hung with chains, long-haired like women in spite of the Apostle's reproof, bearded like the goat, black-robed and barefooted in spite of cold. All these are signs of the Devil; such were Antimus and Sophronius, under whom Rome lately groaned. Such men creep into houses and deceive silly women laden with sins, ever learning and never able to come to the knowledge of the truth. They simulate sadness and long fasts, yet they protract their furtive meals far into the night; the rest I am ashamed to say, lest I should seem rather a satirist than a monitor. There are others—I speak of men of mine own [priestly] order, who covet the priesthood or diaconate only that they may have the more liberty to see women. All their care is for their clothing, their scents and odours, the close and even fitting of their shoes. The curling-iron has left its traces in their crisped locks; their fingers flash with rings, and they scarce venture to go a-tiptoe lest the puddles in the street should soil their feet. To see such men as these, you would deem them rather bridegrooms than clerics. Some spend the whole care of their lives in learning the names and houses and manners of the matrons. One man, the chief of this art, I will briefly and compendiously describe here, that the master's picture may assist you to recognize his disciples. He rises briskly with the sun; the order of his visits is duly mapped out; he seeks short cuts; and this importunate old man will push his way almost to the bedroom where the master or the housewife is asleep. If he sees a cushion or a tablecloth that takes his fancy, or any other household furniture, he praises, admires, handles it with his hands, complains that he lacks just such an one as this, and at last rather extorts than obtains it as a gift; for there is no woman that dares to offend the man who bears all the tittle-tattle of the town. This man is no friend of chastity or fasting; he judges his dinner by its savouries, and his general nickname is *The Fatted Fowl*, or *Puffing Billy*.[1] His barbarous and wanton mouth is ever primed for railing speech; whithersoever thou turnest, he is the first man to be seen. Whatever news be spread abroad, it was he who made or exaggerated the report. He changes his horses hourly; they are so sleek and fierce that you would take him for the blood-brother of Diomede.

(§ 29) The subtle foe hath many stratagems of war. The serpent was more subtle than any beast of the field which the Lord God had made. Remember that thou walkest in the midst of pitfalls, and that many veterans of virginity have let slip, even on the threshold of death, that crown of chastity whereof they had never doubted. If thou hast handmaidens that share thy holy purpose, rise not up against them, be not puffed up as a mistress over them. Ye have chosen one Bridegroom; together ye sing psalms to Christ and partake of Christ's body; why then should your tables be separate? Let thy life challenge others to share it; so honour thy handmaidens that others may be invited to join them. If ye find any of them weak in the faith, support her, console her, soothe her, and make thine own gain of her chastity. Many do but dissemble, that thus she may escape from servitude; speak to such an one plainly in the Apostle's words: "It is better to marry than to burn." Those virgins, those widows, who loiter curiously from one matron's house to another, whose brazen brow has lost all shame, who are worse than the parasite of comedy, cast them from thee as thou wouldst cast off the plague. Evil communications corrupt good manners; such women care for nought but the belly and the belly's neighbours. They are wont to exhort others, saying, "My love, spend that thou hast, and live while thou art yet alive," or again, "Dost thou lay up for thy children?" Wanton and winebibbers, they insinuate all evil, and soften even hearts of steel to the delights of earth. Having begun to wax wanton against Christ, they will marry, having

---

[1] I have ventured thus to translate the Greek into which Jerome lapses, γέρων ποππύζων, literally "the old man whose mouth makes a sound such as men use to attract birds."

damnation, because they have cast off their first faith. Seek not the reputation of eloquence, nor play with lyric verse. Be thou no fastidious follower of those sickly and slobbering matrons who now mutter from between their teeth, now speak with looser lips, lisping and clipping their words as though all natural speech were mere rusticity, and loving adultery even in the tongue. For what communion hath light with darkness, and what concord hath Christ with Belial? What hath Horace to do with the Psalter, or Vergil with the Gospels, or Cicero with the Apostles? Is not thy brother scandalized if he see thee sitting at meat in the idol's temple? And, even though all things be pure unto the pure, and nothing should be refused if it be received with thanksgiving, yet we should not drink together of the cup of the Lord and the cup of devils. Hearken to the tale of mine own misfortunes.

(§ 30) Many years ago, when for the kingdom of heaven's sake I had cut myself off from home, parents, sister, kinsfolk, and, most difficult of all, from the habit of choicer food; when I was on my way to fight the Lord's fight at Jerusalem, I could not give up that library which I had gotten together at Rome with the greatest labour and care. Therefore, wretch that I was, after fasting I would read Cicero; after many night-watches, with such tears as the memory of my past sins drew from my inmost heart, I would take up my Plautus. Whensoever I returned to myself and began to read the prophets, then their rough speech repelled me; and, because my blinded eyes saw not the light, I laid the blame not on my sight but on the sun. While the Ancient Serpent thus deluded me, at mid-Lententide, a fever crept into my very marrow, seized upon my weakened body, and, leaving me no moment's rest—a thing almost incredible—so preyed upon my wretched members that my bones scarce hung together. Meanwhile they made ready for my funeral; my body was already cold, and my breast alone palpitated feebly with a tepid stream of vital warmth. Then was I suddenly caught up in the spirit and dragged before the Judge's throne, where all was bathed in so clear a light, and those that stood by shone with such resplendent brightness, that I fell to the ground and dared not to raise mine eyes. Questioned, I made answer that I was a Christian. Then said He who sat upon that throne: "Thou liest; thou art no Christian, but a Ciceronian: where thy treasure is, there is thy heart also." I fell forthwith into silence; and, amid the stripes (for He had bidden that I should be scourged) I was still more tormented by the flame of conscience, revolving in my mind those words of the Psalmist, "Who shall confess to thee in hell?" Yet I raised my will and cried, amid my stripes and my groans, "Have mercy on me, O Lord, have mercy on me!" At length those who stood by fell down at the Judge's feet and besought him to pardon my youth and grant me room for repentance, on condition of inflicting further torment if I ever read these heathen books again. I, who under stress of that awful moment would have promised even greater things, began to swear by His name that sat upon the throne, saying, "Lord, if ever again I possess worldly books, if ever I read them, then have I denied Thee." Scarce had I sworn this oath when I was dismissed and returned to the upper air; and to the amazement of all, I opened eyes gushing with such a flow of tears as betrayed a pain which convinced even the unbelieving. Nor was that a mere sleep, or such a vain dream as doth sometimes delude us. I swear by that judgment-seat before which I lay, by that sentence which I dreaded—may I never again hear such a question as that!—that my shoulders were found bruised, that I felt the stripes even in my waking hours, and that from thenceforward I read so eagerly in Holy Scripture as I had never read before in worldly books.

(§ 31) Avoid also the fault of avarice. (§ 32) Nowadays, we see many women load their presses with garments; changing their gowns daily, they are yet unable to get the better of the moths. She who is more religious than the rest weareth a single garment threadbare, and trails in rags while her chests are full of raiment. Their vellum is dyed with purple; the letters are of liquid gold; their books are clad in precious gems, while Christ lies naked and dying at their doors. They sound a trumpet when they dole out alms; when they give a love-feast, the town crier is hired to publish it.

The mention of avarice leads St Jerome to tell a story of a "proprietary" monk, and thence to wander into a disquisition upon monks in general, good and bad. The former he describes very much as they are described in the *Paradise of the Fathers*, tr. Budge, vol. i, p. 99. St Jerome then apologizes for this digression, and returns to his subject.

(§ 37) Although the Apostle biddeth us pray without ceasing, and the Saints pray even in their sleep, yet we should have set hours of prayer, in order that time itself may warn us of this duty if by chance we are detained by any work. All know these hours; the third, the sixth, the ninth, daybreak and eventide. Take no food until thou hast prefaced it with prayer; rise not from the table without thanksgiving to thy Creator. In the night-time rise twice or thrice, and ponder on those Scriptures which thou knowest by heart. Arm thyself with prayer before going forth from thine house; returning from the streets, pray before thou sittest down; let not the body rest until the soul have been fed. At every act, at every step, let thine hand make the sign of the cross.

(§ 39) All these things that I have set before thee will seem hard to one who loveth not Christ. But whosoever holdeth all the pomp of this world as dross, and all things under the sun vain in comparison with the winning of Christ; whosoever is dead with his Lord and hath crucified the flesh with the lusts and desires thereof; such an one shall freely cry, "Who shall separate us from the love of Christ? shall tribulation, or distress, or persecution, or famine, or nakedness, or peril, or sword? As it is written, for thy sake we are killed all the day long; we are accounted as sheep for the slaughter. Nay, in all these things we are more than conquerors through him that loved us. For I am persuaded that neither death, nor life, nor angels, nor principalities, nor powers, nor things present, nor things to come, nor height, nor depth, nor any other creature, shall be able to separate us from the love of God, which is in Christ Jesus our Lord."

(§ 40) Nothing is hard to those that love; no labour is grievous to him who is consumed with desire. Behold what travail Jacob endured for Rachel his affianced bride: "He served," saith the Scripture, "seven years; and they seemed unto him but a few days, for the love that he had to her"; yet he himself said in after days: "In the day the drought consumed me, and the frost by night." Let us too love

Christ, let us ever seek His embraces, and all that is hard will seem easy. Unless thou use violence, thou shalt not lay hold upon the kingdom of heaven. If thou knock not with importunity, thou shalt not receive the sacramental bread. Is it not violence, thinkest thou, when flesh desireth to be as God, and to ascend to that place whence the angels fell, to sit itself in judgment upon angels?

(§ 41) Come forth awhile from the body, I beseech thee, and behold as in a vision that reward which eye hath not seen nor ear heard, neither hath it entered into the heart of man. What shall be that day when Mary, the mother of the Lord, shall meet you with her virgin choirs; when, after the passage of the Red Sea and the drowning of Pharaoh's army, she shall take her timbrel and sing aloud to your answering chorus: "Let us sing unto the Lord, for He hath triumphed gloriously; the horse and his rider hath He thrown into the sea." Then shall Thecla[1] fly eagerly to embrace thee; then shall the Bridegroom himself meet thee, saying, "Arise, make haste, my love, my dove, my beautiful one, and come; for winter is now past, the rain is over and gone." Then shall the angels marvel and say, "Who is this that cometh forth as the morning rising, fair as the moon, bright as the sun?" The daughters will see thee, and declare thee most blessed; the queens and concubines will praise thee.[2] Then again shall another chaste company come to meet thee; Sarah with her married folk, and Anna the daughter of Phanuel with her widows. In those two companies shall be your two mothers, Paula after the flesh and Marcella after the spirit.[3] The one will rejoice that she bare thee; the other, that she taught thee. Then indeed shall the Lord mount upon His she-ass and enter the heavenly Jerusalem; then shall the children (whereof the Saviour speaketh in Esaias: "Behold, I, and the children

---

[1] Thecla, the heroine of an apocryphal addition to the New Testament, was supposed to have been a virgin converted by the Apostle Paul, and martyred in Asia Minor. The book of the *Acts of Paul and Thecla* was already condemned as a forgery by Tertullian about A.D. 220; but the story won credit even among the most respectable authors, and enjoyed great popularity throughout the Middle Ages. It may be read in W. Hone's *Apocryphal New Testament* (1820, pp. 99 ff.).

[2] This, again, is almost textually from the Song of Solomon (vi, 9).

[3] For Marcella, to whom Eustochium was greatly indebted for her conversion, see Jerome, *Ep.* 127.

whom the Lord hath given me") bear aloft the psalms of
victory and sing with one voice: "Hosanna in the highest!
Blessed is he that cometh in the name of the Lord!" Then
shall that hundred and forty and four thousand, standing
before the Throne and the Elders, hold their harps and sing
a new song, the song which no man can learn save such as
are sealed unto God: these are they which were not defiled
with women, for they have remained virgins; these are they
which follow the Lamb whithersoever He goeth. Whensoever the vain ambition of this world shall tempt thee,
whensoever thou beholdest something glorious on this earth,
let thy mind lift thee up to Paradise; begin now to be such
as thou shalt be then, and thou shalt hear the Bridegroom's
voice: "Put me as a seal upon thy heart, as a seal upon thy
arm"; and thou, strong in work and in mind, shalt cry unto
Him: "Many waters cannot quench charity, neither can the
floods drown it."

A monk named Jovinian, at Rome, wrote a book in which he asserted, among
other things, that God had no more regard to virginity than to the married
state. He also denied the Virgin Birth of Christ, the special efficacy of
fasting, and the doctrine that the blessed shall enjoy different degrees of
bliss in heaven. Jerome's friend Pammachius procured the condemnation
of Jovinian's writings at the synods of Rome and Milan about A.D. 390, and
afterwards persuaded Jerome to answer them (393). This pilloried Jovinian
as the apostle of self-indulgence; and as such the whole Middle Ages knew
him. Readers of Chaucer will remember how he is quoted by the Wife of
Bath, the Summoner, and the God of Love (*C.T.* D, 675 and 1929: *L.G.W.*
281 a), and how much the Wife of Bath's clerkly husband drew from
"Theofraste." This treatise of Jerome, and the arguments which he borrows
from Theophrastus or from Solomon, supplied quite as much material to
solemn monastic disciplinarians as to satirists like Chaucer; it is indispensable
for the comprehension of one side of the coenobitic spirit; but considerations
of space permit only brief extracts here. (*Adv. Jovinianum*, § 47, Migne,
Pat. Lat. vol. 23, col. 276; ed. J. Martianay, 1706, vol. 4, col. 189.)

4. THE MONK'S VIEW OF WOMANKIND

THERE is a golden book current under the name of the
philosopher Theophrastus; it is entitled *On Marriage*, and
the question is whether a wise man would take a wife. The

author concludeth that a wise man would sometimes do so if the lady were fair to see, well bred, and of honourable parentage, and if he himself were healthy and wealthy; but unto this he addeth: "These things are seldom all concurrent in a marriage; the wise man, therefore, should not wed."

First, it impedeth the study of philosophy; no man can serve his books and his wife with equal zeal. A married woman hath many needs; precious robes, gold and gems, great expenses, handmaidens, furniture of all kinds, litters and a gilded car. Then he must listen, all night long, to her wordy complaints: "This woman goes abroad better clad than I; that other hath universal honour; I, poor wretch, must hang my head down among my fellows. Wherefore hast thou made eyes at that woman over the way? What hadst thou to say to the maidservant? What didst thou bring home from the market?" We may not have a friend or a companion, the wife suspects our love to others, our hate to herself. However learned a teacher there may be in any city, we may not leave our wife, nor can we burden ourselves with her at his lectures. If poor, she is hard to feed; rich, she is most grievous to suffer. Moreover, we have no choice of wives, but must take such as we come across. Whether she be wrathful, foolish, deformed, proud, unsavoury—whatever be her faults, we learn them first when we have married her. A horse or an ass, an ox or a dog, or even the commonest slaves, are tried before we choose to buy them; so also with clothes and kettles, chairs and cups and earthen pipkins; a wife alone is not to be had on approval, lest she be found wanting before we marry her. We must study her face from hour to hour, and praise her beauty, lest, if thou do but look at some other woman, thy wife should think herself neglected. Thou must call her *My Lady*, solemnize her birthday, swear by her health, and wish that she may survive thee. Thou must honour her nurse and nursemaid, her slave, her [foster-brother?] and pupil, her comely follower and the curled manager of her affairs—names which do but cloke her adulterers. Whomsoever she may choose to love, these must have thine unwilling affection. If thou have given over thine whole house to her rule, then art thou her servant. If thou reserve any part for thine own choice, she thinketh herself distrusted; hence come hatred and quarrels and, unless thou see to it quickly, she will brew poison for thee. If thou open thy doors to her old women and fortune-tellers, to her jewellers and silk-merchants, there is another danger to her chastity; forbid them thine house, and she is injured by thy suspicions. But what availeth even the strictest watchfulness, when a wanton woman cannot be kept, and a chaste one ought not? For necessity is an uncertain guardian of chastity; she alone can be called truly chaste who, if she had wished, might have sinned. A fair woman is easily loved, a foul woman easily falls into concupiscence. It is hard to keep a thing that many men covet; it is burdensome to possess that which no man deigneth to have. Yet it is less misery to possess the unshapely wife than to guard the shapely; for nothing is safe when all men sigh after it. One man woos with his comely person, another with his understanding, a third with his wit, a fourth with his liberality. In one way or another, when a fortress is so wholly beset, it must at last be taken by storm. If, however, a man marry for the sake of a well-kept house, or for solace in sickness, or to flee from solitude, yet shall a faithful bondman keep house far better, more obediently, and more buxomly, than a wife; for she holdeth herself to be truly mistress only when she doeth contrary to her husband's will, following not his commands but her own fancy. In sickness, again, we have far more help from friends and grateful servants than from a wife who imputeth to us every tear-drop; whose eyes overflow with the necessary hope of a legacy; and who, by boasting her anxiety, troubleth the sick man's soul to desperation. If she for her part be sick, we must be sick with her, and never depart from her bedside. Or if our wife be good and kind (and such birds are rare indeed!) we groan with her in childbirth, we are tortured when her life is in peril. Moreover, no wise man can ever be in solitude; for he hath all that ever were good, or that ever shall be; and his free mind roameth at will throughout the universe. That which he cannot embrace in body, he can grasp in mind; and, where men are lacking, he speaketh with God. Never will he be less alone than in his solitude. What, again, can be more foolish than to marry for the sake of children, that our name may not perish or that we may have props for our old age and fixed inheritors? What is it to us, when we must leave this world, that another be called by our name—even if the son took his father's name at once, and if there were not countless others of the same name? How can it prop our age if we foster a child who may perchance die before us, or shame us by its wickedness? If again they grow to riper age, they will certainly think thee too long-lived. Better and more certain heirs may be found among thy friends and kinsfolk, deliberately chosen, than among children whom thou must take without *yea* or *nay*. Moreover, the best certainty with our inheritance is to spend it well while we live, rather than to leave for uncertain uses the wealth which our labour has acquired.

Such then, briefly, are the reasons of [the heathen] Theophrastus; do they not put us Christians to shame, who have our conversation in heaven, and whose desire is to depart and to be with Christ? Shall he, who is a fellow-heir with Christ, desire a human being for his own heir? Shall he yearn for children, and delight in a long line of descendants, when he knoweth that these may perchance be possessed by Anti-Christ?

Jerome then goes on (§ 49) to quote further from Aristotle, Plutarch, and Seneca. Above (§§ 28, 29) he has already collected two columns of misogynistic quotations from Solomon's Proverbs and Ecclesiastes, from which he draws the following moral:

Lo, here also (Prov. xxx, 21 ff.) a wife is put among the greatest evils. If thou answer: "Solomon speaketh well only of an odious woman," then I reply (as before) that the mere possibility of such a peril is grievous in itself. For he who taketh a wife knoweth not whether she be odious or lovable. If odious, she cannot be endured; if lovable, then her love is compared to hell, to a parched land, to burning fire. [He quotes farther Prov. ix, 13; xxx, 16.]

In the Second Book of this work, after labouring to refute Jovinian's other tenets, Jerome gives a personal description of his adversary which, it has been suggested, is based merely upon hearsay, or upon the saint's conception of the type of man who was likely to teach such doctrines as Jovinian's. In any case it is a lifelike portrait of an unmonastic monk, true to type if not to the person; and we see whence Chaucer got his conception:

> Me thynketh they been lyk Iovinyan,
> Fat as a whale, and walkynge as a swan,
> All vinolent as botel in the spence.
> Hir preyere is of ful greet reverence
> Whan they for soulès seye the Psalm of Davit,
> Lo, *buf*, they seye, *cor meum eructavit*.

This last extract I have abridged very severely.

And now we must speak plainly to our new Epicurus, wantoning in his gardens amid youths and silly women. I will say to him: Thou hast in thy party the fat, the sleek, the whitewashed sepulchres. Thou mayest add if thou wilt, according to Socrates's taunt, all the swine and dogs; and, (for thou lovest the flesh,) vultures, eagles, hawks and owls. Whomsoever I see comely, curled, with hair trimmed and set and ruddy cheeks, these I know to be of thine herd; those grunt among thy swine. Of our herd are the sad, the pale, that go in mourning array; their tongue is silent, but their habit and bearing proclaims them pilgrims and strangers in this world. Boast not thy multitude of disciples: the Son of God taught in Judea, and was followed only by twelve Apostles. "I have trodden the winepress alone," said He; "and of the people there was none with me." The many that receive thy doctrines, are a proof of voluptuousness; they do not so much approve of thine eloquence as they love their own vices. We see daily, in the streets, some cheating soothsayer be-labouring the posteriors of the fools that frequent him, and twisting his staff to shake the teeth of those who bite upon it; yet there are always fools enough to serve his purpose; so also dost thou take it as a tribute to thy wisdom if a herd of swine followeth after thee, whom thou art feeding into pork for hell. It is always false prophets who promise sweet things, and who please for a time. Truth is bitter, and they who preach it are fulfilled with bitterness; for Christ's Passover is kept with the unleavened bread of sincerity and truth, and it is eaten with bitter herbs.

Moreover, thou hast in thine army many lieutenants; thou

hast thy body-guard at thy side and thy skirmishers thrown out
—well-fed, trim in apparel, sleek, loud of voice, ever ready
to fight for thee with fist or with heel. The noble make room
for thee in the street; the wealthy kiss thy head; for, if thou
hadst not come, the drunken and the surfeiting [*ructantes*]
would not have been able to enter into Paradise.

The last glimpse we get of Jovinian is from a treatise written in 409.
Here Jerome attacks Vigilantius, who had written against relic-worship
and the exaggerated cult of virginity; and in the opening sentences
the saint claims that the earlier teacher's soul had passed by trans-
migration into this new heretic (ed. Martianay, t. IV, col. 281).

This Vigilantius, or rather Dormitantius, hath suddenly
arisen, fighting with unclean spirit against the Spirit of Christ.
He would forbid our revering the tombs of the martyrs, condemn our wakes, have no *Alleluia* sung except at Eastertide,
judge our continence as an heresy and our chastity as a hotbed
of lust. And, even as Euphorbus is said to have been re-born
in the person of Pythagoras, so in this man hath the evil mind
of Jovinian arisen again; so that we are compelled to answer
the Devil's wiles no less in this new heretic than in the old.
Jovinian, condemned by the authority of the Roman See,
breathed out his soul—or rather belched it forth—among
pheasants and swine's flesh.[1] This tavern-keeper of Calagorra
...mixeth wine with water; and, by his old craft, would fain
blend the poison of his own treachery with the Catholic faith.
He assails virginity and hates chastity; at his worldly feasts
he declaims against the fasts of the Saints; he philosophizes
in his cups, and slabbers up his junkets to the sweet sound of
psalmody; as one who should disdain to hear the sweet songs
of David and his fellow-prophets except his belly feast meanwhile. I say this rather in sadness than in ridicule; for I
cannot restrain myself, nor shut my ears to these contumelious
assaults upon the Apostles and Martyrs. For (I shudder to say
it), he is reported to have bishops that abet his crime, if
indeed we may call those bishops who ordain no deacons but
such as have first taken wives; who credit no celibate with
chastity; nay, who show their own sanctity of life by suspect-
ing ill of all the rest, and who, unless they see the wives of

---

[1] Inter phasides aves et carnes suillas non tam emisit spiritum quam eructavit.

their clerics to be big with child, or hear the infants crying in their mothers' arms, will not impart to them the Sacraments of Christ. What can the Churches of the East do? or the Egyptians and those of the Apostolic See, who take for their clerics either virgins or continent folk, or such as, though married, are as though they were unmarried? Such is the teaching of Dormitantius...that men may be as swine, as brute beasts, as horses, whereof it is written: "They were as fed horses in the morning: every one neighed after his neighbour's wife."

St Jerome wrote his famous letter to Eustochium from Rome in A.D. 384. The following paragraph (§ 34) exemplifies the ill-regulated enthusiasm of some early monks, in correction of which legislators like St Benedict framed their admirable Rules.

5. FASTING AND REACTION

IN Egypt are three sorts of monks; coenobites, or dwellers in common; anchorites, who live alone in deserts and take their name from their retirement; the third sort is called *remnuoth*. These last are the worst and most neglected; yet in our province [*i.e.* Rome and Italy] they are the principal, if not the only sort. These live together by twos or threes, seldom in greater numbers, at their own will and government; whatsoever they earn is put together to pay for their common food. They live for the most part in cities and towns; and (as though profession, and not life, made a man holy) they sell all that they make at a higher price than others. There is frequent strife among them, since they live by their own food and suffer no man's authority. In truth they fast in rivalry with each other; Christ bade us do this in secret, but these men fast for victory. In them, all is affectation; loose-sleeved, slipshod, coarsely clad, sighing and groaning, they visit virgins and backbite the clergy; and, whensoever a great festival is held, they eat and drink till they vomit.

6. MONASTIC POVERTY

From St Jerome's letter to Eustochium, § 33 (Migne, *Pat. Lat.* vol. 22, col. 418).

LET me tell you what befell a few years ago in the monastic desert of Nitria. One of the brethren—rather sparing than avaricious, and ignorant that his Lord had been sold for thirty pieces of silver—left at his death a hundred pieces which he had earned by weaving linen. The monks held a council—for some 5000 dwell at Nitria in separate cells—to decide what should be done. Some were for giving the money to the poor, or to the Church, or to the monk's kinsfolk. But Macarius and Pambos and Isidorus, and the rest of those who are called Fathers, were inspired by the Holy Ghost to decree that the coins should be buried with their owner, saying, "Thy money perish with thee." Nor let any man tax this deed of cruelty; so great a fear came upon all who dwelt in Egypt, that it was held a criminal thing to leave a single piece of money at death.

Since relics were almost essential to the ordinary worship of the Middle Ages, and especially to the monks, it was natural that men should everywhere seek and find. The following instance is chosen, out of scores or hundreds which might be found, on account of the celebrity of the saint, the reasonable tone of the narrative itself, and the respect with which it is treated by so great a scholar as Mabillon.

The possession of St Benedict's corpse was disputed for many centuries (and, in a sense, is still disputed) between Monte Cassino and Fleury, or, as it is often called, St-Benoît-sur-Loire. Mabillon, in 1685, printed the following "brevis narratio" from a MS. at St Emmeram, which he judged to be "900 years old, and therefore contemporary with the translation of the saint's body" (*Vetera Analecta*, t. IV, 1685, pp. 451, 453).

7. THE INVENTION OF A RELIC

IN the name of Christ. There was in France, by God's gracious providence, a learned Priest who set about to journey towards Italy, that he might discover where were the bones

of our father St Benedict, no longer worshipped by men.[1]
At length he came into a desert country some 70 or 80 miles
from Rome, where St Benedict of old had built a cell whose
indwellers had been bound together in perfect charity. Yet,
even then, this Priest and his companions were disquieted by
the uncertainties of the place, since they could find neither
vestiges of the monastery nor any burial-place, until at last
a swineherd showed them, for hire, exactly where the
monastery had stood; yet he was utterly unable to find the
sepulchre until he and his companions had hallowed themselves by a two or three days' fast. Then it was revealed to
their cook in a dream, and the matter became plain unto
them; for in the morning it was shown unto them by him
who seemed lowest in degree, that St Paul's words might be
true (1 Cor. i, 27), that God despiseth that which is held
in great esteem among men; or again, as the Lord Himself
foretold (Matt. xx, 26), "Whosoever will be great among
you, let him be your minister." Then, searching the spot
with greater diligence, they found a marble slab which they
had to cut through. At last, having broken through the slab,
they found the bones of St Benedict, and his sister's bones
beneath, with another marble slab between; since (as we
believe) the almighty and merciful God would that those
should be united in their sepulchre who, in life, had been
joined together in brotherly and sisterly love, and in Christian
charity.

Having collected and washed these bones, they laid them
upon fine clean linen, each by itself, to be carried home to
their own country. They gave no sign to the Romans lest,
if these had learnt the truth, they would doubtless never have
suffered such holy relics to be withdrawn from their country
without conflict or war—relics which God made manifest,
in order that men might see how great was their need of
religion and holiness, by the following miracle. For, within
a while, the linen that wrapped these bones was found red
with the saint's blood, as though from open wounds on living

---

[1] Monte Cassino, St Benedict's own monastery on a spur of the Apennines
between Rome and Naples, had been destroyed by the Lombard barbarians in
580, and was not inhabited again until 718 A.D.

bodies; whereby Jesus Christ intended to show that those whose bones are here so glorious would truly live with Him in the world to come. Then they were laid upon a horse, which bore them over all that long journey as lightly as though he had felt no burden. Again, when they journeyed through forest ways and on narrow roads, neither did the trees impede them nor did any ruggedness of the path obstruct their journey; so that the travellers saw clearly how this was through the merits of St Benedict and his sister St Scholastica, in order that their journey might be safe and prosperous even into the realm of France and the monastery of Fleury. In which monastery they are now buried in peace, until they shall arise in glory at the Last Day; and here they confer benefits upon all who pray unto the Father through Jesus Christ, the Son of God, who liveth and reigneth in the unity of the Holy Ghost, world without end. Amen.

For a collection of miracles wrought by these bones at Fleury, see *Miracles de St-Benoît*, ed. E. Certain (Soc. d'Histoire de France).

It will be remembered that Chaucer's monk emphatically repudiated, among other ideas that were "old and som-del streit," the Augustinian doctrine of manual labour:

> What sholde he...swynken with his handes, and laboure
> As Austyn bit? How shal the worlde be served?
> Lat Austyn have his swynk to him reserved!

The allusion is to St Augustine's *De Opere Monachorum*, which has always remained the classical work on this subject. St Augustine himself describes the genesis of this book in his *Retractations* (II, 21): "When at Carthage there had begun to be monasteries, some maintained themselves by their own hands, obeying the Apostle; but others wished to live on the oblations of the faithful....Whence also among laics of inferior purpose, but yet fervent in zeal, there had begun to arise tumultuous contests, whereby the Church was troubled, some defending the one, others the other part. Add to this, that some of them who were for not working wore their hair long.... On these accounts the venerable old Aurelius, Bishop of the Church of the same city, desired me to write somewhat of this matter, and I did so."

The book is of very great value in the light it throws on early monasticism. Although no later writer (so far as I know) ventured openly to combat St Augustine's position, it will be seen that in the later Middle Ages, when monastic labour was practically obsolete, the Religious fell back upon practically the same excuses which Augustine explodes. The following extracts are from the *Library of Fathers*, Oxford, 1847, *Seventeen Short Treatises of St Augustine*, pp. 470 ff.

8. MONKS AND LABOUR

(p. 471) FIRST, then, it is to be seen what is said by persons of that profession who will not work; then, if we shall find that they think not aright, what is meet to be said for their correction. It is not, say they, of this corporal work in which either husbandmen or handicraftsmen labour, that the Apostle gave precept, when he said, *If any will not work, neither let him eat.* For he could not be contrary to the Gospel, where the Lord himself saith, *Therefore I say unto you, be not solicitous for your life, what ye shall eat, neither for your body what ye shall put on....Sufficient unto the day is the evil thereof.* Lo, say they, where the Lord biddeth us be without care concerning our food and clothing: how then could the Apostle think contrary to the Lord that he should instruct us that we ought to be in such sort solicitous, what we shall eat or what we shall drink, or wherewithal we shall be clothed, that he should even burden us with the arts, cares, labours of handicraftsmen? Wherefore in that he saith, *If any will not work, neither let him eat*; works spiritual, say they, are what we must understand....So, say they, do we also. We read with the brethren who come to us fatigued from the turmoil of the world, that with us, in the word of God, and in prayers, psalms, hymns, and spiritual songs, they may find rest. We speak to them, console, exhort, building up in them whatever unto their life, according to their degree, we perceive to be lacking. Such works if we wrought not, with peril should we receive of the Lord our spiritual sustenance itself. For this is it the Apostle said, *If any will not work, neither let him eat*. Thus do these men deem themselves to comply with the apostolic and evangelical sentence....First then we ought to demonstrate that the blessed Apostle Paul willed the servants of God to work corporal works which should have as their end a great spiritual reward, for this purpose that they should need food and clothing of no man, but with their own hands should procure these for themselves: then, to show that those evangelical precepts from which some cherish not only their sloth but even arrogance, are not contrary to the apostolical precept and example. Let us see then whence the Apostle came to this, that he should say, If any will not work neither let him eat, and what he thereupon joineth on, that from the very context of this lesson may appear his declared sentence....

The saint has no difficulty in proving that St Paul, while he claimed the *right* to live by the preaching of the Gospel, thought it a higher degree of evangelical perfection to support himself by manual work. He then proceeds:

(p. 493) For what these men are about, who will not do bodily work, to what thing they give up their time, I should like to know. "To prayers," say they, "and psalms and reading and the word of God." A holy life unquestionably, and in sweetness of Christ worthy of praise; but then, if from these we are not to be called off neither must we eat, nor our daily viands themselves be prepared, that they may be put before us and taken. Now if to find time for these things the servants of God at certain intervals of time by very infirmity are of necessity compelled, why do we not make account of some portions of time to be allotted also to the observance of apostolical precepts? For one single prayer of one who obeyeth is sooner heard than ten thousand of a despiser. As for divine songs, however, they can easily, even while working with their hands, say them, and like as rowers with a boat-song so with godly melody cheer up their very toil. Or are we ignorant how it is with all workmen, to what vanities, and for the most part even filthinesses, of theatrical fables they give their hearts and tongues, while their hands recede not from their work? What then hinders a servant of God while working with his hands to meditate in the law of the Lord and sing unto the Name of the Lord Most High? provided of course, that to learn what he may by memory rehearse, he have times set apart. For to this end also those good works of the faithful ought not to be lacking, for resource of making up what is necessary, that the hours which are so taken up in storing of the mind that those bodily works cannot be carried on, may not oppress with want. But they which say that they give up their time to reading, do they not then find that which the Apostle enjoineth? Then what perversity is this, to refuse to be ruled by his reading while he wishes to give up his time thereto; and that he may spend more time in reading what is good, therefore to refuse to do what is read? For who knows not that each doth the more quickly profit when he reads good things, the quicker he is in doing what he reads?

Moreover, if discourse must be bestowed upon any, and this so take up the speaker that he hath not time to work with his hands, are all in the monastery able to hold discourse unto brethren which come unto them from another kind of life, whether it be to expound the divine lessons or concerning any questions which may be put to reason in an wholesome manner? Then since not all have the ability, why upon this pretext do all want to have nothing else to do? Although even if all were able, they ought to do it by turns; not only that the rest might not be taken up from necessary works, but also because it sufficeth that to many hearers there be one speaker. To come now to the Apostle; how could he find time to work with his hands, unless for the bestowing of the word of God he had certain set times? And indeed God hath not willed this either to be hidden from us. For both of what craft he was a workman, and at what times he was taken up with dispensing the Gospel, Holy Scripture has not left untold.... *After these things*, it says, *he departed from Athens and came to Corinth; and having found a certain Jew by name Aquila, of Pontus by birth, lately come from Italy, and Priscilla his wife, because that Claudius had ordered all Jews to depart from Rome, he came unto them, and because he was of the same craft he abode with them, doing work: for they were tent-makers.* This if they shall essay to interpret allegorically, they show what proficients they be in ecclesiastical learning, on which they glory that they bestow all their time. And at the least, touching those sayings above recited...and the rest of this kind, let them either expound otherwise, or if by most clear shining light of truth they be put to it, let them understand and obey; or if to obey they be either unwilling or unable, at least let them own them which be willing, to be better, and them which be also able, to be happier men than they. For it is one thing to plead infirmity of body, either truly alleged, or falsely pretended: but another so to be deceived and so to deceive, that it shall even be thought a proof of righteousness obtaining more mightily in servants of God, if laziness have gotten power to reign among a set of ignorant men. He namely, who shows a true infirmity of body, must be humanely dealt withal: he who pretends a false one and cannot be convicted, must be left unto God: yet neither of them fixeth a pernicious rule; because a good servant of God both serves his manifestly infirm brother, and when the other deceives, if he believes him because he does not think him a bad man, he does not imitate him that he may be bad; and if he believe him not, he thinks him deceitful, and does nevertheless not imitate him. But when a man says, "This is true righteousness that by doing no bodily work, we imitate the birds of the air, because he who shall do any such work goes against the Gospel": whoso being infirm in mind hears and believes this, that person, not for that he so bestows all his time, but for that he so erreth, must be mourned over....

(p. 502) Wherefore, that I may briefly embrace the whole matter, let these persons, who from their perverse understanding of the Gospel labour to pervert apostolical precepts either take no thought for the morrow, even as the birds of the air; or let them obey the Apostle, as dear children: yea rather, let them do both, because both accord. For things contrary to his Lord Paul the servant of Jesus Christ would never advise. This then we say openly to these persons: If the birds of the air ye in such wise understand in the Gospel, that ye will not by working with your hands procure food and clothing; then neither must ye put any thing by for the morrow, like as the birds of the air do put nothing by. But if to put somewhat by for the morrow, is possibly not against the Gospel where it is said *Behold the birds of the air, for they neither sow nor reap nor gather into stores*; then is it possibly not against the Gospel nor against similitude of the birds of the air, to maintain this life of the flesh by labour of corporal working.

For if they be urged from the Gospel that they put nothing by for the morrow, they most rightly answer, "Why then had the Lord Himself a bag in which to put by the money which was collected? Why so long time beforehand, on occasion of impending famine, were supplies of corn sent to the holy fathers? Why did Apostles in such wise provide things necessary for the indigence of saints lest there should be lack thereafter?"...These and much else they most copiously and most truly bring forward. To whom we answer: Ye see then, albeit the Lord said, *Take no thought for the morrow*, yet ye are not by these words constrained to reserve nothing for the morrow: then why do ye say that by the same words ye are constrained to do nothing? Why are the birds of the air not a pattern unto you for reserving nothing, and ye will have them to be a pattern for working nothing?...

(p. 508) Since these things are so, suffer me awhile, holy brother (for the Lord giveth me through thee great boldness), to address these same our sons and brethren whom I know with what love thou together with us dost travail in birth withal, until the apostolic discipline be formed in them. O servants of God, soldiers of Christ, is it thus ye dissemble the plottings of our most crafty foe, who fearing your good fame, that so goodly odour of Christ, lest good souls should say, *We will run after the odour of thine ointments*, and so should escape his snares, and in every way desiring to obscure it with his own stenches, hath dispersed on every side so many hypocrites under the garb of monks, strolling about the provinces, no where sent, no where fixed, no where standing, no where sitting? Some hawking about limbs of martyrs, if indeed of martyrs; others magnifying their fringes and phylacteries; others with a lying story, how they have heard say that their parents or kinsmen are alive in this or that country, and therefore be they on their way to them: and all asking, all exacting, either the cost of their lucrative want, or the price of their pretended sanctity. And in the meanwhile wheresoever they be found out in their evil deeds, or in whatever way they become notorious, under the general name of monks, your purpose is blasphemed, a purpose so good, so holy, that in Christ's name we desire it, as through other lands so through all Africa, to grow and flourish. Then are ye not inflamed with godly jealousy? Does not your heart wax hot within you, and in your meditation a fire kindle that these men's evil works ye should pursue with good works, that ye should cut off from them occasion of a foul trafficking, by which your estimation is hurt, and a stumbling-block put before the weak? Have mercy then and have compassion, and show to mankind that ye are not seeking in ease a ready subsistence, but through the straight and narrow way of this purpose, are seeking the kingdom of God. Ye have the same cause which the Apostle had, to cut off occasion from them which seek occasion, that they who by their stinks are suffocated, by your good odour may be refreshed.

We are not binding heavy burdens and laying them upon your shoulders, while we with a finger will not touch them.... I call our Lord Jesus, in Whose name I fearlessly say these things, for a witness upon my soul, that so far as it concerns mine own convenience, I would much rather every day at certain hours, as much as is appointed by rule in well-governed monasteries, do some work with my hands and have the remaining hours free for reading and praying, or some work pertaining to divine letters, than have to bear these most annoying perplexities of other men's causes about secular matters, which we must either by adjudication bring to an end, or by intervention cut short. Which troubles the same Apostle hath fastened us withal (not by his own sentence, but by His who spake through him), while yet we do not read that he had to put up with them himself: indeed his was not the sort of work to admit of it, while running to and fro in his Apostleship....

The saint then comes to the subject of long hair.

(p. 512) For there is less sin, if people do not praise the sinner in the desires of his soul, and speak good of him who practiseth iniquities. Now what is more an iniquity than to wish to be obeyed by inferiors, and to refuse to obey superiors? The Apostle, I mean, not us: insomuch that they even let their hair grow long....For whereunto, I pray thee, pertaineth this also, that people so openly against the Apostle's precepts wear long hair? Is it that there must be in such sort vacation, that not even the barbers are to work? Or, because they say that they imitate the Gospel birds, do they fear to be, as it were, plucked, lest they be not able to fly? I shrink from saying more against this fault, out of respect for certain long-haired brethren, in whom, except this, we find much, and wellnigh everything to venerate. But the more we love them in Christ the more solicitously do we admonish them. Nor are we afraid indeed, lest their humility reject our admonition; seeing that we also desire to be admonished by such as they, wherever we chance to stumble or to go aside. This then we admonish so holy men, not to be moved by foolish quibblings of vain persons, and imitate in this perversity them whom in all else they are far from resembling. For those persons hawking about a venal hypocrisy, fear lest shorn sanctity be held cheaper than long-haired; because, forsooth, he who sees them shall call to mind those ancients whom we read of, Samuel and the rest who did not cut their hair....

And then that further device of theirs, (if words can express it,) how painfully ridiculous is it, which they have invented for defence of their long locks! "A man," say they, "the Apostle hath forbidden to have long hair: but then they who have made themselves eunuchs for the kingdom of God are no longer men.".…With which sleight these persons deceive ignorant people, with which cunning craftiness and machinations of the enemy both they themselves are whirled round, and in their whirling essay to make the minds of the weak which cohere unto them so (in a manner) to spin round with them, that they also may not know where they are.…

Wherefore, they which will not do right things, let them give over at least to teach wrong things. Howbeit they be others whom in this speech we reprove: but as for those who by this one fault, of letting their hair contrary to apostolic precept grow long, offend and trouble the Church, because when some being unwilling to think of them any thing amiss are forced to twist the manifest words of the Apostle into a wrong meaning, others choose to defend the sound understanding of the Scriptures rather than fawn upon any men, there arise between the weaker and the stronger brethren most bitter and perilous contentions: which things perchance if they knew, these would correct without hesitation this also, in whom we love and admire all else.

The monastery of Novalese, under Mont Cenis, was founded A.D. 726; its well-known *Chronicle* was compiled by one of its monks in the first and second quarters of the eleventh century. References are to Pertz's smaller edition (*Chronicon Novaliciense*, Hanover, 1890).

9. A FIGHTING MONK

(*Chron. Nov.* pp. 13, 28.)

IT is said that there dwelt in this monastery in early days an ancient monk named Walther, of noble race and royal blood, who is said to have been a most famous and mighty champion... who, after many wars and battles which he had fought doughtily in the world, feeling his body now almost broken down with old age, and remembering the burden of his sins, thought within himself how to come to right penance; and, having resolved in his mind that he could best do this in the monastery wherein the monks kept their Rule most strictly, forthwith he sought out a staff of most cunning workmanship, at the head whereof he bade fashion many rings, and to each of these rings a little bell; then, taking a pilgrim's habit, he wandered thus throughout almost the whole world to explore with this staff, whensoever he came to a monastery, what zeal of common life the monks had and how they kept their Rule. So then he set out upon this pilgrimage, whereof the tradition survives; and to whatsoever monastery he came, he would enter at the hour when the monks themselves came into the church to praise their God— for this he marked very narrowly—then would he smite his staff twice or thrice upon the church pavement, that he might mark the strictness of their discipline by the sound of the bells that hung thereon; for the man's mind was most subtle and crafty to discern by this means between the discipline of divers monasteries. So when, as we have said above, he had wandered almost over the world, he came at length to Novalese, then most renowned for its zeal of sanctity; and, having entered the church, he smote his staff, as he was wont, upon the sanctuary floor, at which sound one of the boys looked backwards to see what this might mean; whereupon the master of the novices leapt upon him and smote this boy, his disciple, upon the cheek, which when Walther saw, he groaned within himself and said: "Lo, here is that which I have sought for so many days and throughout so many lands, and as yet had never found." Wherefore he went out forthwith from the church and besought the abbot that he would deign to speak with him; and, having told him of his wish, he presently took the monastic cowl and was made forthwith, by his own choice and will, the gardener of our monastery. In that office he was wont to take two cords of exceeding length and stretch them across the garden, one lengthwise and another crosswise, whereon in summer-time he hung all baleful weeds, stretching out their roots to the heat of the sun that they might never live again.

The chronicler goes on to describe the vast trains of waggons which brought grain to the monastery from all its farms, led by an empty waggon with a bell on a pole to mark out the sacred convoy, which no man ever

A FIGHTING MONK

ventured to touch; until at last one day the king's servants robbed one of
these convoys. Walther was deputed by the abbot to go and recover it, as
far as possible by gentle means.

...So Walther, going forth from the abbot's presence, and
bearing in mind what so great a master had said unto him,
enquired of the servants of the monastery whether there were
any horse there which was inured to war in case of necessity;
and, when the servants answered that they had good and stout
cart-horses, he bade them be brought forthwith to his presence.
There he considered each one, mounting it with spurs on his
heels to prove its mettle; and, pricking one after another, he
was displeased with all and refused them, and told forthwith
their faults. Then he remembered how he had once brought
with him into that monastery a most excellent charger, and
said to the servants: "That steed which I brought hither
when I became a monk, liveth he still or is he dead?" They
answered: "He liveth, lord, but he is old, and hath been given
over to the baker, for whom he beareth the corn daily to and
from the mill." Then said Walther: "Bring him hither and
let us see how his mettle is." The horse was brought, and
Walther, mounting him and spurring him on, said: "The
horse beareth still in mind those steps and paces which I
sought to teach him in his younger days." Then the abbot
and all the brethren blessed Walther; and he, bidding them
farewell, took with him two or three servants and hastened
to meet the aforesaid robbers. When, therefore, he had
humbly saluted them, he began to warn them that they should
not again do God's servants such harm as they had even now
wrought. But they answered him with hard words, whereupon he rebuked them all the more sternly and more frequently. They therefore, moved with wrath at this proud
spirit of his, compelled Walther to strip him of the garments
which he wore; and he obeyed them humbly in all things,
according to his obedience, saying how the brethren had laid
this command upon him. They therefore, in course of stripping
him, began to despoil him even of his shoes and his breeches;
but when they had come to his breeches, Walther resisted long,
saying that the brethren had by no means commanded him
to suffer those garments to be taken from him; whereupon

they answered that they cared nought for the bidding of the monks; but Walther withstood them to their face, saying that it was not seemly that he should abandon these garments. When therefore they began to lay violent hands upon him, Walther withdrew secretly from the saddle the stirrup wherein his foot had rested, wherewith he so smote one of these ruffians on the head that he fell lifeless to the earth. Then, seizing his arms, the monk struck right and left. ...(Now some men say that when one of them had pressed upon him with more importunity than the rest, and was bending down to draw his shoes from his feet, this Walther smote him with his fist so sore upon the neck that his neckbone brake and fell into his gullet.) Many therefore were slain, and the rest took to flight and left all that they had. Walther therefore, having gained the victory, took all that was his and theirs to boot, and returned forthwith to the monastery laden with the spoil. But when the abbot had heard of these things and saw what had been done, he groaned and gave himself up to lamentation and prayers together with the rest of the brethren, rebuking him sore. But Walther took his penance forthwith from the abbot, lest he should grow proud of his evil deeds in this life and suffer harm in his soul.

From Sigebert of Gembloux, ann. 865 (Pertz, *Mon. Germ. Hist.* vol. VI, p. 341).

10. A ROYAL MONK

THE king of the Bulgarians, being converted with his people to Christianity...became so rooted in the faith that he soon set his eldest son on the throne and renounced the world to become a monk. But when his son, with a young man's inconstancy, would fain have returned to heathen worship, then their old king resumed his knightly belt and his royal robes, pursued after his son, took him and put out his eyes and cast him into prison. Afterwards, having set his younger son upon the throne, the king took back his sacred habit, and persevered therein even to his last breath.

A MONASTIC BACKWOODSMAN

The *Life* of St Sturm or Sturmi was written about A.D. 820 by his pupil Eigil, who succeeded him after an interval as abbot of Fulda. The following description of the choice of a site for this great abbey (about A.D. 840) is abbreviated from chaps. 4 ff. (*Mon. Germ. Hist. Scriptt.* vol. II, p. 367). A few similar instances of the monastic attitude towards nature may be found in L. Zoepf, *Das Heiligen-Leben im* 10 *Jahrhundert*, Leipzig, 1908, pp. 219 ff.

11. A MONASTIC BACKWOODSMAN

WHEN St Sturm had thus spent three years preaching and baptizing among the people, by God's inspiration his heart was stirred to a stricter life, and he longed for the mortification of a hermit's cell; and the Spirit impelled him to reveal this to his spiritual master St Boniface. The saintly bishop gave him two companions, and, having diligently instructed all three, he prayed over them and blessed them, saying: "Go ye into that wilderness which men call Thuringia, and seek out a place fit for the dwelling of God's servants; for unto such God can prepare a fit habitation even in the desert." So these three went forth into the wilderness, and entered into a rural solitude where they scarce saw aught but earth and sky and vast trees. Here they besought Christ earnestly to direct their feet into the way of peace. On the third day they came unto the place which is now called Hersfeld; and, after diligent view and exploration of this spot, they besought Christ that it might be blessed unto them for a habitation. Here they settled upon the site of the present monastery, and made themselves narrow huts covered with the bark of trees; wherein they dwelt for no small space of time, serving God with holy fasts and vigils and prayers.

Then, after a while, Sturm was filled with holy zeal and went forth from this wilderness to the holy archbishop Boniface, to whom he described in order both the site and the quality of the land, and the river-courses and springs and valleys, and all that pertained to this place. This holy man, having listened diligently and pondered these things prudently in his mind, spake as follows: "I am loth that ye should dwell in this place by reason of the neighbourhood of that barbarous race; for, as thou knowest, the wild Saxons dwell hard by.

Seek therefore some remoter habitation in the depths of that wilderness, wherein ye may dwell without peril." Then the blessed Sturmi returned and repeated to his companions the words of the holy bishop; and, with two brethren, he took a boat and ascended still higher. Thus they began to navigate the river Fulda, scanning the ground narrowly at the mouth of every torrent or brook. Then they disembarked and, roaming and looking in all directions, exploring the mountains and hills from top to bottom, if by chance the Lord might show His servants some spot well suited for their habitation in the wilderness, at length on the third day they came to where the river Luder pours itself into the Fulda. Thence they turned back and rowed home to their cell, finding nothing that satisfied their eyes, except that they stayed for a while at the spot called Ruhenbach, where it seemed that God's servants might perchance dwell after a fashion, yet they doubted whether St Boniface would have approved it. Wherefore, having returned to their cell, they besought Christ daily that He would show them that dwelling-place which they longed for in the wilderness, wherein they might serve God free from care, and in obedience to the blessed bishop Boniface.

Meanwhile Boniface sent for Sturmi to hear his report, and promised that he should find some better spot.

Sturmi therefore, having come back to the cell and rested for a while among his brethren from the weariness of his journey, saddled his ass and took a store of provisions and set forth alone, commending his way to Christ, who is the way, the truth, and the life. Thus, seated on his ass, he set out alone to traverse the horrid tracts of this wilderness. Thus did this greedy explorer advance, scanning on every hand, with eager glance, both the rough land and the smooth, gazing around upon mountains and hills and valleys, and narrowly considering the brooks and torrents and rivers. All this while he had the Psalms in his mouth, lifting his soul to God with prayers and groans, and never resting but where night constrained him to stay. When he thus rested for the night, he would cut boughs with the steel which he bore in his hand,

and order them as a fence around him in defence of his ass, lest she should be devoured by the wild beasts which swarmed in those forests. For himself, after he had signed his forehead with the cross in God's name, he lay down without misgiving. Thus did this holy man go forth to fight against the Devil with spiritual weapons, covering his whole body with the breastplate of righteousness, fortifying his breast with the shield of faith, protecting his head with the helmet of salvation, and with the sword of God's word at his side.

One day, as he went thus, he came to the road whereby traders come from Thuringia to Mainz, at the spot where it crosses the river Fulda. There he found a great multitude of Slavonians, who had plunged in for the sake of washing and were swimming up and down the stream. His beast, fearing these naked bodies, began to tremble, and the man of God himself loathed the stench that proceeded from them. They, after their pagan fashion, mocked the man of God and would have done him harm, but that God's power subdued them and held them back. One, however, interpreting for the rest, asked whither he went; to whom Sturmi answered that he was making for the upper parts of that wilderness.

Thus went the man of God, alone, through that gloomy waste, seeing nought but beasts (whereof there was an innumerable multitude in the forest) and birds and vast trees and wild and solitary glades. At length, on the fourth day, he passed beyond the present site of the monastery and found that spot where the stream called Gysilaha flows into the Fulda. Thence he pressed a little higher, and after sunset he reached the footpath which in old times was called *Ortesweg*, intending to fortify himself and his ass against nightly attacks. But, while he was thus busy over his nightly bulwark, he heard afar a sound of splashing in the water, whether of wild beasts or of men. He stood in silence and listened with all his ears, until he heard that splash again. Then, unwilling to cry aloud, the man of God smote a hollow tree with the steel which he held in his hand; for by God's inspiration he knew that this was a man. The stranger, hearing the sound of this stroke, hastened thither and cried aloud. When he was come near so that they could see each other, they exchanged greetings; and the stranger said that he was come from Wetterau to lead his master Orb's horse. Thus they spent that night in talk and in rest; for this man knew well all parts of that wilderness. When therefore the man of God had disclosed his thoughts and intentions, the stranger named every spot to him, and recited in order the brooks and torrents; for they lay there in the spot which in old times was called *the Oakgrove*. On the morrow they arose thence, and each blessed the other, and the stranger went on his way to Grapfeld.

Then St Sturm turned back, commending his way and all his hope to the Lord Christ, and went alone on his way through that wild. Having traversed Oakgrove and found the soil unfit for his purpose, he came to the torrent now called Grenzbach; and, having viewed the lie of the ground and the quality of the soil, he paused awhile in that spot. Thence he went backward for a while, until he came to the site of the present monastery, blessed and prepared long since for that purpose by the Lord. When he was come hither, the holy Sturm was filled with immeasurable joy and went forward in cheerful exultation; for he knew that this spot, through the merits and prayers of St Boniface, had now been revealed to him by the Lord. Wherefore he went round and round, thanking God for all that met him at every step; the more he wandered far and wide, the deeper was his gratitude. At length, having spent a great part of the day in this perlustration and examination of the chosen spot, he blessed it and marked it diligently for recognition, and went on his way rejoicing.

He returned to Boniface, who went straight to Carloman, king of the Franks, and son of Charles Martel.

"We have found" (he said) "in the wilderness of Thuringia, hard by the river called Fulda, a place fit for the habitation of God's servants; which spot is upon your lands. Now, therefore, we beseech your lovingkindness, that we may have this spot as a gift, in order that we may there serve Christ under your protection." At these words, the king was inspired by God to rejoice; wherefore he called together all the princes of his palace, to whom he benevolently repeated the bishop's petition and then bestowed that ground publicly upon the Saint in these words here following: "With regard to that place which thou requirest, and which, as thou sayest, is called Oakgrove, on the banks of the river Fulda—whatsoever I may be found to possess for mine own in that spot, I do now wholly and entirely transfer from mine own hands into those of God; and I decree that the bounds of that possession shall stretch four miles round that place in every direction —eastward and westward, northward and southward." Whereof the king caused a charter to be made, and signed it with his own hand.

Cluny, in Burgundy, beginning A.D. 909 or 910, became the greatest monastery in Europe within four or five generations of its foundation, mainly through the virtues of its abbots. The following is abridged from M. Marrier, *Bibliotheca Cluniacensis*, 1614, pp. 2 ff.

12. A FOUNDER'S PRECAUTIONS

THE Testament of William, surnamed the Pious, Count of Auvergne and Duke of Aquitaine, concerning the building of the convent of Cluny.

It is manifest to all who rightly consider, and God's Providence doth so counsel all rich men, that it is in their power to earn everlasting rewards by a good use of those things which are now in their transitory possession. This indeed is shown most persuasively by God's word in the thirteenth chapter of the Proverbs: *The ransom of a man's life are his riches.* Therefore I William by God's grace, Count and Duke, carefully weighing these things, and willing to provide for mine own salvation while there is yet time, have thought not only fit but most necessary to spend for the benefit of mine own soul some little part of the goods which have been granted to me in this world. Be it known, therefore, to all who live in the unity of the Faith and who beseech Christ's mercy, and to all who shall come after, even unto the end of the world, that for God's sake and our Saviour Jesus Christ I grant of mine own free will, to the holy Apostles Peter and Paul, certain of my rightful possessions; namely Cluny, with its court and manor, and its chapel in honour of Mary the holy Mother of God and St Peter, Chief of the Apostles, together with all that pertaineth unto the said village—manors, chapels, serfs of either sex, vineyards, fields, meadows, woods, waters and waterways, corn-mills, issues and returns, tilled fields and waste, in all completeness; all of which are situate in the County of Mâcon or thereabouts, and shut in within their own boundaries. All this do I William, and my wife Ingelberga, give to the Apostles aforesaid; first, for God's love; then, for the souls of mine ancestor King Eudes, of my father and mother, and for the soul's and body's health of myself and my wife; for the soul of Avana also, who left me all this by testament; for the souls of our brothers and sisters, nephews and nieces, and kinsfolk of either sex; for the faithful vassals who cleave to our service; and for the estate and integrity of the Catholic religion. Lastly, even as all we Christian folk are held together by the bond of one charity and faith, so let this donation be made on behalf of all orthodox of past or present or future times.

On this condition, that a regular monastery be built at Cluny in honour of the holy Apostles Peter and Paul, wherein monks may assemble and live according to the Rule of St Benedict, which monks shall possess, hold, have, and ordain these possessions aforesaid, to all time. On condition also that the venerable House of Prayer there be faithfully frequented with vows and supplications, and heavenly conversation be sought and followed with all desire and heartfelt ardour. Moreover, let busy prayers, petitions and supplications be directed to the Lord, both for me and for all those persons above rehearsed. We prescribe also that this our donation be for a perpetual refuge to those men especially who come forth in poverty from the world, bringing nothing but good-will with them; thus shall our gift be for their abundance....And, for five years, let the said monks pay ten sols to the shrines of the Apostles [Peter and Paul] at Rome for the maintenance of the lights there; and let them have the protection of those Apostles, and the Roman Pontiff for their

A FOUNDER'S PRECAUTIONS

defender; and let the said monks build the monastery aforesaid to the best of their knowledge and ability, with heart and soul. We will also that, in our days and in those of our successors, in so far as the occasions and power of the said monastery may extend, works of pity may daily be wrought upon the poor and needy, strangers and pilgrims, with the utmost earnestness.

Moreover, it is our pleasure to insert in this our Testament, that from this day forth the said monks congregated at Cluny be subject neither to our will nor to that of our parents, nor to the king's most solemn majesty, nor to the yoke of any earthly power whatsoever. Nor let any secular Prince nor Count, nor any Bishop, nor even the Pontiff of the Roman See aforesaid—by God I pray it, and in God and all the Saints, and by that fearful Day of Judgment—let no man invade the possessions of these servants of God. Let no man take therefrom nor diminish them nor change them, nor endow any person therefrom, nor set any Prelate over the monks against their will.[1] And, that this crime may be the more strictly forbidden to all rash and wicked persons, I hereby add and inculcate the same prohibition; beseeching you, O holy Apostles Peter and Paul, and thee, Pontiff of Pontiffs of the Apostolic See, that, by the canonical and apostolic authority which thou hast from God, thou shouldst banish from the fellowship of God's Holy Church, and from their part in the life everlasting, all robbers and invaders and wasters of these possessions, which to you monks I now give with glad mind and ready will....If perchance—which God forbid!—...any man whether of my kindred or not, of what condition or power or cunning soever, attempt any trespass upon this Testament....First, let him incur the wrath of God Almighty, and may the Lord take away his part from the land of the living, and blot his name from the book of life. Again, let his part be with such as have said to the Lord God: *Depart from us!* and let him incur everlasting damnation with Dathan and Abiram, whom the earth opened and swallowed, and sent down alive to hell. Again, let him be made fellow to Judas who betrayed the Lord, thrust into bonds and eternal

[1] *I.e.* they are to have free election of their own abbots. Neither Popes nor Princes respected this for long.

49

torments. Moreover, lest even in this present life he might seem to human eyes to pass unpunished, let him experience in this body the pains of future damnation; let him be doubly racked with Heliodorus and Antiochus, whereof the former was chastised so bitterly with rods that he scarce escaped with his life, while the other was struck by God's judgment, and died with rotting limbs amid swarming vermin. Let him be a partner with all others who have presumed sacrilegiously to violate God's treasury. Let him (unless he amend his ways) find the Doorkeeper of the whole kingdom of the Churches, and Paul with him, to forbid and deny him all entrance to the bliss of Paradise; these Apostles whom, if he had so willed, he might have gained as his most kindly intercessors. Moreover, by the laws of this world, let him be compelled by the judges to pay an hundred pounds of gold to the monks against whom he has trespassed; and, if they have consented thereto, let this consent be null and void....

Ekkehard (surnamed *Junior*), fourth of the five writers of that name at the famous monastery of St Gall, lived from about 980 to about 1060. He wrote a *History of the Vicissitudes of St Gallen*, which is full of human touches, and was freely used by Scheffel in his novel of *Ekkehard*. A good deal of the matter contained in the first pages here given may be found in S. R. Maitland's epoch-making *Dark Ages*, which has destroyed for ever a number of important misapprehensions concerning the Middle Ages, and only falls into the almost unavoidable error of exaggerating in the opposite direction. The Notkers, like the Ekkehards, were numerous at St Gall. One earned by his peculiarities the nickname of *Peppercorn* (*Piperis Granum*); another was *Lippy* (*Labeo*); and the hero of the present extract was the *Stammerer* (*Balbus*). He it was who wrote the immortal funeral sequence, "In the midst of life we are in death." His tomb was worshipped for centuries in his own monastery, and he was formally canonized in 1513. The text is that of Goldast, *Rerum Alamannicarum Scriptores*, Frankfort, 1730.

13. THE THREE INSEPARABLES

(c. iii, p. 23.)

I WILL tell now of Notker, Ratpert, and Tutilo, since they were one heart and soul, and formed together a sort of trinity in unity.... Yet, though so close in heart, in their natures

THE THREE INSEPARABLES

(as it often happens) they were most diverse. Notker was frail in body, though not in mind, a stammerer in voice but not in spirit; lofty in divine thoughts, patient in adversity, gentle in everything, strict in enforcing the discipline of our convent, yet somewhat timid in sudden and unexpected alarms, except in the assaults of demons, whom he always withstood manfully. He was most assiduous in illuminating, reading, and composing; and (that I may embrace all his gifts of holiness within a brief compass) he was a vessel of the Holy Ghost, as full as any other of his own time. But Tutilo was widely different. He was strong and supple in arm and limb, such a man as Fabius tells us to choose for an athlete; ready of speech, clear of voice, a delicate carver and painter; musical, with especial skill on the harp and the flute; for the Abbot gave him a cell wherein he taught the harp to the sons of noble families around. He was a crafty messenger, to run far or near; skilled in building and all the kindred arts; he had a natural gift of ready and forcible expression whether in German or in Latin, in earnest or in jest; so that the Emperor Charles [the Fat] once said, "Devil take the fellow who made so gifted a man into a monk!"[1] But with all this he had higher gifts: in choir he was mighty, and in secret prayer he had the gift of tears; a most excellent composer of poetry and melodies, yet chaste, as became the disciple of our Master Marcellus, who shut his eyes against women. Ratpert, again, was midway between the other two. Master of the Schools from his youth, a straightforward and kindly teacher, he was somewhat harsh in discipline, more loth than all the other Brethren to set foot without the cloister, and wearing but two pairs of shoes in the twelvemonth. He called it death to go forth, and oftentimes warned Tutilo to take heed to himself upon his journeys;[2] in the schools he was most assiduous.

---

[1] A couple of pages later, the chronicler records an exploit of Tutilo's against two robbers who set upon him in the forest.

[2] See chap. LXVI of St Benedict's Rule: "The monastery, if possible, should be so built that all things necessary—that is, water, the mill, the garden, the bakery, and the different arts—may be exercised within the precincts, so that the monks be not compelled to wander outside, which is altogether unprofitable to their souls. We will that this rule be oftentimes read in the congregation, lest any Brother excuse himself on the plea of ignorance." Chaucer has immortalized

He oftentimes omitted the services and the mass, and would say, "We hear good masses when we teach others to sing them." Though he would say that impunity was the worst plague of cloister-life, yet he never came to the Chapter-house[1] without special summons, since he bore that most heavy burden (as he called it) of reproving and punishing.

These three senators of our Republic being such as they were, yet they suffered constantly (as learned and strenuous men must ever suffer) the detractions and backbiting of such as stagnated in sloth or walked in frivolity; more especially, since he was the less ready to defend himself, that saint (as indeed he was) Dom Notker; for Tutilo and Ratpert, who were of sharper temper and less patient under contumely, were more rarely attacked by such folk. But Notker, the gentlest of men, learned in his own person what insults meant: I will here cite but one example, wherefrom thou mayest judge the rest and know how great is Satan's presumption in such things. There was here a certain Refectorer named Sindolf, who afterwards by feigned obsequiousness, (for there was no other use in the man,) and by bringing false accusations against the Brethren, wormed himself into the grace of Abbot Solomon, who promoted him to the Clerkship of the Works. Yet even as Refectorer he showed evil for good so far as he had dared, and more especially against Notker. Now Solomon was busied with many things and unable to look closely into every matter; wherefore many of the Brethren, seeing their food sometimes withdrawn and sometimes tainted, would accuse him of injustice; among whom these Three seemed sometimes to have said something [of the kind]. But Sindolf, who ever fomented discord, knowing that ancient spark which had kindled ill-will between these school-fellows,[2] wormed himself into Solomon's confidence as one who would tell him

St Antony's saying that a monk out of his cloister is in as grievous peril of death as a fish out of water: yet few points of the Rule have been more persistently neglected during the past thousand years. A few pages farther on, we find Tutilo carving statues at Metz.

[1] In which faults were daily confessed or pointed out, and "discipline" inflicted in public, after morning mass.

[2] The four had been school-fellows in the monastery under Marcellus; and Solomon, the aptest of them all for worldly business, was now promoted far above the others' heads.

a matter concerning his own honour; and he, though he knew that nothing is more harmful for prelates than to give ear to whisperings from their subjects, yet asked of Sindolf's tidings. Then the liar told how those Three, ever wont to speak against the Abbot, had on the day before uttered things intolerable to God. The Abbot believed his words, and conceived against his unsuspecting fellows a grudge which he soon showed openly. They, unable to learn aught from him concerning the ground of their offence, guessed that they had been ensnared by Sindolf's wiles. At length, when the matter had been debated among the Brethren, and they, with the concurrent testimony of the rest, had convinced the Bishop[1] that they had said nothing whatever against him, then all demanded vengeance upon the false witness; but the Bishop dissembled, and they tacitly acquiesced. Now these Three inseparable Brethren were wont to meet in the Scriptorium, by the Prior's permission, in the nightly interval before Lauds, and there to hold debates of Holy Scripture, most suited to such a time. But Sindolf, knowing of their colloquies at this time, crept stealthily one night to the glazed window by which Tutilo sat, whereunto he closely applied his ear and listened whether he might catch something which he might twist to evil and bear to the Bishop. Tutilo became aware of this; and, being a resolute man who trusted in the strength of his arms, he spoke to his companions in the Latin tongue (for Sindolf knew no Latin), saying, "The rascal is here, with his ear glued to the window! Thou, Notker, who art a timid fellow, go into the church; but thou, my Ratpert, seize the Brethren's scourge which hangeth in the calefactory,[2] and hasten forth. I, when I hear thine approach, will suddenly open the window, catch him by the hair, and drag him to me here by main force; and thou, dear friend, be strong and of a good courage, and lay upon him with all thy might, that we may avenge God on his body!" So Ratpert, who was ever most ready to discipline, crept softly forth, caught the scourge, and hastened swiftly to the spot, where he found the fellow caught up by the head, and hailed blows upon that defenceless

---

[1] Solomon's final promotion was to the see of Constance.
[2] Chamber in a monastery heated with a fire or by hot air.

back with all his might; when lo! Sindolf, struggling with arms and legs together, caught the scourge as it fell upon him and held it fast. But Ratpert was aware of a rod that lay hard by, wherewith he now laid on most lustily again; until the victim, after fruitless prayers for mercy, thought within himself, "Now is the time to cry!" and roared aloud for the Brethren. Part of the convent, amazed to hear these unwonted sounds at such an hour, hastened up with lanterns, and asked what was amiss. Whereupon Tutilo cried again and again, "I hold the Devil, I hold the Devil, bring hither a light, that I may see more clearly in whose form I hold him." Then, turning that unwilling head hither and thither to the beholders, he asked as though in astonishment: "What! Is this Sindolf?" "Yea, indeed!" cried they, and prayed for his liberty: at which Tutilo released him, and said: "Woe is me! for I have laid hands upon the bishop's intimate and privy whisperer!" But Ratpert, when the Brethren hastened up, had gone aside and withdrawn himself privily, nor could the victim know who it was that had smitten him. When, therefore, some enquired whither Dom Notker and Dom Ratpert had gone, Tutilo answered, "Both departed to worship God when they heard the Devil, and left me alone with that fiend prowling in the darkness. Know ye all, therefore, that it was an angel of the Lord whose hand dealt him those stripes." The Brethren therefore departed, and the matter was much debated (as was natural enough) by the partisans of either side; some said that it had befallen by God's justice, that privy eavesdroppers might be brought to light; others, again, argued that such a man should not thus have been handled unless it were true that an angel of God had smitten him. Meanwhile he crept away and hid himself, broken down by bodily pain and grief of mind together. At last, after a few days, the Bishop asked where his tattler [*famidicus*] lingered so long (for thus he was wont to name this fellow that ever brought him by stealth some fresh tidings), and, having learned the truth of the matter, he would not impute any guilt to so dignified a person as Tutilo in defence of a man guilty of such shameful faults, but called Sindolf to his presence and consoled him with these words: "Since these men, who have ever envied me from my boyhood, have now done thee this evil, therefore I, if I live, will take care to confer on thee some greater benefit." Not long afterwards the occasion came, and he made him Clerk of the Works, in spite of the protests of many, nay of all, who besought him not to degrade so worthy an office by giving it to such a man.... To return to our matter and to follow this Sindolf, prowling like a licensed wild beast under Solomon's rule. One day, which was the Refectorer's day, when Notker and Ratpert were on duty in the kitchen, this Sindolf, whose office it was to pour the measure of drink into their glass, this fellow, I say, murmuring curses under his breath against them (for they were yet absent), rather cast the liquor than poured it forth, so that the vessel fell from the table to the ground, and lay on its side while the cover rolled across the room; yet it held the wine firmly, as though it could not spill. Then Sindolf, coming grudgingly back and picking it up—for he had hastened some paces away from their place; and, as those who had seen it from afar hastened to the spot, and looked on the ground to see whether any wine had been spilt—then said he, "Marvel not if the Devil, from whom they learn their black books at night, hath hindered the cups of his wizards from spilling!" When this had been repeated to Hartmann, he went up to that wayward wretch, and said, "My good fellow, take heed lest thou presume too far at last against such men who so patiently bear thine insults." Sindolf answered again with his customary wanton and reviling words: wherefore Waltram, the Dean, submitted him to regular discipline in the next Chapter of the Brethren....

When at last the holy man Ratpert, smitten with sickness, crept about the cloister of St Gallen and yet ceased not to teach; and when forty of his disciples, now canons and priests, came to the monastery for the holy feast, then he committed his soul to each of them singly, and each promised to sing thirty masses for him on his deathbed. Whereat he was exceedingly rejoiced, and prayed God to cook him longer in the flames of that sickness, whereby he was made into a radiant bread and passed between the hands of his disciples into Paradise, as we firmly believe. Notker and Tutilo, mourning for him beyond all the other Brethren whom he had left behind, wrought much for him also.

When Tutilo was busied with carving in the city of Metz, two pilgrims stood by him as he made a graven image of the Blessed Mary, and besought him for alms, which he gave to them in secret. They therefore departing from him, said to a certain clerk who stood by: "The Lord bless that man who hath so well comforted us to-day. But" (said they) "is that his sister?—that radiant lady who setteth the tools so ready to his hand and teacheth him what to do?" The clerk, marvelling at this speech (for he had but lately come thence, and seen no such lady), went back; and for a moment, for the twinkling of an eye, he saw the truth of their words. Then said the clerk and the pilgrims, "Father, blessed art thou of the Lord, in that thou hast such a lady to help thee in thy work!" But he, having denied all knowledge of the matter, adjured them vehemently to spread no such report abroad. Yet on the morrow, hearing many men repeat this to his glory, he withdrew and passed through the midst of them, and would by no means work longer in that city. But on the gilded halo which he had left plain, this verse was afterwards graven (I know not by whose hand):

Mary herself vouchsafed to carve all this work.

Moreover, the image itself, seated like a living woman, is revered even to this day by all that see it. . . . Many other things have we heard of Tutilo; yet, because we fear lest this age of ours, such as it is, may refuse credence thereto, we have chosen rather to pass them in silence. Since, therefore, we have found no certain record of his death, we can certainly assert no more than this, that we steadfastly believe him to have gone to God's bliss.

Of Notker we will tell boldly what is left to tell, doubting nothing but that he was a chosen vessel of the Holy Ghost. That most holy man lingered on, widowed and orphaned of his own Brethren in the spirit; and at length an evil befell him which cut him to the heart. He had copied, with the sweat of his brow, the Canonical Epistles in Greek, which he had borrowed from Liutward, Bishop of Vercelli; when, behold!

Sindolf—who, as we have said, was already a great and mighty man in the monastery—fell by chance upon that delicately-written book and stole it. Then, cutting away each quire with his knife (as may be seen even to this day) he plucked them apart and ruined them, and, folding them up again, laid them in the place whence he had stolen them! [Ekkehard here passes on to other matters: but his later successor, sixth of that name, describes Notker's blindness and peaceful death in chapter xxxii of his *Vita B. Notkeri* (p. 245).]

The hero of this story is Ekkehard II, nephew to Ekkehard I, Dean of St Gall. The chronicler is here more discursive than usual, especially when he deals with the quarrel between the abbeys of St Gall and Reichenau; therefore I have abridged freely (Ekkehard IV, *Casus S. Galli*, *Mon. Germ. Hist. Scriptt.* vol. II, p. 122). Scheffel has utilized it in his novel of *Ekkehard*.

14. PRIVATE TUITION IN A CASTLE

SINCE this seems a proper occasion to speak of his sister's son Ekkehard, whom he himself and Gerald brought up strictly, I will now enter upon that difficult task—difficult, since such men are few or none in our days, wherefore I fear my words may find no credence. He was so comely of face as to ensnare by his grace (as Josephus writeth of Moses) all that beheld him. Otto the Red of Saxony [the Emperor Otto II] said once of him: "The cowl of St Benedict never sat more fittingly upon any man, than this." He was tall of stature like a champion, and proportionately stout; his eyes flashed, even as a certain man said to Augustus: "For I may not bear the lightning of thine eyes." In wisdom and eloquence, and more especially in council, he was behind no man of his time. In the flower of his age he tended more to glory (as was natural in a man of such make) than to humility but not so in later years; for discipline, wherein pride hath never any part or lot, was note-worthy in this man. He was a strict and prosperous teacher; for, when he ruled both the schools [inner and outer] at St Gall, none except the smallest children dared to speak to his fellow save in Latin; and, if he found any too slow for literary studies, he busied them with writing and illuminating. In both those arts he was himself most eminent, especially in capital letters and in gilding, as may be seen in those verses of his on the vault of the church:

> *Templum quod Gallo Cozbertus struxerat almo,*
> *Hoc[1] abbas Ymmo picturis compsit et auro:[2]*

which letters Ekkehard had carved with his knife and painted. In Latin, he taught nobles and commoners[3] alike; many of whom he brought to the highest places here and elsewhere; for he saw several of them as bishops; and once at Mainz, at a general council, when Ekkehard came in, six of his old pupils rose from their episcopal thrones and greeted their master. Then the archbishop Willigis beckoned the man to him; and, kissing him, said: "Worthy son of mine, thou too shalt one day sit on a throne with such as these"; and, when Ekkehard would have sat at his feet, Willigis graciously took him by the hand and raised him up. But, not to forestall our purpose by relating his later fortunes, let us come back to his earlier deeds.

Hadawig, daughter to Duke Henry [of Bavaria], and duchess of Suabia after the death of her husband Purchard, dwelt in her castle of Hohentwiel; a lady of rare beauty, most severe with her own men, and feared in all countries far and near.[4] She, as a little girl, had been affianced to Constantine king of Greece,[5] who sent his eunuchs and taught her excellently the Greek language. But when another eunuch, a painter, looked earnestly in her face, that he might make an exact likeness of her to send to his master, she (who hated the marriage) distorted her mouth and eyes, and thus stubbornly thrust this Greek husband from her. After which she studied in Latin literature; and Duke Purchard took her with a rich

---

[1] A still existing St Gall MS., no. 152, describes itself as "hoc opus exiguum puerili pollice scriptum."

[2] This temple, which Cozbert had built for the gracious St Gall, Abbot Ymmo adorned with paintings and gilding.

[3] *Mediocres*; the really poor seldom found their way into the community, especially of a great abbey like St Gall.

[4] In fact, Hadawig seems rather to have neglected her wider duties, though her name may well have been terrible in the not far distant regions of St Gall.

[5] Probably to Romanus II, son of Constantine VII.

dowry for wife. But the duke was weighed down with age; and, though she shared his couch, it is said that he knew her not; and, dying within a brief space, he left the girl with her dowry and the duchy. One day this noble widow came to St Gall to pray; Abbot Purchard received her bounteously as his kinswoman and would have sent gifts with her at her departure; but she refused all gifts except that of Ekkehard for her teacher, if the abbot would grant him to her for a while at Hohentwiel; for he was then porter of the abbey, and the duchess had privily concerted it with him, not against his will, the day before. Ekkehard's uncle the dean would have dissuaded this; yet the abbot granted it, however unwillingly, and Ekkehard himself had consented to the lady's request.[1] At Hohentwiel his coming was eagerly awaited, and his welcome more honourable than he had hoped; for she led him by the hand to a chamber adjoining, as she pointed out, to her own. Thither the duchess would come to read by night or day, with some familiar waiting woman; yet she ever kept the door open; so that, even if a man had dared to whisper against her, there might be no room for suspicion. There she and her teacher were oftentimes found busied in reading or in counsel, by ministers and knights and even princes of the earth. Yet she often offended the monk by her harsh and savage manners, so that he sometimes wished himself at home far rather than with her. For example, he in his humility had bidden the servant take down the hangings [behind his seat] and the curtain of his bed; yet she had the servant scourged for removing them, and, if he had not prayed her long and earnestly, she would have had him shorn also.

When he went back to the abbey for fast days or at his own will, it was a joy to see at what cost she would send him by ship to Steinach [our port on the lake], always sending with him some costly offering for his own or the Saint's use, which she chose with great skill and forethought. Among them were silken chasubles, copes and stoles, an alb em-

[1] The editors point out grievous anachronisms in all this story; but this scarcely diminishes its importance for the social historian, as a specimen of what the best-informed monks of St Gall believed in 1050.

broidered in gold with the Nuptials of Philology,[1] and, lastly, a dalmatic and a tunicle almost solid with gold; but these two the cunning and wayward woman took back when Abbot Ymmo would not give her an antiphonary which she had desired.

In those days, envious folk opened their mouths, as at all times, against the monks, as though they lived after their own desires. To leave the rest, and speak only of our own fortunes, a monk of Reichenau[2] was chosen abbot of his own house, Ruodmann by name. This man dealt tyrannically with his own monks; for he had not the sense to shear the fleece without tearing the skin; and he now began to let his tongue loose against us, as not living according to our Rule. St Gall had in those days, besides this Ekkehard the teacher and many younger monks bred in the house, Ekkehard the most valiant dean, Gerhald, Notker, Cunibert of Altaich, who was afterwards abbot, and Walto the Second; all these, by their abbot's command, approached Ruodmann through our Ekkehard [II] and prayed him in brotherly fashion to restrain his tongue. Though he made little of their plea, yet, for the honour of Ekkehard's own person, and for fear of the severe duchess, to whom he was then going, he treated him worthily. So Ekkehard, having vainly striven throughout this colloquy to convert this froward man who would hear no reason, was moved by his bitter threats and returned secretly to the abbey, sending a messenger to tell the duchess why he could not

---

[1] *I.e.* Martianus Capella's allegory, which enjoyed great popularity in the Middle Ages; see Rashdall, *Univ. of Europe*, vol. I, p. 35 n. I.

[2] Reichenau, on a fertile island in the lower Lake of Constance, was a rival and often an enemy of St Gall. Lord Acton, in his own copy of *Geschichtschreiber d. deutschen Vorzeit, Ekkehard*, ed. G. Meyer v. Knonau, p. 255, has pencilled for emphasis the following passage. The St Gall annalist is describing the events of the year 1079 and writes: "The monks and men and manors of the two abbeys came to such bitter mutual hate and enmity that they oftentimes stirred up greater quarrels and battles against each other, than the two rival kings themselves. So the two parties came together in arms at Veltheim, and there a battle was fought; many on either part were wounded and slain." The Reichenau annalist, coming to the reign of Ruodmann, notes briefly, "this man was hated by the brethren of St Gall." From independent evidence we know that he was held in considerable esteem within and without his own house; but he was one of the movers of an imperial commission to enquire into the state of discipline at St Gall; this visitation Ekkehard describes with bitter humour and undisguised partisanship on pp. 126 ff.

come back at that time, and not deigning to accept Ruodmann's offer of servants to escort him. Then Ruodmann,
conceiving him to have returned to the duchess, mounted his
horse and entered St Gall by night, creeping secretly into the
cloister, that he might stealthily spy out whatsoever he might
find that smacked of guilt. Knowing our cloister well, he
crept all round and peered in every corner; then, finding
nothing of what he had hoped, he went up to the dormitory
by the stair from the church, crept softly to the brethren's
rere-dorter, and there sat down.[1] But Ekkehard, ever
watchful, forthwith rose from his couch and followed this
unrecognized stranger; and, seeing that the man was alone,
he marvelled which of our brethren could have chosen to
slink by that unwonted way; for he sat hidden in the shadow
of the lamp that lighted the dormitory [as St Benedict pre-
scribes in his Rule]. But, having paused awhile in doubt,
he knew Ruodmann by his nostrils (for the man, when moved,
was wont to snore in his breathing); wherefore he bade one
of the brethren bring secretly the abbot's lantern; this he laid
at the man's feet with a wisp of hay, and stood silently apart,
waiting upon him as the abbot's chaplain waits. When the
brethren came near, he warned them as usual by signs to hold
their peace, while they marvelled at the lantern, which is
borne before the abbot only, yet their abbot was then from
home. After long tarrying Ruodmann arose, not knowing
what else to do; then Ekkehard raised the lantern, led him
back by the same way by which he had seen him come in;
and, when they were come to the church door, where the
parlour is,[2] he signed silently to Ruodmann to seat himself
until he could bring his uncle the dean and other brethren,
who would not wish to ignore the presence of so distinguished
a guest. And lo! by this time some were already gathered
together at these marvellous tidings; especially from among

[1] Meyer v. Knonau points out that the ancient plan of St Gall corroborates
this description; a stair at the corner of cloister and church led up to the dormitory,
from whence the rere-dorter was reached. That plan, however, is now acknowledged to be greatly idealized: in many respects it represents not so exactly what
St Gall was, as what men dreamed it might become.

[2] The plan of the abbey does in fact show the parlour adjoining the church on
the south.

the younger brethren; one of whom, seeing how matters stood, seized a scourge from the calefactory and would have fallen upon him, crying out upon him as a guilty wretch; and, if the elders had not withheld his uplifted arm, he would have smitten him to his heart's content. Then Ruodmann, finding himself at his last shift, cried aloud: "O excellent young men, if flight were open to me, I would flee forthwith; but now, seeing that I am in your hands without further choice, it behoveth you to deal more mercifully with me, and to await the coming of your dean and the elders." At length, after a brief consultation, the dean and the elders arrived. Then Notker the Physician (he who was called Peppercorn [*Piperis Granum*]) inveighed bitterly against him, saying: "O man full of guile, O lion seeking whom thou mayest devour, woe unto thee now, for thou hast fallen into the hands of those brethren whom, like another Satan, thou goest about to accuse!" Ruodmann, trembling at such words from such a man, and knowing well how merciful our dean was, besought him saying: "Most prudent father! suffer me not to be indecently handled by the devices of thy namesake who hath thus circumvented me, lest thou repent when it shall be too late." Then, falling at his feet, he added, "Lo! I ask pardon from you all, that I may have your grace and abstain henceforth from all such dealings." The more prudent among the brethren were moved at this sudden humbling of so powerful a man; but others, as was natural, murmured for harsher measures. The elders, softened at length by Ekkehard's counsel, reconciled Ruodmann to the whole assembly, and the dean led him forth to his own men who were waiting in the place assigned to them by their master; before whom he put on a good face and parted from us with happy words, and praying Ekkehard instantly that he would not neglect to visit him on his way back to Hohentwiel, to the brethren he promised through Ekkehard two barrels of wine, which indeed he sent by ship to Steinach without further delay. But Abbot Purchard, who was abroad when he heard of this broil, lamented on his return that Ruodmann had got off scot-free; wherefore he complained to the bishop of this unheard-of trespass. Then Ekkehard went on his way to

Hohentwiel, with his namesake [Ekkehard III] who was afterwards dean, and the boy Purchard [II] who was afterwards abbot; for both were his cousins. On his way he spake again with Ruodmann, as had been accorded between them, at Reichenau; in which colloquy that fox tried all his wiles, but found his match. For, when Ekkehard hastened lest he should appear too late in the presence of that strict lady, Ruodmann gave him an excellent steed; and, when Ekkehard had sent this on with a part of his company, Ruodmann purposely kept him awhile with jocund words and familiar thrusts of wit; then at last, dismissing him with embraces and kisses, this trickster whispered in his guest's ear, "Happy man, who hast to instruct so fair a pupil in grammar!" Whereunto the other, smiling as if in cordial assent, retorted in the ear of this adversary-friend: "Even as thou, holy lord, didst once teach dialectics to thy beloved disciple, the fair nun Kotelinde." Then, quicker than thought, he broke off from that which Ruodmann would have whispered back, and, mounting his horse, rode off in wrath. Then Otker, Abbot [Ruodmann's] knight and brother, seeing his indignation, said: "My lord, meseemeth that thou hast wholly lost this horse." And when the two brethren of whom we have spoken, [Ekkehard III and Purchard II,] bowed down and prayed Ruodmann's licence to depart, he himself (as we have heard from their own mouths) turned away from them and said unto his brother: "Prithee, send hasty messengers after him to bring back that noble steed." But Otker made answer, "Nay, for he and his are now on their way to that lady; wherefore I dare not command any of my men to touch aught that belongeth to them." So those two mounted their horses and rode tranquilly after their master. Having ascended the mountain, they appeared before the duchess as she went to vespers. She, who had already heard of Ruodmann's first trespass, greeted them, saying: "I hear, my master, that thou wast no easy lantern-bearer to the wolf which crept into the fold." Then, seeing him smile, she added with her accustomed oath: "By the life of St Hadawig! I should not have been sorry if one of the less experienced in that cloister had scourged him shrewdly." And on the morrow, having first kept her

regular and wonted silence, whereof she was a strict exacter
—for she had now begun to found a monastery on the
mountain—she came in to read with her master. [The boy
who was there went out presently, and] they remained reading
alone, as usual. Vergil was in their hands, and that verse "I
fear the Greeks, even when they bring gifts" (*Aen.* II, 49).
"My lady," said Ekkehard, "I had good reason yesterday
to remember those words"; and he told her how Ruodmann
had invited him to Reichenau and given him that horse,
yet not without crafty speech even at the moment of his gift;
nevertheless he told her nothing of the last words which each
had whispered into the other's ear....Afterwards, the duchess
proclaimed a public conference at Walwies for this and other
matters of government, whereunto she commanded the
bishop and the abbots to come. Now Ruodmann's heart
melted within him, for he suspected that Ekkehard had told
the duchess of that last exchange of words; wherefore he sent
him up a letter to the mountain by the hands of a certain
prudent pilgrim. After pleading for a renewal of friendship
he wrote: "I wonder whether my friend, so sagacious in all
things, has poured into the ears of the duchess those last
words whispered between us; if so, I pray thee to let me know."
To whom Ekkehard answered through the same messenger,
at the end of his letter: "Nay, for I never trusted so far to
my most fair lady as to venture such words in her strict ears."
These words I have excerpted, for brevity's sake, from amidst
the two men's letters.[1] Ruodmann therefore, freed from his
worst fear from the man whom he most dreaded, addressed
himself to Kaminold our bishop.

The matter was settled in favour of St Gall: Ruodmann was to pay
publicly 100 pounds for his trespass, at the castle gate of Hohentwiel; the
Abbot of St Gall was to remit 50 of these for the bishop's sake. After this
reconciliation, according to our chronicler, Ruodmann revenged himself
by persuading the Emperor to order a visitation of St Gall for the reformation of irregularities, as described in the next two extracts here following.

[1] It appears from these words that Ekkehard II had left a written record of
this affair.

THE UNWELCOME VISITOR

Ekkehard gives a very long and involved account of the visitation of St Gall by an imperial commission by order of Otto the Great (pp. 126–33; tr. Meyer v. Knonau, pp. 147 ff.). Much of his story seems almost intentionally obscure; he represents the commissioners as delighted with the discipline in the abbey, yet he shows us plainly that monks habitually broke the Rule in matters of flesh-eating and private property, and that these abuses were not really remedied. An immediate forerunner of this commission had been the visit of Sandrat, a monk whom the Archbishop of Cologne had sent from his own city to bring the St Gall monks to a stricter observance of their Rule. We know nothing more of this monk than what the chronicler tells us; the latter's story is inserted here not as an impartial narrative of facts, but as characteristic of the friction between monks who were wedded to their own ways, and visitors whose business it was to bring those ways into conformity with the Rule and with church law. It is abridged from *Casus S. Galli, Mon. Germ. Hist. Scriptt.* II, 142 ff. A similar story of monastic vengeance from Ekkehard's chronicle is translated at length in this present volume, pp. 52 ff.

15. THE UNWELCOME VISITOR

ABBOT NOTKER, to whom the plenteous harvests of his years of rule brought rich abundance, began and completed many works which none of his forerunners had ever dared. The ramparts which his uncle Anno had begun, Notker crowned with stone walls having towers and gates at intervals.[1] In addition to these lavish expenses, he gave to all the servants, who had corrodies with us, to the number of 170, pure wheat instead of the oats which alone they had eaten hitherto. And, what is more (for such was the man's nature), he built that new barn beside the brethren's barn for the sole use of wild beasts and monsters and birds, domestic or tamed; and of this he made a magnificent work. Yet, while he swam in such prosperity, he was not without some leaven of adversity; for (to say nothing of the many fiefs which the kings compelled him unwillingly to bestow upon vassals, as a man of great wealth and much fame for liberality) Ruodmann accused him again, after his wonted fashion, at court; and, since this was behind the back of Ekkehard [II, who was then court chaplain], he found himself in evil savour before he dreamed of any such thing.

[1] These towers were assigned, then or not long afterwards, to different obedientiaries of the abbey; hence their names of Spiserthor (Cellarer's Gate), Kuchimeisterthor (Kitchener's Gate), etc., etc.

Then, lo and behold! on the very eve of the feast of St Gall, one Sandrat, without the knowledge of Ekkehard or of prince Otto, [afterwards Otto II,] bringing imperial letters, came at the beginning of vespers into our church among the layfolk, thinking to escape notice as an unknown stranger while he pried about everywhere; for, (as he afterwards confessed,) he intended during those holy-days to find lodging where he could and get his food from the market;[1] so that, having first spied in all directions in preparation for his wiles, he might the more freely burst into our midst. But the dean of Murbach, who was by the abbot's side, said: "My lord, if ever I saw Sandrat, there he is now, creeping furtively among those folk. That is the man, that despicable-looking fellow upon whom thine eyes now rest." Then said the abbot: "I see him; but, if this be Sandrat, he is not one whom I can despise." Then, calling one of the brethren, he pointed him out and bade that he should be brought and given a place in the choir. He, whether he would or no, must needs follow his guide with a blush of shame; for he saw himself caught, and concealment impossible; yea, all men's eyes were now upon him. After the service, our abbot went out and greeted him in the parlour, saying among other things: "We marvel that one who hath been so publicly promised to us should come so secretly at last." He, not knowing what to answer, held out his letters, saying: "Let this missive of the great Otto speak for me." The abbot took and kissed the letters, saying: "I hold it not safe to read my lord's letters amid the distractions of this holy-day, which occupy all my leisure; but I will bid the porter seek to procure thee every comfort in thy lodging; and (since perchance thou art weary with thy journey) thou mayest rest a few days in the house of quiet, and take all possible care of thyself; for it is my duty to provide for guests and others, whether in or without the cloister. Wherefore (he added) I will that thou come not to our refectory during these days, lest thou find something there to wound thine eyes." "When thou hast read my lord's missive," said Sandrat, "thou mayest speak unto me as thou wilt; I only hope that I may not find

---

[1] *I.e.* to live incognito in the town, without lodging—as any cleric would naturally lodge—at the abbey. Meyer v. Knonau seems to miss the full sense here.

myself compelled to suffer anything contrary to the Rule at my very entrance among you." With these words they parted; and Sandrat was housed in the upper chamber which Sindolf enclosed for saint Notker, [author of the anthem *Media Vita*].

They kept Sandrat thus apart for three days, until the feast was over, to his great indignation as royal commissioner. After this interval, the abbot admitted him into the chapter-house, harangued him with cold and patronizing politeness, enquired into his business and credentials, and waived his protests aside though accompanied with tears of rage and gnashing of teeth.

Finally, he bade that Sandrat be given a place and authority next to those of the deans, and to spend the next week quietly in watching all our ways; after which he might reasonably, with the Rule for his authority, change whatsoever displeased him. At the end of the week he sat with us in Chapter and said that many things offended him, more especially our vainglorious and most unmonastic exaltations of voice in the church services,[1] and many other things which he would tell afterwards; besides which he saw Sunday daily celebrated in the church, and Friday in the refectory. Also, that his nostrils could not endure the odour of pork-lard; and that he had the emperor's commands to forbid flesh and lard to all, both sick and sound.[2] Of wine, on the other hand, (for he was himself a winebibber,) he complained that it was dealt out too sparingly, and that our goblet served rather for a solace than for a draught. Of his other deeds and sayings I will treat no more, save of certain principal matters; the rest (whereof I might make a whole volume) came to an ill end. Our abbot warned the ten [deans][3] and all the other

---

[1] There was a fine musical tradition at St Gall; and Ekkehard's story of the imperial commission shows that the brethren felt they atoned for what they looked upon as minor infractions of the Rule by the excellence of their psalmody. St Bonaventura attributes a similar delusion to many of his own fellow-friars.

[2] The Rule expressly forbids the flesh of quadrupeds to all but the sick. For the jesuitry which argued that the fat was allowed while the lean was forbidden, see the extract from Peter the Venerable in *Five Centuries of Religion*, vol. i, p. 330.

[3] The context seems plainly to indicate these officials, of whom, according to the Rule, there was to be one for every ten monks—hence the name *decanus*. Other indications (*e.g.* the 170 servants) point to 100 as a very probable number for the monks of the whole abbey.

monks that, as they loved their own selves, they should obey all his prescriptions, whether befitting or unfitting; for he saw how little constancy there was in the man, and foretold that the rigour of his domination would not long endure. Meanwhile he bade set before Sandrat without stint, at the head of the right-hand table in the refectory, all whatsoever he might demand; moreover, he bade them invite him to drink even when he himself desisted; for our abbot had already seen him at drink and taken his measure. The [senior] dean, again, with the provost, frequently admonished all the brethren to bend his haughty mood by their decorous manners; for he was somewhat too harsh with them in discipline after table, by reason of the wine that he had taken. So it befell upon a day that one of the young monks, to whom Sandrat had been harsher than usual for some days past, waxed impatient when this man inveighed against him after his usual fashion when heated with wine, and murmured: "Here is our half-master again!"[1] Sandrat caught from the young man's mouth this word which he thought to have whispered in secret, and answered forthwith: "I, your half-master, will show you now whether I am mad." Then, leaping upon the monk, who was of gentle birth and no small learning, he smote him violently upon the cheek with his open hand. The other, being far stouter of body, extended his arm quicker than thought and dealt him a crushing blow upon the temple with his fist; Sandrat sank half-dead; and the other was only restrained by his fellows from falling upon him again. The dean and the brethren hastened to the spot; the abbot was summoned and the bell rang for a convocation in the chapter-house. There the abbot bade bind the young man to the pillar of the calefactory and beat him soundly with rods. He, amid the smacking strokes (for he was a man of letters) cried aloud: "Behold a marvel! Christ was bound to a column and suffered by the Devil's wiles; I suffer at this pillar by the acts of a second Devil; and, should Sandrat ever fall into my hands,

---

[1] *Halbmeister* is vernacular also for "torturer, tyrant." It is equally possible to construe Ekkehard's Latin into a more insulting speech: "Here again is our half-master, heated in the wine!"—indeed, Sandrat's reply seems rather to point to this.

think it not strange if the same fate befall him which befell his namesake."[1] While the monk thus prophesied amid his scourging, Sandrat sat still stunned with the blow and in great fear of heart; wherefore, falling at the abbot's feet, he besought absolution, and prayed for the emperor's sake that Notker would teach him what to do now. Then said the dean, "Thou askest too much of our lord abbot; how should he presume now to teach thee, who boastest to have taught so many monks and bishops and abbots, and art come hither to teach us?" But the abbot made answer: "Having sworn fealty, O man of God! to our emperor, it behoveth me to suffer all that thou doest in this abbey, up to this point; for I know not of what Rule thou professest thyself in falling upon my brethren and smiting them with thy hand, as if in boorish audacity. And I say unto thee upon my faith, each of us hath even now wrought contrary to the Rule; thou in smiting my son without judgment, I in scourging him for thy sake." When therefore all prayed the abbot to write word of Sandrat's doings to the Emperor Otto, the culprit rose and, as if to give an example to the rest, stripped off his frock and stretched himself thereon upon the ground, beseeching with groans that he might be punished for his transgression. All wished that he might be taken at his word and scourged; but the abbot bade him put on his clothes, since the royal messenger must be honoured in him. Then he used his authority to make peace between the injured brother and this visitor; yet in his art he withheld him not from doing according to his own desires. Sandrat continued to indulge none the less in wine; and within a few days he was as insolent in his domination as ever, until one night, buried in wine, he disturbed the brethren by his snoring and sneezing. Then, calling for his servant Hatto, who had departed from the abbey not long after his coming, he cried out: "Where art thou, wicked servant?" Raving thus, he arose at length, frockless and barefooted, to make water, and defiled the stool by the bedside of Brother Ruomo [the chamberlain], who had just then left the dormitory by reason of the visitor's uneasiness.

[1] The monks seem to have nicknamed Sandrat, *Satan*, by a not too impossible distortion of names.

On the morrow, being arraigned by the dean in Chapter for drunkenness and filthiness, he again cast off his frock spontaneously as before, and, stretching himself thereon, prayed to be beaten. Then Ruomo, rising without the dean's command, quietly seized upon the brethren's scourge which hung hard by him, and laid lustily upon the recumbent visitor. The dean asked: "What dost thou there?" and he made answer: "I do what thou hast bidden, and what he himself hath demanded"; for he made as though he had taken a sign of assent from the dean; wherefore, all this while, he laid on all the more lustily between his words. Sandrat roared, lamenting that he had ever come to this place; the dean rose, and saved him with difficulty from further penance. Ruomo was a man of such worth and authority that no man accused him for this deed; nay, some even said that he had dealt justly. So at length the abbot, with the consent of the rest, bade them lay a bed for this man in the chamber wherein he had been lodged at first, and give him a careful guardian from among our servants. One day Sandrat came back from compline; and, finding that his servant had prepared flesh for himself upon a little table, he said (for he loved the man and deemed him faithful): "Dear soul! give me too of this flesh, and tell no man."[1] The man readily complied; and, when Sandrat was filled with food, gave him wine also. Thus they did frequently, closing the doors from within; until one day Richer asked how this master of the brethren fared at night. "Excellently," replied the servant, "if only I had more flesh to give him, for we have now consumed all that I could get." "Thou sayest well," said the other, "and thou shalt not lack if I can help it; but, as thou lovest thy life, do as I now tell thee. Make as thou haddest locked the door to-night, yet leave it unlocked; take abundance of flesh from our servants, and prepare it richly for thee and him." So Sandrat came that night from compline; and, as was his wont, this faithful servant laid the table for him, loaded it with

---

[1] It was a great temptation to the monk to indulge, after the last of the daily services, in what his lay contemporaries called a "rere-supper" (cf. *Knight of La Tour-Landry*, E.E.T.S. 1868, p. 8). This illegal and unedifying practice is very frequently noted in visitatorial reports.

flesh, and promised that they should have a merry night. Then, behold! the provost, taking certain of the brethren with him, came upon them eating gluttonously; and, standing over them, said: "In truth, holy master, we have found thee busy with good works! yet, with thy leave, these dishes are more proper for our sick folk than for thee." Then, taking the dish, he threatened to cast it in the other's face, yet held his hand. Then, in feigned indignation, he rated the guardian for a wicked servant, and cast him forth from the lodging, bidding him never again to appear before him. Thus they left this deceiver of kings and the kingdom in solitude, carefully locking the cloister doors after them, lest he should enter again. But he, fearing untold evil for the morrow, fled that night, and cowered all next day in a hiding-place among the thickets of the nearest mountain. The abbot forbade all pursuit; and he, freed at last from his anxiety, joined himself to a band of pilgrims who were going on foot to Rome. What may have been his later fortunes, since we hear conflicting rumours, I gladly ignore in loathing of his very name. This therefore is the tragedy of the hypocrite Sandrat and his machinations against us at the bidding of Otto the Great.

16. ABBEY VISITORS

(Ib. p. 141.)

[ABBOT NOTKER banished certain wrongdoers to other cells]; but, while he kept such discipline in the cloister, he was far different to layfolk and knights[1] and servants. The knights, whensoever he was alone without his monks, he was wont to keep at duty within and without, as stewards and butlers in weekly turns, for he willed that they should serve him with discipline. In some cases he took their sons who were to succeed to their fiefs, and educated them strictly in

---

[1] *Milites*, "military tenants of the abbey"; though "knights" is the nearest single word in English, it does not fit so exactly in an eleventh century document as it would in a thirteenth.

his house; they sometimes played themselves bare before him at backgammon,[1] but also for hawks and other such things wherein the genius of freeborn youth is wont to be exercised. Those who were found at fault were beaten by their masters; yet when the time came to dismiss them, Notker would give them armour or other gifts in accordance with their age. By these and other works which marked him for a man of good management he so commended himself that his report was everywhere in men's mouths; yea, even before kings he was not named but with the foreword of "the good abbot." Yet, while he was anxious to keep in all things the constitutions of [his predecessor] Hartmuot, he oftentimes went away in order that the brethren might make merry more freely in his absence, saying to the dean and his colleagues: "If we are to keep constant and inflexible rigour for the sake of those whose tongues wag so freely in these days against the monks, we shall either break the bow of the Rule or, (believe me,) we shall snap the string. Wherefore" (said he) "seeing that I dare not suffer it openly, it is my deliberate will to depart for a while from my beloved brethren, that they may live somewhat more at their ease with closed doors. Yet" (he would add) "I beseech you, sirs, upon whom I lean, that they be not too free, and that no layfolk whatsoever be present at their merry-makings, more especially servants, of whom we know by frequent experience that we cannot trust even their oaths [to keep silence]."

It is to the purpose to tell here how the cloister of St Gall hath always, from time immemorial, been held in such veneration that no secular canon or layman, nay, not even of the most powerful, hath ever been permitted to enter or even to peep into it. Upon which matter I must say what I know will be disbelieved by the monks of this day. I myself have seen—before the days of this monastic schism which

---

[1] *Qui coram eo interdum nudi tabulis luserant.* The pluperfect for imperfect is common in Ekkehard; Meyer v. Knonau confesses himself puzzled by the rest; but it was very common in the Middle Ages to play away one's clothes at games of hazard—chess, dice, or *tabulae*. It may possibly mean, however, that they threw off their upper garments to wrestle, leap, etc., for prizes or stakes, either on tables or on a boarded daïs.

we suffer at the hands of the French[1]—how counts and other great men, and the knights of the abbey, for the delight of following the cross in procession with us through the cloister, clothed themselves in the monks' rochets, young and old, even to men whose beards reached to their girdle, and walked with us whithersoever we went.[2] Moreover I have seen eight of these guests, who seemed the most venerable in age, sitting in frock and cowl around the abbot and his deans in the refectory at Eastertide; yea, and let me tell a merry tale of one of these meal-fellows. One Bernhard, who was not accustomed to keep silence at his own table at home, sat here beside the subdean Rupert, who had a measure of unmixed wine set before him. Bernhard, wishing to drink forthwith, as he was wont at home, took the measure in his hands and drained it to the last drop. Rupert therefore, knowing him to be a merry fellow, whispered in his ear: "According to the Rule, that is *ours*."[3] But Bernhard, forgetting how he had been warned beforehand to keep silence at meals, cried aloud in all men's hearing: "If it be ours, then let us drink it!" and, as the cup was at that moment refilled, he cried, again, "Lo, this is ours again, then let us drink this too!" For he was a man of hoarse voice, jocund in speech and in manners, yet he had a strong hand.

[1] The Cluniac reform had recently been introduced into many German monasteries, including St Gall, by the enthusiastic disciplinarian Poppo of Stavelot. Ekkehard, who was of the conservative party, frequently expresses his loathing of this reform; as Pertz put it epigrammatically in his note, "Poppo, whom the Bollandists have put among their saints, is reckoned by Notker Labeo [of St Gall] among the heretics."

[2] It is interesting to note how, in the chronicler's eyes, this occasional adoption of the monastic habit made the laymen for the time into monks, so that their presence in the cloister was no infraction of the "immemorial veneration" of the cloister. For such monks *ad succurrendum*, see my *Five Centuries of Religion* (vol. I, p. 90 and Appendix 10).

[3] *I.e.* one measure was here set for every two persons. This gave opportunities for the Prioress's refinements of table manners, as described by Chaucer.

17. HUNS IN THE CLOISTER

(Ib. p. 104.)

THE Magyars...invaded Alemannia in bands, no man opposing them. Then our abbot Engilbert, patient as he was of evil, showed himself unwearying in fight. For, when these woes were as yet only imminent, and each of his knights was anxious for his own skin, Engilbert bade the more vigorous of the monks take up weapons and armed the servants, while he himself, like a giant of the Lord, put on a coat of mail under his cowl and stole, and bade the rest do likewise: "For" (said he) "we have hitherto fought the Devil spiritually, trusting in God; now must we ask God's help to show him what we can do with our hands." Javelins were forged, quilted jackets of frieze were made, slings were woven, a sort of shields was made from planks and wicker trays; pikes of wood and pointed staves were hardened in the fire.

But at first some of the monks and servants, incredulous of the tidings, would not flee. Yet a spot was chosen, which God seemed to have made for that purpose, for a castle of refuge[1]...here they made a marvellous stronghold...whereunto they bore the crosses, the diptychs with their cases, and almost all our treasures except the books. These the abbot committed to the care of the monks of Reichenau;[2] yet not safely, for when they were brought back the number did indeed agree with those we had sent forth, yet not the books themselves. The old men and children he sent to Wasserburg, and carefully defended them with the servants who dwelt on that side of the lake....Meanwhile the enemy came not all together, but in roving bands, for no man withstood them. They fell upon towns and villages, spoiling and burning; and thus they found us always unprepared, wheresoever they chose to attack us. Again, they would burst forth from the forests in bands of a hundred or less; and no man knew where

[1] Possibly the site of the later castle of Meldegg.
[2] On an island at the lower end of the lake, and therefore comparatively safe from the Huns. Wasserburg was a similar island, but not so far distant from the mainland, near Lindau.

74

their companies were save for the smoke and the red light of fire in the sky.

Now there was among us a simple and foolish brother named Heribald, at whose words and deeds we oftentimes mocked. When the brethren first began to depart unto the stronghold, and some, in terror, bade him flee with them, then he made answer: "Nay, let him flee who will; I stay here, for the chamberlain hath given me this year no leather for my shoes." And when the brethren, in the last resort, would have compelled him by force to go with them, he withstood them with all his might, swearing that he would not budge a step until he had his yearly dole of leather in his hand. Thus, undismayed, he awaited the onslaught of the Huns. At last the brethren fled, some almost too late, while now at last even the incredulous began lamentably to cry that the enemy were upon their heels; he alone remained obstinate and undismayed, walking to and fro at his ease. At length these wild archers rushed into the abbey, bristling with darts and arrows. They busily searched the whole precincts; it seemed certain that they would spare neither age nor sex. Then they found Heribald standing alone and fearless in the midst of the cloister. They marvelled what he meant, and why he had not fled; meanwhile, those who would have slain him were restrained by the rest; until their captains, questioning him through their interpreters, and discovering his portentous folly, spared him as a laughing-stock to the whole company. They disdained to touch the altar of St Gall, having oftentimes proved to their disappointment that such places contained naught but bones and ashes. At length they asked of their fool, where the abbey treasures were laid. He led them willingly to the hidden door of the treasury, which they broke open; but, finding only the gilt candlesticks and the great hanging candelabra, which our brethren had left in their haste, they hailed him as a deceiver and buffeted him on the cheek. Two of them climbed the bell-tower; for they took the weathercock for pure gold, thinking that the tutelar deity of the abbey (for so they called it) must needs be made of the most precious metal; but while one stretched boldly forward to tear it away with the point of his lance, he fell from that dizzy height and was shattered upon the stones of the court-yard. Another climbed to the summit of the eastern spire; where, preparing himself in beastly fashion to defile God's temple, he fell backwards and was dashed to pieces. Both of these, as Heribald told us later, they burned between the doorposts of the church; the great pile flamed up beyond the lintel and even unto the ceiling; yet, though many of the Huns vied with each other in stirring the fire with poles, they failed to burn St Gall's temple, as they had failed with that of St Magnus. Now there were in the common cellar two barrels of wine filled even to the top, which had been left there because no man, in that last hour of peril, had dared to harness or drive the oxen. Yet none of the enemy opened these; by what chance I know not, unless it were that they had abundance already among their waggon-loads of booty. One of them raised his axe and would have cut the hoops; but Heribald, who was now familiar and domesticated among them, cried aloud: "My good fellow, leave that alone; for what would ye have us drink when ye are gone?" Hearing these words from the interpreter, the Hun fell a-laughing and prayed his fellows, saying: "Touch not my fool's casks." Thus were they kept until the Huns departed; and our abbot found them safe.

Meanwhile they sent scouts to search narrowly through the forests and all other hiding-places, and to tell what tidings they could find. At length, after they had slain [the anchoress] Wiborad [in her hermitage], they scattered themselves over the cloister-garth and the meadows to an abundant repast. They stripped the silver plates from the shrine of St Othmar, which our brethren had not had time to bear away. Their captains feasted with all profusion in the cloister-garth; and Heribald, (as he was wont to tell in after years,) ate and drank his fill with these Huns as he had never eaten and drunken before. They, after their own fashion, lay at meat on the green hay-grass, each by himself, without seats; but Heribald laid chairs for himself and a certain captive cleric. The Huns, using no knives, tore and devoured with their bare teeth the half-raw shoulders and other joints of the cattle which they had slain; after which each would cast the gnawed bones in sport at another. The wine was set in the midst, in full goblets, and each drank at his own will. Then, as they waxed warm with drink, they all cried most horribly upon their own gods, constraining the cleric and the fool to do likewise. The cleric, who knew their tongue well (for which reason they had spared his life), cried lustily with them; and then, when their mad tongues had run on enough, he began with tears to sing the anthem of the Holy Cross (for this was the eve of the Invention of the Cross); and Heribald, though hoarse of voice, chanted with him. All flocked together at this strange chant of their captives; then they danced in wild joy before their captains, and wrestled one with the other; nay, some contended in arms, and showed their utmost skill in the art of war. Meanwhile the cleric, thinking that this merriment betokened a happy moment for beseeching his own release, implored the help of Holy Cross and fell, with lamentable tears, at the feet of the captains; but they fiercely hissed and grunted the purport of this prayer to their satellites, who flew to the spot in mad fury, seized upon the poor wretch, and drew their knives in order to mock his shaven crown with that which the Germans call *picchin*,[1] before he should be beheaded. [A timely alarm saved him: the Huns set fire to the suburbs and rode off under cover of falling night.] Meanwhile Abbot Engilbert, who had led this assault upon the Huns, left the rest behind and rode warily on to the monastery with a handful of men as bold as himself, spying to see whether any were left in ambush. They compassionated the folly of Heribald (for he was a man of noble birth) and sought narrowly for his body, that they might give it burial. But the cleric had persuaded him, though with difficulty, to flee to the mountain top hard by, where they lay hid among trees and bushes; and the abbot, not finding him, was still more grieved to think that the enemy had carried away the poor fool as their slave. Then he marvelled to find the wine untouched by this drunken crew, and gave thanks unto God. [Next day he returned to this mountain stronghold, where Heribald and the cleric presently joined him.] Then, having heard how the Huns sometimes came suddenly back, they again cut

[1] *Picking*, *i.e.* "scalping or scoring his tonsure with their knives."

a stockade of trees over against the entrance to their strong-hold, dug a deep moat, and bored so far under the ground where the sedges grew that they found a well of purest water. Then they brought back, in such pitchers and vessels as they could find, the wine which the Huns had left to Heribald, creeping furtively to and fro by day and by night; thus they lived in their stronghold and called assiduously upon the Lord.

18. AN ABBOT'S BIRTH
AND ELECTION

(*Ib.* p. 119.)

ULRICH, Count [of Buchorn], of the lineage of Charles the Great, took to wife one Wendilgart, granddaughter to King Henry [the Fowler], and begat upon her Adalhard (who afterwards gave the township of Altstetten to St Gall) and a daughter. This Ulrich, hearing in his castle of Buchorn that the Magyars were breaking into Tirol, where he had posses-sions, fell upon them with other confederates, but was con-quered and taken captive. (Note, that those who take the Magyars for Saracens go far astray.[1]) It was noised abroad that the count was slain; and his widow Wendilgart was sought in second marriage, but by God's inspiration she re-fused; nay, she besought abbot Solomon's permission and took up her abode at St Gall, where she built a chamber hard by Wiborad's[2] cell—and lived upon her own possessions, giving freely to our brethren and to the poor for the soul of her husband whom she deemed to be dead. But she had a craving for sweet things, and loved all that was new, as one who had been delicately nurtured and accustomed to luxury; wherefore Wiborad rebuked her, saying that it was no sign of modesty in a woman to long for various meats. One day, therefore, as she sat talking at the holy virgin's window, she besought her for sweet apples, if she had any in store. "Yea," said

[1] This criticism is directed at the *Great Annals of S. Gall*, which Ekkehard constantly uses, and in which the Magyars are frequently called *Agareni*.
[2] The recluse whom the Huns afterwards killed.

Wiborad, "for I have very fair apples, as poor folk count them fair"; whereunto she brought forth some apples from the wood. Wendilgart snatched them greedily from her hand; but, having scarce eaten half an apple, with a wry face, she cast the rest from her, saying, "Austere thou art, and austere thine apples"; and, being a learned lady, she added, "if the Creator had made all apples like unto these, Eve would never have tasted thereof." "In naming Eve," answered the other, "thou hast well said; for she, as thou, was so greedy of food that she sinned in eating a single apple." The noble lady departed in confusion at the words of this humble virgin; and thenceforward she forced herself no longer to lick up all dainties that fell in her way, and made such progress under this monitress, in so short a time, that she besought Bishop Solomon, with the favour of the synod, to clothe her in the holy veil which she had hitherto refused. After which, she so far cast off her lay mind that she inured herself to the virtues of the recluses; and chose to be immured next after Rachilda (who had died daily and visibly of ulcers that overspread her whole body, and more especially her breasts...and at whose tomb (*experto credite*) it availeth much to pray in sudden motions of anguish). Thus came the fourth bitter anniversary of her husband's reputed death; and Wendilgart went to Buchorn, as was her custom, to disperse her goods among the poor. And behold! Ulrich, who by chance had escaped from his captivity, mingled secretly among the rest in rags, and besought her for a garment. The lady rebuked him for his too bold and instant petitions, yet gave him the garment in spite of her indignation; whereupon he seized both it and her hand, and, drawing her to him, embraced and kissed her sore against her will. Then, when some threatened to smite him upon the cheek, he raised his hand and threw back his long hair upon his neck, saying, "Smite me not, for I have suffered many such blows, but know now your Ulrich again!" Then his amazed knights, hearing their lord's voice, and recognizing under those unkempt locks the face of him whom they had once known, greeted him with shouts of joy and congratulation. Meanwhile Wendilgart had sunk upon a seat in amazement, as one who had suffered disgrace from this stranger, crying:

"Now at last I feel that Ulrich is dead, when this man can outrage me thus!" Then, when he showed for her comfort his hand, bearing the scar that she knew so well, she awoke as from a dream and cried: "It is my lord, dearest of all men! Hail, lord, hail, ever-sweetest!" Then, amid their kisses and embraces: "Clothe ye now your lord, and hasten this moment to make ready his bath!" When she had clothed him, "Let us go," said he, "to the church"; and, as they went, "Prithee, who hath veiled thee with this veil?" Hearing that the bishop had veiled her in full synod, he said within himself: "Then I may not embrace thee now, save by his leave." Then the clergy, who had flocked thither in great numbers on that day, began to sing hymns of praise and the people took up their part. They celebrated joyful masses, not for the dead, but for the living; and the count went to his bath. The thing was noised abroad, and brought the wonted concourse of people. The day's feast was richly enjoyed, and many other days were spent in rejoicing. The synod soon met; Ulrich sought back his wife from the bishop who had vowed her to God, and the synod decreed that the bishop should give the veil to be kept in the cathedral chests, in order that, if Ulrich died first, his widow might wear it again. Then their marriage was renewed; the lady conceived, and paid a votive pilgrimage with her husband to her beloved St Gall and to the anchoresses; there she pledged herself, if she bore a male child, to devote him as a monk to St Gall;[1] and thence they went home. Her time drew near; she fell into a sore sickness before her time, and died a fortnight before the expected birth. The child was cut from her corpse and wrapped in the fat of a new-born pig, until his skin should grow; and, since he promised well, they baptized him and called him Purchard. At length his father took him from the nurse's breast, and fulfilled his own and his wife's vow by laying the child on the altar of St Gall, together with the manor of Höchst and certain tithes, and bitter tears for the dead mother. The boy, who was most comely, was delicately nurtured in the abbey. The brethren called him "The Unborn"; and, seeing that his birth was

[1] For these *oblates*, or child-monks, see my *Five Centuries of Religion*, vol. 1, pp. 81 ff., 326 ff., and index.

thus untimely, and that no fly ever bit him without drawing blood, therefore in his case the master spared even the rod. Grown to manhood, he ever cherished his inborn virtues in spite of the frailty of his body; and his ripened soul was lord of his unripe frame. To such a father in God as this Purchard, whose virtues time was turning into ingrained habits, Ekkehard [the dean] offered the honours proffered to himself, with the assent of all. So Purchard, with certain chosen brethren in his company,[1] went to seek the great emperor Otto [I], and found him at Mainz, whither he returned from Schleswig after his victory over King Cnut. The king, seeing from afar this familiar face, cried, "Come hither, little nephew, and kiss me" (for he was small of stature and fair of face) and took him under his cloak and showed him great tenderness. Then, seeing how Purchard bare the abbot's staff, he said, "What! is that blinder of monks dead?"[2] "O king!" said he, "our abbot is dead; what he was, God alone can judge." Then the king kissed each monk in turn, saying: "What ye desire, I see; but I know not whom ye desire." "O king!" said they, "we desire the very man who is under thy cloak, our lord Purchard"; and with those words they fell with one accord at his feet. He bade them rise; and they spake again, saying: "Moreover, our father Ekkehard, who intercedeth for us, sendeth his greeting and his prayers that ye will remember your frequent promises to help him in this one matter." "Yet I fear," said the king, "lest ye be weary of the stricter discipline which your fathers ever loved, and have therefore given the abbacy to this little man, as one whom ye will find mild and pliable. Why have ye not rather elected that [Ekkehard] of whom ye spake even now, a man of lofty mind?" Then they rehearsed unto him the whole tale of their election in every particular, and added: "Moreover, O king! this Purchard hath never hitherto been so mild in his discipline as to give promise of later neglect." These words allayed the king's doubts; and he, taking Purchard by the chin, said lovingly: "Wilt thou then be my little abbot?

[1] Cf. the account of Samson's journey to the king in Jocelin of Brakelond in Carlyle's *Past and Present*.

[2] Abbot Thieto, Purchard's predecessor. The allusion is obscure.

If it be the Lord's will, so be it; for it shall be my will also."
Then he led him to the church, to Queen Edith,[1] saying:
"To thy grace I offer this nephew of mine, who shall soon,
with thy leave, be made abbot." Then the collect was said,
the emperor demanded the staff, and restored it to Purchard
with the customary words for such a grant. He himself began
the *Te Deum*, and bade all present to join in the hymn of
praise....

Purchard was dismissed by the emperor with all loving-
kindness, and went on his homeward way. How great an
abbot he showed himself, with the help and counsel of Ekkehard, the poor are wont to testify, and many of the brethren
and the servants whom we still see to-day; some bear witness
even with tears.[2] But since, as we have said, he was delicate,
therefore he ate flesh at the bidding of Conrad our bishop....
From his childhood he had been used to give alms, which he
now gave all the more fully and gladly as his wealth was the
greater, distributing openly and secretly not only to the poor
and the pilgrims, but to all that were needy among the monks
and their servants. So busily would he give, by day and night,
that he would sometimes come home barefooted or half-
naked; wherefore his chamberlain Richere, his own brother's
son, oftentimes rebuked him in secret; for, (said he,) the
chamberlain's office could not bear such expenses, with an
abbot who had no sooner given than he demanded again
wherewithal to give. The abbot, therefore, would privately
rebuke his nephew for thus gainsaying him; "for," said he,
"if thou give not what I ask, I know one who will help me
whereinsoever he may"; to wit, [Ekkehard] the dean. "For
he supplies me with more gifts for the poor than thou—coats
and shirts, hosen and shoes, and other garments, even unto
belts, he giveth me in secret; but he hideth them where
I may find them under my bed covering."

[1] Ekkehard is here mistaken; the English Edith was dead more than ten years
since, and the present empress was Adelheid.
[2] Purchard resigned in 973 and died 981; few could have had first-hand
memories of him when Ekkehard IV wrote; most must have spoken from tradition.

A MONASTIC PHYSICIAN

The frequent modern assertion that the monks were the ordinary physicians of the Middle Ages will not bear serious examination. The true facts are stated by Dom Mabillon (*AA.SS. Ord. S. Bened.* vol. I, 1668, p. 665 n.): "Custom sometimes allowed clerics and monks to devote themselves to medicine until the time of St Bernard of Clairvaux, as may be seen in that holy father's 67th and 68th epistles....But this art was forbidden to monks and clergy alike by the 9th canon of the Council of Rome held in 1139 under Innocent II." When we find monastic physicians—an infrequent phenomenon—it generally transpires that the man had learned and practised his art before he became a monk. The following case has a special interest. One of the three Notkers at St Gall was nicknamed *Peppercorn*, on account of his severity in discipline. The chronicler makes him a contemporary of Abbot Purchard (see No. 18). This story comes from Ekkehard IV, *Casus S. Galli, Mon. Germ. Hist. Scriptt.* vol. II, p. 136.

19. A MONASTIC PHYSICIAN

OF this Notker, teacher, painter and physician, we must speak but briefly and hasten on, for we have matter for a great volume. After the Great Fire at the Abbey, he made many pictures for St Gall, as may be seen on the doors and ceiling of the church, and in certain of our books; but what are these in comparison with the thousand other things which he performed as writer and physician?...In medicine he wrought marvellous and amazing cures; for he was singularly learned in medical aphorisms and spices and antidotes, and in Hippocratean prognostics, as appeared in that matter of Duke Henry [I of Bavaria], who sought craftily to deceive him. The duke sent to Notker, as his own urine, that of a lady at his court; which when our brother had inspected, he said: "God is now about to work a portentous and unheard-of miracle, that a man should give birth to a child. For it shall come to pass that, about the thirtieth day from this present time, the duke shall be brought to bed of a son and lay the child to his breast." The duke blushed to find himself discovered, and sent gifts to the man of God that he might not refuse to heal him—for to that purpose was he brought thither; moreover, at the lady's humble supplications, Notker brought her into favour again with the duke; for he had held her for a virgin, yet she brought forth even as Notker had prognosticated. Moreover, he quickly healed our bishop [of

83

Constance], Kaminold, who suffered from a long-standing haemorrhage of the nose; for, smelling the blood, he predicted an attack of small-pox within three days. When, on the day foretold, the pustules broke forth, then the bishop besought him to restrain them; whereunto he made answer: "Nay, my lord, I could but I would not, for I could not bear all the days of penance that the church hath decreed for murderers of bishops; as indeed I should be your murderer if I restrained these pustules." Yet he healed them so quickly that the bishop bore not a single mark upon his face.

The Bavarian Othloh was born about A.D. 1010, of a well-to-do family in the diocese of Freisingen. He received his first education among the monks of Tegernsee, and promised "while yet a small boy" to take the full monastic vows. His father, however, persuaded him back into the world; but in 1032, after two dangerous illnesses, he at last took the irrevocable step. His autobiography tells us how many books he copied, and how many he composed himself, during his monastic life. This was spent in the abbeys of St Emmeram (Regensburg, 1032), Fulda (1052), St Emmeram again, Fulda again (1062), Amorbach (1066) and St Emmeram (1067: here he died about 1070). It was not usual for a Benedictine to change convents so often.

His autobiography was written first in poetical form, and then more fully in prose. The most interesting parts are here translated and put together, without marks of omission, from the text in J. Mabillon's *Vetera Analecta*, t. IV (1685), pp. 404 ff. (ed. 1723, pp. 107 ff.). It has been reprinted in Migne, *Pat. Lat.* vol. 146, cols. 30 ff. The extracts given in Mr H. O. Taylor's *Medieval Mind* are in many parts very loosely paraphrased, though they are not so often disfigured by actual mis-translations as are most of the renderings in that very unequal book. There is an excellent paper on Othloh by E. Dümmler in *Sitzungsberichte d. k. p. Akad. d. Wissenschaften zu Berlin*, 28 Nov. 1895.

20. OTHLOH'S TEMPTATIONS

THERE was a certain cleric given up to manifold sins [*vitiis multis modis deditus*], who was oftentimes warned by the Lord for his amendment, and at last was converted and took the monastic vows without the knowledge of any of his friends. In this monastery whereunto he entered he found many men of divers kinds, some reading heathen books and others the

Holy Scriptures;[1] wherefore he set himself to follow only those whom he saw to be busied with divine readings. Yet, the more steadfastly he applied himself to these readings, the more cruelly he found himself beset by diabolical temptations; but, trusting in God, to whose grace he ever committed himself, he strove to persevere in his holy studies with the same mind wherewith he had begun them. And, after a long while, finding himself freed from the assaults of these temptations, he bethought himself how he might edify not himself only, but others also, through his own sufferings. To this end he hath committed to writing not only the grievous temptations which beset him, but also those words of Holy Scripture which came into his mind through God's inspiration, and whereby, as with a shield, he defended himself against the Devil's wiles. Here beginneth the story of his grievous temptations.

Waking and sleeping, I endured divers diabolical delusions, more than I can tell. Yet some at least are so fixed in my memory that I will recount them as best I may. This, methinks, must be counted as the first of those frauds which I have suffered both before and since my monastic profession, that my will to be converted[2] was most foolish and imprudent. For, whereas the Scripture saith *Do thou nothing without counsel* [Ecclus. xxxii, 19], I desired to enter the monastery without the counsel of my parents or any of my friends, suddenly and in the full heat of youth; and it would be too imprudent that one such as I was should undertake so perilous a vow. Wherefore it would have been far better to defer this unto a riper and more perfect age; after which, as one full-grown in virtue, I might at last have treated of my own accord for the conversion which I desired. This, then, and such as these I endured from the Devil's illusions, under the guise of compassionate and good counsel.

Next, that foul tempter aroused himself to assault me yet

---

[1] Which, in medieval language, generally (though not always) included the Fathers as well as the Bible.

[2] *Conversio*, in medieval Latin, is comparatively seldom used in the exact sense which a Bunyan attached to it; in nine cases out of ten, at least, it signifies the taking of monastic vows, just as *religio* is constantly used of a monastic order. It was naturally assumed that such vows did connote a real conversion of mind.

more wickedly, seeing that (by God's grace withstanding him) he had failed of his desired effect with me. For, with his wonted cunning, he sought to tempt me to despair, suggesting the uselessness of all my attempts to turn back, since I was involved in such offences as must make me hateful not only to the rulers but also to the rest of the people, and even to my parents and kinsfolk. "Thinkest thou," said he, "that so wicked a man as thou can earn the pardon of God, that most strict Judge, seeing that Scripture saith: *The righteous shall scarcely be saved*? Cease therefore to desire these things which are not for thee, but rather labour for those things which thou mayest obtain. For if, as in thy folly thou meanest, this were open to all men—if not the righteous only, but the wicked also might come to the kingdom of heaven— then that most excellent apostle Paul would never have said: *For all men have not faith*; and again: *They have not all obeyed the gospel*; nor would our Founder and Saviour Himself, who was the very Truth, have taught this to His disciples and to the whole world at the very threshold of His doctrine: *He that is able to receive it, let him receive it*; in which sentence He signified beyond all doubt that it is not in every man's power to do good." Tortured by such delusions, how think ye was my mind all this while? Truly I could do naught but weep, and, as saith the Psalmist, my tears were my bread by day and night. I acknowledge from the bottom of my heart that no man can overcome these temptations, but by God's grace alone.

Wherefore this cunning and treacherous spirit, unable to draw me into consent with that despair which he brought upon my soul, sought by other false arguments to bend me to blasphemy of God's justice, no longer assaulting me with terror or reproach, but rather as one who had pity and compassion upon my sufferings. For he would put into my heart such thoughts as these: "O youth worthy of all compassion, whose pain no man deigneth to heed! For what man could imagine this great affliction which boweth thee down? To thy fellows it must not be imputed; for, where they cannot know, how should they be able to help? The Lord alone knoweth all thine affliction; to Him alone can we impute whatsoever may seem foolish and disordered in this world. All-knowing, Almighty, wherefore hath He no succour for thee in thy tribulation? for thee, who for His sake hast first forsaken the world, and dost now endure such continual and unspeakable torment. What reason can we find for this strictness, which doth heap every pain upon those who call daily upon Him? Do as thou wilt; leave these vain prayers and lamentations; for He endureth ever in His former severity; it is a mere fool's part to pray and pray for that which thou knowest to be impossible....Dost thou not mark those words of the prophet Ezekiel, *The soul that sinneth, it shall die*? If therefore all shall die who commit sin, then shall none be saved, for none can be found without sin....O undiscerning severity! O miserable justice! for He followeth only the dictates of His own will, nor doth He deign to receive those who flee unto Him. Then, truly, is a discipline most intolerable, and deserving of no man's commendation." These delusions, even as the others, long haunted my thoughts; whereby it may well be seen how great was the peril of my soul.

This, again, would seem to pertain to these same delusions. Oftentimes it came to pass that, when I would have risen from my couch at the first stroke for Matins, as the Rule teacheth, I was awakened long before the time by a ghostly bell, and came with untimely haste to the church. This also, for a while, I thought to be from God; until I found that this loss of my timely sleep compelled me to sleep untimely [in choir]. This also I suffered for some years at the night-hours, that, although I lay so sound in my bed, yet when the time came to rise for Matins all my limbs seemed to be bound with weakness as with an iron chain, and I could scarce stagger to my place in choir.

I must recount yet another temptation and delusion which is the more difficult to relate, that I have never heard or read of any such in the case of any other man. For, after the assaults of the above-named temptations—and many others which I have partly forgot, partly omitted for weariness' sake to my readers—amid all which temptations, by God's grace, I never quite lost my faith or my hope of succour from heaven—then I was long tormented by temptations which compelled me utterly to doubt of the knowledge of Holy Scripture, and of the essence of God Himself. And whereas, in my other temptations, there had ever been some respite and refreshment between fit and fit, and some refuge of hope, yet here, for hours and hours without intermission, I knew scarce the smallest shred of comfort. In my other pains, I had been somewhat strengthened by authorities from Holy Scripture; these had armed me with the armour of faith and hope against the fiery darts of death. But, in this trial, I was compassed about with utter perplexity and blindness of soul; for I doubted altogether whether there were any truth or profit in Holy Scripture, and whether God were indeed Almighty. In other temptations, I say, the assault was in a manner tolerable and temperate; but this burst out upon me with such violence as to bereave not only my spirit, but even my bodily senses of their accustomed vigour; for it seemed sometimes that my eyes were veiled and my hearing dulled, so that I could neither see nor hear in comparison of my wonted perceptions. Meanwhile I heard as it were a Voice that spake with me, and lips that even whispered right into mine ears, saying, "Wherefore dost thou so travail in vain? Where is that hope that thou hadst hitherto in Scripture? Canst thou not see in thine own case, O fool beyond all other fools, that there is neither reason nor order, whether in the testimony of Scripture or in the imaginations of men? Knowest thou not by plain experience that pious books tell us one tale, and men's lives and manners tell another? Dost thou think that all these thousands are mistaken, who (as thou thyself sawest when thou wast yet dwelling among them) cared neither to observe nor even to accept the teaching of Holy Scriptures?" At this, I pondered long and sadly within myself, seeking for questions and objections, and saying, "If this be so, why then is there such accord among almost all these God-inspired Scriptures, that they speak as with one voice about God who made us and about the keeping of His commandments?" Then, as it seemed, that Voice would whisper again in mine ear, "O dullard! if the Scriptures wherein thou trustest speak of God's person and of so many religious matters, it is only because the men who wrote these things lived, in their day, even as men live around us now. In these days, as thou thyself knowest, this is the fashion of men's lives, that they speak words of all honesty and religion, while their deeds are far different, even as it is expedient and as human frailty requireth. Canst thou not see daily how these things are so? From this thou mayest gather that the writers of ancient Scriptures did indeed indite words of honesty, yet they lived not according to the purport of their own words. Know, therefore, that all the books of God's law were thus written, by men who had an outward semblance of religion and virtue, while within they nourished other reasons and another understanding. For indeed we may easily find in many books, more especially of divinity, sentences which signify one thing in the letter, but another thing in truth. This may be proved by that one text of Paul: *The letter killeth, but the spirit* (that is, the true sense) *giveth life.* Do not these words of the Apostle teach us clearly that, by following what is written in books, thou shalt run into great peril? Likewise must we think of God's essence also. Otherwise—that is, if there were such a person or such a power as God Almighty,[1]—be sure that we should see no such confusion, no such diversity, in all things around us. Be sure that no such trials would then beset thee; nor wouldst thou be haunted by the doubt that thou now endurest."

Thus, then, I was assaulted with incredible fury by such delusions as these; and the assaults were of so unheard-of a sort that I feared to show them openly to my brethren, thinking that no man could believe or hear such words. Wherefore, falling upon the ground and sighing deeply in the bitterness of my spirit, and gathering together all the forces of my mind, thus I spake with my lips and from my heart. "O Almighty (if such indeed there be) and Omnipresent (if there be one Omnipresent, as I have oftentimes read in my books), now show me, I pray, who Thou art and what Thou canst do, by saving me without delay from the perils that beset me; for indeed I can no longer bear such trials as these." Then, within the twinkling of an eye, I was not only freed

[1] *Si aliqua persona aut virtus Dei omnipotentis esset.*

by God's grace from all this mist of doubt, but also such a light of knowledge shone forth in my soul that I never suffered again from such deadly darkness of doubt; nay, I began to comprehend what I had never known before; and at this same time that grace of understanding so increased within me that I had much ado to keep it secret....

Since, therefore, I have given a brief account of the diabolical delusions which my sins bred and brought upon me, it seems right and fitting that I should write also of those manners of divine inspiration whereby my mind was fortified to fight against them. Otherwise these delusions, recorded by themselves and without simultaneous record of the divine help which stood by me, might lead the reader to think that I ascribed the victory, which never was mine, to mine own strength; or, again, that I had lacked God's protection in my troubles, and that he himself also might lack the divine help in like case. Therefore, to remove such suspicion once for all, I confess that I was always equipped by God's grace against the Devil's snares; and, again, that I was never so utterly sunk in sloth or wantonness but that I fought the good fight with such strength as I had, whether by watching or by fasting or by continence of all kinds. Therefore, (to omit all mention of the gifts of liberal knowledge bestowed on me, which are themselves a great help to prudent conduct,) I remember that an unseen spirit went oftentimes by my side. For, especially when I rose from my couch for Matins, it seemed that One arose with me, and went with me step for step, and spake to me in such wise as no words can tell—now rebuking, now gently admonishing, often intreating me most humbly to mend my ways and shun my faults—especially those which perchance I had committed the day before, and had ignorantly made nothing of....And when, compassed about with this inspiration and this hidden voice, I had entered the church, and had bent or prostrated myself in suppliant fashion for prayer, then it seemed to me (God knows I lie not!) that the Voice besought me with no less fervour of prayer, saying: "Even as it is thy pleasure to obtain that which thou askest of me, so also it is precious to me that thou shouldst obey my requests."

The Voice, at great length, reasons with Othloh concerning many of his thoughts and deeds, some of which have real autobiographical interest.

(p. 412) "Where now is that patience and constancy and struggle for perfection which thou hast oftentimes promised to God, if He would deign to save thee from those imminent perils, to bring thee safe under the monastic habit? Behold, God hath fulfilled what thy soul hath so often desired; why then art thou so slow to perform thy vow? Thou didst beseech Him to bring thee to a place where thou mightest find great plenty of books; now have thy words been heard; now thou hast books of all sorts wherein thou mayest learn the way of life everlasting; why then dost thou let thy mind wander vainly over matters of no account, instead of hastening to grasp this great gift? Moreover, thinking thyself prompt and ready to endure adversity, thou didst instantly beseech me to suffer some grievous temptation to assail thee; whereby thou mightest deserve to be in some sort purified from thy sins. This again I have granted, suffering thee to be tried not as that wicked Tempter would have wished, but according to the strength that hath been given unto thee; yet, now that these enemies assail thee, wilt thou yield and flee like a fool or a coward?...(p. 414) Forget not this, that many men, for sins far lighter than thine, have by God's just doom been glad to redeem their lives by suffering grievous torment or by shameful loss of limb....(p. 418) Who was it, I pray thee, upon whom thou wast wont to call in those days long past, when thou hadst but newly been sent to learn thy letters at school? When thou didst sit among masters and boys, in constant fear of the rod, upon whom then didst thou call to smooth thy path to learning, and He heard thee?...Since then, as a little schoolboy, thou hadst so lively a proof of God's grace and power, wherefore hast thou now so much less faith in Him, grown at last to manhood, and assured of God's pity not only through the gift of learning but also by many proofs of experience?...

(p. 423) "Marvel not if thou hast been tried by new temptations...by the thought that I, God, am not almighty, and that all my graces bestowed on thee are but a dream....For the Devil, clearly perceiving that all who flee to me may obtain mercy, doth by every sort of delusion draw them back from the gateway of this mercy, that is, from faith. To which purpose, with his accustomed falsehood, he instils these thoughts following into men's souls; either that I deign not to justify any wicked man, or that I am so stern a judge as no sinner can bend to mercy, even though he chastise himself in penance from day to day; or else Satan persuadeth men to doubt of the everlasting bliss of the righteous or the eternal pains of the ungodly, or even to blaspheme my judgments; or, again, to twist Holy Scripture with evil purpose from its true sense; or, lastly, he robbeth men of the certain knowledge of me, even as thou also wast deprived of such knowledge even now....(p. 432) There remaineth yet one temptation, which is the long-drawn suffering of carnal concupiscence, wherein thou believest thyself to have been tried more especially, for which cause thou must listen here, as in other matters, to examples from the Lives of the Fathers. [Here follow four classical examples—that of Equitius from St Gregory's *Dialogues*, of Serenus from Cassian's *Collations* and of Sara and Mary the Egyptian from *Vitaspatrum*; after which our text proceeds:] Hast thou, therefore, [like Mary the Egyptian,] laboured now for seventeen years in fight against the thoughts of carnal desires? Far from it; thou hast not yet suffered a whole year....If so great a saint as Paul was buffeted by carnal desires, lest he should be puffed up by the spiritual favours that he had received, is it not right that thou shouldst be wearied with adversity, lest thou shouldst presume to glory of what thou also hast received?"

...(p. 438) All these things have been written by the Clerk aforesaid, in order that those who at the beginning of their conversion desire to read Holy Scripture may learn to recognize and beware of the Devil's unfathomable wiles, wherewith he is wont to lay snares for all such as read those same Scriptures; and in order also that they may recognize the grace of divine inspiration, and call upon God for help.

From Mabillon, *Annales Benedictini*, vol. v (1740), p. 136. (From an ancient charter.)

21. A SCENE

LANCELIN OF BEAUGENCY granted to the monks of Vendôme the privilege of a fair to be held on St Beatus's day, at Beaugency, in the court of the monastery, in front of the Galilee door of St Sepulchre's church, in presence of the lord Abbot Robert, which said abbot sat there on his palfrey, in the year 1052.

22. MONASTIC CONVERTS

(*Ib*. p. 22. Abridged from an original charter.)

IN this year [1070] Gerard Brunel gave his whole estate of Sconville to St Martin and the monks of Marmoutier, who showed their gratitude by admitting him to the brotherhood of their prayers, and promised also that they would admit him without payment if he should wish to become a monk, and, if not, they would bury him in their monastery. To this compact his wife Ermengarde assented with her three sons, the monks giving them twenty sous to procure their more willing and stronger assent; moreover, to his fourth son they gave a psalter, and promised to feed him for two years at Châteaudun, if he were sent to school there.

23. A CHARITABLE FOUNDATION

(*Ib*. Appendix xiv, p. 606, an. 1080 (original charter).)

I, GERALD, by God's providence first abbot of Seauve-Majeure, and all the congregation of the brethren, have decreed that, for this gift [of the manor of Seauve-Majeure] and many other benefits bestowed on us, the Lord William Duke of Aquitaine shall always be remembered in our prayers, even as he doth deserve to be rewarded by Christ. We have decreed that a special mass be sung for him every week, and that the daily portion of a monk's food be set aside daily to be given to the poor for him. Moreover, even as this is done during his lifetime, no less zealously shall it be continued after his death, so long as our monastery shall stand.

24. MONASTIC RELICS

(*Ib.* p. 28.)

In or about the year 1070, Archbishop Anno of Cologne brought back from Rome certain precious relics which he gave to the convent of Siegburg. These included an arm of St Caesarius, and at the same time "he told the following tale to show how meritorious was the invocation of that saint. There was in Rome (he said) a man named Andrew abounding in all riches, but too loose in his life; for he seemed to have nothing of the Christian about him save the name; with this one exception, that he was devoted to the blessed martyr Caesarius, whose church he was wont to frequent with offerings of wax tapers. Death, who spareth none, seized upon this man, who repented too late and gave up the ghost. His body was laid on the bier, awaiting burial on the morrow; and, while his kinsfolk watched by him even unto midnight, the bier was suddenly moved, and the corpse began to raise its head. Then some fled for fear, but others of firmer mind held their ground, doubting whether he were dead. At length, with grievous sighs, he said: 'This is no shadow of death, but death itself which hath come upon me; and I should have been damned to all eternity.' Here he added many things which had befallen him before the judgment seat of God; after which he exhorted his hearers to caution and penitence, lay down again upon his bier, and gave up the ghost." Mabillon, who gravely reproduces this story, surmises that it may have led to the conversion of St Bruno, which took place about this time.

25. MONASTIC SERFS

(*Ib.* p. 26.)

ANSELM OF RIBEAUMONT, in 1070, granted the serfs of his manor of Hertin to the monastery of St Amand "on condition that each serf pay a poll-tax of two pence to the monastery on St Remy's day; that each should depend for licence to marry upon the abbot or obedientiaries of the said monastery; and that, if he married a wife from any other class than his own, the monastery should take as a mortuary whatsoever chattels he might possess."

The purest side of monastic religion cannot and need not be quoted here; it is to be found in the *Imitation of Christ* of Thomas à Kempis, which, to an attentive reader, shows traces everywhere of its monastic origin. The historical value of that book is enhanced by the fact that there is scarcely an original sentence in it; whole pages (as Vacandard has noted) are practically centos from the mystical writings of St Bernard. The work is original in the highest sense, since Thomas had made all these readings and meditations into his own flesh and blood; but, as an evidential document, its highest value lies in the fact that it is the quintessence of all that was truest and purest among the thoughts of many monastic generations in the past.

The *Imitation*, therefore, must all along be borne in mind; and the present compilation must try to balance that picture by showing some of the greatest saints, and some of the most typical monastic instructors, in their more ordinary moods. Thomas à Kempis will answer all those who are inclined to wonder why monasticism was so great a power in the past; some of my other extracts are designed rather to display those limitations (it may almost be said, those fundamental limitations) which explain the comparative powerlessness of the monk in modern society.

The following extract is taken from St Anselm of Canterbury, *Meditatio V* (*Opera*, ed. Gerberon, 1721, p. 211).

26. THE MONK'S GOD

LAST THINGS

BUT now, my soul, let us strive to see clearly in what fashion the soul of him who hath lived well is led to heaven by his good works; and how his evil works drag the sinner's soul down to hell. The pure soul, leaving the body, sees at a glance all his past deeds; and, seeing that all are good, he rejoiceth with a joy unspeakable. Soon his guardian Angel taketh him by the hand; soon he is embraced by him who held his eyes lest he should behold vanity, and who stopped his ears lest he should hear iniquity. He cometh under the wing of him who kept his mouth lest he should speak lies; he is the joy of him who shielded him from sin in smelling or touching. Thus doth the Angel encompass him on every side with joy and gladness, and bringeth him before the throne of God's light, where he may find bliss without end. Then other Angels and Saints come to meet him, who wait there before the face of God's majesty. They greet him as their fellow and friend in all good works; they embrace him joyfully with the arms of sincerest charity; they open their lips, and show him all the joys of the whole fellowship of heaven. "Lo here" (they say), "our friend! seeing that thou hast served God faithfully, and hast laboured manfully to keep His commandments, now at last come and rest from thy labours, and enjoy with us, from this time forth for ever more, the bliss that hath no end."

Look now on the other part, how the sinner's soul is compelled to come forth from his body. In a moment the Angels of Satan lay hands upon him; they bind him with fiery chains, and urge him still more pitilessly on all sides, and bear him off to the torments of hell, where Satan himself lieth in the pit wherein God hath cast him. There is weeping and gnashing of teeth, there are flames and snares; storms and tempests, those are his portion to drink. Then doth Satan himself seize him to his bosom, and belch forth upon him fire mingled with stench, and biddeth his servants bind him straitly hand and foot and cast him among the torments wherein he shall be tormented world without end, dying everlastingly, yet living in eternal pain. Then that wretched soul, amid such pains and torment, agonized on every side by those infernal furies, cometh at last to himself and seeth all the evil that he hath done. Then doth he cry aloud in his anguish: "Wretch, wretch that I am! wherefore came I ever to life? miserable, and miserably tormented on every side by so many manners of torture! O worms, worms, who gnaw so cruelly upon me now, spare me, I pray, in my misery; spare him who suffereth so many and so great torments beside all this! Alas, misery, misery! I yearn to die, and, dying ever, I must ever live. Now, poor wretch, must I receive back all whereinsoever I have sinned in seeing, in hearing, in taste, in smell, and in touch." Yet all this wretched lamentation, all this late repentance, all this unhappy confession, all this sadness and self-reproach, availeth naught for this unhappy soul; but, whatsoever he earned while he was yet alive, that doth the sinful wretch now receive in the pains of very hell.

Mabillon, *Annales Benedictini*, vol. v (1740), p. 152, an. 1080. Foundation of the monastery of Seauve-Majeure near Bordeaux by Gerald, who had been Abbot of St-Vincent at Laon, but had resigned because his monks "were disobedient to him as to giving up their private property and other misdeeds" (p. 100); Gerald therefore came to Aquitaine and founded a small monastery on stricter principles. Mabillon, abbreviating from the contemporary biographer, thus describes the eight associates who joined him in this venture.

27. A GROUP OF CONVERTS

HIS companions and coadjutors in this work were eight, who had followed him from the Île-de-France to Aquitaine; the first three had been under him at St-Vincent, but the other five were laymen who followed him as master and father for the love of God. The first was Martin, who afterwards became abbot of St-Denys near the hills of Hainault; the second Ebroin, who exchanged his knighthood for the cowl, then became an anchorite, and thus fought on manfully until his death;...the third was Aleraunus, Gerald's own nephew, who became third abbot of Seauve-Majeure. Of the other five, the first was Berlege the Frenchman, of a noble family at Noyon, and brother to the castellan of that city. He, in his youth, deserted the study of letters for the profession of arms, wherein he long practised himself; but at length, inspired by God's grace, he cast aside his arms, gave up all his possessions, and, washing himself clean at the fount of tears, followed after Gerald, or rather, after Christ. The second was Guy of Laon, a very wealthy knight of the Bishop's household, of tried valour and probity. The third was Terzo, a doughty knight in the world, but doughtier still in Christ's service, who was born at Coucy near Laon. The fourth was Walter of Laon, a knight, most prudent in all his works. The fifth and last was also from Laon, Litherius by name, prompt to all good works and to bind all men to himself by kindness. These all, treading underfoot the allurements of the world, went forth from their own land and kindred to follow Christ; they who had been valiant warriors became up-rooters of forest trees, exchanging their costly robes for the vilest and most unsightly garments.

Few things are more characteristic of the old monastic ideal than the institution of oblates—children offered by their parents to be monks or nuns. The age of seven seems to have been generally considered the earliest at which this ceremony might take place: but the Canons Regular of Porto admitted children "three or four years after they had been weaned." In the Benedictine Rule (c. 59) such an oblation is characterized as absolutely binding on the child; to decide, with growing years and experience, against the monastic life, was to commit apostasy with all its temporal and spiritual penalties. So, at least, the majority of expositors interpret it, though St Bernard evidently did not; and this doctrine of the irrevocability of a vow made on the child's behalf, being still the almost unquestioned doctrine in the twelfth century, was naturally introduced into Gratian's *Decretum*. But the following hundred years brought a reaction, and four Popes at last admitted the oblate's strict right to make his final and irrevocable choice in his fifteenth year. From this time forward the custom gradually decayed, especially as many monastic disciplinarians were keenly sensible to the moral evils which it often entailed; and it is maintained by some scholars that the Council of Trent intended to abolish it altogether. (See J. N. Seidl, *Die Gottverlobung von Kindern*, Munich, 1872.) The following extract is from the Custumal of Lanfranc's and Anselm's abbey of Bec, as printed by Dom Martène (*De Antiquis Monachorum Ritibus*, Bassano, 1788, p. 230—lib. v, c. v, § iii).

28. CHILD MONKS

WHEN any boy is offered for the holy Order, let his parents bring him to the altar after the Gospel at Mass; and, after the Cantor hath offered as usual, let the boy also make his offering. After which let the Sacristan take the offering, and let the parents, drawing near, wrap the boy's right hand in the altar-cloth. Then, having kissed it thus enveloped, let them give it into the hands of the priest, who shall receive the boy and make the sign of the cross over his head. If they wish to make him a monk on that same day, let the Abbot bless his crown, saying: *Let us pray, beloved Brethren*; then let him pour holy water on his head and, making the sign of the cross over it, crop his hair with the shears round his neck. While the boy is being shorn, let the Cantor begin the antiphon, *Thou art He Who wilt restore*, the Psalm *Preserve me, O God* (another antiphon is *This is the generation* and the Psalm *The earth is the Lord's*); then let him pray, *Grant, we beseech Thee, Almighty God*, then let the Abbot bless his cowl, saying the prayer, *Lord Jesu Christ, by Whom the garment*. After this aspersion and benediction, let the boy be stripped of his clothes, and the Abbot say, as he strips him, *May the Lord strip thee*; then let him clothe him in the cowl and say, *May the Lord clothe thee*, and say over him as a prayer, *Lord, be present at our supplications*. . . . When the boy be come to the age of reason, let him make his profession after the same order as the other monks, except for the benediction of the cowl, which he hath already received as an Oblate.

Martène then subjoins, from the Custumal of St-Bénigne at Dijon, a series of rules for the education of these oblates, from which the following extracts are taken.

At Nocturns, and indeed at all the Hours, if the boys commit any fault in the psalmody or other singing, either by sleeping or such-like transgression, let there be no sort of delay, but let them be stripped forthwith of frock and cowl, and beaten in their shirt only . . . with pliant and smooth osier rods provided for that special purpose.

And because, so long as the Abbot is in his bed in the dormitory, none may make the sound whereby the Brethren are awakened to rise in the early morning . . . therefore the Master of the Boys should rise very softly and just touch each of the children gently with a rod, that he may awake from sleep; then let them rise as quickly as possible, and, leaving the dormitory, wash and comb and say their prayers. . . .

Let the masters sleep between every two boys in the dormitory, and sit between every two at other times, and, if it be night, let all the candles be fixed without on the spikes which crown the lanterns, that they may be plainly seen in all that they do. When they lie down in bed, let a master always be among them with his rod and (if it be night) with a candle, holding the rod in one hand and the light in the other. If any chance to linger after the rest, he is forthwith smartly touched; for children everywhere need custody with discipline and discipline with custody. And be it known that this is all their discipline, either to be beaten with rods, or that their hair should be stoutly plucked; never are they disciplined with kicks, or fists, or the open hand, or in any other way....

When they wash, let masters stand between each pair at the lavatory.... When they sit in cloister or chapter, let each have his own tree-trunk for a seat, and so far apart that none touch in any way even the skirt of the other's robe... let them wipe their hands as far as possible one from the other, that is, at opposite corners of the towel....

If any of them, weighed down with sleep, sing ill at Nocturns, then the master giveth into his hand a reasonably great book, to hold until he be well awake.... Nor doth one ever speak to the other except by his master's express leave, and in the hearing of all who are in the school.... When there is in the refectory a loving-cup of piment or other drink, then the refectorer-master, if he be of mature age and manners, may let the boys hold out cups and pour them out some drink. ...One reporteth whatsoever he knoweth against the other; else, if he be found to have concealed aught of set purpose, both the concealer and the culprit are beaten.[1]... [At Matins] the principal master standeth before them with a rod, until all are in their seats, and their faces well covered. At their uprising likewise, if they rise too slowly, the rod is

---

[1] Espionage and the rod were the two main pillars of monastic and scholastic discipline in the Middle Ages. The scholars of Pembroke College, Cambridge, held their scholarships on the express condition of acting as faithful talebearers (Rashdall, *Universities*, vol. II, p. 617); and a frequent complaint recorded by Odo Rigaldi against the monasteries which he visits is *non clamat unus alterum*—"they do not inform against each other."

straightway over them. After Matins, when they are to sleep again, if it be not yet dawn, then the master standeth before them as they take off their clothes, with a rod in his right hand and a candle in his left, and they are quickly in their places.... In short, that I may make an end of this matter, meseemeth that any king's son could scarce be more carefully brought up in his palace than any boy in a well-ordered monastery.

Compare with this a passage from the Constitutions of the monastery of Hirschau, about A.D. 1000 (Migne, *Pat. Lat.* vol. 150, pp. 939 ff.). "But all such [boys] if (as men commonly say) they wish their backs to be spared, must beware with all possible diligence and in all places lest they stand or sit together without [some] elder between, or touch each other or suffer their clothes to come into contact in any way; and that none ever presume to make any sign, or even to wink his eye, at any other youth (whether under the same guardianship as himself or no), or to smile at him, or simulate any familiarity, or even sit so that their faces are turned towards each other and each can see the other." Such discipline naturally produced some of the greatest saints and sinners in the monastic orders: the Cluniacs therefore modified the custom, while the Carthusians and others abolished it altogether. Most interesting in this connection is the following passage from *Eadmer* (lib. 1, c. iv), which gains additional significance from the fact that St Anselm was at this time Prior, and afterwards Abbot, of Bec.

29. TRAIN UP THE CHILD

ONE day, when a certain Abbot, much reputed for his piety, spake with Anselm concerning divers points of Monastic Religion, and conversed among other things of the boys that were brought up in the cloister, he added: "What, pray, can we do with them? They are perverse and incorrigible; day and night we cease not to chastise them, yet they grow daily worse and worse." Whereat Anselm marvelled, and said, "Ye cease not to beat them? And when they are grown to manhood, of what sort are they then?" "They are dull and brutish," said the other. Then said Anselm, "With what good profit do ye expend your substance in nurturing human beings till they become brute beasts?" "Nay," said the other, "but what else can we do? By all means we compel them to profit, yet our labour is unprofitable." "Ye *compel* them, my lord Abbot? Tell me, I prithee, if thou shouldst plant a sapling in thy garden, and presently shut it in on all sides so that it could nowhere extend its branches; when thou hadst liberated it after many years, what manner of tree would come forth? Would it not be wholly unprofitable, with gnarled and tangled branches? And whose fault would it be but thine own, who hadst closed it in beyond all reason. Thus without doubt do ye with your children. They have been planted in the Garden of the Church by way of Oblation, there to grow and bear fruit to God. But ye so hem them in on every side with terrors, threats, and stripes, that they can get no liberty whatsoever; wherefore, being thus indiscreetly afflicted, they put forth a tangle of evil thoughts like thorns, which they so foster and nourish, and thus bring to so thick a growth, that their obstinate minds become impenetrable to all possible threats for their correction. Hence it cometh to pass that, perceiving in you no love for themselves, no pity, no kindness, no gentleness, they are unable henceforth to trust in your goodness, believing rather that all your works are done through hatred and envy against them; insomuch that (I grieve to say it), even as they grow in stature, so doth this hatred and suspicion of all evil grow with them; for evil ever bendeth and glideth downward and downward into vice. Wherefore, having nowhere found true charity in their bringing-up, they cannot look upon any man but with scowling brow and sidelong glance. But I prithee tell me, for God's sake, wherefore ye are so set against them? Are they not human, sharing in the same nature as yourselves? Would ye wish to be so handled as ye handle them? Ye will say, 'Yes, if we were as they are.' So be it, then; yet is there no way but that of stripes and scourges for shaping them to good? Did ever see a goldsmith shape his gold or silver plate into a fair image by blows alone? I trow not. What then? That he may give the plate its proper shape, he will first press it gently and tap it with his tools; then again he will more softly raise it with discreet pressure from below, and caress it into shape. So ye also, if ye would see your boys adorned with fair manners, ye should not only beat them down with stripes, but also raise their spirits and support them with fatherly kindness and pity." To whom the Abbot replied, "What sayest thou of raising their spirits and supporting them? We labour to constrain them to the heavy burdens of riper age." "Well indeed," replied Anselm, "for bread and strong meats are good and profitable to all who are able to eat them; but, if ye take milk from a suckling to feed him on strong meats, ye shall see him rather choked than refreshed thereby. Why so? I disdain to say it, for it is clearer than daylight. Yet mark this, that even as a weak or a strong body hath each his own proper food, so also weak and strong souls have their different measures of nourishment. The strong soul delighteth in and is nourished by strong meats, such as patience in tribulation, not to covet other men's goods, to offer the other cheek to the smiter, to pray for his enemies, to love them that hate him, and many like virtues. . . . But the weakling soul, yet tender to the service of God, hath need of milk; that is, of loving-kindness from others, of gentleness, mercy, cheerful address, charitable patience, and many such-like comforts. If ye thus suit yourselves to the strong and to the weak, then by God's grace ye shall win them all to Him, so far as in you lieth." The Abbot, hearing these words, groaned and said, "Truly we have erred from the truth, and the light of discretion hath not shone upon us!" and, falling at Anselm's feet, he confessed that he had sinned, and that the guilt was his; beseeching pardon for the past and promising amendment for the future. This we have written, that it may thus be known how pious was the Saint's discretion to all, and how discreet his piety.[1]

---

[1] It must be remembered that *pius* and *pietas* have also the connotation of *pitiful*, *pity*.

St Hugh, the sixth Abbot of Cluny, ruled from 1049 to 1109. He had entered the monastery in his fifteenth year, and lived to the age of eighty-four. The earliest *Life* of him, by the monks Gilo and Ezelo of Cluny, was written within a few years of his death. Hugh was one of the greatest churchmen of his day, who held his own with the Emperor and even with such a Pope as Gregory VII. The original may be found in *AA.SS. Boll.* April 29th (1675, vol. III, p. 656, § 6).

30. THE SIN OF LAUGHTER

ONCE, when the holy Father was asleep, he dreamed that a multitude of serpents and wild beasts lay beneath his head; wherefore, having shaken his pillow, he found a volume of Vergil lying by chance beneath it. Then, casting aside this secular volume, he slept in peace, and saw how closely the matter of the book agreed with his vision—a book filled with obscenities and heathen rites, and unworthy to be laid amid the bedclothes of a holy man.

There was a certain brother named Durand de Brodon, who first seemed an idiot,[1] but afterwards grew to be not unworthy of Abbot Moses,[2] and was thence promoted for his wisdom to the Archbishopric of Toulouse, where he distinguished himself by his anxious labour in God's vineyard. This monk, though circumspect in other matters, oftentimes incautiously uttered words that moved to laughter. For this cause the venerable father Hugh oftentimes rebuked him, yet with no full effect; wherefore he thus threatened him in the spirit of prophecy: "Be sure, beloved brother, that if thou, in thy lifetime, dost not put away these words of jest, which are altogether forbidden to monks, then thou shalt appear in monstrous form after thy death." Which prophecy was fulfilled at his decease; for to one Siguin, St Hugh's chaplain, the Archbishop's soul appeared foaming at the mouth, and miserably beseeching the help of that Abbot whom in life he had disobeyed. When the lord Abbot heard this from Siguin, he commanded that seven of the brethren, for a whole

---

[1] *Idiota*: possibly simply "stupid," "unlearned."

[2] Moses the Robber, one of the most celebrated of the early anchorites. See Extract 2: also Dom Cuthbert Butler's *Lausiac History*, 1904, p. 197, and the index to *Vitaspatrum* (Migne, *Pat. Lat.* vols. 73, 74).

week, should devote the silence of their own mouths for the good of the Archbishop's soul; which seven he himself chose out from the rest of the convent. All obeyed him save one, who brake silence in contempt of his vow. The Archbishop, appearing again to Siguin, complained bitterly of that treacherous brother who, by speaking, had frustrated his cure. The most pious Hugh, hearing this, commanded that this breach of silence which one man had perpetrated should be patched up by a silence of seven days more. After which the Archbishop's soul appeared for the third time, in apostolic guise, and thanked his purger, this aforementioned and ever-memorable Hugh, for his release [from that punishment].

St Bernard of Tiron, a native of Abbeville, started a reformed congregation in the forest of Tiron (Picardy). He laid great stress on width of vocation and on manual work, recruiting many artisans and artists of different kinds and continuing each at his own special job; so that, in this monastic group, there reigned at first the spirit which St Benedict had inculcated but which the vast majority of Benedictines had long abandoned. St Bernard himself died after three years of this work (1117) but his congregation grew until it comprised about 100 monasteries. After a few generations, the monks of Tiron were practically indistinguishable from the other Benedictines. The following account is from the contemporary *Life* (Migne, *Pat. Lat.* vol. 172, col. 1441).

31. DIVINE CHARITY

LET him tell who can, whether he ever read or heard of any man whose breast overflowed with so extraordinary an abundance of charity; for I myself am not only insufficient to tell it in words, but even fully to grasp the marvel in my mind. For he sent no man away who ever came to him, nor ever rejected any who desired to live with him, neither blind nor lame nor halt nor crooked nor maimed; but all alike were fostered in the wide bosom of his mercy. He shrank not from receiving men with their womenkind bearing sucklings on their backs; none was driven away, however mean or contemptible or poor. Wherefore pupils or orphans hearing this —such as beg their livelihood from door to door, or tend other men's flocks in the fields—hearing this (I say), they would comfort each other, saying, "Let us also go to that haven where all are received." And, when St Bernard sat in the midst of them—let me not be ashamed to say, brethren, or you to hear these things which this most merciful servant of God was not ashamed to do, for he held nothing shameful except sin—let me say then, when he sat in the midst of them, and saw all these halt or lame, these limbless trunks of men, these blind or scrofulous or maimed or wry-grown creatures, then he would silently consider within himself that these are perchance those weak things wherewith the Lord confoundeth the strong, and of whom He saith that of such is the kingdom of heaven. For God hath chosen the weak things of this world to confound all strong things. Therefore he would comfort them, exhorting them to bear patiently for a while the evils of this brief life, and saying: "Dear sons, suffer ye for a little while and faint not, and comfort yourselves with hope in God, who never deserteth those who hope in Him.... Sing therefore in your hearts unto the Lord, saying: 'Lord, all my desire is before Thee, and my groaning is not hid from Thee. Hear our prayers, and bring us up out of the horrible pit, out of the miry clay.' And God shall wipe away all tears from your eyes; and your sadness shall be turned to joy; and ye shall be satisfied when this glory shall appear."

Mabillon, *Annales Benedictini*, vol. V (1740), p. 508, quotes from a contemporary chronicle, under the year 1109, the answer of Otto, Bishop of Bamberg, to those who asked him why he spent so much money on founding monasteries, which were already so numerous everywhere.

32. THE MONK'S VOCATION

THIS whole world (he would say) is a place of exile; and, so long as we live in this life we are pilgrims to the Lord;[1] wherefore we need spiritual stables and inns, and such resting-places as monasteries afford to pilgrims. Moreover (he would add), the end of all things is at hand, and the whole world is

[1] Mabillon reads *a domino*, but it is difficult to accept this.

seated in wickedness; wherefore it is good to multiply monasteries for their sake who would flee from the world and save their souls. And, lastly, I do all this for the full honour of God and for the succour of my neighbours.

Vitalis of Mortain was one of the great monastic reformers of the late eleventh century. At his instigation William Count of Mortain, grandson to William the Conqueror, founded an abbey of nuns. The following letter to Vitalis from Marbod, Bishop of Rennes, tells its own tale (Mabillon, *Annales Benedictini*, vol. V (1740), p. 444, an. 1104; cf. also p. 293).

33. THE NUN'S DOWRY

MARBOD, least of bishops, to Vitalis the servant of God, wishing all perseverance in good works. We have heard that thine Order is studiously bent upon winning souls. We hear that thou seekest not thine own, but others' profit, that their souls may be saved, so that thou art reported to have founded, with God's help, a nunnery, wherein thy compassion faileth not even to that frailer sex of women. Wherefore, beloved brother, I appeal with all supplication to thy holiness, that thou wilt deign to receive into thy flock a certain girl under wardship, who desireth to serve God in virginity but is destitute at present of all human help. For her father in the flesh hath been converted from the world and taken the monastic vow, and her mother is too poor to dream of buying her daughter a place in any rich nunnery. For, albeit the maiden is not without tincture of letters, yet in the ancient monasteries of our parts we have the evil custom that money is preferred to knowledge. For this cause I have thought fit to take refuge in supplication to thine Order, which is doubtless free from this contagion. Grant me therefore this request, beloved brother, not so much for mine own sake as for His who is father of orphans and judge of widows; yet be assured that I also will gladly grant unto thee whatsoever thou mayest think fit to require of mine humility.

34. AN AGEING WORLD

(Dugdale-Caley, *Monasticon*, vol. v, p. 247.)

IN the name of the Father and of the Son and of the Holy
Ghost, and in honour of St Mary the mother of our Lord,
I Stephen, Count of Boulogne and Mortain, providing and
consulting in God's hand for the salvation of my soul and
of that of my wife the Countess Matilda, and for the soul of
my lord and uncle Henry, King of England and Duke of
Normandy, and for the souls of all faithful people, both quick
and dead, in this year of our Lord's incarnation 1126—seeing
that the bounds of this our age are breaking and falling daily
into decay—seeing, again, how all the transitory pomp of
this world, with the flowers and rosy chaplets and palms of
flourishing kings, emperors, dukes and all rich men do wither
from day to day;[1] how, again, death casts them all into one
mingled mass and hurries them swiftly to the grave—seeing
all this, I give, grant, and make over to God and to St Mary
of Furness, and to the abbot of that monastery, all my forest
of Furness and Wagney with all hunting rights therein, and
Dalton, and my whole domain in Furness, with all men and
other appurtenances, in wood or plain, by earth or by water,
and Ulverstone, and Roger Bristoald with all that pertaineth
to him, and my fishery in Lancaster, and Guarin the Little,
with all his land, and soc and sac and toll and theam, and
infangthefe, and all that is contained in Furness save only
the land of Michael Fleming. All this I give for the purpose
and tenor that monastic and regular order, by God's grace,
be kept in that house. This gift, therefore, I decree with all
my princely authority to be kept inviolate for ever; moreover, I maintain and ordain that all else be kept equally inviolate, which the present or future devotion of the faithful
shall contribute to them in Christ. Moreover, that these
things may remain unshaken and unbroken throughout all
eternity, I myself here make subscription with mine own

---

[1] "Perish the roses and the flowers of kings," Wordsworth, *Excursion*,
Book VII.

hand, and fortify this present charter with the sign of the holy cross.

> The sign of Henry, King of England and Duke of Normandy ✠ The sign of Thurstan Abp of York ✠ The sign of Bishop Audin ✠ The sign of Richard Bp of Bayeux ✠ The sign of Richard de Seale ✠ The sign of Robert Earl of Gloucester.

For Peter the Venerable, St Bernard's friend and contemporary, the reader should consult chaps. xxi–xxiii of S. R. Maitland's *Dark Ages*, or the monograph by M. Demimuid, *Pierre le Vénérable* (Paris, 1895). He was one of the greatest abbots of the greatest monastery in Christendom; and we have precise evidence of the reasons why he wrote his *Book of Miracles* and why Balthasar Beller printed them at Douay in 1595.

Peter writes in his first Prologue: "Seeing that the grace of miracles hath a place of no small dignity among the gifts of the Holy Ghost, as a grace of such profit to other men that it hath been the chief means of liberating the world from the darkness of infidelity and of bestowing the eternal light of truth; since, moreover, even now in the hearts of many of the faithful, to whom it hath been given to see this light, faith is increased by this grace of miracles, and hope grows, and truth is confirmed; for these reasons, I am often indignant to think that those wonders which are wrought in our days perish and are buried in barren silence, no man applying his mind to write them down, though, if published abroad, they might profit all that read them. Therefore, since I could compel no man to this task but myself, I have chosen to undertake the task in such style as I could command." In the Prologue to his Second Book, he speaks far more bitterly of the neglect of such writings and studies in his own time as compared with the past, and in Latin Christendom as compared with Egyptians, Greeks, and Hebrews.

Beller, his printer and editor, dedicates the book to the Abbot of St-Vaast d'Arras, Privy Councillor to Philip II of Spain. He had planned a series of the most noteworthy books of the Middle Ages,[1] "of the older fathers, who not only lived in better ages than our own, but strove to leave the purer thoughts of their minds to posterity...among whom not the least place is due to this Peter, whose learning and piety have rightly earned for him, side by side with the blessed Bede, the title of *Venerable*." In these days "wherein Catholics decay by their own fault, and heretics

---

[1] This he partly fulfilled in his editions of Vincent of Beauvais, Thomas of Chantimpré, Jacques de Vitry, etc.

grow from day to day in unbridled fury," he thinks it will be of great profit to prove how richly Catholicism, and Catholicism alone, is endowed with the grace of miracles. We have here, therefore, a book which both twelfth-century and sixteenth-century monasticism recognized as typical and authoritative.

The following extract, from Book I, chap. xiv, is characteristic of the frequent presence of visible demons in the monasteries (Migne, *Pat. Lat.* vol. 189, col. 877). It is also interesting through Peter's answer to a question which besets the modern reader on almost every page of these medieval records, but which it required some real spirit of criticism to raise in the twelfth century.

35. THE BESETTING DEMONS

AT another time another brother, who was a carpenter,[1] lay by night in a place somewhat removed from the rest. The place was lighted with a lamp, as is customary in the dormitories of monks. While he lay on his bed, not yet asleep, he beheld a monstrous vulture, whose wings and feet were scarce able to bear the load of his vast body, labouring and panting towards him, until it stood over against his bed. While the brother beheld this in amazement, behold! two other demons in human form came and spake with that vulture—or rather, that fiend—saying, "What doest thou here? Canst thou do any work in this place?" "Nay," said he; "for they all thrust me hence by the protection of the cross and by sprinkling of holy water and by muttering of psalms. I have laboured hard all this night, consuming my strength in vain; wherefore I have come hither baffled and wearied. But do ye tell me where ye have been and how ye have prospered." To which the others made reply: "We are come from Châlons, where we made one of Geoffrey of Donzy's knights fall into adultery with his host's wife. Then again we passed by a certain monastery, where we made the master of the school to fornicate with one of his boys. But thou, sluggard, why dost not thou arise, and at least cut off the foot of this monk, which he hath stretched in disorderly fashion beyond his bedclothes?" Whereupon the other seized the monk's axe which lay under the bed, and heaved it up to smite with all his force. The monk, seeing the axe thus raised

---

[1] He was therefore probably a lay-brother.

aloft, withdrew his foot in fear; so that the demon's stroke fell harmlessly upon the end of the bed; whereupon the evil spirits vanished forthwith. The brother who had seen this vision related it all forthwith, next morning, to the aforesaid father Hugh,[1] who sent to Châlons and to Tournus to assure himself of the truth thereof. Here, searching narrowly into those things which the demons had asserted, he found that these ministers of lies had told the truth.

But some man will say: "Seeing that the evil spirits far surpass all human cunning in the subtlety of their malice (for their natural nimbleness is clogged by no bodily weight, whereby they are rendered free in all their motions and all the more sagacious by long experience), how is it that they betray their wicked designs or deeds to men's ears?[2] Do they not understand how often men are saved from their most subtle snares by these revelations of their wiles, and the demons are thus frustrated of their purpose? Wherefore, then, did they betray their evil deeds in the hearing of that brother, and confess themselves unable to work the wickedness that they desired?" To this we must answer that, great as are their powers for evil, and prompt as is their will to deceive us, yet by God's hidden disposition they are oftentimes so wondrously and incomprehensibly caught in their own false wiles, that they are sometimes compelled unwillingly to serve that human salvation which is always contrary to their desire.

---

[1] Fifth Abbot of Cluny, sainted by the Roman Church. It will be noted that Peter, at this second mention, betrays the actual name of the monastery where the scandal had taken place.

[2] It needed a narrator of Peter's intellectual distinction to raise this question in the twelfth century, though it is suggested to the modern mind by almost every medieval miracle in which demons are represented as playing a visible or audible part.

36. CHRISTMAS DAY

(Ib. c. xv (Migne, *Pat. Lat.* vol. 189, col. 880).)

I T is the custom of Cluny to celebrate the Saviour's Nativity with singular affection, and with more devotion than any other solemn feast; not only with melody of song, with longer lessons in church, with the light of multitudinous tapers, but (far beyond all this) with special devotion and copious shedding of tears, in joyful unison with the Angelic Host.

It is scarcely possible to exaggerate the emphasis which monastic writers lay upon the value of helping monks, and the danger of vexing them. In the *Miracles de St-Benoît*, which Gabriel Monod rightly singled out as one of our most important sources for French social history from the ninth to the eleventh century, about 150 miracles are told with a good deal of detail. Of these, just about half point a selfish moral, recounting the punishments which fell upon men who neglected St Benedict or his monks, and the inexorable vengeance which pursued all who had done them actual wrong. The two following passages from Peter the Venerable are chosen because they illustrate this not in its crudest but in its least objectionable form; to these I subjoin one of the *Miracles de St-Benoît* as a specimen of grosser egoism, yet far more interesting than the common tales of mere celestial retaliation.

37. THE FATE OF SACRILEGE

(a)

Petri Venerabilis *De Miraculis*, lib. I, c. xxviii (Migne, *Pat. Lat.* vol. 189, col. 903).

T HERE is in Spain a noble and famous town called Stella,[1] and methinks not inaptly, whether we consider its position or the fertility of its adjacent lands or the multitude of its inhabitants, wherein it surpasseth all towns in that neighbourhood. Therein dwelt a burgher named Pedro Engelberti, who, famed for his strenuous life and abounding in worldly possessions, passed almost his whole life, even to old age, in the world. At length, touched by Him who bloweth whither He listeth, he renounced this world and took the cowl in

---

[1] This would be either St James of Compostella, or Estella.

the Cluniac monastery which had been built at Nazara. Thither I came two years after this man's conversion, and heard that he had told a memorable vision whereof the report had come even unto us, yet without the name of its author. Having heard this, I enquired anxiously after him who had told this marvel, and learned that he dwelt in a certain cell hard by the monastery of Nazara, whereunto it was subject. My journey and my business took me to this place, where I found a man marked out for complete faith by his ripe old age, and the gravity of his manners, and the witness that all men bore of him, and the snowy whiteness of his own hair. Nevertheless, willing to drive all scruple of doubt not only from mine own heart but from all others also, I summoned him before my companions, the venerable Bishops of Oloron and Osma, men of much piety and learning, and before others also.[1] Then, showing him how He who is the Truth damneth all such as speak lies, and adding many words more of the same sort to deter him from falsehood, I then not only exhorted him to tell me what he knew for certain concerning that vision, but also commanded him to do so, in virtue of that obedience which he, a monk, owed to me as Abbot. To which he replied, in words which taught us that which we had never guessed before, saying: "These things that ye ask of me I have not heard from another, but have seen, from beginning to end, with mine own eyes." Whereat we rejoiced all the more, knowing now that we had no repeater of others' words, but him who had most certainly seen the thing in itself. Wherefore, being all the more eager to question him and the more intent upon his words, we could brook no longer delay, but all enjoined him strictly to relate what he had seen. I will here introduce him as speaking in his own person, that ye who read or hear this story may have not only the sense of his words, but the words themselves as they came from his lips.

In the days (said he) wherein Alfonso, King of Aragon, sat on the throne of Alfonso the Great, lately deceased, it

---

[1] Peter took great care, according to the ideas of evidence current in the twelfth century, to verify the miracles he relates. See, for instance, lib. I, cc. vi, ix, x, xxvii, and the Prologue to lib. II.

came to pass that he raised an army against his adversaries in the kingdom of Castile. He decreed, therefore, that each household of his kingdom should send one horseman or one footman to that host. In obedience to that command, I myself sent one of my hired servants, Sancho by name, to fight. After no long absence, he came home again with the rest of those who had taken part in that expedition; and, within a short while after, some natural sickness fell upon him which, after a brief struggle, carried him off. It might have been four months after his death that I lay in my bed at Stella beside the fire in winter-time; and suddenly, about midnight, this Sancho appeared to my yet waking eyes. He sat down by the fire and, turning the coals hither and thither as though to obtain greater warmth or light, he showed himself all the more unmistakably to mine eyes. Now he was unclad, with no garment but a vile and scanty rag to cover his nakedness. At this sight I said, "Who art thou?" and he humbly answered, "I am Sancho, thy servant." "What dost thou here?" said I. "I am on my way," said he, "to Castile, and a great host with me, that we may pay the just penalty of our misdeeds in the very place where we wrought them." "Why then," said I, "hast thou turned in hither?" "Because," said he, "I have yet some hope of pardon, and thou, if thou wilt have pity on me, canst the sooner procure my repose." "How then?" "I will tell thee how. On that expedition that thou knowest of, inspired by warlike licence, I and certain of my fellows broke into a church and robbed it of all that we found; and I carried off the priestly vestments; for which sin I am tortured with especial and horrible pains, which I pray thee, as my master, with all possible earnestness, to remedy; for thou canst succour me if thou wilt strive on my behalf with spiritual benefits. Moreover, I beseech thee to pray the lady thy wife, as from me, that she delay no longer to pay the eight shillings [*solidos*] which she legally oweth for my service; that the money which, in my lifetime, would have been given to my bodily necessities, may now be spent upon the poor for the sake of that soul of mine which hath yet sorer need."

Peter enquired after the state of one or two other citizens of Stella, lately dead, and at last after "King Alfonso, dead these few years past."

THE FATE OF SACRILEGE

Then answered another voice, from the window-seat hard by my head: "Ask not of this man, who hath but lately come among us and knoweth not, seeing that he hath not yet had time to learn these things. But I died five years ago, and have dwelt ever since with those spirits, and can tell you much that is unknown to this new-comer." I was amazed to hear this second voice; and, wishing to see the speaker, I turned mine eyes towards the window. There, by the light of the moon, which clearly illumined the whole house, I saw a man sitting on the lower window-ledge, and clad in the same garb as the other. "And who art thou?" said I; whereunto he made answer: "I am the companion of this other whom thou seest; with whom, and a whole host more, I am on my way to Castile." "Dost thou, then, know aught of King Alfonso of whom thou speakest even now?" "I know where he was; but where he is now I know not. For he lay once in bitter torment among the guilty souls; but the monks of Cluny have since taken him away from thence; and I know not what is now become of him." With these words he turned to his fellow by the fire, saying: "Arise now, and let us go on our way. See now how all the ways, both within and without this town, are thronged with the host that came after us; and how many have gone swiftly by, and there is sore need that we should press hard after them." Thereupon Sancho arose, and repeated in lamentable tones his former prayer, saying: "Master, I beseech thee not to forget me, and do thou instantly exhort my lady thy wife to pay that unto my wretched soul which was owing unto my body"; with these words he vanished in the twinkling of an eye; and I cried hastily to waken my wife who slept beside me in the bed. Before telling her what I had seen and heard, I asked whether she owed anything to Sancho, our common hired servant, for his wages; to which she replied that she owed him eight shillings. Seeing then that I had never heard this before, save from the dead man's lips, I could doubt no longer; for my wife's tongue had confirmed the ghost's story. Wherefore, at daybreak, I took those eight shillings from my wife, and added a congruous portion of mine own; all which I distributed partly among the poor, partly for the succour of holy masses

115

which, at my prayer and by my care, should work to the fuller remission of his sins.

Here then have I written down this noble and noteworthy vision, word for word, for the edification of faith and morals among men both of our own time and of the days to come [*tam modernis quam posteris*]; thus declaring, by the testimony of the dead themselves, how great caution is necessary to men. But it is no small testimony—nay, it is the clearest of all testimonies—to the truth of this vision, that the dead man should have told how King Alfonso had been taken up by the monks of Cluny, and snatched away from the torments wherein his guilty fellows lay. For it is known wellnigh to all men in Spain and France, that this king was a great friend and benefactor to the monastery of Cluny. For, to say nothing of his other innumerable acts of piety towards us, this most magnificent and famous king made himself and his kingdom tributary to Christ's poor, for that same Christ's sake, paying yearly to our monastery a tribute, founded by himself and by his father Fredelan, of 240 ounces of gold. Besides which, he built at his own cost two monasteries in Spain, and allowed other men to build others, and himself gave help thereunto; in all which he set monks of Cluny, and gave abundantly of his royal liberality that they might have wherewith to serve God Almighty according to the Rule. Moreover, he restored the fervour of monastic religion, which had almost died out in Spain; by which zeal it may justly be believed that, after his kingdom on earth, he earned for himself an everlasting kingdom also. For he obeyed that benign precept of the Eternal King, and made himself friends of the mammon of unrighteousness, by which friends (according to the tenor of this vision), when his earthly stewardship was past, he was not only snatched from torment but received into everlasting habitations. For what could be more congruous to that eternal justice which rendereth to every man according to his works, than that he should be visibly taken forth from those pains by the men whom he had helped? that they should have mercy upon him, upon whom he himself had taken pity? that they should restore him to the life of the blessed, whose life he had sustained by abundant largesse amid the miseries of this present world? Truly that was no voice of deceit that St John heard from on high, saying, "the works of the dead follow them"; for was not the truth thereof made manifest in this king, whom God snatched from torments, and rewarded with the rest due to the spirits of the blessed, on account of his works of mercy, and as it were through the hands of those to whom that mercy had been shown?

(b)

Duchesne identifies the villain of this story with William, surnamed *The German*, Count of Burgundy 1097–1107, and quotes from an earlier chronicler what is probably the source of the legend: "William Count of Mâcon, nicknamed *Greasy-Mouth*, was excommunicated by the Abbot of Cluny because he vexed the monks of that abbey; wherefore, when he strove to walk, he was unable to set one foot before the other." (*Ib.* lib. II, c. i (Migne, *Pat. Lat.* vol. 189, col. 909).)

First then, to the terror and correction of evil princes, let us relate that which came to pass at Mâcon, where almost all the inhabitants tell frequently and publicly of a strange event, such as I think was never heard in any other place since the world began....It befell upon a time that a certain man took the government of this city under the style of *Count*, and exercised an execrable tyranny over ecclesiastical persons and possessions. He went far beyond the wickedness of other such robbers, not merely robbing portions of the church goods, but seizing to himself, with tyrannical violence, all their wealth and revenues. For, casting canons forth from their churches, and even monks from their monasteries, he mercilessly took to his own use all those lands and revenues which our forefathers had given to sustain them in this present life. The men of that province still show the ruins of ancient churches from which he expelled the men of holy religion, making a waste and a wilderness of those venerable places, once thronged with a multitude of God's pious servants. Thus this Count withdrew himself altogether from God, forgetting hell and the terrible judgments of the Almighty, like unto that judge of the Gospel who feared not God, neither regarded man. Thus for many years he abused the power committed unto him, waxing from day to day in wickedness; until there was now no hope of his amendment, so that he kindled against himself the irrevocable wrath of God Almighty, and learned by dire experience that Scripture truth: *It is a fearful thing to fall into the hands of the living God.* Moreover, seeing that his iniquity had not been hidden but public—seeing that he had provoked God not fearfully but boldly, not stealthily but openly, not in the closet but on the housetop—he was made a terrible example to tyrannical princes. For, on a solemn day, as he sat in his own palace at Mâcon, amid a multitude of knights and men of all ranks, suddenly an unknown man rode on horseback through the palace gate, and, while all gazed upon him in amazement, came riding thus to the Count's own throne. Then at last he drew rein, saying, "I would fain speak with thee, O Count," and commanding rather than exhorting him to arise and follow. The prince, drawn by some invisible and irresistible power, arose and went to the palace door, where he found a horse ready; upon which, at the stranger's command, he mounted. The other forthwith seized the reins, and rose upwards like a mighty rushing wind before the eyes of all men. Then the whole city was moved at the wild and horrible wail that burst from their Count; and, flocking together to this unexampled spectacle, they stared upwards in horror, and followed his airy flight to the utmost limit of human vision. Long they heard his cries: *Help, my citizens, help!* Yet they were powerless to succour him; until, vanishing at last from the sight of man, he received his reward and entered into the everlasting fellowship of demons. From this horrible sight all men went back to their homes, having learned, as aforesaid, by this unheard-of and lamentable example, how fearful a thing it is to fall into the hands of the living God.

Not only doth common report of all men testify to the truth of this story, but also a wonderful, though less miraculous, event of our own day. For that devil-rapt Count aforesaid, when he left the palace with his fellow-demon, passed through a door in the wall hard by; which door the citizens built up as a memorial to posterity of their horror at this event. It is not long since Otger, seneschal to Count William, wished to restore this doorway and to pierce it again for some purposes which seemed to be dictated by private or public profit. One day, therefore, he hired labourers and began to remove the blocking stones from the doorway. Now this man also was, according to his power, a bitter persecutor of churches; and, whensoever a small occasion presented itself, he strove in divers ways to vex them. While, therefore, he busied himself in this work, behold! he was caught up by an invisible fiend and lifted far into the air, in the sight of those who were there with him; after which the fiend let him quickly fall, to the grievous bruising of his whole body and the breaking of his arm by this sudden shock. His companions, seeing this, blocked the doorway again, and condemned it to perpetual closure as an eternal memorial of these two miracles.

(c)

A young noble of the Nivernois attacked some of the dependent posses-sions of Fleury, where St Benedict's body was said to lie. In the course of a raid which he had made upon the conventual serfs and flocks, he was killed by one of the vassals of the monastery. The chronicler proceeds to describe the misery of his parents. (*Miracles de St-Benoît* (ed. E. de Certain, 1858), p. 335.)

The father and mother, seeing that their son was dead, and all their hopes with him—for he was their only son—mourned for him with groans and tears which can scarce be described, bewailing with inconsolable grief that child whom they had loved with supreme affection. Then, fearing the future examination of the Just Judge in Heaven—for they were God-fearing folk—they considered how they should provide for the soul, now that all bodily hope was lost, and how indulgence might be found for him who had so wickedly provoked his own perdition. Therefore they brought with them the venerable Bishop of Auxerre and their son's corpse, and sumptuous preparations for his funeral. Thus they came to Fleury, fell at the feet of Abbot Hugh and all the con-gregation of monks, and implored that the prayers of the monastery might deliver their dead son from that guilt; since they held it for certain that this crime would be blotted out from before the face of the Supreme Judge, if those who had suffered from it would first forgive it with all their heart.

To which end they laid in their son's right hand a chalice weighing a pound of gold thrice refined, offering it as a pledge and hoping that he might earn a readier pardon for his offence if his parents paid some compensation for his rash deed. For, as they believed, so often as sacrifice were made in that chalice to God on high, so often would their son have some share in that holy oblation. The brethren therefore, moved with pious pity, sang mass for him with one accord to the Lord Almighty, beseeching that his offences might be pardoned, and themselves remitting the offence against them in accordance with the power that Christ had granted to His own faithful servants. Then, after all funeral offices had been performed with due honour to the dead, his parents and the noble folk who had come with them were sent back to their homes, carrying with them a strong and consoling hope of the son's salvation.

From the *Chronicle* of the Abbey of Morigny, in F. Duchesne's *Historiae Francorum Scriptores*, vol. IV, p. 360. The date is about 1120.

38. A FAITHFUL STEWARD

ARNALD DE CORBEIL gave us the church of Bolret; and thus we obtained the village called Mesnus—nay, no village, but a desert. The land belonged to the nuns of St-Eloy, but it had been devastated by the multitude of invaders and the frequent incursions of robbers. We therefore gave the Abbess and her nuns a proper sum, with a specified yearly rent, and obtained grants from all who could demand dues therefrom, and took for cultivation this long-untilled land. And, when we vainly sought in all our congregation a man fit for this great task, then that Baldwin aforesaid, whose great labours in the matter of the monastery and the dormitory I have already related, offered himself of his own accord, and undertook this almost unbearable weight of care for his brethren's profit. How shall I tell of this man's fresh labours in the restoration of the village? I believe that even he, who endured them, could not easily recount them. This long-untilled land he tilled to the full. Briars and thorns, flints and bushes, and other refuse clinging to the very entrails of the earth, he tore up now with the plough, now with the hoe, now with other tools of the husbandman. He collected there near fourscore dependent peasants.[1] Then certain injurious folk, seeing how the place prospered, began to harass us and to instigate claims upon us. Some threateningly demanded bran for their hounds; others claimed a tribute of our hens; another, that tribute for his protection which men call *tensamentum*;[2] "mine," said a fourth, "are the highway-dues." One demanded this, another that, tormenting our Baldwin (who was ours indeed) with continual vexation. He resisted with all his might, one man against so many; and, now by pleading in the courts, now by giving money, he withstood the assaults of these adversaries. In this sore need, he would go round almost all the land of Beauce in harvest-time, and beg corn from all men with brazen brow, whereby he would gather together a little money to soften the tyranny of his adversaries and to redeem the land from these customary burdens. One harvest-time, when he suffered such pain in his legs or ankles or feet that he could neither ride nor go afoot, he did not blush to be driven round Beauce in a two-wheeled cart, to beg for corn with his pious audacity—or, to speak more truly, he blushed rather than cease from his appointed task. Such was the devotion of this Baldwin to our monastery; may God repay him all his good, honest and faithful deeds; nor to him alone, but to all others also who have built or helped or protected us, or in any other wise sustained us; God have mercy on their souls!

---

[1] *Hospites oblatiarios*: peasants who gave up themselves and their goods to a monastery in return for protection.

[2] Land in the Middle Ages was burdened with an infinity of little dues, often arising from encroachments. Ducange quotes several cases where the monasteries themselves had inherited from different lords this right of claiming tribute from holders of land in return for the protection they were supposed to give: *e.g.* I, Simon lord of Rochefort, "have sold to the religious men, the Abbot and monks of Bonneval, for £4000, all the *tensamenta* which I had in the village of Bonneval and in other villages."

From MS. in public library at Berne, no. 568, f. 7*a*; printed by H. Hagen in his *Carmina Medii Aevi*, Berne, 1877, p. 178. The MS. is of the twelfth century, and the author, though writing in Leonine verse, and taking a good many grammatical liberties, shows on the whole a command of Latin worthy of that golden age of medieval scholarship. When we have made all allowance for his natural self-justification, the story bears every mark of substantial truth, and supplies an interesting contrast to the other cases in which we have seen grave transgressions pass unpunished. Monastic by-laws as to uniformity of dress, occupation, etc., were minute and inexorable; in a strict house, therefore, it was very easy to earn severe punishment. It is not out of place to note here that J. A. Symonds seems over-hasty in assuming the monastic origin of pp. 174-9 of this same volume; an assumption on which he bases important generalizations (*Wine, Women and Song*, 1884, p. 14).

39. THE SHADOW OF THE ROD

I CALL God to my witness; I had put on my robe, as, on holy-days, we are wont to clothe ourselves in white albs. I lie not, it came into my head to go thus to my bed, wherein I am wont to sleep, to fetch a book [which I had left there]. Wherefore dally I with trifles? This was my constant meditation that, if I performed not the fantasy of the moment, I should be nought. O levity of mind tottering on the verge of an abyss, if sudden death had then come upon me for a punishment, and my life had been cut short! Whensoever my mind desires anything, it burns madly and rages wildly, consuming my wretched heart; it is sweeter than honey to me to fulfil my heart's desire; therefore I planned within myself how I would go for that book. It was too much trouble to take off my alb and put on my black frock—all the more burdensome, because the thing seemed of no account.[1] While then I am thinking and debating of this deed in mine own mind, guile cometh to be partner of my meditations, and pleaseth me forthwith above all else. I make for a safe corner, where I slip my frock over the alb, and cover my head with an ancient goat-skin. Thus clad, yet not in safety, I seek my couch. Insecure I walk; care pierces my breast; thieves, at the time of their misdeeds, quake with no

---

[1] This is the best I can make of the verse "venit et hoc oneri, rem pro nihilo remaneri."

more fearful thoughts than I had. Face, head, eyes I keep under strict command; I seize the volume; on leaving my bed, I look back again and again!

O God, O pity! was there ever an order or an age wherein human fortunes were not subject to vanity! Wretch that I am! my hot-headed fault could not truly shun the snares that beset me; I was espied when I thought to walk unseen. For another of the brethren—whom may some black spirit crush and bring to sorrow!—another, I say, was led of the Devil across my path. He saw, he marked all; he laughed within himself and put on a fierce face to me. He took the matter for a crime; he turned my deed into a grave transgression. Worse still, and far worse; his face fell, his colour changed, and he drove me from him with threats; then was I assured that he would never spare me.

Tortured with horrid fear, I hasten back; I cast off my alb, calling no man to be my companion or my witness. Alas! how dark and gloomy was the rest of that day to me! That was no bright or tranquil sunlight; nay, the light itself was darkened by fear, embittered by tears; that daylight lacked all the light of God. O Phoebus, may thy shining orb deny its beams to the world this day! Such were the last hours that I led before sunset; but more funereal than these, and fraught with fiercer terror, were the pains that I felt when night came on. That was one long starless and moonless night, dreary and sleepless beyond all others; since, in passing, it was destined to bring me a second death. For, with the rising of the day-star, my mind was tortured with redoubled pains; the whole weight of the planet lay upon me; I shuddered to see the sun. Soon the bell rang even as the customs of our Order prescribe; now is the hour when the fatal doom hangs over all guilty heads. We rise without delay; to be brief, the time is come when all erring minds and souls quake for fear; we enter that house[1] where all things are hard, without justice or law, the house of a thousand fears. First walks the abbot; after him follow the congregation. We enter; the abbot first reads the chapter from the Rule; then *Benedicite*; then pours forth a flood of words without reason. The

---

[1] *I.e.* the Chapter-House.

brethren care little to speak of things in general; all the sharper is their discussion of special points; most garrulous and most insistent now are those whose learning is least. While thus they debate, they lay upon their fellows with the rod; and now, in the midst of these things, a dirty fellow, the very dregs of our congregation, sets himself to make known what he saw of me yesterday. The convent hears all; the younger monks smile; but other grim brethren murmur hoarsely and gnash their teeth, until the debate is almost become an open quarrel. To the young it is sport, for young men turn lightly to laughter; but the withered old lips flow with their wonted venom, "O deadly deed! never was such a thing done before! Who shall endure such actions from any man? O, how grievous! O, how nefarious!" and again, "This mad deed must be sorely punished, lest others should think such things to be lawful." With such words doth the pitiless faction cry down the more merciful. To the judgment-seat I come, and fall prostrate and raise my head again, confessing my fault and asking for no indulgence. Why indeed should I beg mercy? I lost nothing by my silence; I lost no chance of pardon that might otherwise have been vouchsafed to me. Why seek we compassion from those who have none in their hearts? We should seek in vain; therefore I stand stoutly by myself. These were the years wherein savage tyranny reigned in our Chapter-House; no love of honour, but fraud and strife and clamour; harshness beyond measure, a burden intolerable to be borne; a doting mind that dreamed of forming us to good by cutting away all that was unspoken of in the Rule; gravity that strove to constrain all our lives under the weight of the Order. There stood I, poor wretch, waiting before the Crucifix for mine own excruciation, and loathing the light of day. What could one do whose life pleased not himself? Yet with pure heart I stood up before them all, yea, before the Prelate himself, as God stood before Pilate. They whose misdeeds are most grievous are they who come near and bark against me now. I call God Almighty to witness that, even as the wolf before the lamb, so stood I unmoved before my judge. Then at last the doomsman pronounced the strict doom of the law; the very memory of that penance doth wellnigh renew its pain; my heart and my ribs grieve whensoever I think thereon. The Father gave the horrid hateful doom that I should forthwith be stripped of my garments. Hard was the sentence, yet, willy-nilly, I obeyed; for God Himself hath bidden that the condemned man should obey his angry judge. There cleave I naked to the ground; upon me they begin to wreak their heavy vengeance; I am scourged, poor wretch, until I almost give up the ghost in my misery. The two stout arms that smite upon me are ready to fail for weariness. What can I say or do? Nought availeth me; neither cross, nor image [of Christ] thereon, before whose face I suffered such grievous torment this hour. Who would not marvel that none could be found to pity this poor wretch? Unable to bear the stripes, I cast myself to the ground; tortured and fainting, while my blood flowed on every side. I had given up the ghost, had this wrath endured but a little longer; yea, I had become an unprofitable carcase. But, when my blood began to flow, then the Lord, who healeth all wounds, touched the heart of these butchers, and unnerved their pitiless sinews; wherefore the brethren left me there bruised and scourged to the utmost—brethren, say I? nay, for they never were my brethren, nor ever shall be!

40. MONASTIC QUARRELS

(a) FROM THE PAPAL STANDPOINT

From E. Pérard, *Recueil*, 1664, p. 105.

BISHOP INNOCENT [II], servant of the servants of God, to Hugh [II] the illustrious Duke of Burgundy, health and his Apostolic benediction. The controversy which hath long raged between our sons Herbert Abbot of Dijon and the monks of St-Seine hath now been decided by the prudent discretion of our dear brother Stephen, Abbot of Cîteaux, to whose wisdom we committed the case to be concluded by way of justice or of concord. But the aforesaid monks, intoxicated with the spirit of pride, have not only neglected to keep the agreement prescribed by this our brother aforesaid, but have done the flat contrary. For, invading a certain manor pertaining to St-Étienne [de Dijon], they poured forth the wine of the brethren of that monastery, broke the wine-casks, and despoiled the whole manor both of its beasts and of its other goods. This doth the more grievously affect us, insomuch as we have heard that these things have been done under cover of thy favour....Wherefore we command thy nobility to cause the aforesaid concord, made by this wise and careful man, to be observed; and to take all care that the said abbot be no more molested on this account. Otherwise, we fear lest it be imputed to thee if, being able to hinder this evil, thou hinder it not. Our dear daughter the duchess, thy spouse, we salute and bless in the Lord. Given at our palace of Lateran, June 18 [1134].

(b) FROM THE MONASTIC STANDPOINT

Edmund of Hadenham, a monk of Rochester, seems to have died about 1307, at which point his work breaks off. This is a world-chronicle containing nothing original except a few notices of his own convent, which are printed by H. Wharton in *Anglia Sacra*, vol. I, pp. 341 ff. The following episode is from p. 353.

1291. This year died Master Thomas of Inglethorpe of pious memory, Bishop of Rochester, and was buried on the 16th of June....A few days after his funeral, the whole community went out in procession to Frendesbury to pray for rain. But the wind was contrary to them, so that the dust was whirled into their eyes and their processional ceremonies could scarce be seen. When they had sung mass at Frendesbury, the Prior prayed the Master of [the hospital of] Strode that he and his monks might be suffered to go through his orchard. The master acceded at once, adding: "Yea, and beyond mine estate also, if need were." But two of the brethren of that hospital, hearing these words, were filled with indignation. Deeming that this would turn to the prejudice of their house, they hastened with certain ribalds at their heels to the postern-door whereby the monks must go out, seeking to impede their passage. So our brethren, coming to that postern, found no free egress; wherefore one of them asked of the master: "Didst thou not grant us a free passage?" to which he made answer: "Yea indeed, and again I grant it." Then one of the monks broke down the postern door and seized upon one of the brethren of the hospital, John of Ash by name, whom he cast upon a dunghill; and other monks, bearing banner-poles, drave away the guards of the postern. Others wrested cudgels from the hands of the ribalds, and smote a certain married clerk of the opposite party, whom they absolved from guilt but not from punishment.[1] In truth they denied this clerk a plenary indulgence, and the Archbishop's absolution followed. After which deeds the monks went on their way chanting the litany *Domine miserere Christe*, followed by the greater litany, *Out, out, out!* This then was the end of that procession, unto this present day.

The offensive use of banner-poles on ecclesiastical processions was already of ancient date. There was a yearly congregation of all the parishes of the diocese at each cathedral church, at which the clergy and select parishioners went in procession, each with the banner of his own church. (E. L. Cutts, *Parish Priests and their People*, 1898, p. 121.) This sometimes led to struggles for precedence, and fights with banner-poles. Bishop Grosseteste, in his synodal statutes for Lincoln diocese (about A.D. 1236), thus directs his archdeacons and parish clergy: "Moreover, cause strict prohibitions to be published in every church, forbidding certain parishes to fight with their banners for precedence over other parishes, during the processions at the annual visitation and veneration of the mother-church; seeing that such fights are wont to result not only in quarrels but even in cruel bloodshed." This is repeated still more emphatically in the synodal decrees of Bishop Langham of Ely in 1364: "Seeing that this is wont to result not only in fights but in deaths" (Wilkins, *Concilia*, vol. III, p. 61; cf. a similar quotation given by Cutts from Bishop Storey of Chichester in 1478. Bishop Giffard of Worcester, in 1292, complains that even swords were drawn in such fights; see his *Register*, ed. J. W. Willis-Bund, 1898, p. 422). These documents show that the exploits of Frère Jean des Entommeures with the staff of his processional cross were drawn from the life.

[1] An allusion to the technical phraseology of full ecclesiastical absolution, as granted (*e.g.*) by a plenary indulgence, *a culpa et a poena*.

Abbreviated from a contemporary letter of Marsilia, Abbess of St-Amand at Rouen, to Bono, Abbot of St-Amand in Flanders, printed by Du Moustier in his *Neustria Pia*, 1663, p. 187. Considerable fragments of the convent of St-Amand still remain at Rouen, not far north from the cathedral.

41. A NUNNERY MIRACLE

IN the year 1107, in the village of Lissy, a woman was so hard beset by the Devil that she was first distressed by various fantastic and malignant cogitations, and then, losing her natural senses, set all her wits to work to make an end of herself by hanging or drowning or in some other fashion, in the absence of her attendants. This she would have done, but that her husband had oftentimes come in suddenly and hindered her. For she had been deluded by a silly woman, restless and garrulous, who had beset her with her lying stories at home, in the fields, and in the streets, persuading her that her husband hated her and loved another woman with whom he sinned in secret. She, believing these lies even as our mother Eve believed the serpent, fell into a deadly melancholy; and, forgetting God and the Christian faith, she set all her purpose on ending her wretched life by some diabolical artifice. But the merciful God, who would that all men should be saved, forbade this project to the greater praise and glory of His confessor St Amand.

They took the wise resolution of bringing this madwoman to our church, which is believed to have from our Saviour a special grace of miracles which no demoniacal power can resist. In this place she was visited and exhorted by friends of both sexes and of sound faith, who besought her earnestly to fortify herself with the saving sign of the cross; which however she utterly refused, saying that she was predestined to hell, and hourly complained of the delay that kept her from perdition. Then it was resolved by those whose faith was pure and whose understanding was more perspicacious than the rest, that a barrel should be filled with holy water, and that on the morrow she should be plunged therein by the hands of the priests, with invocation of Christ's name and power and might. She, carefully noting and understanding these things, was sore dismayed, and began to fall into a hotter fit and to sigh more heavily than ever. But then, looking round on the company, her diabolic cunning impelled her to put on an outward show of moderation, while within she seethed with the Devil's own fury.

Wherefore, at eventide, she was brought forth from our choir, and set before the altar whereat St Amand himself had been wont to sing Mass. Then, as the shades of night began to fall, her friends departed and left her to the appointed guards. But—O devilish subtilty! O treachery of that Ancient Serpent against mankind!—this wretched woman, finding the moment propitious, fraudulently persuaded her guardians to rest now from all the watchings and labours wherein they had wearied themselves on her account, and now to refresh their worn-out bodies with sleep. She feigned also that she herself was sore wearied and in need of rest; for now seven days and nights had gone by since she came to us. They therefore made themselves couches, and lay down in some comfort, and gave themselves for a while to sleep. She then, seeing that she was alone, rose in her bare shift and climbed softly to the highest part of the wall, where she bound half of her head-cloak to the top of a pillar, and made the other half most subtly into a running noose, into which she slipped her neck. Then, falling heavily forwards, she stretched her neck with such violence that a gout of blood gushed forth from her throat and stained the wall over against her. And now it was past midnight, and one of the guardians awoke and rose from his couch; who, finding her gone, searched around the church until he found the place where she hung, and, with great horror, discovered her stiff and lifeless corpse.

This man cried aloud, and shouted the untoward event to his companions. At this, the nuns rushed in from all the convent; the church was filled with cries. They mourned for the miserable corpse, and called on St Amand, with many groans and tears, that he should not suffer the worthiness of his house to perish, but should deign in his clemency to succour those who flocked unto him. Then a light was kindled, the hanging neck was set free from the noose; and the lifeless corpse was cast down upon the church pavement.

Then three of the sisters, bolder or wiser than the rest (for it was still night), sought out the Archdeacon, and besought him with tears to tell them what was to be done. He, answering, advised them to drag the body forth from their church before dawn, and to cast it into the first pit they met. Moreover, he came back with them, and mingled among the clamorous throng, marvelling at this extreme and diabolical cunning of the woman. Meanwhile some of the nuns drew near, and one marked how a little breath struggled for revival in her breast, and saw how her face flushed faintly now and then, and her eyes opened, and at intervals she sighed deeply. Then the bystanders, marking all this more closely, raised a great cry for the succour of their patron St Amand; and, beating their breasts, multiplied their prayers. Then they suddenly saw how, by the power of God Almighty and by the intervention of His glorious and admirable Bishop St Amand, the soul was come back into her body. Yet on that day of her resurrection, and throughout the following night, she remained speechless; nevertheless her bodily strength was such that four men could scarce hold her. On the morrow, at dawn, her first words were, "Holy Lady, loving Mother of God, Mary, be thou my help!" after which she opened her mouth to praise our Saviour and His holy confessor [St Amand], and from her inmost heart poured forth plenteous thanks to Almighty God.

This wondrous miracle hath been noised abroad far and wide, so that our glorious and marvellous God is magnified in the person of His holy bishop, through whom so many miracles are marvellously wrought. For as St Amand, in this life, raised up by his prayers a dead robber hanging upon the gallows, so now in heaven, living with Christ, by His precious merits he recalled to life this miserable hanged woman, to the praise of our Lord Jesus Christ, who alone liveth and reigneth everywhere with the Father and the Holy Ghost, one God, world without end.

42. THE BANDIT CLOISTERED

Abbreviated from Bk II of the *Chronicle of Morigny* (A. Duchesne, *Hist. Franc. Scriptt.* vol. IV, 1641, p. 365).

THEOBALD, Count of Chartres and Blois, [and nephew to Henry I of England,] being a Count Palatine, and next to the King himself in possessions within the kingdom of France, began from his youth upwards to trouble King Louis [le Gros] with war, as though he had an hereditary right to rebellion. By reason of which scandal all France was kindled to warfare, by the wilfulness of the princes on either side, who inflamed the minds of King and Count against each other. Hugh de Creciago was the chief fomenter of all these evils, exceeding the rest in impious counsels and crimes. He was a man of boldness and promptitude, a feigner and a dissembler in all matters, grinding the faces of the poor and slaying the peasants to satisfy his cupidity, as one who would willingly run through the whole course of misdeeds and crimes in a single moment. This man treacherously seized Milo of Montlhéry, a young man of excellent disposition and warlike courage, his kinsman and his feudal lord; whom he then bound with chains and cast into prison. But, in the Psalmist's words, he fell into the pit which he himself had digged. For, being unable to keep him longer in chains, and daring not to release him or take a ransom (as one who thenceforward would be his mortal foe), after dragging him hither and thither in continual doubt what part to choose—at last, led on by the enormity of his own crimes and inspired by the demon of violence, he put an end to his prisoner by that death, most wicked and abominable of all, which the common folk call *murt* [murder]. For he strangled this innocent man by night, and cast the corpse stealthily down from the window of the wooden tower wherein he lay bound; as though Milo had attempted to make his escape. There the body was found in the morning, to the utter amazement and unspeakable grief of all who saw or heard. Then the traitor, with bloodless cheeks and trembling lips, showed outwardly upon his face the manifest signs of his inward torment and his hellish conscience. By God's judgment, to hasten his own ruin, he suffered the corpse to be carried away and buried at the abbey of Longpont, which had been founded by Milo's ancestors. The story was noised abroad in the twinkling of an eye; men and women flocked thither from the neighbouring cities, towns and villages. All were amazed, shedding floods of tears for this new and unheard-of crime, and crying to heaven. The King hastened thither from Paris with a great multitude of princes and knights; at the sight of whose tearful face the crowd multiplied their own wailing, lamentations and groans; and all that multitude cried with one voice for vengeance. Wherefore, after burying Milo honourably in the abbey, all ran impetuously to arms; and, by God's providence, they assaulted and took the Castle of Gumet which stood hard by. Then a great fear fell upon Hugh; accursed of all, deserted by his own men, his heart was filled with amazement and the testimony of his conscience bound his hands and sapped his strength. O marvellous and most happy change of fortune! The traitor was summoned to purge himself by ordeal of battle at the court of Amaury de Montfort, the most noble of all men in that province after the Counts Palatine; and, though Hugh had married Amaury's little daughter, yet he found himself now abandoned by that man wherein lay his only hope, and he dared not to risk the ordeal. Then, being convicted and publicly confessing his guilt, he fell at the King's feet, besought his pardon, gave up all his lands into the royal hand, and took the monastic habit then and there. [Mabillon suggests that he may have become a monk at Longpont, where his victim was buried.]

Guibert de Nogent, from the first publication of his works in the seven-
teenth century, has been known as one of the most interesting auto-
biographers of the Middle Ages: his *Treatise on Relics* and *God's Dealings
through the Franks* [*in the Holy Land*] are no less interesting. His style,
especially in his *Own Life*, is involved and obscure, quite apart from
corruptions of the text; but he was one of the most honest and learned
writers in an age of great intellectual activity; and, though he took
St Bernard's side against Abelard, he shows a critical acumen which can
seldom be paralleled in any period of the Middle Ages. Born near Beauvais in 1053, of noble blood, he lost his father in childhood and his mother
at the age of twelve by her retirement to a convent. His old master having
at the same time become a monk, Guibert ran wild for a few years. At
last, through his mother's and master's influence, he took the vows at
St-Germer, that magnificent abbey-church which may still be seen between
Gournay and Beauvais. The regularity of his life and his fame as a student
earned him the honourable position of abbot at Nogent-sous-Coucy.
After playing a conspicuous part in the Church politics of 1106 and
succeeding years, he retired again to the peace of his abbey, wrote several
books of great value, and died between 1121 and 1124. More specimens of
Guibert's work would be given here, but that his autobiography has recently
been translated in full by Mr C. Swinton Bland (Routledge & Co.).

43. AN ABBOT'S AUTOBIOGRAPHY

(Guibert's *Own Life*: Migne, *Pat. Lat.* vol. 156, col. 856.)

MY mother, while yet scarce of marriageable age, was given
to my father, then a mere youth, by my grandfather's provision. Though intelligence was written plainly on her face,
and nobility shone through the natural and decent gravity of
her features, yet from her earliest childhood she conceived
the fear of God's name. For she had learned so to loathe sin,
not by experience but by a certain impulse of divine dread,
that (as she was wont oftentimes to tell me) it had so steeped
her mind in the fear of sudden death, that in her later and
riper age she mourned to have lost those pricks of godly fear
which had been so lively in her rude and ignorant childhood.
Now it befell that, at the very beginning of her married life,
her husband was so bewitched that their matrimony was not
consummated. For it was said that this union had aroused
the envy of a stepmother who, having herself very many fair
and noble nieces, strove to cast one of these into my father's

arms; failing which, she is said
to have bewitched him by her
magic arts. Wherefore, after
three years of silent suffering,
my father was at last summoned
by his kinsfolk and compelled to
reveal the truth. Think now in
how many ways his kinsmen
laboured to procure his divorce;
moreover, they would have urged
my father to enter a monastery,
little as they spoke then of such
religious Orders; a counsel which
was given not for the sake of his
soul's salvation but in the hope
of succeeding to his possessions.
When therefore this suggestion
proved vain, then they began to
bark daily at the girl herself;
that she, far away from her own
kindred, and harassed by the op-
pressions of others, might at last
grow so weary of this injustice
as to depart from him without
formal divorce. Meanwhile she
suffered all; bearing all the words
that were aimed at her with un-
wrinkled brow, and, whensoever
they led to strife, dissembling as
though she knew it not. Besides
which, some of the richest of our
neighbours, seeing her subject to
this mockery of married life,
began to work upon her mind;
but Thou, O Lord, from Whom
cometh the purity of the soul,
didst breathe into her a holiness
foreign to her nature and her age;
of Thy gift it was that she passed

NOBLE LADY OF THE
TWELFTH CENTURY

From J. Quicherat's *Costume en Fran*
p. 162. A statue of about 1150, proba
representing the Queen of Sheba, forme
at Corbeil and now at St Denis.

through the fire unscathed... Lord, Thou knowest how hardly —nay, almost how impossibly—that virtue [of chastity] is kept by women of our time: whereas of old there was such modesty that scarce any marriage was branded even by common gossip! Alas, how miserably, between those days and ours, maidenly modesty and honour have fallen off, and the mother's guardianship hath decayed both in appearance and in fact, so that in all their behaviour nothing can be noted but unseemly mirth, wherein are no sounds but of jest, with winking eyes and babbling tongues, and wanton gait, and all that is ridiculous in manners. The quality of their garments is so unlike to that frugality of the past that the widening of their sleeves, the tightening of their bodices, their shoes of cordovan morocco with twisted beaks—nay, in their whole person we may see how shame is cast aside. Each thinketh to have touched the lowest step of misery if she lack the regard of lovers, and measureth her glory of nobility or courtliness by the ampler number of such suitors. God is my witness, that there was in those days more modesty in marrying men (who would have blushed to be seen among such maidens) than now among marrying women, who certainly love the market-place and the public all the more for these shameful matters. Wherefore should this be so, my Lord God? but that no man blusheth at his own levity and wantonness, seeing that all the rest are branded with the same mark, and knowing that he himself followeth the same affections as his fellows. Whence, prithee, could he feel shame at such pursuits whereunto he seeth all around him aspiring at the same time? But why speak I of *shame*, when such folk are ashamed only of falling below the rest in indulgence of their lusts?... Thus and in such-like ways is this our modern [*modernum*] age corrupted, thus again doth it spread corruption, scattering broadcast the seed of its own evil conceits; while, by an infinite progression, all such seed doth transmit its own filthiness by propagation to the rest....[1]

(col. 839) I have already related, loving and holy God, my gratitude to Thee for Thy benefits. First and foremost, therefore, I thank Thee that Thou didst endow me with a

---

[1] After more than seven years,..."when a certain old woman had broken those evil charms," the life of Guibert's parents became more peaceful.

mother fair indeed, yet chaste, modest, and God-fearing: for indeed it would have been worldly and foolish in me to write that word *fair*, had I not confirmed this idle epithet with the stern aspect of assured chastity. For as, among the poor, fasting would seem mere compulsion, and therefore the less laudable (since they have no sufficiency of food to do otherwise), yet again the frugality of the rich, in the face of their great abundance, hath its own price; so also beauty, the more desirable it may be, the more highly must we extol it with every title of praise, if it harden itself as a flint against all seducers.... And certainly, although this fleeting beauty be ready to turn with the shifting currents of our blood, yet we cannot refuse to call it *good*, according to the wonted measure of goodness, after the fashion of an image. For if whatsoever hath been ordained to all eternity by God is beautiful, then all that is temporally beautiful must be as it were a mirror of that eternal beauty: since the Apostle saith: "For the invisible things of Him, from the creation of the world, are clearly seen, being understood by the things that are made: His eternal power also and divinity; so that they are inexcusable." Moreover the angels, in appearing to human sight, have always borne a most comely countenance, as Manoah's wife said, "A man of God came to me, having the countenance of an angel, very awful." Therefore the devils, on the other hand (of whom St Peter saith, "These are fountains without water and clouds tossed with whirlwinds, to whom the mist of darkness is reserved"), are wont to appear under the blackest faces (except indeed when they transfigure themselves treacherously into angels of light); nor is that unfitting, since they have fallen from the glory of their noble fellow-citizens [in heaven]...For this cause, O God, I thank Thee that Thou didst instil virtue into her comeliness; for the very gravity of her demeanour might have suggested contempt of all earthly vanity, since a sobriety of glance, a scantiness of speech, and a motionless calm of the features, doth by no means condescend to the levity of onlookers. Thou knowest, O Almighty, that Thou hadst imbued her with the lifelong fear of Thy name as a bulwark against all seductions of the soul. Moreover she had one quality which is seldom or never found among women of great profession; for, by how much she was more chaste through Thy grace, by so much was she the more sparing in her blame of the unchaste; nay, when such tales were sometimes spread abroad by strangers or by those of her own household, she would avert her face, move away from the speaker, and show as much pain at such whisperings as though her own person also were at stake. O God of Truth, Thou knowest that I tell this not from private love, as of mine own mother, but that the thing itself was greater than these poor words of mine could express; especially seeing that the rest of my race were either brute beasts that knew not God, or fierce soldiers stained with blood-guiltiness, and such as must become utter strangers to Thy face, unless Thou have great mercy upon them according to Thy wont.

From this lady then, the truest (as I firmly believe) of all women, Thou didst grant me to be born, the worst of all her offspring. I was her last child in both senses of the word; since my brothers and sisters of better promise are dead and I alone survive whose life was so sorely despaired of.... Wellnigh all Lententide my mother had passed in unwonted anguish before my birth, (an anguish which she would oftentimes recall to my shame when my wayward youth erred in devious paths,) until at last the solemn Sabbath of Easter Eve dawned upon the earth. She therefore, shattered by her long pains, and torn with more bitter agony, as the hour drew near, even when men hoped in the course of nature for my birth, felt her travail to be more and more in vain. My father, and his friends and kinsfolk, were in despair, since they feared no less for her life than for mine. It was a day whereon no private services were held beyond the one divine office that was celebrated at its own fixed hour; wherefore necessity, the mother of good counsel, drove them to the altar of God's Mother, to whom, the Only Virgin before and after her Son's birth, they made these vows and laid this oblation as a gift upon the altar that, if the child should prove to be a male, he should for God's sake and his own be shorn a cleric; but if of the less noble sex [*sin deterior*], that she should be sealed to a suitable [religious] profession. Whereupon, at that very hour, a sort of sickly abortion was born, so abject that men rejoiced only at the mother's deliverance. For this new-born creature was so miserably lean that it seemed like a corpse born out of due season; so lean indeed that the frail rushes of those parts (for it was then almost mid-April) were laid side by side with my fingers, and seemed less meagre. Nay, on that very day, as men bore me to the baptismal font, a certain woman turned me from hand to hand (as hath oftentimes been told me in sport during my boyhood and youth), saying, "Think ye that this creature can live, whom half-hearted Nature hath put forth almost without limbs, and with a thread rather than a body?..."

(col. 843) Thus then I was born; and scarce had I begun to play with childish toys, when Thou, loving Lord—for Thou wast thenceforth to be my Father—when Thou didst make me fatherless. For, after the lapse of some eight months, my fleshly father gave up the ghost; wherefore I thank Thee most heartily that Thou didst make this man to die in the mood of a Christian, who, had he lived, would doubtless have hindered Thy purpose in me. For, seeing that my childish prettiness, and a certain vivacity natural to that tender age, seemed proper and fit for this world, therefore no man doubted but that, when the time for school-learning should come, he would break the vow which he had made for me. But Thou, in Thy good providence, didst wholesomely dispose that I should not lack this early teaching in Thy laws, and that he should not break the vow once made to Thee.

Thus she, Thy widow indeed, nurtured me with painful care. When I was set to learning, I had indeed already touched the rudiments, yet I could scarce put together the simplest elements when my loving mother, eager for my teaching, purposed to set me to Grammar.[1] There had been a little before, and there still reigned partly in my time, so great a scarcity of grammarians, that scarce any could be found in the towns, and few indeed in the cities; moreover, even such as could be found were of slender learning, not to be compared even with the wandering hedge-clerks of modern days. This man therefore, to whom my mother was purposed

---

[1] In the extended sense, of course, in which it still survives in our phrase, *Grammar School.*

to give me over, had begun to learn Grammar at an advanced age, and was so much the more rude in that art, that he had known so little thereof in his youth. Yet he was of so great modesty that his honesty supplied his lack of learning.... When, therefore, I was set under his care, he taught me with such purity, and guarded me so sincerely from the irregularities which are commonly begotten in that tender age, that he kept me altogether from the general games, never suffering me to go forth unaccompanied, nor to eat away from home, nor to accept any gift without his leave; he broke me in to all temperance in word, in look, in deed, so that he seemed to demand from me that I should live not only as a clerk but as a monk. For, whereas the others of my age wandered everywhere at their own will, and the reins were loosed in all due liberty with respect to their age, I for my part was shackled by constant restraints, sitting in my little clerical cloak and watching the bands of playing children like some tame animal.... While, therefore, he lay so hard upon me, and all who knew us thought that my little mind must be sharpened to its keenest edge by these incessant pains, yet all men's hopes were frustrated. For he himself was utterly ignorant of the arts of composition, whether in verse or in prose; so that I was smitten with a grievous and almost daily hail of fierce words and blows, while he would have compelled me to learn that which he himself knew not. With him, under this vain struggle, I spent almost six years, wherefrom I gathered nothing worthy of so great and long-standing labours.... For weary nature should sometimes find her remedy in some diversity of work. Let us bear in mind how God formed His world not in uniformity, but with vicissitudes of day and night, of spring and summer and autumn and winter, thus refreshing us by the changes of the seasons.... Wherefore that man loved me with a cruel love.... When he took so bitter a revenge upon me for not knowing that which he knew not himself, he might clearly have seen how great evil he had done; since he demanded more from my frail little mind than he himself possessed. For as a madman's words can scarce be understood, if at all, even by wise men; so when a man knoweth not, yet saith that he knoweth, and would

fain teach another, then his words are but darkened by the
very earnestness of his explanation.... Yet, though my master
chastised me with such severity in all other ways, he made
it plain that he loved me almost as he loved himself.... And
I, though dull and childish for my age, had grown to love him
so in return, although he so often and so undeservedly bruised
me with his rods, that I utterly forgot his severity and regarded him not with fear, as did other boys of my age, but
with a deep and heartfelt love. Often indeed, and in many
ways, my master and my mother proved me (seeing that I paid
them both a due and equal reverence) to see whether I should
presume, under any compelling circumstance, to prefer the
one to the other. At length opportunity brought experience,
so that neither could doubt thenceforth. One day I had been
beaten in my school, which was none other than a hall of our
house; for my master, in his care for me alone, had now left
the teaching of those others whom he had formerly undertaken, as my wise mother had required when she increased
his salary and honoured him with her patronage. So, after
a few of the evening hours had been passed in that study,
during which I had been beaten even beyond my deserts,
I came and sat at my mother's knees. She, according to her
wont, asked whether I had been beaten that day; and I, unwilling to betray my master, denied it; whereupon, whether
I would or no, she threw back my inner garment (such as men
call *shirt*) and found my little ribs black with the strokes of
the osier, and rising everywhere into weals. Then, grieving
in her inmost bowels at this punishment so excessive for my
tender years, troubled and boiling with anger, and with
brimming eyes, she cried, "Never now shalt thou become a
clerk, nor shalt thou be thus tortured again to learn thy
letters!" Whereupon, gazing upon her with all the seriousness
that I could call to my face, I replied, "Nay, even though
I should die under the rod, I will not desist from learning my
letters and becoming a clerk!" For she had promised that,
if I would be a knight when the time came, she would endow
me with arms and all that I needed for such a life. When,
however, I refused all this with bitter scorn, then, O God,
that maidservant of Thine took so gladly these insults in-

flicted upon her, and was so rejoiced at this contempt of herself, that she revealed to my master this very answer and refusal of mine; and both exulted together that I should seem to aspire with all the ambition of my soul towards that life which my father had vowed for me.

How Guibert's mother, anxious to fix this vocation, entered into a simoniacal bargain which was to thrust this boy of eleven into a rich canonry, and how the married canon who had been thus extruded regained his benefice by excommunicating the pious lady, should be read either in the original or in Mr Bland's translation (Routledge & Co.).

Guibert gives precious glimpses also of his relations with his fellow-monks; the following extracts begin in Migne at col. 847 (lib. 1, c. 6). Guibert had just left his widowed mother rejoicing at his resolve to abandon the idea of knighthood, and take clerical orders.

44. MONASTIC INTERIORS

YET Thou knowest, O God, that this resolve sprang not so much from deep religion and reflection, as from boyish impulses which swayed me at the moment. But, so soon as my youth, big with that which it had conceived from original sin, brake forth into all loss of shame, then that early devotion of mine withered utterly away....

At length my mother began to strive that she might bring me, by hook or by crook, into some ecclesiastical benefice.[1] The first case of this kind was not only evil, but even wicked. One of my youthful brothers, who was a knight and castellan of Clermont-en-Beauvaisis, was awaiting a sum of money from the lord of that town, either as a donation or as a feudal due. The lord put this off and off, being unable, as I believe, to spend so much. Wherefore certain of my kinsfolk took

---

[1] Bourgin here notes: "The papacy, at this very time, was forced to accept the results of these family intrigues. The fifth chapter of the Council of Rome in 1099 runs: 'With regard to those whom their parents' cupidity has thrust by simony into churches or benefices while they were yet of tender age [*parvuli*], if they are now willing to live therein with canonical regularity, and will first formally resign them, we grant of our mercy that they may then retain them'."

counsel and suggested to him that he should give me a canonical prebend in the church of that place; which prebend lay in his gift, contrary to Canon Law; whereby my brother might no longer be pained to pursue him for that debt. In those days, the Apostolic See had made a fresh assault upon the married priests;[1] by reason whereof the common folk, jealous of the clergy, were roused to such a pitch of madness against them, and so bitter an enmity, as to insist that the married priests should either be deprived of their benefices or should abstain from their sacerdotal functions. Whereupon one of my cousins, a man of great power and worldly prudence, yet so beastly in his sensual indulgence that his promiscuous amours were notorious, raged as fiercely against the clergy in virtue of these decrees as though his detestation of their fault had been due to his own singular chastity....Therefore, seizing an occasion of aiding me at the expense of a certain fat[2] priest, as the vulgar saying goes, he went straight to the lord of the town, over whom he had power enough and to spare. From him he obtained that I should be called, in the absence of this cleric and without warning given, and invested with the man's canonry....He, thus despoiled of his prebend by which alone the hierarchy had a hold upon him, began earning his living as a free mass-priest, keeping his wife all the while. Presently it was noised abroad that, at these masses, he was wont daily to excommunicate my mother and all her family. She, who was ever fearful of holy things, dreading the pains of sin and all offences whatsoever, renounced forthwith that ill-gotten canonry, and hired me another from the lord until the cleric who held it should be dead. Thus we fled from the iron spear and fell upon the brazen bow; for to give money in expectation of another man's death is no other than to command daily homicide.

(col. 849) But let me now, so far as it is germane to the story of my own time, touch somewhat more deeply upon the affairs of those religious Orders and those conversions which I have seen, taking example from this monastery [of St-Germer]

---

[1] See Council of Amalfi (1089), cc. ii and xii, and of Clermont-Ferrand (1095), c. ix.

[2] *Loculosi*, literally "money-bagged."

and from many other salutary changes of life. That the monastic purpose flourished in ancient days is certified by abundant written evidence....But, according to that word of the truthful poet, "Things cannot stand long at their highest point"; and (far more truly still) by reason of the world's decline, giving free rein to iniquity, the charity of holy conversation grew cold. Wherefore it came to pass that some monasteries gradually lost that affluence of riches which they had enjoyed; and, seeing that manual work itself decayed, those that were of good conversation became rare. Wherefore, in my days, some most ancient monasteries, reduced by time to scanty numbers (though of old they had superabounded with wealthy gifts), were content with small congregations, wherein very few could be found who had turned their backs on the world through loathing of sin. Nay, the monasteries were for the most part in the hands of such as had been devoted thereunto by their pious parents, and had been nourished therein from their childhood. Such monks, by how much less they feared for their own sins, which they never believed themselves to have committed, by so much more remissly did they pass their lives within the monastic precincts. These men, getting possession of administrations and external offices either from the necessity or from the caprice of their abbots, and being greedy to follow their own will, while they had little experience of liberty outside the convent walls, were wont to fall easily into dilapidation of church goods; after squandering which, they would draw from the regular income. And, even though the Rule was so little kept among them, yet monks were then the more precious for their very fewness.

Guibert then passes on to relate two notable revivals which took place towards the end of the eleventh century, connected with the names of Everard, Count of Breteuil, and St Bruno, founder of the Carthusians. He tells also how his mother, in her widowhood, built herself a house at the gates of the great monastery of St-Germer-de-Fly, near Beauvais; here she gave herself up to prayer and penance.

(col. 863) My mother, while yet dwelling in the village of Catenoy, had resolved to devote herself to the monastery of St-Germer. Therefore she built herself a little house hard by the monastery and, under the guidance of my former master of whom I have spoken, she at length left her former abode. Thenceforward, knowing me now to be wholly an orphan, with no other help or shelter—for, though I had many kinsfolk, near and far, yet was there none who would care intimately for this little boy, tender even beyond the wonted helplessness of his years; who, though lacking neither food nor raiment, was yet constantly vexed for want of those fore-thoughts which his tender age demanded, and which women alone can supply—knowing me, I say, to be given over to such negligence, yet her heart was hardened, O God, by fear and love of Thee. Wherefore, when her journey to St-Germer took her under the very walls of the town wherein I dwelt, the very sight of it filled her with intolerable grief, so was her heart torn with anguish, and so bitter was her pain at the thought of what she left within those walls....

(col. 865) She then, as I have said, thus gave a bill of divorcement unto the world; and I was left alone without mother, without teacher, without master. For that [priest] who, next to my mother, had so faithfully taught and brought me up, had now betaken himself to the monastery of St-Germer, impelled thereunto by the example, the affection, and the advice of my mother. I therefore, left in evil liberty, began most intemperately to abuse this power over myself. I scoffed at churches, I hated the schools, I sought the company of my lay cousins, who were bent upon knightly sports. I cursed the mark of my clerical state, promised myself that my sins would one day be forgiven, indulged in that sleep of which so little had been allowed me in the past, and began to stagnate in this unaccustomed sloth....My mother heard that I now bore myself so much the more dissolutely,—nay, madly—as I had lived before under stricter discipline. Impatient of these tidings, she betook herself unto the abbot, who, at her prayers, granted that my old master should teach me again. For he had been taught in my grandfather's castle and had received many benefits from that court; wherefore he readily acceded to my mother's request; he welcomed my coming, received me kindly, and treated me thenceforward with greater affection. O God, by whose good providence these things came to pass, I call Thee to be my witness here; from the very first moment that I entered this conventual church, and saw the monks sitting in their order in the choir, the sight of these men kindled in me a desire for the cowl which never cooled again; nor had my soul rest until its desire had been fulfilled....At length I disclosed this to my mother; who, fearing my childish levity, reasoned so strongly against my purpose that I was heartily sorry to have told her my mind. I spoke to my master, who rejected me still more unceremoniously; which two refusals vexed me so sorely that I resolved to turn elsewhere. Therefore, bearing myself as though I desired the cowl no longer, I waited from the octave of Whitsunday until the feast of Christmas. Then, burning still with desire to fulfil this purpose, and impatient of the heart-pricks with which Thou, O Lord, didst ply me, I cast off all reverence for my mother and fear of my master, betook myself to the Abbot, and fell at his feet, and besought him with bitter tears to receive me, a sinner, into his flock. He, meanwhile, had desired this no less fervently, yet had never been able to draw from me a clear promise in spite of all his solicitations; wherefore he gladly granted my petition. The necessary garments were prepared in all haste; he brought them forth the very next day; and, in the sight of my mother who stood and wept afar off, he clothed me as a monk and bade that alms should forthwith be distributed that day.

Meanwhile my former master, whom the strict Rule forbade to teach me further, strove nevertheless to spur me on to discuss the Holy Scriptures which I read, to reflect with the help of the more learned brethren on the less familiar phrases, and to compose anthems and verses; whereunto he laboured the more strictly to persuade me, in proportion to the carelessness of the others concerning my education. And, O Lord, O true Light, I remember well the inestimable bounties which Thou didst then shower upon me. For no sooner had I taken Thy dress at Thine invitation, than a cloud seemed forthwith to have been lifted away from the face of my heart, and those things soon began to grow clear, among which until now I had groped like a blind man. Moreover,

I was suddenly inspired with such a desire to learn that my whole heart was set upon this one thing, and my life seemed vain if I spent a single day without some such labour. How often was I thought to sleep, and to rest my tender limbs beneath the bedclothes, when either my mind was struggling with the pains of composition, or I was reading a book under the blanket, hidden from the censure which I feared from others!

And Thou, loving Jesus, knewest well my purpose in this matter; for I did it in the hope of praise and of greater honour in this world. In this, my foes were my friends, who did indeed persuade me to do well, yet constantly suggested to me the praise and glory of letters, whereby men may come also to wealth and to dignity; wherein my friends laid hopes worse than the eggs of asps in mine improvident heart, and deluded me with vain expectations, since I thought that all their promises would quickly be fulfilled. They set before me not only that learning wherein (with Thine aid) I was daily increasing, but also my noble birth in the world and my shapely form; but herein they forgot that Thou hast forbidden us to go up to Thine altar by such steps as these; for thus is our nakedness discovered. For he who climbeth up some other way into the sheepfold, the same is a thief and a robber (Exod. xx, 26; John x, 1).

But the Devil, who by long experience hath learned how to deal with each soul according to its state and quality and age, prepared new assaults against me in consideration of my disposition and my tender body. For he brought the shapes of dead men oftentimes before my sleeping eyes, and especially of such as I had ever seen slain with the sword or any other deadly weapon, or such as I had heard of as having been slaughtered. By such visions did he terrify my helpless drowsy spirit, that by night I could neither be kept in my bed, nor held back from crying aloud—nay, I could scarce command my senses, unless my master were there to watch and guard me....O Lord God, I then bore myself not as I bear myself now; then I lived altogether under great reverence for Thy law and infinite execration for all sorts of sin; and I drank in with the utmost eagerness all that could be said and heard and known of Thy word.[1] I know, Heavenly Father, that the Devil was goaded to madness by this boyish zeal of mine, and that he was destined to be placated by my later lukewarmness. It came to pass one night, (in winter, as I think,) that I woke up in anxious misery and lay in my bed, thinking myself more safe by reason of the clear light that came from a lamp hard by.[2] Suddenly, hard by, there rose a cry of many voices in the deadness of that night— voices, it seemed to me, of the elder monks. There was no sound of words; but by the mere force of that calamitous cry, that seemed to smite my temples into deadly sleep, I swooned away; and there I seemed to see a dead man who (as they cried aloud to each other) had died in the bath.[3] This vision filled me with horrible fear; I started from my couch with a loud cry, and, looking behind me at that first moment, I saw how the lamp was out and how, in the midst of this vast and shadowy darkness, a devil stood by me in bodily form. At this foul sight I was almost mad with affright; until my masters, who often watched by me to moderate these terrors, had by their prudent care brought me back from this frenzy to a whole mind....

(col. 869) When therefore, with the gradual growth of my body, my soul also was tickled by worldly temptations, according to the measure of its concupiscence and itching desires—then, I say, revolving frequently in my mind how great a man I might have been in worldly life, I brooded daily over the same thoughts, and oftentimes imagined things far greater than truth would allow....And, being troubled at times with the spirit of *accidie*[4] (for I suffered many manifestations of envy from my superiors and mine equals), then I began to seek, with the help of my parents, for the means

---

[1] We must, of course, beware of taking too seriously what Guibert says here and elsewhere of the contrast between his early fervour and his gradual coolness in later age. In imitation of St Augustine, he makes his whole autobiography into a confession of sin.

[2] It was a general regulation that a lamp must burn all night in the dormitory.

[3] The bath was a comparatively rare event; see my *Five Centuries of Religion*, vol. I, p. 215 and Appendix 27.

[4] An untranslatable term of medieval casuistry, answering most nearly, perhaps, to *melancholia*. It implies inertia, despondency, and almost despair. See Chaucer, *Parson's Tale*, "Accidie...maketh [a man] hevy, thoghtful and wrawful."

of migrating to another monastery. For some of those at St-Germer, seeing how in times past I had been far beneath them in age, in learning, in power and in knowledge—seeing, again, how (by His only gift who is the key to all knowledge) the thirst for learning did so spur my senses on that I was now their equal, or even, if I may dare so to speak, their superior—these, I say, were so furious against me, and so inflamed with wicked indignation, that they wearied me with frequent controversies and quarrels, and oftentimes made me sorry to have ever seen or known my books. For these men so troubled my studies, and took occasion of our book-learning to move so many quarrels by their continual questions, that their whole aim seemed to consist in driving mine intention away from this study, and in shackling my mind. But, even as oil thrown upon a furnace to extinguish it will but burst out with fiercer flame, so my reason, like a burning fire, did but flame forth stronger and hotter from such attempts to smother it. The questions whereby they thought to crush me did but whet mine understanding and give it a keener edge; the difficulties that they objected would drive me to constant conjecture and reflection and turning over of various volumes, whereby I discovered many interpretations and gained a readiness of reply. Thus, though I was an object of grievous envy to them, yet Thou, Lord, knowest that I bore little or no envy against them; and they, unable to compass their desire of branding me with disgrace, slandered me everywhere as one who was puffed up with his little learning.

The Virgin Mary, however, appeared separately both to Guibert and to his mother, and turned him aside from this un-Benedictine project of changing his monastery.

(col. 872) Meanwhile, I had plunged immoderately into the pursuit of verse-making, so that I laid aside all Holy Scripture for the sake of these childish vanities; and, with mine own self-will for guide, I had come to such a pitch of presumption as to imitate Ovid and the *Bucolics*, and to practise amatory trifles for wrapping sweetmeats or for folding as missives. So, forgetting my strict duty, and casting aside the modesty of my monastic profession, I was allured by the bait of this poisonous licence, only considering whether such courtly speech could be brought within any poet's diction, and never thinking how grievously the purpose of my holy Order was violated by this pursuit to which I was devoted.... Hence it came to pass that my madness so worked within me as to break out into immodest words; so that I composed certain letters that were too thoughtless and intemperate— nay, altogether contrary to honesty. This came to the knowledge of my master aforesaid, who took it very ill....Yet mine irreverence remained the same; for I kept myself to myself, and tempered no jot of these jesting and scurrilous writings. Nay, I wrote such songs still, but secretly, for I seldom dared to show them to my fellows; but oftentimes I ascribed them falsely to other authors, and recited them to such as I could, and rejoiced that they should be praised by those who shared my vows, even though I thought not fit to confess them for mine own; thus, while the author himself reaped no fruit of praise, nought remained for him but to enjoy the fruit—nay, rather, the shame—of his sin. But Thou, Father, didst punish these things at Thy proper time. For, when I fell into misfortune for such work as this, Thou didst then encompass my wandering soul with grievous adversities, and didst crush me under the load of bodily infirmities. Then did Thy sword pierce my soul, and vexation reached unto mine understanding.

He began then to study St Gregory with especial care, under the guidance of Anselm, afterwards the saintly Archbishop of Canterbury.

(col. 875) Hence it came to pass that, when I went with my abbot to a certain monastery of our province, and suggested to him, as a man of great religion, that he should preach a sermon to the brethren in Chapter there, he transferred this task to me, first praying and then commanding that I should take his place....Then the Prior of that house, a man much given to the study of Holy Scriptures according to his power, besought me in friendly fashion to write for him a treatise wherein he might find material for composing sermons of all kinds. But I, knowing that mine own abbot, in whose presence I had preached, would take it ill that I should write such a treatise, approached him with caution, and besought him that he would grant this permission—not as though I cared greatly for myself, but for the sake of this [Prior], to whom he professed affection.[1] He therefore, thinking that it would be but a brief treatise, acceded thereunto; and I, having thus snatched consent from his lips, set to work on the task which I had proposed to myself. [This was the *Moralizations on Genesis*, which stands first in all editions of his works.]...But when my abbot saw that I had commented on the first chapter, he looked most unfavourably on my work, and warned me frequently to cease from writing. I, therefore, seeing that these beginnings of mine were as a thorn in his eye, and taking precautions not only against him but against all others who might thus strive to hinder me, finished my work thenceforward in secret. For I wrote not only this book, but others also, not in a first rough copy on waxen tablets, but straight upon the unchangeable parchment, mentally composing each sentence in its final form. So long as that abbot lived, therefore, all my writings were kept secret; but at his death, seizing the moment when we had as yet no successor, I pressed on rapidly and quickly finished my book....

(col. 879) At length the fire of my desires waxed hot; and, considering that Thou hadst inspired my mind with zeal for every tittle of knowledge, and hadst endowed me with an outer person very proper for worldly honours, and with a lineage not high indeed, yet honourable—these things considered, my own mind and my familiar friends, cruel to me in this one thing, would have persuaded me that I might fitly be promoted to some high or honourable office in the world. And, among these my ambitions, by the stirring of my kinsfolk, rumours of such high promotions came oftentimes to mine ears. Many men flattered me; either as wishing contentiously to fathom my mind, in order that they might then report their treacherous discoveries to mine envious brethren, or as thinking that such zeal for mine honour would please

---

[1] Monod (pp. 72–3) takes it that Guibert preached the sermon in St Anselm's place, and used St Anselm's name to cover his request; but it does not seem possible to get this meaning out of the text. He seems also to misinterpret the abbot's attitude towards Guibert's literary activities.

me, or that my welfare would promote their gain, so that they hankered after better and better things from my fortune. But I, as Thou knowest, O my Creator, recovered from my sickness at Thine only touch and by Thine only inspiration, to the end that Thy fear should make me scorn to seek from men, or to consent or parley with any man who offered unto me such gifts as are in Thine only hand; that is, honours in Thy Church....But, O God my God, by how many adversities and by how much envy was I then oppressed! so that my mind surged secretly towards these outward suggestions as to a refuge from temptation; yet did this inward seething ambition never come so far as to pass my lips. For, though I was troubled, I spake not.[1] Thou knowest, O Jesus, that to one man who devised such a plan as this, yet not at my instigation, I was once so sinful as to say, "What thou doest, do quickly"; yet Thou knowest how I repented thus to have spoken....At length, God not willing that I should be farther deluded, I persuaded these men, who thus solicited on my behalf, that for the sake of their own souls they should turn elsewhere; so that the monks of certain abbeys, who trusted in these men to procure my election, must needs at length apply in other quarters....Then, for the first time, I learned inwardly to taste unity and purity of will, and the felicity of a mind fixed without afterthought upon perpetual poverty. Yet, O Lord, how momentary was this paradise! How small this respite, how short-lived and uncertain was this deep sense of sweetness! Scarce had I tasted it for a few months; scarce had Thy good Spirit, which had led me into the right land, brooded for a brief space upon my newly-enlightened reason, when lo! it was as though Thou hadst said: "When thou willedst, I would not; now thou wilt not, and the thing displeaseth thee; yet, willingly or unwillingly, now must thou take it!" for suddenly I was elected by monks in far-off parts, hitherto unknown to me.[2]...The small learning that I had acquired, and the hope of possessing a person who taught, as men said, outside his own monastery, had dazzled and bleared the eyes of my electors....But Thou knowest,

---

[1] The quotation is from Ps. lxxvi, 5, Vulg.
[2] Nogent-sous-Coucy is about eighty miles, as the crow flies, from St-Germer.

O God, how hardly and how ill my mother took this election. Where others saw honour, she saw horror; for no such promotion as this had been in her thoughts for me. Therein she feared the perils that would beset mine unripe age, the more so as I was utterly ignorant of law and worldly business;[1] for, having given all my time to letters, I had never heeded to learn these other things. Yet she, in common with all my familiar friends, had constantly dinned into my ears that I should not long remain without promotion of some sort.... O God, by how many warnings did she strive to banish all greed from my mind! How certainly did she foretell those adversities and evil fortunes which have in process of time fallen to my lot! how did she warn me against the desires of unstable youth, and refrain my mind that wandered from maze to maze in thought! so that, to hear her thus discourse, thou wouldst not have thought her an unlearned woman but a most eloquent prelate.

Guibert goes off here into long stories of strange events that happened at St-Germer in or about his time; these should be read in Mr Bland's translation.

He then gives an early history of his new monastery, of the common legendary type—a place sacred even before the Christian era—legends of "a woman not yet born, who was destined to give birth to God and man" (a similar story is told of Chartres), a far-off king of the Britons who brings relics from Jerusalem thither, etc., etc. The story becomes historical only with Guibert's penultimate predecessor, Abbot Henry, towards the end of the eleventh century. Then came Godfrey, who was promoted to the see of Amiens in 1104; and then Guibert was elected.

(col. 894) This village of Nogent is under the little fortified town called Coucy, which is a new place built, it is said, by the husbandmen of this land, who are full of wealth and pride, for defence against their enemies. The town of Coucy, therefore, is of no antiquity. But Nogent, whereof we now speak, was surrounded in old days by woods rich in all game, and watered by the river Ailette, rather profitable than great; for it is more plentifully stocked with fish than other more famous streams. This river wanders in no fixed bed, like others,

---

[1] *Ignarus rerum forensium penitus.* A great deal of the abbot's work, as we learn explicitly from other chroniclers and implicitly from a host of other documents, demanded a considerable business knowledge, especially of Canon and Civil Law.

but stretches in a succession of dead waters, still and broad as fish-ponds. The hills that rise on either side are clothed on their steep slopes with vineyards; the soil is rich everywhere in corn and wine and all good fruits, while the river waters and fertilizes the meadows far and wide....(col. 898) When Godfrey was elected to rule this abbey, seeing that he bore himself with much prudence, and that both nobles and common folk had both the will and the power to endow abbeys, many lands and revenues flowed in unto him in these years. For he was one who knew well how to suit himself to the quality of the laity, showing himself ever affable and liberal, and helping them in matters of law and public business whereunto he had given no small attention. For indeed the men of those days whereof I have spoken at the beginning of this book were most liberal-minded in endowment of monasteries, giving much land and money, and giving their goods more cheerfully to such purposes than their sons will give us now a bare good word.[1] Since therefore in the monasteries around us the Rule was less strictly kept than it should have been, and since Godfrey with his monks showed to great advantage in this matter, even as the smallest light will shine in the midst of darkness, so the time was opportune for conferring fame on this abbot by the display of his own self-command, and by his good command over the monks whom he ruled. He would neither commit himself, nor suffer in others of this monastery, the guilt of simony; he would have no money bargain, but chose his monks only for grace, esteeming the deed of filthy lucre to be as execrable as is its name.[2] Therefore, since this man obtained a greater reputation than his fellow-abbots for public business, and was therefore better known in cities and towns, his name was first talked of for some richer abbey, and then for a bishopric. At that time the see of Amiens had been vacant nigh upon two years; and this Abbot Godfrey had been the proctor of a certain archdeacon of that city

[1] This is not merely the usual medieval regret of the good old days; the eleventh century had in fact been a time of most exceptional liberality and activity in monastic endowment.

[2] Canon Law strictly forbade the reception of monks or nuns for money; but this is only one of many passages indicating that obedience on this point was exceptional enough to call for special notice.

who had the favour and suffrages of a part of the clergy and people.[1] Thus, what with his astuteness in worldly matters, and what with the advantage which his monk's cowl gave him, he himself was chosen for bishop....His beginnings there were in accordance with his reputation, and for some years fame trumpeted his praises abroad; but now it may be plainly seen that his glory, once red-hot among men, is now grown not only lukewarm but cold....To this abbey, then, which Godfrey left, and wherein, if he had been content with his present fortune, he might have lived in all freedom and prosperity, without raising any adversary—to this, as I have said above, was I now called by a chance election.... And, howbeit we are wont to pay greatest reverence to those whom we least know, and yet that none of my monks' consciences were hidden from me at my first entrance, but that they opened their minds to me in faithful confession, by that openness they did so bind themselves unto my soul that I, who thought myself to have seen [many] monks elsewhere, knew none who could be compared in this particular with these of Nogent.

This is practically the end of Guibert's autobiography in the strict sense. The rest of his *De Vita Sua* is taken up with a few stories of occurrences at his different monasteries, and with the history of the first attempts to form a "commune" at Laon—an account which is of great value in the history of civilization, but which tells us next to nothing about Guibert except showing him as, politically, a strong conservative. This story may be found in A. Thierry, *Lettres sur l'Histoire de France*, letters 18 to 20.

[1] *I.e.* his proctor at the Roman court. Favour at the royal or papal court, or both, was very necessary for a great bishopric; and a candidate who had no special reason to trust his own skill in Canon Law, or the length of his purse, would commonly employ a proctor to manage the affair for him.

The great royal abbey of France was that of St Denis, standing to Paris as Westminster stands to London. It is pretty certainly to the abbots of St Denis that St Bernard refers in his letter to Guillaume de St Thierry in 1125: "I lie, if I have not seen an abbot riding with a train of sixty horses and more; on seeing such men pass by, thou wouldst say that they are not fathers of monasteries but lords of castles; not rulers of souls, but princes of provinces." Mabillon suggests that this, and other writings of St Bernard, contributed no little to the conversion of Abbot Suger, who in his later days combined the qualities of a good monk with those of a very great royal minister. St Bernard welcomed this conversion in his 78th epistle, written to Suger himself about 1130, from which the following is abridged.

45. A ROYAL ABBOT

A GOOD report hath gone forth into our land, which will doubtless turn good to greater good in all souls whom it may reach. For all God-fearing men, hearing how great things God hath done for thy soul, rejoice and marvel at so great and so sudden a change of the right hand of the Most High.[1] Everywhere thy soul is praised in the Lord; the humble hear thereof and are glad; and even those marvel who know thee not, yet who hear by bare report of the change from what thou wert to what thou art, and who glorify God in thee.

Who hath suggested this perfection to thee? For myself I confess that I yearned indeed to hear of such a change, yet dared not to hope for it. Who would have believed that thou wouldst reach the summit of virtue at one leap, so to speak, and touch the very topmost height of good works? But God forbid that His infinite mercy should be measured by the narrow rule of our faith or hope! God worketh as He will in whomsoever He will, hastening the work and lightening the burden. If thou hadst corrected thine own self alone, nought would have been left for us to carp at. Our one and only complaint was thy bearing and pomp on thy journeys, which showed somewhat too overweening; wherefore thou hadst but to dismiss this pomp, to change thy bearing, and

---

[1] Ps. lxxvi, 11, *haec mutatio dexterae Excelsi*, where the A.V. (Ps. lxxvii, 10) has, "the years of the right hand, etc." This Vulgate text was, very naturally, a stock quotation for any sudden conversion.

thou couldst easily have allayed all men's indignation. But thou hast not only satisfied those who blamed thee, but hast added a reason for praise [by reforming not only thyself but thy fellow-monks]. Among the angels there is great joy at the conversion of one sinner; what then of a whole congregation? What of such a congregation as this?

This had long been a noble monastery, of royal dignity; kings were wont to use it for their tribunals and assemblies. The things that were Caesar's were rendered unto Caesar without fraud or delay; yet the things that were God's were not so faithfully rendered to God. I speak of what I have not seen, but heard; men say that the cloister was oftentimes thronged with knights and troubled with worldly business; it echoed to the sound of quarrels, and was sometimes opened even to women. Under such circumstances, what room was there for thoughts of heaven or of God or of spiritual things? But now God is contemplated there, continence is studied, discipline is guarded with care, and holy books are read. A continual silence, and a quiet unbroken by any din of secular folk, compel men now to meditate on heavenly things. Moreover the travail of continence and the rigour of discipline are relieved by the sweetness of psalms and hymns; and shame for the past tempers the austerity of this changed life. The fruit of a good conscience which is now reaped in patience doth also work the desire of future good—a desire which shall not be frustrated, and a hope which maketh not ashamed.

The Saviour rebuked certain men who made of the house of prayer a den of thieves. He therefore will doubtless be commended, who on the contrary hath laboured to save holy things from the dogs, and pearls from the swine; he by whose zeal and industry Vulcan's smithy seems to have been reclaimed for heavenly studies, and God's house to have been restored to God, and this church, which had become a synagogue of Satan, to have been brought back to its first state. Not that we have disclosed these past evils for the confusion or rebuke of any man, but in order that the glory of this new state may shine forth the fairer and more pleasant by comparison with the old. Lest any occasion of offence or confusion creep in, we may repeat unto you those words of the Apostle: *And such were some of you; but ye are washed, but ye are sanctified.* No secular folk have access now unto God's house; no curious folk can pass into the holy place. There is now no confabulation with idle persons; the wonted hubbub of boys and girls is no longer heard. While ye beat your breasts with your hands, and the church pavement with your knees; while the altars are heaped with vows and prayers of devotion, and your cheeks are tarnished with tears, and your chambers re-echo with groans and sighs, while, instead of the din of legal pleadings, your sacred vaults ring with spiritual songs, then there is no sweeter spectacle to the angels of heaven, nor no more grateful sacrifice to the King of Kings. When, in former days, I saw thee so greedily sucking the bait of death, the nourishment of sin, from the lips of those who fawned upon thee, then was I wont to pray for thee and to groan within myself, *O that thou wert as my brother, that sucked the breasts of my mother!* (Cant. viii, 1). Now indeed my desire is fulfilled.

Suger's own *Story of mine own Administration* exemplifies admirably both the economic value of relics in the Middle Ages, and the admirable use to which an able administrator might put his revenues and his opportunities. Suger, in rebuilding his great abbey-church, is commonly counted as the pioneer of the true Gothic style in Europe; the following extract shows how much good he was able to do in a smaller sphere (A. Duchesne, *Scriptores*, vol. IV, 1641, p. 339).

46. MONASTIC THRIFT

[I N the parish of Essone] the tyrannical lords of the castle of Corbeil, frozen hard in their own wickedness, had so miserably subdued all things to themselves, that they left scarce anything upon the bare ground and sacrilegiously converted the parish to their own uses as though it were lawfully theirs. One chapel remained, which was said to be dedicated to St Mary; a smaller I never saw. It stood half in ruins, in a place called *Les Champs*; and therein was an ancient altar overgrown with grass, whereon the sheep and goats would

often feed. In this place, as many folk testified, burning
tapers were oftentimes seen on Saturdays,[1] betokening the
holiness of that place. This had impelled many sick folk, first
from the neighbourhood and then from other parts, to flock
hither in the hope of healing; and they were healed. When
therefore, by God's providence, the place was frequented by
so many folk from far and near, we sent thither our venerable
brethren of blessed memory, Hervé the Prior and Eudes de
Torcy, to serve our Lord and His blessed Mother there, and
to do all they might for exalting that little chapel and fitting
it to prayer. Then forthwith, within a brief space, so great
an abundance of miracles blossomed forth, to the admiration
of all men, that the two monks were beloved of all, extolled
by all, and their possessions were by some men increased. For
a multitude of sick folk laid down their infirmities at that spot
—men vexed by unclean spirits, blind and lame and withered.
[Here follow two specimen miracles, of an ordinary type.]

This place, therefore, divinely ennobled by these and other
signs of miracles and prodigies, we strove to honour and exalt
for the love of the Mother of God. Wherefore we began
forthwith to prepare for building, and chose twelve brethren,
with a prior, to form a convent there. We built a cloister,
refectory, dormitory, and other offices demanded by the Rule.
We furnished the church decently with ornaments, priestly
vestments, robes and copes.[2] We sent thither two texts, our
old daily text [of the Gospels], and the grail that the Emperor
Charles had given us. We put there a comely Bible in three
volumes. Nor were we less solicitous for the brethren's
livelihood. We endowed them with two ploughlands on our

---

[1] The day sacred to the Virgin; Saturday afternoons were sometimes kept as
a holiday in her honour.

[2] *Palliis et palliorum cappis*, an instance of the loose and general use of the word
pallium. The *grail*, or *gradual*, was a book containing the music of the mass. In
this connection it is worth while warning the reader against a strange misstatement
upon which Cardinal Gasquet has based one of the main conclusions of his *Old
English Bible*. On p. 169 of the 1st ed. and p. 148 of the 2nd, he argues, without
attempting to quote any authority for his assertion, that the phrase *aliquem
textum* "can only mean *any passage*," as opposed to *any complete book*. Yet not
only is *textus* the regular and consecrated word for a book containing the four
Gospels, but in this present passage, as elsewhere, we find it used of other complete
books.

own estate hard by the convent.[1] We planted for them a flourishing vineyard fit for a great abbey, and procured abundance of vines for them in many ways. We built among them, on their own ground, four winepresses, fit for some five hundred gallons of wine,[2] without any cost to them; so plentifully did we provide for them, that they get some years a full 1600, sometimes even 2000 gallons. Moreover, we dyked round a sufficiency of pastures for them from our own meadows, and furnished them excellent gardens with plenty of seed. Again, there was another farm of St Denis which had long been abandoned and reduced to waste, without a single peasant to till it. This had been tilled by some alien peasant from other villages, who had given us perchance a bushel or less of wheat, perchance two or three measures of nuts; yet on this ground we now set out for the monks three ploughlands with a new farm and grange. We gave them sheep and cows and fodder for their need, for the richness of their pastures and the amendment of their lands. Moreover we endowed them of our own free-will with another possession of St Denis hard by Brunet, wherefrom they often draw eighty bushels of corn, and about 640 gallons of wine, and hay for the fodder of their beasts. Of the mill also, which we had lost some 60 years since, we gave them all that we could recover, but on condition that on the day of St Denis then following they should pay 20 sols[3] to the refectory of St Denis. Moreover, in that same village they receive taxes and dues amounting to 100 sols. At Corbeil, in their own district, they have 17 livres of their own revenue, beyond other dues both on sales and on markets and other customary rights; add to this a mill and an oven,[4] and eight modios of oats, and the tribute of hens, and the whole endowment of the church of St Exsuperius.

[1] The ploughland, or *carucate*, was sufficient to keep one peasant with his wife and family.

[2] *Fere quater-viginti modios vini.* The *modius* of Paris, as Ducange shows, contained by vintagers' reckoning 18 *sextarii* of wine; or about 64 gallons.

[3] The *sol* of Paris was the equivalent of 4*d.* sterling about this time: the *livre* being worth 6*s.* 8*d.* sterling.

[4] The oven, like the mill, was a seignorial monopoly in medieval France; these were two of the most burdensome taxes which were swept away by the Revolution.

I put together here several documents concerning St Bernard and the early history of his Order. They are taken mostly from vol. 185 of Migne's *Patrologia Latina*, which contains the almost contemporary *Lives* of St Bernard, and the valuable collection of early records compiled under the title of *Exordium Magnum Cisterciense* by a monk of Clairvaux, who had known intimately several of the saint's companions. They admirably illustrate monasticism at its best, and may be compared with the extracts to be given later on from Caesarius of Heisterbach, a Cistercian of the next generation.

Ralph Higden, a monk of Chester, died in 1364. His *Polychronicon* is not only a digest of such chronicles as the author could get hold of, but also a popular encyclopaedia: it has no original merit, but is most valuable as showing a learned man's outlook on the world during Chaucer's boyhood. The book was translated in 1387 by John Trevisa, chaplain to Lord Berkeley, and is printed in the Rolls Series.

47. ST BERNARD'S CHARACTER
(Trevisa's *Higden*, R.S. vol. VIII, p. 17.)

THAT year [1153] died St Bernard, abbot of Clairvaux, that was born in Burgoyne, in the castle of Fontaine; he was a noble knight's son, and was first fed with his own mother's milk, and afterward nourished with greater meats.[1] Then the year of our Lord 1112—after the beginning of the Order of Cistercians (that is the Order of white monks), fifteen, of his own age, two and twenty—he entered into Cîteaux with thirty fellows; and after the fifth year of his conversion he was abbot of Clairvaux; there he used waking passing the usage of mankind; he said that he lost no time more than when he slept, and he likened death to sleep; unnethe he might suffer them that snored and fared foul in their sleep; he went to meat as it were to torment. For great abstinence that he used, he had lost his taste and savour of meat and of drink, so that he would take oil instead of wine and blood instead of butter.[2] He would say that he savoured water, for it cooled his mouth and his jaws. All that he learned of Scripture he drank it [especially] in woods and in fields in his meditations and prayers. He acknowledged none other masters but oaks

[1] It was unusual for mothers in high life to suckle their own children: cf. vol. III, no. 22.

[2] Trevisa here unwittingly distorts the occasional misapprehensions of the saint into a settled habit.

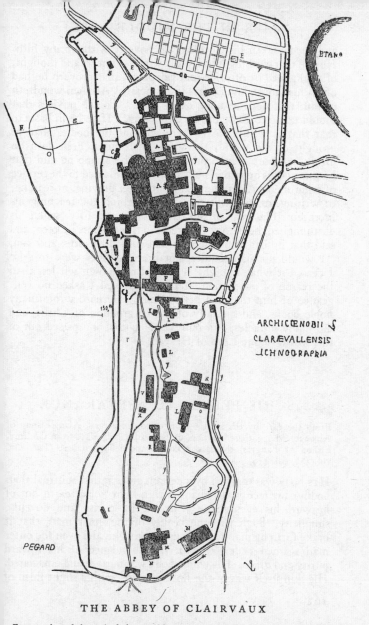

ARCHICŒNOBII
CLARÆVALLENSIS
ICHNOGRAPHIA

PEGARD

THE ABBEY OF CLAIRVAUX

From a plan of the end of the twelfth century, reproduced in Viollet-le-Duc's
Dict. de l'Architecture, t. 1, p. 266.

and beeches. In his clothing was poverty without any filth. He said that clothing is judge and witness of heart and thought, of negligence or of pride and vainglory; that proverb he had oft in his mouth and always in his heart, "All men wondreth of him that doth as none other doth." To the novices that should come to Religion, he would say, "If ye be in haste to that that is within, leave here without the bodies that ye brought of the world; the spirits shall enter, flesh doth no profit." As oft as men prayed him to be bishop he said that he was not his own man but that he was ordained to the service of other men. Alway he was wont either praying, or reading, or writing, or in meditations, or preaching and teaching his brethren. The year of our Lord 1102 and fifty, when his death nighed, he betook his brethren three points to keep, and said that he had kept them in this wise all his life, and said, "I would no man slander, but if any slander were to arise I ceased it what I might; I trowed mine own wit less than the reason of other men; if I were grieved I asked no vengeance of him that had grieved me." Bernard wrote many noble books, and specially of the Incarnation of Christ, and did many miracles, and built sixty abbeys, and passed out of this world to our Lord of Heaven.

48. HIS PERSONAL APPEARANCE

From the *Life* by the saint's younger contemporary, Alan, Bishop o Auxerre, who gathered notices of Bernard's early days from Godfrey, Bishop of Langres, the saint's cousin and fellow-convert (*Pat. Lat.* vol. 185, col. 479).

His body was marked by a certain grace rather spiritual than bodily; his face was radiant with a light not of earth but of heaven; his eyes shone with angelic purity and dovelike simplicity. Such was the beauty of the inner man, that it brake forth by manifest tokens to the sight, and even the outer man seemed bedewed with the abundance of his inward purity and grace. His whole body was meagre and emaciated. His skin itself was of the finest texture, with a slight flush of

red on the cheeks, seeing that all the natural heat of his frame
had been drawn thither by constant meditation and the zeal
of his holy compunction. His hair was of a yellow inclining
to white;[1] his beard was auburn, sprinkled towards the end
of his life with grey. His stature was of an honourable middle
size, yet inclining to tallness. Nevertheless, whereas his flesh
(first by the gift of preventing grace, then by the help of
nature, and lastly by the holy use of spiritual discipline) scarce
dared to lust now against the spirit, yet the spirit lusted so sore
against the flesh, beyond the man's strength and above the
power of flesh and blood, that the frail beast fell beneath the
load and could not rise again.

49. HIS AUSTERITIES

From p. 422 of the *Anecdotes* of Étienne de Bourbon, who tells us that he
learned many particulars from the mouth of Lord Calon de Fontaines
St Bernard's grand-nephew.

I HAVE heard of the blessed Bernard of Clairvaux that in
youth he so afflicted his flesh as to be unable to bear the
common [monastic] life in his old age: wherefore his Abbot-
Superior commanded him to obey, in his bodily diet, certain
Brethren that were assigned to him. It came to pass, therefore, that King Louis VII came once to Clairvaux when the
saint was already an old man dwelling in the infirmary; which
when the king heard, he sent him a present of fish. But his
messengers found St Bernard sitting before roast capons' flesh,
and reported the matter to the king, who would not believe
it of so great a man; wherefore afterwards, in familiar speech
with him, he told him what his servants had said. Then the
saint confessed it to be true, saying that, so long as he was in
health and had felt the power of endurance in his body, he
had worn it down with abstinence; until, being unable to
bear its accustomed burthens, it must at last be supported and
sustained, whereunto he was now compelled by his Superior.
At which words the king was much edified.

[1] *Caesaries ex flavo colorabatur et candido*: probably the *blond cendré* of modern
French.

50. ST BERNARD AND THE SHEPHERD BOYS

From Jacques de Vitry, *Exempla*, fol. 150, ed. Crane, p. 120.

FOR the prayer of innocents is most acceptable to God. Wherefore we read of St Bernard that, when he rode abroad in the morning and saw boys keeping their flocks in the fields, he would say to his monks: "Let us salute these boys, that they may answer to bless us; and thus, armed with the prayers of the innocent, we shall be able to ride on with an easy mind."

51. A CONVENT TRAGEDY

From the *Life of St Bernard*, by John the Hermit (about 1180). (*Pat. Lat.* vol. 185, col. 546.)

A CERTAIN monk, Christian by name, planted a vineyard on the crest of the hill hard by Clairvaux. Then came Guy and Gerard, blood-brethren of the venerable Father [St Bernard] and cursed this vineyard, saying unto the monk, "Brother Christian, where is thy mind and where is thine heart? Wherefore hast thou not considered the Scripture which saith that wine is not fit for monks?"[1] But he answering said: "Ye

---

[1] The reference is to chap. 40 of St Benedict's Rule, which runs, "Every one hath his proper gift from God; one after this manner and another after that: wherefore we have some scruple in fixing a measure for other men's meat and drink. Yet, considering the fragility of the weaker brethren, we hold that an *hemina* of wine daily is enough for each monk. But let them to whom God giveth power to abstain, know that they shall have their own reward. If, however, either the need of the monastery, or the labour, or the summer heat, call for more than this, then let it be left to the Prior's choice, who shall take heed at all points lest satiety or drunkenness creep in:—although, indeed, we read that wine is altogether unfit for monks. But because the monks of our age cannot be persuaded of this, let us at least accord in this, that we drink not to satiety, but somewhat sparingly, since wine maketh even wise men fall off. Where, however, the need of the monastery maketh it impossible to find the aforesaid measure, but only far less, or even none whatever, then let the monks of that place bless God and murmur not. For this we prescribe above all things, that there be no murmurs among them." The exact measure of the *hemina* has been hotly debated, and at great length. Dom Martène, after summing up the conflicting arguments, agrees with Mabillon in estimating it at 18 ounces. The Rule of St Benedict, which is most interesting and instructive, may be found almost entirely translated on p. 274 of Mr E. F. Henderson's *Historical Documents of the Middle Ages* (Bell, 1896).

indeed are spiritual brethren, who eschew wine; but I am a sinner, and would fain drink somewhat." Then said Gerard, "I tell thee, brother Christian, thou shalt not see the fruit thereof": after which they returned to the monastery. So he digged his vineyard and tilled it many seasons: but at last he died and saw not the fruit thereof. Wherefore, after a long while, the keeper of the vineyard came and spake to St Bernard: "Father, our vineyard is accursed, and can bear no fruit." "Why so?" said he: and the keeper answered, "Thy brethren cursed it, and thenceforward it bare no fruit." Then said St Bernard: "Bring me water in a bowl": and so he did. Then the Saint, having hallowed the water with the sign of the cross, said: "Go, my son, and sprinkle this over the whole vineyard." So the brother went and did as his Abbot had commanded him; and the vineyard grew and multiplied so that all marvelled to see it.

52. RELIGIOUS DESPAIR

(*Ib.* col. 419, c. vi.)

A CERTAIN monk, subject to this holy father, had come to such poverty of spirit, partly through the Devil's wiles and partly through his own simplicity and want of sense, as to assert that the bread and the watered wine which are shown on the altar could not possibly be transubstantiated into the true body and blood of our Lord Jesus Christ: wherefore he scorned to take the life-giving sacraments, as unprofitable to his soul. At length the Brethren took note that he never shared in the Sacrament of the Altar, and the elder monks summoned him to private speech. They enquired the cause: he for his part denied not, but confessed that he had no faith in the Sacraments. In spite of all their teaching and admonitions, since he still refused his assent and maintained his disbelief in the proofs which they adduced from Holy Scripture, therefore the matter was reported to the venerable Abbot, who summoned him to his presence, and confuted his unbelief with all that wisdom wherewith he was endowed. But the other answered, "No words can bring me to believe that the bread and wine set forth on the altar are the true body and blood of Christ; wherefore I know that I must go down to hell." At which words the man of God (who was ever wont to display a marvellous force of authority in matters of extreme difficulty) cried aloud, "What! a monk of mine go down to hell? God forbid! If thou hast no faith of thine own, yet in virtue of thine obedience I bid thee go take the Communion with my faith!" O pious father! O truly wise physician of souls, through the anointing of grace which taught him in all things how to heal the temptations of the weaker brethren! He said not, "Hence, heretic!—Begone, thou damned soul!—Away with thee, lost wretch!" but said boldly, "Go and communicate with my faith," firmly believing that this his little son, whom he brought to the birth with the pangs of spiritual yearning until Christ should be fulfilled in him—that this son, I say, even as he could never be separated from the bowels of his charity, neither could he from the foundation of his faith. The monk, therefore, constrained by the virtue of obedience, though (as it seemed to him) utterly without faith, came before the altar and communicated; whereupon, being straightway enlightened by the holy father's merit, he received a faith in the Sacraments which he kept unspotted even to the day of his death.

53. ST BERNARD AND THE NOVICE

(Ib. col. 422.)

THIS faithful and prudent steward of the Lord's substance had once stayed abroad longer than was his wont for the Church's sake: for he was oftentimes compelled by the Pope's mandate to travel abroad, sorely against his will, for the making of peace, or the healing of schism, or the confuting of heresies. At length, having unravelled the tangled threads of the matter which had taken him abroad, he came back to the monastery, and seized the first occasion of entering the cell of the novices, in order that these young and tender sucklings might be refreshed all the more abundantly with the milk of his consolation, as they had lacked for so long a time the sweetness of his divine exhortations. For whithersoever the holy father went forth, he sowed the Lord's word over all the waters, so that he scarce ever returned without the usury of spiritual gain, filling the Cell of Probation with a multitude of novices, oftentimes to the number of a hundred; so that, at the hours of divine service, the novices filled the choir, and the monks (save for a few elder brethren who kept discipline) must needs stand without.

When therefore, as aforesaid, he had come to the Cell of the Novices, and with his pleasant and edifying tongue had rendered them all more joyful and fervent in the observance of their holy purpose, then he called one novice aside, saying: "Dearly-beloved son, whence this sadness of thine, which gnaweth so fatally at the innermost folds of thine heart?" The novice, for very shame, scarce dared to speak a word. Then said that truly meek and humble man, knowing well how to show himself to all men as a true shepherd, and no hireling: "I know, dearly-beloved son, I know well all that concerneth thee; wherefore I pity thee even as a father pitieth his own children. For in this long-delayed absence of mine, wherein I must needs lack that bodily presence of my Brethren which I ever desire above all other earthly things— in this my absence (I say), God of His grace vouchsafed to me that I might supply in the spirit all that my body was powerless to accomplish: in the spirit, I returned hither and passed through every corner of this house, enquiring with all diligence how my Brethren bare themselves. Then also I came to this Cell of the Novices, wherein I found all the rest exulting in the fear of God and with their loins girt to the labours of penitence, yet I groaned to see thee alone languishing in immoderate sadness. When therefore I tried to entice thee to me by blandishments, thou didst turn thy spirit and thy face away from me, weeping so bitterly that my cowl was drenched with thy tears." With these words, and with other spiritual warnings, the holy father pressed hard upon the novice, and so subdued him as to put all his grief to flight, recalling him thus from the melancholy in which he had been almost altogether overwhelmed, to the liberty of spiritual joy.

54. THE LAY-BROTHER'S WORKFELLOW

(*Ib.* col. 1106.)

A CERTAIN lay-brother in one of the granges[1] of Clairvaux, whose office was to drive the oxen, was a man of pure heart and great simplicity, who performed promptly and devoutly all that his masters enjoined upon him, and bore his daily toil with all patience, looking ever to his heavenly reward. One day this man saw in a dream how the Lord Jesus walked by his side, bearing in His sweet hand a goad, and helping him to drive the oxen as he walked on the other side of the waggon-pole: with which vision he was over-joyed beyond measure. When therefore he had awaked and called to mind the gentle-ness, kindness, and sweetness of this his dearly-beloved fellow-worker, suddenly his heart was inflamed with the fire of vehement desire: he sighed after Him, he longed to see Him face to face Who had vouchsafed Himself as his yokefellow. When, therefore, he longed vehemently to depart and be with Christ, then the loving Lord, who walketh with the meek and whose converse is with the simple, would no longer defer the desire of his poor servant; but soon this same brother was laid upon a bed of sickness, so that death freed him on the seventh day from his labour and pain, and he happily laid hold on eternal life, with that everlasting rest which is Christ the Lord. As he lay in his last agony, his most revered abbot the Blessed Bernard came in to visit him, and to bid farewell to his son on the way to his long home (whose conscience he knew to be pure and simple), and to fortify him with a bene-diction, even at his last setting-forth, against the evil purposes of ghostly robbers. The saint rejoiced greatly to learn this vision from the sick man's own mouth; after whose death he proclaimed with all boldness that God had taken him to Himself for that he had walked with God, Who had in truth wrought in him; for it could not be that the Almighty and merciful God would desert in his last agony that servant whose most condescending companion and fellow-worker he had been in the days of his toil.

[1] Out-lying farm or manor belonging to a monastery.

The letter, or "Apologia," to William, Abbot of St Thierry, from which this extract is taken, was written by St Bernard about A.D. 1125, when the Cluniac Order was at the height of its fame. Founded as a reform of the Benedictine Rule, the Cluniac congregation had by its strictly disciplined life earned a popularity and wealth which soon reacted against strictness and discipline: hence the fresh reform of the Cistercians. The Cluniacs had formed a great school of architecture, sculpture, and painting, which profoundly influenced the whole course of medieval art. "So far" (writes Prof. E. S. Prior) "the Benedictine reformation seems only to have accentuated the luxuries of architecture."[1] This may be clearly seen in the great Cluniac portal of Vézelay, built during St Bernard's lifetime, and in the reflected glories of the same art which still remain, for example, at Glastonbury. The Cistercians, although the next two generations brought them to the front with that splendid style which may still be studied at Tintern and Fountains, began (like the Carthusians) by a protest against all magnificence in architecture, and kept a certain severity even through the long period of power and wealth which so soon succeeded to the strict poverty of St Bernard's day. In his time, however, sculptures and paintings were expressly forbidden by the Constitutions, "because, when we busy ourselves with such things, the profit of good meditation is often neglected, or the discipline of religious gravity." Even in 1213, the General Chapter protested against all "notable superfluity and curiousness of carving, building, pavement, and such-like things, which deform the ancient honour of our Order and suit ill with poverty." This poverty, however, was already only a tradition among the Cistercians: in a few years the Franciscans and Dominicans were again to protest by the meanness of their chapels and the purity of their religious zeal against the splendour of the older Orders; but only to follow the same example themselves before a generation was past. The glories of Gothic Art which perished at the Dissolution of the monasteries would, in themselves, have been little regretted by the greatest monks of the Middle Ages. St Bernard begins by rebuking his fellow-Cistercians who carp at the Cluniacs out of pure jealousy, and then passes on to note the real faults which could be justly urged against these latter (chaps. viii–xiii).

55. ST BERNARD AS PURITAN

I MARVEL how monks could grow accustomed to such intemperance in eating and drinking, clothing and bedding, riding abroad and building, that, wheresoever these things are wrought most busily and with most pleasure and expense, there Religion is thought to be best kept. For behold! spare living is taken for covetousness, sobriety for austerity, silence for melancholy; while, on the other hand, men rebaptize

[1] *Cathedral Builders in England*, p. 40.

A

THE PORTAL OF VÉZELAY

From Viollet-le-Duc's *Dict. de l'Architecture*, t. VII, p. 388. The work of Cluniac masons, and our best guide to the now destroyed sculptures of Cluny itself.

laxity as "discretion," waste as "liberality," garrulousness as "affability," giggling as "jollity," effeminacy in clothing and bedding as "neatness."....Who, in those first days when the monastic Order began, would have believed that monks would ever come to such sloth?...Dish after dish is set on the table; and instead of the mere flesh-meat from which men abstain, they receive twofold in mighty fishes. Though thou have eaten thy fill of the first course, yet when thou comest to the second thou shalt seem not even to have tasted the first; for all is dressed with such care and art in the kitchen that, though thou hast swallowed four or five dishes, the first are no hindrance to the last, nor doth satiety lessen thine appetite. ...For (to say nothing of the rest) who may tell of the eggs alone, in how many ways they are tossed and vexed, how busily they are turned and turned again, beaten to froth or hard-boiled or minced, now fried and now baked, now stuffed and now mixed, or again brought up one by one?... What shall I say of water-drinking, when watered wine is on no account admitted? All of us, forsooth, in virtue of our monkish profession, have infirm stomachs, and are justified in not neglecting the Apostle's salutary advice as to "drinking wine"; yet (I know not why) we omit that word "little" wherewith he begins....Men seek for their garments, not the most useful stuff they may find, but the most delicately woven....."Yet," sayest thou, "Religion is not in the dress, but in the heart." Well said. But thou, when thou wilt buy a frock, thou goest from city to city, scourest the markets, searchest the fairs from booth to booth, scannest the merchants' shops, turnest over each man's store, unrollest vast bales of cloth, touchest with thy fingers, bringest close to thine eyes, holdest up to the sunlight, and rejectest whatsoever is seen to be too coarse or too slight; on the other hand, whatsoever taketh thee with its purity and gloss, that thou seekest to buy forthwith at any price: I ask thee, therefore, doest thou this from thy heart, or in mere simplicity?...Yet I marvel, since the Rule saith that all faults of the Disciple concern the Master, and our Lord through His prophet threateneth to require the blood of such as die in their sins at the hands of their Pastors— I marvel how our Abbots suffer such things to be done; unless it be perchance (if I may risk the word) that no man confidently rebuketh that wherein he trusteth not himself to be without blame.... I lie, if I have not seen an Abbot with a train of sixty horses and more; on seeing such pass by, thou wouldst say that they are not fathers of monasteries but lords of castles, not rulers of souls but princes of provinces....

But these are small things; I will pass on to matters greater in themselves, yet seeming smaller because they are more usual. I say naught of the vast height of your churches, their immoderate length, their superfluous breadth, the costly polishings, the curious carvings and paintings which attract the worshipper's gaze and hinder his attention, and seem to me in some sort a revival of the ancient Jewish rites. Let this pass, however: say that this is done for God's honour. But I, as a monk, ask of my brother monks as the pagan [poet Persius] asked of his fellow-pagans: "Tell me, O Pontiffs" (quoth he) "what doeth this gold in the sanctuary?" So say I, "Tell me, ye poor men" (for I break the verse to keep the sense) "tell me, ye poor (if, indeed, ye be poor), what doeth this gold in *your* sanctuary?" And indeed the bishops have an excuse which monks have not; for we know that they, being debtors both to the wise and the unwise, and unable to excite the devotion of carnal folk by spiritual things, do so by bodily adornments. But we [monks] who have now come forth from the people; we who have left all the precious and beautiful things of the world for Christ's sake; who have counted but dung, that we may win Christ, all things fair to see or soothing to hear, sweet to smell, delightful to taste, or pleasant to touch—in a word, all bodily delights—whose devotion, pray, do we monks intend to excite by these things? What profit, I say, do we expect therefrom? The admiration of fools, or the oblations of the simple? Or, since we are scattered among the nations, have we perchance learnt their works and do we yet serve their graven images? To speak plainly, doth the root of all this lie in covetousness, which is idolatry, and do we seek not profit, but a gift? If thou askest: "How?" I say: "In a strange fashion." For money is so artfully scattered that it may multiply; it is expended that it may give increase, and prodigality giveth birth to plenty: for at the very sight of these costly yet marvellous vanities men are more kindled to offer gifts than to pray. Thus wealth is drawn up by ropes of wealth, thus money bringeth money; for I know not how it is that, wheresoever more abundant wealth is seen, there do men offer more freely. Their eyes are feasted with relics cased in gold, and their purse-strings are loosed. They are shown a most comely image of some saint, whom they think all the more saintly that he is the more gaudily painted. Men run to kiss him, and are invited to give; there is more admiration for his comeliness than veneration for his sanctity. Hence the church is adorned with gemmed crowns of light—nay, with lustres like cart-wheels, girt all round with lamps, but no less brilliant with the precious stones that stud them.[1] Moreover we see candelabra standing like trees of massive bronze, fashioned with marvellous subtlety of art, and glistening no less brightly with gems than with the lights they carry. What, think you, is the purpose of all this? The compunction of penitents, or the admiration of beholders? O vanity of vanities, yet no more vain than insane! The church is resplendent in her walls, beggarly in her poor;[2] she clothes her stones in gold, and leaves her sons naked; the rich man's eye is fed at the expense of the indigent. The curious find their delight here, yet the needy find no relief. Do we not revere at least the images of the Saints, which swarm even in the inlaid pavement whereon we tread? Men spit oftentimes in an Angel's face;[3] often, again, the countenance of some Saint is ground under the heel of a passer-by. And if he spare not these sacred images, why not even the fair colours? Why dost thou make that so fair which will soon be made so foul? Why lavish bright hues upon that which must needs be trodden under foot? What avail these comely

---

[1] The contemporary Abbot of Cluny, Peter the Venerable, ordained that "the great crown of lights, most delicately fashioned of gold, bronze, and silver, which hangeth by a strong chain in the midst of the choir, shall not be lighted except on the five principal feasts of the year." A less magnificent one, which still survived in the eighteenth century in St-Remi, at Reims, held seventy-two wax candles.

[2] Horstius has here collected in a note a number of parallel passages from St Ambrose, St Jerome, St John Chrysostom, etc.

[3] It must be remembered that the modern use of the handkerchief was practically unknown in all ranks of society until the end of the Middle Ages.

forms in places where they are defiled with customary dust? And, lastly, what are such things as these to you poor men, you monks, you spiritual folk? Unless perchance here also ye may answer the poet's question in the words of the Psalmist: "Lord, I have loved the habitation of Thy House, and the place where Thine honour dwelleth." I grant it, then, let us suffer even this to be done in the church; for, though it be harmful to vain and covetous folk, yet not so to the simple and devout. But in the cloister, under the eyes of the Brethren who read there, what profit is there in those ridiculous monsters, in that marvellous and deformed comeliness, that comely deformity? To what purpose are those unclean apes, those fierce lions, those monstrous centaurs, those half-men, those striped tigers, those fighting knights, those hunters winding their horns? Many bodies are there seen under one head, or again, many heads to a single body. Here is a four-footed beast with a serpent's tail; there, a fish with a beast's head. Here again the forepart of a horse trails half a goat behind it, or a horned beast bears the hinder quarters of a horse. In short, so many and so marvellous are the varieties of divers shapes on every hand, that we are more tempted to read in the marble than in our books, and to spend the whole day in wondering at these things rather than in meditating the law of God. For God's sake, if men are not ashamed of these follies, why at least do they not shrink from the expense?

The abundance of my matter suggested much more for me to add; but from this I am distracted both by my own anxious business and by the too hasty departure of Brother Oger [the bearer of this letter].... This is my opinion of your Order and mine; nor can any man testify more truly than you, and those who know me as you do, that I am wont to say these things not about you but to your faces. What in your Order is laudable, that I praise and publish abroad; what is reprehensible, I am wont to persuade you and my other friends to amend. This is no detraction, but rather attraction: wherefore I wholly pray and beseech you to do the same by me. Farewell.

At the Council of Sens (1140), St Bernard formally accused Abelard of heresy; but the latter, preferring not to defend himself before a court which he believed to have prejudged the case, left the Council and appealed directly to the Pope. The following account of part of the proceedings is from a pamphlet addressed to St Bernard by Abelard's pupil Berengarius (Migne, *Pat. Lat.* vol. 178, cols. 1857 ff.); its purpose is frankly satirical, but on the whole it bears the stamp of truth.

56. BISHOPS IN COUNCIL

THOU hast set up Peter Abelard as a mark for thine arrows, to vomit forth the venom of thy bitterness against him, to take him away from the land of the living and set him among the dead men. Thou didst call together bishops from all sides and condemn him as an heretic in the Council of Sens; thou hast separated him as an untimely birth from the womb of Mother Church. Though he walked in the way of Christ, yet thou, like a murderer coming forth from his ambush, hast robbed him of his seamless robe. Thou didst preach to the people, bidding them pour forth prayers to God for him; yet in thine heart thou didst purpose to banish him from Christendom. What could the multitude do? How could the multitude pray, knowing not for whom they were to pray? Thou, the man of God, the worker of miracles, who sattest with Mary at Jesus' feet, who didst keep all these words in thine heart, thou shouldst have offered the purest incense of holy prayers before the face of God, that thine accused Peter might return to his right mind, and become clean from all suspicion. Yet perchance thou wert more willing to find an apt occasion of blame against him! At length, when [the bishops] had dined, Peter's book was brought out, and one was chosen to read forth his writings in a loud voice: but he, urged on by hatred of Peter, and well-watered from the vine-stock (not indeed from Him who said *I am the true vine*, but from that vine which stretched the patriarch Noah naked on the floor), bawled even louder than he had been bidden. After a while the prelates might be seen leaping up from their chairs, stamping their feet, laughing and jesting; so that all men might mark how their vows were paid not to Christ but to Bacchus. Meanwhile cups are saluted, goblets are celebrated, the wines are praised, and the prelates' throats are well moistened. Then might a man have cited...from the satiric poet:

"Betwixt one goblet and the next,
The fuddled pontiffs con the sacred text!"[1]

At length, when the reader mouthed out any subtle points of divinity, unwonted to these episcopal ears, then the hearers were all cut to the heart, and gnashed with their teeth on Peter: considering the philosopher with mole-like blindness, they cried: "What! shall we suffer this monster to live?" and wagging their heads like the Jews, they said, "Vah! thou that destroyest the temple of God!..."

Meanwhile the heat of the wine had so crept into their brains, that all eyelids drooped with the heaviness of sleep. Still the reader bawls; but the hearers snore. One leans on his elbow to slumber; another nods and winks on his soft cushion; a third dozes with his head on his knees. When therefore the reader had stumbled upon some sufficiently thorny passage, he would cry to the deaf ears of these prelates: "*Damnatis?*"[2] Then a few, barely awakening at the sound of the last syllable, murmured with slumberous voice and nodding head: "*Damnamus!*"[3] while others, aroused by the chorus of the rest, caught only the last syllable and droned out —"*namus,—namus!*"...To what end did such men do thus? To what purpose is this decree of the lawyers? There is consolation in the Gospel story. "The chief priests and the Pharisees" (saith the Scripture) "gathered a council, and said: 'What do we, for this man doth many miracles? If we let him alone so, all will believe in him.' But one of them named Abbot Bernard, being the high priest of that council, prophesied, saying, 'It is expedient for us that one man should be cast forth from among the people, and that the whole nation perish not.' From that day, therefore, they devised to condemn him."

---

[1] Persius, I, 30:

                —inter pocula quaerunt
      Pontifices saturi quid dia poemata narrent.

Berengarius has substituted *Pontifices* for *Romulidae*.

[2] "Do ye condemn it?"   [3] "We condemn it!"

57. THE HEAVENLY REAPERS

(*Pat. Lat.* vol. 185, col. 1062.)

In the monastery of Clairvaux was a pious monk named Renaud, worthy to be remembered by all good folk.... This man of God, although before his conversion he passed thirty years in the habit of the world, yet he lived no worldly life, but busied himself with deeds of piety, solicitous to glorify God and to bear Him in his soul. For, among other pious motions of his chaste heart, he even dedicated his bodily purity to the Lord, by Whose helping grace he passed by all lewd temptations and filth of the flesh, treading an undefiled path from his mother's womb to the day of his own death. This man took the monastic habit in the monastery of St-Amand, where he dwelt more than twenty years in holy conversation, and gave abundant proof of his sanctity to all men. Then was he inflamed with so much greater love of virtue, that his holy zeal took him to Clairvaux, after long premonition of many revelations from God. What labours, what troubles this saintly man suffered from the Brethren of St-Amand, who grudged at his blessed conversation and would fain have turned him aside from this purpose, I will here pass by for the reader's sake and for very weariness. When, therefore, he was received at Clairvaux, he forthwith girded himself like a man to this new warfare, and, veteran as he was already, showed himself a sturdy novice among us; all day long he mortified himself with labours and watchings, fasts and all other duties of holy discipline. His zeal for prayer was incessant, and in all his praying he had a marvellous gift of tears.[1] One day, therefore, that he was gone out with the other monks to labour at the wheat-harvest, he stood a little apart from the rest and began to rejoice in soul at the sight of the reapers, marvelling deeply to consider all these wise and noble and delicately nurtured men who exposed themselves for Christ's sake to so great toil and vexation, and who suffered this burning sun as cheerfully as though they were plucking apples of heavenly fragrance in some garden of

[1] For this coveted gift of tears, see *From St Francis to Dante*, 2nd ed. pp. 317, 405 (1).

delights, or feasting delicately at some table loaded with the most exquisite meats. At last, raising his eyes and hands to heaven, he thanked the God who had brought him, unworthy sinner as he was, into so holy and numerous a fellowship. While he pondered these and such-like thoughts, scarce able to contain himself for excess of joy, he was suddenly aware of three worshipful ladies, glorious with rosy cheeks and snow-white garments, whereof one walked before with brighter robes and fairer form and loftier stature than the rest. These three came down from the mountain hard by, and drew near unto the Brethren as they toiled in reaping on the steep hillside. He, therefore, troubled and amazed at so strange a sight, cried aloud to himself: "Lord God!" (quoth he) "what may these ladies be, so fair, so worshipful, who draw near unto our convent contrary to the custom of other women?" Even as he spake, he was aware of a reverend white-haired man, clad in a long white mantle, who said unto him, "That taller lady, who goeth before the rest, is Mary herself, the Virgin Mother of Jesus Christ; behind whom follow St Elizabeth and St Mary Magdalene." As soon therefore as he heard the name of God's Mother, then all his bowels were moved for devotion to her name whom he loved so vehemently; and he asked again, saying, "And whither, my lord, whither doth our Lady walk?" "To visit," said the other, "her own reapers": and so saying he suddenly vanished from him, whereat this man of God marvelled the more in his own mind. Then he looked again towards the holy Mother of God with her fellows, and gazed upon them with amazement; for they paced slowly forward, one behind the other, until they came at last to the Brethren. Then they entered in among them, threading their way backwards and forwards among the monks and lay-brethren, as though they would have overseen their work; until, even as they moved, they vanished from his eyes, and returned unto the heaven whence they had come. Meanwhile this man of God stood rooted to the spot, nor could he move until this miracle was altogether past.

Extract 58 is from the *Life* of St Stephen of Obazine in Baluze-Mansi, *Miscellanea*, vol. I, pp. 154, 169, 171. St Stephen, with a few like-minded companions, founded, near Limoges, in the then desert spot of Obazine, a monastery of which he became abbot. About 1148 he procured the incorporation of his abbey into the Order of Cîteaux, then in its full glory. This *Life*, written by a disciple and fellow-monk, is full of interesting information upon twelfth-century monasticism in its strictest forms.

58. MONASTIC DISCIPLINE

THIS [Stephen] was strenuous in discipline, and most severe to correct the failings of delinquents. For, as we have said above, if any raised his eyes but a little in church, or smiled but faintly, or slumbered but lightly, or negligently let fall the book which he held, or made any heedless sound, or chanted too fast or out of tune, or made any undisciplined movement, he received forthwith either a rod on his head or an open hand upon his cheek, so loud that the sound of the blow rang in all men's ears; a punishment which was especially inflicted on the younger boys, to their own correction and to the terror of the rest. When one of the honoured novices held a book in church, and, calling the fellow-novice who sat by him, showed something with his forefinger in that same book, the holy man, seeing this, would not avenge it upon the [offending] person, but caught the book from his hands, brake it asunder upon the desk in all men's sight, and thus returned to his own place; whereby he struck such fear into the rest that scarce any dared to open a book in choir even in cases of necessity. But such discipline as this reigned especially when the monastery itself flourished in its glad beginnings, if I may so speak; when the monks were fewer in number and more perfect in life. For, since there was no law of any Order yet determined, therefore the master's precepts were as a law, teaching naught else but humility, obedience, poverty, discipline, and above all continual charity.... But we [nowadays], straining at the gnat and swallowing the camel, seeking to tithe mint and rue and all manner of herbs, make light of righteousness and faith, neglecting things of more importance under the cloke of every trifle, wearied, moreover, with the long time [of our service] and harassed by the multitude of

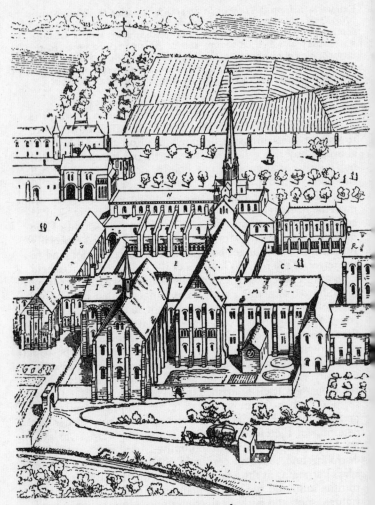

THE ABBEY OF CÎTEAUX

From an old engraving reproduced in Viollet-le-Duc, *Dict. de l'Architecture*, t. 1, p. 27?

those who live with us,—we have fallen away from our earlier vigour, and treat ourselves with more remissness and negligence; so that, while we would fain condescend to the weaker brethren, we hasten rather to follow their negligence than to draw them to perfection: a necessity which in those days existed not, since the men of that age were more perfect, and there were few or none to trouble their purpose....

(p. 169) And, while I write of children, let it not seem absurd if I record some examples of their simplicity, whence it may be seen how pure was their upbringing, and how foreign to all cunning of worldly wisdom. A certain boy was brought up by his mother in a convent of women; and when he was now past the limit of five years, (beyond which age none are permitted to dwell there,) he was removed from thence and sent to the boys' quarters.... But, while he was yet on the way, the Brother who led him enquired of him how the women bore themselves among whom he had been brought up; whereunto he replied that he had never seen women (for those of whom the Brother enquired were to him not *women*, but *sisters*, as he always heard them called). The Brother, therefore, willing to prove whether he said this of his simplicity, or in a figure of speech, asked again: "Wouldst thou then see clearly what *women* are?" "Yes," quoth he: and the other, seeing certain goats that fed afar off, said: "Lo, those are women." The boy believed implicitly as he had been told; wherefore, when he came among his boyish fellows, he boasted (among other things) that he had seen women grazing in the field; whereat the simpler marvelled, and others laughed who more certainly, yet not more happily, knew women by sight.

A boy from another cell was sent by his prior to bring green hay from the meadow. The servants loaded this upon an ass which, on the way homeward, passed through a certain sunken way, where the load was caught between the banks on either side and the ass, slipping away, came home without the boy's knowledge. Yet he stood meanwhile by the hay, smiting it oftentimes and threatening it as best he could; nor did he stir from that spot until the Brethren came out to seek him, who could scarce persuade him that the ass was clean gone, and that the hay could not walk without a beast of burden....

(p. 171) [The Blessed Stephen] would oftentimes correct certain excesses without vengeance of punishment, and by mere terror, as will be clearly seen from the following example. One Saturday, after Compline, as he went round the monastic offices according to his wont, he found the bakers in the bake-house rejoicing in the completion of their week's work; for they had taken certain poles and were striving together in a mock tourney. This he saw through a hole, himself unseen; whereupon he made a noise in his throat that they might know him to be there, and passed on, leaving them in such terror that one of the crew prepared forthwith to flee from the monastery, not daring to face the tribulation to come; but his fellow with much ado was barely able to keep him. On the morrow, therefore, both came into the Chapter-house, and besought mercy of their own accord without waiting to be accused. When, therefore, they stood thus dumb before the judgment-seat, and the Saint asked them what cause they had to accuse themselves, they answered, "You know!" He, therefore, as if in indignation, sent them back to their seats. Wherefore then did he condemn them no further, but that he knew with how sore a terror he had smitten them the night before? He would not heap grief upon grief, as many do, who, the more they are feared of their subjects, bear all the harder upon them, not as being more guilty but as being less formidable.

Another Brother, one of the most dignified, had been grievously chastised with rods in the Chapter-house; after which, as he sat alone and full of bitterness without the door, the Saint saw him and, willing to heal his wound, passed by of set purpose. He, though unwillingly, rose and went with the Abbot, not daring to refrain from following him when he passed by. Then the Saint turned unto him and said: "Perchance thou hast followed me that we may make peace." "Nay!" answered the other, "God forbid! I had no such thought." Whereat the Abbot caught him by the neck and, embracing and kissing him closely, turned his heart to such sweetness that he fell forthwith to the earth and clasped his feet, weeping and praying forgiveness for that former wrath.

Another monk, again, unwilling to quit the monastery without leave, and having importuned the Saint daily for such permission without ever obtaining it, besought this favour one day in Chapter.[1] But the holy man, neither willing to consent unto him nor able to break his evil purpose, answered at length as though overcome with weariness, "If therefore you will by all means go forth, first render that which you owe." "What is that?" quoth he. "Make yourself ready," quoth the Saint, "for Discipline." The monk obeyed, and the Abbot caused him to be so grievously chastised that there was no man there present but shuddered to see it. When therefore he was risen to his feet, then said the Abbot, "Now you may depart, if it pleaseth you." Yet he, (though men thought him all the more troubled at that time, and the more incited to depart,) answered: "Lord, God forbid that I should go hence or leave you all the days of my life. For that whole temptation is now so utterly uprooted from my mind that I desire nothing less than to depart." Who can doubt that the Devil had been troubled and driven forth from him in that hour, even as though he himself, in the monk's body, had received these stripes?

Hugh of St-Victor, to whom Dante assigns one of the highest places in his paradise, "was, with his contemporaries Abelard and St Bernard, one of the most influential theologians of the twelfth century.... He must be regarded as the real founder of the medieval mysticism of France, for Bernard of Clairvaux is dependent upon him for the essential features of his mystical speculations. The same may be affirmed of Peter Lombard." The following extract from his *Rules for Novices* (chaps. xii–xxi: Migne, *Pat. Lat.* vol. 176, col. 941) should be compared with the *Babees Book*, edited by Dr Furnivall for the Early English Text Society, and the similar rules for friars' behaviour in chap. vi of *From St Francis to Dante*.

59. MONASTIC ETIQUETTE

First therefore, the novice must diligently observe that all his limbs follow their proper office.... He must keep discretion of action, so that every limb may do the work whereunto

---

[1] The assembled body of monks or canons. In monasteries, this meeting was held daily for the correction of faults, etc.

it hath been framed; that his hand may not speak, nor his mouth hear, nor his eye usurp the office of the tongue. For there are some who cannot listen but with gaping mouth, opening their palate to the speaker's words as though the sense could penetrate to their hearts through their mouths. Others, worse still, when they work or listen thrust forth their tongues like thirsty dogs, and twist it around their lips like a millstone in accompaniment to their actions. Others, in speaking, thrust forth their finger, raise their eyebrows, and show their inward efforts to magnify themselves by rolling their eyeballs or casting them down as though in profound thought. Others toss their heads, shake their hair abroad, smooth out the folds of their garments, and make a ridiculous figure of ostentation by setting their elbows to their sides and turning out their feet. Others, as though both ears were not made for hearing, twist their neck so as to offer one only to the speaker: others again, figuring I know not what symbol, shut one eye and open the other to look. Others, still more ridiculously, speak with half a mouth. There are a thousand other grimaces, a thousand grinnings and wrinklings of the nostrils, a thousand writhings and contortions of the lips, which disfigure the comeliness of a man's face and the decency of discipline. For the face is the mirror of discipline: and we must guard it all the more strictly as we are the less able to conceal any fault therein....Others swim with their arms as they walk, and, by a twofold portent, tread with their feet the earth below while at the same time they fly with their arms in the air above. What, pray, is this monster which presenteth at one and the same moment a walking man, a rowing boat, and a flying bird?...

The author passes on to deal with behaviour at table (chap. xviii).

Let nothing be done with uproar or tumult, but keep all thy limbs disciplined with modesty and tranquillity: not as some do, who are no sooner set down than they show the intemperance of their soul by the unquiet agitation and confusion of their limbs. They wag their heads, stretch forth their arms, raise their open hands on high; and, with their struggles and indecorous gestures, make a most hideous show of swallowing up the whole feast at one gulp. They pant and groan for anguish, seeming to seek some wider entrance to their roaring maw, as though the throat were too narrow to minister in sufficient abundance to their ravenous appetite. While their body sits in its place, their eyes and hands rove everywhere abroad, far and near; at one and the same moment they crumble their bread, pour wine into cups and beakers, spin the dishes round on the table; and, like a king about to assault a beleaguered city, they doubt at which quarter they shall make their first onset, since they would fain rush upon every point at once. It may be that we ourselves have too far forgotten our modesty in writing thus: but impudence oftentimes knoweth no shame unless it be put to public confusion....

There are some whose throats are sick of a ridiculous disease; for they can swallow naught but fat and delicate foods; and, if ever spare or frugal nourishment be offered, such men pretend forthwith either the indigestion of their stomach or the dryness of their chest, or a certain creeping in their head, or any other such frivolous excuse. Some again despise delicacies and luxuries of the table with great constancy, yet these same will utterly scorn, with a petulance no less grievous and unbearable, to eat the common foods. They seek some new and rare sorts of meats, so that oftentimes a whole crowd of servants must scour all the villages round for one man's belly's sake; and scarcely at length can the wantonness of a single appetite be quenched by tearing up unknown roots from wild and distant mountains, or by drawing a handful of fishes, with painful search, from the deepest abysses of the sea, or by picking untimely berries from their withering thorns. Indeed, I know not well what vice impels such folk, unless it be that, with a certain insolence of mind, they rejoice to see many busy in their service; or that, in their swelling elation, they would fain seem to differ as far from the rest in merit as they differ in their food. Others have a most excessive care for the preparation of their meats; excogitating infinite varieties of seething or frying or seasoning: to-day soft, to-morrow hard; now cold, now hot; now boiled, now roast; first seasoned with pepper, or again with garlic or cummin or salt; for such folk have their own fancies like women great with child....

Concerning uncleanness at table, there is no need of many examples; but, when it hath been shown forth in some points, men may easily avoid the like on every point. Some men at table, in their haste to empty the dishes, wrap in the table-cloth, or even cast upon it, four-square fragments of crust still moist and dripping with the fat or gravy; until at length, having eaten out the bowels of the pasty, they cast back these remnants into their former place. Others, as they drink, plunge their fingers halfway into the cup. Others, wiping their greasy hands on their frocks, turn again to handle the food. Others fish for their pot-herbs with bare fingers in lieu of spoon, striving (as it would seem) to wash their hands and refresh their bellies in one and the same broth. Others dip again into the dishes their half-gnawed crusts and bitten morsels; thus, in their haste to make a sop for themselves, plunging that which their teeth have spared into the dish. These things, as I have said above, would be shameful for us to utter, but that others presume to do them: now, therefore, let those blush to hear who would not follow discipline in their actions.

60. RELICS RE-FOUND

From the contemporary *Life*, written by a disciple, of St William, Canon of Ste-Geneviève at Paris, and afterwards Abbot of Eskilsoe in Sweden, and of St-Thomas-du-Paraclet. The event here recorded happened in 1162, shortly after William had been saved by the personal intervention of the Pope from the persecutions inflicted on him by his fellow-canons on account of his inconvenient strictness and probity (*AA.SS. Boll.* April 6th, vol. I, p. 626).

WHILE a deep silence reigned everywhere, and every gust of storm in the monastery seemed to have been laid to rest, then a murmur arose among the people that the Head of the Blessed Geneviève had been taken away from the sanctuary. This spirit of blasphemy came at last to the king's ears; at which rumour the Lord King Louis was provoked to wrath and fury beyond all measure, swearing by the Holy One of Bethlehem, that, if this proved true, he would scourge all the

Canons and thrust them forth from the monastery. Wherefore, having appointed guardians to keep watch over the treasure and relics of that monastery, he sent letters to the Archbishop of Sens and his suffragans, and to the abbots and priors of that province, bidding all come together at Paris, on a day fixed by himself, to enquire into the truth of this thing. The Brethren, hearing of the King's oath, were troubled and dismayed; fear fell upon them; and, sore as they dreaded the royal wrath, yet they grieved more for that treasure, more excellent than gold or precious pearls, which they feared might have been abstracted. William above all men was grieved in spirit; for he, this long time past, had kept all the caskets of relics and the treasures of the church under his own charge.

The appointed day dawned; the King came with his courtiers, the Bishops with the Abbots, and no small multitude of others who wished to learn the issue of this matter. At last, when some had been appointed and assigned to go up with the Archbishop and his suffragans to the holy place of the sainted virgin, William would fain have gone with them, but they suffered him not. Wherefore, seizing a taper or a censer (I know not which) he said within himself: "If no other way be allowed me, at least I will go up as an attendant"; and thus he went. When therefore the shrine had been opened, behold! there lay St Geneviève's head, the jewel of France, with the other relics of her limbs, which when William saw—the faithful servant of that virgin saint—then he contained no longer the joy which his soul had conceived; but, forgetting those who were of greater authority than himself, he burst forth into sounds of exultation, and boldly raised the *Te Deum*, so that the whole church resounded with the might of his voice; whereupon the whole people, who had come together to this solemn day, took it up with no less alacrity than he, and sang it to the end; after which the Archbishop continued with the collect for the saintly virgin's day.

When, therefore, all these voices had ceased, then the Bishop of Orleans cried in exceeding indignation: "Who is that ribald who, against the authority of the lord Archbishop and the other Bishops, for the sake of the head of some old woman which these Brethren here have fraudulently imposed on us, hath so rashly presumed to raise the *Te Deum*?" To whom William made answer: "If you ask who I am, I would have you know that you have calumniated me, who am no ribald, but a servant of St Geneviève; and, whereas you accuse me of presumption, it was no rash presumption but the sincere love of the holy virgin which hath ever possessed me, that urged me to this deed. The head which ye have seen is (as I confess) that of an old woman, who kept the flower of virginity to her death; for St Geneviève lived seventy years and more in this world, a virgin ever clean and immaculate, until she gave up her soul to heaven and her material body to the earth. But, lest any scruple of doubt cling yet to your hearts, let now a furnace be heated seven times; and I, taking this head, will enter it without hesitation to make known the merits of that blessed virgin." To whom the Bishop scoffingly replied: "I for my part would not enter into a cup of hot water with this head, and wouldst thou enter into a burning fiery furnace?" Whereupon the Archbishop, no longer suffering this prelate's excessive babbling, signed to him to hold his peace, for he approved this devout Brother's pure and sincere devotion to the holy virgin. Moreover, that folly which the Bishop's foul mouth had vomited against the blessed virgin could by no means remain unpunished; for God shall destroy them that speak leasing; wherefore this Bishop in later days, involved in many crimes, was cast forth from his see and wretchedly ended his unworthy life by a death worthy [of his sins].[1]

---

[1] The good canon's zeal misleads him here: this sceptical Bishop of Orleans enjoyed an excellent reputation, and died peaceably in his bishopric more than twenty years after this event.

Mon. Germ. Hist. Scriptt. vol. XVII, pp. 232 ff. The editor, Dr Jaffé, notes
that this description was evidently written towards the end of the thirteenth
century: it contains several allusions to events which happened close upon
1290, but none later. The writer was probably a Dominican Friar.

61. ALSACE IN A.D. 1200

ABOUT the year of our Lord 1200, there were few priests
in Alsace; and it sufficed that one priest sang mass in every
two towns, or (if they were small) one in every three or four.
For many of the priests sang two masses almost daily, one in
one town and one in another; they also said the office in a
third; and, if there were a funeral or an espousal or a concourse of pilgrims, then they sang a third. Many priests had
but little learning, wherefore they were the less able to give
prudent counsel. Moreover the priests had concubines almost
as a general law [*quasi generaliter*], for the country-folk commonly persuaded them to this, saying, "The priest cannot
contain; wherefore it is better that he should have a single
wife than that he should do worse." Canons and knights were
wont to live with nuns of noble birth. The lord Henry,
Bishop of Bâle [A.D. 1215–1238], left at his death twenty
fatherless children in the hands of their different mothers.
Moreover in those days the clergy wore parti-coloured garments [like the laity]. . . . The town priests would preach the
Lord's Prayer and the creeds to their flocks on Sundays in the
German tongue; but few knew or could preach of Holy
Scripture. A single mass was sung about the hour of tierce, or
two in great towns and cities; one betimes for wayfarers,
another about tierce for the ladies. The kiss of peace[1] was
given at every mass; and the use of great candles at the canon[2]
of the mass was unknown. Few compilers of books could be
found; but afterwards many composed works in different
branches of learning. Master William was the first who wrote
questions and a complete book on the Sentences [of Peter
Lombard]; then Brother Albert [the Great]. . . Moreover
Brother Bonaventura, of the Order of St Francis, wrote
praiseworthy questions on the Sentences, and also Brother

[1] See note to *pax*, in vol. III, no. 23.
[2] The most sacred part of the mass.

Thomas [Aquinas].... Moreover Brother Vincent [of Beau-vais], of the Order of Friars Preachers,[1] wrote a Mirror of the World in four books, wherein he enclosed many [marvel-lous] and profitable things.... The wandering scholar Primas published many masterly verses.[2]...

Moreover the Friars Preachers built certain convents of women in Germany, which afterwards grew in all things to profit and honour; the beginning whereof is thus related by our fathers: When first the Brethren came into Germany, they found certain women shut up as recluses hard by chapels: these they multiplied and changed into convents.... Some of these convents gave all their lands out to be farmed by husband-men at a yearly rent, which they collected in due time through their lay-brethren and Béguines and man-servants and maid-servants; others again tilled their own land through their own lay-brethren, through whom also they directed their farms and granges, and had heavy cares. They directed all these things through their windows; for the Friars Preachers had no authority over them in the direction of their temporal affairs; through their windows also they spake with whomsoever they would, seeing, and being seen of those who were without.... The Friars Minor,[3] again, founded con-vents of ladies of their own Order, which also made good progress in all things. These Friars enclosed their nuns so straitly that they could never, or scarce ever, come abroad. They spake to men from their cloister, but were never seen; for they spake through a window of three or four feet square, which was closed by a sheet of iron pierced with a few small holes. Moreover this iron shutter was studded with many spikes, finger-long, so that none might put his eye to the holes in the iron: furthermore, a black cloth covered them from within. Whensoever any lady was received into their con-vents, she mounted a high ladder and thus entered the convent by the true door. They had an abbess, who instructed the rest in religion. Their food was cooked without the convent, and

---

[1] Dominicans.
[2] This witty vagrant wrote the most popular of those medieval satires which were ascribed in England to Walter Mapes.
[3] Franciscans.

sent in to the sisters within. Two or more Friars Minor lived outside for the time, one of whom directed them in spiritual matters, and the other in temporal, ministering to their bodily necessities. They had many lay-brothers and lay-sisters or Béguines,[1] with men-servants and maid-servants, who tilled their fields and vineyards and rendered them other services.

There were few monks in Alsace except the Black Monks and Black Nuns, and the Canons Regular of St Augustine. The Hospitallers and Templars and Antonines had houses or granges with chapels, which were ruled only by servants or few brethren of the Order. The Hospitallers of Bâle had two chapels which were served by one Gallus, a priest, whose necessities were ministered unto by a brother of St Antony's spital. The Cistercians, the Black Monks, and the Canons Regular wore the dress of their Orders, kept their constitutions, and abounded in riches. The Black Monks and Nuns who were not of the proper Rule of St Benedict, but subject to the immediate authority of the Pope,[2] kept the church service of St Benedict well according to the proper rite; but very many scorned to keep the dress and constitutions[3] and manners of Religious. There were hermitages hard by chapels, wherein were single women, or two or three enclosed together; of whom some were subject to the Black Monks, some to the White, some to the Cistercians, and others to other Religious, whose constitutions and customs they kept. The Friars Minor and Preachers and the Teutonic Knights were not as yet, but sprang up some eleven years later;[4] after whom sprang up many other religious Orders also, all of which Pope Gregory [X] is well known to have suppressed [in 1274].

In those days the University of Paris flourished and was renowned. The cities of Bâle and Strasbourg were but meanly walled and ill-provided with [public] buildings, but their private houses were yet more mean. Even strong and good

---

[1] Associations of women for the religious life, generally in a common house, but without absolute lifelong vows.

[2] *E.g.* the Cluniacs, who were exempt from ordinary jurisdiction.

[3] Ecclesiastical bye-laws.

[4] The first Franciscan settlement in Alsace was in 1222; the Dominicans arrived about the same time.

houses had few windows, and those of small size; and they lacked light. Colmar, Schlettstadt, Ruffach, Mühlhausen, and other small cities were not in those days. The nobles had in their towns towers of small size, which they could scarce defend against their fellow-nobles.... The knights spent their days in hunting, fishing, tournaments, jousts, and debauchery.[1]... The Knights wore body-armour of great and close-set and heavy rings. Abbots and clergy took goods on pawn from the poor, and thought that they did no sin. There were few merchants, almost all of whom were reputed rich: master-workers in mechanical trades were few also, and were counted among the rich. Surgeons were few, physicians yet fewer, Jews few also. Heretics swarmed in very many parts; but these were stamped out by the Friars Preachers, with much help from the lay lords.... There were few waggons, and the Alsatians used carts made without iron. Iron-shod or iron-bound carts came later into Alsace from Suabia. Men had but one kind of fowls, and those small; the great tailless fowls with crests and beards and yellow toes were brought in by travellers from distant lands. There was but one sort of doves or pigeons; the Greek pigeons with feathered feet, and many other kinds, were brought later into Alsace. Pheasants were brought by a certain clerk from beyond the seas....

The altars were small; they were three feet high and three in breadth and three in length, as in the ancient church of the apostolic times. The altar-slab jutted forth four finger-breadths beyond the body of the altar.... The fashion of building houses with plaster was not yet come into Alsace; for the earth called *gypsum*, from which plaster is made, was first found by the Alsatians long afterwards, in the year 1290, at Dürckheim. And the earth called *marl*, wherewith the country-folk fatten their fields, was found after the year of our Lord 1200. Men had then no studs to their sword-sheaths, nor had the monks buckles to their belts. The monks' belts had two long slits at one end, and at the other end they were divided into two long tails [which passed through these two holes]. The collegiate church at Marbach was 60 feet

---

[1] The chronicler here gives a gruesome description of the morals prevalent in high and low society.

broad within, from wall to wall, and twice as long. The chasubles[1] and copes for choir use were seven feet long and circular in shape. The canons' dalmatics[2] were ten feet broad, with sleeves of the breadth of eighteen inches, and they were five feet high. The folds of the canons' corporals[3] were three-quarters of a foot long and [blank in MS.] broad. The tower of their church had seven bells.[4]

The following extract forms the Prologue to the third book of that most interesting practical treatise on painting, enamelling, goldsmith's work, modelling, etc., which bears the name of Theophilus. The author was a monk, Roger of Helmershausen near Paderborn; he died probably about 1120. He certainly knew how to paint in oil, for he describes the process in some detail. The best edition is that of A. Ilg (Vienna, 1874); there is a translation by R. Hendrie; compare my *Art and the Reformation*, pp. 95-99.

62. GOD'S ARTIST

DAVID, that most excellent of prophets, whom the Lord God foreknew and predestined before the beginning of the ages, whom, for his simplicity and humility of mind, He chose as the man after His own heart, and set as prince over the people whom He loved, and strengthened with His Holy Spirit to dispose nobly and prudently so renowned a kingdom—this David, (I say,) collecting himself with all the attention of his mind to the love of his Creator, uttered this saying among others: "Lord, I have loved the beauty of Thine house." And —albeit a man of so great authority and of so deep an understanding called this house the habitation of the court of heaven, wherein God presideth over the hymning choirs of angels in glory that cannot be told, and for which David yearned with all his bowels, saying, "One thing have I asked of the Lord, this will I seek after; that I may dwell in the house of the Lord all the days of my life"; or again [he

---

[1] Sleeveless mantle in which the priest celebrates mass.
[2] Wide gowns used by the clergy.
[3] (Or corporas.) Linen cloth to cover the consecrated elements at mass.
[4] Compare all this with Cacciaguida's description of the simplicity of Florentine life in the early thirteenth century (*Par.* xv, 97 ff.).

describeth it as] the receptacle of a devout breast and most pure heart, wherein God doth indeed dwell; with the desire of which gracious guest he himself burned when he prayed, "Renew a right spirit within my bowels, O Lord"—yet it is certain that he desired the adornment of the material house of God, which is the house of prayer. For he left to Solomon his son almost all the stores of gold, silver, brass and iron for that house, which he himself desired most earnestly to build, yet because he had shed men's blood (that of his enemies, indeed, yet in great abundance), therefore he deserved it not. For he had read in Exodus how the Lord gave Moses a command for the construction of the Tabernacle, and had chosen Masters of the Works [operum magistros] by name, and had filled them with the Spirit of God in wisdom and in understanding and in knowledge and in all manner of workmanship in gold and silver and brass, precious stones and wood and all kinds of arts; also he had known by pious consideration that God delighteth in such adornments, which he purposed to have constructed by the teaching and authority of the Holy Ghost, believing that without His inspiration no man might bring any such thing to pass. Wherefore, most beloved son,[1] make thou no long delay, but believe in full faith that the Spirit of God hath filled thine heart when thou hast adorned His house with so great beauty and such manifold comeliness; and, lest perchance thou distrust me, I will unfold by evident reasons that, whatsoever thou canst learn, understand, or excogitate in the arts, this is given unto thee by the grace of the Sevenfold Spirit. By the Spirit of Wisdom thou knowest that all things created proceed from God, without Whom nothing is. By the Spirit of Understanding thou hast received the talent of invention, to know in what order or variety or measure thou mayest ply thy divers works. By the Spirit of Counsel thou hidest not the talent which God hath granted thee; but, working and teaching publicly yet humbly, thou dost faithfully show these things to such as desire to know them. By the Spirit of Fortitude thou shakest off all torpor of sloth, and, whatsoever thou shalt have steadfastly attempted and begun, the same thou bringest with all thy might to good

---

[1] The pupil, real or imaginary, to whom this treatise is addressed.

effect. By the Spirit of Knowledge given to thee, thou dost lord it through the abundant invention of thine heart; and, by so much more perfectly thou aboundest, by so much the more fully is thy mind emboldened in public. By the Spirit of Piety thou knowest what, to whom, when, how much and in what manner thou shouldst work; and, lest the vice of covetousness or greed creep upon thee, thou dost moderate the price of thy reward by pious consideration. By the Spirit of the Fear of the Lord thou considerest how thou canst do nothing by thyself; and how thou hast nothing, willest nothing, that God hath not given thee; wherefore believing, confessing, and giving thanks, thou imputest to God's mercy all that thou knowest, or art, or mayest be. Cheered by these supporting virtues, my beloved son, thou hast approached God's house in all faith, and adorned it with such abundant comeliness; and, having illuminated the vaults or the walls with divers works and divers colours, thou hast in a manner shown forth to the beholders a vision of God's paradise, bright as springtide with flowers of every hue, fresh with green grass and leaves, and refreshing the souls of the saints with crowns proportioned to their divers merits;[1] whereby thou makest them to praise God in His creatures and to preach His wonders in His works. For man's eye knoweth not whereon first to gaze; if he look up at the vaults, they are as mantles embroidered with spring flowers;[2] if he regard the walls, there is a manner of paradise; if he consider the light streaming through the windows, he marvelleth at the priceless beauty of the glass and at the variety of this most precious work. If the faithful soul chance to behold the effigy of our Lord's passion expressed in all its lineaments, then he is pricked to the heart; if again he see how great tortures the Saints endured in their mortal bodies, and how precious a prize of eternal life they won, then doth he receive encouragement to a better life; or, beholding how great is the joy in heaven, how awful the torments amid the flames of hell, then is he cheered with hope for his good deeds, and smitten with fear at the thought of his sins. Work

---

[1] These were the *aureoles*: see my *From St Francis to Dante*, 2nd ed., pp. 169, 382.
[2] *Vernant quasi pallia*; cf. the Squire in Chaucer's *Prologue*: "Embrouded was he, as it were a meede Al ful of fresshe floures whyte and reede."

therefore now, good man, happy in this life before God's face and man's, and happier still in the life to come, by whose labour and zeal so many burnt-offerings are devoted to God! Kindle thyself to a still ampler art, and set thyself with all the might of thy soul to complete that which is yet lacking in the gear of the Lord's house, without which the divine mysteries and the ministries of God's service may not stand; such as chalices, candelabra, thuribles, chrism-vases, crewets, shrines for holy relics, crosses, missals and such-like, which the necessary use of the ecclesiastical order requireth. Which if thou wouldst fashion, begin after the manner thus following.

[Then follow the several chapters of this third book; the titles of the few first may tempt the reader to pursue this study for himself. (i) Of the construction of the Workshop. (ii) Of the Worker's Bench. (iii) Of the Furnace. (iv) Of the Bellows. (v) Of the Anvils. (vi) Of the Hammers. (vii) Of the Pincers. (viii) Of the Irons for drawing wire. (ix) Of the Instrument called *Organarium*. (x) Of Files hollowed out beneath; etc., etc.]

Eustace, Abbot of St-Germer-de-Fly near Beauvais, died in 1211. His preaching, his sabbatarian letter sent down from heaven, and the jealousy of the English prelates, are described in Roger de Hoveden's *Annals*, under the year 1201 (tr. H. T. Riley, Bohn, 1853, vol. II, p. 526). It was very rare for the medieval *monk* (as apart from *friar*) to preach, except for abbots within their own monasteries to the brethren only.

63. A SABBATARIAN MISSIONARY

IN the same year, Eustace, Abbot of Flaye, returned to England, and preaching therein the word of the Lord from city to city, and from place to place, forbade any person to hold a market of goods on sale upon the Lord's Day. For he said that the commandment under written, as to the observance of the Lord's Day, had come down from heaven.

[Here follows a long document said to have been found upon an altar in the Holy Land.]

(p. 529). Accordingly, through these and other warnings of

this holy man, the enemy of mankind being rendered envious, he put it into the heart of the king and of the princes of darkness to command that all who should observe the before-stated doctrines, and more especially all that had discountenanced the markets on the Lord's Day should be brought before the king's court of justice, to make satisfaction as to the observance of the Lord's Day. But our Lord Jesus Christ, whom it is better to obey than man, and who, by His Nativity and Resurrection, and Advent, and by sending the Holy Ghost upon His disciples, rendered glorious this day, which we, accordingly, name the Lord's Day, and hallowed it as being the most distinguished, aroused the miraculous powers of His might, and thus manifested the same against some breakers of the Lord's Day.

One Saturday, a certain carpenter of Beverley, who, after the ninth hour of the day was, contrary to the wholesome advice of his wife, making a wooden wedge, fell to the earth, being struck with paralysis. A woman also, a weaver, who, after the ninth hour, on Saturday, in her anxiety to finish a part of the web, persisted in so doing, fell to the ground, struck with paralysis, and lost her voice. At Rafferton also, a vill belonging to Master Roger Arundel, a man made for himself a loaf and baked it under the ashes, after the ninth hour on Saturday, and ate thereof, and put part of it by till the morning, but when he broke it on the Lord's Day, blood started forth therefrom; and he who saw it bore witness, and his testimony is true....And yet, although by these and other miracles of His might, the Lord Almighty invited the people to the observance of the Lord's Day, still, the people, fearing more the royal and human favour than the Divine, and fearing those who kill the body, but are able to do no more, rather than Him, who, after he has killed the body, has power to send the soul to hell, and fearing more to lose the earthly things than the heavenly, and things transitory than things eternal, have, oh shame! like a dog to his vomit, returned to the holding of markets on the Lord's Day.[1]

---

[1] *E.g.* the Prior of Walsingham, in the thirteenth century, had "a grant of half the profits of the common place where the market on Saturday and Sunday was kept" (Blomefield's *Norfolk*, 1810, vol. IX, p. 276).

To this may be added, though not directly to the point, an entertaining anecdote recorded in Trevisa's *Higden*, R. S. vol. VIII, p. 247.

Aboute that tyme [1259] at Teukesbury a Jewe fel into a gonge [latrine] in a Satirday, wolde suffre no man drawe hym up for reverence of his holy day. But Richard of Clare, erle of Gloucestre, wolde suffre no man drawe hym up on the morwe in the Sonday for reverence of his holy day, and so the Jewe was dede.

64. THE SAVING GRACE OF THE ROD

From St Antonino of Florence, *Chronicon*, vol. III (1586), p. 636. The Reginald of this story was St Dominic's vicar, and a mission-preacher of extraordinary influence.

THIS Reginald (that you may know how strict he was in Religion) found that a certain lay-brother at Bologna had received a piece of cloth of little value, but without licence from his superior; he therefore burnt the cloth and caused the lay-brother to be sorely scourged in Chapter. The culprit murmured and refused to admit his fault; nay, he would not make himself ready for the rod, so that Brother Reginald caused the brethren to make him ready by main force. Then, laying on lustily, he raised his eyes to heaven and prayed that this discipline might drive the devil out of him, even as St Benedict had done in like case; moreover, he bade the brethren pray also for the sinner. Meanwhile the lay-brother was touched with compunction, and said even weeping: "I thank thee, father, that thou hast indeed driven the devil from me; for I felt sensibly how a serpent hath glided forth from my loins"; and so he became a good Religious.

Another apostatized, and would have fled from the friary, but was caught and brought into Chapter before Reginald, who stripped him and beat him sore, saying: "Devil, go forth!" Then, turning to the brethren, he said, "Pray, brothers, pray!" When this had continued already for a long space, at length the beaten friar cried, "Father, hear me!"

THE SAVING GRACE OF THE ROD

To whom Reginald made answer, "What wilt thou, son?" "Truly," said the other, "the devil is gone forth from me; and I promise that I will henceforth be stable in my profession."

This satire by a churchman on worldly abbots may be compared with the layman's satire in No. 115. It is printed by T. Wright on p. xliii of *Poems of W. Mapes* (Camden Soc. 1841) from the Bodleian MS. Digby 53. I have abridged it very considerably.

65. A WORLDLY ABBOT

ABOUT the second or third hour of the day, when the sun putteth off the cool of dawn and groweth to the strength of a youth, then at last doth the abbot arise from his couch; and, puking still with his supper of yesterday and his potations long-drawn into the night, he doth meditate forthwith how to fill his yet undisturbened maw. For indeed his meditation is more of belly than of God, more of sauce than of sacraments, of salmon than of Solomon; nor need we marvel, seeing that his belly is his god. First, therefore, he putteth on a shirt of finest linen, lest the hard hair vex his soft flesh; yet then, for some show of religion, he layeth a hair shirt over this, not without anxious care lest it wed itself for one moment to his bare body. Then come two fur coats or more, if the weather be cold; upon which he layeth a frock or frocks, adding cowl to cowl if need be. His legs are clad in linen drawers and woollen hosen, with boots not hobnailed but of buckskin, and super-hosen over all. Of over-shoes he hath no certain number; for they vary in accordance with the changes of heat or cold. So this fat and round-bellied abbot, thus stuffed out, goeth into the cloister; and there, seeing the cowled congregation, he throweth back his hood to his ears and thus goeth armed *cap-à-pie*. His manly brow is heavy with menace, his eyes stare forth from bushy eyebrows; his glance wandereth hither and thither like the stars in their courses; his mien is austere; his nostrils gape; and, coughing sharply, he roars and bellows like a tyrant; and thus he goeth ruminating, revolving both in mind and in mouth not the psalms but the sauces of yesternight. With such kindly embraces doth he raise and foster his flock; with such mercy doth he compassionate their infirmities. For he can cry truly with the apostle [Paul]: "Who is weak, and I am not strong? who is offended, and I rejoice not thereat?"[1] Then goeth he into the church, and, walking around, he pauseth not beside the altar but by the brothel;[2] for there will be one at least to whom he may say [with Ovid], "Thou alone art my joy; thou shalt lie with me to-night." Doth she consent? Yea, truly, nor can we marvel; since there is no wench so poor but she may soon flaunt gold on all her fingers, if a monk itch for her but now and then; the monk pays a pound for that which the clerk gets for a halfpenny or for love. O foul and preposterous thing, that maketh God's temple into a brothel; for hither come the she-wolves daily; and again, as saith the poet, "Those gaze who come; the women themselves come to be gazed upon." In short, the abbot goeth back to his fold; there, before the fire, feather-beds are laid for this spouse of Venus, with rugs and quilts so soft and velvety that they seem to swallow him up. After such pastime, my lord abbot's table is laid; but with how many dishes may scarce be told. Yet, innumerable as these are in their abundance, there is naught of four-footed beasts, to taste whereof would be to break the Rule. What then doth he eat? Great fishes, for the small he holdeth in no esteem; fishes boiled and fishes fried, fishes roast and fishes stuffed, fishes gilded with egg-yolk. Doth he then abstain from all flesh-food? Nay, but from the four-footed alone. What, he eateth the winged fowls? Nay: but, once plucked of their wings and cooked, then he may eat them; for they, like fish are born in the water; and of fish he may lawfully eat.[3] Such

---

[1] This is, of course, a parody of 2 Cor. xi, 29, twisting it into the exact opposite

[2] This seems to be intended by *non ad altaria immo lup[an]aria declinat ad latera luparia*, as printed by Wright, seems difficult to reconcile with the context.

[3] The theory that fowls may count as fish is an ancient and respectable evasio of the spirit of the Rule; it may even be found in Rabanus Maurus, who wrote the model monastery of Fulda. Martène, in his *Commentarius in Regulam*, give the authorities on both sides. Rabanus relied, as the satirist implies, on Genesis 20, where fish and fowl are represented as created from the waters on the same da But the large majority of disciplinarians recognized that the prohibition quadrupeds implied that of fowls, which were not only more expensive but "wi

men defend their error with the authority of St Ambrose, who wrote, "Great God! whose mighty power doth raise this kind from the waters, and doth send some of them back to the eddying deep again, whereas Thou raisest others to soar in air." Thou therefore, my lord abbot, dost send into the depth of thy maw both flying and swimming fowls without distinction, since both are sprung from the deep; to those eddying depths of thine, I say, thou sendest peacocks and swans, cranes and geese, hens and capons. Cocks he eateth not; for their flesh is tough and tasteless; moreover, if both cocks and hens were eaten, their progeny would fail; and my lord would rather be roasted at the fire than that fowls should fail. The raven, again, my lord hath sworn never to eat; for the raven sent forth from Noah's ark found a carcase and returned not; wherefore he is a wicked and unprofitable fowl. Owls he eateth not; for that is a foul and hated bird. Of wolves there are two sorts, the wood-wolf and the water-wolf [or pike]. The water-wolf he claimeth for his own, strong in St Ambrose's word; the wood-wolf he loatheth, not only as a quadruped but also as a cruel beast. Of another thing which is raised to hang in the air, of the flitch of bacon, what thinketh he? The flitch itself he eateth not, for that is four-footed; yet, seeing that its flesh is savoury and rich in fat, he doth most diligently comment upon its text, and doth come at last to this conclusion, that if the bacon be so long tormented and tossed in the frying-pan that it be turned altogether to liquor, then (since liquor cannot be eaten), he may lawfully take of that which is now converted into drink.[1] But the twisted osier-rope, whereby the flitch is hung, he eateth not, albeit it be no four-footed beast, and be suspended in the air. Wherefore? First, for that it is of a dry and leathery complexion; and secondly, for that it is not born of water. From the bones also he abstaineth, for these breed gross and indigestible humours; moreover, bones are dogs' food; and our abbot is so religious that he will not unjustly baulk the dogs.

their sweetness and pleasure to the taste, they are wont to provoke carnal temptations" (p. 524).

[1] See the evidence of Peter the Venerable in his private comments on the reformed statutes of Cluny, *Pat. Lat.* vol. 189, col. 1028.

Yet, over and above, he eateth many eggs,[1] for these are according to the Rule, and preservative of health; your egg is a comfortable and digestible meat, and (as Ovid testifieth) provocative of lust, which doth the more commend it. But, seeing that the Rule forbiddeth him to exceed the number five, therefore he eateth five hard eggs, five soft, five fried and five boiled, five white eggs in cummin and five black in pepper, five in meat-pasties and five in cheese-pasties, five scrambled and five half-raw, and five blown into ring-cakes; which, albeit they are collectively fifty-five, yet, taken distributively, they are but five of each. Of sauces and condiments what can I tell? he is indignant if each several dish have not his own peculiar sauce. Wines are set before the lord abbot of divers colours, white and red; the white on his right, as being of greater authority,[2] and the red on his left. From each he taketh the first-fruits, drinking nine times, that he may taste and prove the savour of the wine. Then, drinking with intention,[3] he draineth one draught, single but deep, for the peace and stability of the church, secondly for the prelates, thirdly for their subjects, fourthly for all prisoners, fifthly for the sick, sixthly for fair weather, seventhly for a calm sea, ninthly [sic] for all travellers and pilgrims, tenthly for those that stay at home, eleventhly that his monks may eat little, twelfthly that he himself may eat much, thirteenthly for all Christian folk, fourteenthly for human affairs, fifteenthly that the Lord God may send His dew upon Mount Gilboa, whereby the harvests may whiten and the vines flourish and the pomegranates may sprout; and thus he concludeth his draught with an uneven number, as saith the poet, "God loveth odd numbers." Of the rest, indeed, he drinketh not but sippeth only, that he may temper the inextinguishable

---

[1] In all surviving accounts and rolls we find an enormous consumption of eggs recorded; at Winchester, for instance, on the Monday after Christmas, 1492, the monks had nearly five eggs each, in addition to marrow-pudding, numbles of venison, beef and mutton. One fish day, these thirty monks had put before them four hundred eggs, with salmon, whiting, and minnows (G. W. Kitchin, *Obedientiary Rolls of St Swithun's*, 1892, pp. 67, 314, 326).

[2] Prof. J. S. Reid supplied me with two references for this use of *auctoritas* in the sense of "alcoholic strength".—Pliny, *Hist. Nat.* xiv, §§ 68 and 69.

[3] The satirist here alludes to the intentions with which different masses were celebrated.

heat of his stomach. These are the sufferings which he en-dureth for Christ. When supper is done, and the tables are set aside, he cannot rise from his seat, unless he be raised by both arms, like a cow stuck in a miry slough; and then, coming to the customary grace, he maketh no long prayers, but pretermitteth the "Miserere mei Deus," beginning with a hiccough, "Laudate Dominum, *puf* omnis gens, laudate, *puf* et omnis spiritus laudet, *puf*."[1] For, in his psalmody, he joineth not word to word, but with puking interpolations he stealeth one word and halveth another. When, therefore, after supper, this abbot sitteth in his chair, with one to prop him under each arm, and his belly filled to the very gorge, then beginneth he to bring the winds out of his treasures [Ps. cxxxv, 7]; for else he would burst asunder in the midst; to this purpose he openeth wide his nostrils and gapeth with his mouth; the congregation marvelleth at fumes like the fumes of Enceladus, and blasts as though the prison-house of Aeolus were burst open.

66. THE SERF-MARKET

From T. Madox, *Formulare Anglicanum*, pp. 418 ff.

(i) To all whom these presents may concern, Brother John, Abbot of Bruerne and the monks of that [Cistercian] Abbey, greetings in the Lord. Know that we have sold to William, Squire to the lord Nicholas de Noers, Hugh the Shepherd our serf of the manor of Certelle, with all his chattels and live-stock, and we have quit-claimed him of us and our successors for ever, so that we henceforth may exact or vindicate no right or claim in him. For which sale and quit-claim the aforesaid

---

[1] Compare the quotation from Chaucer which I give in illustration of Extract No. 4, p. 26 (*Cant. Tales*, D, 1929):

> Me thynketh they been lyk Iovinyan,
> Fat as a whale, and walkynge as a swan,
> All vinolent as botel in the spence.
> Hir preyere is of ful greet reverence
> Whan they for soulès seye the Psalm of Davit,
> Lo, *buf*, they seye, *cor meum eructavit*.

William hath given us four shillings sterling; in testimony whereof we have set our seal to this present deed.

(ii) To all whom these presents may concern, Matilda, relict of John the Leech, greeting. Know that I, in my widowhood and my full power, have sold to the Abbot of Bruerne, for twenty shillings, Richard son of William de Eastend of Linham, my man, with all his chattels and all his live-stock; and I have quit-claimed of me and of my heirs for ever all right or claim which I had or might have had in the said Richard or his chattels or his stock, so that I and my heirs may henceforth exact nothing from the said Richard or from any man on his account. And, that none may doubt this, I have published these deeds present, sealed with mine own seal, for a testimony.

(iii) Know all present and future that I, Dame Aundrina de Driby, formerly wife to Robert de Driby, in my lawful power and free widowhood, have given, granted, quit-claimed, and by this my present deed confirmed, for myself and my heirs, to my well-beloved and faithful Henry Cole of Baston and his heirs, for their service, Agnes daughter to Jordan Blanet of Baston, and Simon Calf her son dwelling at Stamford, with all their chattels and live-stock, and suits and issue, and all claim of serfdom and villeinage which I or my heirs have or might have had therein, To be had and held by the aforesaid Henry and his heirs, fully and in peace, freely, quietly and untrammelled of me or of mine heirs from all service or secular exaction for ever, Yet so that neither I Aundrina nor mine heirs, nor any man on my part or theirs, may henceforth vindicate or exact any claim of serfdom or villeinage in the said Agnes and Simon, or in their chattels, stock, suits and issue....In witness whereof, etc., etc.

67. THE POWER OF POVERTY

From St Antonino of Florence, *Chronicon*, vol. III (1586), p. 670.

O N E day that Master Jordan [Minister General of the Dominicans, d. 1237] lodged in a certain Cistercian abbey, and many of the monks sat round him, then said they unto him: "Master, how can your Order endure? seeing that ye have no livelihood but by begging; and ye know well that, however the world may be now devoted to you, yet (as it is written in the Gospel) the love of many shall wax cold; and then shall ye lack alms, and fail." Then answered Master Jordan with all meekness: "I will show you by force of reason, from your own words, that your own Order will fail sooner than ours. Read in the Gospel, and ye shall find that those words, 'The love of many shall wax cold,' are written of those days when iniquity shall abound and there shall be intolerable persecutions. Then shall ye know well that these persecutors and tyrants, abounding in iniquity, shall deprive you of your worldly possessions; and then needs must ye fail, since ye are not wont to go begging alms from place to place. But in those days the brethren of our Order shall be scattered abroad, and shall make all the more fruit, even as the Apostles were dispersed in the days of persecution. Nor will they thus be hindered; nay, rather, they will go by two and two from place to place seeking their livelihood even as they have ever been wont to do. And mark ye this also; that those very men who will take from you will gladly give unto our Order, in so far as we vouchsafe to accept it; for we have oftentimes seen by experience how robbers and thieves are glad enough to give us[1] of those things which they take from others; but we will not receive them."

---

[1] The text has *vobis*, but the sense evidently requires *nobis*; this is one of the commonest of misreadings in medieval documents.

68. ROYAL BLOODSUCKERS

From Additions to Adam of Domerham's *Chronicle*, p. 658. A rough list, for business purposes, of the sums claimed by the Crown from certain abbeys for the intervals between the death of one abbot and the institution of his successor.

REDEMPTIONS of certain Abbeys when vacant.

The abbey of St Edmundsbury rendereth 1200 marks for every vacancy, long or short; and the monks have made fine for £200.

The abbey of [*Ulmo*]? 200 marks for each four months [of vacancy].

The abbey of St Albans, for every vacancy of a year or less, 1000 marks; and, if longer, then more in proportion.

The abbey of Evesham, for every vacancy of a year, 200 marks, and, if for a less time, then in proportion, for the temporalities of the abbey.

The abbey of Tavistock, for each vacancy of four months or less, £40; and, after that period, in the proportion of 100 marks per annum.

69. MIRACLES AND MONEY

From Matthew Paris, *Chronica Majora*, ann. 1223.

IN that year [1223], holy miracles multiplied at Bromholm, to the glory and honour of that saving Cross whereon the Saviour of the World deigned to suffer death for the redemption of mankind. And since this sea-girt isle of Britain hath merited by God's grace to be enriched with so great a treasure, it is most worthy that we should impress upon the memory of posterity by what means this relic was brought from so far to our shores. Baldwin, Count of Flanders, became Emperor of Constantinople, where he lived and did great deeds for many years;[1] after which it befell that he was once grievously troubled with certain treacherous kings. Against these he

[1] He reigned in fact only two years; the Bulgarians defeated him at Constantinople and tortured him to death.

set forth impetuously and without due deliberation, leaving behind the Lord's Cross and other relics which the patriarch and bishops had always been wont to bear before him, whensoever he went out to war against the enemies of the Cross; which neglect he now learned most miserably to his cost. [He was defeated, and never seen again.] But at that time there was a certain chaplain of English birth who, with his clerks, celebrated the divine mysteries in the emperor's chapel; he was guardian of the imperial relics and rings and other possessions. When therefore he heard of the death (as all men said)[1] of his emperor, he slipped away secretly from Constantinople with the said relics and rings and many other things, among which were certain precious stones. Thence he came to St Albans, where he sold to one of our monks a certain cross of silver-gilt, with two fingers of St Margaret and gold rings and precious stones, all of which are held in great veneration in the abbey. Then the said chaplain, drawing from his mantle a certain cross of wood, showed it to certain of our monks, asserting with an oath that this was without doubt of that same tree whereon the Saviour of the World hung for the redemption of our race. But men believed him not; wherefore he departed thence, bearing with him his inestimable but unknown treasure. Now this same chaplain had two small sons, for whose care and sustentation he was most solicitous; and this care of his impelled him to offer the aforesaid cross to many monasteries, in order that he and his sons might be received to be monks. At last, after suffering frequent repulse from rich monasteries, he came to a certain cell called Bromholm, miserably poor and lacking convenient buildings, situated in the land of Norfolk. There he called together the prior and certain of the brethren, and showed them the said cross, made of two pieces of wood fixed transversely, and of about a hand's length; and he besought them in all humility to receive him and his sons, with this cross and the other relics which he had, to the monastic vows. The prior and his brethren, overjoyed at such a treasure, by God's disposition, who doth ever foster honourable poverty,

---

[1] Many believed that Baldwin was still alive, and in 1125 a false Baldwin appeared and claimed the county of Flanders.

gave credence to the chaplain's words; and, reverently taking this divine wood, they brought it into their church and kept it with all possible devotion in the most honoured place. This year then, as we have said, divine miracles began in this monastery, to the praise and glory of this life-giving cross; for there are the dead raised to life, the blind have their sight, the lame walk, the possessed are loosed from their devils; in short, all sick folk who come to the aforesaid cross with true faith go away whole and well. So that this cross is now not only frequented, adored, and worshipped by the English nation, but it is also most devoutly venerated by men from distant lands.[1]

70. HUSH-MONEY

[1260] From Adam of Domerham's *Chronicle* (ed. T. Hearne, 1727, p. 528).

GEOFFREY the Comber of Lym pleaded urgently for payment of the debts of brothers John Barnage, John of Ashbury, and Thomas of Blakealle, who had been cellarers under the aforesaid Abbot Roger [of Glastonbury]. These debts amounted to £51. 16s. 6d.; whereof the said Geoffrey had sufficient tallies, and a recognizance of the debt under the hands of those brethren. But it befell about this time that the said Geoffrey, at the instigation of the Devil and of his own drunkenness, committed a certain transgression in Glastonbury, whereby his good report would have suffered greatly if he had not had the favour of the abbot and his bailiffs; for which cause he offered many gifts. The abbot, therefore, desiring less his own private profit than the liberation of the monastery, took a quittance of the aforesaid money, together with the tallies [that vouched the debt], and hushed up the man's transgression and set him free without more ado.... Moreover, in the days of this Abbot Roger certain uncircumspect persons, taking occasion from a contention which arose between that abbot and his monks, brake feloniously into our

1 Cf. *Piers Plowman*, B, v, 231.

cloister against the brethren, in a great armed multitude, scorning the fear of God and the immunities of the church, and on many other occasions heaped injuries and contumely upon us; wherefore, on the death of the said Roger and the installation of Abbot Robert, the Lord Bishop of Bath bade that the said sacrilegious persons should be publicly banned as excommunicate throughout the diocese, and that their names should be diligently sought out, as indeed he had already done in Roger's lifetime. Wherefore very many of these men, whether terrified by the said denunciation and inquest, or perchance smitten with godly compunction, did devoutly and effectually offer themselves to such satisfaction as lay in their power; by which occasion our abbey sucked no small profit from the satisfaction offered by some of these evil-doers.

The so-called *Lanercost Chronicle*, from which these extracts are taken, was not written at the monastery of that name, as earlier antiquaries supposed, but by a Grey Friar, probably of Carlisle. It extends in its original form to 1307, but is partly based on older materials. Like nearly all compilations by the early friars, it is full of picturesque anecdotes and human touches. It was edited for the Maitland Club by Father Stevenson in 1839. A translation of the greater part of it by Sir Herbert Maxwell has appeared in the *Scottish Historical Review*; though not always accurate, it is very readable and interesting.

71. MONASTIC WIZARDS

(P. 85, A.D. 1268.)

LET the reader remember, for the safeguarding of unpolluted faith in God, that during the ravages of that cattle-plague which men call *Lungessouth* in London this year, certain beastly fellows with the dress, but not the mind, of cloisterers taught the ignorant countryfolk to make fire by the rubbing of sticks and to set up an image of Priapus, and by these means to succour the cattle. Which when a certain Cistercian lay-brother had done at Fenton, before the hall hearth, and had sprinkled the animals with holy water mingled with filthy matters of his own invention, and when the lord of the manor was rebuked by a certain faithful Christian for the invention of such idolatry, then he pleaded in his own defence that all this had been done in his absence and without his knowledge, adding: "And know that, whereas until this month of June other men's beasts were sick and ailing, while mine were ever hale; yet now I lose two or three daily, so that few are left to till my fields."

On p. 109 the chronicler records a far worse instance of the same Priapus-worship, in which the parish priest of Inverkeithing used to muster his parishioners to dance with him round the idol. It may be found in full in the *Scottish Historical Review*, vol. VI, p. 177.

72. THE DEMON MONK
(P. 163, A.D. 1295.)

THERE befell a detestable and marvellous thing in the western parts of Scotland, in Clydesdale, some four miles from Paisley, in the house of one Sir Duncan of the Isles, which should strike terror into sinners and demonstrate the appearance of the damned on the day of the final resurrection. A man who lived wickedly under the habit of holy Religion, and who came to a most evil end under the curse of excommunication for certain sacrileges committed in his own monastery—this man's corpse, I say, long after his burial in the said monastery, haunted many men with illusions that could be seen and heard amid the shades of night. After which this son of darkness transferred himself to the aforesaid knight's dwelling, that he might try the faith of the simple and by his adverse deeds deter them [from evil] in plain daylight, or perchance that, by God's secret judgment, he might thus show who had been implicated in this crime of his. Wherefore, taking to himself a body (whether natural or aerial we know not, but in any case black, gross, and palpable), he was wont to come in noonday light under the garb of a black monk of St Benedict, and sit upon the gable of the barn or corn-grange; and whensoever a man would shoot him with arrows or pierce him with a pitchfork, then whatsoever material substance was fixed into that damned spectre was burned forthwith, more swiftly than I can tell the tale, to ashes. Those also who would have wrestled with him he threw and shook so horribly as though he would break all their limbs. The lord's firstborn, a squire grown to man's estate, was foremost in this attack upon the phantom. One evening, therefore, as the master of the house sat with his household round the hall fire, that sinister shape came among them and troubled them with blows and throwing of missiles; then the rest scattered in flight, and that squire alone fought single-handed with the ghost; but, sad to tell, he was found on the morrow slain by his adversary. If however it be true that the Devil receiveth power over none but such as have lived like swine, then it may easily be divined wherefore that young man met with so terrible a fate.

73. OVERWORKED ST FRANCIS
(P. 183, A.D. 1296.)

F OR few can be found in this age of ours who deserve to taste of the sweetness of divine revelation; not that God is niggardly, but that our spiritual palate is infected: howbeit a certain holy virgin, long consecrated to the life of a recluse, had in this year a revelation which I must not pass over in silence.... [She was caught up to heaven on the Feast of St Francis]... and when she enquired the names [of the saints whom she saw there], and asked wherefore St Francis was nowhere to be seen, then St John Baptist made answer, "He, on this his own holy-day, must needs intercede before God for many that call upon him as a new-made saint; wherefore he could not come on this occasion."

Jacques de Vitry studied at Paris, was ordained priest in 1210, and devoted himself to preaching by the advice of the Blessed Mary of Oignies, whose *Life* he also wrote. After her death in 1213 he preached the crusade first against the Albigensians and then against the Saracens. In 1214 he was elected Bishop of Acre; here he worked many years with his accustomed zeal, until at last, disheartened by the vices and failures of the crusaders, he resigned in or about 1227. Next year he was made a cardinal, and in 1239 elected Patriarch of Jerusalem; but the Pope was unwilling to spare him. He probably died in 1240. A passage from one of his letters, recording his enthusiasm for the new-born Franciscan Order, may be found in Sabatier's *St François d'Assise*, c. xiii, p. 261. His *Historia Occidentalis* and *Historia Orientalis* describe the age in language even more unfavourable than that of Roger Bacon and others quoted in this book; but the main human interest of his works is contained in the *Exempla*, or stories for the use of preachers, published by Professor Crane for the Folk-Lore Society in 1890. A good many of these had already appeared anonymously among T. Wright's *Latin Stories*. Professor Crane's edition, though of very great value, contains a good many misreadings which I have been able to emend by collations procured from the Paris MS. References are to folios of the MS. Lat. 17,509 of the Bibliothèque Nationale, and to pages in Crane's edition.

74. THE ROBBER'S CONVERSION

(Fol. 61, p. 29.)

WE have heard of a certain holy abbot, a most religious man, that when a certain impious brigand, a desperate man and leader of a band of robbers, laid waste the country wherein he dwelt, spoiling and killing many, then this abbot mounted his horse and went to the place where the robber and his band dwelt. They therefore, seeing him from afar, ran together to take his horse and strip him. "What wilt thou?" asked this abbot of the chief of the robbers; and he: "I would have this horse and all thy garments." Then said the abbot: "I have long ridden this horse, and worn these garments, it is not right that I alone should enjoy these goods, wherefore I will give them to thee and thy fellows if thou art in need." Then said the robber: "To-day we will sell the horse and garments, to buy bread, wine, and flesh withal." Then said the abbot: "Son, why dost thou travail so sore for thy livelihood and walk in peril of thy life? Come with me to the monastery, and I will entertain thee better than this for as long as thou wilt, and will minister to all thy needs." "Nay," said he, "for I could not eat your beans and potherbs, or drink your sour wine and beer." Then said the abbot: "I will give thee white bread and most excellent wine, with fish and flesh to thine heart's desire." With much ado, therefore, he yielded, that he might prove awhile what the abbot would do with him. The abbot, when they were come to the cloister, brought him into a most fair chamber and let make a great fire, and a fair soft bed with costly coverlets, and set apart a monk to provide him with all that his soul desired. Moreover he bade that this monk, after serving him daily in all luxury of victuals, should himself eat bread and water in this robber's presence. When therefore the robber had marked for many days how sparing a diet the monk kept, then he thought within himself that the monk must have done much evil to do so sore a penance, and enquired of him one day: "Brother, what hast thou done that thou so afflictest thyself daily: hast thou slain men?" "Nay, my lord..." said he, "God forbid, that I should ever have vexed any man, much less have slain him; for I entered into this monastery from my very childhood." "Hast thou then done fornication, or adultery, or sacrilege?" Then the monk crossed himself in amazement, saying: "Lord, what is this word that thou hast spoken? God shield me from all such iniquity: I have never even touched a woman." "What then hast thou done," quoth he, "that thou dost thus afflict thy body?" "My lord, it is for God's sake that I do thus; that by fasting and prayers and other works of penitence I may earn His favour." The robber, hearing this, was pricked to the heart, and began to think within himself: "Why, what an unhappy wretch am I, that have ever done so many evil deeds—thefts and manslaughters, adulteries and sacrilege—yet have never fasted one single day, whereas this innocent monk doth daily so great a penance." Then, calling for the abbot, he fell at his feet, begging him to receive him among the community of the brethren: after which he long dwelt among them in such affliction of the body as to excel all the rest in abstinence and religious practices. Wherefore the abbot, by the example of the monk who ministered to this robber, not only gained his soul for God, but delivered many from death, whom that robber would have despoiled and slain.

75. THE PERILOUS FAMILIARITY
OF WOMEN

(Fol. 148, p. 117.)

A CERTAIN most religious man told me, how in the parts where he had dwelt it came to pass that a certain honest and God-fearing matron, coming oftentimes to church by day and night, served God with right good devotion, and how a certain monk, the guardian and treasurer of the monastery, had a great name for Religion,[1] and was in truth what he seemed. But as they frequently spoke together in church of things appertaining to religion, then the Devil, envying their honesty and their good report, beset them with vehement temptations, so that their spiritual was turned to carnal love; wherefore they agreed together and assigned a night wherein the monk should run away from his cloister with the treasure of the church, and the matron from home with a sum of money which she should secretly steal from her husband. When therefore they had thus fled stealthily away, the monks, rising to matins, found the chests broken open and the church treasure carried off; and, not finding the monk, they pursued hastily after him. The husband also, seeing his chest open and his money gone, followed after his wife: so that, having caught the monk and the woman together with the treasures, they brought them back and cast them into a strait dungeon. But so great was the scandal throughout the region round about, and so sorely did all men backbite the Religious, that there was far more harm from the evil report and scandal than from the sin itself. Then the monk came to himself, and began with many tears to call upon the Blessed Virgin, whom he had ever served from his childhood upwards, and nought of this kind had befallen him. Likewise also the aforesaid matron began to implore instantly the help of the Blessed Virgin, whom she had been wont to salute frequently by day and night, and to kneel before her image. At length the Blessed Virgin appeared to them in great wrath, and, after rebuking them bitterly, she spake thus: "I might obtain

---

[1] Any Order of Cloisterers (as Monks, Canons Regular, Friars, Nuns, etc.).

from my Son the remission of your sin; but what can I do for so great a scandal? for ye have made the name of the Religious[1] to stink in the nostrils of the whole people, so that men will have no faith in them from henceforth: which is an almost irreparable loss." At length the pitiful Virgin, overcome by their prayers, summoned to her presence the demons who had instigated this sin, and enjoined upon them, even as they had brought Religion into disrepute, even so to put an end to this evil fame. They therefore, unable to resist her commands, found after long and anxious thought a way whereby the ill-repute might cease. They brought back the monk by night to his church, repairing the broken chest and restoring the treasure as it was before; so also they locked again the chest which the matron had opened, and restored the money, and set the lady in her own chamber, in the place where she was wont to pray. When therefore the monks had found the treasure of their church, with the monk praying to the Lord as usual; and the husband his wife and his wealth even as it was before, then all were amazed and bewildered; and hastening to the prison they found the monk and the lady in chains, even as they had left them:—so at least it seemed; for one demon had taken the form of the monk, and another that of the lady. When therefore the whole city was gathered together to see these miracles, then said the demons in all men's hearing: "Let us depart now, for we have deluded them long enough and given cause for evil thoughts enough concerning Religious folk." Having thus spoken, they suddenly disappeared: and all men fell at the feet of the monk and the lady and besought their pardon. Behold how great infamy and scandal and inestimable damage the Devil would have procured to persons of Religion but for the succour of the Blessed Virgin.[2]

[1] The members of a religious Order.
[2] This was a very popular tale in the Middle Ages: see the other versions referred to by Lecoy de la Marche in his edition of the *Anecdotes* of Étienne de Bourbon (1877, p. 449).

76. CHRIST, MARY, AND THE FRIARS

From St Antonino, *Chronicon*, vol. III (1586), p. 636.

THERE was, in the [Dominican] friary at Spoleto, a certain novice of noble birth and of great simplicity and purity. One day, as he repeated that hymn of the Blessed Virgin, "Who rulest earth and sea and sky," and came to these words "holding the world in His fist," he marvelled greatly to think that God was of such great stature that He could hold the whole world in His hand. Therefore, being ashamed to enquire of this matter, he prayed the Lord continually that He might vouchsafe to show him the truth of this matter. So it came to pass that he fell asleep one evening in his prayers; and it seemed that he was suddenly rapt up to heaven. Thereupon there came a multitude of angels carrying a great throne and setting it down in a wide open space; after whom came another band of angels bearing another throne which they set up over against the first. Then, in the third place, an innumerable multitude of the heavenly host bore Christ, as the angry Judge, and set him upon the first throne; upon the second over against him they set the glorious Virgin; and then at last came the multitude of all the saints, each in his own order. There in heaven was such fear and trembling as had never been known since the beginning of the world. So, after all these ceremonies, the Judge commanded that the books should be opened and the good deeds of the world rehearsed aloud; which were found to be but few. Then He bade read the evil deeds; and these were so many that He loathed to hear them all; but, falling into a sudden fury, He seized the world as though it were a tennis-ball, and cast it violently down, saying: "When it is judged, let it be condemned and cast away!"

The novice aforesaid shuddered to see this; wherefore he cried with a loud voice saying: "Holy Mary, succour us in our wretchedness!" At which cry the compassionate Virgin Mary rose from her seat, and caught in her own hand the world that had been thus cast away, and said: "O Son, suffer this world which Thou hast redeemed with Thine

CHRIST, MARY, AND THE FRIARS

own blood to be judged once again;[1] for now have I sent forth my [Friars] Preachers to recall the world to Thee." Marvellous and most stupendous to relate! for, even as that novice cried aloud, there followed an earthquake throughout the city and the whole country round about, so that many towers and buildings were thrown to the ground, and men and women fled forth that night from the city.

There is a similar story in the *Lives of the Brethren* (ed. Reichert, 1896, pp. 6 ff.; tr. Placid Conway, 1896, p 1; abridgment by Myrc in my *Social Britain*, p. 238). In a slightly different form it appears in early Franciscan legend. The self-laudation of these friars' visions is cruelly parodied by Chaucer in his *Summoner's Prologue*; what is perhaps the original suggestion of this parody may be found in Caes. Heist. vol. II, p. 279 (Extract 93 in this present volume).

[1] The text has *judicare* where we should expect *judicari*; but the general sense is plain.

Caesarius of Heisterbach was possibly born, and certainly educated, at Cologne, then one of the richest and busiest cities of Europe. After some inward struggles, he was at last converted by the story of the harvester-monks and the Virgin Mary (No. 57, above); upon which he entered the Cistercian monastery of Heisterbach in the Siebengebirge. In this house, then at the height of its efficiency and influence, he finally became prior and teacher of the novices, for whose special guidance he wrote his delightful *Dialogus Miraculorum*, one of the most intimate documents of the Middle Ages. He also wrote a few biographical and chronological treatises, and a book of Homilies. All these were apparently written between 1220 and 1235: the last dated event he mentions occurred in 1233. The *Dialogue* was printed five or six times between 1475 and 1605; the Homilies only once, in 1615. The author's faults are those of his time; his virtues of earnestness and vividness will perhaps be apparent even from these extracts. Father B. Tissier, reprinting him in 1662 in the *Bibliotheca Patrum Cisterciensium*, praises him as just the author to arouse the slumbering embers of strict Cistercian observance, and adds, "yet it is lamentable that this authority, who has deserved so excellently of the Church, should now at last, after so many centuries, be called not only fabulous but even erroneous; whereas, if he be attentively read even by a jealous critic, nothing can be found in him strange to Catholic doctrine" (t. II, Preface). The modern view is rather that of Father Karl Unkel: "The almost scrupulous love of truth which Caesarius shows in his anecdotes is well known, but equally so is his great credulousness" (*Annalen des Historischen Vereins f. d. Niederrhein*, Heft 34, 1879, p. 5). The interlocutors in the *Dialogue* are Caesarius himself, and a novice whom he is instructing. I quote by volume and page from Joseph Strange's critical edition (Cologne, 1851). The whole book is now accessible in a translation by H. v. E. Scott and C. Swinton Bland—the first translation into any vernacular language (Routledge & Co., 2 vols. 1929).

77. THE ANATOMY OF CONVERSION

(Vol. 1, p. 11.)

THE Monk. Conversion is the *turning of the heart* [*cordis versio*], either from evil to good, or from good to better, or from better to best....There is also another kind of conversion, when a man changes his place and his garb out of zeal for some Religious Order. Such a conversion often cometh to pass without contrition. It is no great thing in God's sight for a sinner to change his place and not his fault, to change his garb and not his mind. It is a monstrous thing to wear a wolf's heart under a sheep's dress.

Novice. Does this also commonly happen? [*contingere solet*].

M. Yes; and here is an example. Brother Gottfried of our monastery, who was formerly canon of St Andreas at Cologne, when he and I were novices together, told me a noteworthy matter. He said that it had been told him by a monk of Clairvaux, whom he knew well, how a certain dissolute clerk, of those who are wont to wander from province to province, came to Clairvaux not truly in zeal for the Order, but hoping to steal something from the monastery under the cloak of religion. He therefore became a novice, and lay in wait for the church ornaments during the whole year of his probation; yet these were so carefully kept that he found no satisfaction for the iniquity of his heart. Wherefore he thought within himself, "When I shall be made a monk, and suffered to minister at the altar, then I shall steal those chalices without suspicion or difficulty, and carry them off with me." With this intention, then, he recited his profession, promised obedience, and put on the cowl. But the merciful Lord (who desireth not the death of a sinner, but rather that he should be converted and live) brought a marvellous change over this wicked will, and mercifully transmuted the poison into an antidote. For, when he had put on the monastic habit, he became contrite and converted; and so far did he profit in our holy Religion that, not long afterwards, the excellence of his life earned him the dignity of Prior at Clairvaux. Wherefore, as aforesaid, his very fault was made a remedy to others; for in after times he was often wont to tell this to the novices, and they were much edified by his story.

N. I would fain learn whence so great and marvellous a change came upon him.

M. In the first place, methinks, by God's mercy; but in the second place by the virtue and blessing of the holy habit; for (as one of the holy Fathers of old hath said), "The habit of a monk hath in it the virtue of baptism."[1] Many men knew Henry, the lay-brother of Hemmenrode, who was Master of the Grange called Hart, and who bare witness that the Holy Ghost alighted in the form of a dove upon the head of a certain novice, when he took the vows and was blessed by the Abbot.

---

[1] Jerome, *Ep.* 25, *De obitu Blesillae.*

N. That is joyful hearing; yet I remember one thing which terrifies me much. For I have heard that some have come to the Order with good intentions, yea, and youths of great innocence, yet in process of time they have looked back from the plough and have perished.

M. Oftentimes have I heard of such. The Lord John Archbishop of Trier, a man of great prudence and familiar with the secrets of our Order, was wont to say that boys or youths who came to the Order, unburdened in their consciences by the load of sin, were seldom fervent monks. Nay (wretched to relate!) either they live lukewarmly and indifferently [*minus bene*] in the Order, or they depart altogether; for, not having the fear of an accusing conscience, they presume on their own virtues; and thus, when temptations arise, they are the weaker to resist. Dost thou know that brother of ours who, not a month since, was seduced by a woman and fled from our grange hard by?

N. I know him well.

M. Yet I know for certain that he was a virgin of his body, a well-disciplined youth, so that none better could have been found, in my judgment, among our lay-brethren.

N. Truly saith the Psalmist [lxvi, 5], "The Lord is terrible in his doing toward the children of men."

M. I will tell thee another also, which befell in the time of our elders (as I know from their own lips) at our own mother-house of Hemmenrode. Thither came a youth of tender years, begging most devoutly and humbly for admission; they received him, and his conversation was blameless. David, the venerable priest of whose sanctity so many tales are told, loved this youth with a special love, and often exhorted him to his purpose of entering our Order. The youth, for his part, oftentimes kindled the old man's devotion by reciting hymns and divers sweet canticles in honour of Our Lady. That year, at the blowing of the North Wind, that source of all evil [Jeremiah i, 14], this novice began to waver, and disclosed to the holy man that he was in perilous temptation. The old man comforted him with many words, yet still the temptation ceased not. Then said the youth, "Lo! I will depart forthwith, for I can no longer endure my torments." To whom the

saint made answer, "Wait while I go to the church and pray."
The other promised; yet, even while the man of God hastened
to prayer, the youth made all haste to flee back to the world,
fearing to be held back by the holy man's supplications. When
therefore the venerable priest was come back from his prayers,
not finding the youth whom he had left in probation, he
groaned within himself and said, "This gift is not given to
all men!" the gift, that is, of perseverance in the Order.

N. These are marvellous things that I hear. That aforesaid
Prior of Clairvaux was converted in and from his own per-
versity; and this youth was perverted in his own conversion!
Teach me how to think of these things.

M. I say, with the holy man, "This gift is not given to
all men." In the first, God's mercy was made manifest; in
the second, let us fear God's secret judgments, Who saith
[Rom. ix, 15], "I will have mercy on whom I will have mercy,
and I will have compassion on whom I will have compassion."

N. Proceed then; for I would fain know by what impulse
or by what occasions secular folk are converted to our Order.

M. Many are the causes of conversion:[1] some seem to be
converted by the sole call or inspiration of God, others by the
sole impulse of the Evil Spirit; some by a certain levity of
mind; very many also are converted through the ministry of
other men, viz. by the word of exhortation, by the virtue of
prayer, and by religious example. There are numberless folk
also who are drawn to the Order by manifold necessities, as
sickness, poverty, prison, shame for some fault, peril of death,
fear or experience of hell fire, and desire for the heavenly
country. To these may be applied that word in the Gospel:
"Compel them to come in."

N. Though your words seem to have much probability,
yet they will have less force unless examples be added.

The monk thereupon enters into a series of concrete examples, which
fill the rest of this First Section of his book. He begins with stories, four
in number, of conversions by the sole vocation of God; the first of these
runs as follows (p. 12).

In the days of Conrad, King of the Romans, when St Bernard was preaching the crusade at Liège, a certain canon of the

---

[1] *I.e.* of leaving the world for the cloister.

cathedral, prostrate in prayer before one of the altars, heard a voice from heaven saying: "Go forth and hear, for the Gospel is come to life again." He rose forthwith from his prayer, and found the holy man preaching the crusade against the Saracens; to some he gave the crusader's cross, and others he received into the Order. This canon therefore, pricked to the heart and led by the unction of the Holy Spirit, took the cross, not for the Holy Land, but for our Order, deeming it more wholesome to impress a long cross upon his mind than to sew a short cross for a time to his garment. For he had read those words of our Saviour's: "He that taketh not his cross daily, and followeth after me, is not worthy of me."[1] He said not "for one or two years," but "daily." Many men, after their pilgrimages, become worse than before, and plunge deeper into their former vices, like unto the dog that returneth to his own vomit again, and the sow that is washed to her wallowing in the mire. But the life of monks who live according to the Rule is all one cross, in that they are crucified by obedience in all their members.

N. Thou seemest to me to set the Order before the Crusade.

M. Not I, but the authority of the Church; for our Order hath this indult from the Pope, that a crusader, or a man bound by any other vow of pilgrimage, is absolved before God and the Church if he will enter the Cistercian Order. But if the Cistercian cross and the crusader's cross were equally wholesome to the soul, they would be equally convertible; instead of which, if a monk should leave his Order and take the crusader's cross, (or even, what is less intolerable, should vow such a pilgrimage without the precept and licence of his Order,) he is adjudged to be no pilgrim of Christ, but an apostate. For Peter's successor, to whom in especial are committed the keys of the kingdom of heaven, knoweth how much more wholesome it is to fight daily within against the motions of vice, than to battle for a time without against the Saracen hosts. Yet to some who would fain have been

---

[1] Matt. x, 38; the word *daily*, however, is added from the similar passage in Luke ix, 23. Caesarius tells us himself that he is accustomed to quote Bible texts from memory. See Strange's introduction, p. vi.

converted St Bernard consented not, but (as will afterwards be related) bade them rather take the crusader's vow.

After the other three tales of conversion by the sole grace of God, there follow three parallel stories of conversion by mere instigation of the Devil. One of these converts was a Master of the University of Paris, who tried a whole year's noviciate at Clairvaux in the hope of tempting some of his old pupils back to the world; the other two were vagabond priests, one of whom stole from the convent and ran away. Caesarius then comes to the third category, which seems to have been more numerous than either of the first two (p. 18).

It is a fairly common [*saepius*] experience that some men come to conversion in a certain levity of mind. There came to us a certain youth, a canon in Cologne, rather in levity of mind than in devotion for our Order, as the event proved. When he told us of his purpose there was great joy, especially among the younger brethren. But the Lord Gerard our Abbot, knowing that this was a mere impulse of levity, seeing that he had gambled away his clothes and came to us in a bare tunic, would by no means consent, even though he was much urged to take the young man. Within a brief space, the postulant returned by the way whereby he had come, nor did he ever breathe a syllable of conversion again. [In the second case a noble youth, burdened with gambling debts, "easily obtained admittance" as a novice; but within a few days his friends persuaded him to pay his debts and leave the monastery, to which he never returned. This leads Caesarius into a digression upon the enormity of returning to the world, even for novices who had never made their full profession. In one such case, the sinner fell into a frenzy which could not be assuaged even by the application of fresh-killed dog's flesh to his shaven head; the other died in the midst of "such a storm of wind, and so vast a multitude of crows settling on the roof, that all fled in terror from his house, save one old woman."

He then passes to the fourth category, of those who are converted by means of others, "as, in God's tabernacle of old, *cortina traxit cortinam.*" Henry the Cripple of Clairvaux, who had been a great knight in the world, was converted by St Bernard, who promised in the spirit of prophecy that he should end his days at Clairvaux, whatever might be his other vicissitudes. Caesarius himself was converted by the story of the Heavenly Reapers of Clairvaux;[1] and it was another of these early Cistercian stories which converted his fellow-monk Gerlach. Others, again, were converted by prayer, as in the well-known case of Prince Henry of France. But most fruitful of all was the force of deeds: as Meister Eckhart wrote a century after this, "besser ein Lebemeister als tausend Lesemeister." "Know this, my son," says Caesarius, "that many are drawn to the Order nowadays without exhortation of sermons, without the help of any special prayers, but by the mere examples of religious life, and by the signs of devotion, discipline, or holiness which they see." Brother Dietrich was converted by the sight of a solemn funeral service at Heisterbach; a story which elicits from the novice a very natural remark; and from his master a very characteristic reply.]

N. I marvel that so small a thing can work so great salvation in the soul.

M. What marvel is there here? In substance, a pill is but a little thing, yet in working its virtue is of the greatest; it runs through every vein of the body, dissolves and casts out the peccant humours, and converts the sick man to health.

[A monk now at Villers was converted in the same way. A noble young canon, now Bishop of Osnaburg, was converted by the readiness with which the monks bared their backs to the lash after mass. Brother Henry, our Chamberlain, went from Trier to Cologne for help from the physicians, stopped a night on the way at Heisterbach, and remained there for life. Brother Gerlach owed his life's vocation to another of our monks, who had the gift of tears whenever he sang mass.

The fifth category is of those who are drawn to the monastery by sickness; such cases we see "every day" (p. 30). The knight Ludwig, who owned that castle which still frowns down on Altenahr, took the vows on his death-bed, and "began forthwith to mend, contrary to the nature of his sickness, without sweating or bleeding or sneezing"; he lived just long enough to take the full vows at Heisterbach. This leads the novice to ask for light; he cannot fathom the mysteries of

---

[1] *Exordium Magnum*; Migne, *Pat. Lat.* vol. 185, col. 1062; fully translated in my *Medieval Garner*, p. 75 and on p. 177 of this present volume.

predestination. "This knot is altogether insoluble" to his Master also; but in this particular instance there is a simple solution (32). God predestines each human being to a certain span of life. Nothing can extend this span; but sins and follies can shorten it; only through virtue and piety can a man enjoy the full tale of years allotted to him. Ludwig, the late Landgraf of Thuringia, was dominated by the too common heresy about predestination; he was wont to say, "If I am predestined to good, no sins can deprive me of the kingdom of heaven; if to evil, no good deeds will bring me thither," to which purpose he would quote Ps. cxv, 16, "The heaven, even the heavens, are the Lord's: but the earth hath he given to the children of men." His physician, a pious man, took advantage of a dangerous illness to show him the logical absurdity of this: "Nay, Lord, if your death-day be come, no care of mine can save you from the grave; again, if you are not destined to die of this sickness, my medicines will be superfluous." The Landgraf admitted his logical error, but failed to amend his life, and is now in hell.]

Even as many are drawn to the Order by medicine for their sickness, so also very many are driven in by the road of poverty. We have often seen, and we daily see, persons who were once rich and honourable in the world, such as knights and burgesses, entering our Order under pressure of want, and choosing rather to serve the rich God from necessity, than to suffer the confusion of poverty among their kinsfolk and acquaintance. A certain honourable man, setting forth to me the story of his conversion, added: "Certainly, if I had prospered in my affairs, I should never have entered this Order." I have known some who, when their fathers or brethren were converted, resisted conversion themselves, and came at last when they had consumed all that had been left to them, cloaking their necessity under the cloak of religion, or rather making a virtue of the necessity itself.

N. There is no need to seek examples of such folk, since we see that many, and especially lay-brethren, come to the Order for such reasons; but blessed are they who had wealth and despised it for Christ's sake.

M. Blessed, not because they possessed wealth, but

because they despised it. The widow's two mites pleased God more than many alms of the rich. Know also that some are converted for shame of some fault, or for the brand of some infamy. There was a young novice in our House who was thus drawn into the Order. He had been Canon of a church in Cologne; and, having committed a theft, though a small one, upon his master, an honourable clerk whose table he shared, he was caught by the servants and felt such shame that he fled from the world to our monastery and became a novice. He chose rather to serve God than to suffer such confusion among his fellow-clergy. I was then attached to the same church as he, and knew the cause of his conversion as aforesaid, and I had some fear lest such a conversion should prove insecure. Another youth seduced a nun; and, urged by shame and fear alike (since she was of noble blood) he was converted among us: and that which the Devil had prepared for his ruin was turned by this occasion into his salvation. While the youth aforesaid, by God's just judgment, deserted the Order, this one yet perseveres, by the saving virtue of God's mercy.

N. As I see, it is not of him who willeth nor of him who runneth, but of God who showeth mercy.

M. Even so. That some also are converted for peril of this earthly life, thou shalt learn by this following example. In the days when King Otto went to Rome to be crowned Emperor, he committed the government of the Moselle lands to his brother Henry the Count Palatine; who solemnly sentenced a certain noble robber to death. But Daniel, Abbot of Schönau, arrived on the spot, and besought the Count Palatine until he granted the robber his life, that he might satisfy God for his sins in the Cistercian Order. This man, therefore, having been condemned to death for his crimes, escaped by the grace of conversion from the sentence of damnation.[1] I have often heard of like cases, when criminals who had been condemned for various crimes have been freed by the benefit of the monastic Order.

N. Though these examples may seem trifling, yet we must not think scorn of them, since they tend to edification.

Ninthly come those who are converted by the fear of

---

[1] Or, possibly, simply *condemnation*.

hell-fire. (36) [A scholar of Paris, though refusing to do formal homage to the Devil, yet used a diabolical talisman to advance him in his studies. On his death-bed, just in time, the priest persuaded him to cast it away. The end came; his fellow-scholars assembled to sing the funeral psalms around his bier in church; but his soul fell into a deep, dark, and sulphurous valley, where one set of fiends tossed it like a tennis-ball, while others caught it with claws which surpassed all possible sharpness of earthly steel. "For he said that his soul was as a globe of glass, with eyes before and behind, wonderful in its knowledge and seeing all things. For, on his recovery to life, he told to his fellow-scholars, in their stalls around his bier, all that each had done. 'You' (said he) 'played dice; you others pulled each other by the hair; but you for your part chanted with all diligence.'" He joined the Cistercians, and was Abbot of Morimund some 24 years ago. The Abbot of Marienstatt knew him in the flesh, and told Caesarius the whole story. "I asked him whether he had ever seen this man laugh; for it is said that no man raised from the dead is wont to laugh. He answered: 'Know that I studied this thing in him; never could I note in him the least sign of levity, so great was his gravity and his forbearance. Never did I see him even smile; never did I hear a light word from his lips.'" The Novice shows some natural pride in the reflection that a man of such experience, with all the world to choose from, should have elected the Cistercian Order for his refuge. Caesarius has two other similar cases to tell him; one brings back from hell the clear and categorical assurance that "among all sorts and conditions of men, there is no sort in which fewer souls are lost than among the Cistercians." (40) The third and last is so interesting on other grounds also, that I give it fully on p. 230.

The last class of converts is worthy to stand with the first; "those who are brought to the cloister not by remorse of conscience, but by the desire of keeping their innocence and the longing for their heavenly fatherland." Such was Gottfried, a Benedictine monk of St Pantaleon at Cologne, who "burning with desire for the life on high, and considering that he could not live [at St Pantaleon] according to the precepts of the Rule, came to Heisterbach and besought admittance." The abbot, fearing levity of mind, refused him; and Caesarius is inconsolable: for Gottfried went on to the Cistercian sister-house of Villers in Brabant, and there lived so holy a life that his bones cease not to work miracles unto this day. He came once for a brief visit;] "and, as those have told me who saw him, God gave him such grace in masstime, that the tears trickled down from his eyes upon the altar and his breast. When Brother Dietrich of Lorch, who was then a novice, enquired of him how to pray, he made answer: 'In prayer you should say nothing, but think only of our Saviour's birth and passion and resurrection, and other things that you know well.'...How many consolations this Gottfried had, and how marvellous visions, He alone knoweth Who sent them all....When this man's corpse was laid out to be washed, they found his back so bruised with stripes that all men marvelled to see it."

[So much for the different motives of converts; and now we turn to their different ways:] "Some come with a certain pomp and worldly show; others exhibit a deep humility. A certain Knight named Walewan, desiring to become a monk, rode to the abbey of Hemmenrode on his war-horse, and in full armour; in full armour he rode into the cloister, and (as I have been told by our older monks, who were present) the porter led him down the middle of the choir, under the eyes of the whole community, who marvelled at this new form of conversion. The Knight then offered himself upon the altar of the Blessed Virgin, and, putting off his armour, took the habit of religion in that same monastery, thinking it fit to lay down his earthly knighthood in the very spot where he purposed to become a Knight of the Holy Ghost. Here, when the days of his noviciate were past, he chose in his humility to become a lay-brother; and here he still lives, a good and religious man. At first he was a novice among the monks; afterwards he became a lay-brother for his humility." [The next story, of a well-to-do scholar who preferred to present himself in the humblest garb, shows that even the Cistercians were not ordinarily willing to receive postulants from the poorest classes; they long refused him because "they took him for a poor and wandering scholar" (46).

This section of the book concludes with three stories of women's conversions. The blessed Hildegund, representing herself as a youth, took the vows among the monks of Schönau, and lived as a man until her death in 1188.[1] Her bones still worked many miracles, and attracted much concourse of people. Such stories are not very uncommon; but the reader will not be surprised to find a strong legendary tinge about all of them. The next three examples show nuns in conflict with the wishes of their parents who were opposed to their retirement from the world. Helswinde, Abbess of Burtscheid, for instance,] "was, and still is, daughter to Arnold the bailiff of Aachen, a rich and powerful man. From her earliest youth she was so zealous for conversion that she would say, 'Mother, make me a nun'; for she was wont to go up with her mother to the Salvatorberg, where then dwelt the nuns of Burtscheid. One day, therefore, she crept secretly through the kitchen window, went up to the dormitory, and, putting on one of the girls' cowls, went into the choir with the rest. Meanwhile her mother would fain have been gone, and the Abbess told her of the affair. The mother, taking it for a jest, answered: 'Call the servant,[2] for we must be going.' Then Helswinde came from within to the parlour window and said 'I am a nun; I will not go with thee.' The mother, fearing her husband, made answer: 'Only come now, and I will pray thy father to make thee a nun'; whereat the girl came forth. But the mother said nought of the matter. Another day, while the child slept, the mother went up again to the hill. Helswinde awoke and sought her mother in the church; then, finding her not, she suspected the truth. Wherefore, stealing forth alone and creeping once more through the same window, she again clad herself in the habit; and, when her mother would have called her forth, she answered, 'Thou shalt not again deceive me,' reminding her of her former promise. The mother went home in grievous fear. The father

[1] Compare R. Edelmaier, *Kloster Schönau*, and my *Art and the Reformation*, p. 36.
[2] *Vocate puerum*. But should we not read *vocate puellam*, "call the girl"?

and brethren came up in fierce wrath, burst open the doors, and led the girl away in spite of all her cries; then he committed her to certain kinsfolk who might turn her from her purpose. But she, who was (as I think) not yet nine years old, answered always so wisely that all men marvelled. In short, the Bishop of Liège excommunicated the father and all who had drawn the maiden forth; she was brought back to the convent, where after a few years she became abbess. Let this suffice for the matter of conversion. Many such marvels doth Christ work in His elect, to the glory of His name; to Whom, with the Father and Holy Ghost, be all honour and power, world without end. Amen."

(40) "This next story I learned by frequent repetition from the venerable Brother Conrad, who is wellnigh a hundred years old. He, born in Thuringia and trained in arms before his conversion, knoweth much of the actions of that Landgraf Ludwig, of whom I have spoken at length in my 27th chapter. This prince left two heirs; Ludwig, who died on the first crusade that was made under the Emperor Frederick [I], and Hermann, who succeeded to his throne and is lately dead. Now this younger Ludwig, who was neither intractable nor inhuman—or, to speak more truly, who was less evil than other tyrants—put forth the following proclamation: 'If there be any man who can tell me by some testimony the true state of my father's soul, to him I will give a rich fief.' A certain poor knight heard this, whose brother was a cleric once well versed in necromancy. The knight told his brother of the Landgraf's words; but he made answer: 'Good brother, I was once wont to invoke the Devil by incantations and to ask him whatsoever I desired to learn; but I have long since renounced those arts and conversations.' Yet, since his brother was instant with him in season and out of season, reminding him of his own poverty and of the honour that had been promised, at last the clerk yielded and summoned the demon. 'What wilt thou with me?' asked the spirit. 'It repents me,' replied the clerk, 'that I have so long deserted thee. Now therefore, I beseech thee, tell me where is the soul of my lord Landgraf.' Said the demon: 'If thou wilt go with me, I will show him unto thee.' 'Willingly,'

answered the other, 'if I may see him without peril of my life.' Then said the demon: 'I swear to thee by the most Highest and by His awful judgment-day, that I will take thee hence and bring thee back unhurt, if thou commit thyself to my plighted word.' The clerk, therefore, taking his own life in his hands for his brother's sake, climbed to the neck of the demon, who within a brief space laid him down at the gate of hell. The clerk, looking in, saw a region of unspeakable horror, and divers kinds of torments, and a certain demon of terrible aspect who sat upon a closed pit. At this sight the clerk trembled in every limb; and this demon cried to the demon that bare him: 'Who is this fellow on thy neck? Bring him hither.' 'Nay,' replied he, 'but this is one of our friends; and I have sworn unto him by thy mighty power that I would do him no harm, but only show him the soul of his lord the Landgraf; after which I will bring him back unharmed, that he may preach to all men of thy boundless power.' So the other rose from the fiery cover of that pit, and rolled it aside, and thrust a brazen trumpet down that gulf, whereon he blew so loud a call that it seemed to the clerk as though the whole world tingled with that trumpet-blast. After the space, as it seemed, of too long an hour, the pit belched forth sulphurous flames; and the Landgraf, coming up amid a shower of rising sparks, showed his head and shoulders to the clerk, saying: 'Here am I at thy beck and call, that wretched Landgraf who was once thy lord; yet would to God that I had never been born!' Then said the clerk: 'Your son hath sent me, that I may bring him word of your state, and that you may tell me if by any means it may be bettered.' 'My state,' answered the Landgraf, 'is plain before thine eyes. Yet know this; that if my sons would restore such and such possessions of such and such churches (naming them by their names), which I unjustly usurped and left as an heritage to them, then they would bring great comfort to my soul.' 'Yea, lord,' saith the clerk, 'but how shall they believe my word?' The Landgraf made answer, 'I will give thee a sign known only to myself and to my sons.' He gave the sign; and forthwith he sank again into the pit before the eyes of the clerk, whom the demon brought back to his home—living, indeed, yet so pale and so languishing that they scarce knew him for the same man. He recited the Landgraf's words and showed the sign; yet it profited him but little; for the sons would not consent to restore the lands. Yet the Landgraf Ludwig said unto him: 'I know the signs; I doubt not that thou hast seen my father, I deny thee not the promised reward.' 'Nay,' answered the clerk, 'keep thou thy fief; I will consider henceforth the profit of mine own soul.' And, leaving all that he had, he became a Cistercian monk, thinking it a small thing to sustain every earthly labour, if only he might escape the pains of eternity."

78. THE FLESH-POTS OF EGYPT

(*Ib.* p. 167.)

A CERTAIN abbot of Black Monks, a good man and a lover of discipline, had subjects who were somewhat wayward and undisciplined. It befell one day that some of these monks had prepared for themselves a feast of divers flesh-dishes and choice wines, which they dared not eat in any part of the house for fear of the Abbot; wherefore they gathered together to enjoy that which they had prepared in a vast empty wine-vessel, of the kind which men call *tun* in vulgar speech. Now it was told the Abbot that such and such monks were enjoying their feast in such a wine-tun: he therefore, hastening thither forthwith in much bitterness of soul, turned by his presence the joy of the feasters into mourning. Seeing them therefore affrighted, he feigned himself to be merry, and said, "Ha! brethren, would ye thus have eaten and drunken without me? Methinks this is not fair; believe me, I will dine with you!" So he washed his hands and ate and drank with them, comforting their alarm by his example. Next day (having forewarned the Prior and instructed him what to do) the Abbot arose at Chapter, in the presence of these monks; and, begging for pardon with much humility and feigned fear and trembling, he brake forth into these words: "I confess to you, my lord Prior, and to all my brethren here assembled, that, sinner as I am, yesterday I was overcome by the sin of gluttony, and that I ate flesh in a secret place, and as it were by stealth, in a wine-tun, contrary to the precept and Rule of our father St Benedict." Whereupon he sat down and began to bare his body for the discipline; and when the Prior would have forbidden him, he answered, "Suffer me to be scourged; for it is better that I pay the penalty here than in another world." When therefore he had taken his chastisement and his penance, and had returned to his place, then these aforesaid monks, fearing to be accused of him if they hid their fault, rose of their own accord and confessed the same transgression. The Abbot therefore caused them to be well and soundly scourged by a monk whom he had already chosen for that purpose, rebuking them bitterly and commanding that they should never again presume so to transgress, under pain of sore vengeance.

79. A MODEL MONK

(Ib. p. 231.)

AT the Monastery of St Chrysanthius [in the Eiffel] there dwelt a schoolmaster named Ulrich, a Frenchman by birth, of great prudence and learning. The revenues of his office were so small that he could not avoid falling into debt. One of the brethren at the Praemonstratensian Monastery of Steinfeld, perceiving that he was a man of great learning, oft-times persuaded him to enter his monastery by grace of conversion. At last this Ulrich, by divine inspiration, answered thus: "I owe a little money; pay that, and I will come to you." When the Provost of the aforesaid monastery heard this, he gladly paid the money, and Ulrich forthwith took the habit. Not long afterwards, he was elected Provost of that house (for there were as yet no Abbots in the Praemonstratensian Order). Considering then that, with this office, he had undertaken the keeping not of flocks and lands but of men's souls, he busied himself with the uprooting of vices rather than with the amassing of money, knowing that covetousness is the root of all evil. Now he had a lay-brother so skilful and circumspect in the management of worldly things, so careful and exact, that everything passed through his hands, and he was almost the only one who provided the monastery farms with all that they needed, both ploughs and cattle and money. He was all in all, disposing everything, neglecting nothing, adding field to field and joining vineyard to vineyard. The Provost, marking this, and reading in the Scriptures that nothing was more wicked than avarice, called the lay-brother to him one day, and said: "Dost thou know, my bearded fellow, wherefore I am come into this Order?"[1] (Now he was uncunning in the German tongue; and therefore to the lay-brethren all his speech seemed crooked and distorted.) The lay-brother answered, "I know not, my Lord." "Then I will tell thee: for I am come hither to weep in this spot for my sins. Wherefore now art thou come hither?" The other made answer, "My Lord, for the same cause." "If then," said the Provost, "thou art come to bewail thy sins, thou shouldest have kept the fashion of a penitent: assiduous in church, in watchings, in fastings: constant in prayer to God for thy sins. For it is no part of penitence to do as thou dost—to disinherit thy neighbours and (in the words of the Prophet Habakkuk) to load thyself with thick clay." Whereunto the lay-brother answered, "Lord, those possessions which I get are continuous with the fields and vineyards of our convent." "Well," said the Provost, "when these are bought, thou must needs buy those also which border thereon. Knowest thou what Isaiah saith? 'Woe unto you that join house to house and lay field to field, even to the end of the place: shall you alone dwell in the midst of the earth?' For thou settest no bounds to thy covetousness. When thou shalt have gotten all the land of this province, thou shalt cross the Rhine at a stride: then shalt thou go on even to the mountains; nor even so shalt thou rest until thou be come to the sea. There at last, methinks, shalt thou halt, for the sea is broad and spacious, and thy stride is short. Abide therefore within thy cloister, haunt thy church, that thou mayest bewail thy sins night and day. Wait awhile, and thou shalt have enough

[1] The lay-brethren, unlike the monks, let their beards grow.

A MODEL MONK

earth beneath thee and above thee and within; for dust thou art and unto dust thou shalt return." Some of the elder brethren, hearing this, said, "Lord, lord, if this lay-brother be removed, our house will go to rack and ruin." Whereunto he answered, "Better the house should perish, than the soul": and he paid no heed to their prayers. ¶ *Novice.* He was a true shepherd, knowing that the sheep committed to him had been redeemed not with corruptible things as gold and silver, but with the precious blood of Christ, as of a lamb unspotted and undefiled. ¶ *Monk.* This appeared plainly enough in his words and actions. For in the days when Reinhold was made Archbishop of Cologne, and found the revenues of the see mortgaged and the farms desolate, he was persuaded to borrow from the different Cistercian houses in his diocese faithful and prudent lay-brethren who might watch over the farms and reform the revenues by their industry. When therefore he had accepted this counsel, and had collected certain lay-brethren from the religious houses both of the hill and of the plain, he was persuaded to take this aforesaid lay-brother also. Wherefore he sent an honourable ambassador, who, after greeting the Provost from the Archbishop, added, "My lord hath a small boon to ask of you which ye should not deny him." "Nay," answered the Provost, "it is my lord's part not to ask me, but to command." Then said the other, "The Archbishop beseeches you earnestly to lend him such and such a lay-brother for such and such uses." Whereunto the Provost answered with all due humility, constancy, and gentleness: "I have two hundred sheep at such a grange, so and so many in such and such others; oxen have I likewise and horses; let my lord take then of whatsoever he will; but a lay-brother committed to my soul he shall never have for such uses, since it is not for sheep and oxen that I am to render account at the judgment-day before the Supreme Shepherd, but for souls that have been committed to my care." He left also another proof of his liberality, a somewhat profitable example against monastic avarice. One day, before that the aforesaid lay-brother was removed from his office, the Provost came to one of his granges; wherein, seeing a comely foal, he enquired of the same brother whose it was or whence it came. To whom the brother answered, "Such and such a man, our good and faithful friend, left it to us at his death." "By pure devotion," asked the Provost, "or by legal compulsion?" "It came through his death," answered the other: "for his wife, since he was one of our serfs, offered it as a heriot."[1] Then the Provost shook his head and piously answered, "Because he was a good man and our faithful friend, therefore hast thou despoiled his wife? Render therefore her horse to this forlorn woman; for it is robbery to seize or detain other men's goods, since the horse was not thine before [the man's death]."

The same Provost, being a man of prudence, was unwilling to take the younger brethren with him when he went abroad on the business of the monastery: for he knew that this was inexpedient for them, by reason of the Devil's temptations. Now it befell on a day that he took with him one of the youths; and as they were together, talking of I know not what, they met a comely maiden. The Provost, of set purpose, reined in his steed and saluted her most ceremoniously; she in her turn stood still and bowed her head to return his salute. When, therefore, they had gone a little farther, the Provost (willing to tempt the youth) said, "Methinks that was a most comely maiden." "Believe me, my lord" (replied the youth), "she was most comely in mine eyes also." Whereupon the Provost answered, "She hath only this blemish, namely, that she hath but one eye!" "In truth, my lord," replied the youth, "she hath both her eyes; for I looked somewhat narrowly into her face." Then was the Provost moved to wrath, and said, "I too will look narrowly into thy back! Thou shouldest have been too simple to know whether she were male or female." When therefore he was come back to the monastery, he said to the elder monks, "Ye, my lords,[2] sometimes blame me that I take not the younger brethren abroad with me." Then he expounded this whole case, and chastised the youth sternly with words and stripes. This same Provost was so learned that

[1] On the death of a serf, the lord of the manor was generally entitled to claim as *heriot* or *mortuary* his most valuable possession, and the priest of his parish the next in value. See vol. III, nos. 55, 56.

[2] *Domini*: the usual title for monks, corrupted into the *Dan* of Chaucer and the *Dom* of modern use.

(as it was told me by an elder monk of that House) he preached a sermon in the Chapter-General of Cîteaux one day when he came thither for the business of his Order.

Novice. It oftentimes happens that great men wrest from their subjects money or possessions to which they have little right, and build therefrom Houses of religion. May the Religious knowingly accept such alms as these? ¶ *Monk.* Whatsoever gnaweth the conscience, defileth the conscience. Yet know that such things are sometimes done by God's just judgment, as thou mayest learn by the following example. A certain great and noble man, willing to build on his lands a House of our Order, and finding a spot suitable for a monastery, drove out its inhabitants partly by bribes, partly by threats. But the Abbot who was to send monks to that place, fearing divine displeasure if the poor were thus deprived of their possessions, prayed to God that He might vouchsafe to reveal His will in that case. Then was that just man not suffered to dwell long in anxious suspense concerning this matter: for one day, as he was in prayer, he heard a voice saying unto him in the words of the Psalmist: "Thou, my God, hast given an inheritance to them that fear Thy name." Rising therefore from his knees, he forthwith understood, through this prophetic voice from heaven, how it was God's will that undevout men should be cast forth from these lands, and that men who feared and praised God should be settled there: as we read that the Lord gave to the children of Israel the lands of the Canaanites and other unclean nations. Yet these must not be construed into a precedent; for all covetousness and injustice should be abhorred by the Religious. ¶ *Novice.* Yea, and scandal should all the more be avoided in such matters, because secular folk are unwilling to have Religious for their neighbours.

80. MONASTIC CHARITIES
(*Ib.* p. 223.)

IN the days when that most terrible famine of the year 1197 was raging and destroying wholesale, our monastery, poor and new though it was, gave help to many. It has been told me by those who had seen the poor flocking round the gate, that sometimes fifteen hundred doles were given in a single day. Our then abbot, the lord Gerard, on every flesh-eating day before harvest, had a whole ox sodden in three cauldrons, together with herbs gathered from all sides, whereof he dealt out a portion with bread to every one of the poor. Thus also he did with the sheep and other food-stuffs; so that, by God's grace, all the poor who came to us were kept alive until harvest-time. And (as I have heard from the mouth of the aforesaid abbot Gerard) he feared lest this store for the poor should fail before harvest-time, wherefore he rebuked our baker for making his loaves too great; but the man replied, "Of a truth, my lord, they are very small in the dough, and grow great in the oven; we put them in small, and draw out great loaves." This same baker—Brother Conrad Redhead, who lives to this day—has told me that not only did these loaves grow in the oven, but even the meal in the bags and vessels, to the wonder of all the bakers and of the poor who ate thereof; for they said: "Lord God! whence cometh all this store?" Moreover, that same year the Lord of all plenty rewarded a hundredfold, even in this life, the charity of His servants. For Master Andreas of Speyer, with the money which he had gathered together at the court of the Emperor Frederick, and again in Greece, bought a great estate at Plittersdorf, which he freely gave unto us; who then could have put this thought into his heart but God?

81. DATE AND DABITUR

(*Ib.* p. 236.)

I HAVE heard from an abbot of our Order that another abbot—I think of the Order of Black Monks—was very hospitable and most merciful to the poor. And, being himself fervent in all works of mercy, he took care to ordain as stewards of the house men who would not hinder his fervour, but rather kindle it. The more guests he received, and the more charity he showed to the poor, the more bountifully did the Lord bless him and his house. But after his death his successor, urged by avarice, removed these merciful officials and set others in their room whom he knew to be more parsimonious, saying: "My predecessor was too lavish and indiscreet; his officials were too prodigal: we must so order and temper the expenses of our monastery that, if by chance our crops were smitten by hail, or if times of dearth were to come, we might yet have wherewithal to succour the poor." Cloaking his avarice with such words, he shut hospitality away altogether, and withdrew the accustomed alms from the poor. When these charities had been cut off, the monastery could not profit in worldly goods; nay, within a little while it fell to such a depth of poverty that the brethren had scarce enough to eat. One day a gray-haired, venerable man came to the porter and sought hospitality; the man took him in secretly and fearfully, and, rendering him such offices of hospitality as at that time he could, added these words: "Let it not scandalize thee, good man, that I minister so scantily to thy needs; for our necessities are cause thereof. In old days I have seen this monastery in such prosperity that, if a Bishop had come, he would have been harboured with great charity and abundance." To which the old man answered: "Two brethren have been expelled from this your monastery: nor will it ever prosper until their return: the name of the one is *Date*, and of the other, *Dabitur*."[1] And so saying, he vanished from the porter's eyes. I think that he was some angel, through whom the Lord wished to recall the first charity of

---

[1] *Give* and *It shall be given*. The porter, as a lay-brother, knew no Latin. Browning, it will be remembered, traced this story back only to Luther.

these brethren. The porter, being a lay-brother, kept those names in his heart, and told the abbot and brethren all that he had heard. They returned to their former hospitality, and soon the Lord began to bless them as before.

82. THE MIGHT OF TEMPTATION
(*Ib.* pp. 243, 253.)

HENRY of Wied was an exceeding rich, powerful, and famous knight, a courtier to Henry, Duke of Saxony. Many are yet alive who knew him, and who perchance remember the fact which I am about to relate. He had a wife whom he loved well; and, as they talked one day of the fault of Eve, she began, as is the wont of women, to curse and condemn her for inconstancy of mind, because for a mere apple's sake, to the satisfaction of her gluttony, she had subjected the whole human race to such pains and miseries. Her husband made answer, "Condemn her not; thou, perchance, in such a temptation wouldst have done the same. I will give thee a command which is less than Eve's, yet even for love of me thou shalt not be able to keep it." "What is that command?" said she; and he replied: "That, on the day whereon thou hast gone to bath, thou shouldst never walk barefoot through the slough in the midst of our courtyard: on other days, if it please thee, walk through it."[1] Now that slough was a foul and stinking swamp, drained together from the filth of the whole court: wherefore she smiled and shuddered inly at the idea of transgressing his command. Then Sir Henry added: "I will that we also add a penalty. If thou obeyest, thou shalt receive from me forty marks of silver; if not, thou shalt pay me a like sum"; and she was well pleased. He therefore, without her knowledge, set men to watch secretly over this slough. Wonderful to relate! from that time forward this

---

[1] Compare Bp Grosseteste's rules of housekeeping addressed to the Countess of Lincoln: "Let there be no cow sold whereof the straw does not remain to strew your sheepfolds daily and to make manure in the court." Many manor-houses were farm-houses also (Walter of Henley, ed. Lamond and Cunningham, p. 143).

lady, honourable and clean as she was, could never go through that courtyard without looking back at the aforesaid slough: and, as often as she bathed, so often was she grievously tempted to walk therein. One day, therefore, as she went forth from her bath, she said to her waiting-maid, "I must needs walk through that slough or die!" and forthwith, girding up her robe and looking around and seeing no man, she sent away the maiden who followed her, and plunged up to her knees into that stinking water, wherein she walked backwards and forwards until she had utterly satisfied her desire. The tale was forthwith told to her husband, who rejoiced and said as soon as he saw her: "How goeth it, lady? Hast thou bathed well to-day?" "Yea!" replied she. Whereupon he added, "In thy bath, or in the slough?" At this word she was troubled and held her peace, knowing now that her transgression was not hidden from him. Then said he, "Where, my lady, is your constancy, your obedience and your boasting? You have been less delicately tempted than Eve: you have resisted more lukewarmly: you are fallen more shamefully. Give me therefore that you owe!" And since she had not wherewithal to pay him, he took all her precious vestments and gave them to divers other persons, suffering her to be sore tormented for a while.

Novice. It is very miserable that man's mind cleaveth ever thus to that which is forbidden!...

Monk. There are two knightly families in the bishopric of Cologne, exceeding mighty and proud of their multitude, their riches, and their honours; one of which is sprung from the village of Bacheim, the other from that of Gurzenich. Now, between these families there were once such sore and mortal feuds, that in those days they could not be quieted by any man save the Bishop, their lord; but daily the feud blazed forth afresh in robbery, burnings, and manslaughter. The men of Gurzenich made on their own frontier a fortified house in the forest, not indeed for fear of their enemies, but in order that they might there assemble together, and dwell at their ease, and sally forth thence in a body to attack their foes more violently. Now they had a certain serf born on the land, Steinhart by name, to whose faith they entrusted the keys of their stronghold; but he, impelled by the Devil, sent a secret message to their enemies, promising that he would betray both his lords and their stronghold into their power; putting forward I know not what excuse against them. The knights of Bacheim, fearing treachery, gave no heed to his words; but when for the second and third time he had sent them the same message, then they armed themselves on the day appointed, and, coming with a great multitude for fear of an ambush, they met the serf in a place hard by the fort. This traitor, therefore, going out to them while they still hesitated, brought all the swords of his masters, who were sleeping their mid-day sleep in the fortress; and thus he certified them of his truth. They therefore brake in fully armed and slew all, receiving the serf into their own party according as they had sworn to him. In process of time the wretched man, terrified and moved with remorse at so execrable a crime, repaired to the Roman Court; where he confessed his fault and received a most grievous penance. Nevertheless, giving way to temptation, he fulfilled not that which he had undertaken; wherefore, returning again to the Pope, he renewed his penance, but again fell away from his obedience. When, therefore, he had thus done again and again, then the lord Penitentiary grew weary, and said (willing to be freed from one who made no progress), "Knowest thou anything which thou canst take as a penance, and keep it?" He replied, "Never could I eat garlic; wherefore I am assured that I shall never transgress the prohibition of that herb, if I undertake it for my sins." Whereunto the confessor answered, "Go! and henceforth for thy great sins' sake eat no garlic." The man, even as he went forth from the city, saw garlic in a certain garden; which by the Devil's suggestion he presently began to covet. Halting therefore to mark this garlic, he was grievously tempted: his growing concupiscence forbade the wretch to tear himself away; yet he dared not touch the forbidden herb. Why should I delay longer in this tale? At length his gluttony overcame his obedience; he entered the garden and ate. Marvellous to relate! this garlic, whereof he could never taste when it was cooked and duly prepared and lawful for him to eat, now that it was forbidden he ate it raw and unripe! So, being foully conquered in this temptation, he returned with confusion to the papal court, and told them what he had done; but the Penitentiary drove him forth with indignation and bade him trouble him no more. What the miserable man did afterwards I never heard.

83. MONASTIC FARE
(*Ib.* p. 248.)

OUR conventual bread, being black and coarse, is rather a necessity than a superfluity: and methinks a monk sins more if he abhors it or requires more delicate fare, than if he eats thereof to satiety. There is sometimes most grievous temptation in [the coarseness of] this bread.... Often also the Devil tempts Religious with flesh-meat, whether asleep or awake, visibly or invisibly. Some he conquers, by others he is conquered.

Novice. Of this I would fain hear examples.

Monk. I will tell thee some true and plain instances. There died not long since among us a monk named Arnold, a canon of the Church of the Holy Apostles at Cologne; for before his conversion he had been a man of great wealth and daintiness. He was wont to tell me that the Devil tempted him much with gluttony, even when he did but doze in choir. Sometimes, as he stood in choir and closed his eyes for weariness, he smelt a plate full of flesh in front of his mouth, wherefrom he ate (as he thought) even like a dog: then, blushing to eat after so beastlike a fashion, he would sometimes throw back his head and strike it somewhat smartly against the wall. Again, a certain lay-brother (as I heard from his own lips), hearing one day a certain private mass, slept a little during the recitation of the Canon:[1] then by a diabolical illusion he began to gnaw with his teeth the wood whereupon he lay prostrate, as though he were chewing food: and the sound of his teeth was as the sound of a mouse gnawing

---

[1] The most solemn portion, including the actual consecration.

through a nutshell. Brother Richwin, our Cellarer, who was serving at that same mass, was hindered in his prayers by the noise. When therefore he could speak with the lay-brother, he asked him what he had between his teeth in the mass, saying: "Ye were cause that I could not pray!" "Believe me," replied the other, "I have eaten good flesh." "Where didst thou get it?" said he. The lay-brother answered, "In the canon of the mass, the Devil had prepared for my mouth a full dish of flesh-food. If ye believe me not, mark the wood whereon I lay: there shall ye surely find the marks of my teeth": and he told how the Devil had mocked him in his sleep. In truth, the wood was all gnawed with his teeth: thus our Enemy seeketh at least to delude in sleep those Religious whom he cannot ensnare with gluttony in their waking hours.

84. SLEEP IN CHOIR

(*Ib.* p. 203.)

ONE of our elder monks, Frederick by name, though a good man in other respects, was somewhat notorious for the fault of somnolence. One night, before our monastery had been sent forth,[1] as he stood sleeping at the psalmody of Matins at Hemmenrode, he saw in his dream a long mis-shapen fellow standing before him, and holding a dirty wisp of straw such as men use to rub down their horses. He, looking audaciously upon the monk, and saying, "Why standest thou here and sleepest all night, son of the Great Woman?"[2] struck him in the face with the filthy straw: whereupon the monk woke in affright and, throwing back his head to avoid the stroke, struck it somewhat smartly against the wall. Lo what merriment among the rest!... In the same house is a monk who

---

[1] The monastery was first founded in 1188, on the Stromberg, one of the Seven Mountains; but the severity of the climate, and the difficulty of procuring food, drove the monks to migrate in 1191 to the adjoining valley of Heisterbach. Caesarius says *stood*, because the choir stalls were made to enable the monks to rest their body while they stood upon their feet to sing.

[2] The Cistercians claimed the special protection of the Virgin Mary: see no. 93, below.

often sleeps in choir, and seldom keeps awake; more noted for his silence than for his singing. Around this monk hogs are often seen, and the gruntings of swine are heard. Methinks they feed on the husks that fall from his mouth.... ¶ *Novice.* From these words of thine I gather that the weariness of spiritual exercises cometh from the Devil. ¶ *Monk.* Thou sayest right; for there are some who have no sooner begun to sing, pray, or read, but they presently begin to slumber: such are wakeful in their beds, but heavy with sleep in the choir. So too with the word of God; they are wakeful enough to hear secular talk, but when the word of God is set before them, they are soon asleep. Gerard, the predecessor of our present Abbot, was once propounding to us the word of exhortation in the Chapter-house. Seeing that many, especially of the lay-brethren, were asleep, and that some were even snoring, he cried out, "Hark, brethren, hark! I will tell you of something new and great. There was once a mighty king whose name was Arthur...." Here he broke off short, and said, "Lo, brethren, we are in a sad pass! When I spake of God, ye slept: but presently when I changed my speech to levity, ye woke up, and all began pricking up your ears to listen." I myself was present at that sermon. Nor is it only spiritual persons, but lay-folk also, who are hindered by this devilish temptation of slumber. A certain knight of Bonn, Henry by name, once made his Lent with us in our monastery. After he had gone home, he met one day with the aforesaid Abbot Gerard, and said to him, "My lord Abbot, sell me that stone which lieth by such and such a column in your church, and I will give you whatsoever price you may demand for it." "How?" said the Abbot, "What profit can it be to you?" "I would fain set it by my bed," he answered; "for such is its nature that if a man cannot sleep, and lay his head on that stone, he will slumber forthwith." Such confusion had the Devil brought upon him in the penitential season that, whensoever he came to our church and leant on that stone to pray, sleep would presently overcome him. Another noble, who came to do similar penitence in Hemmenrode, is reported to have spoken to the same effect, saying, "The stones of your conventual church are softer than any beds in my castle!"

He could by no means refrain from sleep on those stones during the time of prayer. ¶ *Novice*. If sloth during divine service were not a grievous fault, the Devil would not be so busy to tempt us therewith.

85. RICHWIN AND THE NUN
(*Ib.* p. 259.)

I WILL not tell of those who have consented to lechery and fallen, but of those who, tempted and shaken, have yet been preserved by God's grace. A certain rich and honourable knight, being separated from his wife according to Church custom, came to a house of our Order for the sake of conversion. To this monastery he gave all his possessions, on the condition that it should pay a certain life-pension to his wife, who had promised to lead a religious life in some nunnery. (I will name neither the convent nor the knight, lest she be shamed by aught of that which I shall say; for she yet liveth.) When he had become a novice, the Devil so pricked her that she drew back from her purpose, and asked again for her husband, who was now become a Brother of the house. Seeing then that she profited nothing by such means, coming insidiously to the monastery with her friends, she besought and obtained permission to speak with him without the monastic precincts. The knights therefore seized him and, dragging him by force to horseback, sought to carry him off; but he, as fast as they lifted him on one side, slipped down over the other; so that, finding their efforts unavailing, they went home with the lady. Then she kept silence for all that year; but after his year of probation, being driven by some necessity, he revisited his house with a monk for his companion, and there he found the lady aforesaid. She, making as though she would have spoken with him in private, led him to her chamber, closed the door privily, and began to embrace and to kiss him; hoping that, if she might lead him into sin, he would leave the Order and come back to her. But Christ the Son of spotlessness, who freed the innocent boy Joseph from the hands of the adulteress, saved also this knight of His from the unlawful embraces of his lawful spouse. For, shaking himself free from her arms, he went forth unhurt, and unsinged by the fire. This knight, on his return, might have said with Solomon: "I have found a woman more bitter than death, who is the hunter's snare, and her heart is a net, and her hands are bands." And of him we may say that which followeth: "He that pleaseth God shall escape from her." ¶ *Novice.* That was a great temptation. ¶ *Monk.* Greater was this that I will now tell.

A youth of Cologne, Richwin by name, became a novice in our monastery. When he had spent some time devoutly and quietly enough in probation, and was learning to fashion himself after the Order, the Devil envied his peace and salvation, stirring up such war in his heart through a certain nun of St Cecilia at Cologne, and tearing his flesh with such goads of lust, that he could not rest. For she composed and wrote letters of recall, wherein she rebuked him for his conversion, pleaded with him for his return, and said that she herself, her house, her prebend, and all that she possessed, should be in his power for his whole life long if only he would come back. These letters she sent by a servant, who asked for the novice; but Henry, cousin to that same novice, and now our Cellarer, met the servant and, (fearing that which indeed happened afterwards,) would not suffer him to speak with Richwin, but bade him begone forthwith from the courtyard. Yet he came upon the novice in the church, gave him the letter, and departed. When therefore Richwin read it, he was kindled to such white-heat as if a fiery dart had been thrust into his heart. From that moment he was exceedingly tempted, so that he purposed every hour of the day to return to the world; yet the pious prayers and exhortations of the brethren held him back. One day, being alone in his hour of trial, and wavering exceedingly, he fell flat on his face and stretched his feet against the threshold of his cell, and spake, crying aloud in his agony, "O Devil! unless thou drag me hence perforce by the feet, I will never follow thee!" At length by the grace of God he triumphed and became a monk. When I asked him whether he yet felt in his heart any remnants of the aforesaid thoughts, he answered, "In truth, brother, the temptations which in those days tore my heart, can now scarce graze my outer garments." Afterwards he became cellarer-major in our House, and died in that office.

86. RICHWIN'S DEATH
(*Ib.* vol. II, p. 296.)

I T is not a year since Brother Lambert of our monastery, sleeping in choir on a Sunday night, saw a vision of Richwin the Cellarer, dead some years before, who entered the choir and beckoned with his hand, saying: "Come, Brother Lambert, we will go together to the Rhine." But he refused, knowing him to be dead, and saying, "Of a truth I will not go with you." Thus repulsed, he turned to the other side of the choir, beckoning with the same gesture and the same words to an old monk named Conrad, who had fought the good fight [*militaverat*] for some fifty years in our Order; and he, drawing his hood over his head, followed him forthwith. That same day, after supper, the Prior bade some of us to his chamber, and this same Conrad was of the number; to whom, in my hearing, this Lambert said, "Of a truth, Brother Conrad, you will soon die, for in that very cowl I saw you last night following after Richwin"; and told him all the vision in order. Then answered Conrad, "I care not; I would fain be dead at this very moment." On the very next day (if I remember rightly) he fell sick, and within a short while he was dead and buried in that same cowl.

87. THE LAY-BROTHER'S AMBITION
(*Ib.* vol. I, p. 294.)

I N Kloster-Camp, a Cistercian Abbey within the bishopric of Cologne (as I have heard from a certain priest of our Order, a truthful man who knew of the matter), there was a certain lay-brother who had so far learnt letters from the monks with whom he spake, as that he could read a book. By this occasion, he was so enticed and deceived that he secretly caused books to be written fit for this purpose, and began to delight in the vice of private property.[1] When, therefore, this kind of study was forbidden to this lay-brother, as to one too much wrapped up therein, then his love of learning drove him into apostasy. Yet he made but little progress by reason of his advanced age. Then, being driven back to the monastery by repentance, and having thrice repeated this apostasy—now going forth to follow worldly schools, and then coming back again—he gave the Devil an abundant handle against himself to deceive him. For the fiend, appearing to him in visible form as an angel of light, said, "Play the man, learn on! for it is ordained and established of God that thou shouldst become Bishop of Halberstadt." This fool, marking not the Devil's wiles, hoped that the miracles of old times would be renewed in him. To be brief, one day the tempter insinuated himself to the lay-brother, and said with a clear voice and joyful countenance, "To-day the Bishop of Halberstadt is dead. Make all haste towards the city of which by God's decree thou art Bishop; for His counsel cannot be changed." Forthwith the wretch crept silently from the monastery, and spent that same night in the house of a certain honest priest near the town of Xanten. But, that he might come in all magnificence to his see, he arose in the night before daybreak, laid the trappings on his host's horse— which was a right good one—put on his host's cloak, mounted and rode away. At daybreak the servants of the house, discovering this loss, pursued after the apostate, and caught him. By them he was haled red-handed before the secular judge; by whose decree he was condemned, and ascended, not to the bishop's throne, but to the thief's gallows. Dost thou see to what end the Devil's promise tendeth? Another lay-brother, though not so manifestly, yet was no less perilously deceived by him.

---

[1] It was contrary to the strict Rule for a monk to possess anything of his own, but few points of the Rule were more difficult to enforce than this.

88. CUCKOO, CUCKOO!

(Ib. p. 295. Compare the anecdote I have printed in vol. 1, no. 36,
from T. Wright's *Latin Stories,* p. 42.)

THEOBALD, Abbot of Eberbach, of blessed memory, told us
last year that a certain lay-brother, being on I know not what
journey, and hearing the frequent song of that bird which
men call *cuckoo* after the sound of its voice, counted how often
it broke off, and finding these to be twenty-two, and taking
this for an omen, reckoned these repetitions as so many years
of his own life. "Ha!" cried he, "it is certain that I have
twenty-two years yet to live. Why therefore should I mortify
myself so long in this Order? I will return to the world,
follow its devices, and enjoy its delights for twenty years; then
will I do penance for the remaining two years of my life."
Doubtless the same devil who by open speech had persuaded
the aforesaid lay-brother to believe that he would become a
bishop, suggested secretly to this man also that he should put
faith in an omen of this sort. But the Lord, Who hateth all
soothsayings, disposed otherwise than he had proposed; for
He suffered him to live in the world for the two years which
he had set aside for penitence, and withdrew by His righteous
sentence the twenty years that had been set apart for worldly
delights.

89. FASTING AND CONSCIENCE

(Ib. pp. 343, 348.)

NOVICE. Do those men sin who, when monks are out of
their cloister, put before them flesh or fat, or the juice of
flesh, and entice them by some deception to eat the same?
Monk. They would seem not to sin, if they are urged to this
by the needs of hospitality or (what is worthier still) by the
fervour of charity. They who eat are excused from sin by
their ignorance or simplicity; they who give the flesh, as
I have said, by their charity. Here is an example. Christian

of blessed memory, late Dean of Bonn, a man of upright life and great learning, who died as a novice in our convent, was most fervent in the virtue of hospitality. One day he invited to his table the Abbot of Hemmenrode, Hermann, formerly Dean of the Church of the Twelve Apostles at Cologne, a man as learned and discreet as himself; and, since there was no dish prepared without flesh, he secretly bade his servant take out the bacon and set the peas before his guest. While the Abbot simply ate that which was set before him, his fellow-monk, who was less simple-minded, found in his own plate a fragment of bacon and showed it to his Abbot; who, seeing this, forthwith put away his plate for conscience' sake. As they went on their way, the Abbot rebuked the monk for his curiosity, saying, "Beshrew thee, for thou hast robbed me to-day of my mess! If thou hadst kept silence, I should have eaten in ignorance, and the eating had been no sin."

I remember that Daniel, Abbot of Schönau, did the contrary of this. While he was yet Prior of our House, and was dining at Siegburg with a simple and upright monk named Gottschalk of Vollmarstein, the brethren of that monastery set before them pasties fried in lard.[1] The Prior soon smelt this and would not eat; yet he hindered not his fellow who was eating. When the dinner was over, and they were licensed to speak, Gottschalk said, "My lord Prior, why did ye not eat of those pasties, for they were most excellent?" "No wonder that they were most excellent," answered he, "for they were most richly fried in lard!" "Why then did ye make me no sign?" said the other; and he: "Because I was unwilling to deprive you of your food. Grieve not, for your ignorance will excuse you." Now this same Daniel was a learned man, who before his conversion had been Master of the Schools. ¶ *Novice.* I marvel not that monks are sometimes deceived with gravy and the fat of animals: but it is strange that some should be so simple as to be misled by the solid substance: that is, by the flesh itself. ¶ *Monk.* I think that

---

[1] Siegburg was an abbey of ordinary Benedictines, who had long since ceased to keep the strict Rule of St Benedict forbidding all flesh-meat except in cases of necessity. The Cistercians themselves commonly broke this rule in later generations, and the Carthusians were the only Order which maintained it until the Reformation.

this comes to pass sometimes on account of the charity of those who minister to them. One day when St Theophilus, Bishop of Alexandria, invited several of the holy Fathers [of the desert] to dine with him, and set the flesh of fowls before them, they all believed themselves to be eating pot-herbs, until he himself betrayed what was in the dishes: not that they had been bereft of sight and taste, but these had been changed by God on account of the charity of him who set the flesh before them. A like deed was done by the lord Ensfrid, Dean of Sankt Andreas at Cologne, in my own days. Know this also, that disuse will lessen the power of discerning by taste between one food and another; nor is it cause for marvel that Theobald, Abbot of Eberbach, who ate no flesh during the fifty-six years that he spent in our Order, could be deceived when he ate flesh under the name of fish. Now this Ensfrid ...entertained one day some men of Religion; whether Cistercians or Praemonstratensians I know not, and, having no food such as monks eat, and no fish, he said to his cook, "We have no fish; the monks are simple-minded and hungry; go and make a stew, take away all the bones, sharpen well the sauce with pepper, set it on the table, and say to us, 'Eat now of this excellent turbot.'" So it was; and they, as good and simple men, not marking the pious fraud of their good and simple host, asking no questions for conscience' sake and for the sake of the rule of silence at meal-times,—they, I say, ate that which was set before them as fish. They had nearly cleared the dish, when one of them found a swine's ear, and held it up for his fellow to see: whereupon the Dean answered, feigning somewhat of indignation: "For God's sake, eat your dinner! monks should not be so curious; turbots too have ears."

90. THE NUN'S SIMPLICITY

(*Ib.* p. 389.)

IN the diocese of Trèves is a certain convent of nuns named Lutzerath, wherein by ancient custom no girl is received but at the age of seven years or less; which constitution hath grown up for the preservation of that simplicity of mind which maketh the whole body to shine. There was lately in that monastery a maiden full-grown in body, but such a child in worldly matters that she scarce knew the difference betwixt a secular person and a brute beast, since she had had no knowledge of secular folk before her conversion. One day a goat climbed upon the orchard wall, which when she saw, knowing not what it might be, she said to a Sister that stood by her: "What is that?" The other, knowing her simplicity, answered in jest to her wondering question: "That is a woman of the world," adding: "When secular women grow old they sprout to horns and beards." She, believing it to be the truth, was glad to have learned something new.

91. A KNIGHT'S CONVERSION
(Vol. II, p. 49.)

WALTHER VON BIRBECH was born in the town of that name, a man of great wealth and power and nobility, cousin to Henry, Duke of Louvain. He, in the heyday of his youth, being devoted to the knighthood of this world wherein he was most doughty and renowned, was accustomed from his earliest boyhood to call upon our Lady, the Holy Mother of God and Ever-Virgin Mary, whom he loved from the bottom of his heart, honouring her with fastings, almsgiving and masses. For though his body was given up, as we have said, to tournaments, yet his whole heart was devoted to the Blessed Virgin. One day, therefore, as he hasted to a tournament with many knights in his company and came to a wayside church, he begged them to hear the mass. They refused and rode away, giving in excuse that so long a delay would be perilous to them. But he remained, bade the priest sing him a mass of St Mary, and then rode after his companions. After a while he met men riding back from the tournament; and, learning from their speech where they had been, he added: "Is it yet begun?" "Yea," replied they: and he: "Who beareth him best there?" "The lord Walther von Birbech," said they: "his name is in all men's mouths; all extol him and praise him to the skies." In process of time he met others who gave him the same answer, whereat he marvelled, not knowing what this might portend. (Now this was wrought by the insatiable loving-kindness of the Blessed Virgin, that she might honour meanwhile in the tournament her devoted knight who had delayed in her service, and that she might supply his absence by her wondrous might.) When, therefore, he was come to the place, he armed himself and entered the lists, but did no great deed there. At last, when the tournament was over, some of the knights came to his lodging and besought that he would deign to deal more gently with them. "Why?" said he, "What is the cause of your petition?" And they answered: "To-day ye took us prisoners, and we beseech you to treat us well." Which when our Walther denied, saying: "I took you not," then they answered: "In very truth we have held out our right hand to you this day; we have seen your armorial bearings, we have heard your voice at the tournament": whereby he knew forthwith that this had been wrought by the grace of the Blessed Virgin whom he had honoured in the mass. ¶ *Novice.* Since it is a mortal sin to go and joust at tournaments, how could Walther's prayer and offering please the Blessed Virgin?[1] ¶ *Monk.* Two mortal sins are committed at tournaments—pride and disobedience—pride because men joust for the sake of earthly praise, and disobedience because it is done against the prohibition of Holy Church; wherefore those who are slain in tournaments are buried apart from the faithful and without the churchyard. But, since the service of the aforesaid mass if it had been rendered in charity, might have been meritorious to Walther for eternal life, therefore in this case it was transferred to his temporal reward....

This Walther, while he was yet in the world, considering these great loving-kindnesses of the Blessed Mother towards

---

1 "That the Church struggled valiantly against tournaments cannot be disputed by any judge worthy of that name. From Innocent II to Clement V [*i.e.* from 1143 to 1314], we have a series of anathemas and thunderbolts....If St Louis had not hated them, he would not have been St Louis....Philippe le Bel, who was no coward, condemned them not once only, but ten times over....But Popes and Kings could do nothing, and the nobles laughed at their prohibitions" (L. Gautier, *La Chevalerie*, Nouvelle Edition, p. 681).

him, was so kindled with love for her that, in a certain lowly church dedicated to her, with the approval of the priest, he cast a rope round his neck and offered himself to her as a serf upon the altar, paying her such a yearly poll-tax as bondmen born are wont to pay.... At length, hearing that our Order was dedicated to the Blessed Virgin, he left for her sake all things in this world—riches, honours, and friends—and took the cowl in the monastery of Hemmenrode, whose fame was then (as now) most renowned; in which monastery how humbly he conversed, how fervent and obedient he was, and how devoted to the service of the Blessed Virgin, all the monks of that foundation will bear witness. He learned in his time of probation the psalter, the hymns and canticles, and many other prayers to our Lady; all of which he repeated with great devotion. He would ever be present at the daily mass of the Blessed Virgin. Almost every word that fell from his lips was a word of edification. Therefore, because many were edified, not only by his words and by the sight of him but also by the odour of his good report, he was made Guestmaster there.... Not only devils, but even brute-beasts obeyed his holiness. The monastery possessed a most comely colt, so precious that both the Archbishop of Trèves and the Duke of Lorraine offered for him 40 marks (as I think) of money; for that colt showed promise of a most excellent war-horse. The monks, fearing to offend either if it were sold to the other, sent the steed as a gift to the Count of Holland by the hands of this lord Walther and two lay-brethren. When, therefore, they were come to a certain forest, the colt saw a herd of mares feeding afar off; and forthwith, neighing and frisking, he shook himself free from his guardians and galloped off towards them. The lay-brethren followed after him; but the mares fled and the colt left them farther and farther behind. When therefore they had come back empty-handed, Walther said: "Let us go on our way; that horse is lost but if St Mary bring him back to us." Scarcely had they gone two miles of their way when this unbroken colt came galloping back, and submitted his neck like a tame lamb to the hands of his leaders.

The foregoing episode is admirably illustrated by a passage in the life of one of Walther's friends, which I therefore intercalate here from the *Chronicle of the Monastery of Vilars* (Martène, *Thesaurus*, vol. III, col. 1311).

92. ANOTHER

DOM CHARLES, the eighth Abbot of Vilars, once a famous knight and doughty in the world, had passed from the schools to knighthood; wherein he profited so well that he gained the favour and love of kings and princes, so that the lord Philip, Archbishop of Cologne, fearing for his life at that court held at Mainz wherein King Frederick knighted his own sons, chose this Charles for his body-guard. One day when the same Charles was riding with the lord Gerhart Wascard from a tournament at Worms to Mainz, where the lord Philip was, they lighted upon an excellent fair meadow full of flowers of every hue and watered by springs and streams, through which meadow they rode in silence, neither caring to talk with the other. As they crossed the meadow each promised to reveal to the other the thoughts of his heart. One therefore said: "I thought and considered diligently the marvellous and manifold delights of this place, and in the end it was revealed to me that all which seems so green in this world is vain and unprofitable." Then said the other: "Even thus was mine own thought." Then each said to the other: "May these thoughts bring us some profit! let us go oversea to Palestine:—but then the things which we leave here will come back to our minds—our noble horses, the comely ladies, our knightly arms—and our hearts will be sore, and it may be that our chastity will suffer harm. What then? let us go over to these wolf-cowls of Hemmenrode[1] and strike a truce of five years from this haunting of tournaments." So they rode on with one squire only, made their vow under such conditions, and came back to Cologne; where, by the Devil's instigation, the whole city blamed their vow. Then they came to [Manderscheid?], where Ulrich Flasco, who had wished to draw them over the sea, took his vow and received the habit with them.

[1] *I.e.* the grey Cistercian monks.

There Gerhart Wascard lost part of his hand, because he said that this should rather befall him than that the least member of the lord Charles (whom he knew to be a clerk, and by God's grace destined to promotion) should be hurt. After a brief while this lord Charles left his parents and his wealth, and with many companions girt himself with the weapons of sacred knighthood in the monastery of Hemmenrode; and so, by his example and exhortation, did other nobles and great men both of holy Cologne and even of more distant lands: namely, Ulrich Flasco, Gerhart Wascard, Walther von Birbech, and many others doughty in worldly warfare and now no less valiant in spiritual conversation.

93. A MANSION IN HEAVEN

(Caes. Heist. vol. ii, p. 279.)

A CERTAIN monk of our Order, who loved our Lady well, was rapt in the spirit a few years ago and carried off to behold the glory of heaven, where he saw the divers Orders of the Church Triumphant—angels and patriarchs, prophets and apostles, martyrs and confessors, all marked with the plain character of their Order, whether Canons Secular or Regular, Praemonstratensians or Cluniacs. He, therefore, being anxious for his own Order, standing and gazing around and seeing none with the Cistercian habit in all that glory, looked up groaning to the Blessed Mother of God and said: "How is it, most holy Lady, that I see none of our Order in this place? Wherefore are your servants, who honour you so devoutly, shut out from so blessed a company?" The Queen of Heaven, seeing his trouble, answered: "Those of the Cistercian Order are so beloved and so familiar to me that I cherish them even under my arms": whereupon, throwing open the cloak wherein she seemed to be wrapped, and which was wondrous wide, she showed him an innumerable multitude of monks, lay-brethren, and nuns. He, therefore, triumphant and thankful, returned to the body and told his Abbot all that he had seen and heard.[1]

94. AN EVIL WORLD

(*Ib*. p. 364.)

IN Clairvaux is a certain priest named William, of whom I have already told, and to whom many secrets are revealed from heaven. This very year, as he stood in prayer, he fell into an ecstasy of mind and was taken up to Christ's Judgment-seat, where he saw an angel with a trumpet standing at the Lord's right hand; to whom Christ, in a clear voice and in the hearing of all the hosts of heaven, said: "Sound now a blast!" which when the angel had done, so mighty was the voice of that trumpet that the whole world seemed to tremble like a leaf on a tree. When therefore Christ said for the second time: "Blow ye again": then the Virgin Mary, Mother of Mercy, knowing that at the second blast the world must come to an end, and seeing that the other saints held their peace, arose and fell at the feet of her Son and besought Him to defer His sentence and spare the world. To whom Christ answered: "Mother, the whole world is seated in wickedness, and it provoketh Me daily to wrath, so that I may not with justice either suspend My sentence or spare mankind. Not only the lay-folk, but even the clergy and monks have utterly corrupted their ways, and offend me from day to day!" Then said she: "Spare them, my beloved Son, spare them, and if not for their sake, at least for the sake of my friends of the Cistercian Order, that they may prepare themselves.". . . ¶ *Novice.* This vision agreeth with the miracle already told, wherein the image of the Mother of God is said to have sweated for fear of the impending Day of Judgment. ¶ *Monk.* That the Day of Judgment is at our gates is shown by earthquakes in divers places, and other signs whereof we have

---

[1] This is a type of story which was current in more than one Order: the Franciscans sometimes boasted that their own blessed were privileged to nestle within the wound of the Saviour's side. These are unquestionably the stories which are so cruelly parodied in Chaucer's *Pardoner's Prologue.*

spoken above; but it is an exceeding consolation that the
Saviour, when these things begin to come to pass, warns the
righteous, saying: "Look up and lift up your heads: because
your redemption is at hand."[1]

Étienne de Bourbon is one of the many distinguished mission-preachers
who arose among the early Friars. Born about 1195, he was studying at
Paris when the Dominicans first arrived there. He joined the Order about
1223, preached in many places and with great effect for the crusades and
against the heretics, and was appointed Inquisitor shortly after 1235. His
active career seems to have ended in 1249; he died about 1261, leaving still
incomplete his Preachers' Manual, of which its modern editor justly says:
"Whoever wishes to grasp the moral and mental state of St Louis's time,
and all that intimate side of medieval society towards which modern
learning seems most willingly to turn, must henceforth study this collection of anecdotes" (Anecdotes Historiques, etc., d'Étienne de Bourbon, ed.
by A. Lecoy de la Marche for the Société de l'Histoire de France, 1877,
p. iii). Very many of the tales are taken from Étienne's personal experiences; but even those which are patently legendary throw much light on
the ideas of the age.

95. UNWILLING SCEPTICS

(P. 195.)

THE Devil useth grievous and secret temptations, either
subtly in matters of faith or with a spirit of blasphemy, wherewith oftentimes, when other arts fail, he tempteth pious souls,
specially those of simple folk, to drive them to despair or keep
them from the good. I have seen a pious and religious and
upright clerk tempted during his noviciate, first by the doubt
whether the world were other than a mere dream, and whether
he himself had a soul, and even whether there were a God;
whereof he was grieved unto death, and the Devil had thus

---

[1] This vision is a type of many which are recorded in the Cistercian, Dominican, and Franciscan Orders. One even more startling is to be found at the beginning of the Dominican Lives of the Brethren (trans. J. P. Conway, pp. 1 ff.:
better in the original Vitae Fratrum, ed. Reichert, pp. 6 ff.). In these, the part
of the Virgin Mary is still further magnified: in one of them it is she who chooses
out St Francis and St Dominic to save the world, and Christ only asks to see
who it is that she has chosen.

almost driven him to despair or to self-murder, but that he believed the wiser counsels of those who told him that, since that thought—the Devil's rather than his own—pleased him not, but rather utterly displeased him, therefore it was rather a martyrdom than a sin, as we shall say in another place concerning blasphemous thoughts.[1]

96. SATAN AS AN ANGEL OF LIGHT
(Ib. p. 198.)

THE Devil is treacherous, not only uttering lies of false witness, but striving also to deceive men with false deeds, transfiguring himself at times into the likeness of Christ and His apostles and angels and other saints and good men, that by such lies he may seduce the unwary.... Moreover, he doth deceive certain indiscreet folk by such illusions.... I have seen a man, a novice in a Religious Order, who was much troubled, waking by night while the others slept and praying God and the Blessed Virgin to reveal to him how it stood with his dead mother, believing himself to be worthy to whom such revelations should be made, since he waked in his bed at the hour when others slept. Once, when he had thus watched almost until Matins, the Devil appeared to him in the guise of the Blessed Virgin, showing a false vision of his mother under her cloak, and saying that she was freed from purgatory by his prayers. When again he had watched in like manner on the following night almost until Matins, he appeared to him in a less decent form; and at last, leaving foul traces behind him, tempted him to sin; whence the novice grew to such wakefulness and weakness of head that, but for the succour and counsel of discreet men, he might have come to grievous peril of body and soul.

[1] Similar anecdotes are common in medieval records: one of the best known is in Joinville's *Life of St Louis*, § 46.

CHAUCER'S FRIAR IN THE MAKING

Giovanni Fidanza, born in 1221 at Bagnorea in the upper valley of the Tiber, joined the Franciscans at an early age as Brother Bonaventura. He became first Professor of Theology at Paris and then Minister General of his Order. Dante has immortalized his character and genius (*Par.* xii); but his moderation as General rendered him unpopular with the Spirituals; and he is the unnamed Adversary who, in chapter 48 of the *Fioretti*, is represented as persecuting the saintly John of Parma. In concert with his old friend and fellow-Franciscan Odo Rigaldi (see vol. I, no. 44) he led the van of the Reforming party at the Ecumenical Council of Lyons; and died, probably of overwork, before the end of the Council (1274). Professor Thorold Rogers, after enumerating the social virtues of the thirteenth-century monk, adds: "It is not easy to understand how these monasteries declined in character and usefulness, till they came to the condition which is described so indignantly by Gascoigne—a condition which renders probable the charges which Henry the Eighth's Commissioners made against them. But many causes appear to have contributed to the result" (*Six Centuries of Work and Wages*, p. 362). The following passage will go far to answer this speculation (Bonaventura, *Opp.* Mainz, 1609, vol. VII, pp. 336 ff.; *Quaest. sup. Regulam*, abbreviated).

97. CHAUCER'S FRIAR IN THE MAKING

M E N say to us: We see that all Orders of Religious are decaying in religious life, even though they seem to prosper in temporal things and in certain ceremonial uses. I would fain know the principal causes of this decay: for ye ought either not to begin that which ye cannot complete, or else ye should use all possible perseverance in what ye have begun, lest ye be deservedly judged as prevaricators of your vow.

I answer: Everything which draweth not its being from itself, faileth and falleth into non-being, unless it be sustained by that which giveth it being. So it is with all Orders, as with all men. Wherefore the Orders not only of Religious, but also of Bishops and Clergy and Laity, and the whole state, are far decayed, in the gross, from that which they were in the beginning, when all the faithful were so perfect and holy as is now but seldom seen. But, because the evil are now the more numerous, therefore the holy make no show in comparison with the multitude of the rest. For true sanctity consisteth not in bodily exercises but in virtues of the mind: which since they make no outward show (except a slight one through certain indications of works), and the saints seek not to be seen and praised of men, but hide those virtues wherein they surpass the rest, therefore there seem to be few saints nowadays in the Church or in the Orders. But as to the causes of decay in religious communities, these (among others) are the commonest. First, the multitude of those that enter in; for the many cannot be so easily bent as the few, even as a great ship is less easily steered than a small, and where are many heads, there are many brains, which cannot all be bent to one mind. Secondly, when those are taken away who first kept the Order in its vigour, or when these are broken down in body, then they can no longer give the former severe example of rigour to the younger members; and the newcomers, who never saw their proper works, imitate them only in that which they now see in them, and become remiss, and spare their bodies under a cloke of discretion, lest they should destroy their health as the older Brethren did. And, since they see not those inward virtues which their elders possessed, these [latter] are everywhere neglected; for [the younger] neither follow their outward asceticism nor apprehend their inward virtues. Moreover the ancient Brethren, no longer able to set them a strict example, fear even to rebuke them by word of mouth; for the younger are wont to say: "The words indeed are good which ye tell us; but your works show them not"; and thus they are the more scandalized. Thirdly, that which a man never learned, he cannot teach; wherefore, when the government of the Order descendeth to these younger Brethren, they foster others like unto themselves; so that the early Brethren are already a laughing-stock, and no longer a model of life. Nay, these younger are the more prone to think themselves better than their elders, the less they recognize what are the virtues of the perfect; and, whereas they keep certain models in the matter of exterior discipline, as in the choir, or in processional entrances [into the church] and such-like, therefore they dare to affirm that the Order was never in so good a state as now. Fourthly, unedifying customs creep in little by little, which are forthwith taken as examples by others; and if any Brethren, filled with godly zeal, rebuke such customs, then others defend them boldly. "Why" (quoth they) "is that unlawful for me which is allowed unto others?" so that, since custom hath already given it a certain fitness, it will pass for an almost ineradicable law. Moreover our rulers, even though they love not such things, yet fear lest some greater evil ensue, and shut their eyes that they may live at peace with the Brethren. And when one such custom hath become bearable, then another is introduced in its train, as though it followed necessarily therefrom, so that if this be admitted the former one may be tolerated. Fifthly [we see] the distractions which frequently spring up, diverting men's hearts, quenching their devout affections, impairing their morals, inducing occasions of inward faults, and entangling Religious in daily fresh impediments to all effectual thought of self-correction, until at last they grow accustomed to think of outward things alone, and the eye of their conscience is so darkened that, even when causes of distraction are wanting, they shamelessly go in search of such; as Samson, blinded and imprisoned, turned the mill.

There are also other causes special to certain Orders; such as too great poverty, which compels the Brethren to become proprietary,[1] each thinking to provide for himself, since there is no provision for them in common; or again, too much wealth, whereby they become carnal, proud, and vicious in many different ways. Again, familiarity with worldly[2] folk, whence ariseth matter for many temptations of the flesh and of temporal things. Again, the frequent change of conventual officers,[3] which though it be partially good, inasmuch as the evil are thus cast forth, yet herein it is harmful that the good, expecting soon to be displaced, presume not to undertake the reform of the Order, or prosper not therein; and their rebellious subjects strive rather to procure the deposition of

[1] St Benedict prescribed in his Rule, and Innocent III re-enacted under pain of excommunication and damnation, that no monk should possess private money or property. These and other repeated prohibitions were, however, generally neglected in the later Middle Ages. See note to Busch, Extract 117.

[2] In medieval parlance, all were in "the world" who had not bound themselves to some "Religion" (see Extract 75). The Latin word used for *world* in this sense was *seculum*; hence the phrases *secular clergy* for non-monastic clerics, *secular arm* for the civil authorities, etc.

[3] This refers specially to the Friars, who (like modern Wesleyans) elected their officials only for brief periods.

the good than duly to reform their state. Moreover, if one official be sometimes willing to strive for reform, he is somehow hindered by the rest, or at least hath no help from those whose succour he needeth; as for example the Prior hath no help from his Abbot, or the Abbot from his Bishop, and so forth; wherefore the rebellious subjects appeal to those who (as they know) favour them in their disobedience. Again, if some in one monastery have set their hearts upon reform, they are sent to another monastery where they find not what they sought.

From these and other causes Religion[1] so decayeth that it becometh not only degenerate, but even almost desperate; so that, unless God so ordain, it is scarce ever otherwise reformed. But, because all things work together for good to those that love God, that which is not done in general may be done in particular. Each Brother who would profit [spiritually], turneth the loss of others to his own gain; and, by God's grace, he wresteth to his own profit all the paths of others' decay. And, even as the glory of the Elect will be all the greater because, being mingled in companionship with the Reprobate, they yet follow not their example, which is to them a matter of temptation and of exercise in virtue, so also the good Religious would never have deserved so much at God's hands, if the defects of lukewarm Brethren had not impelled them assiduously to gird their loins to the manifold struggle of virtue. Wherefore the Apostle, among his other deserts wherein he excellently boasteth himself as the servant of Christ, numbereth perils among false brethren, which to him and to other good men are a manifold occasion of virtue. First, because their evil examples supply the righteous with a matter of temptation, and thus with a cause of victory. Secondly, these are kindled with a righteous zeal at the others' vices, and burn to see such stumbling-blocks to the weaker brethren. Thirdly, they pity their wretchedness, as the mother pitieth her son hasting to perdition. Fourthly, they labour to correct them by good examples and warnings and prayers and benefits. Fifthly, they bear patiently with such froward manners, and with the injuries which these others inflict upon

[1] See Extract 75.

them for their righteousness. Sixthly, the companionship of such bringeth upon them the scorn of those who are without, as though they themselves also were such. Seventhly, they become more fearful and therefore humbler, and are the more anxious not to fall. Eighthly, they thank God the more heartily, Who of His loving-kindness hath defended them from becoming such. Ninthly, their own virtues shine the more clearly, and with a fairer radiance, from the juxtaposition of the wicked. These and other good things God bringeth forth from the companionship of good and evil. For, even as the accidental joy of the good is heaped to full measure by the sight of the pains of the damned,[1] so also in the Church the uprightness of the good is in some fashion adorned by the deformity of the unrighteous; for so hath that heavenly wisdom disposed which leaveth nothing disorderly in any realm.

Thomas Cantimpratanus (of Chantimpré in Brabant) was the son of a noble who had fought under our Richard I in the Holy Land. A hermit near Antioch, to whom the father had confessed his sins, warned him that some of them would keep him long in purgatory unless he bred up one of his sons to the priesthood. The child Thomas was therefore sent to school at Liège, where (as he tells us in vol. I, no. 69) he spent eleven years. At the age of fifteen he was much impressed by Jacques de Vitry's preaching. In early manhood he became a Canon Regular at Chantimpré, but passed over to the stricter Dominicans about 1231. He became a very distinguished preacher, a suffragan bishop, and a fairly voluminous writer. By far the most valuable of his works is the *Bonum Universale de Apibus*, a treatise on virtues and vices by analogy with the life of the bee, illustrated by personal and historical anecdotes. This was written somewhere about 1260; my extract is from the Douay edition of 1597.

98. THE SAVING VIRTUE OF A COWL
(Lib. II, c. 51, p. 390.)

AND, since there are many who flee to Religion when death is upon them, and many have chosen to doubt how far it availeth them to adopt the dress of the Order in this last necessity, therefore I will tell a most undoubted instance and

---

[1] It was a commonplace of the scholastic theology that the joys of the blessed in heaven would be increased by the sight of their reprobate brethren writhing in hell; see the references in *From St Francis to Dante*, 2nd edition, p. 366, and no. 62 in vol. I, from Bishop Thomas of Chantimpré.

most apposite to this purpose.[1] And indeed some Religious are impiously accustomed to deny their habit to penitents at the end of their lives, on the plea that those who refused to enter in health are unworthy to receive the frock at their latter end. Yet Christ, the pattern of all justice, opened the gates of paradise to the thief who repented at the last moment. I have heard from the lips of the aforesaid Walther von Meisenburg, of the Order of Friars Preachers, how a certain great provost came one evening to the city of Magdeburg, intending to pass onwards again next day. But lo! in his first sleep he was seized with a sudden sickness, and sent hastily for the Prior of the Friars Preachers; whom the Provost besought instantly and with tears that he would receive him into the Order and clothe him forthwith. "Nay," said the Prior, "but this shall be done to-morrow; for herein we must ask the consent of the Brethren." Then said the Provost, "I know, I know what I feel; I shall scarce live unto the morrow. If ye love my salvation, haste ye now to receive me as a penitent; for I am certain that I cannot be saved in the world."[2] When therefore the Prior saw the man's earnestness, he hastened home, awoke the convent, asked their consent, alleging the sufficiency of the man for the Order, even though he should outlive this. The convent consented forthwith; the sick man was brought into the friary; he was received, clothed, houseled, aneled, and gave up the ghost before daybreak. Not long after this, a certain nun in the nunnery hard by that city saw in her dreams a vision of an householder sitting in a convenient place, to whom many Friars Preachers came (as she dreamed) to receive their pennies after the labour of the day; and at the last, a certain unknown Brother held forth a timid and

---

[1] The practice here so ardently defended became a crying abuse. In 1406 the Council of Hamburg dealt with "the pernicious error now current among the faithful that whosoever departeth this life dressed in a Franciscan frock is sure of eternal salvation" (Mansi, *Concilia*, vol. XXVI, p. 1017). In Wright's *Latin Stories*, p. 59, there is an amusing anecdote, nearly contemporary with this in the text, of a woman who took vengeance on her husband by intoxicating him and carrying him off in a cart to the nearest monastery, where she successfully represented him as a patient *in extremis* who wished to take the cowl.

[2] Though never formally insisted upon, the feeling that it was almost impossible to save one's soul in "the world" was very strong in the Middle Ages. Compare St Bernard, *Letters*, No. 2.

trembling hand, that he might receive his penny as a Friar. Then the householder, having looked closely into his face, made answer: "Nay, thou shalt have thy penny, yet not now; for thou must first be purged by many remedies." All this the nun told to the priest of the convent, asking whether any of the Friars Preachers were dead: to whom he answered that he had been in their convent last evening and had found no man dead or sick there. Yet in the morning, after Prime,[1] came the subprior of the Friars who had promised to preach to these nuns, and excused himself saying that he must needs be at the burial of such and such a Friar who had even now died in the House. So then the nun's vision was shown to be true, and it was clearly proved that the penitential frock doth indeed profit much, provided that the change of will be sincere.

The following are from the collection of *Latin Stories* published by T. Wright for the Percy Society in 1842. They are from preachers' manuals of the thirteenth and fourteenth centuries, to be used as illustrations in sermons.

99. THE THREE ABBOTS
(P. 49.)

A CERTAIN abbot gave his monks three dishes [to their dinner], wherefore they said: "This man giveth us but sparingly: let us pray God that he may soon die." And so it was; for within a brief while, for that or some other cause, he died. Then came another abbot who gave them but two dishes: whereat they were sore wroth and grieved, saying: "Now must we pray all the more (since one dish hath been taken from us) that the Lord take away this man's life." At length he died; and the third gave them but one. Then were the monks moved to indignation and said: "This fellow is worst of all, for he will slay us with hunger; let us pray God for his speedy death." Then said one monk: "Nay, but I pray God He may give him a long life and keep him among us." The others, marvelling, asked him why he spake thus; said he: "The first (I see) was evil, the second worse, and this man

---

[1] A canonical hour of prayer, originally 6 a.m.

worst of all. Yet I fear that, when he is dead, another may come who will famish us outright." For as the proverb hath it: "Selde cometh the latter the better."

100. THE NOVICE AND THE GEESE
(*Ib.* p. 71.)

A YOUNG anchorite, who had been nourished from his childhood in the hermitage, went with his abbot to the city; and, seeing women dancing together, he enquired earnestly of his abbot what these might be. "They are geese," quoth he. When therefore the boy was come back to the cloister, he presently fell a-weeping; to whom the abbot: "What wouldst thou, my son?" "Father," quoth he, "I would fain eat of those geese which I saw in the city."

The *Liber Memorandorum Ecclesie de Bernewelle* is a record drawn up by one of the canons of Barnwell Priory, by Cambridge, in the years 1295–6. The author's purpose cannot be better described than in his own words (p. 37): "When the sun draweth towards his setting, the heat of the day cooleth; and, as the world declineth to old age, charity groweth cold. Seeing therefore that (as it is written) wheresoever charity groweth cold there iniquity aboundeth, we must not wonder if fraud and deceit and malice and other vices thrive in the world: but we should rather fear lest, if they still grow, they will infect the whole world with their venom. …Wherefore, in order that the servants of God may the more readily, by the help of God Almighty, escape out of the hands of wicked men, having regard to the fact that human memory is defective, it is worth while to reduce to writing certain things which may be useful to our church, and by inspection of this little book, may help our Brethren, both present and to come, when difficulties arise, and they are persecuted by a cruel world. May the Grace of the Holy Spirit therefore lend his aid to bring this work to a suitable conclusion."

101. TOUCH NOT MINE ANOINTED!
(P. 119, A.D. 1267–8.)

ANDREW HARNEYS, of Wiggenhall, held a certain messuage and 24 acres of land and two acres of meadow from the Prior of Barnwell in that said village of Wiggenhall, paying a rent of three shillings a year, and scutage[1] when it fell due. He died without issue, and was succeeded by James the Chaplain as next heir, being his sister's son. This James, after the death of Andrew aforesaid, came to Jolan our Prior to pay him homage and other dues for the tenement which he claimed to hold of him through the said Andrew's death. But the Prior, considering that a great and ample heritage had come to this chaplain, began at once to busy himself how he might bring it into the possession of his monastery. Wherefore he promised and granted to this chaplain, with the consent of his fellow-monks, two Canons' corrodies[2] and two marks yearly, and competent lodging for his life long. The chaplain consented, the deed was drawn up and sealed with the convent seal, and a day was fixed whereon the Prior should go thither to take possession.

Meanwhile the chaplain departed and came to Wiggenhall, where he soon discovered his counsel to certain persons who quickly changed his purpose. So Prior Jolan came hastily across the country, with his horses and trappings and a great train of servants, to take possession of the lands and tenements which James the Chaplain had granted; and after dinner he sat in his own house there with his friends and neighbours of that village, in great merriment: when suddenly the servants of the lord William Bardolf came in arms and made an assault upon the Prior and his men. At which sight the Prior and all that were with him fled in sore affright, some creeping through the windows and others scrambling over walls. The Prior himself fled to Dereham Abbey; nor did one of his train stand his ground, but all left their possessions and fled. Then the said robbers, servants of the lord William Bardolf, led away with great rejoicing all the Prior's horses which they found there, and their harness to boot, save only one ancient jade; and the number of good horses thus taken away was thirteen. Moreover, taking the Canon's rain-capes, they held

---

[1] A money-tax on lands in place of the original tenure of personal military service.

[2] A corrody was a life-pension granted by a monastery, nearly always in kind and in return for value received. The second canon's portion was no doubt for Andrew's servants; as a rule, the documents show us quite well-to-do people content with a single monastic ration.

them up to laughter and derision as though in mockery of the Canons and their Order. But the Prior and his men found their way home at length in great confusion, bearing their loss and awaiting happier times; for in those days the Prior could not plead in the king's court against the evildoers, since it was then as it were a time of war. Nevertheless from that time forth we never had in our convent of Barnwell so many good horses as we lost at Wiggenhall, in the twinkling of an eye, by this robbery aforesaid. . . .

After peace had been made, the Prior remembered what ills he had suffered at Wiggenhall through James the Chaplain; and, by the lord Legate's authority, he haled him into court before the Prior of Huntingdon. He however, appearing before the court, feigned an appeal, and demanded the Prior of Wormegay as his judge, and served a citation on the Prior to answer to him in the priory church of Wormegay on a certain day. But the Prior, knowing that this was near to the manor of lord William Bardolf, feared to plead there. Wherefore he bethought him how he might cautiously refuse that place, and sent Dom Alger our Canon, with an advocate, as his proctor for the day of trial, and sent another Canon, Dom John de Swaffham, to the Court of the lord Legate in London, to obtain remedy for these appeals. So it befell that, while the one party appealed against the Prior of Wormegay on that trial-day, Dom John de Swaffham got his letters signed on the morrow in the Legate's Court, concerning the said appeals, and came home so hastily that he arrived almost at the same moment as Dom Alger came from Wormegay; and our Prior, seeing the letters drawn up in due form, cited the said James without delay by authority of these same letters. James therefore and those that were of his party, seeing these letters of appeal sealed with the lord Legate's seal, were vehemently amazed, and cried: "The Prior's messengers are swifter than the strong flight of eagles!" So he, unable now to defend himself against such subtleties, was laid within a few days under sentence of excommunication, as well for his contumacy as for his offence; under which he persisted forty days without appealing or praying for absolution. The Prior, seeing this, obtained letters of arrest against him from the Bishop of

Norwich. In brief, within a few days a messenger came to the Prior saying that he had seen James the Chaplain walking in the streets of Cambridge; and he sent forthwith two Canons with the sheriff's officers to arrest him. They found him walking in Jew Lane,[1] and sought to seize him; but James ran swiftly, and fled to the church of the Friars Minor. Thither they followed him, and warned him to come out and go with them; but he would not. Then they bade the friars cast him out, since he was excommunicate: but they made answer, "If ye know him to be excommunicate, do then whatsoever seemeth good to you." So the officers came and laid hands upon him, and dragged him forth from the church by his feet, and cast him into prison, where he must needs lie until he had made his peace with the Prior for fifteen marks sterling, for which he found security, repenting sore that he had gone back from his first bargain.

The lord John de Burgh the elder...sent word in those lawless days [to Prior Jolan], to lend him a horse for bearing his harness to a certain place, but the Prior at that time had no plenty of horses, by reason of the aforesaid robbery at Wiggenhall; wherefore he commanded Master Simon de Ashley, who was then our Treasurer, to furnish the lord with a horse. He therefore, in obedience to the Prior, sent an ancient horse, great and lean, which alone he had then at hand. The lord John and his men, seeing this beast, cried aloud, "Whence cometh this ancient devil?" and they walked round our horse with mighty laughter, some showing his teeth, others feeling his head and back with their fingers, others again dragging him by his miserable tail, others pricking him and provoking him to kick. Some cried: "Let him be flayed!" others: "Let him be burned!" In short, the lord bade them take him back whence he had come; and within a few days he sent a knight of his household with certain others, saying to the Prior: "Our lord, the lord John de Burgh, hath sent us to thee saying that he saluteth thee not, nor giveth thee thanks for that ancient horse which thou hast lent him. He commandeth thee therefore to send him in all haste a good ambling palfrey, not as a loan but as a gift; send

---

[1] The modern All Saints' Passage. See A. Gray, *The Town of Cambridge*, p. 63.

therefore thine answer by us without delay." The Prior, considering the time and the person, strove to answer meekly, saying: "Would that I had a good palfrey, and proper for your lord's need! Once I had such; yet will I now gladly give whereof I possess." Therewith he sent a new-bought palfrey, small of stature but of good pace; which the lord took and hath never sent back even unto this day; nevertheless his fury was appeased.

102. THREE MONKS IN PARADISE

The following anonymous fourteenth-century Italian legend, which should be compared with Dante's description of the *Earthly Paradise*, is printed on p. 489 of the first volume of *Leggende del Secolo XIV* (Florence: Barbèra, 1863).

THE Paradise of Delights is in the eastern region of this earthly world, upon a mountain lifted high above all other mountains and all this earth of ours; from which Paradise spring four rivers which encompass the whole world, and which are called Tigris, Euphrates, Gihon and Pison. Now, beside one of these rivers which is named Gihon, there stood a convent of monks who were great friends of God and lived a truly angelic life. So it came to pass one day that three of the monks went walking through the convent garden and came to the banks of the Gihon, where they bathed their feet and hands. Then they saw drifting down this stream a bough of a tree, enamelled with every colour that is fairest to see; for one of its leaves was golden, another silvery, a third azure, a fourth green, and so forth of all motley hues; and the bough was laden with apples and fruits most fair to the eye and most enchanting to the taste. Then these monks took that bough and considered its beauty, praising and glorifying the name and the power of God who made so marvellous a tree; and, as they saw and considered how marvellous and fair the bough was, and as each fell into a contemplation thereof, then they began to weep at the thought of God's mighty works, and said within themselves, "Truly that is a holy place from whence this bough is come!" And while each pondered thereon with tears, one looked upon the other and said: "Wherefore weepest thou?" "I weep," quoth he, "at the great imagination and contemplation that I have in my soul, thinking and pondering of the place whence this bough is come; for methinks God must be there with all His angels." Then each confessed that the same thought was in his own mind; and one said: "Shall we go to that sacred place, even upwards by the bank of this river, until God lead us to that holy spot?" Then said the others: "Let us go now in God's name!" Thus went they forthwith, without speech of their abbot, so were they inflamed and kindled with the love of Christ. And, as they went up the river banks, they found the herbs all full of manna, whereat they marvelled, for they found this to be the sweetest and most savourous substance in the whole world. Thus therefore they pained themselves to go upwards a whole year long; and they found trees laden with the sweetest fruit and most delicious to the taste, that drooped even to the ground all around them; wherefore they went with such sweetness and delight of soul that their feet scarce touched the earth. When they were come nigh unto that mountain, on whose top lay the Paradise of Delights, then they began to hear the song of the angels in Paradise; whereat all were filled with joy, and went onwards in great desire. Now this mountain was clothed all round with divers sorts of trees, all full of sweetest fruit and most delicious and comforting to the taste, and marvellous withal to the sight; and all beneath grew holy herbs, bearing flowers of marvellous hues and of divers and marvellous scents; and that mountain was an hundred miles high. Yet they went so joyfully that they ascended to the summit and felt no pain; and soon they were at the gate of Paradise, which they found fast closed, and over all an angel of the Cherubim guarding it with a sword of fire in his hand. Then these monks sat them down beside the gate, and gazed upon this Cherub; whereat they felt so great sweetness and joy of heart and soul that they lost all count of this world and the next, so great were the most exalted beauties and marvels of that angel! Thus then they tarried at the gate, contemplating that angel for five days and five nights; for his face shone as doth the sun. Then the angel spake and said,

"What would ye have?" "If such be your pleasure," said they, "we would fain enter therein, and tarry there three or four days." Then the door opened forthwith, and the monks entered in. And as soon as they were within, they heard the sound of the wheel of heaven, that turned round with a music so sweet, so soft, so delightful, that they knew not where they were, but sat them down there within the gate, such bliss and content had they of that sound of the wheel of heaven! Thus then they sat in great joy, until they saw two stewards coming towards them, most comely of face and white as snow, with hair and beards that swept the ground; which were no other than Enoch and Elias, holy fathers whom God set to dwell in His Paradise of Delights until the world's end, to give testimony of the death of Jesus Christ His only-begotten Son. Then said these men to the monks, "What do ye here?" "We are come," said they, "to see this holy place." Then said the holy fathers Elias and Enoch: "Give thanks and praise to our Lord Jesus Christ, who hath granted you the grace and the priceless gift of entering into this sacred place; for never came man hither that was born of woman, but only souls that have been purged and glorified. Since therefore it hath pleased God our Lord, we will lead you all around and show you the exceeding great glories and marvels of holy Paradise, so many and so great as no tongue can tell nor no heart conceive." Then they took those holy monks by the hand and led them throughout Paradise, showing them the great gifts of God and the marvels that sweet Jesus had wrought. While they thus went and sought throughout Paradise, they heard the delightful music and the amorous chants of the angels of heaven; then they wellnigh fainted for delight of that angelic song that was so soft and sweet; and, lifting their eyes and minds and hands to God, they rendered thanks and praise to Him. Then were they aware of a living spring, whereof whoso drinketh can never grow old, and whosoever is already old, he turneth to the age of thirty years. And they saw the tree of good and evil, through which all we were lost for Adam's and Eve's sake that ate thereof. They saw also the tree of our salvation, wherefrom was taken the wood of the Holy Cross; to which sacred tree these monks knelt and did great reverence, adoring God with many tears. Then saw they another tree, whereof whosoever eateth shall never die. After that they

DAVID IN HEAVEN PLAYING ON A ROTE
From a thirteenth-century window at Chartres. Cf. Chaucer's *Cant. Tales,*
Prologue, l. 236.

saw four fountains, whence issued the four rivers that encompass the world. Then again they saw a fountain five miles long and broad, filled with a multitude of fishes that chanted day and night in answer to the song of Paradise; whose chant was more sweet than man's tongue may tell. Then they saw the tree of glory, which was so great that it spread its branches for the space of a mile around; whose leaves were of gold, after the bigness and fashion of fig-leaves, and the fruit seemed marvellously wrought, as it were of sugared confections, of unspeakable softness and delight and sweetness to the taste. This tree was full of small fowls, whose wings were red as burning coals of fire, even as though they had been lamps hanging amid the leaves, and all sang with one voice as though they had indeed been angels of the celestial Paradise. Thus sang they at every hour of the day; so sweet and so soft was their song that every human mind would have been lulled to sleep; all day long they praised the court of Paradise. Then those holy fathers Elias and Enoch led these holy monks unto the gate of Paradise, saying: "Return now to your convent, for thither are ye called by God the Creator Who hath made you." Then said the monks, "O Sirs, have mercy upon us! we beseech you, vouchsafe to let us tarry fifteen days here!" Therewith they wept and wailed and fell on their knees, and said to those holy fathers: "We have not yet been eight days here!" Then they made answer: "Ye have been here seven hundred years." Then those monks began to weep yet more piteously, lifting their eyes and hands and souls to heaven, praising and glorifying the power and wisdom of the true God, and saying: "O sweet Jesus Christ, seeing that this Earthly Paradise is so sweet and delightful, what then must be that life of bliss wherein Thou dwellest visibly with Thy sweet Mother! O sweet Jesus Christ, how great must be the joy and gladness to see the choirs of Thy saints, with the hosts of angels and archangels and principalities and powers. O how delightful must it be to behold the choirs of cherubim and seraphim, and the legions of sainted men and women! O sweet Jesus Christ, shall we too ascend to Thy blessed Kingdom?" Then answered the holy fathers Elias and Enoch: "Go now with God's grace, and in a brief space ye shall come to that realm of eternal life." Then said those holy monks: "How can it be that we have been here seven hundred years?

for we seem to be of that same age whereof we were when we came hither." Then said the holy fathers, "Ye have eaten of the fruit of that tree which suffereth not old age, and ye have drunken of the sacred water of the Fountain of Youth, and have dwelt in this most holy place wherein ye have heard somewhat of the glory of eternal life: now therefore go to your convent." "O holy fathers," said they, "shall we find any yet living of our own company?" "Nay," said the others, "for your brethren and companions live now in eternal life, but their bodies are returned to earth and dust these seven hundred years agone, and your convent is renewed and reformed with fresh folk; seven times have they died and been renewed, and seven ages are gone by since your departure." Then answered the monks, "They who are now in our convent will not receive us, nor believe that we have been Brethren of that house; how then shall we do?" "Ye shall show them this sign: bid them seek in the high altar and find the missal-book wherein are written all monks' names of that house for the last thousand years; then shall they find your names also, with the hour and day and month and year of your departure to come hither. This other sign also shall ye show; that after forty days ye shall return suddenly to dust, neither shall flesh or bone be left of you; and your souls shall go to rest in the holy quiet of eternal life, and the angels of heaven shall see through your souls with their own eyes." Then wept those holy monks for very joy, and went forth from the Paradise of Delights, rendering thanks and honour to the holy fathers. Joyfully they went on their way, and came to the convent, and found the gate open, and entered into the church, where they fell on their knees before the altar, weeping and praising and magnifying the mighty power of God, who had vouchsafed to them to return home and die. At which words came all the monks of that convent and said to these three: "What do ye here?" And they told their story. Then said the Abbot: "Ye say that ye are of this house; yet we, who have been here eighty years or more, have never seen or known you. Why then do ye tell us such follies?" "Nay," said they, "but or ever ye were monks of this monastery, we were monks here before you; seven hundred years have passed since we set out hence for the holy Paradise of Delights, wherefore the Brethren our companions are dead, and this house hath seven times been renewed with fresh folk since then. If ye believe us not, seek now within the high altar, where ye shall find the missal-book and memorial wherein our names are written, with the hour and day and month and year of our departure hence." At these words the abbot and monks marvelled; then without delay they went and searched within the altar, and found how those monks had set forth seven hundred years agone. At which miracle they marvelled, and said among themselves: "How may it be that these men have lived so long, seeing that each appeareth of the age of thirty years?" Then said those three: "Marvel not at God's power, to Whom no thing is impossible. We have been all this time in that holy place, and these eyes of ours have seen the angel Cherub, and we have walked with the holy fathers Elias and Enoch, who themselves have walked and eaten with Jesus Christ and have touched him; after which we heard the sweet and beatific song of the angels, and it seemed to us that we had not been there full eight days. What then must be the life of bliss, and the court of heaven? Moreover, we give you yet another sign: for after forty days we shall fall suddenly dead, and at that moment our bodies shall be dust and our souls shall go up to heaven, to a mansion of quiet, there to rest in the life of bliss and everlasting glory; and the angels of heaven shall see through our souls with their own eyes." Then the Abbot and all his monks, to the number of an hundred, fell to the earth, weeping and doing obeisance to those three monks who told these mighty marvels of God's glory. So it came to pass that, at the end of forty days, these three monks abode on their knees before the altar and wept for very joy of heart, while the Abbot with his monks watched and worshipped with great devotion. Then, when the forty days were fulfilled, those holy monks turned to dust, wherefrom proceeded so mighty an odour as though all the musk and all fragrant things in the world had been there gathered together; and the Brethren saw with their own eyes how the angels of heaven bore away those holy souls with a sound of many songs. At which sight the Abbot and his monks were much comforted, and wept for very sweetness of love; and from that day forward they lived in all holiness, even more than in the past, by reason of these great marvels that they had seen. Thus they lived in God's grace and love; and at their deaths they came to life everlasting. *Amen.*

The *Gesta Abbatum S. Albani* is a chronicle of the abbots of that great house compiled about 1350 by Thomas Walsingham, precentor of the abbey and last of the great English chroniclers. The writer had access to the wide collection of documents in his abbey; the *Gesta* extends from 793 to 1349, and Walsingham's own *Historia Anglicana* goes down to 1422. The edition of the *Gesta* here used is that published in the Rolls Series; it is brilliantly summarized by Froude in one of his *Short Studies* (Annals of an English Abbey).

103. A CONVENT ELECTION
(Vol. II, p. 107.)

ALTHOUGH Abbot [John IV, 1302–8] had himself gained much wealth, as aforesaid, yet he left no certain moneys for the ordination of anniversary masses, even as his predecessor Dom John of Berkhampstead had left none; which gives cause for much wonder and blame. When therefore he had ruled the Church of St Alban for six years and three quarters, as a good and prudent prelate, having already been Prior of the same for fourteen years... [*sentence left unfinished by scribe*]. He strove duly to keep the Rule, to love his brethren as he ought, and to keep them at unity; and in worldly matters he purposed to order his House well, so far as in him lay. But the billows of this evil and treacherous age, thwarting him daily and in divers ways with the spirit of a stepmother, hindered him from the accomplishment of his purpose. His mind was constant, his words few; a man of exceeding honesty, religious and circumspect. He moved St Alban's tomb and shrine, decorating it with all honour, and paying the expenses himself, not to speak of many generous gifts, more than 160 marks of coined money: but from the sub-sacristans he took what offerings he well could. Feeling then, from his growing pains and sicknesses, that he could not live much longer, he summoned the Prior and the elder brethren to his presence in his own chamber, speaking of the state of the monastery, which was in debt to divers creditors to the extent of £1300, and to the lord King 1000 marks for the last vacancy; and 17 marks were found in his room, which the Prior of Tynemouth had sent him a little while before— "But this silver cup, and this ring, ye must give after my decease to our lord the King."[1] And he warned them not to elect for their Abbot, after his decease, a proud and pompous man, but some good and simple person; and so, by God's providence, it came about. So he was carried in the brethren's arms to the Chapter-House, where he besought the community to pray devoutly to God for the church and for himself, adding: "Whosoever shall be Abbot after me, must needs report to the Lord Pope how great are the debts of this House, and plead our poverty"; which in process of time came almost to naught, for the greed of the Roman court. Then he added in lamentable tones: "If I have sinned against any man, or treated any contrary to his deserts (which indeed I know not) then let him say so." But the brethren, mourning, said the *Confiteor* in turn; whereupon he kissed and took leave of them. Then he was brought to the shrine, begging pardon and leave to depart, and praying thus: "O glorious Alban, whom I have loved and sought, and who hast been my best helper, as I have been thy servant; O most holy Alban, defend me from the pains of hell!" So he died on the 23rd day of February, 1308, and was honourably buried, as was fitting, by the venerable father Richard of Hertford, by God's grace Abbot of Waltham; and he was laid with his fathers in a marble tomb before the high altar, as may be seen from the inscription which he prepared for himself while he yet lived; to the honour and glory of God, Who is blessed world without end. Amen.

After the burial of Abbot John, of good memory, who had obeyed his Maker's call on St Matthias' eve, then they proceeded on the day appointed to elect a new abbot. Thereupon by general consent Brother Hugh of Eversdon was elected, who had borne the office of Cellarer; a man of stature con-

[1] All these sentences are loose and incoherent in the original Latin.

spicuous even among the most comely; fair to look upon, and liberal to his companions. None could surpass him in the English or French tongue, yet he had but little Latin. When therefore he had been elected, and had consented thereto, he is said to have spoken thus in full congregation: "I know indeed, my brethren, that ye might have chosen a more subtle and more learned man for your abbot; but I am very sure that ye could have chosen none more companionable [*socialem*] out of all this number."

When therefore the proctors were come to Rome, and had set the notice of his election before the Lord Pope, after tarrying long and vainly in the city, and incurring horrible expenses upon divers gifts, at last they must needs return with the most odious answer that the Abbot-elect must by all means cross the sea and present himself in person to the Supreme Pontiff, who (as he said) would fain see that man face to face, on whose behalf so many lords, so many prelates, the King—nay, even the Queen—had written to him with such devout supplications! Wherefore notwithstanding the moneys already vainly spent, he was constrained to go to the Roman court— he, who feared nought more than the Latin tongue, wherein he had but little skill. When therefore, after many chances, he was come thither, his first care (after saluting the Lord Pope) was to grease the palms of his examiners,[1] that they might deal more gently with him. After which, his personal fitness having been favourably represented to the Supreme Pontiff and duly accepted, and his election having been confirmed, he showed himself so lavish of presents to the Lord Pope and the whole Court, that those most covetous of men extolled his magnificence. Yet he expended on his journey to and from the Court, together with the gifts that he made, more than a thousand pounds,[2] besides the tax which he paid to the Lord Pope and Cardinals under the name of *firstfruits*, which amounted to [*sentence unfinished*].

[This foregoing passage may best be illustrated by the full and formal account of expenses incurred at Rome for the confirmation of Hugh's predecessor, John IV, in 1302 (p. 56).]

---

[1] *Examinatores suos emollire.*
[2] *I.e.* nearly £20,000 in modern money.

To the lord Pope, for his private visitation, 3,000[1] florins, that is to say, 1,250 marks sterling.—*Item*, for the public visitation, 1,008 marks: in sum, 2,258 marks to the lord Pope and his Cardinals.—*Item*, to obtain a respite, 200 marks.—*Item*, to the Examiners; viz. to the Cardinal of Albano a goblet worth 40 florins, or 10 marks; to Dom J. the monk a cup of the same value; to Cardinal Napoleone [Orsini] a cup worth 32 florins, or 8 marks.—*Item*, to two other Cardinals, viz., to the lord Francis, nephew to the lord Pope, a platter worth 42 florins, or 10½ marks, and to the Referendary, Master P. de Hispania, another of the same price. —*Item*, to the advocates of the lord Pope's doorkeeper 34 gros tournois.[2]— *Item*, to Master Jacopo da Casula, 19⅔ gros tournois.—*Item*, to Albertino 26½ gros tournois.—*Item*, to the proctors, viz., to Master Corsini 12 florins, and again 20 gros tournois; and to Master N. of Naples, who was the treasurer's proctor, 12 florins, [with] a palfrey and other necessaries to the price of 40 florins.—*Item*, to Albertino da Casula, advocate, 6 florins.— *Item*, in presents to the Cardinals 14⅝ gros tournois.—*Item*, by the hand of Corsini in the matter of obtaining the bulls, and for writing the said bulls for the first time, 63 gros tournois. To Master Blondino, who corrected the annulled letters, 2 florins. To the scribe, for the second time, 60 gros tournois.—To Master P., that they might the sooner be enregistered, 4 gros tournois. For three supplicatory letters 65 gros tournois. —To the clerks who sealed the bulls, 12 florins and 2 gros tournois.—For the registrar, 60 gros tournois.—For the sealing of his own supplicatory letters, 1 florin.—*Item*, through Master Reginald, to P. del Mare, 2 florins; for a copy of the obligation, 2 florins and 4 gros tournois. To the notaries, 50 florins, and 8 florins for the note. For the executory letter, 35 florins. For a ring as a present to Albertino, 6 florins.—[Total, 2,561 marks sterling, *i.e.*, about £34,000 modern money.]

104. AN UNWILLING CONVERT

From *Urkunden und Regesten zur Gesch. d. Rheinlande a. d. Vaticanischen Archiv*, Band II (1903), Letter of Pope John XXII to the Archbishop of Cologne, Dec. 29, 1327. There is a similar case of a nun reported on p. 73 of *Yearbooks of Richard II*, 1388–1389 (Ames Foundation); cf. Eileen Power, *Medieval English Nunneries*, pp. 33 ff.

Arnold von Straten, of thy diocese of Cologne, in our presence, hath shown unto us that long ago, in the thirteenth[3] year of his age or thereabouts, by the direction, guidance, and

---

1 "Probably 5000, as four florins are throughout made equal to one mark."— Editor's note in Rolls Series.

2 50 gros tournois went to the English mark: see Rogers, *Hist. Ag. and Prices*, vol. II, p. 631.

3 The text has *infra tertium undecimum annum*.

impulse of his parents, he entered into the Cistercian monastery of St Mary at Campen in the said diocese and then took the habit of a novice, yet with no intention of abiding in the said monastery, since he could not bear the rigour of that Order. Moreover, at different times and occasions he asked for his secular garments, which however the inmates of the said monastery would not restore unto him, but kept the said garments from him. Then the said Arnold, having finished his year of probation, and being asked by the said parents to take the vows in the aforesaid Order, refused to do so and persevered in this contradictory will of his. Yet in process of time, through force and fear not only of his parents aforesaid but also of the authorities [*praelatorum*] of the said monastery, which may affect even a constant purpose, he took the said vows with tears and grief, not without first protesting that he would by no means abide in the said abbey, but would take the first occasion of flight. Then again, in process of time, the said parents made him take the order of subdeacon, despite his unwillingness and resistance. And the said Arnold, both before and after this his ordination, at divers times, caught such occasions and chances as favoured him, and absented himself from the abbey by the refuge of flight; and his parents and the aforesaid authorities took the said Arnold and cast him into prison; from which prison, catching at an opportune moment and an hour of freedom, he took to flight again and betook himself far away, living in freedom and following secular occupations for the space of six years or more, as a soldier against the enemies of the Church.... Therefore We, albeit nature would incline Us to follow the Rule of the Order, yet seeing that the law doth make divers provisions for such cases as spring from force and fear...do commit unto thee that thou shouldst, by Our authority, grant dispensation of his vows to this Arnold aforesaid.

From No. 50 of the *Scelta di Curiosità Letterarie Inedite o Rare* (Bologna, 1864). The MS. is in the National Library at Florence (Magliab. XXXI, 65). For the story of these *Fraticelli*, freely treated, I may be permitted to refer to a little book of my own, *Friar's Lantern* (Barnicott and Pearce, Taunton, 1906). Scientific studies on the subject may be found in H. C. Lea, *Hist. of the Inquisition in the Middle Ages*, vol. III (esp. pp. 160 ff.), and A. G. Ferrers Howell, *S. Bernardino of Siena*, 1913, chap. I. Most early Franciscans had believed that Christ and His Apostles had possessed nothing, either individually or corporately, and the Popes had for some time favoured this doctrine. But John XXII (1316–1334) was a lawyer and a disciplinarian; the extreme doctrine of the poverty of Christ lent itself too easily to propaganda against a possessionate clergy; and in 1323 he condemned it as heretical, thereby plainly contradicting the decision of his predecessor Nicholas III in 1279. This, with other earlier and later acts, convinced a large number of zealous (or "spiritual") Franciscans that John was himself heretical and that his adherents formed no true Church. This, of course, was flat rebellion; and it is these rebels who are called *Fraticelli*; men whose loyalty to the strictest Franciscan ideal (a loyalty, to be sure, often narrow and exaggerated) brought them into conflict with the official Church. In Italy they flourished chiefly in the mountain districts, more especially in St Francis's own county of Umbria and the adjacent Mark of Ancona. Many of them were burned as heretics in different countries of Europe—even in England, where the conflict was less bitter than elsewhere. The little treatise here translated in an abbreviated form gives by far the most curious and intimate picture which has survived of any of these executions.

105. HOW FRIAR MICHAEL WAS BURNED

THE poor Brethren of St Francis, dwelling in the Mark of Ancona (who have now and for some time past been persecuted for Christ's poverty's sake), sent thence to Florence, according to custom, Brother Michael and a companion, to edify the faithful of that city; and they arrived there on the 26th day of January, 1388.[1] And on Olive Sunday,[2] in Lententide, the said Brother Michael, having satisfied all the needs of our souls, and blessed the olive and distributed to all present, gave out that the poor folk should not (as he thought) wait longer upon him, and that he would fain depart. But considering, on the other side, that Holy Week was at

[1] A slip, as presently appears, for 1389.
[2] *I.e.* Palm Sunday: this is commemorated in different parts by branches of different trees or shrubs.

hand, and the holy day of Easter, therefore he and many others determined that he should not depart until after the Paschal Feast, that is, on the Monday morning, April 19, 1389. Therefore on Easter morning, many persons having communicated, he said (standing at the altar, on the north side, with many and almost infinite admonitions) that he would depart on the morrow, seeing that there was nothing else to be done; and he besought us to have him excused and to pardon him if in aught he had erred, knowing no better; all which words he spake with much humility, and took leave of each in turn.

Then on the Monday morning, at daybreak, being minded to depart, and having already set out with certain companions, Brother Michael began to say that he could not find it in his heart to go. And, after many words, we left it in his choice, and he determined not to depart that day, but said that he would fain lodge that night without the city, that so he might arise early on the next morning; and, having thus determined and ordained, he could not yet depart. So in that interval of time, as it seemed so ordained, certain daughters of Judas, who had already more than once shown themselves backsliders, being instigated of the Devil, besought him now most instantly that they might confess to him for the good of their souls, and so forth; wherefore he resolved to go unto them. And, as he was being led to the women aforesaid, whereof two were Béguines and three widows, as they went by the way, his companion said unto him: "Give me some means of speaking with these women": whereunto he made answer, "I will say that which cometh to my lips, and do thou speak as God shall inspire thee." So, being come into their house, he began to speak unto them, saying: "I hold with the Apostle Paul, who saith that it is for him to do not as other men do, not with observation of omens and days and so forth (Gal. iv, 10); but rather in Christ's name speak I unto you, and I will expound unto you that word of the holy Gospel: *Beware of false prophets*, and so forth." And thus he spake many words of truth unto these women, setting before their eyes the innumerable persecutions which fall upon whosoever shall seek in these days to follow closely and strictly after the commandments of God and of Holy Church, saying, "Believe not us, but believe the Holy Scriptures; for indeed, unless the saints deceive us, this is the truth." When therefore he had long spoken to them of the terrors and dangers of these days, then they besought him, saying: "Ye have proclaimed unto us the pains, speak now somewhat of the reward." But it seemed that he could say no otherwise than of these dreadful things, to prove their perseverance; so that they seemed sore dismayed, and two of them would by no means come to confession. But, having attended to their confessions, and being prayed again to speak of the comfort that availeth all who follow the truth, he spake that which was needful on that point. Then these women, with incredible treachery and devilish enticements, under a cloak of great charity, persuaded him to stay the night, seeing that there still remained two to be confessed. So he abode still with them; and, after that they had supped, they set him again to speak of God. Yet all the while, intending upon this their treachery, they strove to humour him and his companion until after midnight, in order that, being overcome with sleep, they might not perceive these machinations.

When the day dawned, these daughters of Judas feigned that the two who had remained to be confessed last night had had many conflicts of mind, saying: "It is even as you said to us, these things are not to be lightly taken up." So they made as if they would have a respite in this matter, being in haste to leave the house. Then they asked with great hypocrisy that he would leave them some rule of life; and the holy man made answer, "Keep ye the commandments of God," and so forth. Then, at the end of all their hypocrisies, one of them (who had looked through a grating in the entrance) threw open the door with a great noise. And, when they were come out (for the day was beginning to break), there issued forth from a house over against them many soldiers and constables, and fell upon our friars; there were sixteen of them, all armed, and raven friars among them.[1] Then, while some tied our two Brethren's hands, others entered to search the house; and,

---

[1] *I.e.* Black friars, Dominicans. The Dominicans were not only the chief inquisitors, but had often strong feelings of rivalry against the Franciscans.

as they set about this with boisterous rage, Brother Michael pained himself much to comfort his companion. Thence they were taken to the Bishop's palace and cast into prison, and all writings were taken from them; moreover, although Brother Michael prayed with much humility and meekness that they would be pleased to leave his breviary that he might say his hours, yet they would not hear him, but cast him with much contumely into a dungeon. Then Brother Michael, with much praise and thanks to God, as one wholly confounded with the great favour that he had received of Him, made the sign of prayer and turned to his companion and spake with great fervour of spirit and fire of charity, kneeling and oftentimes falling on his face. "O," he said, "what grace hath God shown us, and what are we to be so honoured! O, how many of the poor Brethren have long yearned for this, with much travail of watchings and bodily pains!" And, naming some of them by name, and reciting their perfections and their ardent desire for martyrdom, with much self-reproach he said: "And to us, mere two days' novices, who desired to return awhile to the Mark for a little sleep and bodily rest, hath God willed to vouchsafe a little taste of so great a favour!" All this he said with words and gestures that can scarce be expressed; and then he set himself to say his daily office, and was in prayer; and then he spent all day in speaking of God and of the examples of the saints, for charity and solace of his companion; manifold words he said and more than may be written, but we shall touch upon some if occasion offer itself.

Then, at the hour of vespers, the Chief of the Pharisees[1] sent for Brother Michael, examining him and saying, "What sort of folk are ye, and what laws do ye hold, and what doctrine do ye sow, and where and with whom have ye been?" The holy man replied meekly that he was a sinner, holding to the law of Jesus Christ, and sowing no other doctrine but that of Christ and His Church. Then he, interrupting, asked whether he were a priest, and who had ordained him, and where? to which Brother Michael answered in all truth, save that he said not *where*. Thereupon the Chief of the

---

[1] The Bishop of Florence; cf. John xi, 47 and Dante, *Inf.* xxvii, 85.

Pharisees (or perchance his Vicar), with certain notaries, drew forth a confession of 17 or 18 articles, the effect of which was an avowal made by certain of the poor folk, but stuffed out with many false and heretical consequences; and it was, as it seemed to us, the former condemnation of Lorenzo Gherardi. This they read chapter by chapter, asking, "What think ye of this?" and he answered fully and truly of all that he held, reproving those false conclusions which they drew. And the effect of this confession aforesaid was that Christ, as a mortal man in this present life, even as His Apostles, showed the way of perfection by possessing nothing by way of property, either singly or in common, nor any civil or worldly lordship; all which confession of his was written down by his notary, to whom the holy man protested many times that he should write no word save only what he himself spake. And then, at the end of his confession, he protested and said that, if ever he should say the contrary of these things, it would be for fear of death, and these words now spoken would be true in spite of all. Then said the Pharisees, with many scoffs and gibes, "So the Church has remained among you!" And thus they sent him back to prison.

Next day the Bishop called together his college of Pharisees, among whom were many university masters; and, when these were gathered together in the council chamber, Brother Michael was again sent for and drawn forth and brought before them. Then, after many insults and scoffs, his confession of the day before was read aloud, with the addition of many false conclusions, whereunto he answered, saying: "Wherefore have ye written falsehoods which we never said? Ye shall render account for this at the Last Day." But they mocked and made light of his words, saying, "The man is more headstrong than before!" or again, "The more we pray and beseech them, the hotter they become!" And, for all that he could say, they wrote down whatsoever they would. Then, after reading his confession (as his companion told me) they asked him whether he would hold to the doctrines which were held by such solemn masters and by all the people of Florence. Whereunto he made answer that he held Christ crucified to have been poor, and that John XXII was an heretic, since he said the contrary; and that all his successors who had held and still held and defended his decretals were heretics also. Then, alleging the decretal of Pope Nicholas III, they began to answer confusedly, saying, "We will show you how the words of Nicholas III may be accorded with John XXII." And, as they thus spake with much confusion among themselves, Brother Michael alleged the Rule of St Francis (for there were certain professors of that Rule in the judgment-hall), saying to them, "See ye not that ye deny the very words whereunto ye have made profession?" One of the friars, writhing under these words, said, "I will give no judgment against our Rule," and would have gone on to speak; but they suffered him not, but the Chief of the Pharisees turned upon him with great force and fury, saying, "Tell the man to abjure his error." And he, being afraid to see such fury, said, "Son, I pray that thou acknowledge thy faults before God, and I pray God to give thee a true understanding"; and therewith he held his peace. Then one of the masters alleged a certain point of the Gospel concerning the poverty of Christ;[1] but Brother Michael made answer: "We will not interpret Holy Scripture from our own head, but let us come to what Holy Church hath determined on this point and what the saints have said." And, when he would have alleged the decision of the Church and a text from the saints, they mocked at him and said in great fury: "Dost thou believe thyself deeper in understanding of the Scriptures than we, who are Masters of Divinity?" And thus, mocking the holy man with many scoffs and gibes, they said unto him clearly and without more ado: "It is our will that thou shouldst hold that Christ was proprietary, and Pope John XXII a

---

[1] These texts would doubtless be those quoted by the Blessed James of the Mark, who wrote a treatise against the Fraticelli and was, after St Bernardino of Siena and St Giovanni Capistrano, their most determined opponent. The angel said to St Peter (Acts xii, 8), "Cast *thy* garment about thee, and follow me." Christ had previously said to him, "Put up again *thy* sword into his place" (Matt. xxvi, 52), and to the Apostles generally, "He that hath no sword, let him sell *his* garment and buy one." This (argued the papalists) proves conclusively that the Apostles had a certain amount of private property, and thus knocks the bottom out of the Fraticelli's case (Baluze-Mansi, *Miscellanea*, vol. II, p. 606). By the *Holy Church* in the following sentence, Michael means the solemn pronouncement of Nicholas III.

catholic and holy man."[1] Unto this our holy brother, as one standing among wolves, answered: "Nay, but he is an heretic," making no account of their words and threats. And, as one zealous of holy martyrdom, and fearful of losing his crown, having heard one of them say, "He seemeth a worthy young man," and others, "It is as though he spake with God's mouth rather than man's," therefore the holy man did thus that they might judge him a fool; being in the midst of these Pharisees, he made as though he went through the room in jest, looking at one after another and scorning their folly.

Then these Pharisees, waxing worse and more perverse at every moment, fell into great fury and caused him to be bound straitly in the prison, with his feet in the stocks.

Here he remained for three days longer, under the warning that this respite was given him for repentance, and that the law must take its course after that date. The narrator describes at some length his ill-treatment in prison, and his re-examination on the fourth day, under the same unjust conditions as before, his evidence being further falsified in order to prejudice the general public against him:

(Pp. 19, 22) And to this the holy man answered point by point saying, "Wherefore have ye thus written, for I said not so; wherefore write ye these falsehoods to blind the people?" And, as the notary still read on, the holy man protested over and over again, saying, "Thou shalt render account for this at the Last Day."....And, at the end of the writing, he wrote, "I say with St Augustine: *We may indeed err, but heretics we cannot be*, since we submit ourselves and all our words to the correction of Holy Church, and to the holy Pope that

---

[1] The worldliness of this particular Pope was admitted by his most orthodox contemporaries, quite apart from his heretical speculations as to the Beatific Vision, which, however, were treated as private opinions and which he is said to have revoked on his death-bed. The great Florentine chronicler Giovanni Villani, after recording that his own blood-brother was in communication with the merchants officially deputed to value the Pope's immense possessions after his death, and therefore knew the exact amount, adds: "But this good man thought not of Christ's gospel, where He said to His disciples, *Provide yourselves a treasure in the heavens*, and *Lay not up for yourselves treasures on earth*; nor did he consider what treasure Peter and the Apostles demanded of Matthias when he was chosen into their company in place of Judas Iscariot" (ed. 1834, lib. XI, c. xix, an. 1334). The point of this last remark is, that it was John's systematization of the collection of firstfruits from bishoprics and other rich benefices throughout Europe which enabled him to amass this immense treasure.

shall come." And then the notary came for his writing, and we never saw it again; and in the process which they read when they handed him over to the secular arm, they omitted that writing of his. [He was condemned to be burned on the morrow, and (p. 26)] afterwards, about the third hour of night, came a certain proselyte of these Pharisees, saying, "Alas, vouchsafe now to repent, and know that the Bishop sendeth you word how that to-morrow, at ten o'clock, ye shall be given over to the magistrate to be burned; and I give you to know that the mitres and cloaks are already made, with Fraticelli painted on them in company with devils." The holy man, rather refreshed than dismayed at this speech, made answer, "I will hold no otherwise than as I have said." Then these proselytes, getting no other answer, went their way; and the holy man with much praise and thanks to God turned to his companion in exceeding fervour of spirit. And, when they had retired to a corner of the cell, he began to open his mouth and said: "Henceforward will we speak without any reserve concerning the deeds of truth, both with those within and with those without." Then he fell upon his knees with his companion and said, "Methinks our father St Francis will be there by the stake; and, more than that, I believe Christ's Apostles will be there, and those glorious martyrs, Brothers Bartolommeo and Antonio"; and then again, with words that seemed of consuming fire, he said, "I tell thee yet more; I believe Jesus Christ will be there." This he said with such fervour that it seemed to burn him up. After this he added, "I doubt sore of myself lest, seeing myself doomed to such a fate, I should waver somewhat in my mind, apart from such waverings as I might have in my cave."[1] And again, "May God keep His hand on my head!" And thus he spent all that night, between confession and prayer unto God, with very little sleep.

Next morning he was again brought into the Bishop's Court; and, refusing to abjure, was solemnly degraded from his priestly office, according to the regular routine. When they came to the point of cutting his hair to obliterate his tonsure, and shaving away the skin from his finger-tips where they had been dipped in holy oil at his consecration, "then at

---

[1] The Italian is obscure here: *se non come se fossi alla grotta.*

every point the holy man seemed to say somewhat that his companion could not hear for the great noise which was all about; but it seemed that he said: *It is the Bishop who ought justly to be degraded!* He said much also to encourage his companion, of which the latter could only catch these words often repeated 'We will die for God.' Next morning he was brought, as one no longer enjoying clerical immunity, before the civil magistrate, who could get nothing out of him but 'I am willing to die for the truth'" (p. 32).

Wherefore the magistrate bade that he should again be shackled and cast into prison, wherein were folk who vexed him by day and night with many insults, for that he would not believe in the Pope.[1] And in that prison there was but one plank, whereupon a man might sleep, and they suffered not the holy man to lie there, but on the earth in a corner that was wet with the continual dripping of water; and he was barefooted and bareheaded, nor had he his mantle. And withal he must continually answer the brutalities of the people, who, under cover of great compassion, tormented his soul by day and night....One citizen said unto him, "Why dost thou not as others do?" to which the holy man made answer, "I would rather suffer myself to be cast among lions."

Then, on the morning of his martyrdom, there came unto him a Gonfaloniere,...saying, "Alas, Brother Michael, thou seest how my servants are arming themselves to lead thee to death; I know not what sort of a man thou art; why dost thou not believe even as other men?" He made answer, "I am a sinful man." "If then thou art a sinful man, why believest thou not as other men?" Then answered the holy man, "I believe in Christ, poor and crucified." "So believe I also," said the Gonfaloniere, "and so believe other men." Whereunto the holy man made answer, "Pope John XXII

[1] This phrase, which occurs several times in the story, tells its own tale. Compare a chance remark of the inquisitor Caesar Carena in his *De officio S. Inquisitionis*, pars III, tit. iii, § 10 (ed. 1668, p. 250), where he is discussing how inquisitors ought to deal with equivocal propositions. A citizen of Cremona "being accused of having said, *I believe in God, the Blessed Virgin and the Saints, but not in the Pope*, asserted under examination that he spake not here of our Most Holy Lord the Pope, but of a certain person who in that neighbourhood bore the nickname of *Pope*. Being tortured for this belief [the text has *crudelitate* by an obvious slip for *credulitate*], he abjured without difficulty; for the man was so unlearned, and the interpretation he gave to his proposition was so improbable and incredible."

believed not thus, nor will the Bishop believe it now." Then the Gonfaloniere turned and went his way, saying, "Methinks the man hath a devil."

Nothing remained now but to read his formal condemnation in the judgment-hall and to lead him to the stake (p. 36).

Now, all things whatsoever shall be said hereafter in this treatise, are such as were seen and heard by me who write it, except a few things whereof I shall say in their place that I know them only by hearsay...(p. 43). When his confession had been read, the magistrate went within, not pronouncing sentence according to custom with other folk; for they kept no such order in his case as they are accustomed to keep with others that come before the Court. When the magistrate had gone in, then his minions dragged him boisterously forth from the hall, and he was left all alone among the constables, barefooted and with a gown on his back that was partly fastened with buttons; he walked with somewhat lengthy strides and with his head down, saying his prayers as he went; and he seemed in truth one of the [old] martyrs, among such a crowd of folk as was scarce seen before. And all the people, moved with compassion, cried unto him, "Alas! why wilt thou die?" And he ever made answer, "I will die for Christ." "Nay," said they, "but thou diest not for Christ"; and he, "I die for the truth." Then said one, "Ah, thou believest not in God!" "Yea," said he, "in God and the Blessed Virgin and Holy Church." Then said another, "Wretch! thou hast a devil, who draweth thee with him." "Nay, God forbid!" said he. And thus he answered oftentimes as he went; yet, even so, only to such things as seemed to need an answer, and oftentimes raising his eyes to meet theirs.

When they came to the Canto del Proconsolo, there was a great rumour of people that pressed to see him, and one of the faithful, seeing him, mingled with the rest and said: "Brother Michael, pray God for us!" To whom he made answer, raising his eyes, "Go with God's blessing, Catholic Christians." Again, at the Fondamenti di Sta Liperata one cried to him: "Fool! believe in the Pope!" Then he raised his head and answered, "Ye have made a God of your Pope, even as they still seduce you!" A little farther on, in answer to the same cry, he said with a little smile: "These goslings[1] of yours have fooled you well!" whereat many marvelled, saying, "He goeth merrily to his death!"

When he came to San Giovanni [the Baptistery], one said, "Repent, repent, and choose not to die!" to whom he made answer, "I repent me of my sins." And to others, saying, "Escape with your life," he answered, "Escape ye from your sins."

Just beyond the Bishop's Palace, one said, "Thou dost not ask a soul of us to pray God for thee." Then he cried aloud, "I beseech all faithful Catholic Christians to pray God for my soul!"

Between the Mercato Vecchio and Calimala, one cried, "Escape, escape!" and he answered, "Escape ye from hell, escape from hell, escape from hell."

When he came to the Mercato Nuovo, some said, "Repent, repent!" And he made answer, "Repent ye of your sins, repent of your usuries and your false bargains."

Then, on the Piazza de' Priori, one said, "Repent of this error, choose not death." And he said, "Nay, for it is the Catholic faith; nay, for it is the truth, whereunto all Christians are bound."

And at the Cornmarket there were many ladies at the windows, and tables whereat folk played; who looked up from their play and said unto him, "Repent, repent!" Then said he: "Repent ye of your sins of usury and gambling and fornication." And, a little farther on, some said, "Fool, wherefore wilt thou die?" And he, "I will die for Christ." And one of them went more than a crossbow-shot by his side, contending sore with him and saying, "Thou art a devil's martyr; weenest thou to know more than so many masters of theology? believest thou that if Master Luke[2] knew this to be the truth, he would care to lose his soul? Wilt thou know more than he, who dost scarce know thine alphabet in

---

[1] An untranslatable pun; *papa* = "pope" and *papero* = "gosling."

[2] A celebrated Florentine friar of that day, who was raised to the Cardinalate in 1408.

comparison with him?" Whereunto he answered, "If I remember aright, Master Luke knoweth well that he possesseth certain moneys in contravention of his Rule, and yet he letteth not those moneys go." Then said the other, "O! ye say that we are not baptized, nor true Christians."[1] Then Brother Michael looked him in the face and said, "Nay! I say that ye are baptized Christians; but ye do not as Christians should do." Then said the other, "The people's voice is God's voice." "Nay," said he, "but it was the people's voice that crucified Christ, and slew St Peter." At this there was great contention; one said, "He hath a devil," and others, "He will die in his heresy." "Nay," said he, "heretic I never was nor never shall be." And here one of the faithful called him by name, and bade him think upon Christ's passion. Then he turned with a cheerful countenance and said, "O ye faithful Catholic Christians, pray God to give me strength!"

When he came to San Romeo, seeing one of the faithful in the throng, he said unto him, in the Latin tongue: "Go, hold that fast which thou hast" (Apoc. iii, 11); and then, as he passed on, "I die for the truth."

When he came to Sta Croce [the Franciscan convent] they showed him St Francis's statue hard by the gate of the friary; then he raised his eyes to heaven saying, "Saint Francis, my father, pray to God for me!" Then he turned to the brethren who stood on the church steps, crying with a loud voice, "The Rule of St Francis, whereunto ye are sworn, hath been condemned; and this is how ye deal with all such as will observe it!" These words he repeated as often as he thought the Brethren needed them; of whom some shrugged their shoulders, and others drew their cowls over their faces.

Then, when he turned the corner and went towards the Porta alla Giustizia, many folk vexed him sore, saying, "Recant, recant; wherefore wilt thou die?" To whom he made answer: "Christ died for us." Then said some, "O, thou art not Christ, and hast no need to die for us." "Nay,"

---

[1] This was one of the false and invidious conclusions against which the Fraticelli protested. They held that the Pope and hierarchy, by their adherence to John XXII's heresy, had lost their authority over the souls of the faithful; but they carefully explained that this did not deprive them of *sacramental* power, so that their baptisms, ordinations, etc. were still valid.

said he, "but for Him will I die." To which one made answer, "O, thou art not among heathen folk!" "Nay, but I will die for the truth." "Let us grant, then, that this be the truth; why shouldst thou die on that account?" To which he made answer, "For the truth died St Peter, and St Paul lost his head." Then one of the crowd went by his side vexing him sore, and saying, "Thou diest the death of the desperate."[1] "Nay," said he, "I slay not myself, but it is these who slay me." "But why then dost thou choose death?" "Because I will not speak against the truth." "O," said the man, "St Peter denied the Lord." "True; yet he repented him." "Well, then, thou too mayest repent; for I tell thee, if St Peter were here, he would recant." Then said Brother Michael, "He would not recant; or, if he did, he would do ill." Then said another, "Wherefore dost thou not as thy companion hath done?" "God give him grace," answered he, "that he despair not!" Then said the other, "Brothers F. and G.[2] would not have thee die for this point; and, if they were here, they would recant; wherefore wilt thou do more than they?" To which he replied again, "They would not recant, and, if they did, they would do ill." And when this same man alleged Holy Scripture, saying that Christ fled more than once from death, and other holy men, then Brother Michael turned round and looked upon him and said, "Thou also art responsible, and thou shalt one day render account of these words that thou hast spoken."

Then at the meadow hard by the Porta alla Giustizia, one said, "Why canst thou not do even as thy superior, Brother F. of Camerino,[3] who recanted?" "Nay," said he, "but I will not recant"; and, as the other pressed upon him again, one of the faithful cried, "Recant not, but let this man have his say!" Then he showed him St Francis, painted over the gate, and bade him recommend himself to his holy founder; and he, raising his cowl, besought St Francis's prayers. And, being dry with much speaking, and for the throng that pressed upon

---

[1] *I.e.* This is sheer suicide.

[2] Probably St Francis and Giovanni—*i.e.* John of Parma, the most truly Franciscan of St Francis's successors.

[3] Nothing is known of this friar.

him, he oftentimes lapped the rain-water as it fell. And, seeing that one of the faithful rebuked those who would have had him recant, one of the sergeants and other folk began to take note of this, saying, "These are of his disciples"; wherefore he fell apart from him for a while.[1]

When he was come to the Gate a faithful woman cried aloud, "Stand fast, martyr of Christ, for thou shalt soon receive thy crown!" I know not what he answered; but there arose much talk of this thing.

When they issued from the Gate, the church of Sta Maria del Tempio was shut; this the Pharisees had done, that it might appear that he believed not in Christ. As he drew near to the stake, the outcry became great, for men cried unto him, "Here is the stake; recant here; why wilt thou die?" But he answered them more constantly than ever.

Then, at the stake itself, the sergeants made the folk fall back, and the crier cried that all men should keep their distance. They made a circle of horsemen, whereunto few could enter; and I entered not therein, but climbed upon the wall by the Arno side, whence I could see part that was done, but I could not hear.

When he came to the stake (so far as I could see, and as I heard from others) he went boldly into the hut;[2] and, while he was being bound to the stake, many thrust their heads in to pray him to recant; but he stood firmer and firmer. And, as one told me for certain, he asked him, "What is this for which thou wilt die?" and Brother Michael made answer, "This is a truth which is lodged in my soul; so that I cannot testify to it except in death." Then, to affright him, they made smoke twice or thrice around the hut, and many other frightful things; and the people round besought him all the while to change his mind, save only one of the faithful who comforted him. Moreover, I heard that a youth was brought unto him, with certain of the Prior's servants, sent by the Ten[3] to bring him back safe and sound if he would recant.

---

[1] Was not this the narrator himself, who tells us in the next paragraph that he did not hear Michael's next words?

[2] Apparently the pile was enclosed in a sort of wooden hut, as the narrator always calls it a *capannuccio*.

[3] The Ten Priors were the regular committee of government.

And one of the captains, seeing his constancy, said, "What perversities hath the Devil put into this fellow's head?" and the youth made answer, "Perchance this is of Christ." At last, having besieged him with many arguments, they set fire to the hut from above; and then Brother Michael, having finished his *Credo* (which he began as he entered into the hut) began to sing the *Te Deum*; and, as one told me, he sang perhaps eight verses, and then made a sign as though he sneezed, saying those last words, "Lord, into thy hands I commend my spirit." When the bonds were burned, he fell dead to the earth upon his knees, with his face to heaven and his mouth wide open.

When he was dead, many said, "He seemeth like unto a saint," even among his adversaries. Then some besought of the captain of the horse, as a favour, that they might bury his body. And the captain, having drawn up written evidence of his death, gave them leave and departed with his sergeants. And those young men took away the body, and wrapped it in a linen cloth, and carried it and buried it in a grave at some distance from the stake; and folk returned to their homes; and it was the twelfth hour when he left the palace, and he died a little before the thirteenth hour. And, while folk went homewards, the greater part thought it an ill deed, and they could not say enough evil of the clergy. One said, "He is a martyr," and another, "He is a saint," and another the contrary. And thus there was greater noise of this deed in Florence than there ever had been.

And on Friday night the faithful went, the one not knowing what the other did, and found themselves together at his grave and carried him away secretly. Wherefore on Saturday morning many who went to see him found him not; and, when this was noised abroad in Florence, certain preachers found matter to say thereof in the pulpit, saying that they would fain have set guards, lest folk should canonize the dead man and hold him for a saint.

A SAINT'S CONVERSION

The Blessed Giovanni Colombini, a Sienese merchant of good family, was married to a lady who claimed collateral descent from the family of Pope Alexander III. He passed through many offices in his republic and became at last either Gonfaloniere or one of the Priors. Hitherto he had shown himself only a particularly hard-headed man of business; but his sudden conversion threw him into an equal extreme of self-denial and asceticism. He founded the Order of *Jesuats*, or *Clerks Apostolic of St Jerome*, which received Papal confirmation in 1367. So vast was the number of those who abandoned the world at his persuasion that (according to his biographer) the Sienese authorities banished him in 1357 lest the city should be depopulated. For two centuries the Jesuats remained simple lay-brethren; but Paul V granted them leave to receive holy orders. The Order was suppressed by Clement IX in 1668. The following extract is translated from the ancient *Vita di San Giovanni Columbini* quoted by Professor Del Lungo in his preface to the *Leggende del Secolo XIV* (Florence, 1863), p. xxi.

106. A SAINT'S CONVERSION

In the year of our Lord 1355, Giovanni returned home one day with the desire of eating forthwith; and, not finding the table laid or the food ready as usual, he began to quarrel with his wife and his servant, chiding them for their slowness and saying that he had pressing affairs which compelled him to be solicitous about returning to his merchandise. Whereunto his wife answered benignly, saying, "Thou hast much wealth and few expenses; wherefore dost thou trouble thyself so sore?" Moreover she prayed him to have a little patience, for he would very soon be able to eat; and she added, "while I am setting the meats in order, do thou take this book and read awhile"; and therewith she laid before him a volume containing certain Saints' lives. But Giovanni was wroth and took the book and cast it into the midst of the hall, saying, "Thy thoughts are only upon legends; but I must soon return to my counting-house." This he said, and other words beside; and then his conscience began to smite him, so that he took the book from the ground and sat himself down. Having opened the book, he fell (as God would have it) upon the pleasant story of St Mary the Egyptian, that great sinner who was converted by God's marvellous pity. While Giovanni read this, his wife prepared his dinner, and cried to him that it might please him now to set himself to the table. Then he made answer, "Tarry thou awhile, until I shall have read all this legend!" and, notwithstanding that the story was long, yet being full of heavenly melody it began to sweeten his heart, nor would he cease from his reading until he was come to the end. Meanwhile his wife, considering him in silence, was much rejoiced to see how earnestly he read, hoping that this would profit to the edification of his mind, for it was not his wont to read such books. And so indeed it came to pass, by the operation of divine grace; for this story so impressed itself upon his soul that he meditated thereon day and night without ceasing; and, in this fixed thought, the God of all grace so touched his heart that he began to despise the things of this world, and no longer to cumber himself so much with them; nay, to do the very contrary of that which had been his wont.

The Cistercian General Chapter Acts give us here a good deal of information. There are frequent complaints of non-attendance; in 1303 nineteen abbots—or probably more, for the copyist ends the list of names with an *etc.*—were bidden to send their due complement of students at once, under pain of excommunication. In 1405 come a fresh series of complaints (F. Martène, *Thesaurus*, vol. IV, col. 1544). Benedict XII had commanded that two monks should be sent to Paris by every house of forty and upwards, one by every house of thirty to forty, and one to Paris or some nearer university by every house of eighteen to thirty. The General Chapter of 1387 had extended this, making even houses of twelve liable to send one student to some university. This had been reinforced by threats of excommunication. But, as the General Chapter now complains (A.D. 1405):

107. UNIVERSITY STUDENTS

ALAS! many abbots and officials of our Order—a thing horrible to hear, and suggesting some suspicion of infidelity—shrink not from contemning these statutes by their disobedience, to the offence of God's majesty, and to the contempt of the Power of the Keys granted to the Church, and of our whole Order and its censures, and thus to the enormous peril, the great prejudice and the abominable harm not only of their own souls, but also of those of their subjects who participate with them. We, therefore, abhorring these men's temerity, and wishing to frustrate it as far as possible and to provide some wholesome remedy...lest these statutes and decrees be swallowed by oblivion in the lapse of time, do approve, ratify and renew them, decreeing and defining that they be inviolably kept in this our Order and by our monks, according to the form and order therein contained, for all time.

Abbots who disobey are hereby suspended and excommunicate; priors and subpriors are to report these offenders "in virtue of holy obedience, and under pain of damnation to their own souls," to the General Chapter, and to proclaim this in their own chapters; and the monks are not only absolved from their obedience but forbidden to associate with their peccant abbots: from this sentence the abbots can be absolved by none but the Abbot of Abbots at Cîteaux, except on their actual death-beds. Then, after dealing with other matters of university discipline, the Chapter Statutes proceed (§ 4):

Item, seeing that in times past it hath oftentimes come to pass, in very many monasteries or houses of our Order, that, when scholars are sent from the said monasteries or houses to study at Paris or elsewhere, the choice was made by irregular favour, "flesh and blood revealing it," so that ignorant and ignoble brethren were held to be men of repute, to such an extent that these who, being rude and inept, wasting their time in ease and turning aside from study, were brought to Paris like fourfooted beasts—these same, we say, came home ruder than the very brutes; therefore this General Chapter, willing to abolish this so abusive custom, doth decree, ordain and define that, whensoever a scholar be sent to Paris or elsewhere from any monastery of the Order, there shall be chosen by those same who are competent to elect the abbot, or at least by the sounder part of the whole community, some monk green in years but grey in sense, of good parts and mature manners, of bright intellect, born in legitimate wedlock, and able to study; otherwise let him not be admitted to the said university.

St Lydwine of Schiedam (1380–1433) became ulcerated in her fifteenth year; the sores ate deeper and deeper into her flesh; she was soon bed-ridden, and her biographies are full of painful medical details told with characteristic medieval exaggeration. They may be found, in almost all their nakedness, in J. K. Huysman's monograph, *Ste Lydwine de Schiedam*. She found three distinguished contemporary biographers (see Appendix, s.v. *Brugman*); but, to most readers, the descriptions of her miracles and ecstasies will seem less instructive than the side-lights which these throw on contemporary life in a Dutch town. In explanation of this and other anecdotes, it must be remembered that the church of Schiedam was appropriated to the neighbouring Praemonstratensian monastery of Marienward, so that the parish parson was ordinarily one of the brethren of that house. Apart from Praemonstratensians, the monks of the later Middle Ages were generally forbidden to serve as parish priests, though in Germany even Benedictines did so. *AA.SS.* Ap. II (ed. 1866, p. 275 *a*), *Vita Prior*, c. III.

108. MONASTIC PARISH PRIESTS

SHE had also in her body three deep sores, of about a palm's breadth, from one of which, in the neighbourhood of her stomach, there sometimes flowed forth an abundance of the aforesaid worms, [grey in colour, and full of grey water, of about the bigness of the end of a woman's distaff, and the length of a finger-joint]. Upon this deep ulcer they used to lay a plaster of honey and fresh wheatmeal, whereof the aforesaid worms might suck; for otherwise they would have gnawed her to death; and, if the plaster were made of old wheatmeal, it was found by experience that the worms would not suck it. Moreover, in the making of this plaster, the cream of milk was mixed with the aforesaid ingredients, or the fat of fresh eels or of meat; to which were also added the ashes of ancient ox-flesh, dried in the oven or furnace and ground to powder. By reason of this plaster, there befell an event which I think worthy of mention for ensample's sake, against avaricious and gluttonous men. Dan Andrew, of the Praemonstratensian Order, was parson of the church of Schiedam; of him I shall tell again in Chapters xxxiii and xxxiv.[1] This man, about Lententide, had killed five or more capons, wherewith to

---

[1] All the stories of this man emphasize his unsympathetic attitude towards Lydwine; of the three Praemonstratensians who held Schiedam during her life-time, only the third was satisfactory.

regale the rulers of the city, whom he had bidden to dine with him. When therefore he had come to her house to hear her confession, the maiden began to beseech him that he would give her the fat of one capon for her plaster. When he refused (pleading that the aforesaid capons were very thin, and that their whole fat would not be enough for the basting while they were roasted) yet the maiden besought him the more instantly for the fat of a single capon, in exchange whereof she was ready to give him a whole measure of butter. When he still refused, then the maiden made answer: "God grant that they may all be eaten of rats!" This curse was immediately fulfilled, whereof tidings were joyfully brought to the maiden, not long afterwards, by Sir Ian Pot, priest, who also was at times the said maiden's confessor.

The virgin had also a certain ulcer, which she was wont to alleviate by the application of apples in slices, of that kind which are called *Metzers*; which apples that same parson had in plenty. When therefore he visited her upon a day, and she prayed him for a few of these apples to relieve her necessity, he answered as though in doubt whether he had any, for he was loth to let them go. Yet when he was come home again, and found a plentiful store, and the virgin's messenger came to ask for them, he remembered her former malediction which had fallen upon him in the matter of the capon-fat, and said, "I will give the girl a few, lest they be eaten of dormice." After which digression, let us return to our main story.

About the year 1412, this same parson, doubting the truth of the assertion that St Lydwine was living upon no food but the sacred Host, determined to tempt her by substituting an unconsecrated for the consecrated wafer in communicating her. She spat it out; an angel brought her a true Host in exchange for it; the parson, fearful of the consequences, maintained that he had given her a true Host and that she was possessed with a devil. This caused almost a riot in the town; and Dan Andrew was obliged to crave Lydwine's intercession with his infuriated parishioners (pp. 294 b–296). The biographer then continues (p. 297 a):

After this...the virgin was smitten with an epidemic pestilence, whereof many died at that time in the city. Wherefore, being kindled with the desire of holy communion, she sent her brother William to the church, beseeching him to bring the parson with the sacrament to communicate her. He, though he knew her to be smitten with the plague (for she had two or three black boils in her arm) came nevertheless with the sacrament; and, entering into her cell, he sat by her bedside to hear her confession; after which he gave her the Lord's Body. Then the virgin, turning round, saw how the parson had stopped up his mouth and nostrils, as fearing to be infected by her. Whereupon she said: "Sir, neither you nor any other man shall take your death from me." The parson made answer: "Dearest daughter, would that I might live to see the end of thy life." "Nay, sir," quoth she, "for ye shall not see my death, but I, within a brief space, shall see yours: wherefore I beseech you so to dispose yourself as you would fain be found before the Lord's judgment-seat." The parson was then hale and sound, nor did he feel any infirmity; wherefore he made light of the virgin's words. Yet, within a brief while, he fell into a sickness and remembered her words; wherefore he sent one of his friends to pray forgiveness for his trespasses against her (for he knew that he had not done his duty by her), and that she would pray the Lord to grant him all that he needed for health. Then this virgin, who had ever heartfelt compassion for all men, and especially for the sick, sent word to him that he should prepare himself by true confession, and that he should restore to their rightful owners those ill-gotten goods that he had in his house. He sent back word excusing himself, as though he had had none such in his house; but she, by a second messenger, showed him where he had hoarded them, and the names of their rightful possessors; "unto whom" (said she) "ye must needs restore these ill-gotten goods, if ye would have part in the kingdom of heaven." For this parson, as we have already said, was so infected with avarice that he made light of the virgin's words and would not restore his unjust possessions; and thus he died, with this and other sins upon his soul. After this the virgin, as was her wont, was rapt to the place wherein souls suffered the torments due unto their trespasses; and the holy angel guiding her, showed the manner and quality of the pains wherein this parson was set;

to wit, how devils were casting his soul from torment to torment, as it is written in the book of Job [xxiv, 19, *Vulg.*]: "They shall pass from the snow waters to excessive heat." After this Dan Andrew, came Dan John Angels of Dordrecht, of the same Order and monastery.

Concerning whom the biographer has already written by anticipation (p. 292 *a*). This parish priest, coming into Lydwine's room, was enraptured by the odour of roses which proceeded from the saint's sores: he then confessed her, and was equally amazed at her confessions, which he heard now with other ears.

But she said, "Of a truth, sir, I have oftentimes told you my secrets before." "Alas!" said he, "for all that thou hast told me hath been hitherto as roses cast before fourfooted swine." Wherein he spake of himself; for this parson was so lecherous that, not fearing God's judgments, nor reverencing his order, whether of priesthood or of monasticism, he was accustomed to fornicate with a married woman, a foul creature even according to the flesh. The virgin oftentimes heard him accused of this fault, yet believed not his accusers, seeing that he visited her so frequently and celebrated mass in her presence. Once, however, when he came to her room she told him what she had heard, and accused him of this sin with a married woman. But he began to curse and to swear, denying the crime; wherefore the virgin, as one satisfied by his excuses, dismissed him in peace. Again he was accused to her as one who had relapsed into this sin; again she reprehended him; but again he feared to confess the truth, excusing himself as before with oaths and curses. After this the virgin, rapt to her accustomed heights of contemplation, saw this man sinning in a certain courtyard with this woman aforesaid. Wherefore, when he came to see her, she rebuked him at first as though from the mouths of others; and, when he persisted in his former denial, "Sir," said she, "why do ye so pertinaciously deny it? for I myself, being in an ecstasy, saw you and her in sin on such a day, and at such an hour, and in such a place." Then in utter confusion (for he saw that he was caught), he said: "He who hath revealed this concerning me might have disclosed much more also"; and, going out by a side door into the garden, he wept bitterly. When he had got the better of his tears, he came back and confessed the truth of all her words, promising that he would never do these things again. Then she, seeing how he was illumined by the rays of God's truth, said unto him: "Thou hast committed not that sin only," and rehearsed three or four other faults, exhorting him to amendment. Moreover, she predicted his imminent death, and wounded his mind with so wholesome a spear of compunction that he, after confessing those sins to her in so far as seemed proper, had recourse also to lawful confessors, whom he besought to loose him from the bands of his sins by their ecclesiastical authority. After which, while he was doing penance for his sins, after the space of about eight weeks he was stricken with pestilence...and, in the year 1426, was taken to the place which God's justice had mercifully prepared for him. [Lydwine, in a vision, saw him in a pit so horrible that she thought it must be hell, until her angel told her that it was only a sort of ante-hell into which souls were cast whose damnation was still in doubt. After much suffering for his sake], the virgin brought that soul, by her merits and her prayers, from that special pit into the common purgatory and place of penitent souls.

109. A HARD CASE

From Cistercian General Chapter decree of 1441 (Martène, *Thesaurus*, vol. IV, col. 1602).

THE General Chapter, being legally informed of the honesty of manners and prudence and other virtues of Pierre Porcelle, monk of Poblet, doth by these present letters grant to the said Brother Pierre the following dispensation: Notwithstanding that he is not in Holy Orders, nor can he be promoted to Holy Orders by reason of one of his hands which is as it were withered, yet we grant to the said Pierre that he may and shall, in choir and in all other places, keep the degree and place wherein he entered our Order, so long as this may accord with the will and good pleasure of the Abbot of Poblet.

110. NUNS' DOWRIES

From *Bishop Spofford's Register* (Cant. and York Soc. 1917, pp. 223 ff.). The Bishop has visited at Aconbury, dioc. Hereford, and issues certain injunctions, A.D. 1437/8.

Thomas, by the grace of God, etc., to our ghostly doghters, the prioresse and convent of Acornebury, greeting and Godd's blessynge and oures. Forasmuch as now laat we visitynge you thurgh our authoritee ordinary and the form of the commyn law, and by lawfulle inquisicion fonde certain comperts and defauteis ayens the holy decretis of our holy fadirs and the churches and ayens the hele of your soules and in especial one perlyouse abusyon long tyme afore usid in your place, that no sustyr was receyved into your holy religion bot by trety had first with her frendes and express pact and condicion to yife with hyr certen soome of gude the whilke all the lawes of the chirch dampneth and forbedith as for cursyd symony. And who so thus by symony enters into ony religioun or benefice the law wille and ordaneth that all such persons shuld by the ordinary be prived and expellyd out that monastery perpetually, and to do continual penaunce and be translat in to ane othyr monastery of the same religion. Thereon our holy fader pope Martyn that last was and the Pope Eugeny that now es, considerynge this sinne of simony gretly encresynge, hath ordeigned grevese paynes ayens alle such persons that othir privatly or apertly maketh any such pakteis or condicions, and noght al only the yifers and the takers, but also all tho that bene counsellers or mediatours or assentours to any such unlawfulle werkes, reseyvynge the absolucyon of all such symoners, but only in the article of deth, to the pope's awne person. Wherefore considerynge dewly alle the peryllys of the said unlawfulle receyvynge be pakt or condicion for ony maner of gode herethly gold or sylver or ony othir thyng, litel or much, by our auctoritee ordinary, wee repreve and dampneth by this our opyn decree, perpetually forbedynge of the paynes of the grete curse and of the privacyon of the prioress that now es or after shalbe for the tyme durynge your said monastery of hir estate and office of the prioress and expulsyon and puttynge oute of alle thoese that ever after this tyme ben resaved by ony such pakt or condicion and to be translate and sett in ane othir monastery to do penaunce for the same, that never from hensforward any sustir be receyved by any maner of promess, pact or condicion to yife or to be yifen for hir entre or receyvynge lytel or much; and at by no necligence or ignoraunce this our decree ordinary be brokyn and noght observed, we charge and commaunde by the vertew of obedience that yee pryoress that now es and alle at shallbe in tyme commynge and the covent of the same place that this decree and statut be writen opynly in your martiloge boke and four tymes in the yeer opynly afore alle the convent ane iche sustre of the same be redd, except yoo that err bodyly seeke, called thertoo and pressent, be redd, that is to say, iche quarter of the year ones. Neverthe lesse, if any fader, moder or ony othir kyn or frende of free uylle uithouten such pakt or covenand, uolle yife any thynge of thair devocyon to the monastery profett, wee forbid it noght.

III. A DOMINICAN FRIARY

From *Pierce the Ploughman's Crede*, a Lollard poem of about 1420 (ed. Skeat, E.E.T.S. 1867, p. 7).

THANNE thou3t y to frayne the first of this foure ordirs,
And presede to the prechoures to proven here wille.
[Ich] hi3ede to her house to herken of more;
And whan y cam to that court y gaped aboute.
Swich a bild bold, y-buld opon erthe hei3te
Say i nou3t in certeine si♭♭e a longe tyme.
Y 3emede vpon that house and 3erne theron loked,
Whou3 the pileres weren y-peynt and pulched ful clene,
And queynteli i-coruen with curiouse knottes,
With wyndowes well y-wrou3t wide vp o-lofte.
And thanne y entrid in and even-forth went,
And all was walled that wone thou3 it wid were,
With posternes in pryuytie to pasen when hem liste;
Orche3ardes and erberes euesed well clene,
And a curious cros craftly entayled,
With tabernacles y-ti3t to toten all abouten.

A DOMINICAN FRIARY

The pris of a plouȝ-lond of penyes so rounde
To aparaile that pyler were pure lytel.
Thanne y munte me forth the mynstre to knowen,
And a-waytede a woon wonderlie well y-beld,
With arches on eueriche half and belliche y-corven,
With crochetes on corners with knottes of golde,
Wyde wyndowes y-wrouȝt y-written full thikke,
Schynen with schapen scheldes to schewen aboute,
With merkes of marchauntes y-medled bytwene,
Mo than twenty and two twyes y-noumbred.
Ther is none heraud that hath half swich a rolle,
Riȝt as a rageman hath rekned hem newe.
Tombes opon tabernacles tyld opon lofte,
Housed in hirnes harde set abouten,
Of armede alabaustre clad for the nones,
[Made vpon marbel in many maner wyse,
Knyghtes in her conisantes clad for the nones,]
All it semed seyntes y-sacred opon erthe;
And louely ladies y-wrouȝt leyen by her sydes
In many gay garmentes that were gold-beten.
Thouȝ the tax of ten ȝer were trewly y-gadered,
Nolde it nouȝt maken that hous half, as y trowe.
Thanne kam I to that cloister and gaped abouten
Whouȝ it was pilered and peynt and portred well clene,
All y-hyled with leed lowe to the stones,
And y-paued with peynt til iche poynte after other;
With kundites of clene tyn closed all aboute,
With lauores of latun louelyche y-greithed.
I trowe the gaynage of the ground in a gret schire
Nolde aparaile that place oo poynt til other ende.
Thanne was the chaptire-hous wrouȝt as a greet chirche,
Coruen and couered and queyntliche entayled;
With semlich selure y-set on lofte;
As a Parlement-hous y-peynted aboute.
Thanne ferd y into fraytour and fond there an other,
An halle for an heyȝ kinge an housholde to holden,
With brode bordes aboute y-benched wel clene,
With windowes of glas wrouȝt as a Chirche.
Thanne walkede y ferrer and went all abouten,

And sei3 halles full hy3e and houses full noble,
Chambers with chymneyes and Chapells gaie;
And kychens for an hy3e kinge in castells to holden,
And dortour y-di3te with dores ful stronge;
Fermery and fraitur with fele mo houses,
And all strong ston wall sterne opon heihe,
With gaie garites and grete and iche hole y-glased;
[And othere] houses y-nowe to herberwe the queene.
And 3et thise bilderes wilne beggen a bagg-ful of wheate
Of a pure pore man that maie onethe paie
Half his rente in a 3er and half ben behynde!

The Brigittine monastery of Syon was founded and richly endowed by
Henry V at Twickenham in 1414; it removed to Isleworth in 1432. It
was the only English house of that reformed Augustinian Order which
owed its inception to Queen Bridget of Sweden (d. 1373). These Brigittine
monasteries were always double; the abbess was the head, but about a
quarter of the community were priests or other clerics, to perform the
religious services and to do a good deal of the financial management. This
"Pardon of Shene" attracted many pilgrims and offerings; it is alluded
to as a matter of course in the *Paston Letters*. The following document
was printed by T. Hearne in his Appendix to Fordun's *Scotichronicon*,
1722, p. 1399. A few obvious copyist's blunders have been corrected, and
the spelling has been modernized.

112. RICH INDULGENCES

HERE beginneth the pardon of the monastery of Shene,
which is Syon. First every day in the year whosoever cometh
to the said monastery devoutly giving somewhat to the repara-
tions of the said monastery and sayeth five Pater-nosters, and
five Aves, and a Creed shall have five hundred days of pardon.

And also whosoever saith devoutly our Lady's psalter in
the said monastery shall have five hundred days of pardon.

And, in the feast of St John the Baptist, whoso will come
to the said monastery devoutly, and saith a Pater-noster and
an Ave before the Image of St Bridget and St John, there in
the same place, shall have two hundred days of pardon.

Also whosoever [shall] visit, the said manner or wise, the
said convent or monastery, in the feast of St Matthew the

Apostle, with any deed of charity, shall have one hundred days of pardon.

Also, in the first Sunday of clean Lent, whosoever will visit the said monastery, from Saturday noon till Sunday Evensong shall have three hundred Lents, and the third part of penance released for his sin, if he be in state to receive pardon.

Item In the Feast of the Annunciation of our Lady, what man that cometh to the said monastery shall have one hundred days of pardon and forty.

Item In the Feast of St Gregory, whoso that cometh to the said monastery giving any good to the edifying of the said monastery, shall have seventy days of pardon.

Item On Mid-Lent Sunday, from Saturday noon till Monday Evensong, be done clean remission of all sin, except in the points which are reserved to the Pope, with the third part of the penance enjoined.

Item On Shere Thursday[1] and Good Friday, whosoever cometh to the said monastery, for as many Pater-nosters, and as many Aves as he saith in the said monastery shall have one hundred days of pardon *tociens quociens.*[2]

Item On Easter Day, in the same monastery, is granted to all that cometh thither and saith five Pater-nosters and five Aves in the worship of Christ's resurrection five hundred days of pardon.

Item In the Feast of St George, whosoever cometh to the said monastery shall have one hundred days of pardon for every Pater-noster.

Item In the Feast of the Invention of the Cross likewise whoso saith a Pater-noster or giveth any goods or chattels to the reparation or edifying of the same monastery, shall have one hundred days of pardon.

Item In the Feast of Fabian and Sebastian, he that devoutly visiteth the said monastery shall have the same pardon and indulgence as is granted by divers Popes unto the place of

[1] The Thursday before Easter.
[2] A technical phrase for certain indulgences which might be repeated as often as the pardon-seeker repeated his conditions. In this case, therefore, the only limit to the number of days gained would be that imposed by the impossibility of saying more than a finite number of Paters and Aves during the service at the monastery.

Fabian and Sebastian in Rome, that is to say, three hundred Lents, and two parts of the penance enjoined and four hundred days of pardon.

Item In the Feast of St John the Baptist whosoever will come to the said monastery and devoutly say a Pater-noster shall have ninety days of pardon.

Item Whosoever will come to the said monastery in the Feast of St Peter, for every Pater-noster that he saith, and for every penny or penny's worth that he giveth to the reparation and edifying of the same monastery shall have one hundred and forty days of pardon.

Item Whoso will come to the said monastery in the Feast of St Thomas the Martyr, for every Pater-noster and every Ave Maria that he shall say in the said monastery, he shall have sixty days of pardon for as many as he saith.

Item Whosoever will come to the said monastery in the Feast of St Paul the Apostle, say one Pater-noster and one Ave Maria, shall have one hundred days of pardon.

Item In the Feast of St Bridget whosoever will come to the said monastery, devoutly there visiting the Holy Virgin St Bridget, and giving some alms to the sustentation of the same monastery, shall have pardon and clean remission in all cases, reserved and unreserved, and this pardon endureth from the beginning of the first evensong till the last evensong be done.

Item At the Feast of the Assumption of our Lady, Conception, Annunciation, Salutation and Purification shall have one hundred and sixty days pardon.

Item In the Feast of Pentecost, and every day within the Octave thereof, whosoever visiteth the said monastery with Pater-noster or any other prayer shall have three hundred days of pardon, beside the daily pardon which is one hundred days.

Item Whosoever will come to the said monastery in the Feast of St Luke the Evangelist, and in every feast of the Evangelists shall have an hundred days of pardon with remission of the fourth part of penance.

Item In the Feast of Mary Magdalene whosoever cometh to the said monastery shall have one hundred days of pardon granted by Bishop Stafford Archbishop of Canterbury.

RICH INDULGENCES

Item In the Feasts of St Anne, St Margaret and St James the Apostle, they shall have the same indulgence.

Item In the Feast of St Thomas the Apostle and in the Feast of St Michael the Archangel they shall have three years and forty days of pardon.

Item In the Feast of St Peter which is called *Lammas* or *Ad Vincula* they shall have, from the first evensong till eight days be complete and ended, that is to say, during the Octave, that is to say from the evening of the said *Ad Vincula* unto the end of the said Octave, fully eight days completed and ended, they shall have plenary remission in all cases reserved and unreserved (three out-taken, that is, the vow of chastity, behest to St James, and violently smiting and killing a priest). These except, they shall have plenary remission, and the third part of penance enjoined [shall be] released, with a thousand years of pardon seven hundred days and fifty.

Item In the Feast of St Michael the Archangel, whosoever cometh with devotion unto the said monastery, shall have three years of pardon. *Item* In the Feast of All-Hallows whoso will visit devoutly the said monastery, shall have two years of pardon and forty days for every Pater-noster and every Ave Maria, doing some deed of charity or alms to the sustentation and edifying of the said monastery.

Item In the Feast of St Andrew the Apostle they shall have one hundred days of pardon for every Pater-noster, Ave Maria, and Creed. *Item* In the Feast of St Nicholas the Confessor, they shall have the same pardon.

Item In the Feast of St Catherine the Virgin they shall have one hundred days of pardon. Whosoever will visit the said monastery, doing some deed of alms and charity for the sustentation and helping of the said monastery, shall have the same pardon and forty days granted by a Bishop of Norwich called Lyhart.

Item Whosoever will come to the said monastery in the Feast of Christmas, Easter, Whitsunday, Ascension, shall have every day, and every day within the Octave of them shall have, for every Pater-noster, Ave Maria, and Creed, or giveth any alms or goods with the which the said monastery shall be edified, and God's service therein maintained, shall have seven hundred days of pardon and forty.

The sum of the indulgence and pardon cometh to this, granted by Divers Holy Fathers Popes of Rome, Archbishops and Bishops, Cardinals and Legates (beside the quotidial pardon which is showed in the beginning, and the plenary remission), four thousand years of pardon, ten Lents, and thirteen hundred days.

Abridged from the document printed by G. J. Aungier in the appendix to his *Syon Monastery* (1840), p. 249. Syon, like other great monasteries or congregations, had its own customs or bye-laws side by side with the general Rule of the Order. The section here printed is perhaps the most detailed surviving description of chapter-house discipline for which the community met daily after the conventual Mass. The Brigittine brethren, *mutatis mutandis*, were under exactly the same discipline: certain portions of the women's custumal which are obliterated in the MS. have been supplied by Aungier from the corresponding parts of the men's.

113. NUNNERY DISCIPLINE

Of the holding of the chapter, and how defaults shall be proclaimed and amended, and of the manner of taking of veynes [*i.e.* veniae, *or penances*]

FORASMUCH as we offend in many things, it is needful that in many ways we be corrected thereof. Wherefore when the ordinary chapter is held the president shall come so early thereto that he may correct the lay-brethren ere the clerks come, they being theretofore before and abiding him. And the chapter shall be held with the same observances that the clerk's chapter[1] is held except the reading. And if any of the more grievous defaults be proclaimed in their chapter, it shall be judged and corrected when the clerks are come. When therefore they come before their seats in the chapter-house they shall incline religiously towards the majesty[2] and after

[1] *I.e.* the chapter of the male clergy, who had their separate household in the monastery.

[2] The painting or carving of God the Father, Son, and Spirit, which was doubtless over the president's head.

that they shall incline a little to them betwixt whom they shall sit.

If the confessor keep the chapter all shall rise when he cometh, and as he goeth before them they shall arise but not incline. After this when the president sayeth *"Benedicite"* they, bowing somewhat down their heads, shall answer *"Dominus"* and when the president hath said *"Loquamur de ordine nostro"* all those that feel themselves guilty in any open default, little or much, shall fall down prostrate before the president. To whom the president shall say, *"Quid dicitis?* What say ye?" And then all they so prostrate shall answer as it were but the voice of one, *"Mea culpa."* To whom the president shall say again, *"Surgite,* Rise up." And then forthwith they shall rise up and stand before the president in their order; the eldest in the midst, which, inclining shall acknowledge his defaults, and after him shall each of them do likewise in his order; saying their defaults compendiously, plainly and so audibly that they may clearly be heard of all that are there and also promise amendment. If any searcher[1] have whereof to proclaim any of them so standing before the president he shall...before that the president enjoin any penance to him whom he should proclaim that he be not... [*gaps in text*].

When the president hath given his judgment and commanded them to go to their place, they shall first incline and then go to their place. He that shall proclaim other another, shall not in his proclamation speak darkly or covertly, but he shall say openly and plainly the default and the name of him that did it, having his face and his words direct to the president. None shall proclaim another of pure suspicion nor of hearing only, but if he express the person of whom he had it and also the same person be there present. None shall proclaim another of any crime that he may not prove by three or by two witnesses at the least upon him that he proclaimeth in case that he would deny it; as he will eschew the same pain due to him accused, if he were found guilty by his own confession or by sufficient proof afore expressed. Nevertheless, lest thorough

---

[1] *Circator*, the conventual officer whose business it was to wander about and note lapses of discipline.

hiding of such vices add boldness to sin and the sin not punished for lack of such proof; whereby the vengeance of God may greatly grow, he that seeth or heareth such defaults ought to notify them to the general confessor which may, by other lawful and honest means, wisely and warily cure such sores....And who that is proclaimed he shall not speak in his place but he shall rise anon forthwith and take his *veyne* before the president. To whom the president shall say "*Quid dicitis*, What say ye?" And then he that lieth prostrate if he be guilty, shall answer thus "*Mea culpa.*" And when he is risen he shall meekly say his default and meekly take his correction and go to his place where he is commanded. Moreover if any be proclaimed and is found guilty while he standeth before the president he shall not take his *veyne* again for any default but ever say thus, "It is sooth, *Mea culpa*, I will amend me." Nevertheless if it pass light defaults, or else he will excuse himself of the default proclaimed as to his knowledge therein not guilty, or else whilst he standeth there he trespasseth in his deportment or in his words, in such cases he must take his *veyne* again and not else. In those things that he cannot feel himself guilty, he shall answer thus, "*Domine cum licencia vestra non recordor*, Sir, with your licence I have not in mind that I said or did so." It shall not be lawful to any to excuse him otherwise. But he ought to think in himself that he is guilty before God in full many other sins and perhaps more grievous, which in this life or after must be purged. And therefore he should accept meekly what the president enjoineth him, but if the default put upon him be so grievous that he should thereby be greatly defamed or another greatly hurt in him; for in such cases it shall be lawful to every person so accused and not guilty, meekly to excuse himself in few words and soft. In the chapter none shall defend his own cause, nor the cause of another, nor none shall speak there but the president, the chanter, the searchers and they that confess their own defaults. And also they that are charged to speak or else have licence to speak. And their answer shall be but only in that that is asked of them. There shall no brother speak in a high voice nor inordinately nor dishonestly nor wrathfully nor none shall speak between themselves one to another, even if it be in a low voice, or make any token or beckon from one side to another, or smilingly or wrathfully behold another; who that otherwise doeth, and is perceived, he shall be proclaimed, corrected and punished like as for another default. So that every word in the chapter shall nought else savour but correction of living, health of souls, keeping of the order, and the common profit. None shall be so bold as to absent himself from the chapter or collation without special licence, except the sick lying in the infirmary. Who shall take the long *veyne* he must kneel first upon his left knee and after upon his right knee. And then forthwith lay himself easily down along straight somewhat more resting to the right side than to the left, but not notably much, hanging the outer part of the left foot upon the sole of the right foot and the back of the left hand upon the palm of the right hand, having his hands in this wise between his face and the earth. But he that shall take the short *veyne* must first kneel down upon both his knees, falling down easily upon his elbows, having his face resting upon his hands, between his face and the earth.

Of light defaults

It is a light default...(18) if any take anything out of another's office without leave, or go into any sister's cell except her own without a reasonable cause, or else into any place that it is forbidden to enter.

(21) If any lightly affirm anything with any other, or in likewise deny it though it be true that she denieth or affirmeth. (22) If any mis-keep their things, clothes or other, or else rend them, or break them, or burn them. (23) If any dissolutely laugh, or stir any other by word or by deed to do the same. (24) If any go unconfessed seven days together without a reasonable impediment known and allowed by her ghostly father. (26) If any sister speak irreverently to another, or yet call or name another by their proper name without this word put before, Sister [Sir or Brother], or any such other word according to their state or degree. (28) If any sister look or busily cast her eyes unto the brothers' choir gazing upon them except the time of Communion and elevations of the

Sacrament of the Altar, and other times permitted by the Rule. (29) If any sister, not being in office, offer herself wilfully and without licence to the speech or sight of seculars, when any of those be within the cloister.

Penance

For these, and such other light defaults, to them that wilfully take their *veyne* and proclaim themselves, is to be enjoined the *seven psalms*, or the *common litany*, or the *psalms of the passion*, or a part of the *Lady's Psalter*, or some other thing according thereto, after the discretion of the president.

Another Penance

But to them that proclaim not themselves wilfully, but be proclaimed of another, the penance shall be the greater, and forsooth, if such defaults be had in custom, bodily discipline is to be given; for then they be not to be called light defaults, but in a manner grievous.

Of bodily discipline

Therefore when the default of any sister is such that by regular sentence she deserveth a discipline, the sister, commanded to make her ready thereto, shall stand up in the same place where as she knelt before the abbess doing off her mantle, and let it fall down behind her. And then she, under her cowl, shall take the hinder extremities thereof and lay all honestly in her neck, drawing her arms out of her sleeves to the elbows, at furthest, and baring the shoulders of her back as far as the bare skin, and so kneeling again in the said place, and also inclining, with all meekness shall take her discipline; which she or they shall give whom the abbess biddeth: which yet shall be none of them that proclaimed her but another sister or sisters. And whilst any discipline is in giving for correction all the sisters except the abbess or president and the giver or givers thereof, shall not behold her or them that be disciplined, but cast down their heads and sight towards the earth, as if they should behold it at their feet, having compassion of their sister or sisters. And whilst any is disciplined, she shall nothing say but "*Mea culpa*, I will amend," which she shall rehearse thick and many times and none other shall speak at that time. When the abbess sayeth, "It sufficeth," she or they, that give the discipline, shall cease forthwith at the said word. There shall not be given for the discipline but five lashes, but if the default be of the more grievous defaults, or else that she or they show any token of rebellion, for then the discipliners shall not cease till the abbess chargeth them to cease. And the lashes in disciplines ought not to be too soft or too easy, but moderately sharp, after the commandment of the abbess. And when the discipline is done, she shall clothe herself again, with the help of her, or of one of them that gave her the discipline. But she shall not remove from the same place till she have her full judgment, and till the abbess has said to her, "Go to your place."...

When any therefore is commanded to make him ready to discipline, he shall go to the nether part of the chapter-house, and there, under his cowl, he shall privily draw his arms out of his sleeves and under his cowl make his body bare from his neck unto his middle, and then gird himself strait, that his clothes fall down no lower.[1] This done, he shall turn again to the place where he was before; and there, before the president, casting the outer part of his cowl over his head, he shall fall down upon his knees and elbows for to receive meekly his penance of discipline; and whilst he is disciplined he shall say nothing but "*Mea culpa*, I will amend me," and this he shall rehearse often and thick. And when this discipline is done, he shall clothe himself again in the same place and not go thence till the president hath given his full judgment and said to him, "Go unto your place," for then he shall incline and go to his seat.

I subjoin a few more of the disciplinary regulations from this custumal.

Of opening of the window and sight of seculars (p. 298)

If any sister's friends desire to see her, the abbess shall not lightly grant this but seldom in the year but if the same sister

---

[1] Langland, in *Piers Plowman*, describes the ceremony of penance in a far less deferential fashion than this (B, v, 175).

have a will to be seen of her dear and honest friends. And it is good that the abbess take counsel of the general confessor and know by him when she shall open the window, for he is conservator of the order, and ought to take heed that all points of the Rule be kept. When any sister shall be seen, the abbess shall warn them that, namely [*i.e. specially*] then, they behave them godly and religiously in countenance, in cheer, and in all their meanings. Nevertheless, if they will make themselves a great crown in heaven, let others see them and they see none; for so it is read in the lives of holy Fathers, that when the mother of one came to see her son he went out to her winking [*i.e. beckoning*] that she should see him but forsooth he would not see her in any wise. And it is said in our Saviour's Rule,[1] that if the window be not opened, so much the more plenteous reward is promised to them in time to come.

Of bodily behaviour

Moreover, for by the outward bodily meaning is oft known the inward disposition of the soul, they ought to moderate all their bodily behaviour in such wise that they never exceed the bounds of honesty neither in laughing, standing, sitting, nor going; for, as saith the wise man, the arraiment of the body, dissolute laughing and the entries of a person show what he is. And Solomon saith, "the apostate goeth frowning with the mouth, trampleth and fiddleth with the feet, twinkleth with the eyes and speaketh with his fingers."

Of laughing

None therefore shall use presumptuously to laugh over much or out of measure dissolutely, but when the sovereign, or any of the elder sisters begin to laugh upon any other sister or sisters by way of recreation, courtesy, will, and very love and charity that they smile or laugh again soberly.

Of standing

Wheresoever they stand namely in divine service in the church, they shall not stand upon one foot alone, holding up

---

[1] *I.e.* the Rule of the Brigittine Order.

that other, nor one over another, nor yet hold their chins or cheeks in their hands, leaning notably with their backs or arms, nor cast out their arms or hands, nor shrug with the shoulders, but they shall stand upright holding their hands before them honestly within their mantles or cowl sleeves, scarcely leaning to the stalls, but if need compel them to do otherwise.

Of sitting regularly

Also wheresoever they sit they shall sit upright, gathering the extremities of their mantles and cowls about them that they float not abroad, holding their hands within their cowl sleeves in places of silence, and not stretch out their legs too far, nor lay one knee over another, but cover their feet honestly under their clothes, and not sit fiddling with them. And when they sit between two sisters, they shall sit so ordinately, and so directly, that neither they have their faces to that one, nor their backs turned any deal to that other, nor yet cast lightly their heads about, nor lean to one side more than to another.

Of going and sight-keeping

In their going also, all must behave them so regularly and honestly, that they go no more on the right side than on the left, not too fast, nor too soft, without running and hard going, without getting and moving of the shoulders, without swinging of arms or of hands, not stretching out the neck, nor look about too busily, nor hold too right up the head, but somewhat down to the earth, and go forth simply, showing over all the signs of meekness, remembering the meek publican that durst not lift up his eyes to heaven but he kept his sight down, and smiting his breast, said inwardly, "*Deus propicius esto michi peccatori.*" And so in all their meanings after the rule of Saint Austin they be bound to show their good conversation effectually. Moreover none shall go from this monastery to another though it be of this same Order, but if there be another or more monasteries of this same Order in this realm only of England, built, founded and sufficiently endowed, for then they may go to any of those monasteries after the form expressed in the bull of Pope Martin the fifth and not else. Nevertheless if the monastery (as God forbid) it fall on fire, or be assailed of enemies suddenly, or by every likeliness and certainty, any such peril is to fall, then they may avoid the monastery, if need be, for a while, and turn home again when such peril is past.

Monks and nuns, being forbidden to speak unnecessarily, and even to speak at all except at certain times, evolved a very elaborate sign-language. The following is a selection from about a hundred signs described in the Syon custumal (Aungier, pp. 405 ff.). Further examples may be found in my *Five Centuries of Religion*, vol. I, pp. 86, 473 ff. Giraldus Cambrensis, describing the monks of Canterbury about A.D. 1180, writes that they were "so profuse in their gesticulations of fingers and hands and arms, and in the whisperings whereby they avoided open speech [wherein all showed a most unedifying levity and licence] that Gerald felt as if he were sitting at a stage play or among a company of actors or buffoons: for it would be more appropriate to their Order and to their honourable estate to speak modestly in plain human speech than to use such a dumb garrulity of frivolous signs and hissings" (*Opera*, R.S. vol. I, p. 51).

114. SIGN-SPEECH

A TABLE OF SIGNS

USED DURING THE HOURS OF SILENCE BY THE SISTERS AND BRETHREN IN THE MONASTERY OF SYON

Abbess—Make the sign for age, and also for a woman.

Aged—Draw down thy right hand straight over thy hair and over thy right eye.

Ale—Make the sign of drink and draw thy hand displayed before thine ear downward.

Bed—Make the sign of a house and put thy right hand under thy cheek, and close thine eyes.

Bedes—Fumble with thy thumb upon the forefinger in manner of parting of beads in prayer.

Book—Wag and move thy right hand in manner as thou shouldest turn the leaves of a book.

Bread—Make with thy two thumbs and two forefingers a round compass. And if thou wilt have white make the sign thereof (of white[1]) and if brown touch thy cowl sleeve.

Butter or other Fats—Draw thy two right upper fingers to and fro on thy left palm.

Candle—Make the sign for butter with the sign for day.

Cheese—Hold thy right hand flatways in the palm of thy left.

Church—Make the sign of a house, and after make a benediction.

Chiming—Make a sign as if ye smote with a hammer.

Cloister—Make a round circle with your right forefinger toward the earth.

Clothe—Rub up and down the ends of all thy right fingers upon thy left.

Cold—Make the sign of water trembling with thy hand or blow on thy forefinger.

Drink—Bow thy right forefinger and put it on thy nether lip.

Eggs—Make a token with thy right forefinger upon thy left thumb to and fro as though thou shouldest peel eggs.

Eating—Put thy right thumb with two forefingers joined to thy mouth.

Enough—Close thy fist together and hold up thy thumb, and this may serve for *I know it well.*

Fish—Wag thy hand displayed sideways in manner of a fish tail.

Girdle—Draw the forefingers of either hand round about thy middle.

Glass—Make the sign of a cup with the sign of red wine.

Hot—Hold the side of thy right forefinger fast into thy mouth closed.

I wot never—Move easily the fingers of thy right hand, flatways and from thee and it serveth for *nay.*

Incense—Put thy two fingers into thy two nostrils.

Keeping—Put thy right hand under thy left armhole.

King—Put all thy finger-ends closed together on thy forehead.

Man—Put and hold thy beard in thy right hand.

Mass—Make the sign of a blessing.

---

[1] Written in the margin.

Mustard—Hold thy nose in the upper part of thy right fist and rub it.

Red colour—Put thy forefinger to the red place of thy cheek.

Ringing—Make a token with thy fist up and down as thou shouldest ring.

Salt—Fillip with the right thumb and forefinger over the left thumb.

Saucer—Make a round circle in thy left palm with thy right little finger.

Silence—Put thy forefinger sideways to thy mouth and draw it up and down.

Sleeping—Put thy right hand under thy cheek and forthwith close thine eyes.

Text or Pax—Kiss the back of thy left hand, with a cross on thy breast with thy right thumb.

Vinegar—Make the sign of wine and draw thy forefinger from thine ear to thy throat.

Washing—Rub thy right hand flatways upon the back of thy left hand.

Water—Join the fingers of thy right hand and move them downward droppingly.

The following episode from the story of *Petit Jean de Saintré*, perhaps the earliest real novel in the French language, might be paralleled from official and irreproachable documents. At the back of its obvious exaggerations, it represents undeniable facts. From the point of view of history, it is specially interesting as illustrating the temptations which beset a monk who enjoyed considerable wealth and almost unlimited freedom for social intercourse. It supplies a commentary on the one side upon Chaucer's *Shipman's Tale* and upon some of the most popular of French fabliaux; on the other, upon the vain attempts of official visitors to ensure that monastic officials should always account for the moneys that passed through their hands, and that the rank and file of cloister-folk should leave their superfluous meat and drink to the almoner, instead of carrying it off to regale their cronies outside the precincts.

Antoine de la Sale (1398–1461) wrote several books for the instruction of his royal pupils, Jean Duke of Anjou, and the three sons of the Count of St Pol. Of these, *Le Petit Jean de Saintré* has been called the *Télémaque* of the fifteenth century. It was written in 1459, and describes how a noble widow at the court of King John, the "Dame des Belles Cousines," took a fancy to the little boy of 13 who afterwards, as Froissart tells us, "was counted the best and most valiant knight in France." La Sale is not studious of historical accuracy, and succeeding authors have vainly attempted to identify the "Dame des Belles Cousines" with one of the royal princesses of Saintré's day. The lady trains her little pupil to be her lover; all her moral reflections, and the infinity of Latin adages which she quotes and comments to him, are designed to lead him along the way of Abélard and Héloïse.[1] After sixteen years of happiness, the lady finds herself suffering so severely in health and spirits from Saintré's absence (he is on a crusade in Prussia) that she persuades her doctor to order a change of air, and with some difficulty obtains leave from the Queen to go down for two months to her own mansion in the country. Here comes in the present episode.

La Sale had lived at Rome, where he rubbed shoulders with Poggio and other scholars of the Renaissance. There can be no doubt that his object in this novel was to satirize the platonic love which poets and romancers of chivalry had often preached. The book cannot be better characterized than by Petit de Juleville in his *Hist. litt. franç.* (vol. II, p. 397). In earlier days, "the heroic and chivalrous spirit of the *chansons de geste* and the Breton romances and the lyrics had counterbalanced, so to speak, the *bourgeois*, sneering, mocking spirit of *Renard* and the Fabliaux. In the fifteenth century, the balance was broken; the heroic vein had run dry; the stream of satire overflowed and invaded in all directions. The sense of life was lost; poetry became mere irony, or curious *tours de force* and rhymed acrobatics. Whatever may have been said to the contrary, the old worn-out trunk was by way of giving none but vulgar fruit; and the Renaissance, which renewed it by grafting in a full-sapped branch, was neither fatal nor even useless for the French spirit."

115. ABBOT, LADY AND KNIGHT

(Ch. 69) Let us here omit, then, the names of the county and the land and her own mansion; for the story is silent on these matters for certain causes which will later be seen. But I will imagine that her great house was a league distant from a great city; and at one league from her house was an abbey founded by her ancestors; which abbey, again, was but a league from the city; so that house, abbey, and town were as in a tripod.

[1] See the present compiler's *Chaucer and his England*, pp. 23, 223, and Sir Walter Scott's *Essay on Chivalry* (originally printed in the *Encyclopaedia Britannica*), for a description of Saintré's first relations with his lady.

When it was noised about the county that my lady was come to her house, then did lords and ladies, squires and damozels, townsfolk and their wives, flock to visit her; by whose coming her great grief began to pass and pass away. Now let us leave her, and speak of dan Abbot.

This abbey, as I say, though I name it not here, was founded by my lady's forefathers, who endowed it so richly that it is now one of the ten great abbeys of France. He who was then Abbot was son to a rich burgess of the town, by whose gifts and prayers to great lords, and through his friends at the court of Rome, so much was given that the son was made Abbot. He was five and twenty years of age, big of body, strong and able to wrestle or leap or cast the bar and stone, or to play at tennis; he found neither monk nor knight, squire nor citizen, who could outdo him here when he took his privy pleasures. In brief, he busied himself in all jollity for the avoidance of idleness; and, on the other hand, he was large and free of all his wealth, whereby he was much loved and prized of all good fellows. When dan Abbot heard of the lady's home-coming, it pleased him much; forthwith he let load one of his carts with stags' crowns and bears' heads and ribs, with hares, coneys, pheasants, partridges, fat capons, fowls and pigeons, and a hogshead of Beaune wine; all which he sent as a present to the lady aforesaid, with prayers for her good-will. My lady, seeing these costly gifts, how could she not rejoice? wherefore she bade feast the messenger, and sent her thanks to dan Abbot. Now Lententide was near, and in that abbey were great pardons to be had on the Monday, Wednesday and Friday of every week. My lady, taken with great devotion, proposed to go thither; nevertheless she tarried the first fortnight, that the press and multitude of people might be past. Then she sent word to dan Abbot that she would be at the morrow's mass in his abbey, to gain the pardons. Dan Abbot, who had never seen her, was right glad: then he bade deck the high altar with relics, and the chapel where my lady's fathers lay buried; nor did he fail to send to the town for lampreys, salmons, and the best sea or fresh-water fishes that could be had. Then he bade array his stables, and make ready all manner of meats, and light fires in many of the chambers; for the season was yet chilly. When therefore my lady was come, and had alighted at the abbey gate, there were the officers, the noblest monks of that house, kneeling at dan Abbot's command to offer all the costliest jewels and plate of the house with their services, for which my lady thanked them well. So, having made her offering at the high altar, she was brought into her chapel to hear mass. After

ABBOT AND DEATH
From Holbein's *Dance of Death*

which, when the hours were done, came dan Abbot with his priors and monks, and knelt before her and said: "My most redoubted lady, welcome here to your own house; glad and joyous are we that God hath given us grace to see our patron and foundress here; we offer unto you this abbey, body and goods." Then said my lady: "Abbot, most heartily we thank you; and if there be aught that we can do for you or your community, we will gladly perform it." Then she asked to see the relics; whereupon dan Abbot rose from his knees and took the heads and arms and the saints' bones that were there in great plenty, saying: "My lady, here lies the most valiant prince our first founder, who from the first conquests of Holy Land brought back this head, this hand and these bones of my lord Saint So-and-so; my lord his brother gave us these jawbones and these other bones of such and such a saint, and such and such a lady-saint. And, briefly, all these relics have been given by your forefathers, who made this church and much of the other buildings that you see here; and the rest was built by the Abbots my predecessors and by the lords and ladies my neighbours who lie buried here." When the lady had kissed the relics, she gave a cope and two dalmatics, with a cloth for the high altar, all of fine rich crimson velvet heavily inwrought with gold; after which she would have gone on her way. So, whilst the horses were eating and men hastened to harness them, dan Abbot brought the lady to warm herself in his chamber, which was nobly spread and fair to see, with tapestry and painted glass; and, as one who fared at his ease, and as an excellent good fellow, he said to all the rest: "Let us all withdraw and leave my lady to warm herself and to take her ease awhile in private"; and so it was. Then, when my lady and all the ladies and damozels of her company had well warmed themselves and taken their ease, my lady asked whether the carriages were ready. Then dan Abbot—who had already told the lady's seneschal that she would dine in the house, and that the meat was ready, and had besought him to lend his countenance thereunto—at these words, I say, he came into the lady's presence and led her into his fair closet, a room that was excellently hung with tapestry and spread with carpets and mats, and the windows all glazed, and a merry fire on the hearth, wherein were three tables spread with marvellous fair linen, and the sideboard plentifully garnished with noble plate. When the lady saw the tables thus spread, she said: "What, my lord Abbot, are you now about to dine?" "Dine," said he, "is it not time, my lady? look there at the clock" (which he had set on by an hour and a half, so that it stood upon the stroke of noon). My lady, hearing it strike noon, would have hastened away; but dan Abbot cried, "My lady, by the faith which I owe unto you,

ye shall not go hence without dinner." "Dine!" said the
lady, "certes I may not tarry, for I have yet much to do."
"No! seneschal, and ye, ladies, will ye suffer my request to
be refused?" Then the ladies and damozels, and the seneschal
himself, who were fasting and sharp-set, thinking that they
would here dine far better than they were wont to dine at
home, what with the eyes that they cast upon the tables, what
with the urgency of their words, wrought so in favour of this
first request of dan Abbot that my lady gave her consent.
Then the Abbot, as one overjoyed and gracious and amiable,
knelt down forthwith and thanked the lady, with the other
ladies of her train. Then were the horses sent back to the
stables, whereof the whole company was glad at heart, albeit
they had already well breakfasted. Then said dan Abbot,
"My lady, ye are in the holy season of penitence, wherefore
marvel not if ye are meanly entertained, the more so since
I knew nought of your coming until late last night." "Abbot,"
said the lady, "we cannot fail to find ourselves well here."
Then the Abbot called for water for their hands, which was
all warm rose-water, whereof the lady and her companions
made much joy. My lady would have had the Abbot wash
first, as a prelate of Holy Church; but he would do no such
thing; nevertheless, for the lady's prayers, he went and washed
at the sideboard. Then the table was served, and the lady besought him to be seated; but he made answer, "My lady, ye
are lady and abbess of this house; be seated, and let me go
mine own way." When therefore she was seated, and dame
Jehanne, dame Katharine and the lord of Gency, who was
with her—and, at the second table, the prior of the monastery
and Isabel, with other damozels and two or three esquires,
and my lord Geoffrey of Saint-Amand in face of the said
Isabel—then dan Abbot, with a napkin at his neck, went to
the sideboard and served my lady with toasts of white hypocras,
and likewise to the other tables; then, Lententide figs roasted
with sugar; nor could all the lady's prayers bring him to seat
himself, saying, "My lady, let it not displease you if I keep
company with the seneschal, and show him the way." Then,
when dan Abbot and the seneschal had come and set the
first course upon the table, my lady said, "Truly, dan Abbot,

if ye will not be seated, we will rise from the table." "Well then, my lady, ye should and shall be obeyed." Then the lady would have had the table drawn back; but he said, "God forbid that the table be moved for me!" Then he let bring a stool, and sat in face of the lady, a little lower down. Then he bade bring white wine of Beaune, and then red of three or four sorts, wherewith all were served. In brief, what with many exhortations to make good cheer, and with drinking of healths, the lady had never fared so well for many a day. And it came to pass that, as the lady drank to dan Abbot, and he to her, their eyes, those archers of the heart, began to shoot to and fro; so that their feet (for the tablecloth reached even unto the ground) began little by little to touch each other, and then to tread one upon another. Then did the burning dart of love strike first into one heart, then into the other, so that they ceased to eat; but dan Abbot (for who so glad of this new game as he?) drank first to one, then to another. What then? never was abbot more merry than he; now would he rise and let his stool be brought before the ladies, and sit awhile with them; now would he go before the damozels and pray them to eat and make good cheer; now again to the waiting-women, and drink to them; then again to my lady, sitting down merrily face to face. Then began those archers of love to shoot more busily than before, and foot trod hard upon foot. As for their further good cheer, of wines and meats, lampreys, salmons and other fresh and salt fish, I will say no more here for brevity's sake.

(Ch. 70) When the tables were cleared, and the seneschal and the rest had gone to dinner, my lady thanked dan Abbot for all his good cheer; and thus, from word to word, from step to step, they found themselves at the other end of the room, where they spake of merry matters; and, while the rest dined, dan Abbot let spread his bed with the finest linen for my lady's rest.[1] When, therefore, the seneschal had dined and the lady bade harness the horses, "How! my lady," said the Abbot, "will you break the good customs of this house?" "And what are they?" "My lady, they are such that, when-

---

[1] The after-dinner siesta was a very common medieval custom, even in monasteries, where it is specially provided for by St Benedict's Rule, chap. 48.

soever any dames of lineage or damozels have dined here, they and their company must take their rest, whether waking or sleeping, winter or summer; and, if they sup here, for that night I leave them mine own room and go lodge elsewhere; wherefore, my lady, it is not meet that you refuse the custom of this abbey." So sore prayed this Abbot, and the ladies with him, that my lady graciously admitted this custom; wherefore she entered into her room, and the wine and spices were brought; the door was shut, and the lady took her rest until vespertide.

(Ch. 71) When the dames and damozels were arrayed, then Isabel opened her lips and said: "You say nothing, my lady, nor you other foolish women, of dan Abbot's good cheer." "Certes," said my lady, "he seemeth a man of gentle parts." "Of gentle parts!" cried lady Jehanne, "never saw I so gracious a monk as this!" "And you, my lady," said Katharine, "must you be squeamish of staying here?" "Ha!" said Isabel, "his prayers told me plainly that all went well, and that he prayed from his heart." Then all in chorus, after the manner of women, they praised the largesse, the merriment and the fair person of dan Abbot, in all the words that they could find. The lady, who now was smitten with love and had forgotten her mourning, said briefly, "He hath very gentle parts." And, as they spake thus together, it rang for evensong; and they must needs arise without sleeping to hear that service. When vespers had been sung, and my lady would have mounted her horse, dan Abbot took her by the hand, "Ha! Abbot," saith she, "whither do you lead us?" "I pray you, my lady, let me bring you to a small collation, for it is now high time." So saying, he linked his arm in hers, and, pressing her hand, led her into the lower chamber, well carpeted and warmed, where tables and sideboard were already laid with salads and cress and vinegar, and dishes of lampreys roast or in pasties, and sauces set with great soles boiled or fried or roasted with verjuice of red oranges; barbels; salmon roast or boiled or in pasties, great pike and fat carp, plates of crayfish, great fat eels in galantine, dishes of divers grains covered with jellies of white and crimson and gold, bourbon tarts, cheese cakes and flawns[1] of almond-cream

---

[1] A sort of pancake.

richly sugared, apples and pears cooked or raw, almonds peeled or sugared, peeled nuts with rose-water, figs of Malta and [Alicante?] and Marseilles, dried grapes of Corinth and Orta, and much else which for brevity's sake I omit, the whole neatly arrayed as for a banquet.

(Ch. 72) My lady, who in this fasting-season thought to take only wine and spices, found the tables thus garnished; for the false God of Love had so fiercely assailed her at dinner that his amorous darts had sated her with eating; nevertheless nature acquitted her, giving her such appetite that she needed no pressing. And when the rest of the company saw my lady seated, and dan Abbot over against her in the midst of the table, then all or most of them suffered themselves to be persuaded by the Abbot's entreaties to obey their lady and keep her company. So all sat down at the ends and sides of the table, and, for better sport, four or five of the most gracious monks between every two. There might ye have seen good drinking and liberal eating. What say I? never did so many folk make such sport and good cheer as in this place; yet at length, to the great regret and sighs of my lady and dan Abbot, they must part for this time. But as the lady mounted into her carriage, there were dan Abbot and his priors with their humblest thanks for her, commending their church and their community to her favour. Then said she, "We shall see each other oftentimes; for we purpose now to earn these your pardons more liberally than any others, glad as they have been. But as for you, Abbot, we beseech you to give us no more such great display of meats; for certainly ye have been too outrageous in your expenses, and this is not our will for another time." "Well, my lady, yet a little toast with duke's powder[1] and white wine, or hypocras of muscatel or vernage or malvoisie or Greek wine, as it may please you to take thereof after mass; this ye will not forbid?" "Yes, indeed," said she, "from these days it is our purpose to fast." "Fast! my lady; nay, but that is no breach of your fast, and thereof will I give you mine absolution." With this dan Abbot mounted his horse, and kept the lady company for a while upon her journey; and then he took his leave.

[1] Some spice which I am unable to identify.

(Ch. 73) When dan Abbot was gone homewards to his abbey, then the ladies began again to vie in his praise. Isabel, who was the merriest of mood, spoke first and laughed, "Ha! my lady, how do I praise you for refusing the good that comes in your way!" Then said dame Jehanne, "Truly, Isabel, you mistake; for my lady purposeth to come hither often, yet perchance not always to dine here." "Nay," said dame Katharine, "ye are both in the wrong; why should not my lady take his offers from time to time, since he hath the wherewithal? Say I not right, my lady?" She, who had listened to all, answered, "We must not wholly fleece our sheep; wherefore I go no further than the powdered toasts and hypocras and other choice and delicate wines, wherewith we should be content; but in very truth we purpose to gain all these pardons, or the greater part thereof; for we know not whether we could come hither at another time." Thus came they to her house. The lady, whose heart was aflame with this new fire of love, ceased not to complain, and groan and sigh throughout the night, so yearned she to see dan Abbot and converse with him again. And he, no less inflamed with the soft and amorous glances that had passed between them, rested not that night; for his love suffered no sleep. Then, when the looked-for day was come, the lady said to her ladies, "Truly I will confess now to dan Abbot, who is a prelate of great devotion, that I may the better and more surely gain my pardons." "That was well done," said dame Jehanne, "for my part, I went to confession yesterday." Then the lady sent for little Perrin her page, and bade him take horse and tell the Abbot that she would fain see him without delay. Hastily and diligently did the Abbot obey: and she, when all the ladies had done their reverence, said openly unto him, "Abbot, that we may the more worthily gain your pardons, we are purposed now to make confession." "Ha! my lady," said dan Abbot, "now you are on God's side; and, my lady, who is your confessor? for I might give him further powers, if need be." "Nay," said the lady, "for there is none here more worthy and sufficient than you." "Ha! my lady, then is the virtue in my crozier, for else am I the most ignorant of all." With these words my lady went into the tiring-chamber, that was well tapestried and carpeted, with a fair fire on the hearth; and dan Abbot devoutly followed her; then the door was shut for two hours by the clock, and she spake with all repentance and contrition of her good deeds and loyal loves; and dan Abbot in all goodness and honour, and in gentle sport, confessed her most sweetly. Then, at his departure, my lady went to her coffret and took an excellent great balas ruby set in gold, which she placed on his middle finger, saying: "Dear heart! mine only thought and my true desire! for mine own and only friend I retain you and espouse you with this ring." Then dan Abbot thanked her with all humility; then he bethought him of the common proverb, "he who serveth and not persevereth, loseth his guerdon." Then he gave the lady absolution, and of his charity he kissed her softly and took his leave; and, at his passing through the ante-chamber, he said discreetly to the ladies and damozels, "Let none go in until my lady call; sisters and friends, God be with you until we meet again." The lady, for recovering of her colour, which her penances had somewhat altered, kept for a while to herself, while her ladies and attendants awaited the stroke of eleven to hear mass; then the lady called Jehanne, and attired herself in her simplest attire, with a great kerchief the better to cover her face; in which guise she came forth simple and coy from her chamber, with downcast eyes and mien; thus she went devoutly to mass, and then to dinner; and thus passed that day. The next day, being Wednesday, when the pardons were to begin again, my lady repaired to the abbey to gain them. Dan Abbot, full of joy, caused great plenty of toasts to be made ready, and hypocras and divers sorts of foreign wines, herrings white and red, and other meats for the rest; moreover he bade tend the horses well. When the lady had heard her mass, then dan Abbot took her under the arm, and led her to the fair fire in his own chamber, where breakfast was laid. And when the lady had well broken her fast, he took her and said, "My lady, whilst your company makes good cheer, I would fain show you the new buildings that I have a-making." Then they went forth from the chamber, so far that the ladies found them not. And, as they left the Abbot's privy closet, he gave to my lady a piece of

fine black silken velvet, which she sent for secretly afterwards.
And then the lady came again to the great parlour where were
all the rest, and when her ladies were come back she rebuked
them in feigned displeasure, saying, "Ha! whence come ye
then? I had thought that ye followed me as I had bidden; but
ye loved the good pie and toasts better than my company."
"Nay, my lady, but we lost sight of you, for all our haste."
"Ah! good lady," said dan Abbot, "let them be pardoned
this time." Then the lady fell into great praise of the Abbot's
new buildings, and went forth unto her carriage; and there
he took his leave of her. What more? There was no week
of that Lententide but she went devoutly to gain the pardons,
and oftentimes without great company. There she dined and
banqueted and supped; and, after her sleep, she oftentimes
went a-hunting in the woods after foxes and badgers and other
such small game. Thus then did she merrily pass the whole
of that Lenten season.

Chs. 74–80. The Queen, finding that the lady has long overpassed her
time, writes to recall her to the court. She answers that a few weeks more
will restore her completely to health; the Queen's messenger, however,
told his mistress privately something of the truth. Meanwhile Jean de
Saintré, having distinguished himself greatly at the Emperor's court in
addition to his other deeds of arms, came back to the court at Paris. There
he learned how his mistress had gone home in ill-health, and how, to all
the Queen's letters, "she only answered, 'I come, I come,' and is still
to come at this day. When my lord of Saintré heard that she had thus
been ill, he thought on her words to him, that her heart would never be
at rest until her return; so he guessed (as was truth) that she had departed
to forget her pain of love; and this put great joy into his heart." He put
on his richest robes and jewels, and set off with two knights and twelve
squires all drest in the lady's colours. They found the lady gone from her
house to the abbey, and from the abbey into the fields for hawking. There
Saintré was dismayed by the lady's cold reception, and by her effusive
friendliness for the Abbot, who, however, invited Saintré back to a supper
of the Gargantuan pattern with which we are already familiar.

(Ch. 81) And when the bellies were wellnigh filled, at
the hour when tongues are unloosed, then dan Abbot began to
awaken; and he cried aloud: "Ho! my lord of Saintré, arouse
yourself, rouse! I drink to your thoughts; what are they then?
for you are all in thought." Then said the lord of Saintré, "My
lord Abbot, I am so hard bestead with all these good meats

and wines that stand before me, that I have no leisure for the rest." "My lord of Saintré," said the Abbot, "I have oftentimes wondered, look you, how it may be among you noble men, knights and esquires, who are so busy with deeds of arms, and, when a man comes back, he speaks of that which he hath won." And then, turning to the lady, he continued, "Is it not so, my lady?" "Abbot," said she, "you say truth, and what may this mean? tell us your thought, good sir." "Madam," said he, "if you wish me to speak, it shall be by your leave and at your bidding, and I know not whether my lord of Saintré will be displeased with me; but since it is your will, my lady, this is my thought: there are many knights and esquires in the royal court and in lords' and ladies' courts, who call themselves loyal lovers of the ladies; and to get your graces they weep and sigh and groan before you, and feign such dolour that ye, poor ladies with tender and piteous hearts, surest needs be deceived by them; then ye fall in with their desires and their snares. And these men go on from one to another, taking surety of a garter or a bracelet, or even a thistle-head or a turnip or what not; and then one of these will say to ten or twelve several ladies, 'Ha! my lady, I wear this token for your love!' Then the king and queen and all the lords praise and esteem them, and give them freely of their wealth, to their great profit. Tell me, my lady, is there no truth in this?" The lady, who was pleased to hear this speech, answered with a smile, "Who has told you this, Abbot? For my part, I believe that you say truth." And therewith she trod on his feet; and he continued, "Moreover, my lady, when these knights or squires go forth to do their deeds of arms, and have taken leave of the king, if it be cold weather, they go away to those stove-warmed rooms of Germany and riot with harlots all winter long; and, if the weather be warm, they go to those delicious countries of Sicily or Aragon, where they find good wines and meats, fountains and fair fruits, and delightful gardens; and there they feast their eyes all summer with the fair gentlemen and ladies who give them good cheer and high honour; then they have an old minstrel or trumpeter decked with an old enamelled plate, to whom they give one of their old robes, that he may cry aloud at court, 'My lord hath won, hath won, as a valiant knight, the prize of arms!' Ah, poor ladies! are not ye deceived here? by my faith, I pity you." The lady, who was so tickled with these words that she could not contain herself, turned her head a little and said to the lord of Saintré: "What say you, my lord?" He, sore displeased with these railing accusations of dan Abbot, said to the lady: "If it were your will to take the gentlemen's part, you well know the contrary of these things, my lady." Then said she: "We have indeed seen some who have never done thus, but what know we of the rest? For our part, we are of the Abbot's mind." And with that she trod on the Abbot's foot, smiling and glancing at him. "Ha! madam," said Saintré, "you now speak at your own will; I pray God that He may give you perfect knowledge." Then said dan Abbot, "And what knowledge would you have my lady get of the truth?" "As to the truth," said the lord of Saintré, "to the lady's words I make no answer; she may say what pleases her; but to your words, wherewith you have blamed the knights and esquires, I say that, if you were a man to whom I owed an answer, you would not find me slow to give you one; but, considering your dignity and your profession, I hold my peace here, and perchance you will some day be better advised." Dan Abbot, who was all afire with love, said mockingly to the lady, "My lady, it is on your behalf that I am threatened here in mine own house": and therewith the play of foot and foot went on without ceasing. So, seeing the lady's smiles and glances, he knew how the game pleased her, and said, "Ho! my lord of Saintré, I am neither swashbuckler nor man of arms, but a poor and simple monk, living upon what we have here for God's love; but if there were any man, whosoever he were, that would gainsay me in this quarrel, I would wrestle with him." "Would ye so?" said my lady, "are ye indeed so bold?" "My lady, I can but get a fall; but I trust in God and in my good and honest quarrel that I should get the better; is there any man here who will answer for all these men of war?" My lord of Saintré, at these outrageous words of dan Abbot, felt as though his heart were pierced through and through; and, seeing moreover the favour that the lady showed him, he would fain have died there. She, who marked his silence, said, "Ha! my lord of Saintré, you who are so valiant and who, as men say, have done so many deeds of arms, dare you not wrestle with this Abbot? Certes, if ye refuse, I shall say as he saith." "Ah, my lady, ye know that I was never wrestler, and these lordly monks are masters of that art, as of tennis-play and casting bars and stones and iron staves, wherein they prove themselves among their privy diversions; wherefore I know well, my lady, that I should here be no match for him." "And I," said the lady, "pray you thereunto; now shall we see whether you will play me false; and by my faith, if ye wrestle not here, I will reprove you everywhere and hold you for a truly faint-hearted knight." "Ah, my lady, what say you? I have done enough in my time to content any lady; but, since needs must, I will do your pleasure here." "What saith he, dan Abbot?" "He saith, my lady, that he will not fail you at this need, and that he hath done harder deeds than this." "Saith he so?" said she; "well, we shall see." Then, without further delay—no, not to clear the supper-table—dan Abbot leapt joyously from his seat, and then the lady and Saintré, to the wonder of all that were there. The Abbot led the lady to a fair meadow that was now in evening shade, and said, "My lady, seat yourself here under this fair flowering thorn; for you shall be our judge." So she sat down, overjoyed beyond measure, and made her ladies sit with her; who indeed, for all that they dissembled, found for the most part little pleasure in this matter. Then did dan Abbot that which St Bennet and St Robert, St Augustine and St Bernard, who were prelates of Holy Church, would never in their life have done; for there before them all he stripped to the doublet, untied his hosen (which in those days were not sewn together) and let them fall below his knees; then he came before the lady and made his reverence; after which he caracoled in mockery, leaping in the air and showing his big thighs, as rough and hairy as a bear. Afterwards came Saintré, who had disrobed in a corner of the meadow; his hosen were richly embroidered with great pearls; he came and made his reverence to the lady, dissembling the bitter pain that he felt. Then stood the champions in presence; but, before the bout was begun, dan Abbot turned to the lady, kneeling on one knee and saying in mockery, "My lady, I join my hands and beseech you that ye commend me to my lord of Saintré's mercy." The lady, who well knew the Abbot's vigour, said with a smile, "Ha! my lord of Saintré, I commend our Abbot to you, and beseech you not to handle him too roughly." The lord, who well knew this mockery, made answer, "Ah, my lady, I should rather need his mercy." After these words the two champions caught their hold, and turned round once or twice. Then dan Abbot put out his leg and caught Saintré's form within; then he suddenly unbent and trussed him so that the good lord's feet were even with his head; and the Abbot cried, as he held him down on the grass, "My lady, commend me to the lord of Saintré." Then said the lady, laughing loudly, "Ha, my lord, have mercy on our Abbot!" yet she could scarce speak for joy and for laughter. Then dan Abbot rose to his feet, and the lady said laughing, and loud enough for all to hear: "Yet once again!"

Saintré is forced into a second bout, with the same result as before, which gave the lady an excuse for still crueller insults.

The two esquires, who had stayed to serve him, were almost dead with grief, when they saw how the lady and dan Abbot flouted and derided so honourable and valiant a knight, who had no equal in the kingdom of France; and they said unto him, "You are no man, if you avenge not yourself of this mockery." "Fear not," said he, "but let me go my way and take patience as you see me." Then with all glad cheer he came to redouble the merriment of his lady and of the Abbot, saying, "Alas! my lady, it is great pity of so big and stout a man of body as my lord Abbot is, that he was not put to arms to guard a frontier against the enemies of the realm; for I know scarce two or three men, however stout, whom he would not have conquered." Dan Abbot, hearing this fresh praise, leapt aloft and danced around before the lady and her company; and then he bade bring wine and cherries for their refreshment.

Meanwhile the priors and the ancient monks of the abbey,

who had great displeasure of their Abbot's life, and all the more because they heard now of this wrestling and of the mockery of the lady and the Abbot, who moreover wrought not nor showed not the deeds of a good monk, but a dissolute and evil life—the priors and ancients, I say, ordained that two should go speak with the Abbot in the name of the rest; and these were their words:

"Reverend father in God and most honoured lord, the priors and administrators of your convent, with one voice, after their humble and proper recommendations, have sent us unto you. They have learnt that, on many occasions, ye have given to our most redoubted lady many dinners, suppers and other diversions, whereof the whole convent is content in so far as she is our patroness and foundress; and all the more since ye have this evening brought hither such a lord as this of Saintré, whose fame is spread everywhere and who is so near and familiar to our lord the king. But, in so far as ye have made bold to require him to wrestle, and thrown him more than once, and made sport of him—a thing which pertaineth not to the state of a prelate or of a monk to do as ye have done thus publicly, seeing that it is forbidden to you and to us by our rules and statutes—of this the whole convent is much displeased and angered, praying and beseeching you to leave this course, and to see that he have no further cause to blame you or us before he depart hence; otherwise, the community giveth you to know by our mouth that, if any evil blood arise therefrom, which might do any prejudice or harm soever to the monastery, then must we excuse ourselves and lay the whole blame on you; and herein may it please you to pardon all of us." Dan Abbot, hearing these tidings and words from his convent, made answer: "Priors, go to the monastery and tell them that all I have done hath but been in sport; nor need they be careful thereof, for, before his departure, all shall be rightly ordered."

He took Saintré apart, and invited him to dinner next day. Saintré civilly excused himself on the score of business; with equal tact and politeness he refused three rich presents from the Abbot—a mule, a falcon, and three thousand crowns—but seized the occasion to invite his enemy and the lady to dinner at his own inn. The lady would have refused; but the

Abbot persuaded her that a civil acceptance would arouse less suspicion. Saintré repaired at once to a rich citizen of the town, from whom he borrowed a pair of poleaxes, and two suits of armour. The dinner was good enough to please even the Abbot.

And when all paunches were full, and all stomachs well drenched with wine, my lord of Saintré asked dan Abbot whether he had ever borne armour. "Armour," said he, "nay, truly." "Ha!" said the lord, "truly it were a fair sight to see you armed! What say you, my lady? say I not truth?" "Truly," said she, "I believe and dare aver that, if he bore armour, some who mock him now might lose by that bargain." "Nay, lady, I know no man who mocketh him, but this I say, that I never saw man who would make a fairer show in arms": then he bade his page Perrinet do as had been concerted between them. So Perrinet set up a table at the end of the hall, whereon he laid the greatest and fairest of the suits of armour, without sword or axe. And when dan Abbot saw this fair shining armour, wherein he took great pleasure, and heard himself so highly praised, then he thought that the lord of his largesse would give him these arms, and that the harness had been brought hither for that purpose. So he thought that, if he were prayed to don it, there would be no wisdom in refusing; wherefore, to show his liking, he began to praise the armour to the skies. "Well," said Saintré, "since it pleaseth you so well, if you find it proper to your body, you shall have it." "What, for mine own?" "Yea, truly, dan Abbot, and more still, if ye require it of me." "By my faith, for love of my lady here I will neither eat nor drink till I shall have put that harness on." "Clear" (cried he), "clear those tables, for we have eaten more than enough." Dan Abbot, beside himself with joy, stripped to his doublet; and my lord of Saintré took a bodkin and deftly laced him up, and armed the good Abbot wholly, body and legs, and clapped the bacinet on his head and buckled it well, and then the gauntlets upon his hands. When therefore dan Abbot was thus wholly armed, he turned front and rear, preening himself and saying to the lady and her women: "What say ye to see a monk in armour? is it a fair sight?" "Monk!" said my lady, "nay, but such monks are few and far between!"

"Ha! by God! why have I not an axe in my hands, and a man to chafe me and fight with me!" Then said he jestingly to the lady, "Truly this harness weigheth more than the monk's harness; but it is well enough, since I have earned it." With these words my lord of Saintré said unto him, "Ye have not yet earned it, but ye shall soon have paid the full price"; and therewith he bade bring the other suit, wherein he was swiftly clad. When the lady heard these words, and saw how hastily the lord armed himself, she misdoubted· sore, and cried, "My lord of Saintré, what then is your purpose?" "My lady," said he, for by now he was ready, "ye shall soon see." "See!" cried the lady, "Sir Coward, wilt thou fight with an Abbot?" The lord, by this time being armed, bade his men keep the doors, that none should go in or out from that hall; then said he to the ladies and damsels and monks and all others there present, "Stand ye there by that door; and let no man or woman be so hardy as to stir; for, if any gainsay me, I will cleave him to the teeth." Then might ye have seen these ladies and these monks tremble and weep and curse the hour wherein they had come to that feast. Then came Saintré to the lady, and said, "Of your grace, ye were a willing judge of the wrestling between dan Abbot and me; now therefore I pray and beseech you with all humility that ye will judge the wrestling that I have learned to use, and that ye join me in my request to dan Abbot." "I know not what request," said she; "but this I know; if ye do him the least displeasure, count it as done to me; for I take him under my protection." The lord came then to his adversary, and said: "dan Abbot, at my lady's request and at yours I wrestled two bouts with you, whereof I still feel the effects; nor did any excuse avail me; but, by her request and by yours, I must needs suffer so far. Now then I pray and beseech you, not only for myself but for the sake of this lady whom ye so loyally love, that we wrestle a bout of mine own fashion." "Ha! my lord of Saintré," said the Abbot, "I am not able to wrestle in this harness." Then said Saintré, "You shall pass by that way, or you shall pass through the window." The lady, who saw how Saintré was so wholly purposed to fight, said to him with felon words, "My lord of Saintré, we will and command, on pain of our indignation, that ye two disarm forthwith; and, if ye do not so, your body and life shall be subject to my wrath and punishment as a felon and a coward." When he heard himself thus reviled and threatened, in favour and for love of this Abbot, he cried, "How! false and disloyal woman, such as you are, I have served you as long and loyally as man ever served woman; and now you have dishonoured and abandoned me for a ribald monk, with whom you are so falsely and disloyally fallen into acquaintance: wherefore, that ye may never forget that I am not a man to be reviled and menaced for his love or any other man's, I will give you a guerdon, less indeed than your desert, as an example to other disloyal women." Then he caught her by the top-knot of her tressed hair, and raised his palm to buffet her once or twice; but then he contained himself, remembering the great kindnesses that she had done him of old, and thinking that this might besmirch his honour. Wherefore he cast her upon the bench, weeping and half fainting with grief; and there she sat without daring to stir. Then he let bring two axes and two daggers, first to dan Abbot that he might take his choice; after which he said, "dan Abbot, remember now the injurious words that ye have spoken against knights and esquires who go through the world to gain fresh honours; for ye shall now come to reckoning: stand therefore on your guard." When therefore dan Abbot saw that fate was against him, and that he must needs fight and take this other risk, then he raised his axe, and smote so that if it had fallen fair upon Saintré— what with the bodily force that he had, and all the advantage of his bigger bulk—he would have wounded him sore or borne him to the ground, which indeed the lady would gladly have seen. But Saintré, by God's will, and with the skill that he had in such feats of arms, parried and caught the blow on his axe, and then, with the pike of his axe, he thrust into the other's harness and drove him backwards upon a bench over against the lady's, where the monk rolled backwards with so heavy a fall that the very house seemed to fall with him, crying, "Mercy, mercy, my lady! Ah! my lord of Saintré, for God's sake have mercy upon me!" The lord, who was yet grieved with the villainous mockeries which ye have heard, was purposed to end his life; but, as he raised his axe, he bethought him of the following verses, wherein are contained the holy words which our Lord said in the Old Testament: namely, in the ninth chapter of Genesis: *Whoso sheddeth man's blood, by man shall his blood be shed.*[1] Again He said in His passion: *All they that take the sword shall perish with the sword.* Again to David: *Thou shalt not build an house unto my name, because thou hast shed much blood.* Again He saith by the mouth of David: *Bloody and deceitful men shall not live out half their days.* And again by David's mouth: *The Lord will abhor the bloody and deceitful man.* And again in that same book (Ps. cxxxix, A.V.). And He hath commanded unto us so many other little mercies and loving-kindnesses, and shown the same in His own person, that on this account the said lord of Saintré refrained himself from the death stroke. Yet, seeing that by God's will and vengeance, by reason of his open and notorious sin, such punishment had come upon this monk, he cast away his axe and caught his dagger; then he thrust up the Abbot's visor and said: "Now, dan Abbot, know that God is the true judge, seeing that your bodily strength and your bitter tongue have not kept you from chastisement, even in the presence of her before whom you had vaunted yourself so proudly, and for whose sake you have so dishonourably lied and spoken against knights and esquires: wherefore your false tongue shall pay the reckoning." Then he thrust his dagger through both cheeks and tongue, and left him thus, saying: "Now, dan Abbot, you have well and truly earned your armour." Then he disarmed himself, and, seeing the lady dishevelled with disordered tresses, he said unto her, "Adieu! falsest lady that ever breathed." And, seeing her girt with blue silk laced with gold, he loosed that girdle, saying: "Now, lady, have you the heart to wear this blue girdle? for blue is the colour of loyalty, and truly ye are the most disloyal that I know; ye shall no more wear this." With that he folded it and laid it in his bosom. Then he went to the ladies and monks and others, who were huddled weeping in the corners of the hall;

[1] All these quotations are given by the French author in the Latin of the Vulgate.

and thus he spake: "Ye are witnesses of those things done
and said which, to my great grief, have caused me to do this
deed; and, as for the displeasure that ye have had thereof,
and that ye still have, I beseech your pardon and commend you
to God." Then was the door opened; and, when he was
come down, he said unto the host: "If dan Abbot will have
the great suit of armour, let him keep it in God's name; but
as for the little suit and the axes, give them back to Jacques
and bid him come shortly to see me; now, fair host, have
I contented you?" With these words he mounted his horse
and commended his host to God.

How the lady swore to cleave truly to the Abbot all her life long, and
to be revenged upon Saintré at court, and how Saintré defended himself
and turned the tables on her by means of the blue girdle, may be read in
Chapters 83–86 of the book.

Johann Busch was born at Zwolle in 1399. He showed brilliant scholarship as a boy; but as a youth he chose to join the same congregation of
Austin Canons to which his contemporary Thomas à Kempis belonged.
In 1440 he became Subprior of Wittenburg, and began his long and
arduous career as reformer of monasteries under a commission from the
Pope and the Council of Bâle. In this work he attained more success than
any of his contemporaries except the distinguished Cardinal Nicolaus
von Cusa. His chief writings were (i) a charming chronicle of the monastery of Windesheim, and (ii) the *Liber de Reformatione Monasteriorum*,
a minute and often very humorous record of his life's work. The edition
here used is that of K. Grube (Halle, 1887). A translation of it was begun,
but never completed, in the *British Magazine* for April, 1841, etc.; and
the reader may there find some strange things for which there is no place
here. Miss Eckenstein's account of these visitations in her *Woman under
Monasticism* is quite worthless; she takes it at second-hand from a not
always trustworthy monograph by Karl Grube. See Eileen Power,
Medieval English Nunneries, Cambridge, 1922, pp. 670 ff.

116. A STUDENT'S CONVERSION

(*Lib. Ref.* vol. I, 1, pp. 394 ff.)

So my parents would fain have sent me to the University of
Erfurt, that I might be chief of all our friends and kinsfolk.
But I began to think within myself: "If thou wert already

Doctor, clad in thy many-coloured well-furred gowns, and enjoying the title of thy degree while all men cried: 'Good morrow, Sir Doctor, good day!' and if after this life thou must needs go down to hell, there to burn for everlasting, what profit shouldst thou then have?" So I thought the more frequently on the eternity of hell-pains and the infinity of the heavenly glory, earnestly considering whether my mind could grasp and foresee any end to eternity. When therefore, after many weary rounds of thought, this was still impossible, then after good deliberation I determined firmly in mine own mind that I would desert the whole world with all its delights, and serve God alone for ever in some good reformed monastery. For these words *ewelike ende ommermeer* ["for ever and evermore"] compelled me to do thus and to leave my parents and my friends, whereof I had many, for God's sake and the life everlasting. Hearing this, my parents and kinsfolk strove to turn me aside, and my mother above all; for she said, "Dear son, when thou wert young, thou wouldst fain have eaten in thy bed. Thou canst not fast; wilt thou slay thyself? Moreover, they will not leave thee in one monastery, but will oftentimes send thee to others. Thou shouldst have been the head of us all; wilt thou now desert us?" and much more to the same purpose. I made soft answer to my mother, but in my heart I thought: "These are women's words; none will care to go to hell for me; if I will go to heaven, I must earn that for myself!" So I gave no heed to my father's and mother's tears, but purposed to enter the order of Canons Regular, whereof the reform had lately begun in our parts....

What temptations I suffered as a novice, especially in the Catholic faith, God alone knoweth, from Whom nothing is hid. For God Himself was so great and glorious in my heart, that I could not conceive Him to have put on flesh and walked upon earth so poor and so despised. And when the Gospels were read in refectory, I thought that the Evangelists desired to praise that man, and then my heart cried within me, "Thou knowest, it is not true that this Jesus is God!" Yet I said within my heart, "I will die for it, that He is so." Then my heart cried within me, "Thou wilt die for it, yet shalt thou see that it shall be naught!" But when I found how our father St Augustine and the other Doctors, who lived in the world almost 400 years after Christ, said and wrote and preached that this Jesus was God, then I thought: "It is strange that those wise men were so foolish as to dare to call that man God, Whom they never saw." And, albeit I was thus tempted, yet was I a good and true Catholic; but God Almighty suffered me thus to be tempted, because in later years, taught by experience, I liberated many who were buffeted with the same temptation. How I was liberated from this trial, is contained in the letter which I wrote to one Brother Bernard, of the Order of St Benedict at Erfurt. I had also temptations of the flesh in my noviciate.... My temptations of vainglory, pride, and impatience could easily be driven out, for then I fought one against one; but in those of the flesh two fought against one, for my flesh and the Devil were matched against my struggling soul. When during my noviciate I sang in the service a verse or responsory or versicle, then I thought within myself: "Our layfolk in the nave, prostrate on their knees, are thinking with admiration, 'How good and pure a voice hath our Brother John!'" When another novice sang any part, then I murmured within myself: "Now the lay-folk are thinking, 'That sounds like a rasp!'" Rarely did one of our Brethren leave the choir or do anything, but that I had various suspicions of him, thinking within myself: "He cannot stay longer in the choir, he goeth forth because he would go hither, or thither." One was wont to spit frequently in choir; and I thought that he had many temptations which he drove forth by this continual voiding of his rheum. Thus too I had most frequent suspicions of many others; for a novice is as full of suspicions as an egg is full of meat.

Yet will I sing for ever the mercies of the Lord, Who not only liberated me from many temptations, but through those same temptations rooted me fast in good, giving me a practised tongue that I might sustain the fallen by word and deed. When therefore my profession had been performed, at Epiphany, on the very year-day of mine entrance, by reason of my parents' presence, who brought wine and flesh and white bread for the convent, I was not altogether freed from the temptations aforesaid, wherein I was immersed even to the roof of my cell throughout wellnigh all the time of my noviciate. But on St Agnes' day (for then again we communicated) all my past temptation departed utterly from my heart and senses, and then my Lord Jesus answered: "Now art thou Mine, and I am thine." And from that time until this present it hath ever been well with me, so far as in Him stood; and I began to converse with Him and oftentimes to hear His answering voice, as it may be heard in the heart within.... Whensoever after this I felt inclinations or movements to fault or sin, or when I was offended by others, I conceived certain remedies thereunto which I had found by experience of myself or by study from the Holy Scriptures, which I collected into a certain little book that I might have them at hand; whereby I brought myself back little by little to peace of mind, and withstood such evil inclinations.

The next extract will suffice, out of a dozen equally unfavourable but less entertaining which might be quoted from various sources, to exemplify the difficulties which beset monastic reform in the Middle Ages. The nunnery of Wennigsen, near Hanover, was the first with which Busch dealt; in this and other cases the full context implies, what he says in so many words concerning seven out of twenty-four nunneries which at different times needed his visitations, that the inmates neglected all three "substantial" vows of their Rule—poverty, obedience, and chastity. A strikingly close parallel to all this story may be found in the attempted reformation of Klingental nunnery in 1462, which is very fully narrated by Abbé L. Dacheux in his *Jean Geiler* (Paris, 1876, pp. 310 ff.).

117. A VISITOR'S EXPERIENCES

(*Lib. Ref.* vol. II, i, p. 555, A.D. 1455.)

WHEN first we attempted to reform the convent of nuns at Wennigsen in the diocese of Minden, of the Order of Canons Regular, we found the Bishop of Minden and the great men of the country against us everywhere in the towns, but Duke William the Elder of Brunswick on our side, together with the authority of the Pope and of the Council of Bâle.[1] Wherefore this Duke William entered into the nuns' choir, together with his supreme counsellor Ludolph von Barum, Roger Prior of Wittenburg, and myself. Here the lord Duke, removing his hat, said to the assembled nuns with their Prioress, in our presence: "My lady Prioress, and ye sisters all! It is my will that ye accept the reform and observe your Rule." They, standing with hands folded on their breasts, made answer with one voice: "We have all alike determined and sworn together that we will not reform ourselves nor observe our Rule. We beseech you, compel us not to perjure ourselves." Then said the Duke: "Ye answer ill; be better advised." Then they left the choir, but returned hastily and fell at his feet with arms folded, and made the same answer, "We have sworn together that we will not keep the reform. We beseech you, make us not perjured." Then said the Duke again, "Your answer is nought; wherefore be better advised." Then they went out and returned a second time, and fell flat on their faces in the choir, with their hands folded across their breasts, and answered for the third time in the same words: "Seeing that we have all sworn together not to observe our Rule, therefore we pray you not to make us perjured." Then said the Duke: "Arise, I am not worthy that ye should worship me." With this they arose, and certain from among them began to quarrel with the lord Ludolph von Barum, the Duke's counsellor. Then said I to the Duke: "What profit have we from standing here and chiding with the nuns? Let us quit the choir and take counsel what we should now do." So we left the choir and went about the dormitory; whereupon the nuns lay down forthwith with one accord flat upon the choir pavement, with arms and legs outstretched in the form of a cross, and chanted at the top of their voices, from begin-

[1] This was the frequent experience of orthodox Visitors in all countries and at all times, as the official records show. Apart from the well-earned popularity of the monastic houses at their best, even at their worst they still enjoyed much popularity of a certain kind, both among the neighbouring landowners who used them as dumping-grounds for younger sons and daughters, and among the people who came to the doors for doles; so that even the most lawful and necessary reforms were often the most violently resisted. This undoubted fact has been too much obscured recently by historians of the dissolution of the monasteries in England.

ning to end, the antiphon, *In the midst of life we are in death.* We therefore, hearing their voices, believed that it was the responsory *The heavens will reveal the iniquity of Judas;* wherefore the Duke was afraid lest his whole land should perish.[1] I therefore said unto him: "If I were Duke of this land, I would rather have that chant than a hundred florins; for it is no curse upon your land but rather a blessing and a dew from heaven; albeit upon the nuns it is a stern rebuke and a token that they shall be reformed. But we are few here, for there are but four of us, and the nuns are many. If they made assault upon us with their distaffs and with stones bound up in their long sleeves, what could we do? Let more be called to audience with us." Then the Duke went alone into their choir and said, "Ye sing this upon your own bodies and souls!" And to his servants, who stood with the nuns in the choir, he said, "Come hither to us"; so they hastened forth at once to us.

Then the nuns, who had ended their anthem, followed those servants to us, for they believed that we purposed to break open their chests and boxes and to carry all off with us. When therefore they were all assembled before us, the Duke said, "How dared ye to sing that anthem *Media Vita* over me? Here I stretch out my fingers to God's holy gospels and swear that ye must reform yourselves, or I will no longer suffer you in my dominions. If the Bishop of Minden and your friends will withstand me in this matter, either will I drive them forth in banishment from my land, or I myself will go forth with my [pilgrim's] staff!" The Prioress and her nuns, hearing this, were afraid, and besought the Duke that they might be permitted to call their friends and kinsfolk, by whose counsel they might guide themselves as they should. The Duke at last granted this at our intercession, yet un-

[1] The latter formula is one of solemn excommunication; the former is one of the many ways in which ecclesiastics used the church services for maledictory purposes. The antiphon is of course Notker's beautiful one from the funeral service (see introduction to Extract 13), and the object of the performance was to invoke an evil death upon the intruders. This maledictory chanting of the *Media Vita* had been forbidden by the Synod of Cologne as early as A.D. 1310, but in vain. For similar abuses of solemn services as maledictions see Petrus Cantor's words in vol. I, no. 17.

willingly. So their friends and parents and kinsfolk assembled there to meet us at a certain time which the Duke fixed for us and them; and, even as the nuns had petitioned, in like words did these men petition on their behalf. Twice or thrice we gave them time for deliberation; until, seeing that they persisted in their purpose, the Duke at length said to them by our counsel, "It is my will that ye depart hence. I will not harm them; yet it is my settled purpose that they should reform themselves." Then their friends and kinsfolk ran forth from the convent, followed by young men with bucklers.

Then the Duke commanded that [the nuns] should open the convent door to us. They sent a messenger to say that they had lost the keys. Then at our command (for by his own authority he might not have done it) the Duke seized a long bench and, with the help of certain villeins and countryfolk, he smote so hard upon the precinct-gate that he burst it open together with the steel bolt that fastened it; so that the oaken bar also was driven inwards; and it carried away in its fall, from the wall on either side, certain hewn stones of the bigness of chair-cushions, together with other smaller stones. Thus violently did they break in that door, even as the said Duke had oftentimes done in storming and conquering fortresses of war. The door being thus opened, we entered into the convent and went up to their choir. There they all lay flat in the form of a cross, having round them in a circle little stone or wooden images of saints of a cubit in height, and between every two images a lighted taper; that, albeit neither walls nor bars could defend them against the Duke and us, yet at least the saints, moved by these tapers and prayers, might vouchsafe to protect them.

When therefore they saw the Duke and us standing about them, they all arose and came to us. Then the Duke removed his hood or his cap and said in the hearing of all, "If ye will yet reform yourselves, then will I keep you in my land; otherwise, the chariots are already harnessed to carry you forth from my dominions, never perchance to return." "Nay," said they, "but first cast off these monks from about our necks; then will we gladly perform all your bidding." Whereunto the Duke made answer: "All that I now do and say unto you, I do it after their counsel," pointing to me and Roger the Prior of Wittenburg. Then said I to a nun that stood by me, "Sister! do as the lord Duke desireth; we will deal gently and mercifully with you." Then answered she in indignation, "You are not my brother, wherefore then call me sister? My brother is clad in steel, and you in a linen frock!" for she took it that I had done her contumely in calling her not *Klosterfrau* but *Sister*! Yet, seeing that the Duke persisted in his purpose, they answered at last that they had no Provost; if therefore they had a Provost to begin the reform with them, then all would be ready to begin. To this word the Duke and we all consented. . . .

So Duke William, who had withdrawn about a mile from us in the evening, came to us on the morrow with two or three hundred men, and said to me, "My lord Father and Provost" (for so was he wont to call me), "I would rather that the Bishops of Hildesheim or Minden, or the Counts of Hoyen, had defied me to mortal combat, than that I should thus come with an armed band against women and nuns. But, seeing that this is your counsel, and that it is profitable for my soul's salvation, therefore I gladly do and have done whatsoever ye desire." . . . When therefore all the nuns were come to the Prioress in our presence and were swearing obedience to her, one cried aloud, "This will I never do!" With that she fell forthwith to the earth and lost her senses; and, even though the other nuns cast cold water in her face and unlaced her bodice, if by chance she might get her breath again, yet she remained senseless. When we had thus waited an hour, and she had yet neither voice nor sense, then two men bore her in a litter to the infirmary, where they left her. The other nuns, seeing this, and how the Lord was with us, were afraid and all laid their hands in ours, gladly receiving that which we had willed and commanded. All therefore that could be fetched, and the private vessels wherein they had been wont to eat or drink or cook, they now brought at our command and in our presence to the refectory, to be put into the common stock. Yet some, grieved that they must thus resign their private possessions, cast down their pots so violently that they brake the feet thereof against the pavement. After this, all made confession to me or to the Prior of Wittenburg in their Chapter-House, he sitting in one corner and I in the other; and then they were absolved from the sentences of excommunication which they had incurred through their disobedience.

Though this was not the end of the difficulties, and Busch's own life was twice in serious danger from the outside partisans of the rebellious nuns, yet the backbone of the resistance was now broken, and even the bishop was finally overawed by the duke into helping the reforms. Busch found even more serious difficulties with other visitations, at the risk not only of his life but also of his reputation, since the desperate nuns were ready to catch at any chance of compassing his ruin by slander. With government assistance, he succeeded in working a real reform in a considerable number of monasteries, of which scarcely any fell away again before his death. A generation later, however, the great reformed congregation of Bursfeld, which Busch had helped to found, was already in a bad state again. Johann von Tritheim, or Trithemius, one of the most distinguished monks of any country in his day, wrote in 1493 a long treatise *On the State and Ruin of the Monastic Order*, which he addressed to the abbot president for circulation among the other abbots of the Bursfeld congregation. In this book he repeats more briefly what he had already said at length in his *Homilies and Sermons to Monks* and his *Book of Illustrious Men*. The following extract is from chap. XI of the *De Statu et Ruina*, which is sometimes also called *Liber Pentichus*. We must make some allowance for Tritheim's rhetorical indignation—he complains elsewhere that for the last seventy years scarcely one abbot of his own house of Spanheim had died in harness; nearly all had resigned in despair sooner or later. But his indictment is borne out in substance by equally distinguished and orthodox churchmen of the fifteenth century in England, France, Germany, and Italy, whose repeated testimony is entirely ignored by those who have written on this subject in England during the last twenty years.

118. MONASTIC DECAY

How sorely some diligent reformation of the monasteries in our province is needed, ye yourselves know, my Fathers; for ye are not ignorant of the state of monasticism in our time. I know that ye are aware with how great labour, expense and travail the Fathers reformed our Order in the past; whereof we find few and faint relics in these days. Now, among all the reformations of our Order in this province, three have been specially distinguished above the rest in these days: namely, those called *Castellensis*, *Mellicensis*, and *Bursfeldensis* after the monasteries of their origin. Yet all these, for all their first fervour, have grown cold by degrees and now draw near to their end; for the first two, as though worn out with age, have shrunk to small numbers; while the last, formed after the rest, seemeth as yet to be firmer even as it is also younger; but it too seemeth to grow cold in some of its members, and to decline again to the laxity of its former life. So in old days the world-wide reform of Cluny, while it spread far and wide, failed little by little as though its strength had been spent in its diffusion; for the proverb saith, "All that groweth old draweth near to its death"; so also even the most famous and holy reformation will gradually vanish away unless it be frequently renewed by the wisdom of the prelates; for, the more it groweth in time, the more it is diminished in fervour. For when those were dead whose works showed their zeal for the Order, then new Abbots arose after them, who neglected the holy fervour of reformation and fell back into the old deformities; and (to come to more recent times), where now is that reformation which Cardinal Nicolaus von Cusa, Papal Legate, began [in 1451] with incredible zeal? Where are those terrible oaths of all the Abbots of our province, wherewith they bound themselves to keep the Rule, laying their hands within those of this Cardinal before the altar of St Stephen at Würzburg? Where is their promised observance of the Rule? Behold, Father, ye have 127 Abbots under your Chapter, whereof scarce 70 out of the three above-named Observances have held to their reformation. There are some, I doubt not, who think themselves excellently reformed; but their conversation belieth their claim. Would that our Abbots might heed that repeated commination of our holy founder, who said that the cure of souls doth indeed expose us to a most strict account! See the conversation both of Abbots and monks, whose smoke goeth up round about; which, though it be known, I blush to tell, and ye (most worshipful Fathers) shudder to hear. For the three vows of Religion which for their excellence are named *Substantial*, are as little heeded by these men as if they had never promised to keep them. All is confusion, profanity, presumption. If we look to divine service, they perform this so confusedly and disorderly and dissolutely that there is no sound of sense in their words nor of due melody in their chants; for they lack all erudition in the liberal arts, so that they understand no whit of all that they sing; wherefore they not so much recite, as confound their canonical services, without either affection or devotion or savour of inward sweetness. Never are the Holy Scriptures seen in their hands, never do they do their duty in edifying discourse, never do they take account of training in morals. The whole day is spent in filthy talk; their whole time is given up to play and gluttony; never is a word spoken of reformation; the fury of brawling Brethren rageth in the cloister; cowl warreth against cowl, and the convent is entangled in mad litigation, to the violation of its own laws. Here the javelin is made ready, with the sword and the bow, so that the whole monastery seems in a state of siege. In open possession of private property,[1] in violation of statutes and laws and the Rule, each dwelleth in his own private lodging, wherein they follow the pursuits of clerks rather than monks. They neither fear nor love God; they have no thought of the life to come, seeing that they prefer their fleshly lusts to the needs of the soul. They read not the monastic Rule, they heed not the Statutes, they despise the decrees of the Fathers. They scorn the vow of poverty, know not that of chastity, revile that of obedience; and would that, in refusing chastity, they would at least deign to live in continence! yet the smoke of their filth goeth up all around, and we alone, who are bidden to reform them, ignore that which all the world knoweth.... O holy father Benedict, who wast of old so solicitous for thine Order, why dost thou forsake us at the last?... Who will bring succour among these evils? The Bishop?—Yet he

---

[1] The attempts to prevent monks from possessing private property, renewed from generation to generation for centuries, at last broke down openly in face of steady passive resistance; see for instance the report of the Benedictine Chapter-General for England in 1344 (Reynerus, *De Antiq. Bened. in Anglia*, Douay, 1626, p. 122). Yet Busch, like other visitors, complains that this abandonment of the vow of poverty must always react disastrously upon the other two substantial vows, obedience and chastity. This violation of the vow of poverty was however more flagrant in Germany than in England, or perhaps any other of the great countries of Europe.

careth for his own, seeketh his own profit, and scorneth ours. The Prince?—Yet he selleth his favours, refuseth discipline, seeketh worldly things. There is none to sorrow at the distress of thine Order, none to succour, none to bring help; for all who have power to restore, neglect it; while others, who seem to have a zeal for discipline, do indeed try to help but have no power. O Abbots, Abbots, who are cause of all evils in your convents!...Ye, who should correct the faults of your monks, are faulty yourselves and dissemble the transgressions of others lest your own be reproved. Ye see, most reverend Fathers, the state of your Order, what Abbots ye have and what monks; for there are none to correct the wicked; we only meet with such as should be corrected. Why therefore do ye delay? Wherefore do ye not consider the reformation of such men? Wherefore do ye not restrain the evil lives of your monks? We are confounded by their evil report, and their examples are a stone of stumbling to us; for, the more numerous they are, the more powerful indeed they are believed to be by such as know us not. Rise up now, O Fathers, for the time is short and the days are evil! reform with all your might this deformed Order, raise it up from its fall, restore it from its ruin! for, unless ye bring a remedy without delay, ye shall soon feel some grievous harm.... Even though we may not bring the whole Order to the unity of good life, yet let us do all that in us lieth to reform at least the monks of our own province; and, if we cannot attain to complete conformity in all things, yet at least let them be reformed in the three substantial vows, without which the monastic life can be called naught else but the vile brothel of a faithless soul. The reformation must begin with the Abbots, and then be continued among the monks.

Johann Geiler, born at Kaisersberg near Schaffhausen in 1445, became Doctor of Theology at Bâle and Freiburg, but accepted, at the invitation of bishop and chapter, the cathedral preachership at Strasbourg (1478). Here his spiritual fervour, his hatred of abuses, and the raciness of his style, raised him to a unique position among contemporary preachers. He died at his work in 1510, looking forward to an impending catastrophe from which his strict orthodoxy shrank, while he fully recognized its necessity. Preaching before the Emperor Maximilian, a few years before his death, he cried: "Since neither Pope nor Emperor, kings nor bishops, will reform our life, God will send a man for the purpose. I hope to see that day... but I am too old. Many of you will see it; think then, I pray you, of these words." See L. Dacheux, *Jean Geiler*, Paris, 1876.

119. SEA-SICKNESS OF THE SOUL
(Fol. xxx b of Geiler's *Navicula Penitentie*, Augsburg, 1511.)

THE twentieth condition of a voyage is sea-sickness; for some mariners fall into so great sickness and dizziness of brain that they are compelled to vomit. Why this should be, ask of the physicians. Meanwhile the Shipman and other expert mariners laugh, knowing that they stand in no peril of their lives for such a sickness; yet others who understand this not, and the patient himself in his impatience, are sore cast down thereby, and fear lest they should vomit up their lungs and liver. So also is it with several simple Christians on board of this Ship of Penitence or of Christian Life. They are taken with a horrible spiritual nausea, which tormenteth them grievously, so that they know not whither to turn, and have in horror all spiritual food. For there are some who, though they serve God busily and faithfully, are none the less wearied with temptations of blasphemy, having foul thoughts against the honour of God and His Saints, concerning the Virginity of Mary, and the humanity of Christ, and the sacrament of the Eucharist, thinking that they swallow the Devil when they take it. Moreover they have thoughts against chastity, against the faith, and so forth; so that they are like a man who would fain vomit, twisting themselves to and fro in their souls, until it seemeth to them that death would not be so hard as that temptation. This is called *blasphemy of the heart*, as St Thomas [Aquinas] saith in the *Secunda Secundae*, and the Author of the *Sum of Vices*. Yet the experienced laugh at this, knowing that no evil will come to them therefrom, so long as they have no pleasure or consent therein. Of this we have an example of a certain monk in the desert, who for twenty years was buffeted with such foul thoughts, and dared reveal them to no man for the abomination that he felt in them; yet at last he confessed them to an old and experienced Father, not by word of mouth, for very shame, but in writing. Then said the Father, laughing: "Lay thy hand on my head"; which when he had done, he said, "Upon my head I take all this sin of thine and the whole weight thereof: have thou henceforth no more conscience thereof." Whereat the monk marvelled and would have enquired the cause: then answered the Father and said, "Hath this foul thought ever pleased thee?" "God forbid," quoth he, "nay, it hath ever displeased me sore." Then said the other, "It is plain, therefore, that this is no act of thine, but rather a suffering inflicted by the Enemy, who thus buffeteth thee that he may at last seduce thee into desperation. Now therefore, my son, hear my counsel, and when such foul thoughts invade thee again, say 'To thyself, foul fiend, and on thine own head be this blasphemy of thine! I will have no part in it, for I revere and adore the Lord my God, and believe in Him'." From that time forward this monk was free from this so grievous temptation, for he followed the old man's counsel.

But thou wilt say: Whence cometh then such spiritual sickness or blasphemy, and what remedies shall we apply against it, lest it come to pass that on this account we leap forth from the Ship of Penitence before we reach the haven of eternal bliss? I answer that it cometh from five causes.... First, from the inspiration of the Devil, who by such abominations stirreth the phantastic virtue of simple souls, that he may thus drive them to despair and withdraw them from God's service and the way of salvation upon which they have entered. Whereof we see the proof in experience, in the case of some devout folk, persons of the greatest innocence and chastity, who have never heard with their outward ears such blasphemies and filth as are inspired into them from within; so that it is clear that they could not feel them but by the suggestion of that unseen Enemy; but this is no marvel, seeing that he striveth to set stumbling-blocks not only here but in every divine service, studying how he may hinder in every place the honour of God and the salvation of men's souls. Lo how, at Church Dedications,[1] he setteth up fairs and gluttonous feastings whereby the worship of God may be undermined, as indeed it is, for men busy themselves more with merchandize and feasting than with masses or sermons or prayers; nay rather, all the divine services are so ordered as the Kitchen requireth; the Preface, the Creed, the Paternoster are stretched out or cut short; the Kirk must wait at the Kitchen's heels, so that the feast should rather be called *Kitchenweih* than *Kirkweih*. Moreover the Devil hath set up, in this Holy Week shortly to come, the Fair of Frankfort, that merchants may be hindered from making their communion worthily.[2] Again, in Lententide he hath brought in greater rejoicings, vanities and dances than are wont to be made at other times. So also hath he profaned holy places; and, whereas monasteries were founded in desert solitudes, he hath surrounded them with towns and cities: for hardly shalt thou find a convent, built by holy men in a desert place, but that the Devil hath built hard by a town or city, or at least a King's highway....

Secondly, this blasphemy of the heart cometh from indiscretion.... Thirdly, from idleness...for there is no thought so foul, so abominable, so wicked and execrable, but that this detestable idleness will find it out; as Ezekiel saith: "This was the iniquity of thy sister Sodom; pride, fulness of bread, and abundance of idleness was in her and in her daughters, neither did she strengthen the hand of the poor and needy."... I say thirdly that this example [of St Antony's temptation] should be carefully studied by certain persons who, under a cloke as though they would spend all their time on God and devotion, will do no manual work; yet the Apostle saith that if any would not work, neither should he eat. For although it be not without labour to spend our time

[1] These were yearly anniversaries which still survive in Germany under the title of *Kirmes* (Church mass) or *Kirchweih* (Church dedication).

[2] The large majority of the faithful communicated only once a year, at Easter. This was one of the customs which the Devon and Cornish rebels of 1549 demanded back again: "We will have the Sacrament of the Altar but at Easter delivered unto the people, and then but in one kind."

with God in spiritual exercises, yet it is well sometimes to labour with our hands also. Wherefore it befalleth sometimes that those who neglect this, not indeed from bodily weakness but from sloth and carnal pleasure, fall into great peril to their souls, not only in evil thoughts, but even sometimes in more grievous sins; wherefore St Bernard saith: "Idleness is the cesspool of all temptations and evil or unprofitable thoughts." ...[One remedy] is not to reveal this temptation to all men. A devout person should not confess these grievous temptations to any priest indifferently, even though he be deeply learned, lest perchance he fall into an occasion of despair through the inexperience of many [confessors], as we read elsewhere in Cassian, *Coll.* ii, cap. 2: *Moses.* But let him have recourse to devout, religious, and discreet men, as was that Father of whom I told above. Nor need he when confessing explain in too full detail such foul thoughts as these; but it sufficeth so to say that the confessor may understand his mind, and this once only. If the temptation buffet him still, it is enough that he should confess it again to the same priest simply in general terms....[Let us be as little children learning to walk, who are not too downcast or angry with their falls; but who] humbly and faithfully stretch out their hands to their loving Mother that she may raise them up, seeing that they cannot rise of their own accord.

120. THE EVE OF THE REFORMATION

(Geiler, *Nav. Fat.* turba cii, nola 6.)

O Lord my God, how falsely now do even those live who seem most spiritual—Parsons and Monks, Béguines and Penitents! Their study is not to work God's works but to conceal the Devil's works. Among these all is outward show, and there is no truth, nought else but dung be-snowed or buried under snow; without is the glistering whiteness of righteousness and honesty, but within a conscience reeking with vermin and with the stench of sin. The day shall come when the Sun of Righteousness shall melt the snow, and then

shall the secrets of your hearts be revealed. And would that
the filth of our sins were at least covered with the appearance
of snow, that our sin, like Sodom, were not published abroad
without shame!

More's English Works (as Principal Lindsay writes on p. 17 of the third
volume of the *Camb. Hist. Eng. Lit.*) "deserve more consideration than
they usually receive." Yet he vouchsafes them no further consideration;
and later on Mr Routh mentions one of them only to disparage it (p. 80).
Since they are practically inaccessible to the general reader (for the folio
costs from £25 to £50 according to its condition) I have given in these
volumes some stories which show him at his best as a raconteur, and of
which that which follows is doubly interesting for the use that Shakespeare
made of it. In the *Dialogue* More is arguing in his own person against a
disputant of quasi-heretical leanings, generally alluded to as the *Messenger*
or *your Friend*.

121. AN IMPOSTOR EXPOSED

(P. 134. The Messenger speaks.)

"SOME priest, to bring up a pilgrimage in his parish, may
devise some false fellow feigning himself to come seek a saint in
his church, and there suddenly say, that he hath gotten his sight.
Then shall he have the bells rung for a miracle, and the fond
folk of the country soon made fools, then women coming
thither with their candles. And the person buying of some
lame beggar, three or four pairs of their old crutches with
twelve pence spent in men and women of wax thrust through
divers places some with arrows, and some with rusty knives,
will make his offerings for one seven years worth twice his
tithes."

"This is," quoth I, "very truth that such things may be,
and sometime so be in deed. As I remember me that I have
heard my father tell of a beggar, that in king Henry's days the
Sixth, came with his wife to Saint Albans, and there was
walking about the town begging a five or six days before the
king's coming thither, saying that he was born blind and
never saw in his life; and was warned in his dream that he
should come out of Berwick, where he said he had ever

dwelled, to seek Saint Alban, and that he had been at his shrine, and had not been holpen. And therefore he would go seek him at some other place; for he had heard some say since he came that Saint Alban's body should be at Cologne, and indeed such a contention hath there been. But of truth, as I am surely informed, he lieth here at Saint Albans, saving some relics of him which they there show shrined. But to tell you forth, when the king was come and the town full, suddenly this blind man at Saint Alban's shrine had his sight again and a miracle solemnly rungen, and *Te Deum* sungen so that nothing was talked of in all the town but this miracle. So happened it then, that duke Humphrey of Gloucester, a great wise man and very well learned, having great joy to see such a miracle, called the poor man unto him. And (first showing himself joyous of God's glory so showed in the getting of his sight, and exhorting him to meekness, and to none ascribing of any part the worship to himself nor to be proud of the people's praise, which would call him a good and a godly man thereby), at last he looked well upon his eyen, and asked whether he could never see nothing at all in all his life before. And when as well his wife as himself affirmed fastly No, then he looked advisedly upon his eyen again, and said: 'I believe you very well, for methinketh that ye cannot see well yet.' 'Yes sir,' quoth he, 'I thank God and His holy martyr I can see now as well as any man.' 'Ye can?' quoth the duke; 'what colour is my gown?' Then anon the beggar told him. 'What colour,' quoth he, 'is this man's gown?' He told him also, and so forth without any sticking he told him the names of all the colours that could be showed him. And when my lord saw that, he bade him walk [for a] false fellow, and made him be set openly in the stocks. For, though he could have seen suddenly by miracle the difference between divers colours, yet could he not by the sight so suddenly tell the names of all these colours, but if he had known them before, no more than the names of all the men that he should suddenly see."

References are to pages, unless otherwise stated.
All Saints will be found under St.

INDEX TO PART IV

References are to pages, unless otherwise stated.
All Saints will be found under St.

INDEX TO PART IV

48141871